W9-AHL-674

Adult Children of Alcoholics
Alcoholic/Dysfunctional Families

Since its initial publication in November 2006, more than 40,000 copies of this book have been printed for ACA groups and individuals.

During this time, Adult Children of Alcoholics has experienced a resurgence of meetings and Intergroups worldwide, with more than 1,600 new meetings and groups being formed. The groups have flourished across Europe, Asia, Australia, the Middle East, Africa, India, North and South America and elsewhere.

Currently, the ACA text has been translated into Finnish, Danish, Spanish, and Russian. Ongoing translations include French, Polish, German, Japanese, Hungarian, Swedish, and other languages to bring the ACA message to millions of adult children around the globe.

The ACA Fellowship Text, along with other ACA WSO Conference-Approved Literature helps create unity, identity, and focus for our fellowship. The ACA message is based on the ACA Twelve Steps, ACA Twelve Traditions, Sponsorship (Fellow Travelers) and Reparenting.

With regular use of ACA WSO Conference-Approved literature, we believe recovering adult children can reparent themselves to wholeness with gentleness, humor, love, and respect; integrate the effects of being raised in an alcoholic/ dysfunctional family; achieve emotional sobriety; and experience a spiritual awakening. Within these pages, this life-saving message is inscribed.

ACA World Services Board of Trustees

Adult Children of Alcoholics
Alcoholic/Dysfunctional Families

Copyright© 2006 by

**Adult Children of Alcoholics®/Dysfunctional Families
World Service Organization, Inc.**
Post Office Box 811
Lakewood, California USA 907514
www.adultchildren.org

All rights reserved. No part of this publication may be reproduced,
stored in a retrieval system or transmitted in any form or by any means,
electronic, mechanical, photocopying, recording, or otherwise,
without the written permission of the publisher.

——•——

Adult Children of Alcoholic / Dysfunctional Families

ISBN-13: 978-0-9789797-0-6 (Hardcover)
ISBN-13: 978-0-9789897-8-2 (Softcover)

——•——

Printed in the United States of America
Twenty-First Printing

21 22 23   20 19 18

Contents

Contents

"Adult Child"

"The concept of Adult Child came from the Alateens who began the Hope for Adult Children of Alcoholics meeting. The original members of our fellowship, who were over eighteen years old, were adults; but as children they grew up in alcoholic homes. Adult Child also means that when confronted, we regress to a stage in our childhood."

ACA History – an interview with Tony A., 1992.

EDITOR'S NOTE:

More than three decades have passed since our primary founder, Tony A., was interviewed on the topic of the fellowship that he helped create. For this book we will use Tony's words as the foundation to define the adult child personality. An adult child is someone who responds to adult situations with self-doubt, self-blame, or a sense of being wrong or inferior – all learned from stages of childhood. Without help, we unknowingly operate with ineffective thoughts and judgments as adults. The regression can be subtle, but it is there sabotaging our decisions and relationships.

This revised edition introduces The Laundry Lists and their flip sides, and includes the traits in Appendix D.

We Have Our Book

*T*he 22nd Annual Business Conference of Adult Children of Alcoholics voted unanimously to approve this text as the fellowship book. The ACA "big book"[1] is a meeting book, Steps book, Traditions book, workbook, and group guide.

The idea for an ACA basic text began in 1991 with several ACA members envisioning a comprehensive book that contained the experience, strength, and hope of ACA, in addition to offering all the meeting and service material needed to start an ACA group. ACA members from the Los Angeles/San Fernando Valley Intergroup drew up a table of contents "from blank paper."

One member recalls: "We wanted a book that could be used to hold a meeting anywhere, anytime. We wanted a book that could be used for topic discussions, Step studies, and workshops. We wanted a book that a sponsor could use to guide a sponsee through the recovery process. We wanted workbook items so that members could write down their thoughts and discuss questions with ACA friends. We envisioned a handbook written by adult children."

The ACA Handbook Committee adhered to the 1991 wishes of these visionary members. With spiritual guidance and with humility, we submit this book for fellowship use.

---

[1] The term "big book" is attributed to the basic text of Alcoholics Anonymous, the first Twelve Step fellowship ever established.

We believe this book represents the most complete description of the ACA experience from our fellowship view. In addition to the Twelve Steps, this book contains extensive fellowship writing on the Twelve Traditions, sponsorship, Inner Child, and reparenting. The book also contains 120 shares recorded voluntarily at ACA meetings and events over a ten-year period. These meeting discussions represent the ACA voice, which offers hope for recovery from the effects of growing up in a dysfunctional family.

We realize this is only a beginning. With this book, we hope to begin a discussion on the greater meaning of ACA recovery. We believe this discussion will lead to new levels of clarity for adult children. With this in mind, we leave the reader with a question to consider as you read this book: "What does ACA mean to you?"

ACA Handbook (big book) Committee
September 2006

"The Laundry List"
(14 Traits of an Adult Child)

1) We became isolated and afraid of people and authority figures.

2) We became approval seekers and lost our identity in the process.

3) We are frightened by angry people and any personal criticism.

4) We either become alcoholics, marry them or both, or find another compulsive personality such as a workaholic to fulfill our sick abandonment needs.

5) We live life from the viewpoint of victims and are attracted by that weakness in our love and friendship relationships.

6) We have an overdeveloped sense of responsibility, and it is easier for us to be concerned with others rather than ourselves; this enables us not to look too closely at our own faults, etc.

7) We get guilt feelings when we stand up for ourselves instead of giving in to others.

8) We became addicted to excitement.

9) We confuse love and pity and tend to "love" people we can "pity" and "rescue."

10) We have "stuffed" our feelings from our traumatic childhoods and have lost the ability to feel or express our feelings because it hurts so much (Denial).

11) We judge ourselves harshly and have a very low sense of self-esteem.

12) We are dependent personalities who are terrified of abandonment and will do anything to hold on to a relationship in order not to experience painful abandonment feelings, which we received from living with sick people who were never there emotionally for us.

13) Alcoholism is a family disease; we became para-alcoholics and took on the characteristics of that disease even though we did not pick up the drink.

14) Para-alcoholics are reactors rather than actors.

Tony A.
1978

Welcome to ACA

*N*ever before in the history of Twelve Step programs has a fellowship brought together such a diverse group of recovering people that includes adult children of alcoholics, codependents, and addicts of various sorts. The program is Adult Children of Alcoholics. The term "adult child" is used to describe adults who grew up in alcoholic or dysfunctional homes and who exhibit identifiable traits that reveal past abuse or neglect. The group includes adults raised in homes without the presence of alcohol or drugs. These ACA members have the trademark presence of abuse, shame, and abandonment found in alcoholic homes.

Founded in 1978 in New York, ACA began with a group of Alateens. Alateen is a Twelve Step fellowship made up of children and teenagers of alcoholics. The Alateens were mostly 20 years old and wanted something different from what they could expect in another Twelve Step program when they moved up to that program. They were soon joined by a recovering alcoholic known as Tony A., a New York City stockbroker, who would become the primary founder of ACoA/ACA (both are acceptable usage). At the time, Tony was about 50 years old and had grown up in a violent alcoholic home.

Over the years, ACA has evolved into an established program that offers pertinent resources of recovery for adult children from all walks of life across the world. ACA is an international fellowship with about 1,000[†] meetings in North America, Europe,

Asia, and around the world. Adult children are committed to halting the generational nature of family dysfunction for the greater good of the world. We are not evangelizing against poor parenting nor are we policing the parenting of the world; however, we hope to relieve the suffering brought on by neglectful and abusive homes. We want to join society with our full attention toward making a difference with the help of a Higher Power.

Clinical and medical researchers have measured the causes and effects of growing up in a dysfunctional home and how such trauma continues to affect the adult. Our book offers a medical opinion on this fact in the following pages.

We believe that ACA has the potential to help the suffering adult children of the world on the magnitude that Alcoholics Anonymous brought relief to hopeless alcoholics in the 20th century. Since the founding of AA in 1935, millions of once hopeless drunks have found sobriety, restored hope, and rejoined society in an attitude of love and service to others. With this book on adult children, we are suggesting that ACA has many of the answers to some of the most difficult and threatening mental health problems facing the world today. Our decades of experience has shown that adult children who attend our meetings, work the Twelve Steps, and find a Higher Power experience astonishing improvement in body, mind, and spirit. Ours is one of the few Twelve Step fellowships that embraces the difficult task of trauma work, which can often lead to an exciting journey to the Inner Child or True Self. Along with sponsorship, we encourage informed counseling to help the adult child accomplish the greatest level of emotional healing from an abusive upbringing.

Our fellowship includes members who have been diagnosed with addictions, depression, panic disorders, post-traumatic stress disorder, and various dissociative states. Adult children understand dissociation, codependence, obsession, and compulsion like few others. Many of our members have literally been fetched back from the gates of hell by this simple but spiritual program known as Adult Children of Alcoholics.

The question must be asked: "How does such a diverse group of addicts, codependents, and adult children create a unified fellowship and voice that can attract new members and sustain itself without fragmenting into hundreds of pieces?" One of the main answers lies in identification, the "DNA" of all Twelve Step programs. Adult children of all types identify with one another at the level of abandonment, shame, and abuse like no other group of people in the world. Each day, recovery from the effects of family dysfunction begins somewhere in the world when one adult child sits across from another sharing experience, strength, and hope. We believe that once a recovering adult child meets and shares his or her story with another adult child seeking help, that adult cannot view codependence the same again. This is a potent statement, but our experience shows that it is true.

The proof of identification and ACA unity can be found in ACA meetings and the immediate identification created by the reading of The Laundry List, a list of identifiable traits penned by Tony A. The Laundry List is the basis for The Problem, which is read at the beginning of most ACA meetings. These common behaviors include: fear of abandonment, fear of authority figures, judging ourselves harshly, confusing love for pity, and becoming an alcoholic or marrying one. Self-identification with The Laundry List (Problem) is the glue that holds together our fellowship and its membership. Adult children from addicted homes or homes without addiction, yet dysfunctional, identify with The Laundry List (Problem) in the same degree. We have the same loss.

When read aloud at an ACA meeting, The Laundry List (Problem) produces an immediate sense of curiosity and identification that resonates within the adult child. The feeling is an inescapable sense of clarity and hope that heretofore did not exist for the adult child.

While ACA is similar to other Twelve Step programs, our emphasis on the family system and the Inner Child or True Self sets ACA apart from all other fellowships. In addition to focusing on ourselves through the Twelve Steps, we believe that the family system is open for inspection as well. We believe that each of us is born with a True Self that is forced into hiding by dysfunctional parenting. A false self emerges that protects the hidden True Self from harm, but at a heavy price. Without help, the destructive false self is too much for most adult children to separate from.

ACA holds out hope and acceptance to the hurting adult children of the world, who can "hit a bottom" and reach out for help. Allowing the True Self to emerge in the nurturing atmosphere of ACA is a spiritual experience that awaits any adult child stepping onto the broad highway of ACA recovery.

†By 2018, our fellowship had grown to more than 2,000 meetings.

A Message to Nonmembers

*D*ue to the nature of the Adult Children of Alcoholics program, this book will deal with family matters and family rearing practices. However, nothing in this book is to be construed as ACA taking a position on the family rearing practices or the methods of detecting and treating child abuse.

The primary purpose of ACA is to create a safe setting in which adults who grew up in dysfunctional homes can feel safe and find a way to share their stories with others in a meaningful manner. ACA experience shows that survival traits developed by an abused or neglected child continue to affect the adult in problematic ways that our fellowship understands and addresses. We offer hope and a sense of home for many adult children who live each day in quiet desperation without words to describe such despair. As part of our recovery process, many ACA members take a "blameless inventory" of their parents to understand and stop the generational nature of family dysfunction. The parents are not blamed. However, the adult child examines how he or she was raised in connection with levels of nurturing, discipline, and feeling safe. In homes where obvious abuse and violence existed, the adult child names the behavior as one of the first steps in removing power from such parental acts.

While our individual members are free to choose their own path in life, ACA has no opinion on outsides issues such as child welfare programs, counseling programs, or legislation that might deal with childhood abuse or neglect. There are many legitimate nonprofit and private programs throughout the land which deal with such matters; however, we are not affiliated with such programs.

Finally, this book is not a call to rally against dysfunctional families, parents, or family systems that many would consider problematic. In ACA, we learn to keep the focus on ourselves and live and let live.

Introduction

$\mathcal{H}$aving been a part of the ACA movement since the mid-1970s, it is an honor and thrill to see the development of the ACA Twelve Step community and the potential growth it has as a result of this book. By the time this book is published, decades have passed since the naming "adult child." I can remember seeing The Laundry List in the late 1970s as my professional work was coinciding with the development of this new Twelve Step model. It is my bias that no one deserves to live a life of fear and shame. And it is through the healing of Twelve Step work that today thousands of adult children have found an inner peace. We have stepped outside the shadow of addiction and have choices to how we live our life, versus living a family script.

While I was busy professionally creating therapy models for young and adult children of alcoholics in the mid and late 1970s, I would also be attending one of the first ACA meetings in southern California on a weekly basis. To say, "Hello, my name is Claudia B. and I am an adult child," is and was said with pride. It is a statement that holds great meaning for not just how my growing up years would impact me but for the potential of healing and recovery. Being in those rooms with others who had been raised in similar circumstances, I knew there had never been a place more right for me.

Being in an ACA Twelve Step meeting was being in a place where without speaking I sat with others who genuinely knew me. They knew without judgment and with love how I had felt my entire life. Despite the differences in how our defenses against our pain manifested themselves, we knew we were from the same family system. Rather than to run and hide, to disconnect from each other, to rescue each other, or to control each other, we bore witness to each other's pain and story. We honored each other with acceptance for where we were, precious children and now adults struggling with what is called our false selves. We learned to project this false self to the world in an attempt to hide our inner thoughts and feelings. The preciousness of the Inner Child was tapping from within, asking and hoping to be heard and acknowledged.

Since those early years I have witnessed the struggle and decline of meetings and now a resurgence of ACA. Never during that time would I question the validity of the naming, or the framework of understanding what it meant to be an adult child from an alcoholic or otherwise dysfunctional household. This book will openly discuss how ACA has met growing pains and survived.

In addition to honoring its founders, this book presents the structure of the program beginning with The Laundry List, the 14 characteristics that define the traits from which we need to heal. Other pillars of this structure can be found in chapters titled "How It Works" and "Becoming Your Own Loving Parent." Ultimately, this text delineates the foundation of how the Twelve Steps offer an incredible path that will give the adult child choices, versus living a generational family script. In working the Twelve Steps, the reader has the opportunity to be free from carried pain and shame. This book will allow you to be accountable for choices you make as well. It will truly move you from a place of reactor to actor in life. As said in many Twelve Step programs, "It works if you work it."

Over the years, one of the big questions for this self-help group was whether or not it could or should include people from other types of troubled family systems. When both the therapy and self-help ACA movements began to address these issues, we understood that adult child principles could apply to other people without apparent addiction in the home. Yet to generalize the resources at that time in history would dilute this seed that was only then germinating. People who experienced alcoholism and other addictions in their family needed their own claim. To broaden the concept at that time would have aided in minimizing and discounting the impact that mood-altering substances had on the family specifically. Adult children who were just beginning to be recognized by the therapeutic community could have been pushed to near invisibility again without a specific identifier through alcoholism.

Yet it would not be long before others raised with dysfunction would claim their right to the therapy processes being offered and would find solace and direction in Twelve Step programs that were not directed specifically for them. Today with the structure of the Steps and Traditions, it is believed that the ACA program can be inclusive of others who did not have substance abuse in their family. The common denominator among adult children from a variety of dysfunctional homes is chronic loss and abandonment. What we have learned about addiction in the family is truly a gift to those raised in other types of troubled families. Whether it is due to cultural issues affecting family structure or emotional problems, to be in a family where we learn the primary dysfunctional family rules, "don't talk, don't trust, and don't feel," crushes the very spirit that allows us to thrive. This book will address how ACA met the challenge of inclusion for adult children from homes without the presence of addiction. The ACA fellowship met the challenge with openness and goodwill.

The descriptions can vary among people sitting in ACA meetings listening to the stories of others impacted by chronic loss and abandonment in their growing-up years. The descriptions vary in the source of the dysfunction, which parent was the substance abuser, and whether one is an only child or has siblings. Other factors include birth order, extended family, and community support for the child. Yet, the commonality of the adult child experience overrides any sense of separateness. And that commonality crosses borders. Personally and professionally, I have sat with adult children across the world, throughout the United States, into Western Europe, from Japan, to Iceland, Ireland, Uruguay, Brazil, and Australia. The experiences of growing up with loss and abandonment were universal. The healing that would come with having witnesses to one's pain and an avenue in which to find choice in the present day was exhilarating.

Adult children run the gamut of functionality as adults. Many are high-powered professionals; others are in prison. And certainly some are doing both. Some have very blatant addictions; others have learned to hide them. Some have blatant depression and anxiety disorders; others have compensated in ways that hide their fear and despair. This book will help people define their bottom so that their spiral downward can be halted. When we face a bottom, recovery has a base from which to sprout.

It is a challenge for a Twelve Step program to attend to the multifaceted ramifications of growing up with chronic loss, shame, and fear. Yet, ACA is doing so with a three prong approach, addressing the embodiment of healing the whole person in mind, body, and spirit. The ACA fellowship is also focusing on the family system, which means inventorying parental behavior in addition to inventorying one's own self. ACA is not blaming the parents, but this is a unique Twelve Step approach that is necessary to get at chronic loss and its roots.

To manifest recovery as adult children we need to embrace where fears, misguided perceptions, and distorted thoughts have taken us. The Laundry List will offer that framework. It will help us see and explore how feelings have propelled us into isolation, how we often live as victims, not recognizing choices. We will see how our low self-esteem has us judging ourselves mercilessly, giving others the benefit of the doubt, and tolerating inappropriate behavior. This Laundry List has been with us for decades, and its wisdom holds strong after all these years.

One asks how is the body a part of this healing, and yet that has for many years been the missing piece. The fear response in the brain is fully developed at birth. Yet until children are nearly six years of age they cannot accurately assess danger. They cannot determine what is or is not a threat and to what degree is something a threat. Until they are in mid to late teens the part of the brain that allows them to reason is not fully developed. That is why children need parents to guide, protect, and nurture them, particularly at times of stress. Children raised in troubled families need protection and safety like all children, but they are raised by people who are absent, neglectful, or the cause of stress and pain itself. At times of trauma where does a child run toward? Home. But where do you run when the trauma is within the home? The natural responses to trauma are flight, fight, or freeze. For most kids they need to freeze. They are not able to run, or fight, so in essence they run within. This Twelve Step program honors the trauma responses of its many members. This program goes within to bring true peace for those who want it.

As children growing up in shame, we have fought hard for control whether it was internal or external. It is possible we were given no spiritual guidance, given the dysfunction of our families. Ultimately we came to depend on ourselves, often times questioning or down right challenging any concept of a Higher Power. Yet it is only in letting go of some control that recovery can occur. And when we let go of some control, we have begun a spiritual process. Learning to differentiate between what we can and cannot control is the first step in accepting our humanness. We are not God, we are not all powerful, we are only humans, and our power most definitely has limits. Spirituality is a surrendering process. We surrender the illusion that we must have all the answers, that we must be in charge so we can hide our shame. By becoming aware of the reality of what we are able to control, by facing our old fears of being out of control, we become willing to surrender. We surrender to our inability to change the past and to our powerlessness to control the future. That leaves us with real life in the present. Living in the here and now is another fundamental spiritual concept offered in ACA.

For those new to this recovery I want to address three common resistances to working the program. First is the issue of betrayal. Having worked with both young and adult age children, age is irrelevant when it comes to the issue of loyalty. People of all ages are so afraid of betraying their parents. Speaking your truth, owning your reality is not an act of betrayal with your parents. There is betrayal, but the betrayal is with the disease, the disorder, the dysfunction. To not own your reality or to not speak your truth is the ultimate act of betrayal to yourself.

When you are speaking about what happened you are owning your losses; you are letting go of minimizing, rationalizing, and denial. It is part of rectifying your past. It means you are no longer carrying the baggage that comes with denial. At times adult children have been criticized for blaming their parents. The principles of ACA are not about blame. They are about owning your truth, grieving your losses, and being accountable today for how you live your life.

There are two other primary resistances to this recovery process as well. People want recovery, but they prefer it be pain free. That is understandable, but unfortunately, identifying and feeling our feelings is a part of healing. People are afraid they are too fragile and will fall apart. Where there is loss there will be tears; where there is loss there will be anger. But feelings are cues and signals to tell you what you need. It is the repression or distorted expression of them that gets people sick or into personal difficulty. This program will help you learn to tolerate your feelings without hurting yourself or another. I have been asked many times, does the pain ever go away? I believe the answer is yes.

Another resistance is people want to heal and live in the present, but they prefer to do it alone. This is often based in rigid self-sufficiency. Self-sufficiency is valued in our culture. The rigidity of self-sufficiency is based in mistrust of others and the fear of letting go of control. When you allow others to be a part of your path, that is when it is possible to meet the resistance of fear of feelings. Others will shine the light and offer the hope that we deserve. As adult children, we have lived a life of isolation for too long. Recovery is about connection.

Adult children are survivors and have taken a lot of pride in that identification. Yet I think we all deserve a lot more than that in our lives. ACA is the path to offer that to us. It is not necessarily an easy path. At times, it can be scary, at times painful. But hang on to the vision of where it leads you. Pay attention to the process, but remember to have fun. Recovery is not about perfection. It is in the becoming that we experience the promises of recovery. Learn to validate yourself by becoming your own Loving Parent. Don't judge recovery or yourself. Acknowledge the little steps along the way. In doing so, you will move from shame to self-worth, from secrecy to honesty, loneliness to connection with self and others, and from silence to having a voice.

I believe it is through the Twelve Step program of ACA that we no longer live life from a basis of fear. We live with self-care and love.

Let me leave you with these thoughts as you make your journey through these Steps.

Listen to your Inner Child not with fear but with openness.

Love this child for all she or he has had to defend against.

Know that feelings are to be listened to; they are cues and signals that indicate where you are and what you need.

Mistakes are a sign of growing; remember, be gentle with yourself.

Success is not relative to others. It is a feeling of love and accomplishment for yourself.

Recovery is accepting yourself for who you are, no longer waiting for others to define you or approve of you.

It is safe to take time to play today. Play fuels your creativity, tickles your Inner Child, and nurtures your soul.

May you respond with the vulnerability of your child, but with the strength of your adult.

Surround yourself with people who respect and treat you well.

In faith one finds the strength to survive times of great fear and sadness.

Claudia B.

ACA Disease Model
Adult Child

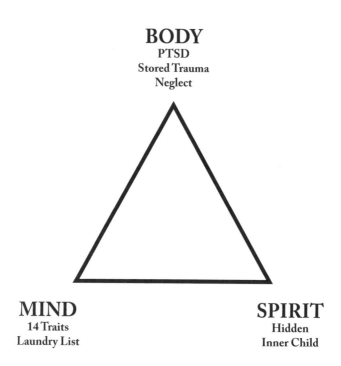

BODY
PTSD
Stored Trauma
Neglect

MIND
14 Traits
Laundry List

SPIRIT
Hidden
Inner Child

This model represents the disease of family dysfunction. The model is a description of our condition and personality. As children, we were affected in body, mind, and spirit by alcoholism or other family dysfunction. Our bodies stored the trauma, neglect, and rejection in the form of Post-Traumatic Stress Disorder. The mind developed the Laundry List Traits or the false self to survive. The Inner Child, the true connection to our Higher Power, went into hiding. ACA recovery can reverse this process.

Prediction factor: If you have any two of the three elements of the model, you have the other.

Example: Trauma/Neglect + 14 Traits = Hidden Inner Child.

The Doctor's Opinion

Looking back, things seemed simpler when Dr. William Silkworth wrote his opinion for AA's "Big Book" in 1939, including his naming alcoholism as a disease.[1] At that time we didn't know what the impact of growing up in an alcoholic or other troubled family would have on its members, especially the children.

Standing on the strong shoulders of those who came before us, today we can see the connections and the territory of trauma, recovery, and healing from an expanded perspective. Over the past decades, research and clinical practice have verified the detrimental effects of growing up in a traumatic and hurtful family. And since 1978, when ACA was founded, countless adult children of alcoholics and trauma have slowly worked their programs of recovery, a nugget of which you are now holding in your hands as the first edition of the ACA "big book."

We have learned several important things. Most families across the world are dysfunctional, in that they don't provide and support the healthy needs of their children. What results is an interruption in the otherwise normal and healthy

---

[1] The disease model of alcoholism has a history dating back more than two hundred years and is considered by many to be the dominant paradigm guiding scientific inquiry and treatment approaches for much of the 20th century. Its origin is credited to Benjamin Rush in the United States and Thomas Trotter in Great Britain. In the late 18th century, these two physicians independently offered the earliest clinical descriptions of alcoholism as a disease. Even so, when Silkworth wrote his observations the disease view was controversial.

neurological and psychological growth and development of the child from birth to adulthood. In order to survive, the traumatized child's True Self (Child Within) goes into hiding deep within the unconscious part of its psyche. What emerges is a false self or ego which tries to run the show of our life but is unable to succeed, simply because it is a defense mechanism against pain and not real. Its motives are based more on needing to be right and in control.

When Dr. Silkworth wrote his opinion for AA, what we now call post-traumatic stress disorder (PTSD) was called "Combat Fatigue" or "Shell Shock," which was thought to be limited to some military combat veterans. Today we know that PTSD is far more common and not limited to these soldiers. Indeed, PTSD may be the most common disorder that befalls adult children of trauma. However, as has been shown by over 330 scientific research studies on well over 230,000 people world-wide, such trauma may also result in hurtful effects that manifest as any one or more of the common so called mental disorders – from depression to addictions to schizophrenia – and an array of physical disorders. Also called "trauma spectrum disorders," these illnesses show a strong link with having a history of repeated childhood trauma. Furthermore, contrary to current psychiatric lore, the evidence for there being a genetically transmitted disorder of brain chemistry between parent and child is weak.

The Stages of Recovery

Most people recovering from addictions and other disorders can recover more successfully by first stabilizing these for a time, since otherwise these problems are usually distractions from being able to focus on ACA recovery issues and work. We call this stabilization period Stage One recovery work, which may take from several months to years to complete.

Many others may have no particular addictions or disorders and come to a recovery perspective because they are hurting or even "bottoming out" from emotional pain and having a desire to change. These can usually enter directly into ACA and trauma effects recovery work, which we call Stage Two, and which usually takes a number of years to complete. The goals of Stage Two work include: 1) realizing our True Self, 2) grieving our ungrieved hurts, losses, and traumas, 3) finding and fulfilling our healthy needs, and 4) working through our core recovery issues.

The final one, Stage Three recovery, is about refining our relationship with self, others, and God from a spiritual perspective. It usually becomes easier to realize a loving relationship with our Higher Power once we have done most of our Stage Two recovery work. This is because the false self or ego cannot experientially relate to or know God, and the only part of us that can do this is our True Self, which we come to know in our Stage Two work. While the false self may at best try to intellectualize a relationship with God, our True Self does it from its heart, with fewer words needed.

Working the Twelve Steps

Stages Two and Three are addressed throughout the Twelve Steps of ACA (Chapter 7). For example, Steps Four and Five are not only about identifying and correcting our "character defects," but also involve finding and working through our core recovery issues. And, when we make our fearless inventory, we can remember to include our personal strengths, and not just our weaknesses.

Most of the Steps involve the core issues of needing to be in control and difficulty handling conflict. For example, the first three Steps suggest that we are powerless over people, places, and things, especially the effects of alcoholism or other family dysfunction, and that we can find assistance to lessen our emotional pain by asking for help, and then surrendering to our Higher Power.

Patience and Persistence

Stage Two recovery is nearly always slow, long, and ponderous. Effective aids include attending ACA meetings, working the Twelve Steps, individual counseling, and Stage Two (or trauma focused) group therapy long term. In my clinical experience, psychiatric drugs do not eliminate the effects of childhood trauma, and seldom result in more than superficial improvement or conclusive, long-term benefits.

Recovery takes patience and persistence. We are naturally impatient to reach the end without delay and skip the hard work of the program. An important part of successful recovery is learning to accurately name the components of our inner life as they come up for us, including our various feelings, and learning to tolerate emotional pain without trying to medicate it away.

One of the most profound principles of healing is embodied in the phrase "one day at a time." Although healing takes a long time, by using this admonition, our outlook can shift immediately, making the journey not only more tolerable, but meaningful, and anchoring us in the present moment. As we grieve our buried pain and work through our core recovery issues, with patience we will slowly release our past unresolved internal conflicts. We gradually discover that our future is a destination not yet determined. Our life is in the present, which is where we can eventually find peace.

– Charles L. Whitfield, M.D.
Atlanta, Georgia
2006

Adult Children of Alcoholics and Its Beginnings

 $\mathcal{A}$ dult Children of Alcoholics officially was founded in 1978 in New York. Tony A. is considered the primary founder along with members of an Alateen group. Alateen is a Twelve Step program for children of alcoholic parents. Alateen is sponsored by Al-Anon.

The Alateens and Tony formed a specially focused meeting that broke away from Al-Anon and became the first ACA group. The new group, Generations, focused on recovering from the effects of being raised in a dysfunctional family rather than the Al-Anon focus of being powerless over alcohol.

Tony is the author of The Laundry List, the first piece of ACA literature. The Laundry List is a list of 14 characteristics or common behaviors that detail the adult child personality. Tony also developed the ACA Solution of attending meetings, focusing on ourselves, working the Steps, and feeling our feelings. Tony died in April 2004 at the age of 77.

Jack E. is given credit for establishing ACA in California and placing The Laundry List in a narrative form known as The Problem. The Problem is read at the opening of most ACA meetings. Jack's recollections of ACA history are included here. Tony's comments on ACA history are from a 1992 interview. This history has been updated based on interviews with Tony's family in 2005. Jack's story was recorded at a different time.

While Tony's story mentions our eventual separation from the Al-Anon fellowship, ACA cooperates with Al-Anon and enjoys a mutual respect of this program.

Hope For Adult Children – Adapted from an Interview With Tony A.

At the end of 1976 or the beginning of 1977, four or five young people who had recently "graduated" from Alateen joined Al-Anon, a Twelve Step fellowship for the spouses, friends, and relatives of alcoholics.

In Alateen, these young people had explored the impact of being raised by alcoholic and co-alcoholic parents now known as codependents. The teens looked at the effects of living in an alcoholic household. Entering Al-Anon, they were faced with the concept of learning to live serenely in a dysfunctional setting. Stepping up to Al-Anon meant they were faced with attending meetings that focused primarily on adult issues or spousal drinking. Some of the Alateens felt unsafe in their homes and believed they could not relate in Al-Anon.

Tony said Al-Anon taught a few skills to the young people, including how to get their own needs met. These bold teens formed their own Al-Anon meeting which they named Hope for Adult Children of Alcoholics. This first meeting met in the Smithers Building in Manhattan. This group used the Al-Anon format but improvised the meeting discussion. The discussions involved the neglect, abuse, and fear that the Alateens thought they could not fully share about in Al-Anon. A second meeting known as Generations would be formed, but it would have no affiliation with Al-Anon.

While the first new group was being formed, the Alateens heard about an Alcoholics Anonymous member sharing in AA about his experiences of growing up in a violent alcoholic home. This was Tony, a 50-year-old recovering alcoholic and New York City stockbroker. Cindy, a member of the Hope for Adult Children of Alcoholics group, heard Tony's AA story and asked him to be a guest speaker at the newly formed group. Tony said he was 30 years older than the Alateens, but their age difference dissolved when he began telling his story. "When we began," Tony said, "there was a wonderful feeling of mutual love, empathy, and understanding."

Hope for Adult Children of Alcoholics was technically an Al-Anon meeting, however, something special was happening with each meeting and with each story being told, Tony said. The founding principles of ACA were being unearthed and spoken in these early meetings. The dysfunctional family rules of "don't talk, don't trust, and don't feel" were being challenged. However, the meeting struggled because of a lack of structure and focus, Tony said. After six or seven months, instead of the membership increasing as expected, the fledgling meeting had dwindled to three or four people. The meeting was about to fold. Out of instinct and spiritual insight, Tony said he invited members of AA to join the little group. He reasoned that some of them, after all, had alcoholic parents of their own. He was right. Seventeen AA members showed up for the next meeting of Hope For Adult Children of Alcoholics. At the following meeting there were 50 people. At the next there were more than 100 people, mostly from AA. The somewhat radical Al-Anon meeting was on its way, with a lot of help from some good AA friends. Yet, the group still lacked consistent structure and clear distinction of its message.

The Laundry List – ACA's First Piece of Literature

A second meeting known as Generations was established, but it had no affiliation with Al-Anon. The group met at St. Jean Baptiste Church. Tony served as the chairman of the meeting, but he also attended the Hope for Adult Children of Alcoholics meeting during this period. ACA was still not officially established yet. Hope For Adult Children of Alcoholics was connected to Al-Anon, and the independent Generations meeting still had no true focus other than the Alateens sharing raw emotions about their abuse and neglect. For about six months, the Generations meeting operated with no format. Tony recalled how the members of the group sternly encouraged him to formalize a format to address the somewhat chaotic group sharing. This confrontation by the group created the moment and circumstances by which Tony penned our first piece of ACA literature.

On the day after Generations members urged him to formalize the group, Tony said he sat down at work and jotted down 13 characteristics of an adult child of an alcoholic. "It was as if Someone Else was writing the list through me," Tony said describing the experience.

The list of common behaviors took two hours to complete, and Tony added one more trait when he edited the traits with Chris, a group member who offered to type up the list. Tony realized he'd forgotten to add a mention of fear. But he had second thoughts. "No, they'd never admit fear," he thought. "Excitement. Yeah, better. They'd accept excitement. We became addicted to excitement," Tony wrote. With that addition, ACA had its 14 characteristics or common behaviors that would be read as The Problem in the Generations meeting. He also wrote the solution edited by Chris.

When Tony read the characteristics at the next meeting, one of the members, Barry, said, "Hey, that's my laundry list!" Since then the 14 common behaviors or traits have been known as "The Laundry List." Tony marks this as the official beginning of ACA or ACoA. It was early spring of 1978. No one quite remembers the exact date of this moment, but The Laundry List (Problem) and the solution would allow ACA to become a worldwide movement of adult children.

At the conclusion of a Generations meeting in late 1979 or early 1980, two women from General Services of Al-Anon approached Tony. They invited the Generations group to join Al-Anon. To join, the meeting had to discontinue reading or using The Laundry List. The group unanimously agreed that it would not give up its Laundry List. The decision marked the beginning of ACA's break with Al-Anon.

Today, Al-Anon meetings that have an adult child focus are not associated with ACA or ACA World Service Organization.

In 1979, Newsweek magazine published an ACA article about Dr. Claudia Black, Dr. Stephanie Brown, and Sharon Wegscheider (now Wegscheider-Cruse). The article was the first nationwide announcement that family alcoholism could and did cause life-long patterns of dysfunctional behavior even for those who never took a drink. The family systems concept of addiction and family dysfunction became more visible as well. Before that time, most addiction or mental health models focused on the individual addict. Black and others were saying that the disease of family dysfunction had long-range effects on the children who became adults. The children were affected by the alcoholism even though they were not putting alcohol into their bodies.

The AA-Adapted Steps for ACA Purposes

At this time, 1979 or 1980, Tony recalls raising questions about the adaptability of AA Steps for ACA meetings. While Tony believed in the AA Steps and their ability to sober up an alcoholic, he had reservations about the Steps being a good fit for ACA. For one thing, the AA-adapted Steps directed the adult child away from looking at the family system of dysfunction. Tony believed this occurred in Steps Four and Five, the Steps on self inventory and an admission of wrongs. In these Steps, the adult child is required to focus primarily on one's self and one's wrongs. The adult child is directed away from raising the question of the effects of being raised in a dysfunctional home. Tony believed that this served as a disconnect between an inventory of the adult child's behavior and the contribution that dysfunctional parents had in planting that behavior. Tony believed in adult children taking responsibility for their behavior and changing; however, he also believed in fairly distributing the cause of an adult child's destructive and anti-social behavior found in Steps Four and Five.

Tony believed that the AA-adapted Steps created a gross vulnerability for adult children in Steps Eight and Nine. In these amends Steps, Tony believed, the adult child could be sent to make amends to violent or abusive parents still in denial about the harm they had rained upon the adult child.

Tony recalled the odd looks he received from AA members as he raised these questions. "They were looking at me like I was a little crazy."

Tony advocated for a departure from the AA Steps. In 1979, with the help of Don D., Tony wrote his own variation of the Twelve Steps, which he believed more fitting for adult children and victims of abuse. These Steps encouraged taking a "blameless" inventory of the parents and focusing on self love. During the next 10 years, Tony refined these Steps, publishing another version of the Twelve Steps in his 1991 book "The Laundry List." In the end, Tony's version of the Twelve Steps balanced taking a "blameless" inventory of the parents with a focused program of self-love and self-forgiveness.

In 1984, the ACA fellowship voted to become an autonomous Twelve Steps and Twelve Traditions fellowship, using the AA-adapted Steps. This was seven years before Tony published his version of the Steps. Some ACA groups use Tony's Steps and his book, which is allowable under the suggested ACA literature policy.

For the most part, the AA-adapted Steps have been accepted by the ACA fellowship. ACA members, in practice, have modified them to allow the person to look at the family system, beginning in Step One. This family history or inventory includes the behavior of the parents in addition to naming family roles, dysfunctional rules, and abuse. Meanwhile, counselors and informed sponsors are aware of the vulnerability an adult child faces when considering a possible amends to a sick or abusive parent or parents. Some parents are too dangerous or too sick to approach.

In ACA today, the adult child looks at the patterns of family dysfunction and is encouraged to talk about all aspects of the childhood in ACA meetings and with a sponsor or informed counselor. At the same time, the AA-adapted Steps require the individual to inventory one's self and to change destructive behavior. We take responsibility for our behavior knowing that some of that behavior was handed off to us by our parents.

Stepping Aside

At one point, Tony stepped away from the fellowship he helped found because he felt as if he was being exalted or placed in a position of authority. At the end of his life, however, Tony continued to practice ACA principles and pass on ACA recovery. In the last days of life, he answered calls from adult children seeking help. The following is a quote from 1992.

I never expected ACoA to become a worldwide program when it began. We were working on trying to keep a little meeting going back then. The first time I got a glimpse that ACoA had national or international possibilities was when Barry said to copyright The Laundry List. He did foresee this, but I had no idea. I felt The Laundry List should be anonymous at that time and never copyrighted it.

The concept of Adult Child came from the Alateens who began the Hope for Adult Children of Alcoholics meeting. The original members of our fellowship, who were over eighteen years old, were adults; but as children they grew up in alcoholic homes. Adult Child also means that when confronted, we regress to a stage in our childhood.

There are three parts of me: the Higher Power, me, and Little Tony. I have to love Little Tony – my child within – if I'm ever going to unite with God. Little Tony is my connection to God.

ACA Came West (1976–1979): Jack E.

Jack E. is considered one of the founding members of ACA in California. ACoA and ACA are the same program. ACA was incorporated in California. ACA groups tend to be located on the West Coast while ACoA groups tend to be established on the East Coast and some Midwestern cities.

Jack's story:

My family was dysfunctional. I believe that alcoholism is truly a family disease. Untreated, it affects all members of the family. Denial was practiced in my family. My mother and father were both children of alcoholic fathers. I did not learn of my grandfathers' alcoholism from either of my parents. Alcoholism was considered then, as it is now by most people, to be shameful. It was not considered to be a disease, but a weakness, so the drinking by my grandfathers was never mentioned.

I grew up to be an alcoholic who drank and married other alcoholics. I was not conscious of wanting to rescue and be rescued, but those feelings were below the surface.

My father was not an alcoholic. My mother was an alcoholic and child of an alcoholic. She was in a severe accident when she was in her teens and was not, in the doctor's opinion, able to survive childbirth. Nevertheless, my mother had two children, a high-risk, heroic act of an adult child of an alcoholic. My mother was a relatively young woman when she died from an accident associated with alcohol. I believe that alcoholism contributed to the accident that killed her. She was not intoxicated at the time of her fatal accident, but without the effects of alcoholism, she would not have had that accident.

In 1976, a friend from AA invited me to speak at a meeting of young Al-Anon members. These members, in their early twenties, decided they were not getting enough solution from a meeting that primarily dealt with spousal problems. I spoke at several meetings, but failed to grasp the issues. After all, I was not in my early twenties. I was interested but not deeply involved. I knew some of the young people from regular Al-Anon. Sympathy existed in my heart, but not empathy.

In late 1978, empathy blossomed. By that time, the young people permitted "older" people to join them in their spiritual investigation. I was holding down two jobs, so my attendance at meetings was limited. My interest became passion by the time I accepted employment in Los Angeles, California, in November 1979.

There was no ACA meeting to attend in L.A. In AA and Al-Anon I shared my experience, strength, and hope, but something was missing. I had discovered a hole in my center, and it hurt. In August 1980, I invited some people from Al-Anon to join me at my home in Santa Monica. We conducted a "feasibility study." We took a look at our family lives, our relationships, and our parents that first evening and decided to formalize the meeting.

I presented The Laundry List that was used at New York meetings of children of alcoholics; no formal name or initials existed at that point. The group did not approve the language on the list of identifying characteristics, and I promised to present a revised list called "The Problem" at our second meeting.

Everyone was surprised to see our numbers had doubled at the second meeting. They doubled again at the third meeting.

In the beginning we weren't sure that anyone shared our curiosity, let alone commitment, but they did. We outgrew my apartment, then outgrew the church in Westwood, and continued to grow. Other meetings sprang up. In sixty days, meetings spread to Hollywood, Mar Vista, and Rolling Hills.

I served as the "Thomas Jefferson" in the beginning. Many drafts of "The Problem" and "The Solution" were presented, often with only a few words changed from the original. We felt a deep commitment to unconditional love of self and parent and Higher Power, just as ACAs do today.

As I write this, an ACA book is envisioned. So is a seminar on the Steps. Both are new undertakings, another part of the constant rebirth of the love reflected in our ACA program and principles. The outreach to the world began very modestly. We did the best we could in the beginning. We overcame a lot of obstacles. We could only dream of the activities you continue to create, year after year. It's just amazing, and it's great.

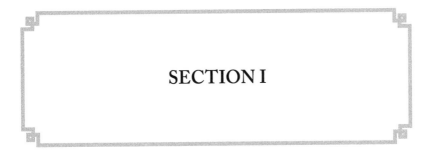

SECTION I

Chapter 1

The Laundry List – Problem

*A*CA cofounder Tony A. wrote the 14 Traits of an adult child of an alcoholic in 1978. When read in New York at the first ACA group, an adult child said: "Oh boy, that's my laundry list!"[†] Since that time, the 14 Traits have been referred to as The "Laundry List."

From the descriptive power of the traits, ACA was born and created. In just 260 words, The Laundry List describes the thinking and personality of an adult reared in a dysfunctional family. A sample of the 14 Traits reveals how we judge ourselves and others harshly. We remain in destructive or loveless relationships because we fear abandonment.

The term "adult child" means that we respond to adult interactions with the fear and self-doubt learned as children. This undercurrent of hidden fear can sabotage our choices and relationships. We can appear outwardly confident while living with a constant question of our worth.

In ACA, we believe the experiences of growing up in a dysfunctional family affect us as adults. Many of us have had successful careers but still felt disconnected from life. Some of us have experienced regular failure. We lived with a self-created calamity mixed with self-harm and self-hate. Many of us have been in the middle of success and failure. We have had fine jobs and homes, but we wondered why others appeared to be enjoying life while we guessed at what was normal. We felt like we were on the outside looking in. Whatever our path, we found no lasting help until we found ACA.

Since its first writing, The Laundry List has been adapted by various groups and authors. West Coast ACA groups placed The Laundry List in a narrative form known as The Problem, which is read at the beginning of ACA meetings throughout the fellowship. The Laundry List traits are also known as the common behavior characteristics among many ACA members.

In this chapter, we offer the original Laundry List as written by our primary founder. We are not eliminating The Problem read at ACA meetings. The 14 Traits are part of ACA's foundational language that creates identity among ACA's varied membership. Adult children who are codependents, drug addicts, food addicts, gamblers, sex addicts, and workaholics relate equally to the personality traits of The Laundry List. It is not uncommon for an adult child to be acting out in one or more addictions or compulsions at the same time. This "addictiveness" is our nature as adult children.

Additionally, The Laundry List attracts adult children from families in which addiction was not an issue. Some of these families include parents who were emotionally ill, hypochondriac, hypercritical, perfectionistic, ultra-religious, or sexually abusive. Adults who have been adopted or who grew up in foster homes relate to The Laundry List as well and recover in ACA.

Many members say The Laundry List is a powerful piece of literature that raised the veil of denial they had lived under as adults. Scholarly studies have shown that many of the traits are specific to adult children. We believe the list is a gateway into a life of clarity and self-acceptance.

The Laundry List
Characteristics of an Adult Child

1

1) We became isolated and afraid of people and authority figures.

2) We became approval seekers and lost our identity in the process.

3) We are frightened by angry people and any personal criticism.

4) We either become alcoholics, marry them or both, or find another compulsive personality such as a workaholic to fulfill our sick abandonment needs.

5) We live life from the viewpoint of victims, and we are attracted by that weakness in our love and friendship relationships.

6) We have an overdeveloped sense of responsibility, and it is easier for us to be concerned with others rather than ourselves; this enables us not to look too closely at our own faults, etc.

7) We get guilt feelings when we stand up for ourselves instead of giving in to others.

8) We became addicted to excitement.

9) We confuse love and pity and tend to "love" people we can "pity" and "rescue."

10) We have "stuffed" our feelings from our traumatic childhoods and have lost the ability to feel or express our feelings because it hurts so much (Denial).

11) We judge ourselves harshly and have a very low sense of self-esteem.

1

12) We are dependent personalities who are terrified of abandonment and will do anything to hold on to a relationship in order not to experience painful abandonment feelings, which we received from living with sick people who were never there emotionally for us.

13) Alcoholism is a family disease; we became para-alcoholics (codependents) [†] and took on the characteristics of that disease even though we did not pick up the drink.

14) Para-alcoholics (codependents) are reactors rather than actors.

Adult Children, Codependents

These 14 Traits describe a personality who cannot truly love another person or truly allow a Higher Power to work in his or her life. As adult children, we have great difficulty accepting love as well. These are not shaming statements or predictions of doom. As children and teens, we were not given a true or consistent example of love. So how can we know love or recognize it as adults? Our parents shamed us or belittled us for being vulnerable children. In their own confusion, they called it love. They passed on what was done to them, thinking they were being caring parents. What many adult children described as love or intimacy before reaching ACA was actually codependence or rigid control.

The adult child syndrome is somewhat interchangeable with the diagnosis of codependence. There are many definitions for codependence; however, the general consensus is that codependent people tend to focus on the wants and needs of others rather than their own. By doing so, the codependent or adult child can avoid his or her own feelings of low self-worth. This is the sixth trait of the 14 Traits. A codependent focuses on others and their problems to such an extent that the codependent's life is often adversely affected. In addition to emotional suffering, codependents can suffer from serious or chronic physical illnesses. The illnesses include stomach problems, severe headaches, insomnia, colon problems, and skin ailments in addition to other physical conditions.

In ACA, we realize we could not have reacted another way given our dysfunctional upbringing. As children, we focused on the odd or neglectful nature of our parents' behavior. We mistakenly thought we caused their moods or attitudes or could do something to change circumstances. We did not realize that we were children and that adults were responsible for their own feelings and actions. Many of us thought we caused our parents' addiction. We took responsibility for their drinking or drugging, thinking we could make them stop, slow down, and eventually love us. As children, we took responsibility for our parents' anger, rage, blame, or pitifulness. We were children, but we unknowingly took responsibility for our parents' feelings and poor behavior. This mistaken perception, born in childhood, is the root of our codependent behavior as adults. By living with a blaming or shaming parent, we developed a dependent, false self. Our false self constantly seeks outward affection, recognition, or praise, but we secretly believe we don't deserve it. Meanwhile, the Inner Child is driven inward into hiding. The false self is the adult child personality expressed in the 14 Traits of The Laundry List.

Many adult children arrive at their adult years with an over-developed sense of responsibility, which they communicate as love or nurturing care. This behavior is a disguise to get the love we never received as children. Before recovery, many adult children had relationships in which they thought they were in love with another person. In reality, they were trapping or manipulating that person to extract affection. This behavior creates the response we fear most – abandonment.

1

By attending ACA meetings, we realize we developed these characteristics to survive our home life. Before recovery, our experience shows that adult children use the 14 Traits frequently. We combine them to meet the demands of life. For instance, a person might fear his boss (Trait 1) and engage in approval seeking behavior (Trait 2) while accepting a high level of abuse on a job that he would feel guilty about leaving (Trait 7). Feeling like a victim, (Trait 5), he goes home to his alcoholic wife (Trait 4) and stuffs his feelings (Trait 10). He takes on an inordinate amount of house chores by being overly responsible (Trait 6). He wants to leave his wife, but he has confused love and pity and fears facing the abandonment that will come from walking away (Traits 9 and 12). The cycle is repeated the next day, the next week, and the next year. The traits are passed on to children in the home.

While these characteristics stunted our emotional and spiritual lives, we must realize they protected us as children. We grip these common behaviors tightly as adults. They are not easily surrendered even though they create the internal pain and isolation that has driven us to Adult Children of Alcoholics. We urge you to be gentle with yourself as you begin to address the most troublesome traits. There is another way to live.

The "Other" Laundry List

Before we write in greater detail about the original Laundry List, we must note that most of the 14 Traits have an opposite. Our experience shows that the opposites are just as damaging as the counterpart. For example, if we feared authority figures, as the first trait suggests, we also became authority figures to our children, spouses, or others. When we stop and think about it, we realize we were feared as authority figures. If we lived our life from the viewpoint of a victim (Trait 5), then many of us have become persecutors or perpetrators who created victims. If we got guilt feelings for standing up for ourselves (Trait 7), we could also feel guiltless by shaming someone verbally. We could take from others what was not ours without feeling guilty.

These examples represent the reverse side of The Laundry List. Many of us would like to deny that we have been a dominating authority figure, but we have. We don't like to think about victimizing others or projecting blame onto them, but we have. Many of us have reenacted what was done to us, thinking we were justified. Some of us have engaged in fights that go beyond mere words. We have slapped and slugged others in a fit of rage. Some of us have used a violent cursing with threats of physical harm to intimidate others. A few adult children have willingly committed crimes. We have stolen merchandise, written bogus checks, or embezzled money for various reasons that don't hold weight in the light of our explanations. We can feel shame or disgust when we think about our actions. This is healthy guilt, which is different from the toxic guilt that we were raised under.

Our behaviors, whether we are a victim or creating victims, highlight an ACA truism: "ACA is not an easy program to work." Yet, the effort it takes to work ACA is far less than the effort it takes to live in codependence or trying to control others or circumstances out of our control. If we apply half the effort to ACA that we apply to living codependently, we will see amazing results. We will find clarity and self-worth.

We will need help. We will need acceptance from others when we cannot accept ourselves. We do not need to shame ourselves or dive into self-condemnation, but we must be honest about our behavior. We sometimes need a reminder that we are acting destructively and should consider rethinking our behavior.

ACA allows us to admit our behavior in a safe place without judgment from others. By working the ACA program, we learn to recognize when we are thinking like a victim or persecutor and to talk about it. We reparent ourselves with gentleness and self-love. We become openminded to the idea that we can change with time and with help.

Chapter One

Reviewing The Laundry List

1

The following text offers greater detail on the characteristics of an adult child. Some traits are presented together to show their possible combinations.

Trait 1:   *We became isolated and afraid of people and authority figures.*

Adult children often live a secret life of fear. Fear, or sometimes terror, is one of the connecting threads that links the 14 Traits together. Two of the first three traits describe our fear of people. While many adult children appear cheerful, helpful, or self-sufficient, most live in fear of their parents and spouses in addition to fearing an employer. Others are constantly afraid of failing finances, imagined health problems, or world disasters. They have a sense of impending doom or that nothing seems to work out. Even the seemingly bold adult child who shows bravado can be covering up a deep sense of feeling unsafe or unlovable.

At the core of these thoughts is usually the fear of being shamed or abandoned. Shame is the deep sense that our souls are inherently flawed. Abandonment means more than being left alone or left at a doorstep.

Shame and abandonment are two of the most identifiable traits of a dysfunctional home. Among other factors, they are two of the conditions that help produce an adult child whether alcohol or drugs are in the home or not. Adult children from all family types not only feel shame deeply, but we believe we are shame. In some cases, adult-child shame is so pervasive that it can paralyze the person's body and mind. Adult children have described "shame attacks," which can cause physical illness or an age regression. During age regression, an adult child can feel physically small. Even vision can be affected when shame is released into the body. An intense shame episode can cause room dimensions to appear warped and lighting to appear odd. Many adult children have difficulty fully breathing during these moments.

Abandonment can take many forms. One form is as simple as the parent leaving the child alone without returning. Or it can involve parental perfectionism in which a child's behavior never measures up. Parents abandon their children when they fail to praise or recognize a child's true effort to please the parent. Instead most parents are quick to criticize and correct a child's behavior but rarely find time to praise the child or to build confidence for good choices. As a result, most adult children have a critical parent inside. The critical, inner parent berates or undermines the person at almost every turn. This critical inner parent is a form of self-abandonment.

Shame and abandonment. That is how our dysfunctional families controlled us as children. We came to see our parents as authority figures who could not be trusted.

We transfer that fear to our adult lives, and we fear our employers, certain relatives, and group situations. We fear authority figures or become an authority figure.

Trait 2:   *We became approval seekers and lost our identity in the process.*

Trait 3:   *We are frightened by angry people and any personal criticism.*

Becoming a people pleaser is one of the solutions that adult children apply to avoid being criticized, shamed, or abandoned. Adult children also attempt to disarm angry or frightening people with approval seeking behavior. We give up some of our identity when we engage in such behavior. We believe that we will be safe and never abandoned if we are "nice" and if we never show anger. However, being a people-pleaser comes with a heavy price. When we please others at the expense of our feelings or needs, we invariably end up hurting ourselves and our relationships. Many adult children vacillate between being sugary sweet and explosively angry. They often explode, feel deep remorse, and

1

promise to change only to repeat the cycle. Many adult children swallow their anger only to produce cases of depression or panic attacks. Whether explosively angry or routinely sorrowful, these behaviors are a vicious cycle that harms our relationships.

At the core, people-pleasing is dishonest and creates the wrong foundation for a meaningful relationship that most adult children really want deep down inside.

Many adult children constantly survey their homes or relationships, looking for situations that could lead to shame or some other public act of criticism. In addition to fearing shame and abandonment, our hypervigilance is intensified by what many therapists call Post-Traumatic Stress Disorder. PTSD is most often associated with combat veterans or survivors of a traumatic event such as a car wreck or a catastrophic event. However, adult children suffer from PTSD as well. A PTSD event or events produce such a high state of threat or danger that experts believe it changes the body chemistry. Long after the threat has passed, the PTSD sufferer remains on "alert" to ward off future events that could retrigger the fear of the previous fearful event.

Trait 4:   *We either become alcoholics, marry them or both, or find another compulsive personality such as a workaholic to fulfill our sick abandonment needs.*

Trait 9:   *We confuse love and pity and tend to "love" people we can "pity" and "rescue."*

Trait 13:   *Alcoholism is a family disease; we became para-alcoholics and took on the characteristics of that disease even though we did not pick up the drink.*

Since alcoholism is a family disease, all family members are affected without having to take a drink. With an amazing predictability, the children grow up to be addicted or marry an addicted or compulsive person. Many adult children become addicted to alcohol or other drugs, thinking their lives will be different than their parents. However, an addicted adult child often surpasses the parents' dysfunctional behavior in drug use and actions. ACA works best for those refraining from alcohol, drug, and prescription medication abuse. We cannot work an effective program if we are stuffing our feelings with alcohol or drugs. At the same time, ACA members should consult their health care professionals about their needs for medication. Any decision to engage in or abstain from pharmaceutical therapy should be discussed with your doctor.

Adult children intuitively link up with other adult children in relationships and social settings. As bizarre as it sounds, many adult children are attracted to an abusive, addicted person because that person resembles an addictive or abusive parent. Before recovery, many adult children tend to choose people who will abandon them so they can feel the familiar pain of being unwanted. We can also switch from feeling like a victim to reacting like a persecutor.

Because we confuse love and pity and have an over-developed sense of responsibility, our abusive relationships "fit" with a subconscious set of traits we are looking for in a mate or significant other. While many adult children would protest that they would not choose such a person, they are actually left without a choice until they get help in ACA. Before recovery, if the adult child manages to leave their unhappy relationship, the person usually selects the same type of abandoning and abusive person in the next relationship. Without help, we are doomed to seek out people who treat us as we were treated as children. Traits 4, 9, and 13 are a factor in these decisions.

1

Trait 5: *We live life from the viewpoint of victims, and we are attracted by that weakness in our love and friendship relationships.*

Trait 6: *We have an overdeveloped sense of responsibility, and it is easier for us to be concerned with others rather than ourselves; this enables us not to look too closely at our own faults.*

Our experience shows that we often lived as victims. By living as victims or with victim characteristics, adult children seek to control others and ward off potentially shaming or abandoning situations. Taking the victim position can be shrewdly manipulative for an adult child who knows how to use it; however, being a victim loses its power when overused. People tire of such behavior and tend to move on. This causes the adult child to select another victim to reenact the behavior. Many adult children, who practice being a victim, often switch over to the super-responsible role in preparation for a return to the victim role. By taking on too much work and responsibility, the person can vault into a fit of rage, collapse, or isolation. The person hopes to garner sympathy and pity. The victim reemerges.

Playing the victim or being overly responsible allows the adult child to avoid focusing on himself or herself. Both roles are saturated with codependent avoidance of feelings and being responsible for one's own feelings. By concerning ourselves with others and their chaos, we avoid doing anything about our own lives. By being overly concerned about others, adult children wrongly think they are involved in life. In reality they are missing life. The enmeshed, codependent ACA can be so wrapped up in another person's thoughts and actions that the adult child has no inner life or outer support when the relationship wanes. Codependent ACAs describe feeling lethargic, disoriented, and hopeless when their partners are gone. This is the high price for focusing on others.

Trait 7:   We get guilt feelings when we stand up for ourselves instead of giving in to others.

Trait 11:   We judge ourselves harshly and have a very low sense of self-esteem.

Who could have his home burglarized and feel like he or she did something wrong? An adult child.

Who could feel guilty about asking a cashier to correct a mistake when the cashier handed back incorrect change? An adult child.

Before recovery, most adult children assume they are wrong whatever the situation might be. If a mistake is made on the job, the adult child takes responsibility for it. If someone feels upset, we think we might have done something to cause the feelings in another. On the flip side we can blame others and avoid taking responsibility for our errors or poor behavior. We can judge ourselves harshly and place blame on ourselves and others willingly when such blame is not necessary.

Because of our shaming childhoods, adult children doubt and blame themselves in a knee-jerk reaction that is predictable and consistent yet rarely observed until recovery is encountered. We react instead of thinking about options and then acting.

The guilty feelings we encounter when standing up for ourselves have their roots in not being allowed to ask for what we needed as children. Judging ourselves harshly comes from abusive and hypercritical parents. As children, we went without basic needs or praise. We were vulnerable children, but we were shamed when we expressed a legitimate need. "You are so selfish," our parents said. "Do you ever think of anyone else but yourself? Do you think I am made of money?"

As adults, we remember such interactions with our parents. We refeel the pain of being dismissed or shamed when speaking up for a want or need. As adults, many of us avoid asking for

1

what we need to avoid old pain. Others manipulate to get what they think they want. They are unhappy a lot. Even when we get what we think we want, we realize it is not enough again.

Trait 8: We became addicted to excitement.

When ACA founder Tony A. wrote this trait, he originally stated: "We became addicted to fear" but changed the wording to "addicted to excitement" for clarity. Either way — excitement or fear — adult children use both to mimic the feeling of being alive when in reality they are recreating a scene from their family of origin. Gossip, dramatic scenes, pending financial failure, or failing health are often the turmoil that adult children create in their lives to feel connected to reality. While such behavior is rarely stated as such, these behaviors are an "addiction" to excitement or fear.

Because we were raised in chaotic or controlling homes, our internal compass is oriented toward excitement, pain, and shame. This inner world can be described as an "inside drug store." The shelves are stocked with bottles of excitement, toxic shame, self-hate, self-doubt, and stress. Other shelves include canisters of lust, fear, and worry. As odd as it sounds, we can seek out situations so we can experience a "hit" of one of these inner drugs. We can create chaos to feel excitement. Or we procrastinate on the job to feel stress. Before finding ACA, we picked relationships that triggered our childhood unrest because it felt normal to be upset, persecuted, or shamed. During these moments, we thought we felt alive with excitement, but in reality we were staying just ahead of our aching childhood. Our actions as adults represent our addiction to excitement and a variety of inner drugs created to survive childhood. Many of our repressed feelings have actually been changed into inner drugs that drive us to harm ourselves or others. Without help, we cannot recognize serenity or true safety. Because our homes were never consistently safe or settled, we have no true reference point for these states of being. Without ACA, we can view emotionally healthy people as boring or confusing.

Trait 10: *We have "stuffed" our feelings from our traumatic childhoods and have lost the ability to feel or express our feelings because it hurts so much (Denial).*

Trait 10 highlights the body feature of the disease of family dysfunction. The ACA disease model addresses the body, mind, and spirit of the adult child. Clinical research strongly suggests that childhood trauma or neglect are stored in the tissue of the children. The emotional or physical trauma does not go away without an effort to address the original cause. In some cases the stored hurt creates a dissociative effect in the adult. The adult child has dissociated from his or her body. The person appears to function quite normally in society; however, the stored trauma is there, creating bodily ailments that can appear as depression, panic disorders, hyperactivity, or sloth. Because of this storing or dissociation, many adult children are truly baffled when a counselor suggests the person is holding down feelings or avoiding feelings.

Trait 12: *We are dependent personalities who are terrified of abandonment and will do anything to hold on to a relationship in order not to experience painful abandonment feelings, which we received from living with sick people who were never there emotionally for us.*

Trait 14: *Para-alcoholics (codependents) are reactors rather than actors.*

1

Adult children are dependent personalities, who view abuse and inappropriate behavior as normal. Or if they complain about the abuse, they feel powerless to do anything about it. Without help, adult children confuse love and pity and pick partners they can pity and rescue. The pay off is a feeling of being needed or avoiding feeling alone for another day. Such relationships create reactors, who feel powerless to change their situation. They freely use the 14 Traits of an adult child to negotiate for crumbs of attention. Others use the traits to create smothering over-dependence by their partners. Until they find recovery, they lack the language and support needed to recognize the problem. A proven solution awaits in ACA.

Am I an Adult Child?

The following questions will help you decide if alcoholism or other family dysfunction existed in your family. If your parents did not drink, your grandparents may have drank and passed on the disease of family dysfunction to your parents. If alcohol or drugs were not a problem, your home may have been chaotic, unsafe, and lacking nurture like many alcoholic homes.

The following questions offer an insight into some ways children are affected by growing up with a problem drinker even years after leaving the home. The questions also apply to adults growing up in homes where food, sex, workaholism, or ultra-religious abuse occurred. Foster children, now adults, relate to many of these questions.

1. Do you recall anyone drinking or taking drugs or being involved in some other behavior that you now believe could be dysfunctional?

2. Did you avoid bringing friends to your home because of drinking or some other dysfunctional behavior in the home?

3. Did one of your parents make excuses for the other parent's drinking or other behaviors?

4. Did your parents focus on each other so much that they seemed to ignore you?

5. Did your parents or relatives argue constantly?

6. Were you drawn into arguments or disagreements and asked to choose sides with one parent or relative against another?

7. Did you try to protect your brothers or sisters against drinking or other behavior in the family?

8. As an adult, do you feel immature? Do you feel like you are a child inside?

9. As an adult, do you believe you are treated like a child when you interact with your parents? Are you continuing to live out a childhood role with the parents?

10. Do you believe that it is your responsibility to take care of your parents' feelings or worries? Do other relatives look to you to solve their problems?

11. Do you fear authority figures and angry people?

12. Do you constantly seek approval or praise but have difficulty accepting a compliment when one comes your way?

13. Do you see most forms of criticism as a personal attack?

14. Do you over commit yourself and then feel angry when others do not appreciate what you do?

15. Do you think you are responsible for the way another person feels or behaves?

16. Do you have difficulty identifying feelings?

1

17. Do you focus outside yourself for love or security?

18. Do you involve yourself in the problems of others? Do you feel more alive when there is a crisis?

19. Do you equate sex with intimacy?

20. Do you confuse love and pity?

21. Have you found yourself in a relationship with a compulsive or dangerous person and wonder how you got there?

22. Do you judge yourself without mercy and guess at what is normal?

23. Do you behave one way in public and another way at home?

24. Do you think your parents had a problem with drinking or taking drugs?

25. Do you think you were affected by the drinking or other dysfunctional behavior of your parents or family?

If you answered yes to three or more of these questions, you may be suffering from the effects of growing up in an alcoholic or other dysfunctional family. As The Laundry List states, you can be affected even if you did not take a drink. Please read Chapter Two to learn more about these effects.

END NOTES

†ON PAGE 3: "Oh boy, that's my laundry list!" was said by Barry at the first ACoA group in the world. (*The Laundry List: The ACoA Experience* by Tony A. with Dan F., 1991, HCI Publications.)

†ON PAGE 6: Para-alcoholic was an early term for those living with an alcoholic and affected by the alcoholic's behavior. The term evolved to co-alcoholic and codependent. ACA founders use para-alcoholism to identify the process by which we acquired certain traits by growing up in an alcoholic family. These are The Laundry List traits, which are acquired in childhood and articulated in adulthood as codependence or unhealthy dependence.

Chapter 2

"It Will Never Happen to Me"

$\mathcal{M}$ost adult children grow up with a pledge they have made to themselves. For some the pledge is a secret promise that is never shared with anyone else. For others, it is a sentence shouted in the storm of a family argument. The pledge is this: "I will never be like my parents. It will never happen to me. I will not treat my children or my spouse in the manner that my family treated me. I will not hit anyone or argue with anyone. I will not be an alcoholic."

There are variations of this pledge, which include a promise to never marry an alcoholic or dysfunctional person. But we do. Some of us have had numerous dysfunctional marriages or relationships before we stopped to consider what we were doing. We had forgotten our promise to ourselves, or we denied that our behavior paralleled the behavior of our parents. This chapter will deal with our promise to be different than our parents, grandparents, or legal guardian. As adults, we may have avoided adopting some parental behaviors, but we passed on shame, self-doubt, and codependence perfectly to our children. Some of us may have avoided abusing others physically or verbally. Yet, our children and relationships were still mired in our dysfunction. We recreated the abandonment and loss of our own childhood. In our relationships, we picked people we could rescue or perpetrate against. We also picked people we could act out our victim role toward. Some of us blatantly abused

2

others in the same manner we were abused or belittled as children. But this is not the end of the road for us. We can change. ACA offers much hope.

Internalizing Our Parents

Family dysfunction is a disease that affects everyone in the family. Taking a drink is not necessary to be affected. This is an ACA axiom, and it serves as a basis for our First Step. The effects of growing up in a dysfunctional family force us to develop survival traits that are known as The Laundry List (Problem). Since the disease of family dysfunction is generational, these traits also represent the internalization of our parents' behavior. As much as we would like to deny it, we have become our parents. If we have succeeded in acting differently than them, we still passed on unwanted traits handed off to us by our parents. We unknowingly passed them on to our children. We did not mean to do this. We tried to be different. We made a pledge.

We used denial to forget our pledge and the fact that we had internalized our parents.[†] Denial is the glue that holds together a dysfunctional home. Family secrets, ignored feelings, and predictable chaos are part of a dysfunctional family system. The system allows abuse or other unhealthy behaviors to be tolerated at harmful levels. Through repetition, the abuse is considered normal by those in the family. Because the dysfunction seemed normal or tolerable, the adult child can deny that anything unpleasant happened in childhood. At the same time, there are many adult children who can recount the horrors of their dysfunctional upbringing in great detail. Yet, many do so without feeling or without connecting the deep sense of loss that each event brought. This is a denial of feelings identified in Trait 10 of The Laundry List (Problem).

These forms of denial allow the adult child to sanitize the family story when talking about the growing-up years. Denial can also lead us to believe that we have escaped our family dysfunction when we carried it into adulthood. Step One of the Twelve Steps states that we are "powerless over the effects" of growing up in a dysfunctional family. The Step calls us to admit that our behavior today is grounded in the events that occurred in childhood. Much of that behavior mirrors the actions and thoughts of the dysfunctional parents, grandparents, or caregivers. Once we come out of denial, we realize we have internalized our parents' behavior. We have internalized their perfectionism, control, dishonesty, self-righteousness, rage, pessimism, and judgmentalness. Whatever the pattern might be, we realize we have internalized our parents. Their behavior and thinking are our behavior and thinking if we are honest about our lives.

It is important to note that we have taken in or internalized both parents. This includes the parent who appears more functional compared to the alcoholic or chemically addicted parent. Our experience shows that the "functional" or nonalcoholic parent passes on just as many traits as the identified alcoholic. This "para-alcoholic" parent also passes on his or her pattern of inside "drugging" as well. The para-alcoholic (the codependent) is driven by fear, excitement, and pain from the inside. The biochemical surge and cascade of inner "drugs" that accompany these states of distress in this parent can impact children as profoundly as outside substances. Our experience shows that the nondrinking parent's reaction to these inside drugs affects the children just as the alcoholic's drinking affects them. We realize this seems technical, but it is important to understand if we are to comprehend the reach of a dysfunctional upbringing. As children, we were affected by the alcoholic drinking from without and by the para-alcoholic drugs from within. We believe that the long-term effects of fear transferred to us by a nonalcoholic parent can match the damaging effects of alcohol. This is why many of us can temporarily abstain from other addictive behaviors after growing up, but be driven by inner drugs that can bring difficulties as we attempt to recover. Our para-alcoholism of fear and distorted thinking seems to drive our switching from one addictive behavior to another as we try to make changes in our lives.

Chapter Two

Another way to think about how we acquired para-alcoholism as children is like this. The alcoholic can be removed from the family by divorce or separation, but nothing in the home really changes. The alcohol abuse or other dysfunction is gone, but the home remains fearful and controlling. Boundaries are unclear. The children don't talk about feelings. They either become enmeshed with the nondrinking parent or alienated from him or her. The rules of "don't talk, don't trust, and don't feel" apply even with the alcohol or other dysfunction removed. The inside drugs of the para-alcoholic are at work, affecting the children. The nondrinking parent's fear, excitement, and pain are affecting the children and are transferred to the children. This is the internalization of the parent's feelings and behavior in one of its purest forms.

Many adult children express anger at the nonalcoholic parent for not protecting them or not removing them from the dysfunctional situation. We felt abandoned watching this parent remain absorbed by the alcoholic's behavior. Ironically, many of us hold more resentment toward the nondrinking parent than the alcoholic parent.

From the nonalcoholic parent we learn helplessness, worry, black-and-white thinking, being a victim, and self-hate. We learn rage, pettiness, and passive-aggressive thinking. From this parent, we learn to doubt our reality as children. Many times we have gone to our nonalcoholic parent and expressed feelings of fear or shame. Many times this parent has dismissed our feelings. We have been called selfish or too sensitive when objecting to our drinking parent's behavior. In some cases, this parent defended or excused the alcoholic's behavior.

The damage that some nonalcoholic parents can do through inaction or by failing to remove the children from the dysfunctional home boggles the mind. Some of these parents have ignored sexual abuse within their homes. In some cases, a child has been accused of being dishonest when the child tried to tell the nondrinking parent about the sexual abuse he or she was facing.

This is difficult to think about or to accept, but for many of us it is true.[1]

From the nonalcoholic parent, we learned to accept abusive or neglectful behavior as a natural part of life. For example, during an argument, some of us left or f led the home with the nonalcoholic parent only to return in a few days as if nothing had happened. From this behavior, we got the message that it was normal to push aside our fear and return to our abusive or shaming parent. As a result, we can have great difficulty walking away from unfulfilling relationships as adults. We know in our minds that we should leave, but it "feels" normal to stay. These are just a few of the examples of being infected by the disease of family dysfunction.

In the interest of fairness, we must realize that our parents passed on what was done to them. They are adult children as well. We are not blaming them for being powerless over the effects of family dysfunction. In most cases, the treatment that they handed out is the treatment they received growing up. Our parents internalized their parents. This has to be true if we are to believe that family dysfunction is passed down from one generation to the next.

Our fairness in looking at our family must also extend to parental alcoholism. If our parents or grandparents are active in alcoholism or addiction, we are not blaming them for that as well. We must understand that our parents are powerless over alcohol and that their lives are unmanageable. This is the disease of alcoholism, which affects a person in body, mind, and spirit. Our parents can suffer from an obsession or compulsion to drink that always overpowers them unless they get help. Some of us have watched our parents or grandparents die agonizingly slow deaths. A few of our parents have been lost to alcoholic insanity or dementia. They have been depraved and pitiful or unapproachable and scary. The alcoholic is powerless over alcohol and has an obsession of the mind to drink or take drugs. The para-alcoholic

[1] While many adult children are sexually abused by a parent, others have been abused by an older brother, sister, or other family member.

2

suffers from a similar condition, yet it is difficult to see since it is on the inside. In essence, the alcoholic and para-alcoholic are the same personality driven by near-identical fear, but one drinks and one does not.

This is where we got confused as children. We thought we were the drinker's problem or some part of it. From the alcoholic's behavior, we assumed that we were no good, unseen, hated, ignored, used, or attacked by the alcoholic because there was something wrong with us. From the para-alcoholic's behavior we assumed we were less important than the drinking. We deduced that we were the problem when in reality the disease of alcoholism was the problem. We take this mistaken belief into adulthood. We can continue to act out our childhood role with our alcoholic parent or someone else. Some of us can remain stuck and feel responsible for our parents on some level. We can act out our role with the nonalcoholic parent as well. If there was dysfunction in the home without alcoholism, we can have the same misperception. We can act out a dysfunctional role with our parents or another person.

Many of us are adults who have not admitted that our parents are alcoholic or that there was dysfunction in the home. Until we do so, we can still feel trapped by our family. We can remain confused about the extent to which we internalized our parents' behavior. We still get pulled into family crises or arguments that lead nowhere. We accept family abuse and neglect, believing we have no choice.

But we are becoming educated about the disease of alcoholism and family dysfunction. We did not cause our parents' drinking, and we cannot control it. Admitting that our parents are alcoholic or addicted does not excuse their behavior or make it less damaging. But we are avoiding an attitude of persecution. In ACA, there is a way to discuss and heal from the events of the past without minimizing these events and without remaining stuck with such memories. ACA offers a proven path that leads to change and a connection to a Higher Power.

Additionally, we must realize that some of our parents and grandparents had positive traits that we internalized as well. Many of our parents had a work ethic, gentle humor, and kindness. They have a selflessness that we can recognize. They taught us right from wrong and how to get along with others. Many of our parents made sacrifices that we benefit from today. The ACA program allows us to acknowledge our parents' support and positive contributions in our lives. With the help of ACA, we are offering our parents fairness as we look at the family system with rigorous honesty. We are looking for the truth so that we can live our own lives with choice and self-confidence. We want to break the cycle of family dysfunction.

Types of Abuse and Neglect

The internalization of our parents' behavior is further brought about by abuse, neglect, or other unhealthy behavior. We believe that hitting, threats, projection, belittlement, and indifference are the delivery mechanisms that deeply insert the disease of family dysfunction within us. We are infected in body, mind, and spirit. Parental abuse and neglect plant the seeds of dysfunction that grow out of control until we get help.

There are different definitions of abuse and neglect or other unhealthy behaviors. Our definition is based on adult children facing their abuse and neglect from childhood. For our purposes abuse can be verbal, nonverbal, emotional, physical, religious, and sexual.

Abuse can be a single traumatic event or it can be cumulative events over time. Some of the signs of abuse and neglect are addiction, codependence, workaholism, and phobias. Because our parents could be chronic worriers or doubters, we can worry obsessively about events that never occur. Regular worrying or anxiety is a sure sign of an internalized parent.

Abuse creates the same feelings of inferiority and constant fear whether it is physical or verbal-emotional abuse. The person who is physically abused and the person who is emotionally abused end up with the same fears, denial, and lost hope. Physical and emotional abuse can both produce post-traumatic stress disorder or stored fear. They create the same wound whether hitting is present or not.

Physical Abuse

Many adult children have been exposed to various forms of physical abuse that include slapping, pinching, slugging, burns, piercing, cutting, and battery. Verbal and emotional abuse usually accompany physical abuse. An amazing number of adult children have been punched and berated by their parents but do not understand this behavior as abuse until finding ACA or an informed counselor. Before finding ACA, many of us believed we deserved what we got or caused the abuse to happen.

Many of us have been severely injured by a rageful or violent parent. Some of our parents have been sent to prison for their abusive crimes. Since abuse is generational, some of us have reenacted the cycle of abuse with our own children. We can carry great shame and despair associated with our behavior. Because we may have tried to change and failed, we can truly believe we are lost souls after an episode of rage. We may have been diagnosed as pathological and unreachable. There is a tired lie that many of us live with: "Batterers rarely change. They cannot control their rage or anger." In ACA, we confront this untruth by offering hope and acceptance. Our experience shows that adult children can change no matter what their dysfunction might be. We have seen miraculous recoveries when the ACA program is worked with willingness and patience.

He Was Abused But Found Out He Did Not Have to Repeat the Vicious Cycle

My father beat my pregnant mother so I have lived with abuse even before birth. I believe that all abuse is physical abuse. Our bodies absorb it. Today when something happens, I feel the same pain that I felt as a child. The experience stays inside my body to be relived again and again. After getting socked across the face and knocked across the room as a child, my body no longer felt the pain of the blow. It made no difference whether I was hit or not. The anticipation of it filled me with terror. When someone raises a hand near me today, I start to cringe. When I see a mother spank her child, I start to cry as if it is happening to me.

In ACA I've discovered I will continue to feel physical pain as long as I am willing to feel it. It stops when I tell the Dad inside my head, "You can't beat me anymore." Memories of physical abuse are stored in my body, both as the receiver of the blows and as a potential perpetrator. I am learning to use my anger constructively so I don't become someone else's abuser.

My Inner Child and I are in the discovery phase on this issue. We know we have been abused. We feel the feelings about that abuse. We are finding new ways to use all the anger constructively. We don't have to recycle it endlessly, and we don't have to hurt someone else with it. We can find good ways to use the energy from the anger instead, until we can hand off our anguish to our Higher Power and forgive those who hurt us.

Verbal and Emotional Abuse

Verbal and emotional abuse can be just as damaging as physical abuse even though there are no visible bruises. The body is badly bruised on the inside. We have been called vulgar names and labeled wrongly. We have been judged as inferior or unintelligent. We have been called no good. Many emotionally abusive parents believe they are disciplining their children with loving instruction. But in reality they are undercutting the child's sense of worth. While the parent seeks to build respect and honesty within the child, the child can feel like a failure.

Many dysfunctional parents use perfectionistic remarks disguised as support to urge a child to do better. For example, comments of perfectionism sound like support, but the child never seems to meet the parent's expectations. This parental behavior is neglectful. The neglect involves the withholding of true praise when the child does meet expectations. Without true praise, the child or teen does not feel valued and safe. The child feels he must perform or do well to earn a parent's love.

Some neglectful parents will use silence to cover up their hurtful behavior. In some cases the parent avoids talking to the child for several days following a family disagreement. Feeling abandoned, the child will apologize even if the parent was clearly hurtful during the argument. This means the parent was clearly wrong, but the child is coerced through silence to apologize.

Adults subjected to this kind of treatment often have difficulty understanding how the verbal and emotional abuse affected them as children and teens. They wonder if they are making a big deal out of nothing, but their addiction, codependence, or many forms of fear are evidence that something occurred before adulthood. They were not born to be addicts or codependents. They had help.

When confronted with the effects of verbal and emotional abuse in ACA, we usually resist. We could not believe that people who said they loved us or cared for us would lie. If we were called lazy, disgraceful, or shameful, it must be true since the words came from the most important people in our lives. If we keep an open mind, we learn that this was verbal abuse presented as love, but a loving parent does not say these things to a child.

The effects of verbal and emotional abuse are hard to comprehend because we never thought to challenge what was said to us or about us until we found ACA. If we were told we were worthless or ignorant as children, we believed it without question. Before finding ACA, we walked about with believed inaccuracies about ourselves from childhood. As part of the internalization process, we began to repeat these inaccuracies to ourselves as teens and adults. After awhile they came to be known as truth when in reality they are not true. We came to believe that we are disgraceful or no good. We believe that something is wrong with us even though we cannot voice what the thing is. With this belief, we can go through our adult lives silently condemning ourselves and doubting ourselves as a normal course of living. We may even begin to act shamefully or outrageously to fulfill our parents' projection that we are bad or inferior. This means the internalization process is complete. We have accepted false labels as truth. We are engaged in thinking or behaviors that support the false labels. But this is not who we are. No matter what we have done, this is not our True Self. ACA helps us find out who we are if we are willing to work the program and talk about what happened to us.

But still, a skeptic of the effects of verbal and emotional abuse might say: "These categories of abuse described by ACA are so general that anyone can qualify as being abused or neglected. It seems like you are saying that anyone who was ever disciplined or corrected by a parent can turn out to be an addict or another addictive type. No parent is perfect. You cannot expect a person to escape childhood without some moments of doubt or fear that are brought by a caring parent who is only human."

To this we say, a caring parent always raises a caring child and adult. A dysfunctional parent always raises a dysfunctional child and adult. There is no gray area here in our experience. Our categories of verbal and emotional abuse are not so broad if we concentrate on the type of abuse and the specific effects on the child. In ACA, we are talking about abuse and neglect that involves belittling, threatening, shaming, hateful, and indifferent behavior by the parents on a regular basis. This behavior produces a felt sense of shame and fear in the child. This type of parenting creates observable behavior that is self-harming and neglectful when the child grows into an adult. These behaviors are codependence, emotional eating, drug abuse, alcoholism, sex addiction, workaholism, debtor's addiction, and gambling addiction. These tend to be the most identifiable behaviors and usually serve as a layer upon other self-harming behaviors. The ACA description of verbal and emotional abuse is based on specific parental behavior with observable results in the adult.

Another skeptic of the effects of verbal and emotional abuse might say: "Yes. My parents could be harsh, but they meant well. They did not mean what they said. I know they loved me and cared about me." In our experience, this kind of selective recall is a form of denial. To think that our parents could shame us or belittle us for being a vulnerable child is too much for us to accept. Like most children, we wanted to believe that our parents cared about us no matter what they said to us. As adults, we search for any kindness our parents might have shown and ignore clear examples of damaging behavior. Societal pressure helps us select the memories that are more presentable. We can fear being labeled as ungrateful or as a grudge holder if we stop to question what happened in the home. So we "forgive and forget," yet, the ingested harms of childhood work behind the scene to sabotage our relationships and careers. Whether we admit it or not the evidence of the childhood verbal abuse is there in our addiction, codependence, or some other method of neglecting ourselves. There can also be chronic depression and extreme anxiety. Some of us can have panic attacks accompanying these behaviors.

We cannot have it both ways. We cannot say that our childhood was perfect, loving, or uneventful and then act out with addiction or other compulsions. People who truly care about themselves will tell you that they learned to do so in childhood. The thought of harming themselves or staying in a controlling relationship does not appeal to them. They do not live as enablers or as people unsure of their purpose in life. If these people could learn to believe in themselves as children, then why is it so hard for us to accept that we learned to disbelieve in ourselves as children? This is near the core of our woundedness. We do not believe in ourselves.

People who truly care for themselves cannot always point to a childhood event that let them know that they were valued by their parents. But their actions show they care about themselves. Conversely, we cannot always point to an incident in our childhood in which we decided we were inferior or defective based on parental messages. Yet, our actions show that we really do not care about ourselves. Despite what we say, we believe that we are incomplete. We compare ourselves to others and usually come up short. There is a hole inside of us that can never be filled with enough food, drugs, sex, work, spending, or gambling. We become more aware of this hole with each failed relationship or job.

If some of us still doubt a connection between childhood events and adult behavior, then why do we identify with a majority of The Laundry List traits? Why do we fear authority figures and remain in unloving relationships when others would leave? Why do we judge ourselves harshly? Why the difficulty identifying feelings or separating our emotions from those of another? Why can't we muster the resolve needed to lay down drugs or other problematic behaviors without switching to another destructive behavior?

If we have related to this chapter so far, we are left with a decision to consider. We either believe that the way we were raised has a direct link to our compulsions and codependence as adults, or we do not believe it. Through denial, we can ignore the evidence and continue to blame others for our decisions and confusion. Yet, if we believe there is a connection, we can choose ACA and pick up the tools of recovery. We can begin the journey toward clarity and being truly responsible for our own lives. If we choose recovery, we need help finding out what happened to us so we can change our thinking and behavior. To make progress, we must want the ACA way of life and all that it has to offer. No one can force us to accept ACA. We have to want it for it to work. ACA is for people who can make the connection between childhood neglect and an adult life of fear and loneliness. ACA works best for people who can name what happened to them and become willing to ask for help.

Chapter Two

They Didn't Leave Marks

Others were physically abused around me in childhood, but I was 'only' emotionally and verbally abused. There wasn't a mark on me. My parents fed us. They kept the lights on and the shingles on the roof. They also verbally assaulted us. Providing the food and shelter for us was a monumental effort, and they let us know loudly we should have been more thankful.

The verbal attacks were demoralizing, and I felt terrible pain and shame because 'nothing' really happened to me. I couldn't validate myself. With no physical marks on my body, no one from the outside world could validate my reality, either. I started to abuse myself as well as others. I thought if I acted crazy enough, someone would know something was wrong. That would validate me. Then I could validate my own belief that I was being abused. It didn't happen that way. People thought I was crazy, and I became even more shame-based. I didn't believe I was abused for a long time. No one would listen to my story, either. I got depressed because I felt I was walking on the shifting sands of reality where I could be certain of nothing. In ACA we spread the message that emotional abuse hurts people, too. I get strong validation from the fellowship. It gives me a sturdy platform on which to stand while I work on my recovery.

No matter what abuse or neglect we endured, ACA helps us figure out what we are carrying inside. We are seeking a full remembrance of the childhood that goes beyond merely recounting the acts of dysfunctional parents. With a full remembrance we revisit the feelings that came with the abuse or hypercritical behavior of the caregivers. We remember the event, and we remember the feelings. We face both with the help of our ACA support group and our Higher Power. By seeking a full remembrance, we break the "don't remember rule" of the family. We begin our grief work that eventually frees us from our compulsive need to control others. We also learn to tell our story with honesty and fairness. We learn to separate ourselves from our parents and find out who we are.

Internalized Modes of Thinking and Acting

For the remainder of this chapter, we will detail four modes of internalized behavior passed on by parents, relatives, or a guardian. We will look at perfectionism, control, all-or-nothing thinking, and judgmentalness, also known as "critical inner parent." These four conditions seem to dominate the ACA personality. After arriving in ACA, we begin to recognize our perfectionism and rigid thinking. If we are honest, we see our control or attempt to control others. Almost all of us can identify a critical inner parent or critical inner voice. This is the voice of self-doubt or self-blame that undermines our relationships and chances of happiness. Recovery from these modes of thinking and behaving can be found in the tools of the ACA program.

We will begin with a look at perfectionism, which can appear as sloth, procrastination, and passive-aggressiveness in addition to perfect acting and thinking. We open the segment on perfectionism with a member sharing his experience on the topic.

Perfectionism
It Did Happen to Me

When I heard that perfectionism was a pattern of my thinking, I didn't think it fit for me. I was never overly neat. I performed below my potential. I didn't think I was judgmental of others. I thought a perfectionist was someone who never made a mistake or who was obsessively clean.

In ACA, I began to realize that I was filled with perfectionism and an inner critic. I could hear my father's critical voice. It would be in my head or in something I would say. There was a lack of self-acceptance in almost every sentence I said. Nothing I did or thought was good enough. I could always find something wrong with what I had done at work or something I had said. Until I found ACA, I never questioned my judgmentalness of myself or others. I just thought that is how life was.

Chapter Two

Identifying Perfectionism

Perfectionism and forms of perfectionism exist in all types of alcoholic and dysfunctional homes. There is a difference between parents challenging their children to reach higher and to improve, and the damaging perfectionism in which the bar keeps being raised beyond reason.

Perfectionism is a response to a shame-based and controlling home. The child mistakenly believes that she can avoid being shamed if she is perfect in her thinking and acting. However, our experience shows that expectations are continually raised in these kinds of homes. Shame or the feeling that we have failed our parents seems to occur no matter what we do. During these moments, a critical inner voice begins to form. This is an early sign of internalizing our parents' hypercritical attitude. These are the seeds that lead to a lack of self-acceptance.

Some perfectionistic homes are violent and oppressive. The children are told to be seen rather than heard. In these homes academics or doing well in school may or may not be a focus. However, the children have to be perfectly behaved to avoid threats and belittlement by parents or the family. Doing house chores and cutting the lawn can be criticized with regularity. Nothing the child does seems right. The child usually gives up and begins to passive-aggressively fail in school or other areas. Some children don't give up. They take the path of trying to please the parent who is rarely satisfied. The parent seems to always find something wrong with the way the laundry is folded or the carpet cleaned. When praise comes from these parents, it usually comes with a qualifier: "You did that pretty good for a screw-up."

In fairness, we must admit that our parents did what was done to them. With the best intentions, they passed on perfectionism or being critical in the manner that they received them. Some parents routinely found fault with our thoughts or accomplishments without any apparent malice. If asked, the parent or caregiver would tell you that they meant well. The parents wanted the children to excel or at least try harder. The parents or relatives really do not see how their second-guessing or regular criticism affects the child's feeling of self-worth or being okay. When the child scores poorly on a self-esteem test, they are baffled. They usually blame the child or peer pressure.

In other homes, the children are like objects of perfection to be displayed alongside dinners centered on tables with fine fixtures, perfect posture, and orderly spoons and forks. Holidays and celebrations bring guests who compliment the parents for sparkling floors and perfect children.

From the outside the parents seem devoted to the children. They faithfully attend sporting events and academic challenges. The caring parents provide fine clothes, computers, and transportation for their children. Yet, our experience shows these homes can be icy and rigid. In some of these homes, the parents withhold praise and affection when a child falls below an elevated mark of achievement. Many parents use their intellect to dismiss any objection by their children. The parent's reasons for the child to achieve more are no match for a child's protest. The child or teen is overwhelmed by the parent's god-like reasoning that calls for behavior without error.

We know of an adult child who brought home perfect scores in her school work. She had earned straight "As" in all of her classes. When she showed her report card to her mother, the mother said: "Is that the best you can do?"

This adult child is now 61 years old and can remember the disappointment she felt upon hearing her mother's remark. Through ACA, she realizes how a lifetime of such remarks left her fearing that everything she did was not good enough. She is a talented woman who performs top-notch work. But she says, "My mother's sense of perfection was basically a simple but subtle withholding of approval for nearly everything I did."

In ACA, we aren't against high achievement and stretching one's self to do better. Yet, we come from homes in which doing our best was never good enough. Or it seemed never good enough.

When we did excel there was usually limited time to rest. We were immediately presented with a new challenge. Looking back, it seemed like our parents could never appreciate what we had done even though they seemed pleased. We can remember them bragging about us to neighbors and friends. In some cases, we received fine gifts or other rewards for our effort. But behind the scene, we knew that we needed to be working on the next achievement to keep the praise coming. Many of us lost our ability to be children and to relax. We knew our parents cared for us, but we were not sure if they would love us if we failed or performed less than perfectly. Their inconsistency in showing their approval made matters worse. We could not tolerate their disappointment. Their silence or turning away from us in displeasure cut deeply. We would do anything to win their approval.

At the same time, other parents were cold and calculating. They planned their hurtful remarks about our appearance or achievements. We learned to not seek praise or encouragement from these parents. We have difficulty accepting praise as an adult as a result. We also have great difficulty accepting mistakes as adults. Mistakes can mean shame or a sense of failure for many of us. In adulthood, we transfer our fear of displeasing our parents to a fear of displeasing an employer, a friend, or a spouse. Most of us agonize over mistakes because we internalize the error. Until we get help, we have trouble distinguishing a mistake from who we are as a person. We believe we are the mistake instead of understanding that we make mistakes.

Perfectionism fueled our people-pleasing trait and fear of authority figures. For some of us, it fueled our workaholism and lust for recognition to soothe our praise deficit. Many adult children have rooms filled with plaques and trophies for achievement, yet, the person never seems at peace. The person is not sure if he or she is competent despite the evidence that would support the competency. These adults are preoccupied with planning the next challenge. They seem to be seeking an achievement high.

Our perfectionism as adults represents an internalization of our parents' attitudes and discontent with self. Many of our parents truly wanted the best for us, but they handed off a sense of being incomplete as a person. We could never win enough awards or finish a project that made us feel whole. For most of us, our parents never said: "You have done enough. Take time to enjoy your accomplishment. Relax."

We were not taught how to have fun.

Perfectionism in dysfunctional homes fuels our control and our attempts to control people, places, and things.

Control

He Missed the Control Angle

When my counselor said that adult children have an issue of control, I didn't get it. I was busy focusing on my drug addiction and trying to stay sober and clean. I entered ACoA counseling because I could not move forward in the Twelve Steps. I was blocked in Steps Two and Three. I saw the Higher Power as a shaming authority figure. I needed help in taking a balanced and fair inventory in Step Four. In counseling, we concentrated on the traits of an adult child. We worked on affirmations, feelings, and the modes of thinking. Control was mentioned with perfectionism. I understood the perfectionism quickly, but it was years before I realized my iron-fisted grip on control.

Identifying Control

Of all the modes of thinking that adult children developed to survive their childhood, control seems to be the most troublesome to address. Fear is the root of this toughened element of our personality. We either seek control or we feel controlled by others. Control affects our choices and our thinking. It affects our interpersonal relationships and our relationship with a Higher Power. To ask an adult child to surrender control is like asking someone to leap from an airplane without a parachute. Without recovery, an adult child can live in terror of letting go of control.

This terror can be unspoken and covered over with people-pleasing, drugs, or another behavior. Living in isolation, shut off from society and friends, is a manner for maintaining control without having to admit what one is doing.

In ACA, we learn to let go of control in stages. Our parachute is the Twelve Steps and a Higher Power of our understanding. By addressing our fear, we release some of our glaring behaviors of manipulation, passive-aggressiveness, and false kindness. These are all forms of control that seem to respond well to early program work. Deeper issues of control respond to focused program work and the spiritual path of ACA.

Our brand of control looks like many things. There is the obvious in which the adult child attempts to control the thoughts and actions of others. This is the adult child who second guesses a spouse's choices, corrects grammar, and uses notes and the telephone to check up on people. This person attempts to disguise the control with phrases like: "I am only concerned for your well-being," or "I was only thinking of you."

There is also the obsessive-compulsive person constantly rechecking door locks, personal appearance, and worrying about leaky faucets and heating bills. There is the person who controls others by being sloppy or aggressive. This person knows that a showdown is coming with a spouse or partner, yet he or she behaves a certain way to remain in control.

Many of us have controlled others from a position of being an enabler or martyr. When this occurs we are usually involved with an addict who needs someone to enable his or her addiction. We pay the rent and utility bills while the addict uses drugs, gambles, watches pornography, or acts out in another form of addiction. We are convinced that we love this person deeply and that we are doing the best we can. We pour out our money and dedication to the person. There are regular episodes in which we complain loudly about the addict's behavior. In moments of despair, we might even read a self-help book that describes our situation precisely, but nothing changes. We are still running on will-power and fear. We remain convinced that we are dedicating our heart to the addict. By every measure of codependence, our behavior is sick, but we do not realize it. We can feel shocked or angered if anyone would suggest that we are getting our own dysfunctional needs met. We are convinced that what we are doing is helpful and loving.

But in reality our enabling behavior keeps the addict crippled and vulnerable to our manipulation. We are convinced that the alcoholic or addict is the problem or more of the problem than ourselves. Without help, we become sicker in these situations. When we look at what is really going on here, we realize that we are addicted to control, yet we are lying to ourselves. We must remember that rigid control to an adult child equates to safety. Learned in childhood to feel safe, we seek control at all costs even if we are trying to tame the uncontrollable, which is addiction.

Our attempts at control bring spiritual death to a relationship with ourselves and others. When we get honest, we realize that paying the bills and complaining about the addict's mistreatment is really a disguise for our fear-based control. Some of us take this learned behavior to the point of martyrdom and actually believe that we have no choice in the matter. While we might feign confusion or helplessness, we think that we know what we are doing. But at the same time, we secretly believe that we cannot change. We cannot believe there is another way to live. With this attitude, we easily push away suggestions for real help because we do not want to give up our focus on another person. At the core of this learned control is a fear that we will not know who we are if we do not have an addict or dysfunctional person in our lives. This is what we learned in childhood. We were raised with alcoholics and addicts, and we do not know how to live unless we have an addict to please or complain about. In ACA, we learn that we can live without an addict to focus on. We can survive the journey of finding out who we are. We can change and know happiness.

2

We can recognize our control by looking honestly at our current relationships or how we began a relationship. We can ask a few questions that deal with trust. Trust is one of the elements that we need to develop to address our learned control. However, trust is not a quick fix, and it does not come without effort.

Here are questions we can ask ourselves to check our level of control: Do I tell the truth about my job, finances, or attitudes when I meet someone I might be interested in for friendship or romance? Do I try to learn things about others so I can anticipate their likes and dislikes? Do I trust the person I am with? Do I trust my co-workers, family, or friends? Do I trust myself?

Withholding the full truth about ourselves or trying to figure out another's likes and dislikes might seem like a small matter. But for the controlling adult child, this behavior usually grows into larger issues of withholding. In our efforts to control outcomes, we withhold feelings and our true motives. We can build up resentments based on our fear of telling the full truth about ourselves. We can feel misunderstood, yet we have not made the effort to find out what we truly need from another person. While we might practice moments of honesty, we still have secrets in our friendships and relationships. Those of us who began a relationship by withholding information never stopped to think when true honesty would become a desired trait of our relationship. Fear and control do not allow such thoughts.

If we begin a relationship by withholding information, when do we expect to be more direct? When would consistent honesty begin and remain a centerpiece of the relationship? For the person who relies on control and the manipulation of others, these questions seem confusing. Yet, if honesty is an important feature of healthy relationships, then why not be honest from the start?

This is not a call for the reader to run out and disclose all to friends, family, or lover. To do so would only be another attempt at controlling others. A burst of honesty before we have a foundation in recovery is not advisable. Others might not understand what we are trying to do. And we might not be able to maintain such honesty without help. We urge caution. We begin being more honest and letting go of control in a safe setting such as an ACA group.

Another method for identifying our control or attempted control of others involves a look at the roles and behaviors that a controlling person uses. We have identified the aggressor, enabler, martyr, and obsessive-compulsive personality. Here are other roles and behaviors that identify control:

Acting like a victim or rescuer

Manipulating or recasting facts

Throwing fits of anger

Intellectualizing

Exaggerate harms done to you

Embellish facts or stories

Gossip

Act incompetent

Act superior

Act confused or lost

Lying

Refusing to talk

Practical joker

Refusing to stop talking

All-or-Nothing Thinking

He Identified the "Thinking" in the All-or-Nothing Thinking

My all-or-nothing thinking can be verbal or it can remain in my head. It shows up verbally when I gossip about someone or judge someone. Before finding ACA, I could make broad or all-or-nothing statements about people without thinking about what I was doing. This was easy to spot once I began attending meetings and learning about recovery. I learned to stop gossiping, and I am better at not judging others without mercy.

The all-or-nothing thinking in my head was a little more tricky. Whenever I would hear something new in a meeting or something different, my mind would slam shut. In my mind, I would say, 'That will never work,' or 'That's not me and my family.' Sometimes these thoughts were so subtle that I didn't know I was doing them. I am so grateful that I kept coming back to the meetings. I learned to identify the 'thinking' part of the all-or-nothing thinking. My hearing, or listening, has improved immensely since doing so.

Identifying All-or-Nothing Thinking

With perfectionism and control as our guide posts, most adult children operate with "all-or-nothing" thinking before finding ACA. This is also known as "black-and-white" thinking. All-or-nothing thinking is common among newcomers and members who relapse into codependence or addiction. In codependence, options melt away and fixation or compulsion takes over the thinking process.

In ACA, we make a distinction between being decisive and all-or-nothing thinking. Being decisive means that we have seriously thought about our options, and we have picked a course of action. In all-or-nothing thinking, we usually do not seriously consider options. We push forward with a sense of fear or closemindedness.

All-or-nothing thinking can be divided into two categories: external and internal. The external involves what we say, and the internal involves our thinking. When we write or speak in absolutes without options, we are usually involved in all-or-nothing behavior. We have given words to our black-and-white thoughts. This is common in unhealthy homes where opinions or thoughts are attacked by the family with sweeping statements.

The internal version of all-or-nothing thinking can be trickier to detect. Since we have lived in our heads so much as adult children, we cannot readily detect a black-and-white thought. The all-or-nothing thinking is there, but it is hidden due to familiarity. The thoughts are so familiar that we have accepted them as fact. Just as a spell checker will learn misspelled words and not recognize them as incorrect, so will our mind not recognize all-or-nothing thinking made familiar by daily living.

We can bring our all-or-nothing thinking into the open by attending ACA meetings. We listen to what we are saying about ourselves. We can also journal or write down our thoughts. With all-or-nothing thinking there is little room for variance. Typically, there is no in-between. The adult child sees himself as all wonderful or as all horrible. He is brilliant or stupid. He is perfect or inadequate. People are marvelous or people are wretched. Such thinking is typified by rigid thinking, changing boundaries, and a hypercritical attitude of one's self or others. With black-and-white thinking, we argue unfairly and unreasonably with others. In most cases, we seek to hurt the other person rather than to seek a solution. Nothing is resolved. Arguments are rehashed infinitely. True emotional sobriety is not possible until this type of thinking is addressed.

All-or-nothing thinking has its roots in the messages and actions of our parents. We can hear a parent's voice when we talk about or decide matters in our adult life. Even if we have made a conscious effort to be different than our parents, we can still hear their voices in our voice. We can recognize their attitudes. This is perhaps one of the most dramatic signs that we have internalized our parents' attitudes and dysfunction.

Many all-or-nothing statements have a serious flaw. The person making the statement usually cannot stand behind it. An example of an all-or-nothing statement is the title of this chapter. "It will never happen to me." We said we would never marry an alcoholic or be an alcoholic, but we did. We said we would never mistreat others or pass on our parents' dysfunction, but we did.

Learned from our parents and relatives, we use all-or-nothing statements for many reasons. We use these statements to control others, push others away, and to avoid asking for help. "Others may need emotional help," we might say. "I will never need that. I am not perfect, but I am okay on my own."

All-or-nothing statements usually contain one of these words: never, must, always, and don't. The statements give us a sense of control or security that does not last. In most cases, we cannot back up our statements with consistent action. After awhile, our word or words mean nothing to those nearest to us. They know we don't say what we mean or do what we say.

Examples of all-or-nothing statements are:

Sure. My parents weren't perfect, but I was just rebellious.

I never listened.

I have always been stubborn. I don't pay attention.

I always find trouble. I always find a way to screw things up.

I have no idea how I ended up in that predicament.

You cannot change your mind once you decide.

I don't know what feelings are. I can't understand feelings.

You must never be angry.

Never trust men.

Never trust women.

You must always respect your parents and elders.

God only loves good little boys and girls.

There are more examples of all-or-nothing thinking, but this is a good start. The first step is recognizing the behavior. A classic example of all-or-nothing thinking involves an adult child feeling alone or abandoned after a disagreement with an authority figure or spouse. The scenario goes like this. A spouse or significant other disagrees with the adult child. The adult child regresses to a stage of childhood and feels wrong, faulty, or undesirable. Because he hears any form of criticism as an attack, the adult child believes there can be only one conclusion: "I am wrong or faulty." This conclusion is not related to the conflict with the spouse, but it now enters the conflict and diverts a workable solution. Blame usually enters the picture. The all-or-nothing statements pop up throughout the argument and the fallout which usually follows.

When we argue, we might say:

You always accuse me of leaving the toilet seat lid up when it is you who never keeps a clean house.

You never listen to me. You will never understand me.

I have given you everything, and you give nothing back.

Without help, we do not argue well with others, and we are doomed to reenact arguments that lead nowhere. We repeat the pattern of hurtful arguing that we witnessed as children. Nothing is resolved, and we harm ourselves and our significant other. If we have children, we affect them as well. We do not mean to do this, but it happens. Our arguing changes our children even when they are not the target. We know this is true since it happened to us, but we are not unique. There are millions of parents in our situation.

With ACA, we learn to fight fairly and to recognize when we are making statements that we cannot back up. We see how our words and old messages can affect others. We learn to stop or limit these all-or-nothing statements. We see them as dysfunctional tools that no longer serve a purpose for us. We learn to fight fairly by becoming willing to practice the principles of self-honesty and self-forgiveness. We will not do this alone.

We will get help from ACA members and from a Higher Power. After awhile, we learn to say what we mean and mean what we say. We begin to trust ourselves to keep our word.

Critical Inner Parent or Critical Inner Voice/ Feeling

His Inner Critical Parent Showed Up At Work

It took awhile for me to identify this critical inner voice that I heard about in meetings. I later realized it was there, but I had become so comfortable with my negative thoughts that I could not see how critical I was of myself. The negative messages had played so long in my head that they seemed normal.

In addition to what I was learning in meetings, a counselor pointed out that I was too negative, but I didn't understand her either. Something happened at work that made me realize how critical I was of myself. I had been attending ACA meetings for awhile, when I made a mistake at work. I immediately heard this roaring voice in my head. 'You damn idiot. You can't do anything right. You never listen.'

I stopped and recognized the voice as my father's voice. I thought to myself, 'that's what they have been talking about in meetings.' During the next few days, I began to recall other times when I had yelled at myself from within. I began to hear my critical inner parent. I could not believe how almost every sentence was negative or doubting myself.

Identifying the Critical Inner Parent

We began this chapter talking about how we have internalized our parents' behavior. Anyone who might doubt that he or she has internalized a parent's behavior only needs to listen to the internal critic. This is the voice in our head that brings self-doubt or second-guessing from within. This is the voice that makes us reactors rather than thoughtful actors in relationships, work, and worship. Spurred on by this inner voice, we can explode with harsh words and threats that can be traced directly to the parents or grandparents. By being open to the possibility of a critical inner voice, we see how our words match the words of the parents. ACA helps us hear what we are saying to ourselves and to others. We realize how harsh we can be toward ourselves.

In other situations, the critical voice can be subtle and more difficult to detect. For example, we attend ACA meetings and observe how well others seem to be doing in the program. Some of us conclude that other ACA members have it all together, but we will never make it. If we are in the later years of our lives, our critical inner voice might say we are too old to benefit from ACA. We can secretly tell ourselves that we cannot recover, or we cannot experience the benefits of the Steps. This is the subtle but critical inner voice, attempting to disqualify us from recovery.

Recognizing this critical inner voice takes awhile. We have become so comfortable with shaming ourselves or cursing ourselves that we cannot hear the extreme negativity. Occasionally, the inner critic is a feeling more than a voice. The adult child feels different, unacceptable, or wrong without knowing why. Yet, the body posture which speaks of nervousness or a sense of poor self-worth is there. There can also be a lack of eye contact when talking to friends and fellow workers. The critical inner parent gives us that guilt feeling when we think about asking for what we need.

When the critical inner voice emerges, it is usually the voice of one parent. In some cases it is both parents. The critical inner parent brings together all the elements of primary modes of adult child thinking and behaving. There is perfectionism, control, and all-or-nothing thinking in this voice. Until we find ACA, we believe that something is wrong with us, and this voice convinces us of such thoughts. Some of us have been told we are too critical of ourselves, but we do not understand the statement. Before finding ACA, many of us have joked about sounding like a parent. "I heard myself say something the other day that sounded like my mother," we have said. Until we find our way to Adult Children of Alcoholics, we do not connect the dots between our parents' critical attitude and the inner voice that pushes us as adults. This is the voice that passes forth the seeds of family dysfunction.

Finding Focus and a Home in ACA

Admitting that you have internalized your parents' behavior is a brave step toward changing the behavior; however, admitting that "it happened to me" is the discovery process. Discovery is marvelous, but recovery is the focus. We can discover many things from insightful self-help books or from a talk-show host. Yet, our experience shows that we cannot read ourselves into true change, and we cannot watch enough television to find healing that lasts. We simply become information gatherers, which is a form of control in itself. If we are simply reading about recovery or watching it on television, we still think we can reason out a solution without doing the actual work of recovery. Our experience shows that we cannot recover alone. We need to interact with recovering adult children to practice the principles that bring real results.

Moving beyond discovery into recovery is not a complex mystery. It takes only one key element: the desire to recover from the effects of the disease of family dysfunction. With desire comes willingness. With willingness, we are well on our way to recovery.

In ACA, we believe recovery takes regular attendance at ACA meetings. We also must work the Twelve Steps and be willing to talk honestly about what happened to us as we grew up in a dysfunctional home. Recovery takes effort. But many of us believe that recovery takes only half the effort that it took to stay stuck in enabling or controlling behavior. That means we can exert our energy toward recovery and have plenty of strength left over to enjoy the new avenues that open up to us due to the ACA way of life.

Our experience shows that many adult children have arrived at an ACA meeting, identified profoundly with our literature, and then drifted away from ACA without following through with the program. They have not moved beyond the discovery phase, but they assume their discovery is recovery when it is not.

We admit that recovery is not easy, but the rewards are great if you can stick with it and stay focused. We will not deny that there is pain and challenge ahead. You will not have to do this work alone. We ask new members to avoid some hindrances to recovery that include: isolating and not asking for help, intellectualizing the program, focusing only on counseling, "falling in love" with another member and avoiding program work, erratic meeting attendance, and taking drugs or drinking alcohol. We suggest that newcomers to ACA stay out of romantic relationships since we need time to focus on ourselves. We are highly susceptible to unhealthy attachments which can divert us from focusing on ourselves. The ACA solution is in the meetings and the Twelve Steps, instead of in someone else. Another stumbling block involves taking on too much program work at once. Some members who smoke, overeat, and act out sexually might attempt to address all of the conditions at once. For these ACA members, we suggest two program slogans: "Easy Does It" and "First Things First." Some of us may be able to work on all of these areas at once, but others need to focus on the most dominant compulsion or self-harming behavior before moving to the next. If we are using alcohol or drugs addictively, we must first find abstinence from these drugs for ACA to work. We build on that success to work on the next area of our lives. Each case is different. Some ACA members can work on more than one area of their lives at once. There is no right or wrong way; however, each ACA member must be honest with himself or herself. Each of us must make a sincere effort to make progress in the program whether working on one or many compulsions or addictions.

Those who find success and healing attend ACA meetings regularly, get a sponsor, and do the Twelve Step work with focus. ACA is a way of life that works if you work it. The rewards and gifts are immeasurable.

Chapter Two

Program slogans that work:

ACA is Simple but it is Not Easy

Live Beyond Mere Survival

There Is Another Way to Live

One Day at A Time

Easy Does It

Keep it Simple

Progress Not Perfection

First Things First

This Pain Too Shall Pass

Let Go. Let God

H.A.L.T. – Don't get too Hungry, Angry, Lonely, or Tired

Keep Coming Back

Name It, Don't Blame It

Ask For Help and Accept It

Pray and Pray Hard

Don't Just Do Something. Sit There

Be Still and Know

There is no Healing Without Feeling

End Notes

†ON PAGE 22: For more information on how adult children internalize their parents' attitudes read: "The Laundry List: The ACoA Experience" by Tony A., with Dan F., 1991, HCI Publications. In this book, Tony created his own version of the Twelve Steps. Step Four from the book states: "We made a searching and blameless inventory of our parents because, in essence, we had become them."

Chapter 3

"My Parents Did Not Drink But I Can Relate"

$\mathcal{S}$oon after the establishment of Adult Children of Alcoholics in 1978, members began arriving at ACA meetings, identifying with The Laundry List traits of an adult child but appearing to have no alcoholism or addiction in the home. Many of these members were in denial about their parental alcoholism.[†] Others were grandchildren of alcoholics who lacked information about family alcoholism. They were not necessarily in denial since their nondrinking parents had failed to give them clear information about the family's addiction. By working the ACA program and by attending meetings regularly, many of these adult children connected the meaning of family alcoholism.

For those in denial, the true nature of family alcoholism emerged as they worked Step One and realized the effects of being raised in an alcoholic or addicted home. They claimed their membership in ACA as well.

However, a reasonable number of adult children truly had no addiction in the home. They were not in denial. They identified strongly with sharing in ACA meetings and with ACA literature. There also appeared to be no addiction in the preceding generation of their families. Yet, their homes had features which created the early loss of security and sense of self-failing that characterize addicted homes. This chapter captures the voice and identification of these ACA members.

Additionally, this chapter will list a variety of families that produce adult children. While some of the family types are different in nature, there is a common thread of shame and abandonment among families. Chapter Three shows that ACA members come from a variety of backgrounds but identify with one another through the Laundry List traits.

Out of the playpen

My parents never drank a drop of alcohol in their lives, nor did their parents before them. They were highly respected members of the church. I read somewhere that our earliest childhood memory is often symbolic of our lives. My earliest memory is sitting in a playpen on a front veranda, feeling alone, trapped, and unable to get out.

I was born and raised in a little farming town. After my parents married, three babies were born in three years, and my mother had no idea how to cope with us. My father worked in the medical field and constantly brought home drugs and pills for mother's nerves and migraines.

In our family, there was a very sharp distinction between the family image in the community and what I actually saw at home. To the community my parents were esteemed leaders and church workers, models of family life and community service. Our family life at home was actually far from this idealistic picture.

My father was a workaholic, always "on-call." When not at work he attended meetings for a myriad of community organizations. One of his addictions was to become president of every organization he joined. My mother struggled at home with her nerves, her migraines, and her children. When I misbehaved, I was beaten, even though my misdeeds were never more than average childhood explorations. Mother's worst threat was that she would walk out of the house and leave us if we did not behave. She often did walk out the door and down the road, taunting us with, "See! I'm leaving you until you learn to behave." Crying, we would plead for her to come back and promise behavioral perfection.

I became a workaholic like my father and almost as neurotic as my mother. I was unable to sustain any kind of meaningful, intimate relationship. By the time I was forty I had the same dual world as my parents: a wholesome public image of success and service and a private life of loneliness, suppressed feelings, and sexual dysfunction.

I found a therapist who helped me explore the long-lost child imprisoned in the playpen of my soul. One day he mentioned that I might find meetings for Adult Children of Alcoholics helpful. I thought he hadn't been listening when I told him of my family's history of proud sobriety. He said I didn't have to join, pay, or say anything, so I went to a meeting. I was shocked. "The Problem" was the story of my life. It all fit. It is five years later now, and I am still working the program. With the help of my Higher Power, I claim my life and spirit separate from the web of past family dysfunction. The miraculous combination of therapy and working the Twelve Steps set me free from the prison of my childhood playpen to explore and experience my real and unique self.

Her grandfather only drank on special occasions

I had been in Al-Anon for a while when the ACA program was first introduced in my area. It started with a series of workshops which a friend said I should attend. However, to be eligible for these ACA workshops, I had to identify as either a child or grandchild of an alcoholic. In thinking about the stories of my mother's childhood, I asked her if her father was an alcoholic. She drew herself up to her total height of 5'4" and said haughtily, "Heavens, no! He only got drunk on special occasions." "Like when?" "Like when he went to town."

There were other clues like this, so I went off to the ACA workshops with a clean conscience, and this huge body of information opened up for me. I discovered that while my mother wasn't an alcoholic, the emotional illness of the family disease of alcoholism manifested in her using food to stuff her feelings. My dad used over-the-counter

Chapter Three

pills for the same reason. I didn't ever see him doing that, but after getting into ACA recovery, I remembered friends of his commenting on his being a hypochondriac. I was coming out of denial.[1]

We are not sure when we – adult children without an alcoholic upbringing – began arriving at ACA meetings. An old timer recalling the early days of ACA describes how the fellowship quickly adopted an attitude of inclusion. "No one was ever asked to leave an ACA meeting even though their primary cause for being in a meeting was not alcohol related. We knew that they were relating to our meetings and that ACA was probably the only real hope for some of these members. We could not turn them away and deny them the chance we were given.[2]

---

[1] More and more people are identifying as grandchildren of alcoholics. Technically, these "GCoAs" are ACAs. They were raised by parents who passed on the disease of family dysfunction without having alcohol in the home.

Many people have said that the disease of alcoholism "skipped" the parents and was passed to the grandchildren, but this is a common misperception that deserves closer scrutiny. The disease did not skip the parents. These parents may have removed alcohol from the home, but they passed on the disease of alcoholism unintentionally. The disease of family dysfunction was transferred from the alcoholic grandparent to the grandchildren through the nondrinking parents. This transfer mechanism is para-alcoholism, which is detailed in Trait 13 and Trait 14 of The Laundry List. Para-alcoholism is primarily made up of the stored fear and distorted thoughts of the person raised in an alcoholic home. In our view, the presence of alcohol is not necessary to transfer the disease of alcoholism since it can occur through endogenous means. The para-alcoholism (the inside drugs of fear and pain) of the nondrinking parents transfers the disease in good form. So the alcoholism of the grandparents is passed through the nondrinking parents to the grandchildren by para-alcoholism. GCoAs identify with ACA recovery and benefit from the ACA program. Many grandchildren of alcoholics express feelings of not being good enough or not having a right to their pain. When trying to understand their story, they wonder if their grandparents' alcoholism or dysfunction matters. They know something is wrong or unsaid. They often wonder if they are making up the pain or confusion in their lives until they find out about the disease of alcoholism and its effects on the family.

The fact that the disease of family dysfunction shows up in the grandchildren offers some level of proof that family dysfunction is generational.

[2] In an interview in 2006, Marty S. recalled a 1983 Service Board discussion about ACA membership. Marty remembered that Jack E., the person who brought ACA to California from New York, realized that many of the hurt, battered, and mostly scared people pouring through the door had not been raised in alcoholic families. Yet, he saw that they had the same mixture of doubt, expectations, and hope as ACAs after reading The Laundry List (Problem). Marty said Jack was one of the first ACA members to give birth to the idea of inclusion.

We are not writing this chapter to set ourselves apart from ACAs who grew up with addiction in the home. Even though we were not raised with alcoholism, we can empathize with the effects of alcoholism described in our meetings. We are grateful to the early ACA members who created this program. We have claimed our place in the ACA fellowship. Our voice is ACA's voice.

In addition to identifying with The Laundry List (Problem), our recovery shows that we identify with an early loss of security like the person raised with addiction. We identify with the mistaken belief that we were responsible to heal or fix our families. We understand the "don't talk, don't trust, and don't feel" rules. We understand the destructive obsession and compulsion of codependence and how it relates in our lives. We work the ACA Steps. We connect with our Inner Child and find hope and lasting peace in ACA.

Family Types That Can Create Adult Children

Since ACA's beginning, ACA groups have seen new members from at least five distinct family types that did not include alcoholism or addiction. While these families are labeled nonaddicted, there can be alcohol or drug use in the family. For example, the adult child from a home with a chronically ill parent may have witnessed the parent misusing drugs even though the parent was ill. This is also true of the mentally ill parent taking drugs prescribed by a doctor. Many clinicians aware of the adult child dynamic believe that most mental health diagnoses are actually adult child related.

The five family types that can produce adult children even though alcoholism is not always present are:[3]

- Homes with mental illness in the parent(s).

- Homes with hypochondriac parent(s).

Chapter Three

- Homes with ritualistic beliefs, harsh punishment, and extreme secretiveness, often with ultra-religious, militaristic, or sadistic overtones. Some of these homes expose children to battery and other forms of criminal abuse.

- Homes with covert or actual sexual abuse, including incest and inappropriate touching or dress by the parent(s).

- Perfectionistic, shaming homes in which expectations are often too high and praise is typically tied to an accomplishment rather than given freely.

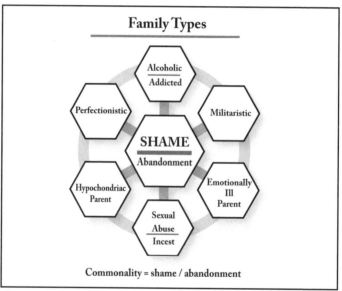

Family Types

Alcoholic
Addicted

Perfectionistic

Militaristic

SHAME
Abandonment

Hypochondriac
Parent

Emotionally
Ill
Parent

Sexual
Abuse
Incest

Commonality = shame / abandonment

[3]In the above graphic, we are including the alcoholic family to show how all the families touch the center point of shame and abandonment. This is the commonality of the families.

Additionally, there are other family types or combinations of these family types. These families produce adult children identifying with ACA principles. Many foster children, now adults, identify with the ACA traits and manners of thinking. Moved from home to home while growing up, they understand abandonment at the same depth as adult children from alcoholic homes. Adults from divorced homes understand shame and confusion and also identify in ACA. There are even a few adults raised by "hippie parents" who abandoned their children while chasing the "peace" movement of the 1960s. These adults find safety and their voices in ACA as well.

Before we talk further about nonaddicted homes that create adult children, we want to briefly address homes where addiction is present, but the addiction is not alcoholism. There are adult children from homes where illicit drugs or prescription drugs were abused. These ACA members can identify with alcoholic dysfunction because alcohol is a drug; however, there are some unique considerations for adults raised by parents who abused drugs. Children raised by parents abusing prescription drugs learned to anticipate when an addicted parent would be loopy after taking a tranquilizer or when the parent would appear "up" after taking a stimulant. The children also became aware of psychosomatic illnesses created by a parent to get drugs. These children heard about endless backaches, headaches, or other ailments that only a pill or shot would fix. The children became aware of their parents using several doctors to maintain a supply of prescription drugs. Some of these adult children have developed an addiction to prescription drugs as well.

Kids raised by addicts using illicit drugs had the knowledge that what their parents were doing was illegal. Many of these ACAs had to hide their parents' drugs if the police showed up at the front door. Some children had to help their stoned parents look for misplaced drugs. Some addicted parents encouraged or forced their children to take drugs with them. In homes where illegal drugs were manufactured, many children have been harmed by dangerous chemicals used to produce the drugs.

We Are More Alike Than Different

While there are many different family types represented in ACA, our fellowship identity is apparent in our meetings and our message. Our message of recovery is consistent and cohesive throughout the fellowship. By listening to adult children share or talk at an ACA meeting, one usually cannot distinguish what type of family the adult child might have been raised in. Unless the person discloses the specific type, the sharing of experiences is almost identical among the various recovering adult children in ACA. While we come from different family types, our ability to identify with the ACA message is amazingly similar if not exact.

We are more alike than we are different. Our experience shows that the codependent rupture, which creates an outward focus to gain love or affirmation, is created by a dysfunctional childhood. It is the same rupture among adult children of all family types. This soul rupture is the abandonment by our parents or caregivers. The abandonment sets us up for a life of looking outward for love and safety that never comes. The codependence of the adult child from the alcoholic or nonalcoholic home is the same and leads to the same loss of self. This codependence or abandonment by the parents is the seed of ACA empathy. The seed bears the fruit of identification and bonds together adult children of all family types. This identification creates a viable fellowship of such diverse people.

As adult children from various families, we focus on ourselves for the surest results. We gradually free ourselves from codependent or addictive relationships. We also address our "addictiveness." With addictiveness, we tend to use almost everything in our path to cauterize our continual bleeding of the soul. Food, sex, drugs, work, spending, religion, and people are fair game for a codependent ACA trying to feel safe or loved. Some of us describe feeling like a black hole pulling everything in our path into us, yet letting nothing escape, not even light. Our addictive relationships represent our impulse to heal our family of origin through our adult relationships. Because we were not consistently nurtured and not made to feel safe as children, ACAs from all families spend their lives chasing love and affirmation in other people, who often cannot give it. The ACA focus on one's self is a proven remedy to this spiritual dilemma.

The foundation of ACA identification comes from The Laundry List (Problem), which describes a personality who fears people, has difficulty expressing feelings, and who can tolerate a high level of abuse or neglect without realizing the effects of such behavior. The adult child personality, the false self, lives in fear of being shamed and abandoned. Yet, the person chooses relationships which do both. These common behaviors are the identifying traits which create ACA identification. This identification makes it possible for adult children from different homes to come together and recover together without fragmenting into different groups. The language of ACA, grounded in our traits and literature, creates the critical mass that changes our thinking and behavior. With the support of the ACA fellowship, the True Self emerges.

History of Inclusiveness

To understand how ACA could attract such a diverse group of adults and how it developed its response of inclusion, we must look at how Alcoholics Anonymous responded to drug addicts, showing up at AA meetings soon after the fellowship was established. AA's focus was alcoholism then and has remained so for more than 70 years; however, history reveals that AA responded to desperate drug addicts needing help with the fellowship's character wisdom.

AA history reveals that a "strange alcoholic" with a problem more stigmatized than alcoholism showed up about 1937 at one of the earliest AA meetings.† At the time AA was in its second year of development. The Twelve Steps and the AA "Big Book," the fellowship text, had not been published. The first two AA

3

groups were struggling to survive. Early AA members struggled together and hammered out the foundational principles that would become AA's legacy.

Several decades ago, early AA members were hypervigilant of the shaming stigma of alcoholism. Early AAs guarded their personal anonymity tightly. Written accounts show that members discussed the status of new group members in a manner that is not practiced by modern AA groups. A new member might be asked many questions about his or her background before the person attended a first meeting. The AA members were cautious of public scrutiny. To be exposed as an alcoholic before World War II could mean ruin in the eyes of an unaccepting public. Meanwhile, the drug addict had a lower standing than the lowly drunk in those days.

This "strange alcoholic," as AA history describes him, was a drug addict as well, according to AA lore. Desperately wanting help, he had found his way to AA because few options existed for addicts during this era. The foundation of Narcotics Anonymous, a fellowship which has offered sure hope for hundreds of thousands of drug addicts, was still 15 years away.

The "strange alcoholic" showing up at AA was honest about his addiction and discussed his dilemma with the AA group. AA history reveals that early AA members were alarmed at the man's condition and what it might mean to their struggling group. The group members feared they could be shunned and their livelihood threatened if word got out they were helping this man.

The story continues and details how the AA members tussled with the decision to turn away the person or to allow him to remain. To turn him away would perhaps doom him to death. After much discussion, a member of the early AA group calmly asked: "What would the master do?" With that spiritual question, the discussion ended. The early AA members knew it would be wrong to turn away this desperate man. With a sense of inclusion, the addict attained sobriety and blossomed. He reportedly attracted many new members to AA, teaching them the program he was so freely given. At the same time, AA retained its focus on alcoholism while also opening the door to addicts with a genuine alcohol problem.

No Fear

In ACA, the fellowship never feared being shamed or ridiculed by society for accepting different types of adult children into our meetings. These potential ACA members were never viewed with alarm by ACA. These potential members were equal in their pain and desire to heal just like the next adult child. The issue was a matter of identification and ACA unity. The solution we found was inclusiveness born from our similarities rather than our differences.

We believe the solution of inclusion rose from the spiritual depths of ACA meetings and group consciences. Following AA's wisdom, the ACA fellowship realized it could not turn away a suffering adult child wanting a solution from the horrors of an adult child life. Intuitively our groups and our members realized we could not turn away an adult child any more than AA could turn away a desperate addict 70 years ago.

Our history shows that as the number of these adult children grew, the fellowship expanded its philosophy to include these remarkable new members. The identification created by the 14 Laundry List traits proved just as irresistible to adult children from nonalcoholic homes as it did to adult children with alcoholism in the home.

In addition to being discussed at the group level, the issue of inclusion was discussed at ACA's Annual Business Conference. The conference represents the fellowship voice and offers direction for the ACA World Service Office Board of Trustees to consider. ACA groups and World Services modified our literature to create greater identification for ACAs from nonalcoholic homes. ACA's First Step was modified as well. ACA's First Step states: "We admitted we were powerless over the effects of alcoholism or other family dysfunction, that our lives had become unmanageable." ACA also modified its Third Tradition to expand the definition of its membership requirement for ACA. The only requirement for membership in ACA is a desire to recover from the effects of growing up in an alcoholic or otherwise dysfunctional family.

We can see how AA's inclusiveness gave rise to the fellowship's simple but brilliant solution to the question of membership requirements. AA's Third Tradition states: "The only requirement for AA membership is the desire to stop drinking." That's it. No pledges to sign and no promises to make to anyone. This was the wisdom of inclusion gained in part by allowing a different kind of alcoholic into early AA meetings. The decision was a foundation stone that simplified AA's requirement for membership.

From AA's experience with the Third Tradition, ACA has taken a similarly inclusive position. We cannot help all people of all times, but we can throw open wide the doors of ACA to willing adult children across the world. In the AA spirit of 1937, we cannot turn away these adult children.

END NOTES

†ON PAGE 53: Dr. Claudia Black estimates that 50 percent of adult children of alcoholics, and 90 percent of children of alcoholics who become alcoholics, deny or cannot recognize problem drinking by a parent ("Healing the Child Within," Page 25, Dr. Charles Whitfield, 1987, HCI publications).

†ON PAGE 61: The Twelve Steps and Twelve Traditions book of AA, Page 141–42, 1952, describes this scenario in which this "strange alcoholic" appeared at one of the early AA groups asking for help.

Chapter 4

Hitting an ACA Bottom

*W*ithin the various Twelve Step programs there is a simple wisdom that rings true and signals a new start for most people seeking help. This starting point can occur before the person enters the doors of ACA. For others, the starting point emerges only after years of anguished ACA recovery with seemingly little results. The ACA wisdom is this: "There is nothing like hitting bottom to motivate someone into action that produces lasting change."

Like members in other recovery programs, the adult child must hit a bottom. He or she must realize the bottom and ask for help to find a new way of life. We are not that different than the alcoholic, who seeks help from the ravages of alcoholism. In ACA we seek help from our false selves and our obsessive nature to harm ourselves. Because of our addictiveness, we choose a variety of methods to do ourselves in. Many adult children use a combination of drugs, food, sex, and relationships to harm themselves emotionally and physically. We have seen adult children addicted to drugs while gambling or eating food out of control. The drugs and emotional eating are coupled with multiple relationships. This can lead to a maddening pace of chasing drugs and sex or romance. Self-abandonment flourishes and eventual collapse occurs. Many consider this hitting bottom, but this is only one example of an array of ACA bottoms and crises.

Chapter Four

In moments of despair, some of us have sought professional help only to be diagnosed with a label that does not empower us to understand what is happening. The awareness of the adult child phenomenon is high among the general public and many helping professionals. Yet, treatment options that we find are not always focused on this aspect of our condition.[†] In some cases, hitting bottom is given a different label that can delay our entry into ACA. Recognizing that we have bottomed out with drugs, control, or another compulsive behavior is a critical first step toward ACA recovery. In ACA, we find a comprehensive message of recovery that involves the Twelve Steps, reparenting one's self, and embracing our Inner Child. The Inner Child is also known as the True Self by some of us.

Defining an ACA bottom precisely is not the goal of this chapter. However, our experience shows that there are general similarities in this important aspect of recovery. Without hitting or naming a bottom, a person can nibble at the ACA program, never fully grasping the gifts of recovery. The person can remain in a place of pain or near pain. We have seen adult children wander in and out of ACA without admitting that a bottom has occurred. Meanwhile, the person's life is stagnant or continues to deteriorate.

Bottoming out can vary from person to person; however, the general consensus reveals that the person usually has exhausted all resources, lacks self-love, and is practicing self-harm. The person may be allowing others to neglect and abuse him. While a bottom is in progress, denial is rampant and relatives or friends may have turned away. At this juncture, the adult child usually isolates or becomes involved in busy work to avoid asking for help. He scrambles to manipulate anyone who might still be having contact with him.

Some adult children are at the other extreme. They have resources and speak of a bright future or new challenge; however, their bottom involves an inability to connect with others on a meaningful level. Their lives are unmanageable due to perfectionism and denial that seals them off from others.

These are the high-functioning adults who seem to operate in the stratosphere of success. In their self-sufficiency they avoid asking for help, but they feel a desperate disconnect from life. Their bottom can be panic attacks without warning or bouts of depression that are pushed away with work or a new relationship.

There are still other adult children who hit bottom with rage or bursts of erratic behavior. This is the adult child who has taken on the persecutor or rescuer role. The person can use aggression or manipulation to avoid dealing with life on life's terms. Dishonesty and distrust usually dominate this person's thoughts and behavior. This person can live alone or live with people who fear him or her. This scenario can evolve into a relationship bottom that is triggered by the obvious: an abusive or empty relationship.

There is the "pink cloud" bottom in which a person finds ACA and makes rapid improvements only to drift away from meetings. By attending ACA, the person feels understood and hopeful for perhaps the first time in life. He or she floats about in meetings in a state of bliss. The person shares openly with others about family dysfunction. He or she begins to see improvements in relationships and thought. After awhile, this person drops out of ACA without truly giving the program a chance to work. Many of these adult children return to destructive behaviors. They forgot that family dysfunction is progressive and sometimes fatal. If they are lucky, some of these members return to ACA. They talk of life being lonelier than before. They talk of progressing in their dysfunction or remaining stuck in unhappiness.

Hitting bottom can be triggered by many things or it can result as the natural progression of the disease of family dysfunction. The disease is progressive and tends to become worse over time. That means our drug abuse, codependence, or other compulsive behaviors become so severe that our lives or sanity are at stake. These behaviors become progressively worse. Or we switch to other behaviors, and the progression to our bottom marches onward.

4

All ACA bottoms have one thing in common: self-abandonment. While our actions can harm others, we ultimately harm ourselves by running from ourselves. We give up on ourselves. We can believe we are not worth saving. Most bottoms are emotionally painful unless the adult child is dissociating from reality. The pain varies due to our ability to switch over to other soothing compulsions.

The level of pain that adult children can tolerate without admitting they have hit a bottom is astonishing. Being adult children, we have learned to endure colossal amounts of abuse and aloneness that only we understand. Even long-time members in recovery have suffered with emotional pain seemingly unable to find relief in ACA. They have held on with sheer grit and forced prayers. We also have members who suffer in silence with psychic numbing, believing they are unable to feel anything.

Whether we are numb or in emotional anguish, we pay an enormous price unless we become willing to move into action. If we have suffered long, we are usually hanging onto some secret or fear that blocks us from working the program. We usually know what the thing is. If we pray and remain still, we will know what to do. We are not alone anymore.

Many of our members who have worked remarkable Twelve Step programs in AA or Al-Anon come to ACA to further address their shame and feelings of being unwhole. They have made good progress elsewhere, but they sense something is missing. While working ACA's Steps, these members may realize a new bottom or the work needed to seize a deeper sense of healing. These members are introduced to a Loving Parent and Inner Child. For these members, ACA meetings can unlock the grief that has not been addressed for years.

While ACA bottoms are emotional and spiritual lows, they are also physical. ACA members have spoken of experiencing withdrawal-like sensations in the body during a bottoming out. There can be mental confusion and loss or increase of appetite. In a relationship bottom there can be an intense feeling of isolation and abandonment. The emotional pain seems like too much. It is that powerful.

We are not judging those who have faced an ACA bottom or a relapse. An ACA relapse can involve a return to sustained dependency on our survival traits or family role. Another type of ACA relapse can involve binging on food, sex, or drugs, or remaining in an abusive relationship without a clear plan to get out. A bottom or relapse can both be addressed by action and asserting one's self in the program.

Secondary Addictions – Drugs, Food, etc.

Many adult children find ACA and begin recovery. A few seem to do well only to act out in addictions such as drugs, alcohol, food, gambling, or compulsive spending. Many of these addictions have been called secondary addictions that emerge as we address our shame and abandonment. Our primary addiction is fear, excitement, and pain in the form of para-alcoholism. Within every para-alcoholic (codependent) is an inside "drug store." As odd as it might sound, we actually can get high or get a "fix" from fear and excitement. With pain, it is a similar experience even though we don't usually enjoy the "high" brought by pain.

For many of us, we have been aware of our secondary addictions but have kept them at bay with distraction and denial. These addictions can lead to an ACA bottom and signal a need for focused Step work and counseling. Our experience shows that the benefits of ACA recovery – self love and peace of mind – cannot be experienced if a person is still acting out with drugs, sex, or other addictions.

These secondary addictions can be overpowering, forcing the adult child to act against his or her will. The ACA believes he or she has no choice in avoiding these self-harming behaviors, but God, as we understand God, is greater than any compulsion experienced by an adult child.

Chapter Four

Most of us have hit a bottom or relapsed to some degree. We have experienced low points and periods in our lives when we were unwilling to take action. The pain of change was greater than the pain of remaining the same so we remained stuck. Some of us received the gift of desperation and reached out for help. Still others stumbled onto ACA only to be amazed that such a program exists. These ACAs were led to ACA without clearly knowing what they were seeking, but they found the fellowship somehow.

Most adult children hitting bottom are in a crisis, feeling hopeless and helpless; however, many of us have failed to realize or admit that a bottom had been reached. As a bottom nears, many of us find the strength to reapply ourselves and appear to be doing well again in the eyes of others; however, we are on course for another bottom or debacle. Nothing has changed. We are the same, chasing something that we don't want once we get it. Our resilience is actually "acting out behavior" in some cases. Such acting out is hard to detect since it is usually socially acceptable to appear self-reliant.

Our primary founder, Tony A., described the ACA bottom as this: "The adult child is an identity crisis having an identity crisis."[1] That means that we were born in crisis and cannot easily recognize another way to live other than crisis. Before arriving at ACA, we can remain in a crisis situation, thinking our lives are normal and manageable.

Red flags that warn that a bottom or relapse is coming involve: dropping out of meetings and isolating; being argumentative or unreasonable; gossiping; losing focus and returning to one of the family roles of hero, lost child, or mascot; general noncommitment to recovery; avoiding the Steps and intellectualizing; failing to give service to ACA; binging on sex, drugs, food, or other compulsive behaviors; and acting with perfectionism and failing to talk about feelings and critical inner messages.

[1]Telephone conversation Feb. 27, 2004.

Body, Mind, and Spirit

The ACA fellowship has not written specifically on hitting bottom until now. We cannot confuse our stories of childhood abuse with the critical step of recognizing and speaking of hitting bottom. The abuse of our childhood is not our ACA bottom. The abuse and neglect helped set up the bottom, but they are not the torment that creates the motivation for meaningful change. The motivation comes from the despair of acting out on the survival traits or common behaviors. These are the behaviors that allowed us to survive our homes through people-pleasing, being invisible, or submissive. In recovery, we want to be different, but it takes effort and focus. We want what ACA has to offer, but we must be willing to do the work and give back to ACA.

We are adults suffering from the effects of alcoholism and dysfunctional families. The childhood abuse and our adult lives created unbearable living conditions in body, mind, and spirit for us as adults. Adult children have been described as the "walking wounded," strutting about in a state of emotional and spiritual bankruptcy while claiming to be "fine."

This is not a shaming analysis. It is written in this manner to raise the awareness of the importance of this critical element of ACA recovery. Adult children who cannot realize hitting a bottom tend to repeat the mistakes of the past and fail to receive the full rewards of the ACA program. They miss out on feeling fully safe or understanding their feelings.

There are several reasons why the adult child bottom seems difficult to recognize or talk about. In addition to self-sufficiency, hitting bottom can be masked by adaptive behaviors that can be misleading to onlookers and to the adult child. Most of these adaptations fall under the category of resilience.

Clinical studies that measure adult child resilience seem to fail to see that such "positive" behaviors are acting out behaviors for some. For example, the adaptive behavior of working grueling hours at the expense of health and social life is usually the fear of authority figures or people-pleasing traits in action. Such traits are often destructive or draining. They keep the adult child in an endless loop of rigid perfectionism or serving others in a passive-aggressive manner. Through the lens of resilience, the adult child appears to have adjusted from childhood abuse. He looks like a faithful worker, but the person could be acting out a defense trait that gains social approval.

Adult child authors Gravitz and Bowden state how ACA adaptive behaviors can make the adult child invisible to himself and to society. This self-invisibility can make the realization of a bottom or relapse more difficult.

"Because their survival behaviors tend to be approval seeking and socially acceptable, the problems for children of alcoholics remain invisible," the authors write. "Many limp into adulthood behind a façade of strength. They survive adulthood, too, but many do not enjoy it."[†]

Not all successful, stable ACAs are in denial about hitting a bottom nor are they acting out their survival traits. Attendance at ACA meetings and contact with a sponsor helps the adult child recognize when she is using a survival trait to shield pain or picking up a tool of recovery to work through pain.

Learning to survive or develop resilience are admirable traits; however, in ACA we learn to go beyond mere survival. We strive for true healing and connection with a Higher Power through the realization that we have worth and that we are lovable just the way we are. However, the process of recovery takes time and patience. This is not easy.

While in recovery, many ACAs will endure many bottoms as they dig down through layers of hurt feelings and feelings of being unworthy. But hope is here. Through Twelve Step work, patient prayer, and mutual sharing with others in the safety of ACA, our child within emerges.

ACA is for people who want it, not who need it. ACA is for the adult child who can get honest about hitting a bottom and make a commitment to attend ACA meetings and work the ACA Steps to find the Inner Child and true connection to a

Higher Power. Many adult children waste years of their lives wandering in and out of meetings without owning the language of hitting bottom. They cannot seem to get focused and committed to this life-giving program. Others come to meetings awhile and feel better and wander off perhaps forever.

While the alcoholic will use up and manipulate others to find money to drink, the adult child will use up himself or herself before reaching out for help. We may remain in a suffocating situation at work or in a relationship before asking for help. This is only natural since we learned to shut down our pleas for help as children of abusive parents. Asking for help as children did not work so we believe the same is true as adults. That means that adult children struggle doubly hard in asking for help. We cannot allow our aversion to asking for help to get in the way of our chance at wholeness.

In ACA, we learn from each bottom we experience if we are focused on attending meetings and spiritual growth. The duration of the bottom or low point is shortened and less painful if we are working an active ACA program.

While ACA cannot remove the pain and fear of facing an ACA bottom, the fellowship can support us emotionally and spiritually. These are the moments that serve as a foundation for a meaningful life of feelings, friendships, and hope.

While facing these times, we learn to talk about our feelings and to be gentle with ourselves. We avoid isolation or becoming inappropriately angry or blaming others. We begin to trust the process of living life on life's terms. We are not alone. We realize that life today really is different than when we were children without a voice.

END NOTES

†ON PAGE 66: Stephanie Brown, Ph.D., November/December 2004 edition of *The Therapist Magazine.*

†ON PAGE 72: "Guide to Recovery: A Book for Adult Children of Alcoholics," page 3, 1985, Gravitz and Bowden

Chapter 5

ACA is a Spiritual
Not Religious Program

$\mathcal{A}$dult Children of Alcoholics "is a spiritual program based on action coming from love." We believe that the disease of family dysfunction is a spiritual dilemma rather than a moral deficiency to be solved by proper living. We don't believe we have a mental health problem to be cured purely by science. We have no quarrel with proper living or scientific solutions. But any solution for the disease of family dysfunction must include spirituality in our view. Spirituality is one of three key elements that underpin the recovery process for the individual. In ACA, we recover in body, mind, and spirit. Through the principles of the program, our bodies are renewed, our minds become clear, and our spirit connects with the God of our Understanding for an inner awakening. This is ACA wholeness for the individual and a sign of wholeness of the ACA program. ACA is a way of life, which can meet all of our emotional and spiritual needs.

ACA is not aligned with any sect or denomination, but we stress spiritual awareness as part of our daily lives. Through the Twelve Steps, each of us finds a spiritual life that works. However, no one is required to prove his faith or to demonstrate dedication to a spiritual life. We humbly live our spirituality without a grand demonstration.

Many of us believe that our actual parent is a Higher Power, who is patient and loving. Most of us no longer believe that God is punishing, abandoning, or indifferent. These were the traits of our parents or caregivers. Through the ACA program, we realize we projected these traits onto God and struggled with a religious version of a Higher Power until arriving at our first meeting.

Before finding ACA, we watched others, who seemed to have faith and favor with God, while we were not sure of our position with the Divine. Some of us tried religion and applied religion's answers in our lives with some good effect; however, the day always came when we felt abandoned, tricked, or rejected by God. We never seemed to measure up to what we thought God wanted us to be. Even when we were told that God was loving and forgiving, there was something inside of us that said, "No. A loving God does not pass this way." Before ACA, many of us had heard of God's unconditional love. But we seemed to drink the lukewarm version that never quenched our thirst for wanting to feel whole. We spit it out.

In ACA, we take a spiritual and not religious approach to healing the effects of being raised in a dysfunctional home. We believe that family dysfunction is a spiritual disease that best responds to surrender, self-acceptance, and a consistent effort by the adult child to make conscious contact with a Higher Power. We don't believe that family dysfunction is a moral deficiency of the parents or that changing our behavior is merely a matter of self-will. Some religious folks take this position. We understand and respect the position, but we disagree.

With this chapter, ACA is not taking issue with the religions of the world. To do so would be religious in nature and not spiritual in our view. In fact, ACA has no opinion on outside issues including religions and belief systems. ACA's primary purpose is to carry the message of hope and recovery to adult children of alcoholic and dysfunctional families. We do not debate religion or religious thought in ACA. Our members are free to seek a spiritual path of their own. For some that will be a religious path.

We encourage ACA members to explore their belief system to find a Higher Power that brings about a personal change and a real connection to life. Before ACA, many of us searched for a connection in drugs, food, sex, and relationships, but it was always a misconnection. We searched the earth trying to connect with people, places, and things who lacked the ability to connect as well.

Those arriving at ACA who are comfortable with their belief are not required to surrender such belief; however, the Twelve Steps will ask these members to reveal how their belief creates healing for them. Many of us with strong religious beliefs had been unable to live by such convictions before finding ACA. We found religions that allowed us to reenact the shame and despair of our childhood. There are many fine religions, but we took what religion had to offer and converted it into a familiar method of self-abuse or self-condemnation. Before ACA, many of us tried to live religious lives, but we were quick to point out our religious failings and to condemn ourselves for falling short. If we weren't condemning ourselves, we were unsure of what we believed. Nonetheless, we acted like true believers, hoping we could have the faith and peace that others appeared to have. Finding ACA and the Twelve Steps allowed us to reap the rewards of our faith, perhaps for the first time.

Many people come into ACA having been harmed or turned sour by the belief systems of any one of a number of religions and dogmas. They stopped believing in God, or they resigned themselves to practicing only the minimum requirements of their faith. Others became skeptics and dropped out of church or worship services. Some of us in this category continued to pray, but we wanted nothing to do with religion.

One of our members describes how she progressed from the religion of her childhood to a spirituality that she is comfortable with.

The religion I was brought up in taught me that God is love. However, it wasn't until I got into ACA recovery that I discovered that my parents had been my "god." Usually they were loving, but anger was there. My parents' inability to handle every day problems in a mature manner was to leave me with the same inabilities. What else could I learn from people who didn't know how to handle life themselves? I lived in the religion of my childhood until I no longer gained value from it, and then left it as an adult. I have found other religions to help me in life's trials, and now I am content with the spirituality I have. I enjoy fellowship, study, faith, hope, and worship. Is it a perfect church? No way, but I am able to understand and accept to a degree when things don't go the way I think they should, or even the way I think God would want.

Many of us have been brought up in a religion that is dogmatic and cannot seem to accept any deviation from the truth taught by that religion. In ACA, we have no conflict with this system. We only ask that ACA members of this belief respect the choice and path of other ACA members. We do not witness, preach, or evangelize in ACA.

On the other hand, many of us are uncomfortable with the word "God" and can recoil at the word's mention. To some, the word "God" is a curse and should not be used at all, except for swearing, ironically. These members often find relief in the thought that G-O-D could stand for "good, orderly direction."

Other ACA members find a hip label for the God of their understanding and affectionately use the initials "HP" to represent their Higher Power. This is derived from our Second Step and shows that these members are comfortable with and on an intimate level with their Higher Power.

Some of our members find the same comfort and intimacy with the word "God" or "God as I understand God." The names for God or a Higher Power are many in ACA. We are free to use the word or words that fit for us.

Adult Children of Alcoholics believes that recovery from the effects of growing up in a dysfunctional home requires spiritual intervention; however we do not propose to be the authority on what works best for each individual. The effects of growing up in a dysfunctional home are so pervasive that it takes regular attendance at meetings, counseling, fellowshipping, and a Higher

Power to bring about lasting relief and hope. Any ACA member avoiding a spiritual path tends to struggle with making progress in ACA.

At first glance, ACA might look like a religious program since the Twelve Steps and Twelve Traditions include the words "God" or "prayer." However, upon closer inspection the Steps and Traditions are worded to leave the matter of faith and belief in the hands of the individual. This is radically different than most religious systems which outline specific rules of worship, salvation, historical religious figures, and religious observances for their followers. In ACA, we have no pulpit, hymnals, or Sabbaths, nor do we align ourselves with a specific meditation style that would commit us to an Eastern or Western form of worship.

In ACA, we honor the sovereign right of every member to believe or not believe as he or she wishes. The atheist and agnostic are welcome in ACA as well. At the same time, ACA makes no apology in stating that spirituality must be sought to fully recover from effects of the disease of family dysfunction. These are the differences between being a spiritual rather than religious program in our view. This is the freedom of choice we offer each ACA member in the matter of belief. For some of us, this choice is the first time we have been allowed to ask questions about spirituality or to discuss spirituality. This is an independence that we want and desire.

The ACA choice on spiritual matters is grounded in our Third Step and particularly the last five words of Step Three. The last five words are "God as we understand God." These words are the gateway to a life of exploration, awakening, and connection to a Higher Power personal to each of us. These words guarantee that each ACA member is free to choose a Higher Power, who is available and personal to the individual. No one will make this decision for us. With Step Three, we get to choose a Higher Power, who works in our lives and who hears our prayers. This decision might seem daunting for those of us who were told what to think about God and what would happen if we thought the "wrong things" before arriving at ACA. For guidance, we attend meetings

5

and talk with our sponsor or a spiritual advisor as we determine the nature of our Higher Power. This is the paradox of independence for some of us. Our spiritual freedom can seem daunting and liberating at the same time. We keep it simple. There are no more big deals. Most of us choose a Higher Power who is loving and caring, but there are no set guidelines on spirituality.

Some of our members share their experiences on seeking a spiritual path.

Spirituality Share #1

For me, spirituality means that I am allowed to explore and learn about the God of my understanding and the mysteries of life. I am using my free will to seek the God of my understanding, and it is a marvelous journey. I was raised in a religion where you could not question or doubt so I have come a long way in ACA. The spirituality I have found in the program has transformed my life. I feel alive. I don't feel constricted. I can recognize the spiritual in people and events.

Spirituality Share #2

So what is spirituality? I believe that it's my connection with my loving Father Mother God. I believe that since I am allowed to think, I get to decide. Learning to accept myself, just the way I am, with the ability to become a better person is one of the biggest things that I have learned in the ACA Twelve Step program. Is that not a spiritual result of my study?

Spirituality Share #3

Spirituality is a continuation of the Twelfth Step in my opinion. The Twelfth Step says we have a spiritual awakening not a religious awakening. When I carry the message to someone else and share my story I get a feeling that can only be described as spiritual. I would never describe the feeling of helping another person as religious. It is spiritual. It is love for another.

Chapter 6

ACA – How It Works

We present the ACA Identity Papers in their original form because of their historical significance. The first two papers appear here and the third appears in Chapter 10. The papers were written more than 30 years ago during the formative years of our fellowship. The Identity Papers include the foundational language, focus, and method of recovery that sets ACA apart from similar Twelve Step fellowships.

The ACA Program and How It Works
The Identity, Purpose, and Relationship Committee
November 10, 1984

In 1983, a committee was appointed by the Interim Central Service Committee (ICSC) to define the ACA program. This report delivered at the first Annual Business Conference (ABC) explains who we are as individuals and how ACA helps us accomplish our goals.

Characteristics

We find that a difference in identity and purpose distinguishes Adult Children of Alcoholics from other 12-Step Programs and underscores the need for our special focus.

The central problem for ACAs is a mistaken belief, formed in childhood, which affects every part of our lives. As children, we fought to survive the destructive effects of alcoholism and began an endless struggle to change a troubled, dysfunctional family into a loving, supportive one. We reach adulthood believing we failed, unable to see no one can stop the traumatic effects of family alcoholism.

Following naturally from this pervasive sense of failure are self-blame, shame, and guilt. These self-accusations ultimately lead to self-hate. Accepting our basic powerlessness to control alcoholic behavior and its effect on the family is the key that unlocks the inner child and lets reparenting begin. When the "First Step" is applied to family alcoholism, a fundamental basis for self-hate no longer exists.

The ACA Program

Two characteristics identify the ACA Program. The program is for adults raised in alcoholic homes, and although substance abuse may exist, the focus is on the self, specifically on reaching and freeing the inner child hidden behind a protective shield of denial. The purpose of ACA is three-fold: to shelter and support "newcomers" in confronting "denial"; to comfort those mourning their early loss of security, trust and love; and to teach the skills for reparenting ourselves with gentleness, humor, love and respect.

Moving Out of Isolation

Moving from isolation is the first step an Adult Child makes in recovering the self. Isolation is both a prison and a sanctuary. Adult Children, suspended between need and fear, unable to choose between fight or flight, agonize in the middle and resolve the tension by explosive bursts of rebellion or by silently enduring the despair. Isolation is our retreat from the paralyzing pain of indecision. This retreat into denial blunts our awareness of the destructive reality of family alcoholism and is the first stage of mourning and grief. It allows us to cope with the loss of love and to survive in the face of neglect and abuse.

Feeling Our Feelings

The return of feelings is the second stage of mourning and indicates healing has begun. Initial feelings of anger, guilt, rage, and despair resolve into a final acceptance of loss. Genuine grieving for our childhood ends our morbid fascination with the past and lets us return to the present, free to live as adults. Confronting years of pain and loss at first seems overwhelming. Jim Goodwin, in describing the post-traumatic stress of Vietnam veterans, writes that some veterans "actually believe that if they once again allow themselves to feel, they may never stop crying or may completely lose control...."[1,2]

Sharing the burden of grief others feel gives us the courage and strength to face our own bereavement. The pain of mourning and grief is balanced by being able, once again, to fully love and care for someone and to freely experience joy in life.

Reparenting Ourselves

The need to reparent ourselves comes from our efforts to feel safe as children. The violent nature of alcoholism darkened our emotional world and left us wounded, hurt, and unable to feel. This extreme alienation from our own internal direction kept us helplessly dependent on those we mistrusted and feared. In an unstable, hostile, and often dangerous environment, we attempted to meet the impossible demands of living with family alcoholism, and our lives were soon out of control.

To make sense of the confusion and to end our feelings of fear, we denied inconsistencies in what we were taught. We held rigidly to a few certain beliefs, or we rebelled and distrusted all outside interference. Freedom begins with being open to love. The dilemma of abandonment is a choice between painful intimacy and hopeless isolation, but the consequence is the same.

[1] "The Etiology of Combat-Related Post-Traumatic Stress Disorders," Goodwin, Jim, Psy. D., Disabled American Veterans Pub., Cincinnati, p. 16.

[2] Post-traumatic stress is the tension of unresolved grief following the loss of fundamental security.

We protect ourselves by rejecting the vulnerable inner child and are forced to live without warmth or love.

Without love, intimacy and isolation are equally painful, empty, and incomplete. Love dissolves hate. We give ourselves the love we seek by releasing our self-hatred and embracing the child inside. With a child's sensitivity we reach out to explore the world again and become aware of the need to trust and love others. The warm affection we have for each other heals our inner hurt. ACA's loving acceptance and gentle support lessen our feelings of fear. We share our beliefs and mistrust without judgment or criticism. We realize the insanity of alcoholism and become willing to replace the confusing beliefs of childhood with the clear, consistent direction of the Twelve Steps and Traditions, and to accept the authority of the loving God they reflect.

ACA is a 12-Step Program of Recovery

ACA's relationship to other anonymous programs is a shared dependence on the Twelve Steps for a spiritual awakening. Each program's focus is different, but the solution remains the same. In childhood our identity is formed by the reflection we see in the eyes of the people around us. We fear losing this reflection, thinking the mirror makes us real and that we disappear or have no self without it. The distorted image of family alcoholism is not who we are. And we are not the unreal person trying to mask that distortion. In ACA we do not stop abusing a substance or losing ourselves in another. We stop believing we have no worth and start to see our true identity, reflected in the eyes of other Adult Children, as the strong survivors and valuable people we actually are.

Identity, Purpose, and Relationship Committee

Finding Wholeness Through Separation:
The Paradox of Independence
The Identity, Purpose, and Relationship Committee
January 19, 1986

As ACA grows to maturity, we see the need to more clearly define our relationship to Alcoholics Anonymous and Al-Anon Family Groups and to acknowledge our special contribution to Twelve-Step Programs.

Separating

As we struggle to form an identity separate from our "parent" programs, we are also becoming aware of the need to separate emotionally from our alcoholic homes. Only in complete separation can we find the freedom to express who we are and to create the experience of intimate closeness we so desperately needed as children.

Results of Abandonment

René Spitz, in his classic study of infants in foundling homes, discovered that babies who were left alone for long periods of time could not tolerate the isolation and lost the will to live.[1] The despair of not being held except during basic care left the infants without hope of receiving the comfort and love they needed to feel safe and secure.

How a Negative Self-Image Begins

Children in an alcoholic home exist in a constant state of basic insecurity which begins when the cry to be held is met with hostility and rejection, or simply ignored. Self-soothing is not possible in an atmosphere conditioned by violence and fear, and children of alcoholics are always close to feeling the despair

[1]Spitz, R.A., and Wolf, K.M. Anaclitic Depression. "The Psychoanalytic Study of The Child," 1946, Vol. 2, pp. 331–42.

which comes from being helpless and dependent in a home without love.[2]

Abuse Seems Normal & Acceptable

An alcoholic home is a violent place. Alcoholism is a violent solution to the problem of pain, and anyone trapped in its lethal embrace is filled with rage and self-hate for choosing this form of denial. Children exposed to such violence come to believe they are to accept punishment and abuse as a normal part of existence. They identify themselves as objects of hate, not worthy of love, and survive by denying their underlying feelings of hopeless despair.

Nurturing Self-Worth

In loving homes, children are eager to see themselves reflected by those around them. A positive self-reflection increases their sense of security and feelings of self-esteem and gives them confidence in relating to others. They see respect for their need to be protected from harm and relate to authority with trust and not fear. They come to believe they have value because they are accepted and loved.

Fitting into the Dysfunctional Family

As children in an alcoholic home, we are horrified by the images we have of ourselves. What we see reflected in the distorted mirror of alcoholism are projected images of hostility and hate. In a desperate effort to connect and belong, we force ourselves to fit these distorted images and become false selves to keep from feeling isolated and alone. Sadly, we often become mirrors for our family, struggling without success to reflect the love we need for ourselves. This tragic reversal further robs us of the chance to form an identity based on being valued and loved.[3]

---

[2]Seabaugh, M.O.L. The Vulnerable Self of the Adult Child of an Alcoholic: A Phenomenologically Derived Theory, Doctoral Dissertation, University of Southern California, 1983, p. 110.

[3]Ibid., p. 108.

The strength of this desperate attachment becomes clear when we attempt to change the family's belief about who we must be and find a less violent identity.

Learning to be Indecisive

Children of alcoholics are paralyzed by indecision when trying to separate emotionally from their homes. They are in conflict about when to approach and when to avoid the very people on whom they depend to give security, comfort, and love because these are the same people who are destroying the children's sense of well-being. They are equally in conflict about leaving home, burdened with shame and guilt and a massive sense of failure for being unable to find a less violent solution to the problem of pain. With few social skills and an inability to discriminate between whom to approach and whom to avoid in the outside world, they are forced to agonize in the middle and to fight falling into despair.

Repressing Feelings to Survive

To survive in the midst of confusion and to have any sense of control, Adult Children must distance or dissociate from their feelings of panic and fear. There are three forms of dissociation. The first uses the functional defenses of the mind to deny or distort the painful reality by repressing, projecting or rationalizing the feelings that are causing the pain. Using a substance to alter the feelings is the second way to dissociate from feeling pain. The most easily available substances are alcohol, sugar, nicotine and caffeine. A final form of dissociation uses negative excitement to keep us unaware of deeper fear. By focusing our attention on phobias, obsessions, dreams and taboos, and compulsively tensing in response to these fears, we force the body to build a protective physical armor and to produce adrenaline, endorphins and melatonin to chemically block the perception of pain. All three

Chapter Six

forms of dissociation keep us imprisoned in a narrow and familiar range of behavior, never reaching the extremes of panicked exhaustion or of collapse into suicidal despair.

Responsibility

Freedom from alcoholic insanity is a question of responsibility. We cannot be responsible for something we did not create. The decision to stop drinking belonged to the alcoholic alone, and there is no need to punish or reject ourselves for the frightening consequences of someone else's decision. As children we are tied to our families by our physical needs. As adults we are held only by the shared beliefs about who we are.

Our mistaken beliefs about who we must be to survive are based on the reality of our having survived in an alcoholic home, where every move or failure to move might bring injury, pain, or death. These beliefs are false only because they continue to give a limited view of the world as a dangerous and hostile place. Our survival beliefs represent our understanding of how to think, feel, and behave in keeping the fragile balance and rigid stability we associate with being alive.

They were essential to our well-being as children. They were formed during times of great fear and distress and are necessarily concerned with extremes. We are unable to imagine or conceive of a less painful, more fulfilling way of living, thinking we live in a world dominated by alcoholism. We are constantly afraid of losing control, of finding ourselves once again in the confusion and chaos of an alcoholic home, of being overwhelmed by feelings of sadness and grief for our childhood.

To Be or Not to Be?

The paradox of independence is that only in separation do we find the courage and strength to live in the world as complete human beings, capable of giving and receiving love, of creating out of a sense of wholeness. In normal separation, children are reassured by leaving and returning to consistent and loving parents, and then carry these parents inside to remind themselves they are safe and loved. As children of alcoholics, we internalize parents who are filled with rage and self-hate and who have projected these feelings onto us. We carry this negative view of ourselves, feeling insecure and frightened of our own self-rejection and of being rejected by others. We remain in the same double-bind we experienced as children, unable to detach from or remain with the people who caused us harm.

Empowered or Powerless?

In a normal home, children also internalize the strength of their parents. They feel securely held by a sense of parental power which gives logic and structure to their lives. With this foundation and strength, they are able to build a self and create loving intimacy through their own sense of power. Children of alcoholics have an overriding feeling of powerlessness for being unable to stop the destructive effects of family alcoholism.

Steps & the Serenity Prayer

The Twelve Steps and the Serenity Prayer remind us we can receive real power and apply it in our lives to things we are able to change. We need to recognize that we gained sufficient strength from our parents, as destructive and confusing as they were, to let go of the false sense of security they provided and to find true security in a new attachment to our Higher Power, who is always accessible and ready to direct our lives in a meaningful, loving way.

Gratitude to AA and Al-Anon

We are grateful to Alcoholics Anonymous and Al-Anon Family Groups for bringing clarity and sanity to our lives. In the clear, consistent mirror of the Steps and Traditions, we finally see who we are – adult children of alcoholics. Our particular need is to create a new identity based on being valued and loved.

Chapter Six

Reuniting with the Inner Child

By accepting and reuniting with the vulnerable child we keep hidden inside, we begin to heal the broken pieces of our shattered selves and become whole human beings capable of interacting in the world with confidence and trust. We need the security, strength, and positive support we find in ACA to grow to independence and to reflect back to our parent programs our own experience of recovery.

Emotional Sobriety & Freedom

What ACA has to share with other anonymous programs is the experience of transformation promised in the Serenity Prayer. By accepting the unchangeable past and changing the beliefs that keep us bound and confused, we broaden and deepen the Steps and Traditions to create the possibility of emotional sobriety and spiritual freedom for anyone affected by family alcoholism.

Identity, Purpose, and Relationship Committee

Chapter 7

The Twelve Steps of ACA

PART I

*T*he pathway to emotional sobriety that endures time is through the Twelve Steps of ACA. This is the heart of the Adult Children of Alcoholics program. Adapted from the time-proven Steps of Alcoholics Anonymous, the Twelve Steps are precision tools that work. The ACA Steps clarify and help resolve a childhood of neglect, abuse, or rejection. With more than 30 years of experience, ACA is a proven program that offers a way out of confusion. The program brings clarity and sanity in measures we always hoped for, but usually could not believe existed as we grew up in dysfunctional homes.

Since their original publication by AA in 1939, the Twelve Steps have relieved the suffering of millions of alcoholics, addicts, codependents, food addicts, sex addicts, and many more obsessive-compulsive types. The Steps, and their various adaptations, have brought sure hope and a better way of life to those who desire change. In ACA, the Twelve Steps also bring recovery to our members who were not raised with addiction in the home. Our experience shows that these ACA members internalized the same abandonment and shame as children brought up in alcoholism or other addictions.

Beginning with Step One, we address denial, which can involve simply refusing to admit that abuse or neglect occurred in our childhood. Denial also includes trivializing behavior or remarks that were obviously harmful to us. If we admit that harmful behavior occurred, we can still be in denial if we fail to acknowledge the effects of the harm in our lives. Additionally, we are practicing denial if we attempt to explain away the behavior or to offer excuses for our family. By breaking through our denial, we seek a full remembrance. We find our loss and learn our story. With help and acceptance, we recognize the false identity we had to develop to survive family dysfunction.

In ACA, we learn to focus on ourselves and find our real identity. We must be willing to work the Twelve Steps so we can grow emotionally and spiritually. These are the Steps we work to address growing up in a dysfunctional family.

1. We admitted we were powerless over the effects of alcoholism or other family dysfunction, that our lives had become unmanageable.

2. Came to believe that a Power greater than ourselves could restore us to sanity.

3. Made a decision to turn our will and our lives over to the care of God as we understand God.

4. Made a searching and fearless moral inventory of ourselves.

5. Admitted to God, to ourselves, and to another human being the exact nature of our wrongs.

6. Were entirely ready to have God remove all these defects of character.

7. Humbly asked God to remove our shortcomings.

8. Made a list of all persons we had harmed and became willing to make amends to them all.

9. Made direct amends to such people wherever possible, except when to do so would injure them or others.

The Twelve Steps are reprinted and adapted from the original Twelve Steps of Alcoholics Anonymous and are used with the permission of Alcoholics Anonymous World Services, Inc.

10. Continued to take personal inventory and when we were wrong promptly admitted it.

11. Sought through prayer and meditation to improve our conscious contact with God, as we understand God, praying only for knowledge of God's will for us and the power to carry that out.

12. Having had a spiritual awakening as the result of these Steps, we tried to carry this message to others who still suffer, and to practice these principles in all our affairs.

The Twelve Steps are simple but not always easy; however, they work if a person truly wants to change and can hang on while change occurs. The Steps sometimes work even if a person picks at them like a finicky child forking at a lump of unwanted spinach. Such half measures often create the personal discomfort that motivates the adult child into greater action and personal growth.

By adapting AA's Steps, ACA is adding its flavor to the Steps while keeping intact the original intent of an admission of powerlessness followed by surrender. Such surrender is followed by a review of spiritual beliefs, self-inventory, making amends, and seeking conscious contact with a Higher Power. We develop a genuine attitude to live in love and service to ourselves and others.

While ACA adapted the AA Steps with few word changes, our experience shows that the adaptation has unique considerations. Because of our inherent sense of being flawed or unlovable, the adult child must be reminded that he or she has worth. We have worth and are acceptable, regardless of mistakes made or accomplishments achieved or not achieved. As adult children we are a traumatized group of adults, who can revert to self-doubt when making errors or sensing disapproval by others. No adaptation of the Twelve Steps for adult child purposes will be fully successful unless it emphasizes self-love. We are God's children despite mistakes made. Through such affirmations and Twelve Step work, we come to believe in our self-worth. We learn to tell ourselves that we are human and have something to offer the world. We face our mistakes and the opinions of others with confidence. In ACA, we get to say who we are, instead of a drunk or dysfunctional parent saying who we are not. This is the great fact for us. We have paid our dues with the countless cursings, threats, and subtle neglectful acts we have endured as children. We stand now as adults, not complaining, but as people seeking to feel and be. We have earned it. This is our claiming of the Twelve Steps and their rewards.

Our solution appeals to cultures across the globe. Our members practice ACA recovery in Europe, Asia, Australia, Pacific Islands, the Middle East, Africa, and North and South America. We have learned that children anywhere exposed to shame and abandonment develop the same soul wound. When given an option as adults, many choose ACA's way of life. The ACA program is a proven way of life that fulfills its members emotionally and spiritually.

The term "adult child" does not mean that we live in the past or that we are infantile in our thinking and actions. The term means that we meet the demands of adult life with survival techniques learned as children. Before finding recovery, we suppressed our feelings and were overly responsible. We tried to anticipate the needs of others and meet those needs so we would not be abandoned. We tried to be flexible or supportive of others as we denied our own needs. We monitored our relationships for any sign of disapproval. We tried to be perfect so we would be loved and never left alone. Or we isolated ourselves and thought we needed no one.

As adults, we have been responsible team players or invisible loners. We are great employees, listeners, planners and party givers, but we respond to adult life with childhood survival traits that leave us feeling unsure of who we are. This is how we survived childhood, and this is how we lived as "adult children."

When faced with working ACA's Twelve Steps, some adult children feel overwhelmed and balk. Others are alarmed and believe they could be encouraged to abandon or confront their families. This is not the purpose of the ACA program. In ACA, we realize that our parents did not have the options that we have in ACA. If we were raised by relatives or grandparents, these people as well did not always have options. Our parents or relatives passed on family dysfunction. We are not minimizing the fact that many of our parents acted hostile, manipulative, or indifferent. Some dysfunctional parents were inebriated and pitiful. We balance our experiences as children with the knowledge that we have a unique chance through ACA to break the cycle of family dysfunction. Even though our families may not seek recovery, we can respect them. We set appropriate boundaries to protect ourselves. We can disentangle our lives from their lives without shutting them out completely.

We ask the adult child considering ACA to look at the program as a way of life that will unfold over time, bringing rich rewards of emotional relief and self-acceptance. There will be transformations and healing grace as well. We suggest that ACA members work the Steps one at a time, avoiding looking ahead and perhaps becoming overwhelmed. In ACA, we learn to slow down, breathe, and ask for help. The Steps work best when we surrender our self-sufficient attitudes and ask for help.

Our experience shows that the Steps are a proven way of life, yielding new meaning and a sense of purpose in one's life. We apply the Steps with willingness and honesty. In addition to addressing dependence and addiction, the Twelve Steps awaken the person to an inner strength that comes with a true connection to his or her Higher Power. We have always had this inner strength. Even when we appeared pitiful and helpless, the strength was there helping us survive until we could find real help. The Twelve Steps bring forth this God-given strength and true choice or discernment. With the Steps and true choice, we can finally breathe deeply and feel joy.

Chapter Seven

Making a Beginning

Beginning with Step One the adult child begins to realize, perhaps for the first time, the destructive malady of growing up in an alcoholic or other dysfunctional home. In addition to shame, our families included perfectionism, rage, mental illness, sexual abuse, religious abuse, or illicit drug use. Some parents were hypochondriacs who abused prescriptions and used an endless number of ailments to control others. By working the Steps and attending meetings, we see that we are not unique and that our family is not unique as well. There are millions of people like us. In ACA, we begin to acquire the language we need to describe what happened to us in a manner that has meaning and resonance. Even adult children with years of Twelve Step experience in other programs gain a new awareness of family-of-origin issues by working the ACA Steps.

By working the Twelve Steps with a sponsor or knowledgeable counselor, the adult child realizes the denial and secrecy that were necessary to survive such an upbringing. Denial, which fosters a lack of clarity, is the glue that allows the disease of family dysfunction to thrive. Cloaked in denial, the disease is passed on to the next generation with amazing consistency. The basic language of denial is: "don't talk, don't trust, don't feel."[1]

With Step One we come out of denial and talk about what happened. We bring details to light. Many of us have smelled our parents' drunken breath. We have found hidden whisky bottles and pill bottles. We have cleaned up vomit. We have comforted a frightened brother or sister. The police have been called to our home. Our neighbors talked about our family. We avoided having friends over because we feared how our parents might act in front of them. We have made excuses for our parents, pleaded with our parents and condemned them with no real change. We have hidden illicit drugs and lied to neighbors. We have slept with our clothes on and ready to run.

[1] It Will Never Happen to Me, by Dr. Claudia Black – 1981.

Some of us have thrown water on a mattress accidentally lit by a passed out mother or father. We have burned with shame after being cursed or belittled. We have listened to a parent's promises to change but have seen no lasting results. We have heard our parents curse one another regularly, swapping insults and hurtful claims. We have listened to them rehash the same blame and threats year after year. Nothing changed. We have seen our parents run up great sums of debt to buy affection or happiness. Our utilities have been cut off for nonpayment. We have lied to the collection agency for our parents. We have experienced divorce or heard talk of divorce that never came. Our siblings may have remembered things differently, but we know our own truth. We know what happened and we are breaking our silence.

Families without alcoholism have similar situations. These families abuse the children through the use of intellect, manipulation, or silence. We know our truth.

By working the Steps, the adult child realizes family roles that were required to approximate protection in an unsafe home. We often feared for our safety and took on roles to disarm our parents. Some of us sought to be invisible. The roles which are usually present in alcoholic and dysfunctional homes include "family hero, lost child, scapegoat, and mascot."[2] Some of the roles allowed us to be a parental favorite. As the favorite, we could temporarily dodge harmful behavior that could be shifted to a brother or sister. However, we were harmed by the process as well or when it was our turn to be abused, neglected or rejected. In addition to physical abuse, we were subjected to emotional abuse. The emotional abuse involved belittling comments or hatefulness aimed at our hearts. The abuse left no visible marks, but it is stored in our bodies just the same as slapping and hitting leave marks on the body.

[2]Roles by Sharon Wegscheider.

Chapter Seven

In addition to creating false safety, our childhood roles had other functions. The hero child of a dysfunctional family might seek to make good grades at school. This is the honors student who shows the world that her family values education and is therefore stable. The mascot, typically the youngest of the family, serves as comic relief for dysfunctional homes that leave little room for joy. The lost or invisible child remains silent. The child knows it is not safe to speak. The lost child retreats to his or her room and remains absorbed in reading books or fantasies of living elsewhere. The scapegoat child lives out the parents' prophesy of being a bad or rotten kid. These are the roles that are almost predictable for any family in which dysfunctional parenting is present.

Such survival roles tend to have a hardy life and remain fixed in our personalities long after we have left our unhealthy homes. Adult children finding recovery learn about such dysfunctional roles. They can look at their families and see the roles in effect decades after the children have grown up and left the family. There is the 50-year-old brother still playing the hero. There is the 40-year-old sister, living out the lost child role by avoiding holiday meals and rarely calling home. This is difficult to watch once we find ACA and begin our recovery journey. The adult child in recovery gets the chance to retire his or her role with dignity. We are never too old to work an ACA program and receive its benefits.

In addition to learning about survival roles through the Twelve Steps, many adult children realize they have absorbed generational shame, abandonment, and rage only to grow up and recreate similar families or relationships. They realize they wanted to fix others. Without focused help, many ACAs spend their lives in adult relationships trying to repair their original family. Who hasn't read a story about a child with an ailing parent growing up to be a doctor in an effort to find a cure for the ailing parent? Adult children are no different. We want to heal our drunken or dysfunctional parents by acting good, silent, or by taking care of them. But the "sickness" the adult child attempts to cure in the parent is the disease of dysfunction, which we have no power over.

The ACA Identity Papers identify this behavior as our main problem – a mistaken belief that we could have changed our parents. Additionally, The Problem, read at ACA meetings, underscores our attempts to heal or rescue others. It states: "We confused love with pity, tending to love those we could rescue." Trying to rescue or heal our parents set the course of our lives. Many ACAs grow up believing they have failed in healing their families without realizing it was never their job to do so. As adults, many of us subconsciously attempt to heal our families in our adult relationships by disguised designs. In ACA, we realize we have no power over alcoholism and family dysfunction. We cannot change anyone but ourselves.

At the same time, some of us were so abused or belittled as children that we felt powerless to have any effect on our parents' behavior. The thought of healing or changing them never occurred to us. However, we grew up with the same loss, shame and self-hate as other adult children. Like others, we turned to control in adulthood for a sense of safety.

Without recovery, we, as adult children, intuitively find dysfunctional people and attempt to heal them or cure them based on our upbringing. We confuse love with pity and get unhealthy dependence. ACA experience shows that such behavior dooms relationships. We cannot change anyone. The only person we can change is ourselves, and an adult child rarely changes unless he or she becomes willing to learn a new way to live. The good news is this: There is another way to live.

The ACA fellowship offers hope to any adult child, who can realize he or she has hit a bottom and become willing to attend meetings, work the Twelve Steps, and seek a Higher Power of his or her understanding. There are many types of bottoms in ACA. Some of our members hit a bottom with alcoholism or addiction. Others hit a bottom in codependent relationships

Chapter Seven

that can be just as addictive as drugs. For instance, some adult children become obsessed and develop a compulsion for another person that is similar to the addict's obsession and compulsion for drugs. The "withdrawal" from an addictive, codependent relationship can be just as painful, if not more painful, as an addict's withdrawal from drugs. ACA members know that codependent pain can grip a person's body with an agonizing sense of abandonment. The fear of abandonment can be so powerful that it makes breathing and concentration difficult. Fear of going insane is not uncommon. Some adult children have been struck with anxiety or panic attacks when going through a codependent separation. For many, it is too much to take without help. Codependent pain of this magnitude is actually our childhood terror of abandonment inserting itself in to the break up. The intense fear of losing our spouse or partner is really our Inner Child reliving the fear of being unloved or unwanted by our family.

There are many definitions for codependence, but for our purposes, codependence means that we constantly look outside of ourselves for love, affirmation, and attention from people who cannot provide it. At the same time, we believe that we are not truly worthy of love or attention. In our view, codependence is driven by childhood fear and distorted thinking known as para-alcoholism. We choose dependent people who abandon us and lack clarity in their own lives because it matches our childhood experiences. In ACA, we learn to love and affirm ourselves and develop relationships with people who can do the same. We learn that our feelings will not kill us. The program works for those who want it.

ACA membership is defined by a wide variety of people. There is the newcomer looking for a sponsor and learning the family rules of "don't talk, don't trust, and don't feel;" the older ACA member who has worked the Twelve Steps and who sponsors others; the ACA member who has significant experience in other Twelve Step programs, yet lacks an understanding of the Inner Child; and the adult child who has lost focus on the ACA program and needs to return to clarity through the Steps and ACA meetings.

Powerlessness versus Learned Helplessness

Many adult children struggle with the notion of powerlessness in Step One since powerlessness is all that many of us have known as children; however, the powerlessness that we describe in ACA is different than the learned helplessness we experienced as children. As children we were overrun by parents who unknowingly taught us to feel helpless or to feel less competent. Some parents accidentally undercut our learning ability and suggested we could do nothing right. Or our parents said we should try harder when we had already reached a level of above average. Some of us learned to be helpless or to give up since we could see no way to please our parents or family. Later on in life, we realized we could do things and learn, but we still had areas of learned helplessness, particularly in relationships. We either gave up or increased our attempts to control others. We could be subtle or aggressive in our attempted control.

In teaching us helplessness, our parents clouded this reality by failing to understand what they had done. They taught us to be dependent and then blamed us for being dependent. When we look at our childhood, we can see how our parents undermined our reality by telling us how we should think and feel when we objected to their treatment of us. As children, we were outmatched. Our parents projected their fears, suspicions, and sense of inferiority onto us. We were defenseless against the projections. We absorbed our parents' fear and low self-worth by thinking these feelings originated with us. Our dysfunctional parents often said: "Why can't you get this?" "I am so ashamed of you." "Why do you act like that?" "You must be the dumbest child in the world." Upon hearing such comments, we felt helpless to defend ourselves. We began to believe we could not trust our perceptions. Some of us knew we could not trust our parents as well, but we believed their words without question. We believed what they said about us was truth, when it was not.

With Step One, the adult child realizes that he or she is now an adult and that the powerlessness mentioned in the Step does not engender a denial of feelings or mean that we are helpless. Powerlessness in ACA can mean that we were not responsible for our parents' dysfunctional behavior as children or adults. It means that as adults we are not responsible for going back and "fixing" the family unit. We are not responsible for rescuing, saving, or healing our parents or siblings who remain mired in family dysfunction. We can detach with love and begin the gradual process of learning about boundaries. We live and let live.

While some adult children confuse powerlessness for helplessness, there are others who dismiss the idea of admitting powerlessness as Step One suggests. These adult children believe they are all-knowing, all-sensing, and all-flexible. They secretly feel powerful in their ability to adapt to any situation or group of people they might encounter. These adult children make great salespeople, planners, and instructors. No situation is too challenging, and no group of people is too complex for these adult children to "conquer" with their adaptive behavior. These adult children usually see no need to ask for help in their lives, believing they are self-sufficient and beyond such a need. They feel powerful in their self-sufficient control. They tend to manipulate others for things they want, but find out they are not happy with themselves when their wants are met by others. These adult children rarely stop to think that self-sufficiency is covering up a fear of rejection which they think could come if they ask for help.

Meanwhile, to ask for help and get it might mean that someone would get to know them, and that is too risky. In such cases, self-sufficient power is really a mechanism to ensure isolation and aloneness. These adult children remain in control and are suspicious or indifferent to notions of powerlessness mentioned in Step One. They don't often trust what they hear in ACA meetings, but they adapt to remain in control.

By admitting our powerlessness over alcoholism and dysfunction, we gradually learn to trust our perceptions and feelings. Whether we are self-sufficient or clamoring about appearing helpless, we can learn to trust ourselves and ask for what we need. We let people into our lives. At the same time, the word "boundary" begins to have meaning and creates a reasonable amount of power for us. We stop giving away our power to others and feeling helpless to change. By admitting our powerlessness, we take our first step toward reclaiming personal power, which is critical for healing our fractured identities. If we are compulsively self-reliant, we take our first step toward trust and asking for help.

With Step One, we also begin to realize that we have a choice. Before coming to ACA and finding the solution to family dysfunction, adult children do not have a choice[3]. While we had the illusion of choice as adults, what we really practiced before ACA was control, which predictably fizzled into binges on food, work, sex, gambling, spending, or destructive relationships. It is not uncommon for us to have had two or more addictive or compulsive behaviors occurring at the same time. For example, we have seen adult children in active drug addiction also enmeshed in a loveless relationship while being sexually compulsive with another partner. These addictions and compulsive behaviors can be substituted for one another in addition to occurring simultaneously. Based on our experiences before ACA, we thought we had made bad choices when in reality we were condemned to repeat the same mistakes of our parents through compulsions or mad dreams of denial. We had no choice, but we judged ourselves without mercy for "choosing" badly.

We can re-experience powerlessness in our daily lives as we try to fix our current relationships based on old ideas of feeling helpless and hopeless. When we realize such powerlessness as an adult we step back, let go, and take a new course of action

[3]Earnie Larsen – Feb. 26, 2005, Las Vegas talk

or take no action. We learn to detach with compassion and to stop trying to repair our family of origin. We also change our current behavior in our current relationships; however, the key words are "slowly" and "gradually" and come from the Twelve Promises of ACA. Promise Eleven states: "With help from our ACA support group, we will slowly release our dysfunctional behaviors." Promise Twelve states: "Gradually, with our Higher Power's help, we learn to expect the best and get it."

Unmanageability

Like powerlessness, the concept of unmanageability in Step One is often misunderstood by adult children. While some of our families were chaotic and unstable when we were children, many homes seemed manageable and productive. But we learn that productivity does not always equal a manageable, wholesome life. For many of us, what we thought was manageable or desirable in our dysfunctional homes was actually oppressive control.

The unmanageability that we speak of in Step One involves our desire to control others and ourselves while having a sense that we are not capable or effective. While we have moments of control, we usually experience painful episodes of losing control. We feel hurt when confronted by our loved ones for our controlling behavior. They act out in anger or abandonment to disrupt our attempts to control them. We may be momentarily hurt, but we usually blame others for this abandonment. We blame them for not reading our minds or not acting in a manner that we would approve. We run about attempting to control others and situations in an effort to avoid our own unmanageable lives. Control is an attempt to minimize uncertainty and to avoid our own uncomfortable feelings about the past and present. Yet, our unmanageability, fueled by our fear-based control, inevitably creates what we fear the most: abandonment.

Many adult children, whether they are a newcomer or a member who has worked another Twelve Step program, miss this subtle distinction between powerlessness and helplessness. They miss fear-based control appearing as manageability.

ACA experience has shown that adult children will cling to controlling behavior and learned helplessness as long as it works for them; however, these learned behaviors can be changed with diligent Step work and regular attendance at ACA meetings.

Lastly, any discussion about ACA powerlessness and unmanageability is incomplete without the disease concept of alcoholism and family dysfunction. When alcoholic or other dysfunction is present in the family, every member of the family is affected. We are affected in body, mind, and spirit. Through the first 18 years of our lives, our families had 6,570 days to shame, belittle, ignore, criticize, or manipulate us during the most formative years of our being. That is 160,000 hours of living in dysfunction with unhealthy parenting. That is 72 seasons of sorrow stored deeply in the tissue of our bodies. The dysfunction is encoded into our souls as the false self. To survive this long exposure to family dysfunction, our minds developed deeply entrenched roles and traits that changed the meaning of words and experiences. Some of us misremembered the damaging nature of the abuse because we depended upon our abusers for food and shelter.

As children, we did not have the option to leave our homes. If our parents slapped us, molested us, or neglected us, we had to live with them. We had to figure out a way to survive. The subconscious survival decisions we made as children involved changing the meaning of words. Because we were vulnerable, we changed the way we perceived the emotional and physical abuse. We feared for our safety or feared we had caused these things to happen. We developed stories that minimized our parents' behavior or which convinced us that we were wrong and deserved their harmful behavior. We came to believe that we deserved to be hit or criticized with brutality. We confused molestation for love because the person molesting us was a relative describing such action as love. Such confused thinking about hitting or touching fueled our denial as adults. The confusion allows many of us to say we had normal childhoods when we have lived through hell.

We never spoke of family secrets. We thought we had forgotten the abuse, but the body and mind remembered. The survival traits we lived by showed a clear path of our terror of abandonment and being shamed. During these years of family dysfunction, our Inner Child or True Self went into hiding and remained heavily fortified under addictions or dependent behavior. This is what we mean when we say the disease of family dysfunction affects us in body, mind, and spirit. The disease survives in the language of denial and is passed on to the next generation through secrets, blame, and confusion.

The disease of family dysfunction is progressive, incurable, and sometimes fatal. The disease becomes worse over time unless treated; however, the malady is often misdiagnosed, causing the adult child to seek remedies that usually fail to bring true relief. Many adult children have taken their own lives or died from complications of drug addiction or physical ailments that can be traced to childhood abuse. These are stark claims, but we have found them to be true in our experience. This is the dire nature of the family disease of dysfunction and its great reach. But there is much hope in ACA and in sharing our pain with other recovering adult children.

We urge patience and gentleness when addressing these areas of our lives. That means we take care of ourselves. We do the Step work and program work necessary to reap the benefits of the ACA Promises.

Examining Spiritual Beliefs

Moving to Steps Two and Three, many adult children are confronted with the issue of faith and a Higher Power. In our anger at our parents and God, many of us thought we had outgrown or moved past this issue in our lives. Frankly, some of us did not like this part of the ACA program. Being told of the spiritual nature of ACA irritated some of us. We wondered about the need for spirituality in recovery. We must remember that ACA is a spiritual and not religious program. Faith and religious conviction are not requirements for ACA membership.

We avoid dogmatism and theological discussions, yet, a Higher Power is a key part of the ACA way of life.

Many adult children have assigned the traits of their dysfunctional parents to God or a Higher Power. If their parents were shaming, vengeful, and inconsistent, then their God tends to be the same. Some adult children describe having a "getcha God." For them, God keeps a record of their behavior and punishes them or "gets them" for making mistakes.

There are many levels of belief among our fellowship members. There are adult children, who are atheist or agnostic, who struggle with the notion of a universal force who will hear their prayers and make a meaningful impact in their lives. Numerous adult children recall praying to God for their parental abuse to stop, but nothing seemed to change. Many of these adult children concluded the Higher Power did not exist. They thought God did not hear their prayers. For these ACA members we ask that they keep an open mind. God, as we understand God, may have bundled up all such prayers from across the world and created ACA.

Other ACAs are staunch believers who cannot seem to allow a Higher Power to work in their lives. They cannot seem to get out of the way. There are also former believers who think they cannot reclaim faith. They feel abandoned by their Higher Power. One purpose of Step Two is to introduce the idea of keeping an open mind on the possibility of a Higher Power who can restore sanity. In some cases, our Higher Power helps us create sanity or wholeness for the first time in our lives.

ACA is a spiritual program that confronts the effects of the disease of dysfunction head on. The disease affects our bodies, minds, and spirits and requires a spiritual solution for lasting impact. Knowing where our perceptions of a Higher Power originated from and if the perceptions are accurate, is critical. We must discern what we believe or do not believe if we are to work Step Two and the remainder of the Steps.

Moving into Step Three, we see the third Step is merely a decision to ask our Higher Power to help us live courageously and sanely on a daily basis. One day at a time, we recover from the disease of family dysfunction. Step Three is underpinned by the ACA Solution, which is read at the opening of most adult child meetings. The ACA Solution is that we become our "own loving parent." Becoming our own loving parent involves seeing our "biological parents as the instruments of our existence." As The Solution states: "Our actual parent is our Higher Power, whom some of us choose to call God."

Working Step Three in ACA means that we realize that our parents brought us into the world. However, we are children of God, seeking to reclaim our true nature or original selves. The Twelve Steps support this journey to the Inner Child or True Self.

Meanwhile, Step Three helps further free us from the generational shame and abuse wrought by dysfunctional parents or caregivers. By realizing that our actual parent is our Higher Power, we complete more of the separation-from-family work. This work is critical so that we can frame the past in its proper perspective while reaching for a brighter future. We gradually realize our painful past can become our greatest asset. We realize we can help others who lack hope and clarity about what happened to them as children. As we learn to tell our story in meetings and in sponsorship, we move from "hurting, to healing, to helping." By practicing Step Three we begin to stand on our own. We are clear on what we believe. We seek God's will with greater clarity. We come to believe that we really are children of God, as we understand God. We come to believe that God hears our prayers. We are less confused on what to pray about. We begin to have true choice.

Inventory Steps and Realizing Generational Abuse

In Steps Four and Five, we review in detail how we were raised. We remember the messages, situations, and feelings. We also look at how we react and think in relationships as adults. We tell our story to another person and to God, as we understand God.

Like Step One, the Fourth Step of ACA distinguishes our fellowship from other Twelve Step programs. In ACA, we inventory our family system in addition to inventorying our own behavior. Other Twelve Step fellowships tend to limit a review of family dynamics. In ACA we look at our parents' behavior, family roles, rules, messages, abuse, neglect, and how that affects us as adults. We balance the inventory of our family system with a thorough inventory of our own behavior.

Many of us peep ahead to Steps Eight and Nine and sense that we have amends to make to various people, including our parents, who have harmed us as children. Oftentimes this harm is the vulgar act of incest, physical abuse, or mental and emotional abuse by sick parents or caregivers.

It is not the purpose of the Twelve Steps of ACA to place blame on the parents or caregivers; however, the adult child also must not shield the parents during the inventory process.

Our cofounder, Tony A., believed that adult children could take a "blameless" inventory of his or her parents. That means the adult child can name the types of abuse that occurred and the role playing necessary to survive the upbringing; however, with a "blameless" inventory, the adult child also realizes the generational nature of such abuse or neglect. The parents were passing on some form of what was done to them.

In preparing to make amends to our parents, we must develop a gentler manner toward ourselves. ACA's Fourth Step stresses this process. We must balance taking responsibility for misdeeds committed as an adult with the knowledge that our mistakes probably have their origin in the abuse we endured as children. We seek balance. We don't want to use our childhood abuse as an excuse to avoid taking responsibility for our actions as adults. But we also do not want to belittle ourselves for these mistakes or abuses. Adult children can be brutally hard on themselves for making mistakes. We condemn ourselves and rage at ourselves with ease. This serves no good purpose and only means that we have learned to abuse ourselves. No one needs to beat up an adult child. We do it to ourselves long after our parents or relatives have stopped. We need to stop this self-condemning behavior. We can take full responsibility for our actions, knowing that our childhood abuse contributed to our abuses as adults. We also know that we are not blaming anyone for our adult behavior. We are learning to love ourselves. We can do this.

Making amends to parents or caregivers is a personal choice, which should be considered with the help of a sponsor, trusted friend, or informed counselor. These issues surface in detail in Step Four along with the conditions of abuse that we endured as children. While we encourage ACA members to avoid looking ahead in the Steps, we believe it is appropriate here to plant the seeds of common sense for later Steps. For too many years adult children have been sent to make amends to abusive parents without being given greater options. This cannot continue. There are conditions of abuse to consider, which will be discussed in greater detail in this chapter. Our experience shows that there is a way to make amends to abusive or neglectful parents while protecting one's self. We can proceed courageously with this knowledge.

In Step Four, we also shatter the cardinal rules of family dysfunction. The "don't talk" rule that most of us learned as children is broken so that a self-inventory can be fully reached. Breaking this rule began in Step One with the admission of being powerless over the effects of alcoholism and family dysfunction. When we work Steps Four and Five, we also break the rules of "don't trust" and "don't feel" by listing and articulating our life story in a structured manner. We learn to trust the person to whom we tell our story. We feel the feelings that arise by sharing such information. This sharing of our story with our sponsor or informed counselor reveals destructive patterns in our adult lives while illuminating abuses from our childhood. We also begin to see our grief or stored loss lying beneath our decisions to wrong ourselves and others.

In Step Four, the adult child learns to "name" the acts of abandonment, shame, and other forms of abuse practiced by dysfunctional parents. At the same time in Step Four, the adult child lists his or her own defects of character, acts of selfishness, and blame that allowed the adult child to rationalize destructive behavior or reject real solutions.

Character Defects Versus Laundry List Traits (Common Behaviors)

In Steps Six and Seven we learn the important difference between defects of character and The Laundry List traits developed as children to endure our dysfunctional homes. The main difference is this: Adult children tend to feel relief when reading the 14 traits of The Laundry List because we realize we are not unique. However, we can feel shame or dread when hearing a list of defects of character.

Our defects of character can include judgmentalness, slothfulness, and dishonesty. These defects can cause great discomfort to others and ourselves. In other cases defects of character can include what society sees as noble traits, but for us they are stumbling blocks. These defects can include perfectionism, obsessive tidiness, and appearing self-sufficient by avoiding asking others for help. Employers praise the self-starter who keeps a tidy work place and rarely asks for help.

For the most part, our defects of character are different than our Laundry List traits because the traits are rooted in the First Step. The Laundry List traits include fearing authority figures, stuffing our feelings, people-pleasing, and feeling guilty when we ask for what we need. The traits are the effects of growing up in a dysfunctional family. These common behaviors have deep roots and could easily be called survival traits. The Laundry List traits are like branches of a tree, while the defects of character are the fruit. The defects of character can be linked back to one or more traits.

We use Steps Six and Seven to remove the defects of character. However, we take a different approach for the Laundry List behaviors. We attempt to integrate them through gentleness and patience. Our traits have great value to us if we can embrace them and transform them.

Until integration occurs, the traits can cause great despair for the adult child. We seem unable to change them until we get help. The Laundry List traits represent the false self, which is convinced that it is real. The false self disbelieves recovery and the loving nature of a Higher Power. This false self once protected us, but it now has to be retired.

We must be patient with ourselves as we integrate the Laundry List traits in Steps Six and Seven. The traits are deeply anchored because they are the defense system we developed as children under difficult circumstances. We must acknowledge a certain amount of respect for the traits and for ourselves for figuring out how to survive our dysfunctional homes. As children, they were the difference between living and dying in some cases. We survived, but in ACA we want to move beyond mere survival.

The safe harbor we find in ACA meetings is the starting point for transforming our survival traits. We listen to others share how they did it. We learn that the integrated trait of people-pleasing might look like this: we do helpful things for ourselves and accept praise, instead of constantly pleasing others and pushing away compliments. By transforming our people-pleasing manner, we do not stop caring about others. However, we stop going over the line to ensure that we are never abandoned.

Many times the Laundry List survival traits will rebel and assert themselves more clearly as we begin to surrender to a new way of life; however, our experience shows that the traits can be softened if not tempered into usefulness. Some of us seem to make no real progress on changing our survival behaviors until we become entirely willing as Steps Six suggests. With more than survival as our goal, we continue to lessen the strength of the traits and gradually lay them down with respect.

Making Amends

In approaching Step Eight and our amends list, we should have a more balanced perspective of what happened to us as children and what we are responsible for as adults. Without this balanced

Step work in the preceding seven Steps, most adult children will take on too much responsibility for their actions as children and adults. Others will ignore the amends process and remain mired in self-pity or protracted guilt that leads to further deterioration of the body and mind. By working the amends steps, Steps Eight and Nine, we are not letting our parents off the hook for their behavior nor are we taking an attitude about our childhood abuse that would excuse or protect our own selfish behavior as adults. We do not allow fear of uncomfortable situations to block us from making amends. ACA experience shows that amends build the character and inner strength that can only be wrought by going through the process.

In making our amends lists in Step Eight, we work closely with our sponsor or counselor to determine the exact nature of our amends. We look at the concepts of forgiveness and self-forgiveness. Many adult children blame themselves for passing on their childhood abuse to their own children. We must understand that we could not have turned out differently as parents. We simply repeated what was done to us because it is all we knew. This is not an excuse but a fact. With this knowledge, we begin to entertain the possibility of self-forgiveness in Step Eight.

Self-forgiveness is an elusive concept for adult children. We ask that the adult child keep an open mind and consider that God has already forgiven the person. God is waiting for the adult child's acceptance of such a blessing. We realize that we are practicing the concept of self-forgiveness when we hear ourselves talking about being gentle with ourselves.

With such an attitude, we learn to protect our emerging Inner Child or True Self when we make amends to parents or relatives who could still be in denial about their family dysfunction. We go into such amends knowing our Inner Child is listening but also knowing we are attempting to correct our damaging behavior as adults. We know we have made mistakes based on bad information from childhood. But we are focusing on our behavior and our need to change. We don't make excuses for our behavior; yet, self-forgiveness gives us a gentler view of who we are and what we are trying to change in our lives. We nurture our Inner Child by forgiving ourselves and turning over our parents and children to God, as we understand God.

Some incest victims have struggled with forgiving an offending parent or care giver. We urge these adult children to speak with other ACA members to find a solution that works for them. Some parents are so dangerous and sick that the adult child must avoid them to remain safe and sane. Surely we would think twice about asking an incest victim to make amends to a perpetrator father, mother, or other relative. The actual amends may be to protect ourselves and know we have done nothing wrong.

At the same time, many other abused adult children believe that the healing process for them cannot be complete until they forgive their worst offenders. The process is not always simple, but it is possible to forgive a sick parent and find peace of mind. Forgiveness does not mean that the parent's behavior was proper or excusable. It means we learn to live freer lives by discharging old trauma in a safe manner.

In Step Nine, there are a variety of amends for a variety of people and relationships. Some amends require a simple apology while others will require changed behavior that can only occur over time and with Step work, meeting attendance, and the help of a Higher Power. In some amends, we must pay back money we have stolen or squandered. Other amends are "living amends" which will require us to leave people alone. Amends to a deceased parent or friend can involve writing that person a letter. We read the letter out loud to our sponsor or ourselves. We can usually find a way to make an amends if we pray and seek guidance.

Daily Inventory, Meditation, and Awakening

In Steps Ten, Eleven, and Twelve, we learn to continue our self-inventory process, pray and meditate, and carry the message of hope to adult children while practicing the principles of the

Steps in our daily lives. ACA is a program for continued personal growth. The Twelve Steps call the adult child to live the ACA program with a range of feelings and self-confidence. ACA is a design for living that works.

In Step Ten, the adult child learns to appropriately inventory thoughts, actions, and motives with an honesty and gentleness that was not present in our families of origin. Step Ten is where many adult children learn to balance their responses to situations. We confront our black-and-white thinking and realize we have choices. We learn to say "no." We can ask for what we need. We become actors rather than reactors.

Most adult children learned to take their own inventory long before they arrived at ACA. However, these negative inventories were usually nothing more than our critical inner parent judging us harshly. Many adult children doubt themselves, criticize themselves, and feel inadequate without much prompting. Steps leading up to Step Ten can expose the toxic shame and abandonment we endured as children and teens. The shame gave us a negative orientation to the outward and inner world. In our minds, we developed the deeply grooved, self-shaming messages that lived on long after we left our homes. For instance, who could have his house burglarized and feel at fault for the burglary? An adult child. Who could feel guilty for asking someone blocking a doorway to move? An adult child. Step Ten helps us address any negative messages held over from previous Step work.

Step Ten does not mean we will never criticize our behavior again or never apologize for obvious wrongs on our part. However, with Step Ten we hopefully will learn to judge ourselves less harshly and forgive ourselves more readily. With such an attitude, we learn the difference between condemning ourselves unjustly and identifying areas to improve. We see how we took on too much responsibility for others' thoughts and actions. That's what we did as children when we filled in the unspoken sentences that fell on the floor when our parents argued or criticized with an unreasonable manner. We were children taking on too much blame for dysfunction that was not our responsibility. In Step Ten, we unhook from the behavior of others. We learn to focus on our own thoughts and actions with balance and self-love.

In Step Eleven, we learn that spirituality is not reserved for those of the clergy or those of religious teaching or temperament. God, as we understand God, is available to all. We seek through prayer and meditation to improve our conscious contact with a Higher Power. We seek the power we need to live in freedom each day. It has been said that a life of prayer and meditation leads to a life of mental stability or emotional maturity. In ACA, we believe this to be true. The power we find in Step Eleven is the true power from our True Parent, God as we understand God.

There are many methods to meditation and many fine books on the subject. In ACA, we have learned to keep it simple. Many of our members find a quiet place in the morning to meditate, but any time will do. We usually sit in a relaxed, upright position for 10 minutes to an hour. The time varies for each member. Some members, at the beginning of the meditation, take several deep breaths and exhale slowly, repeating an affirming message in their minds. As we concentrate on our breathing and on self-love or serenity, we feel a closer connection with our Higher Power. We feel relaxed and safe. Practice is the key to meditation. Make a start and continue to try.

In Step Twelve, the adult child begins to realize the value of his or her personal story. This realization is one of the key elements of undergoing a spiritual awakening and psychic change that brings integration to our fragmented lives. Our stories are often painful. Common logic would suggest forgetting the past, but our experience speaks otherwise. We are survivors with a voice. We are learning to live with self-love and grace. We have found the value in our stories, and we feel motivated to pass on hope to the still-suffering adult child. By working the Twelve Steps, we come to believe that our story has great spiritual value. We don't live in the past, but we know where we come from and how to find clarity and meaning in life. By the time we reach Step Twelve, we know about the negative messages we have confronted and changed. We also recognize self-forgiveness. We feel more sure of ourselves. In ACA, the adult child finds his or her voice.

In carrying the message of hope in the Twelfth Step, our story is the identification tool that allows us to connect with other adult children and bring hope like no one else can. Something marvelous happens when one adult child talks to another adult child, sharing experience, strength, and hope. Both are helped, and the message of recovery experiences a heartbeat.

By carrying the message of recovery through Step Twelve, the adult child confirms his or her commitment to the recovery process and passes on what was freely given to him or her. When we give back, we help ourselves in addition to helping someone else.

PART II

Twelve Steps of Adult Children

This section offers in-depth writing based on ACA principles and experience garnered during a 30-year period. The section includes about 35 shares of ACA members recorded voluntarily at meetings, retreats, and by invitation during a 10-year period. Transcribed mostly from tape recordings, the shares represent an array of ACA Twelve Step experience.

STEP ONE

We admitted we were powerless over the effects of alcoholism or other family dysfunction, that our lives had become unmanageable.

Someone Finally Wrote It Down

The first time I read the common behaviors of an adult child, I felt like a bell that had been fetched up and rang hard. I was calm on the outside, but I was vibrating on the inside. I could not believe what I was reading. I remember looking over my shoulder to see if someone had been reading my mail and had planted this stuff somehow.

I may have rubbed my fingers on the page, trying to feel the words because they seemed so real. The words of judging myself without mercy and being a people-pleaser were describing my thinking and behaving in a language that was clear. I could not deny it. I was cursed harshly and subjected to violence as a kid. I was never listened to. Now, someone who I had never met had written down how I thought and felt without meeting me. Until I found ACA, I had spent my whole life condemning myself and feeling no good. I took drugs and acted out in disgusting ways, feeling lost. I read the traits for the first time 20 years ago. I have been hooked on ACA ever since. The traits and the Twelve Steps have given me a new life and self-love.

My Body Is Remembering What Happened

It took me awhile to understand what I was hearing in ACA meetings. The common behaviors (14 traits) meant a lot, and I got them quickly. But all the talk about being shamed and abandoned seemed to go over my head for many months if not years. I could recall the mechanics of my abuse, which involved hearing my father call my mother vulgar names and being attacked by my father when I was four years old. I even saw blood and teeth fly when my violent dad knocked out men with clubs and pop bottles. But the feelings associated with these events did not register for the longest time. I was so numbed out and so shut down that I could not connect the terror that I must have felt with the recalling of the memory.

I got help from a counselor who would slow me down when I recounted a violent episode in my home. It was the difference in telling the story rapidly without feeling and thinking about it as I talked. She said I had post-traumatic stress disorder. I was skeptical, but I knew my memories were violent and not normal. I had a high tolerance level to seeing violence and not feeling. I also got help from another source: movies. I began to notice feelings and tension in my body if a violent movie scene would occur. I don't watch violence, but the few scenes I would see, even on TV, began to trigger what I had not felt in a long time. It happened on God's schedule. I was not ready for this when I came here, but my body is telling me what happened, and I can handle it.

The Gift Of The Twelve Steps

A friend of mine stopped coming to ACA meetings because he thought the Twelve Steps were a continuation of the dysfunctional family system. To him the Twelve Steps were just a list of things to do to get approval and behave acceptably according to someone else's standards. But Alcoholics Anonymous didn't start out with the Steps when AA was founded in 1935. The written Steps came after the first meetings in an attempt to offer suggestions, not rules, of the recovery process.

Chapter Seven

Someone asked the first one hundred sober alcoholics in AA what they did differently that finally broke the deadly hold of alcoholism, a disease that had defied all medical and religious remedies throughout the ages. The group said they discussed the evolutionary process of their recovery, and then AA cofounder Bill W. documented the process used to obtain sobriety. That was the beginning of the suggested Twelve Steps. In reviewing my own recovery process in Adult Children of Alcoholics, I now see how my Higher Power guided me in working the Steps. The gift of the Twelve Steps resulted in my emotional and spiritual sobriety.

There Is Nothing Noble In The Struggle

I have been in situations where the outcome would have been better if I just said, "I can't do that." Instead I took on the impossible, failed, and beat myself up for it. I would go without recreation, sleep, and food to keep myself focused on the task at hand. Relentlessly, I considered different perspectives until I found a way to get the job done.

This depleted the energy I needed to survive.

I began to withdraw from my family and friends. One day I was sitting on the carpet in my home office looking at piles of paper. I couldn't organize the papers or find the ones I needed. I couldn't get off the floor. I could only cry. I thought my life would never get better, and I wanted to die.

My therapist said, "When you learn you can't do it, then you've got a chance. So far you keep finding more energy to keep trying. The best thing for you to do is to fall apart, realize your life is unmanageable, and understand that you can't do it all."

When my life got as bad as it could possibly get, I started coming to ACA. I discovered I had taken Step One by saying, "I can't do this anymore. I quit." My life got better from that moment on. I had hit a bottom.

While giving all you can is admirable, I have learned in ACA that it's better for me to know my capabilities and limitations. When I can't do something, I need to just let go. When I see my friends struggling now, I don't try to fix their lives for them. When they hit their "bottom" they will let go and reach out for help as I did. I have finally discovered there is nothing noble in the struggle. I surrender.

I Couldn't Do It Alone Anymore

I grew up in what I thought was a normal household. My mother started to work when I entered first grade. With our parents working, my two sisters and I were expected to care for the house. About that time I remember not wanting to go to school and not wanting to leave the house. When I was at school I wanted to go home during my lunchtime to make sure that everything was all right. I thought, "If I do more, my parents will care more about me. I will be good enough to be loved." But I never felt I was good enough.

When I grew up, I became a teacher. As one of the more responsible teachers at the school, I was given extra duties and problem children. For a long time I handled the additional responsibilities. My life revolved around school and home ownership. I was important for what I did. I was my job.

When I realized I could not keep handling the stress, I spoke up at school. I was ignored or told I was "doing a fine job."

I began having panic attacks. When I began tutoring children after school and conferring with parents on report cards, I experienced chest pains and saw my doctor. The following night, I had a huge panic attack and went over to my boyfriend's house.

I visited my therapist and said, "I can't do it anymore." He asked me what "it" was. I didn't know. On the drive home it suddenly occurred to me that "it" was life. I could not go on anymore. My life had become unmanageable. Nothing was fun for me. I saw no future. I needed help just taking care of myself and getting meals.

The rehabilitation evaluator I went to suggested I attend an ACA meeting, even though alcoholism wasn't a problem in my family. I went to a meeting anyway. It was too soon for me to go to meetings because I was in such poor shape. I picked up some literature and recognized myself in the 14 characteristics (The Problem). If there

Chapter Seven

was help anywhere, I thought, maybe it was in this ACA program. I started attending meetings regularly. I have been very grateful ever since for this program.

I Told God How Powerless I Felt

On my last weekly visit to my parents' house, my mother hadn't been pleased to see me. The people-pleasing, approval seeker she used to know was gone. Any hope that I might meet her needs was also gone. She was sulky, shaming, and negative. Perhaps she was hoping that I would give in and try to fix her.

Many years ago I had planned on having kids to fix me and meet my needs, so I could have a sense of wholeness and self-respect, too. My children would have a lust for life that would lift me to realms of happiness rarely experienced by humans. I had planned on being admired by ranks of the "prestigious sane."

My mother must have seen me as a boring cold fish that day. I felt sad and trapped but I chose not to fix her. I told God how powerless I felt, and I began repeating the Serenity Prayer. Suddenly my mother lightened up, and with the opportunity to be happy, joyous, and free, so did I. Sanity replaced insanity. Clarity emerged. The next day I fully understood what had happened. I thanked my Higher Power for the miracle. I realized my past attempts at fixing my mother drained me of my precious energy and demoralized my spirit. I no longer believe I can fix her. I did not cause my mother's discontent.

Step One Summary

These shares represent the basic spiritual principles of ACA's First Step – powerlessness, unmanageability, surrender, and letting go. Step One requires that we admit that our family is dysfunctional and the dysfunction affects our thinking and behavior as adults. We must admit that we are powerless over the effects of growing up in a dysfunctional home. Our lives are unmanageable regardless of appearances of self-sufficiency. Social standing or compulsive self-reliance does not equal recovery. We must realize that will power or self-determination is no match for the effects of growing up in a sick family. We cannot figure it out on our own. We need help. We must shatter the illusion that we can reason out a painless solution.

The shares also represent the critical separation-from-family work, which is necessary to gain clarity about our lives. Separating from our families means setting healthy boundaries and removing ourselves from abusive situations and family crises, which are common for dysfunctional homes. Many times adult children struggle in their ACA program because they cannot seem to break ties with destructive or manipulative relatives. We cannot grow and find our true inner selves as long as we engage in family dysfunction that is draining and unhealthy.

Separating from our dysfunctional family is a healthy act of defiance. By doing so, we are challenging the authority of the family lie. We are making a statement that we will no longer be loyal to denial and dysfunctional family roles. This can seem frightening, but we have the support of our ACA group.

Many adult children separate from their families with love not abandonment. They need time away to focus on themselves and to disconnect from the gravitational pull of a dysfunctional home. At an appropriate time, we review the relationship we want to have with our families. We will choose to avoid some family members because they are draining or abusive. Other relatives will accept us and encourage us on our new path even though they may not understand or be willing to walk this way with us. ACA can improve our relationship with our families with the knowledge that we do not have to participate in their dysfunction. We are free to live our own lives.

Hitting Bottom

ACA recovery begins when the adult child gives up, asks for help, and then accepts the help offered. Some adult children call giving up "hitting a bottom."

Hitting a bottom can occur before the adult child attends his first meeting or it can occur after arriving here and beginning the Twelve Step process of recovery. Some ACA members reach a bottom after years in recovery. Hitting a bottom can involve losing everything and becoming homeless, or it can be a feeling of extreme suffocation brought on by our obsessive need to control others. Some ACA bottoms can be a chronic sense of aloneness in which the adult child never feels joy and never really connects with others in a meaningful manner. Many adult children have become literally paralyzed in recovery because of their inability to let go and trust themselves or others.

Other bottoms can involve a compulsion or obsession for another person. The obsession is so maddening that we think we will go insane unless we have this person in our lives. While we are focusing on another person, the pain we are feeling is actually the abandonment rupture from our childhood. Our compulsion for another person is the refeeling of the original rupture from our parents shaming us or abandoning us as children. The soul wound does not get better with pills, drugs, sex, or other forms of diversion. If we survive this compulsion, we tend to repeat it in the next relationship unless we ask for help and accept it. ACA's Steps get at this wound and heal it with a Higher Power's grace.

All bottoms have meaning, and all bottoms can be a starting point for a new way of life. There is hope. Healing is possible.

Surrender means we become willing to do whatever it takes to recover and find peace and serenity in our lives. We admit complete defeat and give up notions that we can "fix" or control someone else. We become willing to attend meetings, work the Twelve Steps, and break through the denial of family dysfunction. Amazingly, an estimated 50 percent of adult children of alcoholics deny or cannot recognize alcoholism among their families. By growing up in a dysfunctional home we become desensitized to the effects of alcoholism, abusive behavior, and lack of trust.

Recovery from the effects of an alcoholic and dysfunctional upbringing is a process, not an event. We need to be patient with ourselves. We need to be honest about our own behavior and the thinking we developed while growing up in our family of origin. If you find yourself in an ACA meeting, it probably means you are here for a reason. You probably are not the only person in your family experiencing difficulties in relationships, on the job, or in other areas of your life. Your family is not the only family that struggles with denial and silently broken hearts. We have found that family dysfunction is a disease the affects every member of the family. In the individual it affects the body, mind, and spirit. The disease of family dysfunction is pervasive and resilient. The disease is progressive. Our relationships become more violent, controlling, or isolating, depending on which path we take. Our "addictiveness" to work, sex, spending, eating, not eating, drugs, and gambling progresses as well, depending on our path.

Moreover, the disease is generational, which means the traits and thoughts you have at this moment have been passed down from generations hence. Relief from the disease occurs when we do Step work, attend Twelve Step meetings, and seek a Higher Power's guidance. By admitting we are powerless over the effects of family dysfunction and that our lives have become unmanageable, we are ready to move onto Step Two.

Making a Start

When possible, we recommend that you attend 60 meetings in 90 days, get a sponsor, and make a start. For adult children with addiction issues, we recommend that you attend Twelve Step meetings to address those issues as well. While ACA is often the only program for many adult children, ACA is not a replacement for addicts working a program in Alcoholics Anonymous, Narcotics Anonymous, or Cocaine Anonymous.

We also recommend choosing a sponsor. A sponsor is someone in ACA, who attends meetings, works an active ACA program, and is willing to be available in assisting you in your program. The sponsor will not work your program for you, but he or she can offer support, hope and clarity. We strongly suggest getting

Family History Diagram

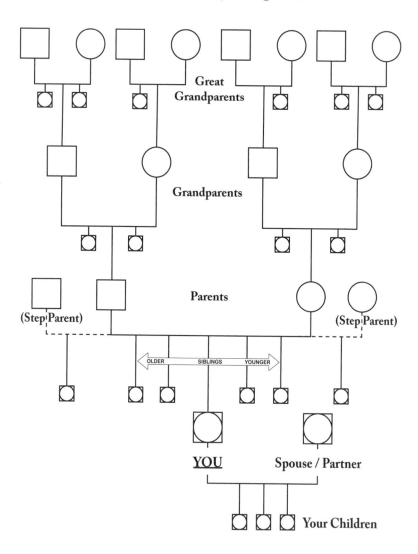

a sponsor early on. Do not go it alone. Our experience shows that you cannot recover in isolation.

Step One: Family History Diagram

We cannot overstate the need for creating an extensive family diagram, which reveals with greater clarity the effects of family dysfunction in our lives today. This is important Step One work.

In this exercise, you will create a diagram of your family of origin by listing your parents, grandparents, aunts, uncles, and other relatives that you can remember or have heard about. By diagramming your family and their personalities, you begin to see the generational nature of addiction and other family dysfunction. The labels that you will use in diagramming your family serve the purpose of helping you find clarity rather than serving as a value judgment. You are not necessarily judging the family. You are looking for patterns and similarities. You are looking for your position in the structure. If done thoroughly, the diagram will demonstrate how you could not have turned out any differently as an adult. If you were raised by addicts, enablers, spenders, and workaholics, you could not have been substantially different as an adult.

You can create a diagram of your family by listing your paternal relatives on one side of the chart and your maternal relatives across from them. A sample diagram is provided here. For more space, you can duplicate this diagram on notebook paper. As you fill in the diagram, refer to the labels in 1 through 26 on page 128.

Family Diagram Labels

Think about your experiences or what you have heard about each relative in connection with addiction, religion, relationships, food, sex, work, etc. Place the name of each relative in the diagram with the label which best describes him or her.

Chapter Seven

The labels for your family members can include one or a combination of labels:

1. alcoholic/addict
2. used alcohol/drugs
3. enabler
4. religious
5. worked a lot (workaholic)
6. undependable, does not follow through
7. heavy debt (always borrowing money) or big spender (flashy clothes)
8. worried a lot (neurotic)
9. perfectionistic (high strung)
10. harsh, always critical, verbally abusive
11. chronically ill, hypochondriac
12. pill popper (always taking something)
13. great cook (always thought of herself last)
14. obese sibling/relative
15. emotionally ill
16. sickly child, too sensitive
17. always had her face in a mirror (thought she was better than others)
18. ladies man, player, gigolo, skirt chaser
19. sexually aggressive, not safe
20. violent, slapped others, pinched, threatened, glorified fighting
21. grabbed or wrestled inappropriately
22. thief, bogus check writer, inmate
23. argumentative (will not be quiet, keeps arguments going)
24. people-pleaser
25. martyr
26. loner

STEP ONE SPIRITUAL PRINCIPLES:

Powerlessness and Surrender

7

Chapter Seven

STEP TWO

Came to believe that a Power greater than ourselves could restore us to sanity.

He Learned That Unhealthy Dependence Is Progressive and Powerful

I am here to tell you that being dependent on others in an unhealthy manner is cunning and patient. After more than 18 years of working the Twelve Steps I thought I could handle a relationship with a woman who I knew was probably a romance addict. The insane obsession I developed trying to rescue and then fix this woman pushed me close to insanity.

In the beginning we had so much fun. I bought flowers and chocolates. She drank wine and regaled me with stories from her homeland in Europe. We even wrote poetry to one another.

The craziness began when I realized we had different ideas of honesty. As an ACA member I wrongly assumed that most people practiced honesty or attempted honesty. Wrong. But by the time I found out, I was too far in. For the next six months I lived in a dependent, obsessive hell. I felt like I was losing my soul each time I compromised one of my program values for this person. When I finally made the decision to break free, I writhed on the floor with emotional pain that I almost could not bear. It is only by prayer, Step Two, and the help of two sponsors that I am here and sane today. I can tell you that dependency is patient, dormant, and progressive. And powerful.

I Was a Bible Teacher But Found a Higher Power Through ACA

When I first read, "a Power greater than ourselves could restore us to sanity," I thought, "I'm not crazy!" I went to church regularly. I knew I was a good person. I even had a personal reawakening of my faith. Nevertheless, I was miserable for many, many years. There was a void within me I just couldn't fill. I am a Bible teacher and did many wonderful things for God, but I still needed to understand why I had been physically and sexually abused.

I was invited to go with a friend to a Twelve Step meeting. I thought the people were odd. I thought they all needed to go to church to find God in a hurry. As I continued to attend those meetings, I learned it wasn't God who was missing. When I got honest with myself, I realized I went to God many times, but I was dishonest. I wanted Him to help me, but I wore a mask of perfectionism. I realized I was not allowing God, as I understand God, to help me. I was telling my Higher Power what to do. I was a little god myself, controlling and abusive. My behavior was insane.

Eight years ago I confessed to my husband and my children that I was a fraud because I had hidden my feelings from them. One of my sons said, "Mom, I thought you had the perfect marriage." I had religion, but I had no Higher Power. Now God, as I understand God, teaches me that I'm not a god, that I cannot control anybody or anything, and that I cannot change anybody except myself.

Seeing Sanity for the First Time

When I first read Step Two, the notion of being restored to sanity confused me somewhat. Yet, I remained quiet and continued to work the Step and got some benefits anyway. I agreed that the insanity I practiced as an adult child in drug addiction and compulsive behaviors had actually been accepted by me as sane behavior. Being a people-pleasing male, my denial allowed me to act irresponsibly. Sometimes, I acted dangerously without comprehending another way to live.

As I remained in the program and studied the Steps, it slowly dawned on me that I had never really known sanity to begin with. My family-of-origin, with its cursings, belittlement, and threats of abuse, was not an atmosphere that would produce a healthy person with a sane view of life. My distorted view of sanity was not totally insane, but it was not sane either. By working Step Two, I first found clarity and then sanity. I gained clarity about the level of abuse I had grown accustomed to. With such clarity, I glimpsed real sanity for the first time. I realize today that I have a choice of handling situations in an insane manner such as cursing, shaming, and blaming, or a sane manner with feelings, prayer, and asking for help. I am being restored to clarity, and I am finding sanity for the first time as well.

When I Lost Myself My Higher Power Took Over

It felt to me as if members of my family were spinning around me faster and faster. My mother's Alzheimer's disease was substantially worse. Her boyfriend was battering her. My mentally disabled younger sister was dying of breast cancer and needed to move into a different board-and-care facility.

In my professional life, I could hardly figure out what to do each day. I was not sleeping well. I would wake up and think about death, not suicide, but what it felt like to be dead and still feel pain. I was acting out violently. I stopped being able to do anything for anybody. I couldn't deal with my mother's situation or my sister's cancer. My husband would no longer tolerate my violence. I had an emotional breakdown.

I truly hoped a Higher Power didn't exist, because if He did, I would be judged, and I would be going to hell, I thought.

My therapist said, "Just let go. If you can't do anything, don't do anything." My husband told me, "You've had a breakdown. Leave this to someone else."

I did little things to help my family, but I had to let go of the big situations concerning my mother and my sister. Immediately my mother was accepted into a convalescent hospital where she will be safe. My sister was placed in a home where she will be comfortable as her cancer progresses. God took care of my family problems; I just did what I could do and let go. My Higher Power took over. I lost myself completely, and He took care of the problems I couldn't.

I Came To Believe

I'm glad Step Two says, "Came to believe…" I am not on good terms with God. There have been times when I believed in God and times when I wasn't sure there was a Higher Power. As to the last part of the Step, "restoring us to sanity," I don't feel insane. I have, however, made an insane world for myself. For a long time I continued the insane pace as if it were normal. Eventually I became overwhelmed and couldn't meet the demands I placed on myself. Then I did only absolutely necessary things. I got up to use the bathroom. I got up to eat.

I have seen some miracles that people in this program talk about, the coincidences that happen too often to be ascribed to chance. In the beginning I thought, "Gee, how did that happen? Wasn't that good planning?" That's when I came to actually believe in a Greater Power who was watching over me.

I still have a long way to go on Step Two. Tonight, for the first time, I heard the phrase "came to believe." I felt awful that I couldn't do Step Two because I didn't really believe in a Higher Power. I thought that meant I couldn't do the rest of the Steps since they all rested on this one, so I could never hope to recover. Gradually I am coming to believe there is something that can help direct my life. This I can do.

I Am Listening

There just has to be a Higher Power to my way of thinking if there is any logic in the world. Over the last month, I have been able to simply be present during moments of quiet reflection. I have not experienced any program miracles yet, but I've come to believe my life can be restored to sanity. I have come to believe in a Higher Power. In my recovery I don't expect or require immediate, dramatic changes or improvements in my profession, my relationships, or my emotional health. I'm not trying to keep myself busy. I'm not trying to suppress or medicate my pain. This is new for me.

Today doesn't feel quite as unnatural as it did when I first began to deal with Step Two. I'm simply asking God to let me know He exists somehow. I've become receptive to having a little faith.

Step Two Summary

These shares illustrate the confusion we have had when it comes to the topic of a Higher Power. Before finding ACA, many of us believe that a Higher Power is indifferent, fake, punishing, or reserved for the true believers of the world. Step Two helps us revisit our earliest messages about a Higher Power to find out what is true for us. We make this journey with an open mind.

A few of these shares detail the insanity or flawed thinking of adult children. The insanity we speak of in Step Two refers to our continued efforts beyond all reason to heal or fix our family of origin through our current relationships. In an attempt to heal our dysfunctional family from the past, many of us set ourselves up as a Higher Power in our current relationships. We played God by being all-knowing or being all-flexible to control or manipulate others. We wrongly believed we solved the problems from our birth family by keeping our own homes in order. We may have even eliminated alcohol or other dysfunction from our home. Our children, who often act out in addiction or aggression, give us a clue to our failing. We unintentionally passed on our family insanity or distorted thinking.

Similar themes arise for the adult child who moves away from a dysfunctional family to find a better life and sanity. Yet, the dysfunction followed us into our lives away from our dysfunctional homes. The thought never dawned on us that we had carried the disease with us in the form of persistent fear and distorted thinking. This is para-alcoholism as we know it.

Meanwhile, some of us set ourselves up as a "helpless God," which is a creative way to manipulate and control others. Before finding ACA, many of us found power in acting helpless, which is a role we learned as children. This is not to say we did not experience real moments of utter helplessness as children, but as adults many of us used helplessness in a learned manner to stay in control.

In addition to the helpless one, dysfunctional family roles include the hero, lost child, scapegoat, black sheep, and mascot. The roles underline our insanity in our current relationships. For example, if we played the family hero as a child, we tend to play the hero or rescuer as an adult. We insanely knock ourselves out in relationships or in the work place, hoping for affirmation and praise, which we don't believe we deserve. Some of us tolerate unreasonable amounts of abuse or neglect in return for meager amounts of attention. We mask our efforts to control another person by appearing helpful. We often do not believe we deserve happiness. We read self-help books and learn about needs and wants and then state our needs in such a demanding manner that we step on the toes of others. We are baffled when they rebel at our efforts. We feel betrayed, but we try again.

The lost child, as an adult, practices insanity by remaining isolated or refusing to ask for help. The lost child appears to have given up efforts to fix his family of origin. Many lost children practice "relationship anorexia." They avoid relationships because they are terrified of abandonment, which has its roots in the childhood years. Like all adult children, the lost child experiences intense abandonment fear. As an adult, he or she chooses to limit chances for such hurt by avoiding relationships. The fear of change seems greater than the fear of isolation. Without help, the lost child passes on this fear to his or her children.

There are other forms of adult child insanity, isolation, and manipulation that we engage in, which usually leaves us feeling abandoned, angry, or confused. Yet, we try again, repeating the same mistakes. Fueled by fear, our false self discounts real avenues of help. The false self chooses to reapply old thinking and behaving that guarantees the same hurtful results we have always known in our decisions.

Many adult children have a poor concept of sanity because our parents did not give us good examples as children. Boundaries were not clear. Punishment or praise were not consistent. Our parents operated from distorted thinking that clouded reality in the home. Their confused thinking created behavior that was inconsistent or uncaring. We came to believe that this behavior was normal when it was insane by the standards of decency or true parental love.

In one respect, Step Two implies that we had sanity and lost it when in reality we may be learning about sanity for the first time in ACA. A helpful tip in working Step Two involves replacing the word "sanity" with "clarity." By working Step Two, we gain clarity about how our family dysfunction affects us in our lives as adults. We gain clarity about our abandonment and internal shame. Many of us find Step Two sanity through clarity.

We know we are drifting back into dysfunctional insanity or unmanageability when we find ourselves relying on the 14 traits of an adult child in our jobs and relationships. These common ACA traits are a great gauge of flawed thinking and reacting. They include fearing authority figures, people-pleasing, judging ourselves harshly, feeling guilty when we stand up for ourselves, becoming addicted to excitement, and becoming an addict or marrying an addict. We confuse love and pity and tend to "love" people we can rescue. We also can be the rescued. Practicing these traits is a form of insane living.

Another brand of ACA insanity involves self-harm and its various forms. We have seen adult children harm themselves in abusive relationships, with drugs, or with a degrading or dangerous behavior. We have seen some adult children repeatedly endure one dysfunctional relationship after the next, thinking it will get better with each new person. The adult child "falls in love" again and again, ignoring red flags involving the object of his or her affection. When the breakup comes, the adult child experiences intense feelings of abandonment, which are linked to the childhood days of neglect and abandonment.

To avoid the devastating pain of a romantic break up, many adult children harm themselves with drugs, sex, gambling, food, or other destructive activities. Others get lost in reading, working, or spending lavishly. Some will fall into the cycle of making up and breaking up with their lover. Others will select a new partner quickly to lessen the pain of a break up.

Some adult children running from the pain of a relationship will create a situation in which he or she can experience a "shame hit." Like the heroin addict who seeks a hit of heroin, the adult child seeks a "hit" of his or her shame. As odd as it sounds, many of us seem addicted to shame or abandonment. Since we grew up with an orientation to fear, shame, and abandonment, we seek out situations that recreate these feelings in ourselves.

This is a shocking claim, but many of us can relate to it. Such activity is akin to the crisis-oriented lifestyle of many newcomers to the various Twelve Step fellowships. A crisis-oriented person feels alive when he is in a crisis he has helped cause. Likewise, many adult children feel alive when they can create shame or abandonment in their lives. Adult children seem to seek the thing they dread the most because it is familiar. This is learned by living in an unhealthy home.

It has been said that "insanity is repeating the same mistake and expecting a different result." That has been our experience. Change does not occur until the adult child does the Step work needed to curb the tendency to reach outside ourselves for love and affirmation. One of the keys to being restored to sanity involves surrendering our need to harm ourselves or to run from our feelings. We must also be honest about our actions and motives. We must name our behavior properly to avoid the delusional thinking that we are "feeling fine" when in reality we are headed for trouble. Such honesty or clarity of thought comes from seeking a Higher Power and by attending ACA meetings. We stop reacting and become actors, choosing a nurturing role in our Higher Power's play rather than a nightmare role in a destructive or unloving relationship.

When we settle down and listen, we begin to realize that the Power that brought us to ACA is still with us today. Where we once thought we found ACA by mistake, we begin to realize that a benevolent Power has been guiding us all along. Discovering this Power is one of the great miracles that many adult children have experienced in working Step Two and the remaining Steps. For some the Higher Power is recognized simply as loving and nurturing. The Higher Power is patient as it seeks to help the adult child find wholeness and integration of a divided self.

STEP TWO SPIRITUAL PRINCIPLES:

Openmindedness and Clarity

STEP THREE

Made a decision to turn our will and our lives over to the care of God, as we understand God.

Let Go. Let God.

Defining God, as I understood God, took a long time. I didn't believe in a benevolent God. I did believe that everything that could go wrong would go wrong. I know it is unrealistic to think the worst would always happen, but it seemed to happen for me.

To recover from my own negativity, I came to ACA. I tried to believe everything wasn't my responsibility. I tried to believe that whatever was going to happen in my life was controlled by some God. This was difficult. I always assumed I was wrong in whatever situation arose. I haven't completely given up all my control, yet. When I encounter obstacles now, I remind myself to "let go, and let God."

Eventually, by working the Steps, I turned my will and life completely over to God, as I understand God. My life is, coincidentally, working better. Today, when I am acting compulsively, I take a breather from that activity to moderate my behavior. Sometimes I have to say aloud, "I'm turning this over to God." Today I believe in a force some people call God. This force makes certain that what is supposed to happen does happen. I am letting go of control more easily.

Control Made Her Feel Safe

I have trouble turning my will and my life over to the care of God. It's difficult for me to "let go" because I feel like I'm not being responsible.

I didn't listen to my body or my thoughts. I ignored my feelings and reactions for so long because I placed no importance on them. My intense fears are what made me start to listen to my body. My panic, I decided, came from things I didn't want to do. I had to be in control to feel safe. When I make a decision now I try not to torment myself with: "I should have," or "maybe if." I do what I need to do, and then I let go. I stop trying to make things come out the way I want them to.

In ACA I'm changing my life. I'm receptive to alternatives. In a sense, I'm turning over my power to this ACA group that is greater than me. I have only just begun my work on Step Three.

Compassion, Forgiveness, Love, And Gratitude

I came to the program after a 7-year relationship ended. When my lover left me, it felt like my whole being left. I experienced more pain than I had ever felt. Every fear I had known was boiling up in me. I wanted to live, but I didn't know how to deal with the pain. I didn't trust God enough to take care of me because I was too busy taking care of everyone else. I finally understood the depths of despair that lead people to commit suicide. I began to understand what ACA means when we say: "We learn to focus on ourselves" so we can get better.

The gifts and miracles of life were not what I had thought they were when I tried to control people around me. My agenda was a ticking biological clock. When I felt pain, I compulsively cleaned my house to stop feeling anything. I could see pain in others, but I used it as a cue to try to fix them rather than identify with the pain in empathy and just listen. Only when I surrendered my life and my will did what I know intellectually become real for me. Compassion, forgiveness, love, and gratitude became real as I worked the Steps and surrendered. By turning my will and life over to my Higher Power, I could see examples of these spiritual principles in the lives of others.

From forgiveness I learned to love. I had this fantasy about love. I didn't know how to love myself, so I always looked for men to be my gods. I did anything a man told me to do: I changed my hair; I changed my makeup; I changed my clothes; and I behaved in the way he wanted me to behave. I thought marriage and children would fix me. When I left the house and went to work I was a totally different person. I didn't know how to be real. I was a fake. I was abandoning myself. I finally learned that abandoning myself would not take care of my abandonment or rejection issues.

Chapter Seven

The ACA program has brought me the miracle of life. I am able to experience compassion, forgiveness, love, and gratitude, the emotions that make my life worth living. I take responsibility for what I want out of life. I am honest and open with other people. I have had this spiritual awakening.

I Found A Voice In My Inner Child

It was hard to turn my life and my will over to my Higher Power. I didn't hear a big, booming voice. I wondered how I would know what to do for God. Somebody said at a meeting, "If I have a result in mind when I pursue a course of action, then I am doing my own will." That was a good tool for me to use.

I also heard about the Inner Child in meetings. I did an exercise once that seemed to connect me with a five-year-old child inside me. The first time I got a sense of doing God's will was when that Inner Child wanted to do something and the critical parent inside my head said, "No, you can't do that." I decided to defy my critical parent again if the opportunity arose. I drove by the supermarket one day when I was on my way to the bank. I wanted to pick up a loaf of bread and some bananas. My critical parent piped up inside my head, "You can't stop. You told the woman at the bank you were coming right over." A child's voice inside my head replied defiantly, "I want to get my bread and bananas now!" I parked my car and got the bread and bananas. As I drove to the bank I worried about what might happen because I didn't do exactly what I said I would do. The woman had gone out to lunch. She had, however, left the paperwork for me. I hadn't inconvenienced her at all.

I find it interesting now, that I get to do things I want to do that seem completely illogical. I give myself permission because that's the message God seems to send me about what He wants me to do. He excites my Inner Child. More often than not someone seems to benefit from my Inner Child's yens. I believe this is why I get the messages.

"Getcha God" Or Actual Parent

I struggled a lot with the Third Step because I had confused my violent and shaming father with God. I thought God was a super powerful being living in the far reaches of outer space, keeping score of all my bad thoughts and actions. I had a "getcha God" who I believed would "get me" for my imperfect behavior. I gave up on God and told people I was an agnostic because it sounded cool. I lived my life in an endless cycle of harmful relationships, lost jobs, and lost friends. I could never be a friend, actually. I stopped getting into relationships to stop the pain. I had no choice. I was compulsive and getting more out of control with each passing year.

When I came to ACA I saw the Third Step and wanted no part of God. I worked Step One and attended meetings. I tried to keep an open mind, but I was angry at God. The Second Step and The Solution helped me open up my mind more about God. Step Two mentions a Higher Power and asks me to consider the notion of a loving, benevolent force. The Solution says that "our actual parent is a Higher Power, whom some of us choose to call God." It says the Higher Power gave us the Twelve Steps of recovery.

Through the years I have come to believe that I am loveable. I have replaced my "getcha God" with the "actual parent" who will never abandon me. My parents were the biological couple bringing me into the world. My actual parent is a God of my understanding. I have a choice today when I put my will and life in the hands of this God. This God listens.

Step Three Summary

ACA is a spiritual and not religious program, which means we avoid dogmatism, theological discussions, or grand testimonials about the miracles of God. We are not aligned with any religious, mystical, or spiritual systems of belief; however, we believe it is imperative that the recovering adult child find a Higher Power to help him or her find healing from growing up in a dysfunctional home. We make no apologies for this great fact of our recovery program. But we also understand the struggles that many adult children have had with belief and faith. We are not pushing religion or spiritual beliefs upon anyone. We use the Twelve Steps, professional help, and a Higher Power to reclaim our wholeness. This is the ACA way.

These Step Three shares represent the sovereign right of every adult child to choose the God of his or her understanding. For the first time in our lives we can finally think about what a Higher Power means to us rather than relying on what we have been told. Step Two gave us insight into how many of us came to perceive a punishing or indifferent God. In Step Three we open our minds to new possibilities. Some of us are comfortable with the word "God" for a Higher Power. Others will use Spirit of the Universe, Father of Light, Earth Mother, or the Divine. Some ACA members still investigating their spiritual path choose an ACA group as a power greater than themselves. Whatever we choose to call our Higher Power, we make a decision to turn our will and life over to its care on a daily basis.

We turn over everything without bargaining with God as we understand God. We don't release some things to a Higher Power and hold onto others. If we struggle with turning over our will and life to a Higher Power, we can begin by turning over our self-hate, self-doubt, or fear. We can ask God to take our compulsions, resentments, and learned rage. Some of us will work up to turning over our will and life to the care of God. This is a process that we learn to trust.

These Step Three shares also represent a deep well of hope and patience created by a loving God who has given us a program to restore our lives. It is a well of grace we can return to again and again and dip out self-acceptance, self-assurance, and love. Each time we take Step Three, we drink down God's love. We replenish our Inner Child or True Self. We come to believe that God hears our prayers and loves us always.

ACA's Third Step typifies our spiritual approach to the disease of family dysfunction. In ACA, we view our compulsive thinking and dependent behavior as a spiritual dilemma rather than a mental illness. We have no quarrel with science and medicine, which have made great strides in mapping and studying the brain. Such clinical work is of great importance in understanding human behavior and brain functions. We freely use such clinical labels as depression, panic disorder, bipolar, dissociation, and post-traumatic stress disorder. Some ACA members have been diagnosed as multiple personalities and as schizophrenic.

We do not believe our brains are missing any elements. We start with the premise that we are whole and that we had a normal reaction to an abnormal situation of being raised in a dysfunctional home. Our normal reaction to protect ourselves has created survival traits, compulsions, and self-harming behaviors, which respond to the ACA Steps and spiritual remedies. We are not minimizing the severity of our situation as adult children. The disease of family dysfunction manifests itself in dependency, addiction, and dissociative personalities. The disease can kill. Every day, adult children commit suicide, die in addiction, or die one day at a time in silent isolation, thinking they are hopeless. In ACA, we believe we were born whole and became fragmented in body, mind, and spirit through abandonment and shame. We need help finding a way to return to our miracle state.

Whatever mental diagnosis we may have, we seek a Higher Power in prayer and ACA meetings to relieve our chronic nature of feeling different. We believe God understands the root of mental health labels and freely offers help to those seeking God's love and light. We believe in a spiritual solution for the disease of family dysfunction.

In addition to a deep sense of shame and abandonment, we believe that most of our emotional and mental distress can be traced to our steadfast nature to control. In ACA, we realize that control was the survival trait which kept us safe or alive in our dysfunctional homes. We controlled our thoughts, our voices, and many times our posture to escape detection from an abusive parent or care giver. We knew our parents were looking for imaginary cues to criticize us or verbally attack us. As adults we continue to control ourselves and our relationships in an unhealthy manner. This brings abandonment or predictable turmoil. We make promises to do better but eventually return to our obsessive need to compulsively arrange, question, worry, dust, wash, lock, unlock, read, or hypervigilantly survey our thoughts and actions to feel safe. But it is never enough. Experience shows there is little hope and little spirituality in homes governed by smothering control.

By making a decision to turn our will and lives over to the care of God as we understand God, we are actually making two decisions. By deciding to ask a Higher Power for guidance in Step Three, we are also deciding to back away from control. We are surrendering our plans to run our own lives on self-will. We are asking God for help, which strikes at the heart of our instinctual reaction to solve problems on our own.

The decision we make in Step Three represents one of our first true choices.

Asking a Higher Power for help is not easy for adult children for many reasons. We knew asking for help as children was risky and could be quashed by parents who would not allow such talk. We were told we were selfish or immature if we asked for help. We were told to be quiet. At other times we were taught to doubt our perception of what was happening. As we grew older, the option of asking for help or thinking we could ask for assistance dissolved. By the time we reached adulthood, most of us avoided asking for help, thinking we were self-sufficient and beyond such needs. This attitude can be a major stumbling block for adult children trying to call upon God to heal the disease of family dysfunction in their lives.

This is the same attitude that often stands in the way of us asking a sponsor for help in working the Twelve Steps. If we are to get better, we have to quit playing God, ask for help, and ride out the uncomfortable emotions that accompany this risk. We play God and avoid asking for help in the strangest ways. Many adult children can play God by being philosophical about the origin of people, the cosmos, and mysticism, but we use this knowledge to avoid getting involved in our own lives. People come to us for our knowledge on spiritual matters, but we may feel phony because we realize we are not getting our own needs met. We only have ourselves to turn to for help. We cling to control. We have become knowledge Gods sealed off from others.

Others can play God and avoid asking for help by appearing agnostic or atheistic. They seem put off by talk of spiritual matters. This does not mean that the views of the agnostic or atheist mean less. These views are respected in ACA. But to use such positions to remain in isolation is a tough path to follow. We must ask for help if we are to break out of isolation and join humanity. We can't just talk about it. We have to let go of control and do it. We make a decision to ask someone to help us and then accept the help once it is offered. We cannot recover alone.

We have to change this attitude of not asking for help if we are to make progress with Step Three and all of the Steps. We understand that simply going to an ACA meeting and sharing our fears and hopes does not immediately produce a desire to ask a Higher Power for help. Many of us still wonder if we deserve help and others wonder if we will be rejected if we take the risk and ask. Other adult children are still angry at God for seemingly not intervening in their abusive or neglectful homes. Still others wonder if a Higher Power exists at all. There is one way to find out. Make an effort and try. There is another way to live.

Endless Supply

Don't worry about wearing out Step Three. This Step is a bottomless well of hope, which is needed to deal with our fear-based attempts to control ourselves and others. As we work the remainder of the Twelve Steps, we will invariably struggle with control and self-doubt. Such struggles are only natural since we relied on controlling our feelings and emotions to survive in our homes and relationships. Control meant a sense of safety and predictability; however, we surrendered much of our personality and spirit through this manner of living. In Step Three we begin the gradual and gentle process of easing off of stifling control and replacing it with emotional freedom.

Each time we encounter the cliff face of control and feel overwhelmed by steep walls, we must remember we can draw on an endless well of God's grace. The Third Step, coupled with our association with other recovering adult children, is an endless resource of hope and reassurance. We can tap it indefinitely, one day at a time.

Letting go of rigid control is possible in our experience. However, we first must realize what letting go means. Some of us equate letting go to dying or potentially being harmed in a severe manner. Many adult children can be filled with panic at the thought of loosening their grip on an addiction or harmful behavior that they believe keeps them alive or safe. We have seen adult children grip a harmful behavior until the end. Some will die because they cannot find the willingness to let go. Others will let go and live. This is not easy but we can do it – let go – with the help of our Higher Power and our ACA support group.

In Step Three, we are not suggesting that we live without some restraint. We are not suggesting living in anarchy without real choice. To the contrary, by identifying our fears and dependent traits we take several steps away from control. We step toward our Higher Power and true freedom.

In Step Three, we deepen our knowledge of how we have battled with control and with a Higher Power most of our lives. Many adult children hoped for God's grace or intervention, but we never seemed capable of truly letting go and letting God work in our lives. We shamed ourselves for being unable to let go and truly have faith and belief. We thought we were incapable of having meaningful faith. We forgot what many of us heard as children: "God loves us always."

We realize we are letting go of control when our prayers bring a settling effect to our spirit or emotions when we are troubled. We realize we are letting go when we break our isolation and ask another adult child to listen to our fears or hopes. We choose company instead of finding comfort in isolation. We let go of control when we become honest about a troublesome behavior we want to change. We pray and ask for help to be willing to change. We let others share our lives.

The Gift of Choice

Choice is God's gift for letting go. Many of us practice letting go by drawing a continuum chart and placing it on the refrigerator door. We mark our daily progress along a horizontal line. On some days our control registers to the far end of the continuum and we feel alone and isolated. On other days we let go of control and catch a glimpse of God's will for us. We feel freedom. We learn to discern what events or decisions need greater attention and which items can be ignored. We let go of control by asking for what we need instead of manipulating others for things we really don't want. By letting go of control, we continue on the path to greater choice. With choice, we find out what we like and dislike. We feel less compelled to repeat rituals of control to make it through the day. We choose a new coffee shop, or we enroll in a college course and learn to explore the world around us. We choose to take singing lessons or volunteer for a worthy cause. We get our hands dirty in gardening or we let dust collect on the ledge longer without dusting compulsively. We see the art in spilled milk on the counter top. We learn to listen to our Inner Child and to be spontaneous. These are the choices that stretch out before us. There are countless more, but they are missed if we cling to control.

Before we arrived at ACA, we had no real choice. We were dependent or addicted to drugs, food, sex, or work, without a sense of direction. Most of us were reactors locked into unchangeable behavior. With ACA's spiritual focus on addressing the disease of family dysfunction, we break the cycle. We replace rigidity and fear with hope. We create an opening for change.

We choose to turn our will and lives over to the care of our Higher Power on a daily basis. We realize that the path of greater choice is a spiritual path that begins at denial and no choice and progresses through greater levels of choice to discernment. The level of choice we develop in ACA is proportional to the integrity of our boundaries. The more we let go, the stronger our boundaries become. This is an ACA paradox: Letting go creates stronger boundaries.

A Word About Religious Abuse

ACA respects all the religions and spiritual belief systems of the world. We make no judgment on which religion is better than the next. Our Third Step opens wide the path of exploration on spiritual matters. We encourage our group members to seek the fullest spiritual life possible to make the greatest gains in recovery.

That said, many of our members have suffered from religious abuse that can include harsh treatment at the hands of well-meaning people. Other adult children have been sexually abused by a priest or other church figure.

While we realize God's love in Step Three, we acknowledge that many adult children have been spiritually abused and struggle with a concept of God in addition to struggling with control. The emotional and spiritual damage created by such acts of betrayal are staggering for some. We urge these ACA members to keep an open mind and to be gentle with themselves as they work the ACA Steps to find a God of their understanding. We believe our best hope is seeking a spiritual solution in concert with other recovering adult children.

Other forms of spiritual abuse include the adults in our lives appearing righteous in public while hateful and abusive behind closed doors. This is yet another conflicting view of God in which the child is confused and believes this to be the actual face of God. However, we must remember what the ACA

Solution states: "Our actual parent is a Higher Power whom some of us choose to call God. Although we had alcoholic or dysfunctional parents, our Higher Power gave us the Twelve Steps of Recovery."

The Solution also states that our parents were the biological agents bringing us into the world. A loving God is the actual parent for many of us choosing the ACA way of life.

Finding a God of our understanding is essential for long-term recovery and real, inner change. We cannot shrink from the task of seeking God earnestly, regardless of what we may have been taught about God as children.

ACA is a spiritual program, which offers the power and grace needed to help heal these spiritual and emotional wounds. There is power in the ACA Steps and the fellowship created by such Steps. ACA work, coupled with focused counseling, can help the religiously abused adult child find a way to work Step Three. We can find a way to connect to the True Parent, our God of our understanding.

Third Step Prayer

Many ACA members use the Third Step Prayer to formalize their Third Step and to move on to Step Four. Some of us say this prayer with another person. This person can be your sponsor, counselor, spiritual advisor, or close friend. We offer this action for the purpose of learning to ask someone to participate in your new life. Sharing a prayer with another person lets us know we are making a connection to life and others in a meaningful way. Here is the ACA Third Step Prayer.

God. I am willing to surrender my fears and to place my will and my life in your care one day at a time. Grant me the wisdom to know the difference between the things I can and cannot change. Help me to remember that I can ask for help. I am not alone. Amen.

STEP THREE SPIRITUAL PRINCIPLES:

Willingness and Accepting Help

STEP FOUR

Made a searching and fearless moral inventory of ourselves.

A Picture Is Worth A Thousand Words

There was so much to learn in ACA when I got here. I identified with the common behaviors in counseling and at my first meeting but the talk of a Child Within and shame and abandonment was more than I could understand at first. My ACA counselor understood what I was trying to do. She helped me understand my loss or the pain of my "stuck grief" through the Fourth and Fifth Steps.

She used the Twelve Steps, ACA books, feelings exercises, affirmations and one other thing that helped me see my shame and abandonment underneath my experience of being an abused kid. She said that when my father cursed or threatened me that he was shaming me and abandoning me. I didn't understand that until I looked at my childhood pictures that the counselor asked me to bring to a session. I had seen these pictures before, but now I could really see them. There was a picture of me when I was 5 years old. Before I found ACA, the picture meant nothing to me, but my mother always seemed to cherish it. She kept it on the television. My counselor had me hold that picture in a session and look at it without speaking. I could finally see how sensitive and gentle I looked as a child. I never realized how bright my eyes were. My smile was true. After this, shame and abandonment began to mean something. I took my first step toward my Inner Child.

The Healing Was In The Balance

I found ACA when I was just getting sober and clean. I felt insane. I had done things and thought things that made me fear for my sanity. I could not stop these voices in my head that told me I was insane or going insane. When I saw Step Four, I could not accept that I might have good qualities. I was convinced I was becoming evil. I felt like a Jekyll and Hyde. I was calm on the outside but terrified of my thoughts or obsessions on the inside.

I avoided relationships because I was afraid I would act out somehow and harm someone. As a teenager, I had committed shameful acts against a younger niece. As a newcomer in ACA, I recalled my behavior. I felt disgusting and wondered if the Steps were a solution for me. I took my best shot at Step Three and started Four. Because I had learned to judge myself harshly, I listed mostly negative actions and thoughts on my first Fourth Step. I waited for judgment. The thought of balancing my Fourth Step by listing positive traits never crossed my mind. The thought of looking at generational shame and parental abandonment was equally off the table in Step Four.

A caring counselor looked at my Fourth Step and suggested that I write down 10 positive traits I might have. I almost refused because I sincerely believed that to write out any good qualities would be a lie. In my crazy thinking, I believed honesty was my salvation and to write down a trait I did not believe in would be dishonest. Willingness prevailed, and I did the assignment, which included reading my list of good traits in counseling sessions. I stumbled with the reading, but the effect was profound. Even though I did not believe in the affirmations, I found myself thinking about them often. I did my Fourth Step and Fifth Step and thought that I got little relief. But something happened. After my Fifth Step, I could still judge myself harshly at a mistake, but that affirmation list would pop into my head almost immediately and cause me to pause.

That was 20 years ago. I can now list my positive traits in my head and believe them. The affirmations and my other ACA work gave me enough breathing room to give myself a break. I thought all the disgusting things I did started with me, but I had help from generational shame. I thought I was no good, and I found out instead that I have worth.

Step Four Is The Shame Buster

For me, Step Four was the "Shame Buster." I had a pervasive feeling of inadequacy and a sense of being defective. The Fourth Step "busted up" that shame.

Having my needs ignored or my vulnerabilities abused as a child created shame. As a child, I was not capable of figuring out that my parents' illness and abusive behavior were the reason for my sense of abandonment and neglect. I thought I was not good enough to deserve the emotional support and care I needed. I survived by being good, perfect, and always right. I behaved in ways I knew would receive approval. I thought if I could be good enough, I'd be safe.

I did Step Four by making a list of my good and troublesome behaviors. This helped me look objectively at my strengths and areas to improve. My shame started to dissolve as I started to see myself as I am. I no longer had to defend and rationalize my behavior to cope with shame. Shame is the lie that tells me I am bad. I've done some bad things, and I've done some good things. Step Four allows me to see the actual truth. It tells me I am human. I have strengths and areas to improve. Step Four brought me a measure of self-worth, so I could start to let go of my compulsive need to be perfect, to be right, and to seek approval.

The Long and The Short of It

My inventories need not begin with, "Oh God, what's wrong with me?" I have to own what is good in me, as well as those things that are not. I don't need to bludgeon myself further by focusing only on what is wrong with me. I need to be rigorously honest and thorough in both my short and long inventories. I need to balance my good qualities with areas that trouble me.

In addition to the long inventory in Step Four, I use a short inventory to explore daily events. When I cooked oatmeal for my husband one morning, he announced that he used a double boiler when he made oatmeal so the cereal cooked evenly and there was no residue left on the sides of the pan. I glared at him. But instead of echoing one of my mother's retorts – "If you don't like the way I do it, do it yourself!" – I took some slow breaths and looked at the situation more calmly. The analysis was fairly simple. When I was a child, whatever my mother did was important and could not be interrupted. My anger came up when my husband crossed what I thought was a boundary. My fury arose when the rules that applied to my mother did not seem to apply to me as an adult. My cooking got interrupted by my husband. I wanted to respond like my mother, but I applied my recovery. I asked him to get my attention and then ask me if I could take a short break before he began a conversation when I was cooking or doing another activity. He said he would, and he did.

My long inventory, Fourth Step, poses questions on all aspects of life. I have done three different inventories to date, once in a Step Study group, once with a sponsor, and once alone. By answering the questions in the inventories I discovered who I was, where I had been, where I was right at that time, and where I was going.

Through the various inventories, I discovered I was a real person with likes and dislikes, vices and virtues. In revisiting my family-of-origin, I learned that the shame I carried wasn't mine. It was merely a technique used by a dysfunctional parent to control her world. Using this Fourth Step method, I have grown emotionally and spiritually. I now know how to be the person I want to be.

Getting Started on Step Four

In approaching Step Four, many adult children have said: "Why dredge up the past? What is done is done. I am forgetting the past and moving forward."

For these statements, ACA has an answer and a guarantee. Most people don't arrive at ACA's door by mistake. You are here for a reason, so keep an open mind. Our experience tells us that our past can be our greatest asset if we are willing to ask for help and do the work to find out what happened. Even the adult children who can recount abuse or incidents of rejection without working a single Step can benefit from Step Four. Simply recounting the past is not always enough to bring about healing and self-forgiveness. Without knowing the meaning of the abandonment encoded within the past, the adult child is doomed to repeat it. The unexamined past becomes the future of the next generation. Dependence, addiction, and hellish living are passed on to the next generation with amazing accuracy. We ask you to work this Step and all of the Twelve Steps to find your True Self and break the cycle of family dysfunction. If the Steps do not bring relief or clarity to your life, we will refund your old way of life in full. This is the ACA guarantee.

ACA Relapse

If we skip this Step or Step Five, we risk relapsing into unhealthy dependence and self-harming behavior. An ACA relapse always features a recreation of the fear, self-hate, and abandonment from our childhood. Through relapse, we reenact roles and dependent behavior that we learned from unhealthy parents. A relapse can take many forms, but all ACA relapses have this center point.

One form of an ACA relapse involves an adult child acting out destructively for several weeks with one or more of the survival traits. The traits are known as The Laundry List (Problem) or common behaviors. Another form of relapse could involve remaining in a physically or emotionally abusive relationship without a clear plan to get out. Relapse could also involve practicing self-harming behaviors. The behaviors include alcoholism, binge eating, taking drugs, gambling, or promiscuous sex. When we relapse we can return to a life of fearing authority figures and judging ourselves harshly. We can feel "hung over" emotionally when we engage in unhealthy dependent behavior. We see our boundaries weaken, and we find ourselves manipulating others for what we think we need. At the same time, others in relapse will assert themselves as a controlling authority figure upon children or a spouse. With indignance, we dole out abuse through moments of rage and dishonesty. We might feel remorseful, but we feel powerless to change. When this occurs, we usually have not given ACA or the Steps a fair chance.

Still others may have stopped some of their more destructive behaviors in ACA. Yet, we switch to another compulsion or behavior that is just as damaging. This can be a relapse as well. For all ACA relapses, denial returns in some form, and we find ourselves choosing to use the behaviors detailed in The Laundry List to survive. We forget that we have a choice. We return to one of our dysfunctional family roles. We stop feeling. We usually have stopped attending meetings.

In ACA, we seek "emotional sobriety" by making a commitment to love ourselves and be good to ourselves. We stop harming ourselves by attaining ACA emotional sobriety.

Reviewing Steps One, Two, and Three

Many of us begin Step Four by reviewing the first three Steps. In Step One, we realize we are powerless over the effects of family dysfunction and that our lives are unmanageable when we try to control others or get our inner needs met by outside sources. We are powerless over the survival traits we developed to live through our upbringing; however, we learn that we can fade or soften some of these common ACA behaviors over time.

In Step Two we learned about coming to believe. We learned that we attached our parents' traits of indifference, shame, or harshness to a Higher Power. We begin to separate the behavior of our parents from God in working Step Two. We begin to see our parents as the couple who gave us life. We also begin to see our Higher Power as the Actual Parent who will not abandon us.

In Step Three we learned that our compulsion to control others and ourselves blocks God's will for us, which is to live in peace with our feelings, creativity, and spirituality. We learn that real choice is God's gift to us for letting go. We learned that our attempts at choice before recovery were actually veiled control. In Step Three, we learned that choice often begins by facing our denial. As we grow in the program, our decisions include true choice that progresses to discernment. We learn to be still and know that God is God.

The difference between a searching and fearless moral inventory in Step Four and the Step One identification of our thinking and behaving involves balance. In Step One, we assessed the effects of an abusive childhood and how that abuse played out in our daily lives though defense traits developed as children. To a degree, we took our parents' inventory. We determined what happened so that we might find clarity on how to proceed in the moment and the future. In Step Four, we will balance our knowledge of the effects of family abuse in our lives with our own troublesome behavior as adults. As adults, we have harmed others. We have made flawed decisions based on our family background and blamed others when they challenged us to change. Many of us committed the same mistakes repeatedly, feeling hopeless to change. We secretly believed we could not change. We could assume the posture of a victim, which we thought helped us escape criticism but which brought a greater sense of helplessness. We sank to greater depths of self-hate and despair. Or we became a martyr, blaming others in detail for their abuse but refusing to accept responsibility for doing recovery work. Many defiant adult children have used their childhood abuse as an excuse to defend outrageously sick behavior and push away suggestions for help. We must find a way to surrender and to become teachable. We must understand that suggestions for help are not criticism or personal attacks.

Many of us have children who will possibly qualify for ACA one day due to transferring our disease of family dysfunction to them. This was not our intention, but it has often happened. We feel ashamed and alarmed at some of the things we have done to ourselves and our children. But we have hope in ACA. With the help of an ACA support group and our sponsor, we can change. We come to believe there is another way to live.

If we are diligent in working ACA's Twelve Steps, miracles occur that we could not imagine. Healing and a deeper sense of God's presence are often the result of working Step Four. Our sense of shame is dissolved and that feeling of being unforgiven fades with this Step's freeing power. This freedom grows with the completion of each succeeding Step.

Blameless

The key word to remember in working ACA's Fourth Step is "blameless." ACA founder Tony A. believed that adult children should take a "searching and blameless inventory of our parents because in essence we had become them." Tony believed that we internalized our parents. We had become them in thinking and action even if we took steps to be different.[†] While we focus primarily on ourselves in Step Four, we have added an inventory of the family to the process. ACA believes that we cannot take a searching and fearless inventory if we leave out the family.

Blame is not the purpose of Step Four or any of ACA's Twelve Steps. However, we can hold our parents and family accountable for their action and inaction. Blameless and accountability are the guideposts that steer us toward a balanced but searching inventory.

We hold our family accountable by naming what happened to us without fear of being ridiculed or disbelieved. In Step Four, we name the threats, the hitting, the inappropriate touching, or whatever else might have happened to us. We talk to our sponsor or spiritual advisor about what happened in our childhood.

We avoid blame because we are aware of the generational nature of family dysfunction. Our parents passed on the seeds of shame and fear given to them. They were once children without a choice. They survived as we survived. While some parents were obviously sadistic or unrepentant, others did the best they could. These parents made a conscious decision to raise their children differently than they were raised. Many of these parents abstained from alcohol, yet passed on problematic fear and shame just the same. Some of these well-meaning parents learned to say affirming statements of love and encouragement. Yet, they still transferred their own self-doubt and lack of self-love in large measures. Many of us are the adult children of these parents. We have acted out with addiction or another self-harming behavior, continuing the disease of family dysfunction.

Nondrinking parents raised in an alcoholic home are essentially unrecovered adult children who unintentionally pass on family dysfunction. These parents are typically a dependent personality driven by the inside drugs of fear, excitement, or anxiety. This is para-alcoholism. It affects the children in the same manner that the alcoholic drinking does if it is present. This means that our nondrinking parents were dependent people driven by a hundred forms of fear and self-doubt. They projected their fear and anxiety onto us with the same damaging effect that alcoholic drinking can have on a child. They passed on addiction or unhealthy dependence without taking a drink.

We avoid blaming the drinking parent as well. The alcoholic suffers from an incurable disease that progressively worsens. The alcoholic is very sick in body and mind. We cannot reach the level of spiritual growth that we are seeking by blaming sick people.

Avoiding blame does not mean that we avoid being angry or disgusted. Many of us feel rage when we talk about the abuse and neglect in our homes. These are normal feelings for the abusive and unhealthy parenting we lived through.

We also avoid sinking into a victim mindset. This mindset can disqualify us from the emotional and spiritual gifts of ACA. If we learn to accurately name what happened to us rather than blaming others for what happened, we find the truer path to healing and self-forgiveness. There is power in naming the exact nature of our abandonment and shame. We move out of the victim role and claim our personal power by taking this path. Step Four gives us a chance to identify what happened and transform our painful childhoods into our most valued asset. When we know what happened to us, we can help other adult children as no one else can, including some of the most dedicated professionals and clergy. We can finally say with humility: "This is what happened to me. This is my story. There is another way to live."

We stress fairness with our parents while holding them accountable for another reason as well. Many of us working Step Four realize we have harmed our own children. We have passed on what was done to us. Many of us have changed our behavior and made amends. However, some of us could one day be the focus of an inventory of our own children arriving at the doors of ACA. This is another reason to take a blameless, yet fair, inventory of the family and parents. If we give fairness, we can hope for fairness.

While we will look at the generational nature of family dysfunction in Step Four, we must remember that the Fourth Step is our inventory. In ACA we learn to face our denial and focus on ourselves. That means we will look at our parents' behavior in conjunction with our own behavior. We keep the focus on ourselves and on efforts to find clarity and be free of family dysfunction. We want to stop trying to heal our family-of-origin through our current relationships. We want to stop isolating and repeating the same patterns that bring about our worst fears of abandonment and self-hate. We want to reclaim our wholeness.

While working Step Four and all of the ACA Steps, we encourage you to nurture yourself. We must balance this probing look at our behavior with gentleness. We must protect our Inner Child or True Self vigorously. At the same time, we cannot let discomfort or fear stop us from getting honest about our own behavior.

Step Four Worksheets and Assignments

The following worksheets and assignments will help you detail the effects of being raised in a dysfunctional family. The worksheets include an inventory of survival traits, secrets, harms, resentments, sexual abuse, and post-traumatic stress disorder. Most ACA members have some form of PTSD, which is often expressed in our hypervigilance of our surroundings or our acute monitoring of comments or actions of others. This behavior is a carry-over from growing up on guard much of the time.

The spiritual principles of Step Four are self-honesty and courage. We urge you to be honest and thorough, but also to be gentle with yourself during the inventory process. Most adult children have no problem listing their faults and feeling overly responsible for the actions of others. The key is to balance your positive qualities even if you think you have none. You have positive traits. These exercises will help you nurture yourself and balance your defects and your assets.

We recommend that you stay in contact with your sponsor or counselor as you go through these Step Four exercises. Use ACA meetings, the phone, and e-mails to remain centered and focused on what you are doing. Step Four is your chance to detail what happened to you as a child. We go through this process in an atmosphere of love, understanding, and support. That's what is different today compared to when we were children and could not talk, trust, or feel. In Step Four, we get to do all three with the support of ACA and God as we understand God.

Distinguishing Our Feelings

Before starting your Fourth Step exercises, review the following list of feelings. The definitions describe where and how different feelings are felt in the body. This should be helpful in the exercises ahead.

In addition to stuffing or dissociating from our feelings, some of us have great difficulty understanding feelings and their definitions. Many of us have been shown a long list of

7

feeling words only to stare away, wondering what the words mean. We are confused about feelings because naming and feeling our own feelings is new to us. As children and teens, we based our feelings on our parents' moods and actions. We were hypervigilant to a parent's tone of voice, body language, and gestures. We watched a parent's behavior to determine how we should feel or not feel. By the time we arrive at ACA, many of us do not know that it is okay to have feelings that are different than those of people we care about. In ACA, we learn that it is okay to have our own feelings. If someone we care about is sad or angry, we can empathize with him or her, but we do not always have to feel sad or angry with the person. We can support the person in his or her feelings without having to feel or fix the person's feelings. This is an awakening for us. This is a key step in recognizing our own feelings and learning how to truly support another without unhealthy dependence.

Additionally, our parents or relatives used feeling words in ways that did not match the definition of the words. This inconsistency distorted reality and made identifying our feelings as adults almost impossible. Many times our parents abused us verbally or physically and called it love or care. "I only do this to you because I love you," some parents might say. "Don't feel that way" was another way we were talked out of our feelings or told our feelings did not matter.

Many ACA members speak of "bundling" their feelings before coming to ACA. They describe expressing all their feelings in a bundle or as one indistinguishable feeling. For example, anger, shame, joy or worry are expressed by tears. They speak of crying when they are angry and crying when they feel elated. They talk about their feelings "being all together and indistinguishable."

At the same time, many ACA members tend to deny the existence of feelings or have difficulty identifying feelings at all. They talk of feeling numb inside or being confused by the mere mentioning of feelings. The list below offers a general definition of about a dozen feelings as they pertain to ACA. The definitions come from ACA fellowship experience.

1. **Loved** – A sense of feeling valued, understood, and heard. Listened to. Feeling safe with another. Warmth in the heart. Lightness of body.

2. **Fear/Anger** – Fear is usually masked by anger. Fear – pounding heartbeat, dilated pupils, increased breathing, tightened skin, extreme alertness. Anger – tightened jaw, upwelling in the chest, gritted teeth, dilated pupils, angry thoughts.

3. **Shame or Ashamed** – An intense sense of being faulty, wrong, or inferior at the core of our being. A feeling of being ruptured. A burning feeling in the stomach. A sensation of the body shrinking. Spiraling inward in the stomach or chest or both. Constricted throat. Difficulty in speaking. Heaviness on the chest and difficulty breathing. Feeling glared at by others.

4. **Guilt** – A sense of unease or regret for a wrongful or neglectful act against another. Different from shame because guilt is usually about something we have done rather than a statement of who we are.

5. **Amused** – A light feeling of humor or good spirit. Grins and smiles. God's medicine.

6. **Abandoned** – A sense of loss, being left, pushed out, forgotten, minimized, betrayed, feeling vulnerable. Feeling physically small. A dot. Lost at sea.

7. **Embarrassed** – An emotion arising from being exposed, caught in the act, confronted, ridiculed. Feeling flushed. Heat or redness in the face. Shortened breath. Involuntary stomach flutters.

8. **Betrayed** – Similar to abandonment; lied to, being deceived in meaning, feeling fooled, Spiraling inward. Weakness in the limbs. Praying is difficult.

9. **Satisfied** – A sense of feeling full inside, rested, not worried, trustful thoughts. Being in the moment. Not wandering. Being in the body. Centered to earth. Grounded to earth.

10. **Hopeful** – An expectation that things will work out, trusting oneself and others, energy level rises. Breathing is easier. Hitting all green lights.

11. **Inspired** – A sense of hope and wonderment of people and things, colors seem brighter, problems seem to find their right size. More energy in the body. Lightness of foot. Obstacles are secondary to solutions.

12. **Humiliated** – A sense of having the inner self exposed, abused, or taken away by the act of another or self. Vacuumed out. Void. Soul theft.

13. **Loss or Grief** – A sense that something has been taken, a longing for feeling, given the answers to life but unsure of the questions. A school yard without children.

14. **Joy** – A sense of integration of the survival traits/ common behaviors. Coming out of the dark night of the soul with sureness of foot. Divided self reunited. Inner peace. Recognizing the True Self within. Knowing you can trust yourself. Seeing light in self and others. Energy and warmth throughout the body.

Feeling Intensity Scale

In preparation for the exercise ahead, select three feeling words. Rank each feeling on a scale of one to 10 with 10 being the most intense. The feeling can be in the present or from the past.

Use various cues to recall the feelings. Think about the scene or location in which the feeling occurred. What was said and how was it said? What occurred? What was the hour of the day or the temperature? What were you wearing?

If you have difficulty identifying feelings, think about a movie that has stirred feelings of sadness, joy, or anger. What was the scene? What happened to cause you to feel?

By working this exercise, one of our members said he felt his childhood aloneness when he visited an abandoned schoolyard. Another member said some feelings could be triggered by colors, smells, and shadows.

Example of feeling intensity scale:

Feeling word _____.

| 1 | 2 | 3 | 4 | 5 | 6 | 7 | 8 | 9 | 10 |

Step Four Exercises:

1) Inventory of Laundry List Traits (survival traits)

The following are the 14 traits or common ACA behaviors of an adult child. Identify or circle the number of traits you identify with and describe how that trait manifests itself in your life today.

Example:

Trait 1: We became isolated and afraid of people and authority figures.

"My mother was always drunk and hateful and I feel intimidated when I am around angry or rude people today."

Begin (circle the traits you identify with):

1. We became isolated and afraid of people and authority figures.

2. We became approval seekers and lost our identity in the process.

3. We are frightened by angry people and any personal criticism.

4. We either become alcoholics or marry them or both or find another compulsive personality such as a workaholic to fulfill our sick abandonment needs.

5. We live life from the viewpoint of victims and we are attracted by that weakness in our love and friendship relationships.

6. We have an overdeveloped sense of responsibility and it is easier for us to be concerned with others rather than ourselves; this enables us to not look at our own faults.

7. We get guilt feelings when we stand up for ourselves instead of giving in to others.

8. We became addicted to excitement.

9. We confuse love and pity and tend to "love" people we can "pity" and "rescue."

10. We have "stuffed" our feelings from our traumatic childhoods and have lost the ability to feel or express our feelings because it hurts so much (Denial).

11. We judge ourselves harshly and have a very low sense of self-esteem.

12. We are dependent personalities who are terrified of abandonment and will do anything to hold on to a

relationship in order not to experience painful abandonment feelings, which we received from living with sick people who were never there emotionally for us.

13. Alcoholism is a family disease; we became para-alcoholics (codependent) and took on the characteristics of that disease even though we did not pick up the drink.

14. Para-alcoholics (codependents) are reactors rather than actors.

Laundry List Worksheet

Using the Laundry List, fill out as many of the columns as you can. The "event" column is the childhood incident that comes to mind that might have helped create a Laundry List trait. Some traits are developed over time. You are looking for incidents, verbal spats, or conversations in which the parents projected their own sense of self-doubt, fear, and flawed thinking onto you. This is one of the places where para-alcoholism and the transfer of dysfunction occur. Para-alcoholism is the chronic fear and distorted thinking of our family transferred to us. It fuels codependence.

Do not be discouraged if you cannot fill out all of the columns. If you struggle with filling in the columns, get a notepad and write down things your parents said about you, family members, or other people. Keep the notepad with you and write things as you remember them. You can use the feelings list from the previous pages to help with the "how I felt" column."

Event	Cause of Event	How I Felt (feelings word)	Inner Child Reaction	Type of Trait Developed (from 14 Traits)

Example:

How the trait of fearing an authority figure might have developed.

Event	Cause of Event	How I Felt *(feelings word)*	Inner Child Reaction *(general reaction)*	Type of Trait Developed *(from 14 Traits)*
Father yelling at me or blaming me for a mistake.	He said I did not listen.	afraid/ physically small	knot in stomach/ breathing difficult	fear of authority figure and criticism

2) Family Secrets Inventory

Almost every dysfunctional family has a story or image that family members present to friends and outsiders. For example, "The Rodriguez family believes in education and challenge. We never give up," the family says. Another family says "The Wilson family works hard, and we stick together no matter what comes our way."

Beneath the story line is the reality of the dysfunctional home. There are secrets, inconsistencies, and wrongs that are contrary to the family image. Family denial supports the family image and denies the hidden story. In this exercise, we ask you to list family secrets. The secrets can involve attempts by parents to hide addiction, inappropriate touching, mishandling of money, lying, and infidelity. In some cases, seemingly insignificant events can also be secrets. On a piece of notebook paper list all memories, incidents, and messages that were considered family secrets or inconsistent with the family image.

3) Shame Inventory

The Big Book of Alcoholics Anonymous states that "Resentment is the number one offender. It destroys more alcoholics than anything else."[†]

In ACA, we believe shame claims the Number One spot. We believe that shame is so potent that a few drops can create a lifetime of lost self. Shame often was on the scene before abandonment, which is perhaps the second most troublesome abuse we have faced as children of unhealthy parenting. Shame and abandonment serve as the fear-based launching pad for an outward search for love and security which we never find in other people, places, or things. Shame blinds us to the fact that love is inside each of us waiting to be discovered.

To shame a child is to abandon the child. A parent can shame and abandon a child without ever leaving the room because a shamed child feels unlovable and alone at a deep level.

Adult children not only feel shame at the molecular level, but we also carry inherent shame. That means most of us carry around a deep sense of inadequacy, embarrassment, or uniqueness without having to interact with another person. We not only feel shame. We believe we "are" shame. When shamed as an adult, we can literally vibrate with shame as if being struck like a bell. We can feel the shame burning in our stomach and our face. When shamed, we can spiral inward to an unreachable spot. In some cases a shame spiral is so intense that the adult child's vision is distorted and perceptions change. Room lighting can seem more intense or dense and the expressions on people's faces seem over exaggerated. Shame of this nature has accumulated over many years, but it can be lessened and made more bearable in ACA and with God's help.

Shame List

List incidents in which you felt shamed by your parents or care giver. In addition to sexual abuse or harsh cursings, shame can come from calm statements by parents about appearance, speech, dress, and mannerisms. Some shame can be uttered in tones of sarcasm, overly critical judgments, and hurtful comments veiled as teasing or jokes.

The difference between appropriate parenting that corrects with love and affirmation, and shame which destroys the spirit, is how you feel about the act or comment. Shame tends to make you feel isolated, inferior, and unwanted. Discipline from loving parents can cause discomfort, but you still believe that you have worth and that you are loved despite your mistakes.

On a piece of notebook paper, list examples of shame. Try to include as many details of the incidents as possible, including your age, where you were, what was said, and how your body reacted to the shame.

4)   Abandonment Inventory

Abandonment is the bookend to shame when growing up in a dysfunctional family. Abandonment can be a physical abandonment in which our parents left us with friends, relatives, or day care centers while they practiced their addictions or dependence. Some children have been left alone at home for days while a parent or parents stayed away partying or chasing a loveless relationship. However, abandonment can also involve shaming statements as you learned in the previous exercise. We know of an adult child who cut her finger badly as a child and hid in the bathroom instead of running to her mother for comfort. The little girl intuitively knew that her bleeding finger would bring a harsh and blaming response from her mother, and it did. Instead of comforting the child, the overwhelmed mother howled at her husband and her child as he rushed the girl to the emergency room. The frightened mother shamed the injured child while also abandoning her emotionally.

Abandonment List

List the times you felt abandoned by your parents or care giver. List your age, the location of the abandonment, and any other details you can remember.

5) Harms Inventory: Generational Transfer

In this exercise, we inventory how we have abandoned or neglected other people in our lives. If we have children, we also look at how our actions and words served as the transfer mechanism for the disease of family dysfunction. This transaction is brokered by what we tell our children. We may hear ourselves saying things to our children that our parents said to us. Our words, flawed thinking, and reactions to life transfer dysfunction to the next generation. This was never our intent. Indeed, many of us swore to be different than our parents. Many of us have said: "It will never happen to me." But it did.

We know in our hearts that we would not have harmed our children purposely. We must remember we are facing our actions with courage and honesty. This is not easy, and we should give ourselves a break. We are not alone here. We have the support of our ACA group, a sponsor, and our Higher Power as we face the consequences of our behavior. The guilt we might experience in this exercise is healthy guilt.

Harms Worksheet

Those I have harmed, abandoned, neglected, mistreated	What I did, my behavior	Results, or memory of incident	My memory of having been similarly harmed as a child

Gentleness Break

The ACA Fourth Step involves a balanced look at our family of origin and our own behavior and thoughts. The emotions, events, and self-blame stirred by this Step can seem overwhelming for some. As you work Step Four, we urge you to be rigorously honest, holding nothing back, but we also remind you to be gentle with yourself. Remember you are not alone, and you have not done or thought anything that someone else has not done or thought. You have character assets and abilities that help balance disturbing aspects of your life.

In Step Four, we ask you to balance any shameful or fearful memories that might arise with the knowledge that you have honesty and courage in your life. ACA is not an easy program to work, but your courage is apparent and shows in working this Step and the Twelve Steps of ACA. Adult children have an inner strength that has always been there. That inner strength, which some choose to call a Higher Power or Divine Spirit, is with you now as you face this liberating inventory of your life. We suggest that you remain focused during this process, but take gentleness breaks and stay in contact with your sponsor or counselor. During this break read the Eleventh Promise of the ACA Promises out loud. Also read the ACA Fourth Step Prayer. (You will find the ACA Promises at the end of Chapter 15).

Promise Eleven: "With help from our ACA support group, we will slowly release our dysfunctional behaviors."

Fourth Step Prayer:

Divine Creator. Help me to be rigorously honest and to care for myself during this Fourth Step process. Let me practice gentleness and not abandon myself on this spiritual journey. Help me remember that I have attributes, and that I can ask for forgiveness. I am not alone. I can ask for help. Amen.

6) Stored Anger (Resentment) Inventory

In ACA we want to "lift up" resentment and see what is underneath. We believe resentment is stored anger caused by innumerable losses as a child. Such loss creates grief appearing as depression in addition to creating stored anger. We will cover grief work in Step Five.

Most adult children deny they have anger and therefore deny they are angry. On the other hand, there are some adult children who can explode with anger but never seem to tap the stored anger deep within them. Without naming their childhood loss, they can "recharge" and explode repeatedly, feeling ashamed or confused by their behavior. They really want to change or curb their anger, but they feel powerless to do so.

In the "affects my" column below, losses can include the loss of the sense of safety in the home. There is also the loss of identity and the loss of childhood experiences of learning to play, imagine, and be spontaneous. Many adult children also lost friends due to a dysfunctional parent's behavior. Others had to stop a favorite sport in high school due to a parent's intolerance or nonsupport. The goal of this exercise is to find your anger and lift it up and see the loss beneath it.

Stored Anger (Resentment) Worksheet

I resent	The Cause	Affects *(my self worth, friend-ships, safety, ability to imagine)*	My reaction *(anger, rebellion, withdrawn, passive/ aggressive, or other)*	Inner Child's reaction *(don't trust, don't talk, don't feel, or other)*

7) Relationships (Romance /Sexual/Friendships) Inventory

As adult children, most of us have used a variety of relationships in an attempt to heal ourselves from the chronic sense of aloneness in our lives. We have used sex, romance and friendships to feel safe or not alone. This sense of aloneness has its roots in abandonment by our family. Until we get help, we continually look outside ourselves for drugs, gambling, sex, work, or people to make us feel whole, but it never works. This is the codependent germ appearing as addictiveness in us.

List your relationship partners, friends and other people you have had relationships with. Watch for patterns that emerge in your relationships. (Note: Some adult children practice relationship "anorexia," which means they avoid relationships to remove any chance of being abandoned or hurt. For these adult children we ask that you inventory the relationships or relationship that brought about this scenario in your life).

Relationships Worksheet

Person	What I expected to get	What I got	My dependent behavior	How relation-ship ended

8) Sexual Abuse Inventory

This exercise helps some adult children identify sexual abuse. For many incest survivors, this exercise can stir strong memories. We urge you to stay in contact with your counselor or sponsor. It is important to remember that you did not cause the sexual abuse. Many adult children are confused on this issue because they were children when the abuse occurred. They lacked the ability to think objectively about what was happening to them so many children assumed they caused it or asked for it. As adults, these childhood assumptions can linger and undermine the adult's review of what happened. If you were touched, fondled, forced to perform sex acts, asked to perform sex, or watch sex acts as a child, it was not your fault no matter what the circumstance or no matter what was said by the adult or teen abusing you.

Some adult children have grown up to be perpetrators by reenacting what was done to them. These acts can be disturbing and painful to admit, but you are not disqualified from being an ACA member. You are not disqualified from the healing grace of your Higher Power or the acceptance of the ACA fellowship. We ask you to modify this inventory to include these acts; however, we caution you on how much detail you would share in an ACA meeting about such acts. If you are acting out and feel out of control, we ask you to seek professional help.

Sexual Abuse Worksheet

Abuser	What happened	My age	Who I told or did not tell	Who got blamed?	How did abuse stop?

Gentleness Break

During this gentleness break, read the Twelve Promises of ACA found in Chapter 15.

Affirmation: *The promises of ACA are for me, and they are being fulfilled in my life. I am discovering my real identity. I am facing shame and uncomfortable feelings without running or acting-out. I have positive attributes that I am discovering. God, as I understand God, hears my prayers. I can ask for help.*

9)   Denial Inventory

For ACAs, denial lives in the way we recall the abuse, neglect, or rejection we suffered as children. Denial is the mechanism which protects and helps plant the seed of family dysfunction in the next generation. For help with this exercise, look at some of your descriptions in the worksheets involving sexual abuse, stored anger, and Laundry List traits. There is no need to embellish or understate what happened.

Categories you might be in denial about include the manner of punishment used by your parents or how your parents or siblings teased you. Constant arguing by the parents also is a form of abuse that many of us grew accustomed to, but which we do not see as abuse. Many times our parents argued abusively or cursed in front of us without regard to the impact it had on us as children. Their arguing changed us.

You may also be in denial about your behavior as an adult. We ask you to look at your manner of language and actions in dealing with your children, employer, or spouse or partner. What language do you use? What is your tone? What messages do you give other people about their worth? Do you ask for what you need straight out or do you manipulate to get what you want?

The denial worksheet has two exercises. The first one deals with how your parents or relatives treated you. The second involves how you treated others as an adult.

In the first exercise, in the "what happened" column, many ACA members list incest, touching, harsh spankings, and threatening talk, but this column is not limited to these types of events. The worksheet involves unhealthy actions by your parents and how you remembered the incidents. The exercise helps you see how you recall the incident years later. Denial can flourish when we recall a harmful or abusive event without the full details. We can blame ourselves for the abuse or explain it away if we leave out details. If you were abused by a sibling or other relative, include that person's behavior in this exercise. This exercise will help you determine the facts of an event and how it was described later with accuracy or inaccuracy.

Denial Worksheet:
Your Parents' Behavior
(include other relatives)

What happened (facts)	My age	How I felt about what happened	Parents' message of what happened	How I later described what happened

My Behavior: The Laundry List Reflection

In this worksheet, you are looking at your own hurtful, neglectful or possibly abusive behavior. This is not an easy exercise since most of us would not like to talk about our own neglectful acts. We need God's help with this exercise to avoid condemning ourselves. We must remember that we have inner courage and that we are not evil or beyond recall. Given our dysfunctional upbringing, we must realize we could not have turned out differently. Our behavior as adults was scripted from our childhood. We repeated what was done to us by our parents but there is a big difference between ourselves and our parents. We are facing our shameful actions and abuse with ACA and with a Higher Power. We are owning our behavior with help and prayer.

In this exercise we are looking for the reflections of the Laundry List traits. Most of these common behaviors have a reflection that is just as damaging as the original trait. For example, we have lived as victims, but many of us have victimized others in an attempt to control them or harm them. We have feared authority figures, but we have become authority figures who have been feared. Some of us have been perpetrators, acting against our will. We have perpetrated abuse and abandonment.

In the "what happened" column, list incidents with relatives, co-workers, and spouses or partners. How have you victimized others? How have you been an authority figure? How have you judged others harshly? Do you gossip? Malicious gossip can be a form of perpetration.

Denial Worksheet:
My Behavior

What happened (facts)	Who was involved (child, spouse, other)	My perception and feeling of what happened	How I later described what happened

10) Post-Traumatic Stress Disorder: Body Work

In ACA, we believe that the disease of family dysfunction affects the adult child in body, mind, and spirit long after the adult has left his or her family of origin. Our bodies are composed of bones, tissue, and a central nervous system connected to our brain. We think it is reasonable to believe that the body remembers much of what it experiences, just as the brain remembers what it has processed and responded to.

Who among us has not performed a certain task for many days or months, but we repeat the same hand motion or same reflex when the task has changed. For instance, if we stored our favorite pair of shoes in a certain area of our closet for many months, then move them, we may reach into that section of the closet before realizing we have moved the shoes to another place. The mind and the body react automatically to a remembered task. The arm is extended into the closet before the mind realizes the shoes are at the other end of the closet. This may happen two or three times before we rewire ourselves to remember the new location of our shoes. The same response holds true for those of us writing checks and making an error by writing out the wrong year after January 1st. Many of us automatically write in the wrong year before realizing it has changed. These are simple examples of stored memory in our minds and bodies.

Medical research reveals that the brain and body are inseparable as we live, breathe, feel, and sense our surroundings as children and adults. As the brain remembers and reacts automatically, so does the body.

Post-traumatic stress disorder involves the mind and body and remembered responses to severe trauma or near trauma. PTSD is a documented disorder that affects adult children in addition to war veterans and victims of traumatic events. PTSD symptoms can include hypervigilance of surroundings, unexplained body sensations, increased heart rate, and being startled easily. In adult children PTSD tends to manifest itself in hypervigilance, compulsive behavior, and hard-to-detect body sensations. It is as if our bodies have "rewired" themselves to protect us from severe harm or severe harm that almost occurred.

Many adult children are skeptical or confused about PTSD, and we understand. We can see how our minds would store memories and adapt with survival traits to live through a dysfunctional upbringing. However, it is difficult to understand that our bodies would remember or store trauma. This skepticism is often underlined by the fact that most adult children are shut down emotionally or "numbed out." We have become adept at shutting down our feelings instantly. It is difficult for us to realize what our body is trying to tell us. We ignore our body or misinterpret its language.

The body's language can take on many forms that include backaches, headaches, stiff necks, tastes in the throat, genital pain or numbness, arm pain, foot pain, or a sense of disorientation when feeling stressed or fearful. Others have sharp or dull sensations in the legs or feel a lump or obstruction in the throat. There can be diarrhea, stomach pain, or flashes of panic. With PTSD work, some ACA members will realize they hold their head a certain way or sleep a certain way. Some adult children realize they cannot sleep facing a doorway while others must check and recheck locks before going to bed or leaving for a trip. Most, if not all, adult children have some degree of PTSD; however, not all such symptoms are indicators of a PTSD incident. Symptoms in the body can be caused by medical conditions, aging, or disease that are not PTSD related.

PTSD caused by battering and incest is typically easier to detect or suspect. Subtle, but just as telling, forms of PTSD are more difficult to recognize. PTSD caused by years of parental neglect and hurtful acts intermixed with moments of nurturing can be tricky to detect and understand.

We know of an adult child who seemed to love canned potatoes. She felt "comfort" just knowing there was a single can of potatoes in her cupboard. As this person began addressing her ACA issues as an adult, she realized that the canned potatoes meant something more than a fondness for a peeled vegetable in a can. She realized, or her body remembered, that canned potatoes were the difference between going hungry or having something to eat when her alcoholic mother went out for days without coming home.

By doing ACA work, she realized that her body remembered the hunger pains brought on by an abandoning mother. As a child, while feeling fearful and hungry when her mother was gone, she found a can of potatoes. She ate the potatoes and felt full. Her hunger left, and she could sleep. At a young age, she felt comforted by the potatoes for two reasons: She solved her immediate problem of hunger, and she knew she did not need her mother to take care of her. She could now take care of herself. She would take care of her sister, too. She learned to drag a chair to the edge of the stove to warm up soup and drag the same chair to the sink to wash dishes. She no longer had to feel hurt or abandoned by a mother she loved and adored. The child could take care of herself and not show her love for her mother because it hurt too badly when her mother left home for days. The canned potatoes represented her introduction to adulthood before she attended her first day of school as a first grader.

This is a subtle example of PTSD buried deep but which produced a real action in the adult child's life. The memory contains PTSD elements of fear, threat to survival, and feeling alone, perhaps destitute. The memory resided in her mind and stomach. As a 30-year-old woman, she shopped for canned potatoes and thought of it as a funny nuance in her life. She was a successful professional, divorced and raising her own daughter without relying on help from her family. However, 25 years after the original incident, this woman's body, her stomach, remembered that hunger pain but transformed it into a comforting memory of canned potatoes with the help of her brain. Through ACA work, she also realized she had a hunger for her mother's love, a hunger she could never completely swallow.

Was this adult child starved by her parents as a child? No. But there were moments of extreme hunger and a feeling of terror when nightfall would come and the house would grow dark without the mother coming home. The child's father was often away as well on business. This adult child missed enough meals that she had to find a way to take care of herself and a sister. There were other acts of neglect and abuse in this woman's life: harsh whippings, threats of beatings, and incest. As an adult, she tended to have enmeshed relationships, focusing on others and feeding them first before she fed herself. She typically placed herself last and lived with an unnamed sense of having little value as a person. When she finally walked away from an abandoning and loveless relationship, she felt like her world had ended. She was sure she was guilty, wrong, and defective. Her own alcoholism, exposed publicly by her own behavior, caused much shame. However, she has found the ACA way of life and realized she has an inner strength and real connection to God. She now reaches into her cupboard for a variety of food to nourish her body and soul.

A Word of Caution

PTSD work, coupled with ACA meetings and quality counseling, can produce powerful clarity and healing for adult children. Yet, we offer a word of caution. Not all actions or thoughts you had as a child have a deeper meaning. Some do and some do not. Our parents were only human, and they made mistakes. A harsh comment or being left for the afternoon with a babysitter does not equal PTSD or abuse. An occasional swatting on the behind without malice is not always abuse. A parent threatening to leave you at the grocery store to scare you into leaving with them when they have finished shopping may not be traumatic.

However, at the same time, one vicious whipping or battering can be stored in your body and memory for decades. Certainly, incest, rape, and inappropriate touching are trauma by their very nature. Also, a parent who chronically left you in day care or with relatives without returning home for days begins to venture into neglect. From this scenario, you can have cumulative abandonment or a PTSD memory as a child. These memories can produce stress chemicals and brain pathways that underline the formation of stored trauma known as PTSD.

The difference between neglect or abuse, which can produce stored trauma, and a parent being human is usually a matter of degree and longitude. When a parent misses enough birthdays, curses loudly and hotly long enough, and constantly blames the child for normal needs, then you have an area to review.

We ask that you find a qualified professional to help you sort out what you experienced as a child. Listen to your body and write about funny habits or rituals that seem innocent yet persistent.

While counseling is supportive and meaningful, we have found that counseling alone is not always sufficient for lasting internal change. ACAs need a place to sound out their experiences and thoughts among people who give support and lasting meaning

7

to such experiences. Attendance at ACA meetings help clarify actions and thoughts that seem mundane. Keeping a journal of your daily thoughts and feelings helps as well. Thoughts, actions, and sensations that tend to have a pattern could be the tip of a PTSD iceberg. We urge caution and prudence.

ACA members completing the PTSD exercise have sought helping professionals who have helped them detect and free up stored trauma and neglect. We do not recommend specifics on which type of body work is best. Experience shows that ACA members have received good results from massage (deep tissue), nondominant handwriting exercises, and guided meditation. Guided meditation and nondominant handwriting tend to offer clues on where stored trauma exists while deep-tissue massage often releases that trauma.

We have seen some adult children benefit from deep-tissue massage without knowing the exact location of an old abuse wound. When we speak of trauma we are not limiting the trauma to hitting, slapping, or vulgar acts of incest. Trauma and neglect can occur and be stored by subtle but longitudinal acts of neglect and blame. Parents who never admit being wrong and who heap heavy doses of perfectionistic language and expectations upon their children create stored trauma without lifting a hand. This type of shaming and abandoning behavior produces the fatigue of spirit that can be misdiagnosed as depression or lethargy. We ask that you keep an open mind as you do this worksheet. (p. 184)

This exercise is not meant as a replacement for a diagnosis from a qualified therapist or counselor. If seeking a massage therapist for PTSD or grief work, we suggest that the therapist be educated and experienced in working with trauma survivors if possible. There are issues of touch and boundaries that should be honored.

Trauma/Neglect Inventory

For the PTSD worksheet, begin by writing down any traumatic or neglectful act you can recall. Was there hitting, cursing, threats, or talk of threat in your home? Were you injured? Write down the area of your body that was injured. These places can hold PTSD triggers.

There are also elements of PTSD not caused by overt trauma. For example, a child growing up in a home with perfectionism and unreasonable expectations can feel anxious turning in a project at work. This is a form of PTSD caused by being undercut by a parent who usually found fault in our housework or schoolwork even when it was above average.

Next, write down PTSD symptoms you might have. They might include headaches, backaches, throat problems, tense shoulders, genital sensations, dull pain, twitches, or numbness. You might also list funny or noticeable habits, rituals, and routines.

As you recall information for this worksheet, think about your posture, breathing, or feelings associated with the items you list. Think about whether you were sitting, standing, or lying down. Was the room lighted or dark? Were you outside? Did you place your hands anywhere or squeeze your eyes shut during the trauma or abuse? Did you rock yourself in a chair after the event? Did you take a walk or hide in your closet after abuse or anticipating abuse?

Try to fill out all the categories in the worksheet, but if you draw a blank, put the worksheet aside for a day or two and return to it. This worksheet is not a replacement for a professional evaluation, but it can help you get started on this important aspect of ACA recovery.

When you have recalled some experiences or memories, fill in the categories of the worksheet with your listed items.

As a hint, write a sentence about a current incident that might have caused you to react a certain way. Using the labels from the PTSD worksheet, label the parts of the sentence as

7

you trace the event back to your childhood if it relates to your childhood. For example: "My body tensed up (symptom), and I felt frightened when I overheard an adult scolding a child (event/trigger). I can recall my parents standing over me and yelling at me when I was young (my reality). My parents said I was a rotten kid (parents' message about what happened). I just always felt like a screw up. I must have been six years old (my age)."

A more subtle example of PTSD might be the symptom of hoarding food or never throwing anything away. For example: "I realize my intoxicated parents rarely fixed us a meal (event). We were hungry a lot growing up (my reality). We never had decent clothes and kids at school laughed at us. I get anxious (sensation) when I think about throwing anything out. My parents said we were a proud family and relied on no one for help (parent's message). I say we were poor due to alcoholism (my reality)."

After identifying the items in the sentences you write about yourself, place them in the worksheet categories where they fit. This exercise will help you see the trigger, your reality, and other important information.

PTSD Worksheet

Event or trigger	My age	My reality of what happened	Parent's message of what happened	Symptom or ritual, funny habit	Where stored in my body, type of sensation

11) Feelings Exercise

The Step Four feelings list helps adult children build on the feelings exercise at the beginning of this section. This exercise addresses the "don't feel" rule developed while growing up in a dysfunctional family. By talking about our feelings we address the "don't trust" and "don't talk" rules as well.

Many adult children are unsure of their feelings or cannot distinguish feelings, so this exercise helps you get started identifying emotions and becoming more comfortable with using feelings words.

Most adult children are terrified of feelings and believe they cannot withstand them. In ACA, we must remember that we are not alone. Recovery is different than when we were children and had to face the feelings of isolation and despair alone. When feelings arise in ACA, we learn to "sit" with them without acting out. We hug a pillow, lie on the floor and breathe deeply, take a walk, or simply sit still and hang on. Our feelings will not kill us. We can name our feelings and understand them. This is an ACA promise. We learn that we can pick up the phone and call someone to listen to us. Feelings pass. We can survive our feelings.

Many adult children have "frozen" feelings in addition to being confused about feelings. Our feelings are like a great glacier, which appears stationary, but which moves with great force and sureness. Hidden within the glacier are huge boulders that scrape the earth leaving deep scars and ruts. Occasionally, one of these huge rocks works its way up, piercing the icy surface of the glacier. Release occurs.

Addictiveness and unhealthy dependence are often attempts to ignore a frozen mass inside. ACA Step work helps locate trapped feelings and melt the glacier of our soul. At some feelings we shiver, but there is release that brings healing. By claiming our feelings, we step out of the shadowy chill of a glacier into sunlight. We feel the warmth of acceptance in ACA. We are finally home.

Identifying our feelings and talking with others about how we feel is a critical step in breaking the isolation we have lived with for so long.

Talking about our feelings is a risk; however, this is a risk worth taking because the rewards are great. When we let others know about our feelings, we connect with people on a spiritual and equal level instead of a dependent and manipulative level. We learn to not fear our emotions in ACA.

Many adult children learn how to identify and distinguish feelings by practicing the feelings sentence. Select one of the feeling words and complete the sentence. Complete three sentences each day for two weeks and then continue to practice the sentence regularly.

Feelings Sentence:

I feel_____when _____ because _____.

Example:

"I feel hopeful when I attend an ACA meeting because I know I am heard."

Word selection:

loved	joyful	ashamed	humorous	irritated
angry	embarrassed	trusted	betrayed	pleased
satisfied	ambivalent	hopeful	inspired	loving
frustrated	disappointed	grief	accepted	excited
grateful	confident	humiliated	guilty	serene
rested	shame	abandoned	pleasure	safe
tenacious	thoughtful	playful	fascinated	enthralled

12) Praise Work

Most adult children constantly seek affirmation but do not truly believe compliments and praise when they come. In this Step Four exercise, we are introducing the practice of praising or affirming ourselves. Most adult children have a praise deficit, which can never be solved by an outside source. Before recovery, we tended to operate with closed feelings and dismissed any affirmation coming our way from others. Or we manipulated others into praising us while we still felt inadequate and inferior. The affirmation work here is more involved than self-esteem work, which tends to be topical in nature in addressing mannerisms, attitudes, and dress. With praise work, we go further inside and confront ourselves about pushing away compliments and sincere attempts by others to affirm us. Because we shut out our parents when we were children, we tend to shut out people as adults. If we were not affirmed or praised as children, we are typically uncomfortable with praise as adults. Ignoring praise or failing to see our accomplishments as adults can help disqualify us from loving relationships.

Learning to accept praise is different than the ACA trait of constantly seeking affirmations. When we constantly seek affirmation, we set ourselves up to live a goal-oriented life. By living such a life, we tend to feel fulfilled only when we complete a project and only when affirmation comes with such tasks. We lack the inner voice to tell ourselves that we are okay when others don't deliver the affirmations that we were seeking.

By learning to praise ourselves and accept praise from others, we are less prone to suffer the debilitating effects of being a people-pleaser. We tend to stand more steady and affirm ourselves when external praise does not come. Our mistakes, while still unsettling, are more tolerable.

In addition to introducing affirmations, this exercise is presented here because it is a balancing exercise. These affirmations will help you understand that you have good qualities as you inventory your past behavior.

Praise Exercise

Below is a list of 25 assets, which will help balance positive and spiritual qualities while working Step Four. Circle at least 10 attributes even if you do not believe you possess all of them. Because we operate from a praise deficit, we often do not realize the assets we have in our lives. This is the start of the praise work. There will be a praise exercise in the Step Ten daily inventory as well.

strong	compassionate	spontaneous	trustworthy	prompt
humorous	courteous	creative	tenacious	kind
sensitive	talented	loving	judicious	hard working
willing	honest	a listener	accepting	a friend
intelligent	organized	spiritual	modest	an ACA member

After circling your assets, sit quietly and affirm each one by saying: I am_____(repeat for each asset you have circled). Hang onto the list to help balance the defects of character that you will find in your Fourth Step inventory. It is essential that you remember that you have positive qualities and spiritual direction in your life. You are not a defective character. You have defects of character.

STEP FOUR SPIRITUAL PRINCIPLES:

Self-honesty and Courage

You have finished the Fourth Step outline. Congratulations. You have taken a searching and fearless look at your family-of-origin and your own thoughts and actions. You have also balanced this look with positive traits that include the courage you exhibited by completing this challenging Step. Your journey is still unfolding. You are not alone. Ask for help and accept it.

Set an appointment with your sponsor or counselor to work Step Five: "Admitted to God, to ourselves, and to another human being the exact nature of our wrongs."

My Fifth Step Date is: Day _____ **Time** _____

Important Note

Before your Fifth Step date arrives, read all of the section on Step Five and learn about the exact nature of your wrongs. In Step Five, you will also find instructions on what to do when you have finished Step Five. Many ACA members work Steps Six and Seven immediately following their Fifth Step. These instructions in Step Five will guide you through the sequence of Steps Six and Seven.

7

A Fifth Step Tool For the ACA Sponsor

Appendix B has an outline for your sponsor or the person hearing your Fifth Step. This outline helps the sponsor, spiritual guide, or mentor guide you through Step Five and prepare you for Steps Six and Seven.

Chapter Seven

STEP FIVE

Admitted to God, to ourselves, and to another human being the exact nature of our wrongs.

He Expected Condemnation And Got Fairness

When I did my Fourth and Fifth Steps with an ACA counselor, I had to be reminded to be gentle with myself while also being rigorously honest about how I had harmed others. I started in a Twelve Step program that did not allow you to look at another person's behavior. Looking at family dysfunction was out of the question there. I was told to forgive my parents, which I did, but I was left with a sense of not being whole inside.

When I worked the ACA Steps, I got to look at shame, abandonment, and loss in addition to inventorying my own selfish behavior. I got to find out about the exact nature of my abandonment by my parents. They tried to love me and protect me, but in reality they passed on low self-worth and self-hate. I used to say they did the best they could, but now I say they passed on what was given to them – family dysfunction.

Being gentle with myself or writing down my assets was odd or even weird at first. My counselor encouraged me, and I continued to do this. After awhile I began to believe that I have good traits as well as areas I can improve. My Fifth Step gave me a balanced look at my life. I wasn't looking for that. I was expecting condemnation, but I got fairness.

Exact Nature Of His Wrongs

I went into Step Five holding back nothing. I figured I had nothing to lose. The best I could do with my life got me to my first Twelve Step meeting 22 years ago. If I got arrested again for DUI, I was going to prison back then. I found sobriety and then I found ACA. My life and the Twelve Steps took on a new meaning that has continued to grow inside of me more than 20 years later.

In Step Five I found out the exact nature of my wrongs. For instance, when I stole something, I found out there was a legal wrong and a spiritual wrong. The legal wrong was that my petty theft was against the law. The spiritual wrong meant my theft separated me from my Higher Power. When I stole or acted out with drugs or sex, I was separating myself from my Higher Power and other people.

After I took my Fifth Step, I did not feel alone all the time like before. I have had my moments of feeling alone since then, but they are not as powerful. I finally feel like I fit somewhere. I am a member of ACA.

The Most Important Lesson: Listening And Trust

I guess the most important lesson I can take away from Step Five is that I finally trusted someone enough to tell him my story. I finally got to tell someone about all of the thoughts and behaviors I thought made me beyond help.

I remember feeling odd about talking about some things, but my sponsor just listened and nodded his head in agreement. Sometimes he talked about an incident that he had done that was similar to mine. He did not judge me. That was a huge relief.

I have since sponsored others and listened to their Fifth Steps, and the rewards have been great. I have been able to return the gift of listening to someone and not judging him. This is the heart of ACA in my opinion. We could never do this as children. We could never trust or just have someone listen to us. I thank God every day for this program.

She Followed Through With Step Five

I once thought I could skip admitting the exact nature of my wrongs to God and myself since I seemed to be doing that in writing my Fourth Step inventory. Looking back, I can now see that the Steps separate Step Four and Step Five so there is enough time for real progress to happen. We need time to recall what happened. We also need to talk to a trusted sponsor or counselor about our story.

The benefit of Step Five is improving my relationships with my Higher Power as well as myself. I do this through trust and honest communication.

She Broke the "Don't Talk" Rule and Found Freedom

The Fifth Step was by far my most difficult Step. I remember when I grew up my father would explode emotionally, and we'd walk on eggshells. Afterwards, no one would ever talk about the incident. There was never an apology. My father frequently said to me, "No one wants to hear what you have to say. Nothing you have to say is valuable. You're not learning anything when you're talking. Shut up."

To ask someone I barely knew to listen to me talk about my problems for even a few minutes was very difficult. To ask them to listen to my entire Fifth Step was much harder. I overcame my father's admonitions when I worked Step Five. My sponsor and I spent two afternoons, for three hours each time. I told her about my character defects, my life, and what I had contributed to my problems. I felt guilty because I made a lot of mistakes, but admitting my mistakes made me feel incredibly free.

The Fifth Step process has been very challenging. The reward, however, is freedom from the past.

Step Five Summary

By working Step Five we are challenging the three main rules entrenched in our souls as a result of growing up in a dysfunctional home. The rules are: "don't talk, don't trust, and don't feel." Growing up in a dysfunctional family meant not trusting what you were seeing or what your parents said. Abuse was often minimized or blamed on another cause, which resulted in the child not trusting his or her perceptions.

The "don't talk" rule has its origins in homes where children were often told to "shut up" or "be quiet" whenever they attempted to speak or express a thought. Others were ignored under the "don't talk" rule and therefore stopped talking. The "don't talk" rule also means the family does not talk about things that are important such as feelings or spirituality. The rule is also a method of keeping sick family secrets.

The "don't feel" rule of dysfunctional homes often means that feelings were unimportant or too scary to address. Before recovery, we could be accused of being too sensitive or being immature if we expressed feelings in a dysfunctional home. To avoid such ridicule, we usually shut down our emotions. The "don't feel" rule is the rule that underlies our ability to stuff feelings such as fear. Some of us lived in constant fear of being ridiculed, teased, or battered by an abusive parent. By the time we reach recovery, many of us are numb from living with fear. We cannot call the feeling of fear into focus, but it is there, driving our hypervigilance.

In Step Five, we talk about what happened, and we trust another person to hear us without judgment. We feel the feelings that come up with the help of our ACA support group and a sponsor or counselor.

In Step Five, we finally get to talk about what matters rather than denying or filtering what happened. This is a critical step for any adult child hoping to face the effects of a dysfunctional upbringing and to continue to grow in the ACA program.

We know that breaking dysfunctional family rules does not come easy for adult children. These rules are similar to the survival traits we used to live through our childhoods. We learned to trust these rules and use them in our daily lives; however, the rules have outlived their usefulness. They are strangling our lives and our relationships. We have to find another way to live with feelings, trust, and voice.

For some ACAs, the Fifth Step will be the first time they have told anyone some of their most troublesome memories of abuse. We know the courage this will take to move forward with Step Five. We know you will be letting someone into compartments of your mind that you may have thought would remain tightly shut forever. But these are the very secrets and problematic memories that need letting out. You are finally safe to take this action in ACA with a sponsor, trusted counselor, or spiritual leader.

Avoid Half Measures

To skip over this Step, or to employ half measures in the Steps, has proven disastrous for adult children. By not following through with Step Five, these adult children seem to never grow spiritually in the program. They have exposed painful behavior and secrets in Step Four only to hold onto such pain by not doing a Fifth Step. They are stuck. They have meeting knowledge and ACA knowledge, but they hang onto some of their most painful behaviors. They often sound polished at ACA meetings, but they have not faced their worst fears or secrets. The clues are there. They continue to reenact the abandonment of their childhoods, or they position themselves for constant chaos or heavy doses of shame. They still feel responsible for their parents' dysfunction on some level.

By avoiding Steps Four or Five, many of these adult children seem to practice greater degrees of dysfunctional control and are cut off from God. Many drop out of meetings never to return. Others attempt to work a program but feel somehow cheated by a Higher Power and ACA. They lead a double life outside the meetings, stopping by ACA occasionally to check in but avoiding the necessary actions to change. Our hearts go out to these suffering adult children. They need to complete the Steps. Step Five shows us the value in following through with the Twelve Steps.

If we skip Step Five, or attempt to somehow minimize it, we may never claim the promises of the ACA program. The Twelve Promises involve learning to live with inner peace and a grateful sense that we have survived an ordeal. We have something to offer the world, but we must put forth effort to claim it. With this effort, we realize how our stories and experiences matter.

In reality, going through Step Five is the easier, softer way compared to codependent living, which brings constant torment or chaos. The emotional and mental effort it takes to run our lives by dysfunctional control or through loveless relationships is enormous.

Go Through the Pain

There is no way around Steps Four or Five. We must go through them to get to the other side, to find the God of our understanding waiting there with a timeless embrace. This is our experience. Thousands of adult children have completed Step Five and found a peace and serenity not known before. They are waiting for you on the other side of Step Five. They called upon the inner strength which helped them survive a dysfunctional upbringing. They used that inner strength to make it through Step Five with room to spare. You have this inner strength by the very fact you have completed the first four Steps of the program.

Step Five gives us a chance to finally talk about what matters to someone we trust. We give our Fifth Step without grand promises to be perfect or strive for perfection. We tell our story to another person with honesty and sincerity and leave the results to God as we understand God. We can finally give ourselves breathing room to change one day at a time. We claim our humanness and our position in the world.

Reparenting Ourselves

In addition to breaking dysfunctional family rules, Step Five is another significant step in learning to reparent ourselves and to face the exact nature of our childhood abandonment. This abandonment is linked to the wrongs we have committed against others. We take a balanced look at how we have harmed ourselves and others as well. Reparenting tools include addressing the hypercritical voice in our head that fuels our self-doubt or self-harm. With reparenting, we begin to accept the fact that we have good qualities. The qualities have been understated, but they are there. We fail to see our internal goodness because we tend to focus on a mistaken sense of being flawed or hopelessly wrong. In Step Five, we must be honest about our selfish behavior and claim it. We also must lift our eyes to see our kindness and our love, which is there and which was first. Some ACA members find it difficult to identify or to claim their good qualities, but we have them. Through reparenting, we challenge our inner critic by reminding ourselves of our strong points. By doing so, we realize that we are not as bad as we thought we were nor are we as noble. We have a balance of positive and problematic traits that we are learning to accept or to address.

We approach Step Five with an attitude of self-love and trust that our Higher Power is with us and will not abandon us. We have taken a hard look at ourselves and our family of origin in Step Four. We have held nothing back. We are now preparing to release years of stored grief, shame, and hurtful secrets to God and to someone who understands.

Many ACA members choose their sponsor or counselor to hear their Fifth Step because they have developed trust with this person. It is important that the person hearing the Fifth Step understand what we are trying to do. It is not our job to explain the Fifth Step process or to educate the person about ACA when we sit down to tell our story to him or her. We choose someone we can relate to and who will not pass judgment on our inventory of our lives.

The spiritual principles of Step Five are honesty and trust. We must have self-honesty about the effects of growing up in a dysfunctional home. The effects are our survival traits, which include people-pleasing, becoming addicted or marrying an addict, fearing authority figures, and feeling guilty when we ask for what we need. We often confuse love and pity, and we tend to "love" people we can rescue. We also can be the rescued. We stay in abusive relationships because they resemble how we were raised. We are terrified of abandonment so we tolerate high levels of abuse or neglect as adults. The abuse seems normal.

In Step Five, we must also have self-honesty about those we have harmed, including ourselves.

When looking at the exact nature of our wrongs we must be honest about our motives and designs. We must take ownership of our wrongs without minimizing our errors or exaggerating them. Many adult children commit wrongs against others based on a sense of being defective or unwanted. Driven by an unnamed hurt inside of us, we harm others so that we might feel powerful. Or we recreate the isolation we became comfortable with as children. We harm others, which is wrong, but the exact nature of our wrong is that we have harmed ourselves. In harming another, we usually have acted out on a survival trait. With such behavior, we miss a chance to address our isolation and the feeling of being defective.

The old saying goes: "Hurting people hurt others," and that appears to be true for adult children. The script goes like this: "If I can hurt you before you hurt me then I will feel powerful or in control."

Our inside hurt does not give us the right to harm others, but understanding that pain can begin the process of freeing us from its grip. Realizing such pain is the starting point for change and learning to love ourselves. We listen to our hurt and reparent it toward self-love.

If we minimize our wrongs or fail to see their exact nature, we fall short of the mark of self-honesty in Step Five. Self-honesty does not mean self harm. We want rigorous honesty, but we do not want to abuse ourselves by being rigorously scathing. If we overstate our wrongs and beat ourselves up, we tend to drift into an attitude of martyrdom, or we assume the victim posture.

At the same time, we cannot be too lenient on ourselves for harms committed against others. Being too lenient can lead to an attitude of being "damaged goods" without hope for repair. This can lead to the victim plateau as well and mire us in self-pity or push away the true path to self-discovery in Step Five. The key to rigorous honesty that steers between self-abuse and leniency is this: We become willing to face whatever we have done and then do the footwork to change. We work the Steps, we listen, and we talk to others about our feelings. If the pain of feeling defective or shamed emerges, we sit with it instead of acting out. The pain will pass. We pray, and we seek the truest course with input from our sponsor, counselor, or ACA group members. Our answer will emerge, and we will recognize it.

Step Five is where we embrace a more balanced view of who we are as sons, daughters, citizens, employees, business owners, and spiritual seekers. Since we come from homes that were out of balance with abuse or hypercritical attitudes, it is not easy for us to embrace our positive qualities. But we have such traits as compassion, trust, intelligence, and spirituality. Other positive traits are friendliness, honesty, and tenacity. We are not the disease of family dysfunction, but we have acted on harmful traits developed in that family when we were children. We are facing our behaviors in Step Five and making an honest attempt to change. We can feel good about this effort and our good character no matter what our story reveals.

Exact Nature

When we look at the exact nature of our wrongs, we see that we have harmed ourselves based on our sense of being unacceptable, inferior, or lost. Further examination of our wrongs reveals there can be both legal and spiritual consequences to our actions. When we break the law there is a legal wrong, but we also see a spiritual separation as well. We separate ourselves from our Higher Power with our behavior. We experience spiritual loss.

Some adult children have committed crimes that have caused them to spend time in prison or lose their family and job. Others have been so caustic or difficult to live with that they end up alone. Still others remain on the job and in relationships but are not connected to life in a meaningful manner. Each of these adult children has committed a wrong and should stand ready to make amends.

But the adult child should also realize that the exact nature of a wrong can also involve loss. That is the secret in understanding Step Five. All of these harmful acts add up to loss. Each time we harmed another person or ourselves, we lost a piece of ourselves. Each time we shamed our own child or spouse, there was loss. Each time we judged ourselves without mercy for common mistakes, there was loss. Each day we remained in an abusive, dependent relationship there was loss.

Before finding ACA, we grew more weary each day, but we continued to try. We were the walking wounded with a smile. We were always on the verge of grief.

Grief: The Onion and Time

Every adult child has unexpressed grief, which is usually represented by the symptoms of depression, lethargy, or forms of dissociation. The grief that we speak of in ACA is the cumulative loss of childhood. Grief is loss that is stuck beneath denial, willful forgetting, and the fear of being perceived as dramatizing the past. Grief is the built-up defeats, slights, and neglect from childhood. We carry this grief with us as we create careers, raise families, or trudge through life as best as we can. Keeping ourselves busy or focusing on others seems to help us avoid looking at our childhood grief/loss, but it is there. Until we find ACA, we rarely understand the exact nature of our loss or how we can address it. If we sought help before ACA, our childhood loss was usually diagnosed as depression and commonly treated with ineffective methods.

Chapter Seven

The losses we speak of in ACA include the actions and inaction of our parents or family. Being shamed by our parents or a relative represents the loss of being able to feel whole as a person. Shame tramples a child's natural love and trust and replaces it with malignant self-doubt. With shame, we lose our ability to trust ourselves or others. We feel inherently faulty as a child. As adults, we can have a mistaken sense that something is wrong with us without knowing why. Other childhood loss includes being unfairly criticized by our family or being compared to a brother or sister and coming up short. This represents a loss of feeling valued as a person by our family. When our parents project their own lack of self-worth onto us, we experience loss as well. If our parents have said we are bad, dumb, or inferior, they were actually projecting what they believed about themselves. As children we were defenseless to throw off these projections. This is loss and grief carried into our adult years. These are examples of loss in addition to the early loss of security brought by trauma and neglect.

We introduce grief work in Step Five, realizing that such work is a lifetime journey. Long-time ACA members understand the importance of claiming grief or loss. Many older members will speak of finding their grief by working the Twelve Steps or by sitting alone quietly and feeling the feelings that arise. Experienced ACA members speak of grief with a sense of serenity rather than with sorrow or resentment. They have made peace with their losses and found wholeness. They know that grief exists in every adult child. They know that time will reveal it. Time will heal it.

While grief can be perceptible through writing and talking about our memories, some grief is not always visible. We indirectly address our childhood losses each time we attend an ACA meeting and listen to the experiences of other adult children. We also address our grief each time we work a Tenth Step inventory or practice an Eleventh Step meditation. Our experience shows that grief is there between the lines and the thoughts waiting to be released. Emotional release and meditating on what we have lost are certainly part of addressing grief, but there is more.

With Step Five, we are ready to remove deeper layers of the "onion," which is analogous to our recovery journey. We are removing layers of shame and despair to find our True Selves. We began peeling back layers of the onion in Step One with the admission of being powerless over the effects of family dysfunction. Just as an onion can bring tears, our grief work will help us find our tears.

Our experience shows that grief is often stored in our minds and bodies, waiting to be purged when the time is right. We understand that grief is cumulative, which means all the neglectful and shaming acts of our past are piled up. We had not forgotten them as we had thought. Our bodies remember. Our minds remember. Our Inner Child knows. In addition to addiction or depression, many of our members believe grief helps fuel our compulsive acts of cleaning, perfectionism, sex, binge eating, work, and gambling.

Addressing grief is not self-pity. Self-pity is a refusal to accept real help while clinging to denial and a dead way of life. Seeking our grief is an honest effort to go inward to find the God of our understanding waiting there with release.

To place a foot on the path of grief work, we need a balanced view of who we are and what happened to us. We cannot come to grief work weighing in too heavy as a victim or weighing too light as the hero child. The victim aspect of our personalities can take the road of self-pity and refuse true help. The hero believes he or she has placed childhood abuse in the past and is no longer affected by such memories. We must avoid these two paths if we are to accurately identify and purge our stored grief.

Steps Four and Five give us the balanced view of ourselves sufficient enough to go after stuck emotions and feelings and find our productive tears. Before grief work, our tears were unproductive. Before recovery, many adult children eventually stopped crying because their tears did not bring relief from relentless despair and abandonment. Grief work restores the power of tears. We cry deeply knowing that we are finally safe and that we are finally understood. By finding our grief, we come to believe on a deeper level that our parents' dysfunction was not our fault. We did not do anything wrong as children to cause their sick behavior. We are not bad, defective, or imperfect. We are human. We are focusing on our lives and moving forward. We want to make things right and to understand who we are.

By addressing our stuck grief with the Steps, we get a better understanding of our assets as individuals and our problematic behavior. We do not take too much responsibility for our family's dysfunction, but we do not shrink from taking responsibility for our own harmful behavior. We are gentle with ourselves, but we don't make excuses for our behavior. We pray, make amends, and continue to change our behavior in the Steps going forward from here. We no longer judge ourselves without mercy, but we are saddened by our losses as children. This is the bittersweet taste of grief work. We also see the losses that our parents must have endured as children. In grief work, we find it easier to have forgiving thoughts of our parents because we begin to have forgiving thoughts of ourselves. We have separated from our family without abandoning our family. We also have found a safe family in ACA.

What to Expect in Addressing Grief

Grief work can take many forms and can bring some of the greatest rewards of the program. Some grief work involves journaling in which we write about incidents in our life and reflect on the feelings we had at that moment. Many adult children can recall childhood acts of abuse, neglect, or rejection without emotion. Others will talk about the abuse or neglect as comical or unimportant. Our experience shows that the emotion is there, but it is stuck behind our ability to deny the past or to recall it without clarity. We can have the memory of the event, but we block the feeling associated with it. This is a form of dissociation. When we journal about a childhood incident, we slow down and think about how we must have felt at that time. If we struggle with this exercise, we think about how one of our children would have felt in that situation. If we have no children, we think about how a child would feel in our place as a child. We ask members to do this exercise several times over many days and to be patient.

The "picture" exercise is another proven method to help recognize and release stored loss or grief. Some counselors will ask a client to round up several childhood pictures and bring them to a session. An ACA sponsor can do this type of work as well with a sponsee. Many of these snapshots are grade-school pictures that we had forgotten. The pictures come into sharper focus when discussed in therapy. Observing ourselves in the second or third grade, we notice how shy, giggly, and sensitive we had been as children. We had feelings. We had loss.

Another form of grief recovery is known as "sculpting" or role playing. This is also known as experiential therapy. In this type of grief recall, we are usually in a counseling setting with other clients helping reenact a troublesome scene from our past. This is a profound and powerful tool to tap hidden loss and shame.

Finally, some grief work takes time. After years of recovery, we may find ourselves weeping over a movie scene that reminds us of a childhood stage of our lives. Or we find ourselves watching a child play quietly in a schoolyard. We observe how the child is focused inward and full of imagination. We think about our own childhood and innocence. We make a connection to our Inner Child. The tears come.

As a result of working Step Five, we seem to breathe easier and judge ourselves less harshly. For some, our posture changes. Our head is up, and we make eye contact with people. We feel lighter in our step and in our breathing. We feel a greater connection to our Higher Power.

Pinpointing and Measuring Loss/Grief

We offer this exercise to help you recognize childhood loss, which is associated with the shame and abandonment exercises in Step Four. Adult children can recount the abuse or neglect of childhood, but this does not complete the understanding of childhood loss. In exercises no. 3 and no. 4 in Step Four, you identified incidents of shame and abandonment, which are loss.

We find our loss and stored grief by naming what was taken away from us as well as what we did not receive as children. We can pinpoint and measure our loss by comparing the treatment we received as children in dysfunctional families with the care we could have received if raised by loving, consistent parents. It is important to measure our loss so we can experience it and release it.

Our search for our grief/loss can begin by asking this question: "What did I receive from my dysfunctional family and what would I have received from loving parents in the same situation?'

The difference between what you got and what you could have received is the measure of loss or grief. This loss adds up over time.

For example, many dysfunctional parents scold a child when the child accidentally harms himself or herself while playing. The frightened parent lashes out in anger instead of with affection. What would a loving parent have done if you cut yourself or skinned your knee?

In another example, a dysfunctional parent will manipulate a child into taking sides against the other parent when the parents argue. What is the loss for the child in this situation? What would a loving parent do in the same situation?

An Important Note for The Step Worker

In Step Five, we have looked at the exact nature of our wrongs in addition to the exact nature of our childhood abandonment. We have been introduced to grief work and reparenting as well. You are now ready for your Fifth Step appointment. You will take your Fourth Step worksheets and writing with you to your sponsor or the person hearing your Fifth Step. The listener should be someone you trust and who understands what you are trying to do. You should allow at least two to three hours to do your Fifth Step. Do not hurry the process. This is your chance to tell your story and to find greater levels of freedom. Your listener will understand.

Also, be ready to immediately do Steps Six and Seven when you have completed Step Five. Step Six – were entirely ready to have our defects removed – and Step Seven – humbly asked God to remove our shortcomings – were meant to be worked together during this phase of Step work.

Steps Six and Seven will not require a lot of writing, but there are some instructions to be read on the removal of defects of character. In Step Six, you will also read about integrating The Laundry List traits. Here are instructions on how to proceed with Steps Five, Six, and Seven.

Summary for Steps Five, Six, and Seven

1. Take your completed Fourth Step worksheets with you to your Fifth Step appointment.

2. Say the Fifth Step Prayer in this section before doing your Fifth Step.

3. After completing your Fifth Step, return home and read all of the section on Step Six in this book. There will be information on becoming entirely ready to have God remove your character defects and to integrate Laundry List traits (survival traits). There will be information here on how to proceed with Step Seven as well.

Chapter Seven

Fifth Step Prayer

Divine creator. Thank you for this chance to speak honestly with another person about the events of my life. Help me accept responsibility for my actions. Let me show compassion for myself and my family as I revisit my thinking and actions that have blocked me from your love. Restore my child within. Restore my feelings. Restore my trust in myself. Amen.

STEP FIVE SPIRITUAL PRINCIPLES:

Honesty and Trust

STEP SIX

Were entirely ready to have God remove all these defects of character.

Making Myself Ready

Part of the process of becoming entirely ready is to feel the painful consequence from my character defects. This naturally follows from admitting my wrongs, which I did in Step Five. As long as I was rationalizing and blaming others for my problems, I had no motivation to change. Once I quit rationalizing and took responsibility for my own behavior, I saw how letting go of my character defects can be of benefit to me. Change can be painful and scary. The process of becoming entirely ready in Step Six means I get uncomfortable enough to allow change to happen.

At Some Point I Just Stopped Fighting

I thought I was a positive, happy, fun-loving person who laughed a lot. In ACA I discovered quite a few defects of character. I am negative, self-critical, self-sabotaging, self-rejecting, afraid of being abandoned, and unfeeling. I never realized my penchant for negativity. I criticized myself unmercifully. I heard people in program say, "Erase the critical parent tapes and replace them with nurturing tapes." I just couldn't do it.

I put myself in the position of my critical parent. I realized that if I had done an excellent job for thirty five years and then someone decided I was no longer necessary, I'd be furious. My critical parent, in fact, worked very hard to sabotage my efforts in recovery. I decided the only way to overcome this self sabotage was to integrate my critical parent into my recovery process. Using self-guided imagery, I pictured my critical parent and complimented her on keeping me alive. I asked her to reallocate her energies from hiding family secrets and suppressing our Inner Child into releasing the secrets and caring for, loving, and nurturing our Inner Child. My critical parent has become my cheerleader. When I say, "That was really stupid," a voice in my head retorts, "It was human, not stupid."

Chapter Seven

I've learned in ACA that when I turn things over to my Higher Power, He takes care of me. So it is with my defects of character. I am no longer negative, self-critical, self-sabotaging, self-rejecting, afraid of being abandoned, or unfeeling. At some point I just stopped fighting and gave God my shortcomings. In ACA, I was able to see things about myself I didn't like and modify them. I don't think we ever change who we are, but we can change how we react.

Integration Led To Freedom

When I first arrived at ACA, I thought I was a defective character instead of having defects of character. Because of my all-or-nothing thinking, I did not give Step Six a serious try at first because I thought the Step meant literally removing all my defects of character. Since I did not think this was possible, I ignored the Step for the most part. What I have learned, for me, is that Step Six is about how willing I can be to have my defects of selfishness, lust, or pettiness lessened. I am sure some people have their defects removed. I have had mine significantly lessened. I remain willing to have them totally removed.

Today I look at Step Six from the standpoint of integrating behaviors I developed to survive my violent alcoholic upbringing. I was a people-pleaser without an opinion. I was never a good friend. I never stood for anything because it might mean I could be challenged or criticized. I used drugs addictively to avoid my childhood abandonment. I was full of hurt, but I unknowingly blamed others until I could find help. Getting clean and sober and going to ACA did not change that overnight

For years, in meetings, I struggled with my survival behavior thinking it was a defect of character. In reality my survival traits were deeply rooted friends. They are the Laundry List traits. They were no longer useful, but they had protected me. The harder I pushed against them, the harder they seemed to push back. I felt hopeless trying to let some of them go. But then I heard about integration. I heard about an exercise in which I could visualize meeting these traits and making friends with them. I could thank them for their work in protecting me, but I could also ask them to step aside. I got results and remained willing to give up these traits on a daily basis.

By viewing my survival traits as part of me rather than something that was awful or defective, I took a softer approach. I humbly asked God to allow me to lay down these survival behaviors and replace them with trust, forgiveness, and self-love. The results have been awesome. I integrated most of the traits into my life, and I feel the most freedom ever.

Step Six Summary

In Step Six we realize that we have defects of character like most of the population in the world. However, our defects of character tend to be entrenched and trap us in unfulfilling relationships and block us from receiving the love of a Higher Power. Our defects can include procrastination, lust, envy, greed, selfishness, and judgmentalness. We also have survival traits or common behaviors. The survival traits are the 14 characteristics of The Laundry List (Problem). These common behaviors represent the effects of growing up in a dysfunctional home. They are in a different category than defects of character.

Our survival traits include people-pleasing, addictiveness, hypervigilance, and stuffing our feelings to avoid conflict or arguments. We often confuse love with pity and tend to "love" those we can rescue. Even though we have identified such traits in Step Four, we are still new at this. We need focus to find our best course of action for release. Many adult children take the path of removal for character defects and take the path of integration for the survival traits.

There is a key distinction between defects of character and the survival traits of The Laundry List. Adult children readily identify with the survival traits; however, they struggle with claiming defects of character. Most adult children willingly admit to being people-pleasers or fearing authority figures but balk at claims of being judgmental, dishonest, or jealous. Adult children tend to feel relief when reading The Laundry List traits because they realize they are not unique in actions or thought.

Chapter Seven

They often feel shame or dread when hearing a list of defects of character. These are the distinguishing points between defects of character and survival traits developed as children.

Admitting defects of character can be terrifying for adult children who have grown up in perfectionistic homes. To admit an error or to appear less than perfect is equated with extreme fear or a feeling of being unduly vulnerable. Some of us experience a plummeting feeling in our stomachs when it is suggested that we have defects of character. Admitting defects had no real value in most dysfunctional homes so we see no value in it before coming to ACA. We must remember that we are recovering in ACA. Admitting our defects of character does not make us inferior or inadequate. In fact, it means we are human.

The key to becoming free of character defects while making peace with our survival traits involves a three-prong approach with willingness, prayer, and time. In some cases we have seen defects of character removed completely in a short time, but for most of us it takes prayer and patience to mark progress. But progress is possible.

We were introduced to willingness in Step Three when we made a decision to turn our will and lives over to the care of God, as we understand God. We also showed willingness in Step Four by inventorying our behavior and thinking.

We will be the most willing to have our character defects removed by a Higher Power after we have completed Step Five. However, we can concentrate on willingness each time we meditate on Step Six or any of the Twelve Steps. As long as we make a sincere effort, we make progress on removing our defects of character with God's help. Willingness is our most powerful ally because it means we are teachable when it comes to addressing our defects of character. By being teachable, we learn to discern how much effort to put into changing our defects and when to get out of the way and let God handle it.

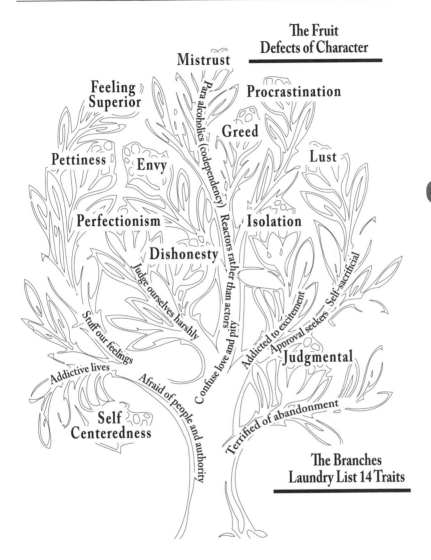

The Fruit
Defects of Character

Mistrust

Feeling
Superior

Procrastination

Para alcoholics (codependency)

Greed

Pettiness

Envy

Lust

Perfectionism

Isolation

Dishonesty

Reactors rather than actors

Judge ourselves harshly

Addicted to excitement

Approval seekers Self-sacrificial

Stuff our feelings

Judgmental

Addictive lives

Afraid of people and authority

Confuse love and pity

Self
Centeredness

Terrified of abandonment

The Branches
Laundry List 14 Traits

Many times we have seen an ACA member fraught with frustration over repeating a defect of character. We have seen the member work diligently to change only to return to old thinking or behaving. Finally, the adult child gives up and God moves in, and the behavior is changed or at least made tolerable.

Most newcomers in ACA can be overwhelmed at Step Six since it is hard for them to believe that God would remove their defects of character. To the new member, we urge you to make a start and keep trying. This is a good use of the will. With the help of ACA, we make progress and avoid perfectionism in Step Six.

The Value of Healthy Pain

Becoming willing to have a Higher Power remove our defects of character can range from being painless, to moments of discomfort to agony. Some character defects such as gossiping and judgmentalness can be stopped painlessly. In ACA we learn to focus on ourselves, which cures a lot of gossip and the judging of others.

We face moments of discomfort and emerging pain with our ACA support group and a sponsor or counselor. Adult children dread emotional pain because we rarely had anyone to stand with us as we experienced anguish as children. Growing up in a dysfunctional home, we often endured unspeakable suffering in silence. We became hypervigilant to emotional pain and sought addiction, work, sex, or drugs to stay "pain" free. Many of us have writhed on the floor with codependent pain; however, pain is different in ACA. We now have friends and a Higher Power to rely on. We are not alone.

Our experience reveals that there is value in emotional pain. With support, and with gentleness, we can find our healthy pain and its healing release, just as we reclaimed our tears. Before we arrived at ACA, our tears seemed unproductive so many of us stopped crying. Through Step work or counseling we reclaim our tears and their value.

Emotional pain is a similar gift. Many of us had a preview of this pain in Step One or Step Four as we detailed the abuse of our lives or the abuse we visited upon others. We realized that we were not alone or unique in our pain. We realized that the pain we will feel in ACA is different than the unproductive pain of growing up in a family wrought with abandonment. In our homes, we learned to seek unhealthy pain that served no real solution and which fed our addictiveness. With the support of ACA, we experience healthy pain and find release.

We have seen adult children struggle in isolation and sorrow when such a solo struggle is not necessary. The emotional pain will end, but it can be prolonged if we fail to ask for help. During these times, we muster all the humility we can and ask someone we trust to listen to us. We become willing to share our fears and doubts about ourselves with another person. We find that ACA members really will help out. We find out that emotional pain can be the gateway to a closer connection with God as we understand God. We learn that the denouement of pain – the winding down of pain – is often where the integration of survival traits occur. After making it through, we feel changed. We embrace the inner strength we have always had, and we see emotional pain in a new light. We see it as one instrument which can temper our diamond hard survival traits.

By facing our pain, we learn that we really are not alone in our suffering. When we find ourselves in this kind of pain in Step Six, we stay close to meetings and keep our faces turned toward God as we understand God.

Entirely Ready

Upon completing Step Five, we return home and find a quiet place to reflect upon what we are doing with our lives. We are on a path of self-honesty and self-forgiveness that will lead us to a new way of life. We are also moving away from our victim, perpetrator, and authority figure roles. We learned in Step Four that our survival traits have an opposite that we have practiced as well. If we feared authority figures, we often became an authority figure who was feared either as a parent, supervisor, or other position in life. If we judged ourselves without mercy, we also judged others just as harshly. We have been victims, but many of us have also been perpetrators. If we have gossiped maliciously, we stop. We become willing to ask our Higher Power to help us forgive ourselves and to change.

We are seeking a life in which we can feel our feelings and talk honestly about what is going on in our lives with the support of our ACA friends. Some of us will reconnect with our family of origin and have the best relationship we can have with them. We will be less judgmental of our family, but we also will know when to disengage if necessary. We are reparenting ourselves as we grieve a lost childhood. We are on a path to the Inner Child or the True Self.

After completing Step Five, we sit quietly and reflect upon our inventory. We notice our breathing and remember to breathe deeply. We have looked at shame, abandonment, sexual issues, and a praise deficit. We have also looked at stored trauma and frozen feelings and our spiritual beliefs. We sense that we have an inner courage that has always been there and which in now emerging. We may have had notions of spiritual beliefs or universal truths before, but we now begin to believe more deeply. With Step Five, we have focused on ourselves. We have done something for ourselves that matters and which has spiritual weight. We have inventoried our lives and taken a risk by telling our story to another person. We have broken the family rule of remaining silent. We realize we are among true friends. We are reparenting ourselves. We are not alone anymore.

With Step Six, you are taking the time to become entirely ready. You are about to humbly ask God to remove your shortcomings with a Seventh Step prayer. Step Seven states: "Humbly asked God to remove our shortcomings."

We have a list of our defects of character. We prepared our list by reviewing our Fourth Step inventory. We also understand our survival traits and their function in our life. These are The Laundry List traits that we respect but which now must be further lessened or integrated.

Our defects of character usually include self-centeredness, judgmentalness, envy, greed, lust, jealousy, feeling superior, dishonesty, and pettiness. As we sit and think about our shortcomings, we do not judge ourselves. Our character defects and survival traits are old friends we are beginning to bid farewell. Some will leave us immediately. Others will fade gradually. Still others will be integrated into our personality to enrich our lives and character. We are seeking our wholeness with what we are about to do.

By now, we have stopped punishing ourselves. We are asking God, as we understand God, to help us become entirely ready to have these defects of character removed. We must realize that good intentions do not work in removing our defects of character. Likewise, will power or self-determination is no match for these flaws in our thinking and reacting. We need help from a power greater than ourselves to achieve Step Six results.

We sit in a relaxed position, but we concentrate on becoming entirely willing to have our character defects removed. When we are ready, we repeat the Seventh Step prayer for each defect or survival trait we wish to have removed or integrated. As we prepare to say the Seventh Step prayer, we review our possible defects of character and survival traits.

Possible Defects of Character:

Self-centeredness, judgmentalness, procrastination, perfectionism, envy, greed, lust, feeling superior, dishonesty, and pettiness.

Laundry List Survival Traits or Common Behaviors:

People-pleasing, fear of authority figures, stuffing our feelings, addiction, and confusing love with pity (The complete list is at the front of the book).

Options for the Removal of Defects of Character and Integration of Laundry List Traits.

Option 1 – Read all of the section on Step Seven. Then say the Seventh Step prayer for the removal of each of your defects of character, and for the integration of each of your Laundry List traits. For example, we might integrate our trait of fearing authority figures into a belief that authority figures are human beings instead of possible abusers or adversaries.

Option 2 – In Step Seven, turn to the heading on "Removal of Defects of Character" and read the information there. Say the Seventh Step prayer for your defects of character and Laundry List traits. Read the remainder of Step Seven the following day.

STEP SIX SPIRITUAL PRINCIPLE:

Willingness

STEP SEVEN
Humbly asked God to remove our shortcomings.

He Finally Gave Up

I can remember how I fussed with a defect of character of jealousy for weeks. I would seem to make progress by talking about it and attending meetings, but I would see this person again and be burned up inside. I also felt helpless and abandoned. I wanted to do harm to this person. I wanted to act out like a little child. I was hurt so I wanted to hurt someone else.

I cared enough about ACA that I did not act on my urge to harm anyone. In recovery, I have learned that my first thought is on God. He takes it no matter how wild the thinking is. My second thought is on me. I am responsible for my actions.

I continued to pray and attend meetings. I called my sponsor and another person regularly. I avoided this person when I could, but I could still be upset when I thought about her. One day, I was struggling with this defect and feeling weary of the effort. I was tired of it, but I did not think I could be free of jealousy. I finally felt tired enough and sat down. I was whipped. I settled back into my chair alone. I raised my head to stare at the ceiling. A simple prayer formed in my mind: "God. Please help me let go."

During the next few days I felt more peace inside. I still had to work at it, but I gave less energy to jealousy and this person. I found out I was giving away my power to someone else.

We Can Take Ourselves Back To God

My aunt once told me, "Humility is truth." For me, Step Seven could be rephrased, "Truthfully asked God to remove our shortcomings." A humble spirit means I've been through my Fourth, Fifth, and Sixth Steps so I know the truth about myself. The truth is that I am a good and loving person who has some flaws. Those flaws are like small cracks in a beautiful vase.

I heard someone ask at a meeting the other day, "What do you do when something gets broken?" Then that person said, "You take it to the manufacturer to be fixed. When we are broken, we can take ourselves back to God."

All I Had to Do Was Ask

I didn't have any defects of character until I came into this program. I thought! The hardest part for me was to admit I had any shortcomings. To survive, I had to believe I was sane, in control, and lucid. Recognizing my defects and then admitting them nearly killed me. Humbly asking God to remove them was easy in comparison.

I wasn't aware of the family secret until I came into ACA. Once I recognized the secret affected both my family and me, I didn't want the character flaws anymore. I had been molested, and in an effort to keep my children safe, I had hurt them. I kept my son at arm's length, but embraced my daughter. My son grew up believing something was wrong with him. I was afraid to get close to him because I did not know what a healthy relationship was between a parent and a child of the opposite sex.

At the same time, my daughter said, "You told me you loved me, Mom. I heard it, but I didn't feel it." With my Higher Power's help I accepted my basic personality and character defects and integrated the ones I could. I made amends to my children knowing they might walk away hating me. God gave me the courage to make amends anyway. When I was done, God removed my defects of character. They just fell away. There were no more barriers between my children and me. The energy and love flowed freely between all of us at last.

Because I was able to ask God to remove my shortcomings, and He did, my children did not have to carry the family dysfunction into their lives like I did. They were young enough to assimilate the information, ask their questions, accept honest answers, and ask for what they needed.

Step Seven Summary

As we approach Step Seven, we take time to notice that we have taken a fearless and thorough look at ourselves and our family of origin. In the First Step, we admitted our powerlessness over the effects of family dysfunction. That powerlessness includes the development of our survival traits that blocked us from a meaningful relationship with God. The traits also caused us to recreate our family of origin in our adult relationships. We focused outwardly on others, trying to control them or to fix our families through them. We developed an over-powering obsession or compulsion for another person. This obsession brought us to "hitting bottom" and asking for help in ACA.

In Steps Two and Three, we revisited our concept of a Higher Power, learning that many of us transferred the traits of our parents onto God. We projected our abandoning parents onto a Higher Power, believing that God was vengeful or indifferent. Even if we thought God was love, many of us secretly wondered if God truly cared or listened.

We also learned that our compulsion to control ourselves or others was a major stumbling block in our ability to let God help us. Many of us exposed our facade of self-sufficiency for what it was: a camouflaged isolation in which we were terrified of asking for help. We were hiding in plain sight from ourselves and others. We chose a sponsor – a fellow traveler – and took the first step to move beyond isolation.

In Steps Four and Five, we made a searching and fearless moral inventory and told someone our story for the first time. While we reviewed our parents' behavior in a "blameless" fashion, we also faced our behavior. We take responsibility for our actions. These are some of the first steps to reparenting ourselves and truly focusing on ourselves and what we can change in our lives.

In Step Six, we learned that willingness is the key to removing our character defects. We also learned that our survival traits from childhood could look like character defects; however, they had much deeper anchors and responded better to integration. We made peace with the traits and asked them to step aside so that we could live our lives in freedom. In Step Six, we learned the value of healthy emotional pain.

In Step Seven, we realize we cannot remove our shortcomings without the help of a Higher Power. We may have had moments of freedom from our defects, but they seem to return or take on a new form if we fail to ask for God's intervention. To our horror, we see a defect reappear in a new obsession or new twist that is torturous to face alone. In Step Seven, we muster all the trust or faith that we can. We rely upon God to remove our defects of character. We humbly ask God, as we understand God, to remove our shortcomings.

Removal of Defects of Character

For the removal of our defects of character, we sit in a relaxed position and concentrate on becoming entirely willing. We also become willing to integrate our survival traits. We may meditate and pray. When we are ready, we repeat the Seventh Step prayer for each defect or survival trait we wish to have removed or integrated. Do not be concerned if you are not clear if you are addressing a defect or survival trait. God will understand. Humbly ask God, as you understand God, to remove your defects of character.

Seventh Step Prayer – Character Defects

God. I am now ready that you should remove from me all my defects of character, which block me from accepting your divine love and living with true humility toward others. Renew my strength so that I might help myself and others along this path of recovery."

Possible defects of character are: self-centeredness, judgmentalness, procrastination, perfectionism, envy, greed, lust, feeling superior, dishonesty, and pettiness.

> *"I humbly ask you to:*
> *"Remove my defect of* _____.
> *"Remove my defect of* _____.
> *"Remove my defect of* _____.
> *"Remove my defect of* _____.
> *Amen."*

Seventh Step Prayer – Laundry List Traits

God. I am now ready that you should integrate my survival traits, which block me from accepting your divine love. Grant me wholeness.

Laundry List survival traits or common behaviors: people-pleasing, fear of authority figures, stuffing our feelings, addiction, and confusing love with pity. (See the complete Laundry List in the front of the book).

> *"I humbly ask you to:*
> *"Integrate my trait of* _____.
> *"Integrate my trait of* _____.
> *"Integrate my trait of* _____.
> *"Integrate my trait of* _____.
> *Amen."*

With our character defects and survival traits addressed, we rely upon our Step Seven humility to prepare us for the amends process in Steps Eight and Nine. Humility will lead us as we find our path of self-forgiveness while making things right for those we have harmed.

Additionally, we realize our humility leads us to creativity and exploration. We realize we have more energy because we are focusing on ourselves instead of others. We have more mental energy available for new interests. Our Inner Child can begin to play and to create during this stage of recovery. This creativity, and accompanying intuitiveness, marks the growth of our real identity.

Working Step Seven: A Step of Action

Step Seven is an ongoing process. We can work this Step almost anywhere and anytime we feel the need to have a character defect removed. If we slip into judging another ACA member wrongfully, we can say "God. Please remove my shortcoming of judgmentalness."

If we are impatient at the grocery market, waiting to check out, again we can pray. "God. Please give me patience. Help me live in the moment without impatience."

Prayers that address our shortcomings should be simple but sincere. Typically, the fewest number of words uttered in humility seem to resonate best with God. A sincere desire to change coupled with heartfelt humility seem to go further with God than breathy and lengthy prayers of woe.

The sincere adult child working an ACA program of meeting attendance and selfless service gets results with Step Seven. This is the sure path when we struggle with a troublesome shortcoming.

We have seen adult children struggle for weeks, if not months, with a particular defect of character. The person prays, writes in a journal, shares at meetings, and gets involved in service work, but still the defect persists and appears to be gaining strength. However, the Higher Power is at work.

During these times, the adult child continues to attend meetings. He or she stands on the program foundation built thus far. The person keeps working the program and doing the things that have worked in the past. The adult child remains focused on being free of the shortcoming while sharing about the effort to bring about change. The days pass. The adult child continues to pray, journal, and seek the help of a Higher Power. Frustration and exhaustion may occur as the person stays focused on being free. This is healthy pain and a good use of the will. At some point the adult child realizes that he or she must seek a Higher Power with all earnestness. The meetings and prayer, have been necessary, but the person must seek God with urgency and intent. With this attitude a moment arises when all the program work, meetings, prayer, and worry have an effect and the shortcoming budges. A sense of calmness comes over the person. The shoulders ease down in a relaxed position, and the person breathes deeply and says: "God. Help me." Relief follows.

True Humility

Humility is not humiliation; however, some adult children have humiliated themselves and found humility. Humiliation tends to come from our need to harm ourselves by reenacting the shame from our childhood. Without help, our toxic shame from the past will find a way to express itself in our adult lives no matter how perfect we act and no matter how hard we try to control ourselves or others. The shame finds a way to well up. We are horrified by its expression in relationships or events and our participation in it.

Humility comes from God and is a sibling of anonymity, a foundational principle of the Twelve Steps and the Twelve Traditions. Through anonymity, we practice service with love. We seek to be of maximum service to our Higher Power and others.

With humility we find that our will aligns with God's will on a more frequent basis. True humility is the willingness to seek and do God's will with our best effort. We know that we are not perfect and know we could fall short. Yet, we try our best to live this Step and obtain its spiritual intent of removing our shortcomings through humility.

With humility, we become more thoughtful in our decisions, and we are slower to anger. We begin to become actors rather than reactors to life's situations. We begin to have greater freedom of choice and feel more comfortable asking for help. In addition to asking for spiritual help with our defects, we begin to pray with a quiet patience for a Divine Spirit to temper our most glaring survival traits. We pray for integration of these characteristics which served us well, but which now must fade. We fear authority figures less. We back away from being people-pleasers. We stop confusing love with pity. We get sober and clean as well.

With humility, we also learn to recognize when we feel "full" in our relationships and in our wants and needs. Because of our core abandonment issue we are not sure when we have had enough attention or praise. With humility we are less restless and know how to be at peace with what we have. We also learn how to ask for what we need, instead of manipulating people for something we don't need. Humility helps us choose between what we really need, and the wants that can be placed on hold.

Without humility, we have seen some adult children place wants ahead of needs with troubling outcomes. Feeling empty inside, they chase after their wants constantly through spending, debting, and comparing their lives to others. Many adult children spend hours looking for bargains or chatting online with little nurturing effect. Other adult children run from store to store craving the latest fashion or technological advancement, but it is never enough. We have no problem with having luxury items after our emotional and spiritual needs are met. We have no problem with online chatting if the chatting is not a diversion to focus on someone else with unhealthy dependence. We tend to give away our personal power by placing our wants first. Humility gives us personal power that can help us feel "full" in our lives and less frantic to chase wants.

In addition to an inner peace and a glimpse of God's will, humility also brings an unexpected burst of creative energy for many adult children. Since we have backed away from trying to control others, we suddenly realize we have more energy to do things for ourselves. We have more time to attend concerts, go hiking, or begin a book of poems or finish one. Many adult children take their Inner Children to the circus, or buy water-colors and spend afternoons painting and mixing colors to see what happens.

Balancing Our Remaining Defects With Our Attributes

Most adult children have a few lingering defects of character after completing Steps Six and Seven. We cannot use this as an excuse to remain in problematic situations or old ways of thinking.

During the next few days, create a list of your remaining defects of character and compare them with your positive behaviors. During Step Five, we identified many of our problematic behaviors. As we told our story, our sponsor or listener helped us identify our defects of character and our positive qualities. We reparent ourselves by listing any problematic thinking or behavior that might linger after completing Step Seven. We strive to be free of these defects of character, but we also remind ourselves that we have positive qualities. Through humility, we can ask our Higher Power to help us avoid picking up and using a defect of character. We humbly ask our Higher Power to help us address our remaining defects. In this exercise we seek balance in our lives. We avoid focusing only on our problematic behavior. List your positive qualities across from problematic behavior that continues to affect your life. We reparent ourselves with the positive qualities.

Example:

Continued defects	**Balance/Reparent with**
Self-centered	Selflessness
Not always honest	Rigorous honesty
Manipulative	Sincerity
Perfectionist	Compromise

7

STEP SEVEN SPIRITUAL PRINCIPLE:

Humility

STEP EIGHT

Made a list of all persons we had harmed and became willing to make amends to them all.

I Loved My Father

When I made my first Eighth Step list, I put my alcoholic father on the list even though he had perpetrated violent and shaming abuse upon me as a child. At the time, I was in another program that told me to avoid looking at his behavior and to focus on mine. I did what I was told and made my amends to him in a letter. I never mailed the letter.

When I worked the Eighth Step in ACA, it was a different story. I had discussion before I considered forgiving my father. I recalled how he once sat me on his knee when I was a child. He was cussing at my mother across the room. He was very drunk and I could smell his three-week-old whisky breath. When drinking, my father would get very drunk and sit for hours cussing or picking fights with my mother, who tried to ignore him.

On this night, my father sat me on his knee and pointed to my mother across the room and bellowed, "Son. Your mother is a whore." It was a lie, but I can remember my mother looking away as my father made me agree with him. After that, I remember my mother's hugs felt different. I felt like a coward for the next 20 years. I thought I should have fought my dangerous dad. I met a counselor, who walked me back through the episode 20 years later. The counselor asked me how much I weighed when this happened. I must have been 10 years old so I weighed about 100 pounds. She then asked how much my drunken father weighed. He was 6-feet 5-inches and 230 pounds. I understood.

I chose to forgive my father after I was able to get angry about what happened and to talk about his sick behavior. I found out I really loved him deep down inside. I thought I didn't, but I did. I loved him, but I could never admit it because everyone knew he was a drunk. I forgave him to move him out of my head. I want to live in peace. I have also forgiven myself. I placed my name at the top of the Eighth Step in ACA.

I Read My List Daily

Like Step Six, Step Eight requires an investment of time to become willing. There's a world of difference between wanting to do something and being willing to do it. I do not want to use a needle to remove a sliver from my finger, but I am willing to do so because it will relieve my pain and suffering.

I made a list. I was willing to make amends to some people as soon as I wrote down their names. For others, it took longer. I used to keep the list in my daily meditation book and tried to remember each person each day during my prayer and meditation time. I was seeking willingness to make amends.

She Became Willing

There were many people I had harmed. I hurt the men in my relationships. I hurt my son and my daughter as well. I hurt myself, too. I remembered my old boyfriends and how I treated them. My way of ending a relationship without having to confront the person was to push his buttons until he left me. That way I didn't have to be the "bad guy."

With my children, I remembered the harm I committed and sought self-forgiveness in Step Eight. I recalled how I made my daughter doubt trusting me. One day when I was trying to change the sheets on the bed, my daughter stood on the sheets. I picked her up gently and moved her so I could get on with my chores. As soon as I moved her, she jumped back onto the pile thinking this was a wonderful game. After two or three repetitions of this I gave the sheets a little yank assuming she would fall on her bottom and that would end the game. Instead she bit through her tongue. The look on her face said, "How could you!" This was her loss of innocence. She knew it was no accident.

Writing out a list of all the wrongs I had done to other people was like taking a stick and beating myself up with it. I felt awful about the pain I had inflicted. It hurt me deeply to keep my silence when I was a child. It hurt me to confront my mother to tell her all the things I felt about her but didn't say when I was growing up. It was devastating to me to know I had passed the family dysfunction on to my children just as my father had passed it on to me. I was a victim of my own dysfunction, too.

It was not difficult to become willing to make amends when I became aware of the havoc I had wreaked, especially upon my children. The weight on my shoulders was immense. I was so grateful to be able to recognize and repair some of that damage early enough so my own children were not permanently scarred.

Step Eight Revealed Inner Courage

I approached my Eighth Step list with willingness, wanting to do what the program asked. I surrendered and put down all the names of the people I needed to make amends to. Even a person I hated. I stopped fighting and blaming. The Step required a list of those I had harmed and willingness to make amends. I did both and found my inner courage when I wasn't looking for it. Serendipity.

Making out that Eighth Step list meant a lot. I knew I was doing something important for me. It was a continuation of Step Four and the actions I took there. That's what all the Steps have meant to me. I finally found a way to do something concrete that was not necessarily easy but meaningful. I had support as well.

Step Eight Summary

In Step Eight we make a list of the people we have harmed and become willing to make amends to them all. While making such a list, we are also mindful of our Inner Child and the need to protect the child within from harm during the amends process. While we will concentrate here on willingness and making the list, we must realize that many adult children have families that remain in denial about family addiction or dysfunction. Walking into your home and announcing that you are an adult child might bring an unintended effect. We urge caution for some circumstances; however, we do not let fear or being uncomfortable stop us from making this important list of our wrongs.

With Step Eight and Step Nine we are strengthening our commitment to changing our lives. We are doing something that is not easy but which will build confidence and set us free. We are moving past our comfort zone. We are moving further away from our dependent, people-pleasing selves toward our new home. We are improving a real connection with our Higher Power.

With new clarity, we see where we want to go, and we believe we can get there. We realize we can change. That feeling that we could never change our lives has been faced by the time we reach Step Eight. The feeling of being unique or defective has been addressed as well. We realize we are human beings and that we make mistakes like the next person. We also realize that our life experiences place us in a unique position. We can be helpful to suffering adult children yet to find a way out. Our stories and our knowledge of the ACA program are golden to a confused adult child feeling alone and often imbalanced.

In Step Eight, we are facing our lives, and we are claiming our future, one day at a time. We know what we are doing. We know it is okay to talk, trust, and feel. We know that we have greater choice instead of decorated control. We know that we are moving forward with the help of our ACA group. We can trust ourselves. We know it is okay to know who we are.

Letting Our Parents Go

Step Eight is where we begin to place a tighter grip on our part in the harm visited upon friends and within our closest relationships. In Steps One and Four, we inventoried our parents or relatives in addition to inventorying ourselves. We saw how our selfish, manipulative, or destructive behavior as adults originated from our parents. We took responsibility for our behavior without blaming others.

In Steps Five through Seven, we began to place more weight on our own responsibility and to separate from our parents and our dysfunctional family role. In Step Eight, we will scrutinize our behavior more than our parents' behavior. We are not forgetting our abusive past, but we are now more ready to face what we have done to others. We are not alone here. We have our sponsors, ACA friends, and a Higher Power who will not abandon us. Step Eight is where we begin to release our parents to God as we understand God. The ACA Solution states: "When we release our parents from responsibility for our actions today, we become free to make healthful decisions as actors, not reactors."

Making an Eighth Step list of those we have harmed and facing our past is an act of courage. This outward courage is a reflection of our inward strength that has been there all along. How could we have survived and arrived at ACA without this inner courage and without a Higher Power? While we once thought we survived by coincidence, we are now beginning to believe in divine intervention at some level. Not all of us can put our finger on it, but many of us know we should not be here. We should not have survived, but we did. We certainly should not have made it to ACA where we now sit contemplating a list of people we have harmed and feeling confident enough to follow through with amends. Some of us know that we should be institutionalized or worse. Many of us who have been locked up or locked down, realize we are lucky as well to have this chance. We want to be sincere. We want to follow through and contribute to society in a meaningful manner. We also want to be the best we can be for our immediate families. We want to finally be emotionally, spiritually, and physically present with them.

Chapter Seven

Many of us prepare our Eighth Step list based on our Fourth Step worksheets. There should be names there that we have looked at in our personal inventory. We will want to work with our sponsor or counselor as we prepare this list. One of the spiritual principles of Step Eight is willingness. We need not look ahead to Step Nine just yet. We are simply making a list of people we have harmed and becoming willing to make amends. Some names will include our children, employers, relatives, friends, and parents. We realize our parents were often the perpetrators of our abuse; however, many of us have acted inappropriately toward them. Some of us have been calculating and have acted with malice of forethought. We have attempted to get even with our parents in one way or another. We hurt them and hurt ourselves emotionally in the long run. Some incest victims have extracted money and gifts as part of the compensatory guilt they use against an offending parent or relative. These are difficult claims to listen to, but we must face them if we are to be different in our dealings with other people. For if we have abused our parents in retaliation, we more than likely have abused others. The abuse started with our parents, and we will start there to change our behavior.

In many cases we have crossed the line, and we must look at that behavior for our own benefit, not our parents' benefit. This is our Eighth Step list, and this is our chance to change. We are the ones seeking change, and therefore we are the ones doing the heavy spiritual lifting. We are sweeping off our side of the street regardless of what another has done or not done. We are giving our parents to God, as we understand God. We are freeing them to their choices and their desires. We are separate from them. They have no power over us just as we have no power over them.

That said, some parents are so dangerous or perverted that the adult child must avoid them to remain safe and sane. Surely we would think twice about asking an incest victim to make amends to a perpetrator. Any amends would obviously involve harmful behavior we have engaged in after growing up and leaving the home. The actual amends may be to protect ourselves and to know that we did nothing to cause the sexual abuse in childhood. Forgiveness of a sexually abusive relative without a face-to-face meeting has been the choice of some ACA members in this situation. We gain personal power by realizing that the dysfunction did not start with us. We release the shame we have carried surrounding the sexual abuse. We know that we can have healthy love in our lives.

At the same time, some incest victims in ACA have made direct amends to a sexually abusive relative. These members report the amends, or a frank discussion with the offending relative, allows real honesty to be introduced into the family. In these cases, the incest victim forgave the offending relative and made direct amends for harmful behavior toward the relative. These adult children say the amends produced a powerful sense of resolution. Resentment and shame were removed.

We leave decisions on these types of amends to the adult child and his or her sponsor or counselor.

Willingness and Self-Forgiveness

If we stumble in placing a name on our Eighth Step list, we ask God for willingness to at least write down the name. This is Step Eight so the amends has not occurred yet. We can at least put the name to paper and show willingness. We will trust our Higher Power to show us the time and place to make the amends. Many of us have been astonished when we watch how God works in creating the situation for an amends.

This type of willingness goes for the person we hate as well. Most adult children, if they get honest, have a person he or she hates. Given our experiences, we would not be human if we did not. Simply thinking about this person can bring great discomfort for some, but we at least consider writing down the name.

In addition to willingness, a key concept of Step Eight is self-forgiveness. We cannot forgive another until we forgive ourselves. This is a spiritual axiom. Many adult children struggle with self-forgiveness because we were oriented to doubt ourselves or to be hypercritical of ourselves as children. In most situations, we instinctively doubted, judged, or blamed ourselves for any problem that might arise. We judged ourselves without mercy even as we appeared to be fighters or debaters on the issues of life. We judged ourselves as we projected blame onto others.

Forgiving ourselves is foreign to most of us because self-forgiveness is nurturing and affirming. In most of our homes, we never heard of such talk. We must seriously consider the concept of self-forgiveness and practice it if we are to make progress in ACA. Without self-forgiveness, we tend to avoid embracing our successes in life, and we feel unworthy of loving relationships. In ACA, we learn to forgive ourselves by degrees until we become comfortable with this spiritual concept. This is a key moment for us and for reparenting ourselves.

In Step Eight, we are still learning to trust ourselves and to stand with ourselves without fading. If we balk at forgiving ourselves, we face this doubt and affirm ourselves. We get back to the business of self-forgiveness. We show self-forgiveness when we place our name at the top of the Eighth Step list. We also show self-forgiveness by listening to the words we use to describe ourselves. Where we once described ourselves as "lazy," "mean," or "incapable of love," we now describe ourselves in a gentler tone and with language that reflects the growing love inside of us. We begin to hear ourselves say: "I thought I was unlovable, but in fact I am a precious child of God. I am a miracle."

Such thoughts or words are the markers of self-forgiveness and true self-love.

STEP EIGHT SPIRITUAL PRINCIPLES:

Willingness and Self-forgiveness

STEP NINE

Made direct amends to such people wherever possible, except when to do so would injure them or others.

I Must Make Peace with Myself to Right the Wrongs

Making amends sometimes means an apology. Sometimes it involves changing my behavior toward a certain person. Sometimes it means telling the truth. For me, making amends always seems to involve forgiveness. I need to forgive the other person for their part before I can make amends. Of course I must make peace with myself in order to have the strength and courage to right the wrongs I've done to others.

Cleaning Up the Wreckage of My Past

The behavior I make amends for in childhood I can name here. I picked my mother's beautiful roses to give to a nice lady down the street for talking to me or in the hope she'd give me some candy. I took money from my mother's purse to pay off a bet I lost to my brother's friend. At the time I justified the act because I'd been tricked into making a wager that I couldn't win. I spent some silver dollars from the collection my parents gave to me and crossed a major highway just to buy candy. I dated two boys at the same time, being faithful to neither. The list goes on and on.

I told my mother that I stole her rosebuds, apologizing, giving her flowers to take their place, and never stealing flowers again. For the one dollar of dimes I stole to pay off the bet, I told my mother and returned the money one thousand fold. I never stole a dime from anyone again. I told my mother about the silver dollars and crossing the busy road. I replaced the silver dollars in the collection, safeguarded the family antiques from that day forward, and kept myself out of unsafe situations thereafter. I never told either boy I dated about the other one, but from that experience I dated only one boy at a time.

That was ancient history. In my adult life, I have done a few things I shouldn't have as well. I broke the moral rule, adultery.

7

I learned my motivation for having broken it, built some self-worth, and apologized in Twelve Step meetings. This is one of those situations where it would have been wrong to contact the people I hurt by my behavior. At least one marriage ended and lives were torn apart. There was far too much pain suffered by too many to open those wounds after the fact so that I could play out my act of contrition.

I wrote a letter to my lover admitting my distorted ideas about love, loving, caring, and relationships. In it I apologized for the grief I had caused him, his family, and me. I burned the letter. I considered suicide, but realized that while it would stop my pain, it would never change the pain I had caused. Only in living and never engaging in this soap opera again could I hope to right this wrong before God and myself.

There Is Always A Way To Make An Amends

As a recovering adult child, I still have a high tolerance for inappropriate behavior, so it is likely that another person had done serious damage to me before I noticed I was being attacked and then defended myself reactively. In recovery, however, I need to make my amends for each and every act of inappropriate behavior of my own. I do this regardless of what the other person did. Whenever possible I make my amends directly and learn a lesson in humility.

When the damage to me would negate the benefit, however, I do indirect amends. Putting myself in harm's way is not required of me to do this Step. I do not have to set up an appointment to make amends with someone who promised to kill me if they ever saw me again. I don't have to apologize directly to drinking alcoholics, people high on drugs, or people wallowing in any form of dysfunction because they won't hear me anyway. In these cases I do have to make indirect amends such as writing a letter that I later burn, volunteering my time to a soup kitchen, alcohol rehabilitation center, or senior center. I can send money to some community or charitable organization as it appropriately fits my misbehavior.

Step Nine Summary

Step Nine can be one of the greatest recovery moments that we will ever experience in ACA. While the Step can appear daunting, Step Nine is one of the fellowship's best kept secrets. The emotional and spiritual rewards of this Step are like a great hidden treasure. We cannot tell you how the amends process will turn out for you, but we can promise fulfillment and growth that will exceed your expectations if this Step is faced with honesty, sincerity, and thoroughness.

We liken the Steps leading up to Step Nine as a spiritual ropes course. The challenge course has involved risk, group support, and the realization of inner courage.

The ropes course began in Step One when we detailed the effects of growing up in an unhealthy family. Our Step One admission of the family dysfunction showed us the layout of the course that we would be encountering. In Steps Two and Three we strapped on the safety belt of a Higher Power for the hurdles and challenges ahead. In Steps Four and Five, we got a taste of trusting ourselves and others as we fell backwards off a high porch into the arms of ACA members. These members had been through these Steps and said we could make it. We felt like we were blindfolded. Many of us could not see the reasoning for inventorying our past and telling someone our story. We could not see to the other side, but we trusted our friends and God to catch us, and they did. In Steps Six and Seven, we sat around a group campfire, listening to stories and relating. We realized we are human and have defects of character like the next person.

In Step Eight, we stand at the base of a 30-foot challenge pole, tilting our heads back to see a narrow but stable perch on top. With our Eighth Step list in hand, we begin climbing the sturdy pole toward freedom and God. As we ascend, we see into the upper branches of trees around us. We stop climbing momentarily to check the "safety harness," which represents

Step Three and our decision to trust a Higher Power. We glance downward into the smiling faces of friends. They know what we are trying to do with our lives. We hear their encouraging words rising from below. We climb higher now above the treetops. Reaching the pole's perch, we carefully stand up, a little wobbly at first, but we soon steady ourselves.

As we stand there with our Eighth Step list, we are astonished by a perspective we never imagined possible. We have finally gotten above it all with clarity. We can see that our parent's dysfunction was not our fault. On the horizon, we see the preceding generations of our family lined up in single file, stretching back for miles. There must be 100 generations or more. At the front of the line, we see our parents as children with their parents. We recognize our grandparents, but visualizing our parents as vulnerable children is a new experience for us.

We notice the generations of our family passing forward a bundle. They move the bundle along by handing it off from one generation to the next. We watch as the bundle moves closer to our grandparents and to our parents. The bundle is heavy and gripped tightly as one generation hands it off to the next. The bundle is held at the stomach level as it is passed forward. We concentrate on the bundle and begin to recognize it. Our eyesight has been improved by our Step work. We can see more clearly. We see our grandparents kneel down to give the bundle to our parents. As our parents receive the bundle as children, we understand what they have taken possession of. It is shame, abandonment, and loss from the ages. We think about what we have seen. We realize we don't have to take possession of the bundle. It is not ours. We are free. We look behind us, over a shoulder, to a clear horizon. There are no families there yet. We realize we have a chance to interrupt the passing on of family dysfunction.

We see no blame for anyone for what we are about to do in Step Nine. We are not blaming our parents or ourselves. We are willing to make amends to those we have harmed so that we can be free to serve God and society. During the amends process, we will protect ourselves and our Inner Child, but we will not shrink from this important Step. We feel as if we are closer to God, and we want to live and let live. We are learning to reparent ourselves with love and gentleness. The sky is clear. We step off into Step Nine.

Moving Forward With Prudence and Courage

Step Nine is about mending relationships with others and ourselves. The Step also involves cleaning up the wreckage of our past and being willing to release resentments. In some cases, an amends will help restore a relationship. In other cases, an amends will bring closure to a past relationship or association.

With our Eighth Step list in hand, we have a good assessment of who we have harmed and who we will be approaching with our amends. While we will make the amends on our own, we realize that we are not alone.

The emotional and spiritual rewards for making our amends are awesome. Many such benefits are intangible, but they assure us that we are finally making greater progress in our lives. We are truly involved in real behaviors that are bringing change into our lives. In Step Nine, we are bringing together the pieces of our spiritual blueprint created by the preceding Steps. We are building our new home. We are turning on switches and opening windows installed by the hands of the Spirit of the Universe. There is still work to be done, but we are on our way. We have our foundation in place.

We approach Step Nine with humility and with a sense that we are about to make a significant shift in our lives. We are breaking the shackles of unhealthy dependence and carried shame. With the support of ACA, we understand we can lay down the guilt and shame we have carried from past behavior. We realize that this is a chance to address behavior that we thought was unforgivable. For years, many of us have carried guilt about some thoughts and actions. Many of these behaviors are a reenactment of what was done to us as children. Some of us have struggled horribly with these behaviors, believing we were evil or hopeless. We may have even tried to change but failed. We thought we were unique. Some of our behavior has been disturbing and perhaps outside the bounds of law. With Step Nine, we are naming what we have done and making amends for what we have done. With the help of ACA, our worst acts become forgivable if we are humble and seek help from a Higher Power. Honesty is a must as well.

With sincerity and effort, we begin to no longer feel ashamed of our past. We gradually release our carried guilt and our carried shame. We feel free. With such freedom, our behavior changes for the better. We know it is okay to trust ourselves. We realize that shame and fear of abandonment drove our harmful behavior. With help, we can stop reenacting what was done to us.

We want all of our freedom. We want to be free of food addiction, sex addiction, gambling addiction, drug addiction, and compulsive spending. We want to sleep well, enjoy our jobs, and contribute to the betterment of the world. We are reclaiming our personal power and taking our place in the world as individuals with something to offer. We have greater choice in our lives. We desire wisdom and discernment. We realize that the ACA way of life is comprehensive, practical, and spiritual. The program is a way of life that works in all areas of our lives. With it, we can face career choices, relationship challenges, and questions of God, in addition to facing our past and recovering from abuse and neglect.

We approach our amends list with an attitude of neutrality. We are not judging ourselves or others for their wrongdoings. We want to focus on our own missteps and not on the other person.

While amends is the primary objective of Step Nine, we want to be clear that we are also taking an important step to change our self-harming behavior. We harmed others in our relationships, but we also harmed ourselves because we were oriented toward abandonment and neglect as children. There was perfectionism, rudeness, and manipulation, which we learned to respond to as children and seek out as adults. As alarming as it sounds, we tended to choose people who abused us or were abusively controlled by us. In Step Nine, we are now approaching some of these people with an attitude of neutrality instead of morbid self-guilt or chipper confidence. There is a strong possibility that many of these people are still in denial. Some will not understand what we are trying to do, but that is not the point. We understand our purpose and our intent.

Sincerity, brevity, and humility are the ideas we keep in mind as we make our amends. We must remember that we are making amends for our benefit. We are not making amends to heal or fix another person. If the person gets benefits from our amends, we are grateful, but that is not our goal. Our goal is to honor our commitment to ourselves and to right our wrongs and continue our spiritual path.

During our amends, we don't attempt to educate people about ACA unless they ask. Even then we keep it brief unless they sincerely want to hear more. We don't recruit people to ACA in our amends process. We also don't bring up our newfound spirituality unless the moment is appropriate. It is not wise to meet someone we have harmed and announce our new or renewed focus on God. To do so places us at risk of being branded a religious crank.

Amends vary in type and form, but keep in mind that amends means making things right. Our first amends should be to ourselves. We have harmed ourselves with codependency, drugs, sex, work, gambling, and food like no other people on the planet. We have abandoned ourselves and judged ourselves without mercy countless times. We have stayed in abusive relationships long past the point of sanity because we were terrified of being alone. We have acted insane. Our behavior has equaled slamming our hand in a car door repeatedly or placing our hand on a hot stove believing we had no other way to live. Many of us have been a berated and castigated person, pushing ourselves far away from God, as we understand God. But no more. We are claiming our spot in ACA. We matter. We can forgive ourselves.

We use our inner courage to make a start. With our amends, we make no excuses for our behaviors, but we promise to do our best to change. We make practical statements about change instead of uttering grand resolutions or windy claims to be different. We want our actions, rather than our words, to show that we have changed.

In making an amends, we keep it simple, but we avoid being dismissive. We also avoid arguments or verbal jousting. We do not want to create additional harm during the amends process. We should have an attitude of humility and a sincere desire to repair what we have done or to restore what we have taken from another person.

During an amends, we might say: "I am involved in a program in which I am learning to change my behavior and to live more honestly and openly. Part of the process involves making amends to people I have harmed with my behavior. I am making amends to you for _____ (name the behavior, action, or other). I want to make it right. I am not making excuses, but I have harmed people based on my lack of knowledge about living. I am changing my behavior."

If we owe money, we need to make every effort to pay it back. If we have shamed someone publicly, we make amends publicly. If we have cheated a governmental agency or an employer, we find a way to make an amends either by working late or donating to a worthy cause. Carrying the ACA message of hope into a prison or treatment center is a good way of paying society back for harms against the greater public. This benefits our personal recovery as well. We get out of ourselves and help create a better society by helping the suffering adult child.

In making amends to our parents, we realize we are returning to the place where our abuse or neglect occurred. If we have retaliated against our parents, abused our parents, or used their grandchildren against them to harm them, we need to consider making amends for such behavior. At the same time, we need to be mindful that our Inner Child is with us as we walk into this amends scenario. Many of our parents have been batterers, blamers, manipulators, vindictive, self pitying, judgmental, silent, petty, aggressive, poor listeners, bossy, bullies, detached, or unloving. Others have been overly sweet, wishy-washy, inconsistent, vague, doomsayers, worriers, hypochondriacs, martyrs, and predictors of great catastrophe of the world or our lives. These are the souls we are leaving in God's hands. We are no longer responsible for them. We did not fail in fixing them. We are powerless over them and their choices.

With parental amends, we have to balance protecting our True Self with our need to fulfill the spiritual requirement of Step Nine. The Step calls us to be honest and to make our best effort to right our wrongs. We remember that our parents are spiritually sick people who repeated what was done to them. We are not minimizing what they have done to us, but we are not judging them. We are giving them to God with our amends, and we are protecting ourselves during the process.

Forgiveness is the key here. We seek forgiveness for ourselves and give forgiveness to our parents. Forgiveness does not mean that we are forgetting or minimizing our parents' behavior. We are forgiving them so that we can move forward with greater freedom in our souls. There is spiritual power in forgiveness. Cultures of all times and places have recorded the inner and spiritual value of forgiving another. ACA is no different.

Our experience shows that some parents will respond with a sincere desire to change. Others will be indignant and attempt to place blame elsewhere. For potentially violent parents, we need to gauge our safety and consider whether or not we can meet with them for amends. Whatever the situation, we make the amends for ourselves regardless of an anticipated response. We want to do all we can to clear up the wreckage of the past so that we can live in the present with honesty, hope, and spirituality. We are living our own lives. We are gaining greater freedom from the effects of growing up in a dysfunctional home.

Amends to Our Children

If we make amends to our children, we need to keep it simple and make sure the language we use is age appropriate. We should have the agreement of our sponsor or counselor on what we will say. Children do not always need all the details about our abuse or neglect. They have lived it and need a demonstration of changed behavior more than psychological or wordy explanations.

We are truly concerned and remorseful for what we have done to our children, but we avoid feeling overly guilty. Such guilt can lead to overcompensating with even poorer parenting skills. Because we feel guilty, many recovering parents allow their children to act out with greater frequency or run over them until the parent explodes in anger. We must remember that we are still parents, and we have some skills. We also have a genuine desire to love our children and help them have a better life than we had growing up. We face our children and their behavior by attending meetings, working the Steps, and seeking help from a sponsor, counselor, or spiritual advisor.

When we focus on ourselves and ask for help, we are more ready when our children want to talk about their feelings and emotions. This is a key point. We try to avoid prodding or prompting our children into talking unless we are clear about our motives. Parents who cajole their children into talking too soon are usually trying to relieve their own uncomfortable feelings of being a dysfunctional parent. Under the disguise of wanting to listen to the child, the parent is actually gathering information about how the child thinks and feels about the parent. If the child opens up, the parent may invalidate the child's thoughts and feelings. In other cases, a child's honesty about unhealthy parenting can overwhelm the parent who can shift into a mode of overcompensation and lose more ground. We need to attend meetings and be on a solid foundation to listen to our children and to take the best course.

Similar experience is offered to grandparents recovering in ACA. These adult children can feel doubly guilty for passing on dysfunction to their children and grandchildren. If this is our situation, we must remember an important distinction about our lives. We are courageous. We are facing our behavior and actions instead of denying them. Adult children with grandchildren bear the brunt of being a pioneer for the family. They are often the first in a dysfunctional family to recover. They can be criticized or not understood by their family of origin, yet they stay focused and remain in recovery.

We must make a focused effort on self-forgiveness to avoid drifting into morbid guilt. If we feel paralyzed by the past, we stay focused on our program and know that we are doing God's will. We must attend meetings, pray, ask for help, and be ready if children or grandchildren want to talk.

Except When To Do So Would Injure Them Or Others

In making amends, we avoid bringing harm to another person by disclosing something that might be unnecessary and off the mark.

For instance, if we are making amends to an ex-wife, we need not bring up the infidelity we might have had with her sister. To do so serves no purpose in the moment. We need to admit our cheating to our sponsor or counselor and know in our hearts that the behavior was wrong. We change such behavior in the future and stay out of the lives of our ex-wife and her sister.

If we have been sexually promiscuous in our current marriage, we need to proceed with caution unless we have contracted a sexually transmitted disease that could affect our spouse or partner. If that is the case, our spouse or partner should know immediately about our sexual activity so they can seek medical care.

A fair number of marriages have been destroyed by disclosing details about extramarital affairs. While it appears noble to tell everything about an affair, we have seen such disclosures cause jealousy that destroys the relationship.

There are at least two options here that meet the rigorous honesty required by Step Nine. Many unfaithful wives and husbands have confessed their infidelity to a sponsor or counselor and changed their behavior without having the spouse involved. Others believe that telling everything to the spouse or partner is the best course. We leave the method of handling infidelity up to the Step worker; however, the key is honesty and a willingness to tell someone about the cheating followed up with a commitment to stop the behavior.

Many adult children owe money and have difficulty handling money. Some of us have absconded money or plunged ourselves so far into debt that we cannot possibly repay all that we have squandered, stole, or manipulated out of people, employers, or relatives. It is not the purpose of Step Nine for you to live in poverty in a noble effort to pay off an impossible debt. However, we cannot use this as an excuse to avoid paying back reasonable amounts of money we have borrowed or accepted. If we can cut back on spending and make payments, we need to do so. We want to change our attitude about spending. Step Nine can help us live within our means and grow spiritually.

If the debt is so large to force bankruptcy or a similar situation, we need to know in our hearts that we would pay back such bills if we had the resources. We also change our behavior by avoiding building up more debt while we still have this large deficit in our lives. To say we would pay off a huge financial burden if we had the money and then continue to spend recklessly or charge up debt is dishonest. This behavior is contrary to the Step Nine amends process.

If you have stolen money or manipulated people for money, gifts, or other items, this must cease as well. To continue such behavior is a relapse of sorts and a sure disconnection from God. To steal or manipulate for money is self-harming behavior in the long run since it shuts down our connection to the Divine.

If we have committed a crime that has been undetected, we need to visit with our sponsor or get legal advice about how to proceed. We need to be willing to go to the authorities and turn ourselves in if that is the course that we choose to take.

There is always a way to make an amends if we are sincere and patient. We can make amends to a deceased person by writing a letter and reading it aloud. If we are unable to locate someone on our amends list, we wait for God's timing to show us how to make the amends. We are astonished how our program works when we become willing and leave the results to the Divine Creator. One of the keys to the amends process involves our attitude and our willingness to make amends when the opportunity presents itself.

Sexual Compulsivity

Many adult children have struggled with sexual compulsivity that has brought great sorrow and a hellish isolation from society. However, the isolation does not stop here. Sexual compulsivity separates the adult child within. The sexually compulsive self is at odds with the True Self, and this serves as a battleground of compulsion versus doing the right thing. In this person, you have the self divided against the self. This conflict is common among all adult children but is highlighted by sexual compulsivity. Sex addicts live in a state of toxic shame fueled by despair. They live and breathe and walk in hell each day. They are driven by compulsions and obsessive thinking that over powers their rational mind. These adult children are deeply hurt individuals, who can get better if they can find absolute honesty and hang on while God acts.

When an adult child progresses into sexual addiction, they become two people. They can be hard-working and creative people on the job and an obsessive sex addict when they are cruising restrooms, parking lots, or bars looking for sex "dope." We are not moralizing on sexual preference here. We are talking about selfish, predatory adult children, who place themselves and others in danger with unsafe or illegal sex. This behavior can occur by gay or straight adult children. Sex addiction does not respect sexual preference. We cannot rule out innocents being harmed by a perpetrating adult child as well.

After acting out sexually, many of these adult children reel in horror with what they have done; however, they return to the same acting out behavior or worse unless help is sought and sought earnestly. These adult children live out a cycle of work, ritualistic thinking, acting out, and remorse. Then the cycle begins again. Some adult children will spend the rest of their lives in prison for a sex crime they felt powerless to avoid.

Most, if not all, sexually addicted adult children were victims of sexual abuse as children. We are not making excuses for their wrongful acts as adults. But they were once children without a choice. They are whole but fragmented just like the next adult child seeking help. They qualify for ACA.

If we have been a sexual predator or sexually compulsive, we must know in our hearts that we were wrong. We cannot minimize our behavior. There are people we can never approach in making amends by the very nature of our acting out with them. Some of us have victims that we cannot approach for legal reasons. God understands what we have done and what we are facing. For support, we talk with our sponsor or a trusted friend and take our forgiveness needs to a Higher Power. We pray and pray hard for forgiveness and the ability to change.

Some of us have progressed to disturbing levels with pornography, multiple partners, dominance, bestiality, compulsive masturbation, and forms of sexual abuse. But we can change. We were not born this way. We are still children of God no matter what we have done. We must remember that God loves us always. This is a matter of grace for adult children facing this kind of agony.

Our experience shows that these adult children typically have good intentions and want to change. They need God's grace and professional help to deal with the sexual compulsion. We must remember that God's grace is limitless for those who truly want to change. The Higher Power is there whether we have failed one time or 1,000 times. Always we are loved by God as we understand God. This is difficult for an adult child raised in a punishing or judgmental home to understand. We think we have limited chances or only one chance. After acting out we want to be punished, but a loving God waits for the right moment of surrender. We must surely try and surely be willing. A Higher Power loves us the same whether we have failed or succeeded. A loving God never abandons an adult child truly wanting change and making an effort.

Surely we need a miracle if we are facing this in our lives. Adult children in this category have had such miracles when they sought God with their heart's desire. Certainly, meeting attendance, prayer, and association with other recovering adult children are important to relieve this compulsion. We pray and pray unceasingly in this situation.

STEP NINE SPIRITUAL PRINCIPLES:

Forgiveness and Courage

STEP TEN

Continued to take personal inventory and when we were wrong, promptly admitted it.

Step Ten Helped Him Find Boundaries

Step Ten taught me more about boundaries than I could imagine. When I first came into the program, I would apologize to everyone and everything at the drop of a hat. One time, I had judgmental thoughts about someone. I began talking about him behind his back. Due to the program I felt guilty, but I was not prepared to take appropriate action on my healthy guilt. In my confused thinking of the Steps, I called this person out of the blue and made amends. It was awkward because he had no idea what I had been doing behind his back. I felt embarrassed as I talked. I realized I crossed someone's boundary even though I meant well. I tried to work the program without a sponsor and it backfired.

With the help of Step Ten and my sponsor, I learned that I don't have to tell everyone what I am thinking all the time to be honest. I can inventory my thoughts and actions at the end of the day and call my sponsor if anything is lingering or troublesome. I have learned that thoughts are just thoughts and not necessarily actions I will take. That was a huge relief for me to know. After reviewing my day, I make amends immediately if I have wronged someone. I understand boundaries. I got one.

Step Ten Pays Big Dividends

Learning to promptly admit when I'm wrong has paid big dividends for me in peace of mind. Learning that the response from others is almost always positive has also made it easier. When I admit I am wrong quickly, I prevent possible grudges from building up. I don't have to expend huge amounts of energy blaming, rationalizing, and covering up. I don't get bogged down with guilt or shame. Being able to admit that I'm wrong when I am wrong makes me feel free. I am very grateful for this wonderful sense of freedom.

He Is Doing Things Right As Well

Step Ten taught me a lot about self-acceptance. It also taught me to stop being so hard on myself. I was hypervigilant in looking for ways to beat myself up or always make myself wrong. By inventorying my behavior regularly, I could see where I was doing a lot of things right. I began to inventory those things as well. In fact, my Tenth Step includes what I do right. I need that. It's a great balance.

Keeping Step Ten Simple

I keep Step Ten simple. It does not have to be a big ordeal at the end of the day. I have a few simple questions that I ask myself at bed time. Was I judgmental today? Did I criticize another or myself today? Am I keeping something to myself I should talk about? Am I loving myself and being good to myself? Did I see how similar I am to others today?

I answer these questions and make amends if an amends is necessary. I keep Step Ten simple. I have received immense spiritual rewards from it. I am more honest and I feel like I can talk about my feelings and behaviors so they don't get bottled up. I am so grateful for ACA.

Every Night I Review My Day

Each night before I go to sleep I read. I also take an inventory of what I have done during the day. When I pray, I plan how I will behave tomorrow.

Step Ten Summary

Step Ten is where we continue to inventory our behavior and thinking. With this Step we continue to let go of control and expose our denial about the effects of being raised in a dysfunctional home. We learn to take a balanced view of our behavior, avoiding the tendency to take too much responsibility for the actions of others. At the same time, we also curb our tendency to blame others when we are obviously wrong, yet are too afraid or ashamed to admit it. In these cases, we keep it simple. There is no need for long analyses of our behavior. We know that we come from wounded childhoods and we are addressing that in the Steps. We don't have to cast every amends or apology in the light of how we were raised or how we reacted before recovery. We know what the issues are for us. We make an amends with briefness in mind but with a sincere desire to change. Keeping it simple is the best course in some matters. Other amends might require background information about our past and a longer explanation. We will discern those situations as they arise.

Step Ten helps us apply what we are learning in meetings and to gauge our daily progress. In Step Ten, we are making a statement to hang onto the hard-won changes we are employing in our lives. We are living with more honesty and affirmation of ourselves. We realize we don't have to act perfect or flawless to be loved or accepted. We can make errors and laugh at ourselves without feeling shame. We are less fearful of people and their opinions of us.

We are trying out new ways of thinking and acting, but we must be diligent if we are to follow through with our recovery process. We will not change overnight, and the tendency to pick up old habits is tempting at times. ACA is not an easy program to work, but the rewards are great for those who try with sincerity.

Step Ten helps us polish the spiritual principles we are learning and using in our daily lives. To remain spiritually fit, we must continue to attend meetings, share our feelings, and help others. By helping others on their path of recovery, we help ourselves and learn to break our isolation. We get out of ourselves and contribute to the well-being of our ACA support group. With Step Ten, our personal and spiritual lives improve gradually.

Step Ten calls us to inventory our use of the ACA program to improve our marriages, jobs, and choices. We must practice the ACA program in the home and in our jobs if we are to be true to ourselves. The home or office is not an easy place to practice the principles of ACA, but we must. We do not preach about ACA or invade boundaries with our program. Yet, we stand ready to apply the principles of honesty, humility, and forgiveness outside ACA meetings as well as inside the meetings. We also ask for what we need and keep our word. This is not easy, but neither was living with our addictiveness. It took effort to support addictive choices. Practicing spiritual principles and inventorying our lives takes effort as well, but this is the labor of self-love.

We have more courage and inner strength than we think. It is essential that we practice ACA in every area of our lives to continue to grow emotionally and spiritually. We cannot let another person's behavior divert us from our program or give us cause to wander and live unfocused lives.

We learn to spot red flags, which once served as excuses to run from our problems. With Step Ten, we learn to recognize the cues that lead to fantasizing or dissociation. Many adult children use fantasy, daydreaming and "splitting off" to avoid being in the moment. We also learn to recognize when we are obsessing on another person or activity to avoid our feelings or staying in the moment. With Step Ten, and with help from our sponsor or counselor, we can disrupt a fantasy or dissociation episode. When these dissociative moments happen, we relax and think about what might have happened leading up to the moment. Sometimes the triggering activity occurred days before or hours before. We stop and breathe and get in touch with what is happening. We give our program a chance to work and to meet this challenge. We can make it. We can do this. We can survive our feelings and memories and heal.

We often cannot avoid triggers, but we can change the way we deal with them. We stop dealing with them in isolation. We have help now. We are not alone. We can talk to another person about our fears and thoughts regardless of what they are.

Chapter Seven

A daily or weekly inventory is different than the hypervigilance we have practiced before recovery. In our Step Ten inventory we judge ourselves less harshly because we know we are human and will make mistakes. We known we can talk about our feelings and our missteps without being judged when we share in ACA meetings. We have shaken hands with our critical inner parent. We are beginning to listen to the actual parent, whom many of us choose to call God.

There are two suggestions for a daily or weekly inventory: Keep it simple, and look at what you are doing right as well as reviewing your shortcomings. Look at what your ACA group is doing right. This is critical in reparenting ourselves with gentleness and patience. When we discover we have harmed someone with our behavior, we promptly admit it and move on. If we have apologized repeatedly in the past, we need to stop apologizing and change our behavior. During these times, we avoid condemning ourselves for making mistakes or acting in a manner that might offend or harm another. We are not perfect and never will be. We are involved in a fellowship of people trying to learn to live decent lives while also addressing troublesome behaviors. ACA is a fellowship of some of the most abused and fractured people in the world; however, we accept each other and focus on helping one another. We give each other support as we try to repair our lives. We do not have any place else to go. We must stick together and love one another and help one another while realizing there will be bumps. We are not complaining about our station in life. We are facing it and taking responsibility for it in Step Ten and the rest of the Steps. What we are doing is not easy, but we accept where we are individually and as a fellowship. We can make a commitment to live life by spiritual principles and to be fair to others and ourselves.

One Day At a Time

Step Ten reminds us to focus on the present and live in the moment. We live one day at a time in ACA. By living one day at a time, we are free to focus on ourselves and handle the challenges of life as they come. Step Ten helps us avoid feeling overwhelmed by staring too long at the past or obsessing on the future. One day at a time we make progress in our emotional, physical, and spiritual lives. Our past can be our greatest asset, but we remember to focus on the present. We begin to actively participate in our lives and in the lives of others seeking fulfilling relationships. As the Twelve Promises of ACA state, we learn how to have fun and play. We fear authority figures less, and we discover our real identities. We feel more connected to ourselves, and we believe that a God of our understanding is available to us. We are learning how to set boundaries and how to keep them. In relationships, we are learning to choose people who love themselves and can be responsible for themselves. Gradually and slowly we are releasing our dysfunctional behaviors with the help of our ACA group and a Higher Power. These are ACA's great promises, which are being fulfilled among us daily.

With a Step Ten inventory, we are learning that we have choices. When we arrived at ACA, many of us used control disguised as choice. In reality, we had no choice before working Step One or the remaining Steps of ACA. Before finding ACA, many of us had control usually followed by loss of control and self-blaming despair that left us confused and lost. Our denial locked us into believing we must reapply ourselves. Before recovery, we did try again – countless times – and we failed again. We repeated the same mistakes expecting different results. We blamed others for the results and failed to change our own behavior. We repeatedly picked people who could not love themselves and attempted to extract love from them. Some of us developed a compulsion so strong for another person that we could not easily break away from that person even when we were clearly involved in a relationship that duplicated the abuse of our neglectful homes. Many of us needed intervention to move on and focus on ourselves.

Real choice means that we give up control and trust our Higher Power to provide the love and help we need to live with flexibility. Real choice is a spiritual continuum beginning at denial and leading to self-honesty, humility, wisdom, and finally discernment. Step Ten is part of that continuum of spiritual discernment. When we inventory our motives and trust our Higher Power, answers seem to emerge. Solutions seem to appear. By practicing Step Ten and all the ACA Steps, we intuitively learn how to address problems which once baffled us. We learn to avoid being enmeshed in the unhealthy dependent problems of others. Gossip is less appealing because we don't have the need to become transfixed on the problems of others to avoid looking at ourselves. We trust ourselves to stand steady and to be patient. We recognize manipulation – our own and others' – more quickly and take a different path. We learn to inventory our motives before taking action. Sometimes we take no action which is the best action. These are the elements of choice and discernment found in Step Ten.

Step Ten is about using the new tools of recovery we have discovered in ACA. In addition to the Twelve Steps, the tools of recovery include attending ACA meetings regularly, getting a sponsor, and associating with recovering adult children. Other tools of recovery include sponsoring new members and getting involved in service work. We volunteer to share our recovery at prisons or the treatment setting. We answer the Intergroup helpline if we have an active Intergroup. We seek to become a trusted servant.

Integration

Step Ten is where we can continue to integrate any left over character defects or survival skills into our emerging identity. As we learned in Step Seven, there will be residual defects and survival traits that won't recede easily. This does not mean we have failed in previous Steps. Step Ten is where we can acknowledge and embrace these lingering but less useful traits. We use humility and consistent effort to integrate these aspects of our personality.

Some adult children describe integration as walking into a dark room, closing the door, and talking to each lingering trait. We visualize such traits as people-pleasing, addictive thinking, confusing love with pity, and judging ourselves harshly. In the darkness, we speak to these traits. We thank them and others for their protection in our lives. We ask them to retire or step back. Some we bid farewell, and some we integrate. We make peace with those parts of ourselves that kept us alive as kids but which now no longer serve a useful purpose. This exercise is called walking into the darkness to find the light. Coming out of the dark room, we stand in the light, knowing we have faced our most disturbing traits again and survived. Facing our "shadow" helps us live in the moment and feel hopeful about the future.

Step Ten Guide

1) Personal Inventory

Here are a few Step Ten questions we ask ourselves daily or weekly. These questions help us live the ACA program in all areas of our lives. Step Ten keeps us mindful of our program.

1. Am I isolating and not talking about what is really going on with me?

2. Did I view anyone as an authority figure today and feel frightened or rebellious?

3. Did I dissociate, fantasize, or become involved in self-harm today?

4. Am I keeping secrets and feeling unique? Am I talking about my feelings?

5. Am I being honest in my relationships or am I seeking approval over honesty?

6. Am I acting "perfect" and obsessing over making mistakes?

7. Do I overreact or isolate from others when I perceive that I have been criticized?

8. Am I attending ACA meetings to nurture myself and to give back what was given to me?

9. Have I acted helpful recently to manipulate others?

10. Am I secretly angry at someone, but I am avoiding talking about it?

11. Have I listened to my Inner Child or True Self today?

12. Did I judge myself or someone else without mercy today?

13. Am I listening to the Critical Parent or Loving Parent?

14. Am I remembering that I can ask for help today and that I can call someone?

2) Choice Exercise

In Step Three we realized that our need or compulsion to control others is a major stumbling block in allowing a loving God or Divine Presence to work in our lives. In Step Ten, we revisit this troublesome survival trait. We are not saying that all control is bad. We must have some order in our lives or risk chaos; however, rigid control can mean death for some ACAs and their loving relationships. If we think about it, we know the difference between compulsive control and practical order in our lives. There is room for spontaneity and imagination in the latter.

With Step Ten, we also realize we have released more of our control, and we are learning the difference between control and discernment. Discernment comes from inside and is the breath of God guiding us to do the right thing. We know what to do in a given situation when our breathing matches God's breathing. In comparison, with control our breathing is often unnatural and short. There is constriction in the body. We feel driven and fixed without a sense of having real choices when we operate from rigid control. We speak without thinking, and we feel embarrassed. We then punish ourselves harshly and apologize to others a lot. We hold unpurged resentments.

With discernment, we refrain from saying something off color or acting impulsively on a given situation. Discernment means we know who we are. We trust ourselves at last. We can relax and be an actor in life rather than a reactor.

In the following exercise, create a continuum of choice ranging from denial to discernment. Place this simple continuum on your refrigerator or at your work station. Each day, pencil in where you think you are in having real choice in your life. Move the mark around throughout the day if necessary because we can change our level of control at any time. That is the beautiful nature of choice. We can have choice at any time and back away from rigid control. There are no waiting lines for choice. You are first in line always.

Choice Continuum

Denial	Some Choice	Greater Choice	Discernment

3)   One Day at a Time Exercise

Step Ten reminds the recovering adult child to live in the moment to enjoy life's gifts and to feel connected to life. List the tools of recovery you are using to help you live in the moment.

4) Feelings And Journaling Exercise

We were introduced to the feelings exercises in Step Four. In ACA, we believe that feelings are one method by which we know ourselves and God as we understand God. Feelings expressed in the safeness of ACA give us a second chance to experience imagination, creativity, and love. We can also experience anger, frustration, and fear in healthy degrees. These once troublesome feelings – anger and fear – lose some of their power over us in ACA. We learn how to express them with the knowledge that they will pass. Experiencing fear and anger in ACA is different than when we were children and saw no end to such feelings or had to repress them. Feelings come and go. We survive them, and we grow emotionally and spiritually.

Because of the important nature of learning to identify how we feel and think, we are including the feelings exercise in Step Ten for regular use or practice. Many adult children are unsure of their feelings or cannot distinguish feelings. This exercise is a simple tool to help you get started identifying feelings and becoming more comfortable with using feelings words.

Talking about our feelings is a risk; however, this is a risk worth taking because the rewards are great. When we let others know about our feelings, we connect with people on a spiritual and equal level instead of a dependent and manipulative level.

Many adult children learn how to identify and distinguish between their emotions by practicing the feelings sentence. Select one of the feeling words and complete the sentence. Complete a sentence each day or every other day to become comfortable with talking about your feelings.

Feelings practice sentence

I feel_____ when _____ because _____.

Example:

"I feel hopeful when I attend an ACA meeting because I know I am being heard."

loved	joyful	ashamed	humorous	irritated
angry	embarrassed	trusted	betrayed	pleased
satisfied	ambivalent	hopeful	inspired	loving
frustrated	disappointed	grief	accepted	excited
grateful	confident	humiliated	guilty	serene
rested	shame	abandoned	pleasure	safe
tenacious	thoughtful	playful	fascinated	enthralled

5) Praise Exercise

We were also introduced to a praise exercise in Step Four. We include this exercise here to remind adult children to celebrate their good qualities as we also inventory our mistakes and missteps. We urge them to note what they do right or how they are thoughtful, caring, and unselfish. We are breaking out of our people-pleasing role and learning to affirm ourselves though self-love.

Following is a list of 25 assets, which will help balance positive and spiritual qualities for your Step Ten inventory. Circle at least 10 attributes. Include those you are unsure of or those you would like to have in your life. Because we operate from a praise deficit, we often do not realize the assets we have in our lives.

strong	compassionate	spontaneous	trustworthy	prompt
humorous	courteous	creative	tenacious	kind
sensitive	talented	loving	judicious	hard working
willing	honest	a listener	accepting	a friend
intelligent	organized	spiritual	modest	an ACA member

After circling your assets, sit quietly and acknowledge each one by repeating:

"I am _____ (fill in the affirmation)."

STEP TEN SPIRITUAL PRINCIPLES:

Honesty and Discernment

STEP ELEVEN

Sought through prayer and meditation to improve our conscious contact with God, as we understand God, praying only for knowledge of God's will for us and the power to carry that out.

Meditation Brought Meaning to the Closing Prayer

When I was introduced to meditation years ago, I was skeptical. I come from a religious affiliation in which meditation was not discussed much less an option for spiritual growth.

I was willing to do what the program asked. I tried it, but nothing seemed to happen for months. I would meditate and become drowsy or be distracted by a buzzing fly or a passing airplane. I continued because I wanted to get the emotional sobriety I heard about in meetings. I liked reading my meditation book, and I thought my daily meditation was relaxing but not too productive.

The first inkling I got that meditation was working occurred at the end of a meeting. It was during the closing prayer. Before I began meditation, I was usually distracted during the prayer. I would shift from foot to foot or keep my eyes open thinking about what I would do after the meeting. Typically, I never listened to the closing prayer.

I don't know which night it was, but it happened during the prayer. As I was standing in the circle after the meeting, I realized that I was motionless. I was present in the moment and listening to the prayer. I was relaxed and allowing the words to enter my mind. I felt at peace the moment I closed my eyes for the prayer. I later recognized this as the relaxed state from my meditation. However, the quickness of the calmness is what struck me. It came immediately as I stood with friends and closed my eyes. I was "in" my body and in the moment, which had not been possible as a child.

The next time I meditated I began with the closing prayer and again felt relaxed. I was making conscious contact with my Higher Power. I was in the moment and "in" my body. I once doubted the value of meditation, but I cannot live without it.

Chapter Seven

Meditation and Motives Lead to Solutions

My meditation and styles have changed during the years, but I have always meditated and gotten great results. I began with simply sitting in a chair and taking slow, deep breaths with my eyes closed. This worked great for years. I could find peacefulness or make conscious contact with my God regularly. I even meditated on problems and relationships and found solutions. The answers or direction I got usually involved me looking at my motives and wants and needs. Meditation could lead me to a direct thought that produced a solution. Sometimes it would lead me to ask myself questions about my motives. A solution or answer would emerge, or I would talk to my sponsor and find a path to take. I feel more emotionally mature when I use prayer and meditation to live my life.

How I Keep a Conscious Contact

I work a spiritual program. I go to God for all the tools and information I need. God, to me, is a higher level of consciousness. Everyday in prayer and meditation I go deep within myself to a quiet place where there's peace, love, light, hope, and joy. I honestly take my daily inventory, I release all my self-will, I turn over my will, and I ask God to lessen my nonfunctional character traits. I commit myself to correcting my previous mistakes. This gives me a conscious contact with my Higher Power.

How Do You Know If It Is God's Will?

I have two channels to God: my Inner Child and my prayers. My Inner Child lets me know what she wants to do. When I pray to my Higher Power, I ask Him to let me know how I should proceed. I get God's answers by looking for opportunities that excite my Inner Child and by observing what happens when I use all my God-given talents.

My Inner Child gets very excited and animated when she has something to say to me. She's the one who feels the feelings, who is closest to God. She insists I stop and watch God's glory in a sunset, a flower bud, and a child chasing a butterfly. She stares in utter fascination and reverence at God's hand at work as an artist paints or a carpenter builds. She is magnetically drawn to the languages, customs, clothing, foods, and crafts of people from all ethnicities, races, countries, and classes. She is amazed at how a bee makes honey or how an engineer harnesses the power of a river. She is amazed at how a 10,000 pound jet lifts itself off the ground. She is connected to the great force that created the wonders all around me, and she touches the hand of God.

Step Eleven Summary

7

Step Eleven is where we travel often to find greater levels of maturity through prayer and meditation. Through meditation, we begin to visualize emotional sobriety. We find out what ACA recovery looks like. We begin to see that recovery is a noticeable freedom from the damaging affects of The Laundry List traits. We realize our Step work has brought some measure of healing from the trauma and neglect of our childhood. We intuitively rely on the Steps and ACA meetings to face every situation in our lives. We rely upon God as we understand God for sure footing. With emotional sobriety, reparenting ourselves becomes a reality in our lives. We love ourselves. The proof of emotional sobriety can be found in our relationships with others and with God, as we understand God. If our relationships are still controlling and without feelings or trust, we must reconsider the strength of our emotional sobriety. True emotional sobriety brings a connectedness to ourselves and to others. This connectedness in relationships is characterized by expressed feelings, trust, mutual respect, and an acknowledgment that a Higher Power is real. We realize we don't need to chase after others to soothe our childhood fear of abandonment. We begin to see that we can bring our True Selves to a relationship. We have something to offer that is different than unhealthy dependence. This is what ACA recovery looks like. It addresses our rupture from our primary relationship with our family. This is the relationship template that has colored every relationship going forward. A demonstration of ACA recovery and emotional sobriety must show that we have changed the pattern of our lives. We live with feelings, spirituality, and with our true identity.

Step Eleven is also where we further address our addiction to excitement. This is the eighth trait of The Laundry List. Through meditation we learn to quiet our minds and to relax. With meditative techniques, we let go of racing thoughts. We learn to be in the moment and to be present in our bodies. We learn that our thoughts can end. This was new to many of us who have been troubled by images and thoughts all of our lives. We learn that thoughts are born, live, and die. We can let troublesome thoughts die a natural death in meditation.

In Step Eleven, we take time out of the day to focus on our spiritual path. We connect with God through our True Self when we find stillness and listen for God's footstep. Our True Self knows God's call. The True Self knows the path that our Higher Power takes to the heart. It is the path of love.

Through Step Eleven, we find God's will and a personal power that we did not know existed. There is real power. We can have it if we make the effort and let our Higher Power lead the way.

Adult children approaching Step Eleven, arrive at the Step with varying attitudes. Some adult children approach meditation with skepticism or disinterest born from the newness of this suggested practice. Many of us were raised with suspicions about meditation or without information about its spiritual qualities. Some may think they can skip this Step or brush by it. Ignoring meditation is not wise if we are to get the greatest gifts of inner peace from ACA.

Some adult children may still be holding onto notions of a Higher Power having the traits of their parents. They tend to wonder if God is indifferent, punishing, or really there at all. Some adult children secretly believe that meditation is reserved for the clergy or for serious spiritual seekers. But aren't we all serious about finding relief and acceptance within ourselves? Is that not spiritual? Can only the clergy want freedom and conscious contact with God?

Some of us have attempted meditation half-heartedly and found it lacking. Others have used drugs to enhance the experience and found that lacking as well. In ACA, we do not need drugs to connect to a Higher Power or the Divine. We are whole. We have all the energy centers, spiritual gifts, and cosmic powers within us. We are spiritual beings opening ourselves up to the Higher Power of the heavens. Through prayer and meditation we find out that we are more than our abuse and neglect. We are miracles asking and praying for an opening. The seekers understand this path.

Each adult child has been a spiritual seeker from childhood without knowing it. We are now realizing it as recovering adult children. When we look back at our lives and see the choices we made leading to this path, we are often astonished. What once appeared as disconnected decisions that may have turned out poorly were actually choices that steered us to our "true north" in ACA. Some of us took the long route, but the steering was there. The seeking was there. The intuition was there. We had a magnetic pull towards ACA that we are now realizing. We had an inner spiritual compass that cannot be denied any longer.

Our primary founder, Tony A., said: "The adult child personality is a personality which doubts God or cannot believe the unseen, but which seeks God who is unseen."[4] We cannot stop ourselves from seeking contact with a Higher Power. It is part of being an adult child, and we must accept this great fact. We are called to God and cannot resist. Acting distracted or indifferent no longer works. The True Parent calls.

[4] Tony A. conversation 2004

Looking at our pathway leading to ACA, we realize the miracle of it. Many of us are adults who should not be here, but we are. Many of us should be dead, institutionalized, or lost at sea. Instead, we are here with our faces turned toward the Creator of Light. We are seekers, and we have always been. We cannot deny it, so why not seek further with one of God's favorite tools – meditation?

History tells us that all great spiritual seekers used meditation and prayer to gain the greatest quality time with a Higher Power or the Divine Presence. The Vedics and Buddhists of the East came this way and received great rewards. Through focused meditation, they were transported into a new dimension and received mystical and spiritual gifts hard to describe yet real. These bodhisattvas and yogis know that the cosmos is endless and blissful. They have experienced consciousness as a different dimension, yet they remain here helping others find it for themselves.

The West also had its share of meditators and seekers. Their dramatic transformations or glimpses of the eternal are well documented. With meditation and prayer, they have received power to focus their talents and to make a better world. These opportunities are open to ACA members as well through Step Eleven.

Getting "In" Our Bodies

Many adult children are disconnected from their bodies without realizing it. Step Eleven is one method to reconnect with our bodies. Our disconnection can occur in the form of frozen feelings, which is also known as "psychic numbing." We become numb to feelings and sensations. This is a symptom of being disconnected from our True Self, which expresses itself in the body through feelings and imagination. That means our disconnection from our body represents a disconnection from our real identity.

Some of us have been so traumatized that we shut down our emotions and cut ourselves off from our bodies. While we still function in our jobs and relationships, we are not totally present in our own bodies. We look at others and wonder what it is like to feel "normal" because we are sure that we don't feel normal. In reality, we are not feeling much of anything. Wondering if we are normal or being confused about feelings are clues to being disconnected from our own body.

Another form of not being in the body involves dissociation or "leaving the body." Many sexual abuse victims describe leaving their bodies during the abuse. Part of the healing process for these adult children involves getting back into the body and reclaiming wholeness.

Many young boys and girls who have been cursed harshly, brow-beaten, cowed, and threatened undergo a similar separation from the body. They experience stuffed feelings, psychic numbing, and dissociation all together. They usually complicate the dissociation with drugs, sex, or another compulsive behavior. Once the addiction is addressed the numbing and dissociation must be addressed in ACA and usually with professional help.

We know of an adult child who sought help for his dysfunctional upbringing. He was sober and clean, but he sensed that something was not right. He compulsively acted out in other areas of his life, but he maintained his drug free lifestyle. His acting out caused him great shame. His issues of frozen feelings and dissociating from his body came up during an early counseling session. During the session, his therapist asked a simple question: "How does it feel to feel loved?"

The adult child struggled with an answer and tried to offer a definition of love; however the counselor gently interrupted and said: "No. I am not looking for a definition of love. I want to know what it feels like in your body to feel loved. When I feel loved, my breathing is easier, and there is a warmth in my face below the skin. I feel like smiling a lot."

Chapter Seven

The counselor repeated her question: "What does it feel like to feel loved?"

The adult child said he stared at her. He could not answer. He later realized he was 26 years old and could not recall feeling loved. He had never stopped to think about it until that day. He knew his parents had cared for him and provided food and shelter. They had said they loved him, but he could not remember feeling safe or loved as a child. His alcoholic father threatened the family and cursed his children.

This simple question about feeling loved raised the question of whether the adult child had truly been loved at all. He was so shut down emotionally that he could not recall the physical reaction – bodily reaction – of feeling loved. He recalled being an object of infatuation in a relationship, but that never seemed to last. He had never felt warmth in his face, and his breathing had not been made easier by the infatuation.

Becoming sober and clean improved his life, but it also allowed his original sense of feeling inferior and defective to emerge. In sobriety, he remained disconnected from his body and struggled with accepting love because of a deep sense of feeling flawed. He thought he could recognize love in others, but inwardly he resigned himself to believing he could never feel it. He had a definition of love from books and movies, but he did not feel loved. Outside observers saw a helpful man who held a job and had friends and a purpose in life. He was a stellar Twelve Step member who helped others. He could be counted on to help out his home group. After this counseling session, he said he understood what it meant when his counselor said: "You are not in your body. You are not feeling your feelings. You are up in your head."

Step Eleven is a point where adult children can get "in" their bodies and into the moment. By getting "in" our bodies we can then go out into the world and make our best contributions. This is important work and should be taken seriously. Taking the time to sit quietly and do simple meditative breathing and concentration is a proven way to accomplish this soul healing exercise. By returning to our bodies or becoming aware of our bodies, we find another piece of the puzzle to reconstruct our wholeness. We have all the parts within us, and we are finding them with God's help.

God Within

In meditation, there are no hard and fast rules that we present here. Typically, a person who meditates finds a room or location free of noise and distraction. The person may sit in a chair with both feet on the floor. Some adult children sit on the floor in the cross-leg, yoga position.

The person usually begins a meditation by taking several deliberate and extended breaths. The breathing is important to slow down our thoughts and prepare us for seeking conscious contact with ourselves and God, as we understand God. As we breathe in deeply and slowly exhale, we listen to the air traveling in and going out of our lungs. This breathing is the language of the Higher Power for many of us. It is the signal to draw the Higher Power from within out. Many ACA members believe this is where the Higher Power dwells and has always dwelt – within. Meditation gives us a chance to find that out.

During meditation, some adult children close their eyes and concentrate on a simple prayer or meditative reading. Others meditate with their eyes open, concentrating on a focal point.

The straightforward purpose of Step Eleven is to improve our conscious contact with God, as we understand God. In meditation, we pray for knowledge of God's will and the power to carry that out.

Some adult children pray for wholeness during meditation, asking the Higher Power for clarity. We were introduced to wholeness in Step Three. In ACA we believe we are whole and have been fragmented by our upbringing. We have all the pieces within us for our spiritual awakening to occur. We are seeking

God's will and the power to carry out the process of wholeness. We are asking God for what we need. We want wholeness and our miracle restored.

As we meditate, we let our thoughts come and go. We let them fade. We concentrate on our breathing, but we don't over concentrate. We breathe naturally and relax the tension in our bodies. At some point in the meditation, many adult children become very still inside. This is the point of being aware of our bodies and being "in" our bodies. It is also our initial contact with God, but there is more. There is much more if we meditate regularly.

During meditation our breathing is calm, and we feel rested. Our shoulders are relaxed, and our legs feel firmly grounded. We are connected to the earth. We realize we are fully in our bodies. We also feel full spiritually and emotionally. We feel loved by our True Parent. During this state of being, we can lose track of time because we have slipped the bounds of physics. We are physically sitting in a chair, but our conscious contact is with God. Some of us glimpse bliss and an ocean of acceptance, forgiveness, and self-love. There is another dimension. This is the God we went searching for without knowing it but knew at some point would be here. This is the Higher Power who formed ACA from the prayers of children and adult children across the world. This is the God who arrests shame.

If we believe we are not reaching a meditative state after many tries, we do not worry about it. We keep trying, knowing we will make it. There is no right or wrong way to meditate. God will not leave us behind. The Higher Power is within. It is our True Self. We cannot be abandoned or left behind.

Whatever meditative style we choose, the goal is to seek God's will and the power to carry that out. With continued meditation, we return to our everyday activities, feeling more emotionally sober. We feel more energy to get involved in life and to contribute in making a better world. By traveling inward in meditation, we find strength to go farther outward than we could have imagined.

As we greet co-workers or friends, we feel that we are changing inside. We begin to recognize a power inside we had not known before. We are less frightened of authority figures, and we see the strengths in people as well as their weaknesses. We are not easily stirred into frantic action when things don't go our way. We begin to back away from situations that once compelled us to argue without cause or do the bidding of another. We are less harsh on ourselves and our mistakes. We want to attend ACA meetings and help others with their journey.

In addition to meditation, Step Eleven also encourages prayer in our search for seeking God's will and the power to carry that out. In ACA, we examine our prayer life and our thought life. Our thought life is the place in our head once dominated with all the negative and minimizing messages from our childhood. This thought life was invisible to others, yet it was real to us because it contained the experiences and beliefs that drove our compulsions and unhealthy dependence. We became addicted to excitement or to our thoughts. While we appeared orderly in the public eye before arriving in ACA, we always had a "script" in our minds. No one else could see or hear the script, but we could hear it and we acted on it. We developed odd obsessions and compulsive behaviors based on this script or thought life. We sometimes felt powerless to change, but we now believe we have found a power to address our destructive thinking. With the help of a Higher Power, we work at freeing ourselves from obsessive and compulsive behaviors. The preceding Steps have gone far to modifying our thought life. We have changed the negative messages, and we are changing our behaviors – slowly and gradually.

Prayer and meditation will take us further. We pray to put into action the principles and concepts we are finding in ACA. We pray for strength and power to work the ACA program and to stay focused. We pray for God to enter our thought life and take out what blocks us from accepting ourselves. We pray to connect with our Inner Child.

While there are few rules on prayer, many ACAs believe prayer is reserved for the end of the day and usually practiced in the home or at a religious facility. We suggest that prayer can be done almost anywhere and any time. We are not confined to praying in one location or at any particular time. Like meditation, prayer has been used through the ages for worship, guidance, intervention, salvation, and to find comfort from aloneness. There is no standard length for a prayer, but some of the most powerful prayers have the fewest words. The Serenity Prayer comes to mind and represents a concentrated measure of serenity, humility, courage, wisdom, and spirituality in 25 words. It is a prayer that has anchored Twelve Step meetings and the development of Twelve Step fellowships for decades across the world. It is a proven prayer which causes anyone hearing it to pause. It has that kind of power.

Some ACA members recall prayers from childhood that served them well and brought comfort on some level. In recovery, they speak of how these prayers were little lights pointing the way to help. One adult child learned a short prayer as a third grader and now sees that prayer as a plea for clarity to decipher the contradictory messages of her severely enmeshed home. She now recognizes ACA wisdom in the prayer.

"God,
When I look let me truly see.
When I listen let me truly hear."

When she found the prayer as a 9-year-old, it resonated with her and brought a measure of comfort in her young life. When she hit bottom at age 33, the prayer rose in her consciousness like an old friend. She believes her prayer for clarity and understanding led her to ACA and guides her in the program.

The simple prayer is an example of seeking and listening, which is the heart of ACA's Eleventh Step. Many ACA members describe prayer as seeking God's guidance and meditation as listening for it. We pray and listen in Step Eleven.

There are no limits on prayer length. Longer prayers have their purpose and serve the seekers well.

With prayer and meditation we find our true inner power. This is the inner strength that we have always had but used limitedly. God has been holding onto it until we were ready to claim it in Step Eleven. This is the power which changes our life and our course of thinking and behaving. This is the power which keeps us going when we lapse into judging ourselves or feel discouraged about making progress in ACA. This is the power that we find when we ask humbly to be used for the greater good of the world.

We feel more alive than ever before with Step Eleven. We are more imaginative and hopeful. A return to prayer and creativity are two of the gifts of Step Eleven in addition to making conscious contact with the God within.

While we have spoken much of God and God's guidance, ACA is not a religious program nor does it represent any religious belief. However, the disease of family dysfunction is a cunning, baffling, and powerful disease. It requires a spiritual solution in addition to our practical efforts to work the Twelve Steps and share our stories in meetings. We believe the disease of family dysfunction is a spiritual dilemma. We need a connection to the God of our understanding for our best hope.

Grief Work Revisited: Connecting With Our Inner Child

In Step Eleven, we will revisit grief work. We recommend guided meditation for this type of grief work. In this exercise, you will travel back into your childhood to connect with your child within.

While grief can stir the emotions, it is not always sad or unpleasant. Many times we recognize the measure of our loss and that is enough. At other times there are tears and a sense of lament and then we feel release. With grief, we are properly labeling a loss or a key event in our childhood. For the best results, we suggest that you tape record the script below and play it back to serve as a guided meditation.

Meditation Exercise

7

Read and record the script here in your voice, or have a friend record it on tape or a CD. When you have recorded the script, play it back to begin the guided meditation.

(Begin recording here)

To begin the guided meditation, find a quiet and comfortable room without distraction. You may sit in a chair or sit on the floor. An outdoor location is acceptable as well. Sit upright but be comfortable. Begin the exercise by closing your eyes and taking a deep breath and releasing it slowly.

As you take four or five slow breaths, let any thoughts you might have fade away. Be aware of being present in your body. If your mind is wandering, gently focus on yourself and be present in the moment and in your body. Continue breathing naturally.

(Let 10 to 20 seconds of the tape lapse here without talking. This will create silence for you to relax and breathe several times before the script continues. Begin recording the script again after the silent delay.)

Imagine that you are sitting on a warm beach. The weather is pleasant and not too hot. The beach is secluded but safe. You can feel the warm sand beneath your feet as you stand up and look out upon a calm, blue ocean. White sea gulls are diving for fish and the smell of seawater is refreshing. You are wearing a T-shirt, loose trousers, and a floppy hat to block the sun.

In front of you, near the shoreline, you see an image of yourself when you were six or eight years old. Your Inner Child is bent at the waist picking up starfish and sea shells. The child notices you and waves you over. You walk up to the child and the child reaches out and places a starfish in one of your hands. You smile and feel the bristles of the tiny starfish tickling you. Your Inner Child smiles and squints to block the friendly sun.

The child reaches out and grips your hand. The child's skin has been warmed by sun rays. You both begin walking along the beach. You notice the child's soft hair and sensitive touch as you walk. The child trusts you and giggles softly each time a wave washes up the shore almost touching your feet.

You walk for many moments, chatting softly, but paying attention to the child's innocence and imagination. You want to protect the child.

You notice two people ahead, and they seem familiar so you keep walking toward them. Your Inner Child squeezes your hand and moves slightly behind you as you move closer to the couple. The child becomes shy, pushing into your leg from behind. You keep walking.

You recognize the couple before you reach them. They are your parents, waiting for you to walk up. They grin at you and your Inner Child. They ask if they can walk with the child.

You feel your stomach tighten, and you look down at your Inner Child to find the child pressed into your legs from the back. The child won't look at you and won't let go of your hand.

You smile at your parents but ask them to wait for another day to walk the child. You and your Inner Child walk up the beach away from your parents and sit down. The child looks over a shoulder, climbs into your lap, and sits down. You hold your Inner Child. You both watch your parents walk away.

The sun is lower now but still warm. Your Inner Child naps. You are safe. Your Inner Child is safe. You are going to make it. You know what you are doing. You can trust yourself to take care of your Inner Child. You can trust yourself to love.

Continue to meditate and hold your Inner Child. When you are ready to stop, gently wake the child, walk the child to your cottage, and tuck it into bed. After putting the child to bed, back out of the room, counting slowly backward from ten. Open your eyes.

(Stop recording)

The recording is complete. You now have a recording to transport you on a guided meditation to the child within. The exercise represents the loss or grief of our childhoods. Our families were not always safe or nurturing. This is loss. The exercise also represents our reparenting choice today. We can take care of ourselves and our Inner Child.

You can use this exercise to revisit your childhood. Upon occasion you can ask the Inner Child how the child feels or what the child is experiencing. Listen and then journal or write about what you hear from the child.

Creativity Exercise: Wallet Card

Create your own Eleventh Step prayer and place it on a wallet card to carry to work or to meetings. Keep it simple, but create a prayer that is specific to you and your relationship with the Divine, Higher Power, or God. This is your own prayer.

STEP ELEVEN SPIRITUAL PRINCIPLES:

Seeking and Listening

STEP TWELVE

Having had a spiritual awakening as the result of these Steps, we tried to carry this message to others who still suffer, and to practice these principles in all our affairs.

Our Story Is Our Greatest Asset

I remember how skeptical I felt when someone said my abusive upbringing would be my most valued asset. I did not see how my experience could help anyone, but I also did not know about ACA either. In ACA, I am not a victim. I have come to believe that my childhood places me in a position to help others when no one else can. I don't live in the past, but I can help myself by helping others. I know this is true because I have been helped by listening to others share about their lives in meetings. It creates identity and unity. I share my ACA story for identity and to help others.

I have seen the results of adult children helping adult children in prison meetings and in treatment as well as regular meetings. I don't have anything against doctors or psychiatrists but sometimes they cannot help. They often don't understand that the adult child needs contact with other recovering ACAs and meetings instead of setting goals and merely changing behavior. Goals and changed behavior are important, but you can't beat the help that comes from relating to others in an ACA meeting. You can see a new person's eyes change when The Laundry List (Problem) is read. This is powerful stuff.

Apply The Wisdom And Share It

The Twelfth Step means I have come so far from the original pain that brought me into the program. I have awareness, strength, and the power to apply this program in every area of my life, not just a specific compulsion or addiction. I can be of service to others, both within and outside the program. I volunteer my time by listening and being supportive. I strive to be an example of a peaceful and happy way of living.

As it says in The Solution, "We progress from hurting to healing to helping." Thank God.

I Give It Away To Keep It

There's a piece of table literature we have, which groups the Twelve Steps into stages. The stages are listed as: Steps One through Three as "Giving Up," Steps Four and Five as "Fessing Up," Steps Six through Nine as "Cleaning Up", and Steps Ten through Twelve as "Stepping Up."

I see Step Twelve as the Step where I begin taking responsibility for this program by sponsoring others, doing service, and serving on outreach committees, and giving talks when asked.

This is the program that saved my life. I owe this program and the people in it my life, my success, my money, and my joy. Because of my love for ACA, I have delivered meeting directories to every library, therapist's office, Twelve Step recovery center, college and university health facility, counseling office, psychology department, business and government personnel office, and church in my city.

The people in my family of origin now communicate and show their love and respect for me. I know others who feel the way I do; they're all giving service in ACA. They're all serving on service boards, putting on special events, sponsoring others, or doing ACA outreach. It goes beyond gratitude. It's the essence of the program.

Keep Coming Back

The program does not end with Step Twelve. I work the Steps to maintain my emotional sobriety and to stay out of unhealthy situations. I don't have to be hypervigilant, but I stay alert to my people-pleasing and rescuing ways. After 20 years, I still attend meetings for myself and to give back what was given to me freely. That's what I heard early on: "Keep coming back no matter what." I did, and I found a new way of life. I continue to get what I need from the meetings and by sponsoring others and being sponsored. I can't tell you how many times I have gone to a meeting and the topic was about a situation or incident in my life. This program continues to amaze me.

When It Counted, My Spiritual Awakening Was There

I remember the first time I read Step Twelve. I was attracted to carrying the message and practicing ACA principles, but I was skeptical of my chances of having a spiritual awakening. Looking back, I can see how I decided that spiritual experiences were for other people. Doing the best I could with my limited faith, I worked all of the Twelve Steps, but I focused on carrying the message in Step Twelve. I mostly ignored talk of spiritual matters. I was willing to settle for earnest Step work, giving service, and helping others. I hoped this would be enough to get me through life. With this approach, my life improved dramatically. I finished college and started a career. I remained active in meetings and sponsoring others. I got honest about my people-pleasing and controlling ways. I could honestly share in meetings about turning my will and life over to the care of God, but I still wondered if I was truly letting go. I hoped God was hearing my prayers, but I was unsure. Looking back, I realize I was bringing my Laundry List "self" to Step Twelve. I was trying to have an intellectual relationship with a Higher Power without actually letting go. This was my pathway to a spiritual awakening that has been dramatic and unanticipated.

I never thought my decision to enter a relationship that turned abusive would lead me to the part of Step Twelve I had been ignoring, but it did. This relationship almost drove me to insanity with its pain and abandonment. I was losing my soul, and I knew it. I was faced with throwing away ACA or breaking free. When I made my decision to leave, I faced panic, obsession, and fear at levels that I never imagined possible. I prayed night and day and stayed close to my sponsor and meetings. For weeks it was touch and go, but I turned the corner. I faced my terror of abandonment from childhood. I knew I could survive my feelings. I continued to pray and stay close to my Higher Power. A few months later my spiritual experience came in a dramatic vision and with synchronicities that prove to me that God is there, and God is loving. This happened in my 20th year of recovery. I was not looking for it, but it happened. I have had a spiritual awakening as the result of facing my fear of abandonment.

Step Twelve Summary

In Step Twelve we claim our program of recovery for ourselves by putting into practice the spiritual principles we have used and continue to use to reparent ourselves. The principles include surrender, hope, honesty, self-forgiveness, humility, and many more from the Twelve Steps.

Step Twelve calls ACA members to carry the message to other suffering adult children in addition to practicing these principles in all our affairs. We can also expect a spiritual awakening as promised in Step Twelve.

There is possibly no greater act of reparenting ourselves than carrying the message of hope to another suffering adult child yet to know of a new way of life. By doing so, we grow emotionally and spiritually. We learn to love ourselves more surely.

Through reparenting, we learn to use spiritual principles in our daily lives to replace old ways of thinking and reacting. The Solution states: "By gradually releasing the burden of unexpressed grief, we slowly move out of the past. We learn to reparent ourselves with gentleness, humor, love, and respect."

In carrying the ACA message of hope to another, we use gentleness, humor, love, and respect in the same manner that we do these things for ourselves. There are other points to consider when carrying the ACA message to those who still suffer, but we begin with this attitude.

We progress from hurting to helping. We awaken to a sense of wholeness we never knew was possible. By working the ACA Steps, we learn that our past can be one of our most important assets in our effort to help others and ourselves. We don't live in the past, but we can help another adult child when no one else can or when sincere attempts by professionals have failed. We use our stories to build identity with the person we are sponsoring or carrying the message to in treatment or elsewhere. Adult children new to the program can be skeptical without showing it. Many are experts at disbelief. They can only be reached by someone who can share about his own family dysfunction in terms that the new person understands. When we talk of being a people-pleaser or confusing love with pity, we see the connection we make with the person seeking help. Before long, the person usually opens up and begins relating similar experiences. That is the power of our story when we tell it with humility and hope for helping others.

The Twelfth Step is our stage where we become actors instead of reactors without solutions. Acting from a foundation of self-love and respect, we offer our spiritual solutions to adult children seeking a better way of life. We also help ourselves.

God Exists

One of the results of a spiritual awakening involves the understanding that God is real. With a spiritual awakening, we move from theories about God to the belief that a Higher Power is accessible and hears our prayers. We know that a loving God or a Spirit of the Universe exists. We have come to believe that God, as we understand God, is the Actual Parent.

Many of us approached Step Twelve realizing there is a general standard for a spiritual awakening. The AA Big Book outlines two types of spiritual awakenings, yet there are many others across cultures and across continents. In AA, there is the dramatic spiritual awakening or "bright light" experience. AA cofounder Bill Wilson had such an experience in 1934 as he faced near insanity brought on by an alcoholic binge.† This experience is not the norm, but it does occur. The dramatic experience can bring about a profound change in attitude and belief in a Higher Power. There is also a spiritual awakening of the "educational variety." This gradual awakening emerges as the person comes to a greater understanding of a Higher Power through Step work, meditation, prayer, and helping others find ACA. A gradual spiritual awakening holds just as much meaning and brings just as much lasting serenity as a dramatic awakening can bring.

ACA members have experienced these types of awakenings. Our experience reveals a third type as well. This third awakening has features of the dramatic awakening and educational variety combined. This "dramatic educational" awakening can involve profound visions and indisputable evidence that God is among us. We know a freedom from dependent thinking and actions that we have not known before. We realize that we are loved and can love others.

Occasionally, the person having the dramatic educational awakening is not sure what has happened. He must educate himself about the event.† We avoid analyzing the experience or over-thinking it, but we do seek information from a reputable source about our spiritual vision or episode.

Education alone is not enough to gain the greatest benefit from our spiritual experience. We also learn that spiritual experiences have greater meaning when matched with a dedication to work the ACA program. Spiritual experiences can be thrilling and consciousness expanding. They become a sustained spiritual awakening through Step work and by relating with the Inner Child. This is the True Self and a conduit to the God within.

With a spiritual experience, we usually realize that we are transformed in some manner. We know something has changed inside of us even though we do not yet fully understand it. For some of us, our spiritual focus seems sharper. We know a peace that we could not imagine previously. We can still have moments of being affected by life, but these moments seem milder and are handled more quickly. We know there is something greater than ourselves at work in the universe. We let go and let God work in these matters with greater ease. For others, there may be an intuitiveness not previously known. There can be a new creativity or energy that flows freely.

The dramatic element of this awakening can come at any time, yet it tends to come when the adult child is faced with a crisis of some sort. Intense emotional pain or an extreme sense of hopelessness can be the gateway to a dramatic spiritual experience. The intensive desperation usually lasts for several hours or several days. This gift of desperation can set the stage for a dramatic spiritual experience if we are humble enough to ask our Higher Power for help. During these moments, this acute feeling of hopelessness represents an abandonment crisis. This is our childhood terror of abandonment welling up in our adult lives. This sense of fear and pending doom reaches back to our deepest fears of being alone. Some of us have dealt with this creature in previous Steps and found relief. For others, a final showdown is necessary to face our fear of abandonment once and for all. If we are willing and sincere, we learn we can survive our feelings and our worst fear. To get through, we pray often, and we pray hard. We call our sponsor, go to meetings, and talk about how we feel. Eventually, we release our terror of abandonment and embrace our Higher Power. We may experience significant dreams or unexplainable events during these times. We come out of this experience knowing we are changed. We feel the difference in our body and our mind.

For many of us, our spiritual awakening began in Step One when we realized that we were not alone or insane with the thoughts we had. We attended our first meeting, believing we were unique or that our family was the only family of its breed or pattern. What an amazing sense of relief washed over us as we heard The Laundry List (Problem) read. The traits of an adult child seemed to crack decades of hardened denial that had built up in our heart and soul. Many of us wept at hearing the traits of an adult child being read. Our awakening at our first meeting continued as we listened to adult children share their experiences as children and adults. As they talked we heard clarity, hope, and the ACA solution. We also heard honesty, openmindedness, and willingness. This is "HOW" the program works. By the end of the meeting, we were changed. We could not be the same again after hearing the message of recovery. There would be tough days ahead, but we were subtly different after that first meeting.

Others experienced an awakening in writing a Fourth Step and telling their story in Step Five. With these Steps, we finally got to see the patterns of our family and to finally talk about what matters in our lives. Many of us trusted ourselves and another person for the first time in Step Five. We bravely broke the family rule of secrecy by telling our story to another person. Who would have thought that talking, trusting, and feeling would equal a spiritual experience, but it does for adult children.

We felt this new spirituality in our breathing and in the sense that we could face life on life's terms. Many of us felt a stronger connection to a Higher Power after Step Five.

There are many more examples of spiritual experiences and awakenings from the Twelve Steps. They all add up to the spiritual awakening we are seeking in ACA. Such spiritual awakenings are necessary for the long haul. We need a spiritual awakening, which creates a personality change that breaks the grip of family dysfunction on the soul. Only God, as we understand God, can bring about this change. Without this personality change, we can be subject to setbacks into people-pleasing, judging ourselves harshly, or remaining in abusive relationships. The preceding Steps made us aware of these survival traits, but in Step Twelve they become unbearable with our newfound awareness. The knowledge we gain in Step Twelve forces us to take action if we feel ourselves drifting into unhealthy behavior.

While spiritual awakenings can take different avenues to emerge, most awakenings tend to have some common characteristics. In addition to knowing that a Loving God exists, a spiritual awakening typically brings an end to the aching sense of being different and alone. Shame, abandonment, and control have been dealt with as well. If they resurface, they are handled in a more efficient manner once we become spiritually awake.

A spiritual awakening simplifies our lives. We intuitively know what we need and what we can live without. We are no longer reacting to people, places, and things. We live and let live.

Spiritual awakenings, regardless of the variety, do not signal an end to personal growth. The awakening is the beginning of new growth for many. We are transformed, but we still can have behavioral and relationship challenges ahead; however, there is new energy and creativity to help us grow. There is the effortless effort that opens up for many of us. By serving others, we tap into an outflow of love and light that attracts others. We give away what was given to us. We know how to use the spiritual principles of the Twelve Steps. We want to mentor that experience for others.

Avoiding a Spiritual Bypass

While some spiritual experiences are miraculous, breathtaking, and bring a sense of awe, they do not equal recovery by themselves. ACA members have had spiritual experiences that bring dramatic visions and powerful dreams. In some instances, the experience transports the person to another dimension of timelessness and pure love. The body ceases to exist in this place of higher consciousness and bliss. Spiritual experiences of this nature help us to confirm our belief in a Divine Creator, but the experience does not exempt us from doing the work of recovery. We must still work all of the Twelve Steps to address the effects of growing up in an unhealthy family. We must attend ACA meetings and give back what was given to us. We must be willing to give service and to help out at our ACA support group. We can know that we have experienced something dramatic and otherworldly while we keep our feet on the ground and live one day at a time.

ACA members who focus primarily on seeking a spiritual awakening without working on the effects of family dysfunction are often involved in a spiritual bypass.[†] A spiritual bypass means that the person is attempting to avoid the pain that can come with working through the trauma and neglect from childhood. In some cases, the person attempts to jump ahead in the recovery process without going through the entire process. This path invariably fails or leads to dissatisfying results. If one does succeed in having a spiritual experience, but avoids program work, the person can still remain mired in addictiveness or problematic relationships. The spiritual experience may bring some forms of enlightenment; however, the person can cling to old ways of living without embracing ACA recovery. Through arrogance and fear, the person appears to work a program that has little resemblance to the ACA program. At the same time, compulsions and addictiveness continue. A spiritual experience without grounded program work can produce an unhealthy ego. With an inflated ego, the person can use the spiritual experience as a shield against suggestions to work a full program.

Spiritual experiences, if handled properly, can lead to a spiritual awakening that brings creativity and serenity. With a spiritual awakening we are willing to practice ACA principles in all our affairs and to carry the message to others.

Service is Love Grounded in Self-Love

Spiritually awake adult children understand the spiritual axiom which states: "We must give away what we have to keep it." This is one of the most selfless acts of love we can offer a confused world; however, we must love ourselves first to have something to give away. Without self-love, the Twelfth Step merely becomes another goal we achieve or a mark we pass on our way to pleasing others or abandoning ourselves. Without self-love, we tend to use service to others as a camouflage to hide in plain sight. Self-love is a result of working the Twelve Steps, being vulnerable, asking for help, and being aware of our bodies through meditation and proper breathing. We love ourselves when we find our pain. We sit with it without acting out on drugs or some other compulsive activity. We go after our stored grief and greet it and feel it. We find our True Selves and sit beside the Divine Light.

In his final days, in the Twelfth Step of his life, our founder, Tony A., focused on self-love. He boiled down his 30 years of recovery into the simple but powerful concept of self-love and self-forgiveness. In his last days, he continued to encourage adult children to love themselves.

Because of his own violent upbringing before World War II, Tony knew that adult children carry inherent shame and abandonment. Without help, we can abandon ourselves in a heartbeat. He believed we can only be healed by self-love and the hand of God called upon by the willing adult child. He knew adult children spend a lifetime running from abandonment or shame disguised as a variety of compulsions and self-harming acts. He knew we never stopped loving our parents even though we thought we had. Through his recovery, Tony realized his parents were the biological couple who brought him into the world. However, the actual parent is a Higher Power who never abandons.

We meet the actual parent through the Twelve Steps. With spiritual help, we stop resisting the idea of loving ourselves unconditionally. In self-love, Tony was not speaking of narcissistic self-centeredness or navel gazing. He was speaking of embracing our wounded inner self and turning to our Higher Power for breath, life, and healing. He knew that when adult children go inside and find their wholeness they can serve God and the world as Trusted Servants. We go outward by going inward. We become inwardly illuminated.

By loving ourselves, we can begin to take down our final wall and let love in. This is the core of the onion – self-love. Letting someone in takes courage because we have been hurt deeply by rejection as children. We loved our parents naturally, but our parents could not accept our gift. They did not love themselves. They could not recognize what we were trying to give them. As children, we were confused by our parents' rejection. We quickly learned to retract our love and bury it deep inside. We created a false self, who chased people and things so we could feel in control but never whole. We thought we had buried our love permanently, but it is there. No matter what we have done in the false self, our love is there. This means we can love others. This means we can be a friend.

By loving ourselves, we see there is more love in the world than we realized. There is still much dependency and addiction, but there is love and we can see it. We recognize it because it is in us. By recognizing love, our false self dissolves. We realize we are not our addictions. We are not drugs, food, spending, gambling, sex, or compulsions. We are love.

As children of God, we want to carry the ACA message to the adult child who still suffers so that we might continue to grow spiritually ourselves. We attend ACA meetings for ourselves, but we also do it to be available to new people making a start in the program. We know what our story is, and we know our loss. We also know hope and forgiveness. We have progressed from hurting to helping.

Meanwhile, those who are spiritually awake accept Twelve Step work with an attitude of service rather than sacrifice. By the time we reach this Step, we know the difference between being a rescuer and giving service with love.

The difference between reacting like a caretaker and lending a hand involves the fact that we are helping ourselves. We are not people-pleasing or fearing authority figures. We do not seek titles or power in ACA. We sincerely want to help out in the spirit of anonymity. We are moving out of isolation by attending meetings and getting involved. We see service work as giving love rather than enabling or manipulation. We also know when to step back or ask for help. We also know that we are going to be all right no matter what happens. We have God and our friends in ACA. We are going to make it.

Step Twelve is a Beginning

Reaching Step Twelve is the beginning not the end. It is a beginning of a new way of life that we can take into our work place, relationships, and on our spiritual journey. We have been applying ACA in all three areas in the preceding Steps; however, in Step Twelve we are making a more formal statement that we have adopted a life of surrender, hope, honesty, humility, and forgiveness.

With the Twelve Steps we have a design for living that we believe will help us face life's challenges and joys. There are no guarantees that the Twelve Steps will straighten out life's meandering path; however, with the Steps, we believe we can take the curves more gently. We believe we have an edge in whatever life deals us. In addition to having a proven program to rely on, we also realize we are not alone. We have ACA friends we can count on. We have meetings we can attend. We have our feelings, and we have prayer. We also know we don't have to be perfect or in control all the time. We keep it simple in matters of living and relating to people. We live one day at a time and handle what is in front of us. What a great relief as we face the future.

Some of us will face relationship challenges, health issues, and death as part of life. ACA members tend to meet these challenges in good form due to their support group and spiritual life. We have seen adult children use the principles of the Twelve Steps to handle family illness, despair, and death with amazing serenity and faith. We have marveled at some ACA members and their ability to stay focused without falling into blame or destructive behavior when faced with an unfairness of life.

These adult children realize the importance of staying active in ACA and remaining spiritually fit to face the vicissitudes of life. Many will say it is easier to stay spiritually fit by taking daily program action than attempting to catch up once a crisis hits. Regular attendance at ACA meetings helps us stay spiritually fit.

Many recovering adult children will need the Twelve Steps to face children who may have been affected by their dysfunction. Many of our members fit into this category. They have children or adult children who are acting out in addiction, dependency, and other forms of self-harm. Some of their children or grandchildren live in another state or area and are rarely seen. All of these circumstances bring great emotional pain to an adult child who has inventoried his life and realizes the generational nature of family dysfunction. It aches to know that he or she is powerless and cannot fix anyone.

These adult children continue to attend meetings and talk about their feelings of guilt and powerlessness. They pray. They do service work or sponsor a new member and stay involved. They avoid isolation. They forgive themselves. Their emotional pain is lessened. Many have positive outcomes over time. They reconnect with their children or see a child find help.

Practicing ACA principles in our relationships with our children and others is possibly one of the most challenging areas of our lives. Relationships are where our survival traits attempt to reemerge. We must remain open to steer our lives away from stifling control. With honesty and kindness, we allow God to work in our relationships. We talk about our feelings in the relationship, and we listen to the feelings of others as well. We check our motives with a trusted friend or with a sponsor. We remember we can talk, trust, and feel instead of control, isolate, and fume. Relationships can be different in recovery. It is never too late to have a happy childhood or relationship.

Chapter Seven

Get Out of Yourself

While much of ACA's program involves the inward journey, Step Twelve reminds us to journey outward as well. We carry the message to other adult children in our meetings, on the telephone, and through service work. We get out of ourselves by sponsoring others, giving rides to meetings, and by getting involved at an ACA event or fund raiser. There are many opportunities if we only look. Most of this activity falls under the title of Twelfth Step work, and it means that we are answering the call to carry the message to others. We cannot use old excuses of feeling ill, not good enough, or unique to continue sitting on the sideline of life. To avoid helping others is to avoid helping ourselves. We can do this. We have our Higher Power and our friends to help us participate in life. We learn how to have fun in addition to contributing to our own recovery. The gratitude we feel is limitless.

In ACA, we carry the message of hope to adult children across the world. There are ACA groups in Denmark, Germany, Italy, Turkey, Russia, Hungary, and Japan, as well as North and South America, Australia, and the Pacific Islands. There could easily be 300 million adult children across the world who qualify for ACA. We doubt there will ever be a shortage of people who could use the ACA way of life. However, we typically carry the message to people who want it and not to people who need it. We have learned that you cannot give ACA to someone who does not want it. But at the same time, you cannot stop someone who wants it from having it. We know of adult children in some of the poorest countries in the world, with minimal amounts of ACA literature, living the ACA way of life. Their willingness, openness, and courage are amazing.

Additionally, we try to answer calls to carry ACA's message of hope into prisons, treatment centers, or mental health care facilities. Adult children are sent to prison every day for harming themselves or others. Still others have psychiatric problems so severe that they require hospitalization. Both the prisoner and the psychiatric patient are adult children and deserve to hear ACA's message. Our program is mature enough, and our members are strong enough, to do this work within the guidelines we have established for these facilities. No one should put themselves in harms way by carrying the message into these facilities; however, there are opportunities to carry the message here. The program has had success in these facilities.

Carrying the ACA message gets us out of ourselves and builds confidence. We see that we can help others as a sponsor or mentor. There is great joy awaiting you to watch a frightened or foggy newcomer attend his or her first meeting and watch that person open up. This is something you do not want to miss. To watch a new person realize that he or she is not alone is heart warming. To hear a new member sharing about finding clarity about his childhood is equally joyous. We really feel like we are a part of life during these moments. We believe we are living the life we always wanted to live. We are finally home. We have found a fellowship of people we have always sought.

In carrying the ACA message to another, we keep it simple. Our stories are sufficient. There is no need to embellish or minimize what we have been through. When carrying the message, we follow a simple formula of building identity, describing the ACA program, and then inviting the person to a meeting. To build identity, we offer a few examples of what our life was like before finding ACA. We talk about our feelings of isolation and uniqueness even as we worked hard at trying to fit in with others. We talk about hitting a bottom in relationships or at work. Next, we let the person we are trying to help read a copy of The Laundry List (Problem). At this point, the person will usually begin to share some of his or her own story if the person is wanting help. We ask the person to attend an ACA meeting as soon as possible.

As ACA members trying to help another person, we know that the program works and what the Steps can do for a person. They offer another way to live for the person wanting to live differently. The message of ACA states that ACA works, and it will work for anyone who can hit a bottom, surrender, and ask for and accept help. That's the tricky part. Most ACA's are self-sufficient. They attend meetings and learn the language but fail to ask for help. They suffer with an entrenched feeling of being different or frightened. But there is hope with willingness and with time.

Our promise is this: Any adult child seeking help from the effects of growing up in a dysfunctional home can find acceptance, honesty, and self-love in ACA. We are the fellowship who reaches out to the self-sufficient adult child winning employee awards and to the adult child in the institutional setting. We judge neither. We love both. We see them as the same because we know what they did not receive and what they seek. We also know what we have to offer. We know what we are doing. We are arresting the disease of family dysfunction at its generational nature. We focus on ourselves in ACA. To each adult child seeking this way of life, we say: "God will be there when you need God."

STEP TWELVE SPIRITUAL PRINCIPLES:

Love and Self-love

END NOTES

†ON PAGE 157: Read Tony's Fourth Step on p. 57 in The ACoA Experience: The Laundry List, by Tony A. with Dan F., 1991, HCI Publications.

†ON PAGE 168: Alcoholics Anonymous "Big Book," Step Four, p. 64, Fifth Edition.

†ON PAGE 283: Bill's Story, Alcoholics Anonymous "Big Book," p. 1, Fifth Edition.

†ON PAGE 284: Tony A. spent much of his life experiencing spiritual and mystical moments that he investigated and used to understand his life journey. One of the most powerful experiences occurred in 1978 when he wrote the 14 traits of The Laundry List. In his book, Tony wrote: "I felt that I was receiving inner guidance and direction as I wrote the words. It was a strange feeling." (The Laundry List: The ACoA Experience by Tony A. with Dan F., p. 12, 1991, HCI publications).

†ON PAGE 287: The concept of a spiritual bypass is attributed to Dr. Charles Whitfield and Barbara Whitfield. The Whitfields have written extensively on spiritual experiences and practical mysticism in addition to adult child recovery.

Chapter 8

The Solution:
Becoming Your Own Loving Parent

While becoming your own Loving Parent is at the core of healing from a neglectful childhood, it is also the gateway to the child within. In addition to the ACA Twelve Steps, this is The ACA Solution. By reparenting ourselves with gentleness, humor, love, and respect, we find our child within and true connection to a Higher Power. This is the God who does not abandon.

Through The Solution, we understand that we can release our biological parents. We can continue to separate from our family in body and mind. This is an important step for us as we develop our own identity that is different than our dysfunctional family role. The roles are family hero, scapegoat, lost child, or some other role. With The Solution, we are on our own, but we are not alone as we were when we were children. We have our ACA group, the fellowship, and a Higher Power to rely upon. With help and support, we learn what it means to be a Loving Parent to ourselves.

Becoming our own Loving Parent means that many of us come to believe that our Higher Power is our actual parent. Our biological parents were the couple needed to bring us into the world. The birth parents passed on the disease of family dysfunction that affects us in our lives today. Our Higher Power is the parent who gives us unconditional love and the way out of confusion and self-abuse. The Higher Power gave us the Twelve Steps.

Chapter Eight

Becoming our own Loving Parent – reparenting ourselves – requires that we accept the reality of the Inner Child. The child within is our original identity which knows how to love and trust freely. We become willing to consistently seek out and integrate the Inner Child into our lives. By making the effort, the child within becomes our guide to feelings, creativity, and spirituality. Through reparenting, we learn to listen for the child within. We can restage our childhood and teen years with gentleness by being a Loving Parent to ourselves. With the help of our ACA friends, we learn how to fill in the nurturing and attention we did not receive as children.

Many adult children can be lukewarm to the notion of a Loving Parent who lives inside of them and who is thoughtful and affirming. They can more easily identify with a Critical Parent who is harsh or who produces consistent self-doubt from within. Many of us can accept the idea of an inner Critical Parent but balk at the notion of a loving one.

Reparenting ourselves in a loving manner is not as unique as it sounds. Most of us were forced to parent ourselves as children. Our parents or relatives were not available. They were often not present with emotion or care. When they were present, they were not attentive. In their absence, we parented ourselves in a caring manner. As children, we met our own needs by preparing our own meals or doing housework. Some of us saved our own money and bought school supplies or small gifts for ourselves or a sibling. We knew our parents would forget or would trivialize birthdays or holidays. In some cases we parented a brother or sister with more care than our dysfunctional parents had to offer. We readied a sibling for school, reviewed homework, bought food, and read to a brother or sister at night. Even if we were not always kind to a brother or sister, we can still see moments when we cared for them or were concerned about them.

In some homes, we were provided with all we needed and told often that we were loved. However, our parents were adult children themselves out of touch with feelings and true intimacy. We seemed to have everything we needed, but we faced unreasonable expectations and cutting criticism. We were forced to parent ourselves into perfectionism to win family approval. We parented ourselves to make perfect grades and to appear self-sufficient and independent.

If we were violent or self-destructive as children, we can still see moments when we hoped for or believed in affectionate care. As adults, we can ask ourselves how a Loving Parent would care for a neglected child. We can do these caring things for ourselves.

Whatever our behavior was as children, we learned parenting skills or have the potential to learn. Our potential is a combination of survival skills and true love for ourselves. Our caring nature is a solid foundation for developing the Loving Parent inside each of us. We were willing to care for others, so why not for ourselves? Why not ask a Loving Parent to help us reclaim our childhood innocence and to live more gently today?

Parenting ourselves as children and reparenting ourselves as adults has important distinctions. We were alone as children, and we were forced to grow up too soon. We are not alone as we reparent ourselves in ACA. Through recovery, we use reparenting to connect with ourselves and others in a healthy manner. Reparenting also gives us a chance to reclaim our childhood years in a more supportive light. We can use reparenting to salvage our displaced childhood years. We can reclaim and restage those childhood years. We do not fictionalize our childhood, but we take the time to see how vulnerable, courageous, and loving we were as children. We can give ourselves the care we gave others. This is how we go forward in life by knowing where we came from and how we survived to get here.

Review of Key Terms

Before continuing with the chapter, we will review important terms that have been introduced thus far and which will be explained in greater detail going forward. The terms are:

1. **Inner Child** – The original person, being, or force which we truly are. Some ACA members call this the True Self.

2. **False Self** – The addicted or codependent self.

3. **Loving Parent or reparenting** – The inner parent we can develop from the part of us that took action to care for ourselves as children and which can be awakened in recovery.

4. **Critical Parent** – The hypercritical and judgmental voice that frequently finds fault in our thoughts and actions. This includes the frequent blaming of ourselves and others.

Loving Parent

What does it mean to become your own Loving Parent? The first step in reparenting ourselves involves recognizing the loving voice inside. Our experience shows that every adult child has love inside regardless of what the person says or believes. Love is there and it is original.

As we awaken the Loving Parent inside, we remember a simple slogan: "First Things First." Many adult children rush into Inner Child work without taking time to meet their inner, caring parent. As a result, some of us will struggle with finding the Inner Child until we take this necessary step. The Inner Child will not usually emerge until we establish our Loving Parent. In some cases, a sabotaging aspect of the Inner Child will emerge if we rush this phase of our recovery. This angry aspect of the Inner Child can overpower the newly developing Loving Parent and delay recovery.

There are many ways to awaken the Loving Parent inside, including writing a letter. We might say, "Dear, Loving Parent. I recognize you, and I am depending on you to help me be gentler with myself and more accepting of myself. Please challenge me to try if I am apathetic, but also help me give myself a break if I judge myself too harshly. Help me focus on progress rather than perfection." We keep the letter handy and read it often until it feels natural to make contact with this loving part of ourselves.

Reparenting ourselves can mean many things, but the central theme is that we are willing to challenge our critical, inner voice and to care for the child within. By reparenting ourselves, we lose interest in harming ourselves with addictions and compulsions. We remind ourselves that we have worth. We do this as often as it takes without thought of the repetition or how it might sound to another person.

With a Loving Parent active in our lives, we stop assuming we have done something wrong when we encounter situations that have no right or wrong outcome. On the other hand, if we are a compulsive blamer, we stop looking for people to blame for our decisions. As a Loving Parent to ourselves, we pause and listen for the things we tell ourselves on a daily basis without thinking about their meaning. Most of us judge, criticize, condemn, or minimize ourselves without realizing the harm we commit against our soul. Even the adult child who seems to blame others without mercy, secretly believes he or she has little value as a person.

If ACA was a fellowship about becoming your own Critical Parent, the meeting rooms would be empty. There would be no need for meetings or Step work because we already know how to be a Critical Parent to ourselves. We need no lesson here. We wrote the book on being hypercritical and abandoning of ourselves.

We awaken the Loving Parent inside by actively listening to what we tell ourselves about ourselves. We stop in mid-sentence if we are putting ourselves down or criticizing our thoughts or behaviors. We identify the source of the negativity which is the inner critic inside all adult children. We face this critical voice with affirmations that state who we truly are. Through reparenting ourselves, we reframe our mistakes as chances to learn or grow emotionally. This is a sign of becoming our own Loving Parent.

Another way in which we can become our own Loving Parent is to realize that we will not recover overnight. ACA recovery takes time. Even when we attend meetings, work the Steps, and use the telephone, we can still struggle at times. ACA is simple, but it takes a balanced effort and patience at times to make it through. We can do everything right and still wonder if we are making progress. A Loving Parent inside reminds us that we are good enough and that we are making progress.

We must realize most adult children arrive in ACA as the result of a crisis. Some of us have pulled down our worlds around us. That is the power of a codependent bottom. We arrive in ACA with relationship troubles, employment problems, or legal problems. Some of us cannot hold a job or we job-hop. We can owe large sums of money in child support, or we have towering credit card debt. Some of us are bankrupt due to our codependent and selfish behavior. Some of us may be facing prison due to our law-breaking ways. We can be impatient. We attend meetings and find some relief, but we struggle with seeing how meetings can pay an overdue electric bill or how working the Steps can fix a blown car engine. We want to talk about our problems rather than talk about the Twelve Steps or taking action. Our sponsor wisely reminds us that recovery comes first. We cannot fix our car, pay bills, or stay out of jail without recovery. We are asked to attend meetings and stay focused on our program. Our Loving Parent inside agrees with the sponsor.

We must be patient with ourselves during these times. If we try to pull it all together again too quickly, we can create stumbling blocks in our program. We can doubt the need to be gentle and loving to ourselves. For example, the adult child who has brought financial problems to the family might want to work overtime to make things right. Spurred by guilt, the mother or father will work extra hours that take away from the person's ACA program and from the family. Long work days without ACA meetings create a sense of isolation for the recovering adult child. We can take back our self-will and begin to run our own lives without asking for help. We forget that we can talk about our feelings. We forget that we are not alone. During these times, the critical inner parent usually reemerges in greater force. Our program suffers and the family or spouse begins to complain as well. We can begin to feel resentment and think about quitting ACA. With this attitude, talk of a Loving Parent seems foolish or unrealistic for some. In these moments we stop. We think about what we really want out of life. Do we want harmful stress and self-will or do we want to work toward self-love and serenity? A Loving Parent reminds us that we have a choice today. We can take care of ourselves. We can be patient with ourselves. We can pick up the "1,000-pound" telephone and talk to someone.

That said, we know that picking up the telephone or asking for help is not easy for us. Most adult children are compulsively self-reliant. We learned in childhood to avoid asking for help or that accepting help came with strings attached. We can try to work ACA alone or with limited input from a sponsor. The program that we fashion for ourselves is different than the ACA program, so we struggle. At the same time, other ACA members can be compulsive talkers who think that calling someone and talking at great length about their issues is asking for help. These adult children rarely take direction or accept helpful suggestions that would lead to change. Typically, these adult children do not consider the need for a Loving Parent or focused Step work.

A stumbling block in awakening our Loving Parent involves false loyalty. By reparenting ourselves, we can believe we are being disloyal to our families. We can think that talking about our lives and our needs is selfish and disloyal. We learned this false loyalty from childhood. Most of us were usually parented to be hypercritical and self-judging. We were taught to doubt ourselves so it became natural to believe that we are wrong, defective, or uninformed. A Loving Parent asks us to think about what we have been told about ourselves. A Loving Parent supports us in breaking the loyalty to unhealthy family messages and beliefs.

Affirmations are a key element in challenging our loyalty to a dysfunctional family and changing negative tapes in our heads. We select a few affirmations at the end of this chapter and write them down. When we begin our day, we can read the affirmations out loud to ourselves. We can take the affirmations with us to work as well and post them inconspicuously where we can see them throughout the day.

The Inner Child – True Self

Once we become comfortable with affirmations and sharing about being a Loving Parent, we are usually ready to make contact with our Inner Child. For many ACA members the child within represents our True Self. This is the part of us that is our original being. The Inner Child has original trust, original belief, and original love. The child within understands feelings and the language of a Higher Power. The Inner Child or True Self is present during our spiritual experiences and underpins our spiritual awakening.

The Inner Child also has all of the mental, physical, and historical memory of the family. One of the surest signs that an Inner Child exists is found in the definition of the term "adult child." An adult child is someone whose actions and decisions as an adult are guided by childhood experiences grounded in self-doubt or fear. Until we get help, we can operate from childhood fear that threatens our jobs and relationships. Under certain conditions, we can revert to childhood states that are age specific. Many adult children have said they feel like a child in a grown-up body. This is a clue to the Inner Child, but there is much more. The childhood fears expressed in adulthood are only a fraction of the full nature of the Inner Child.

Adult children who have experienced their Inner Child describe an inner being that is joyful and playful. There is a feeling of lightness and great optimism when the Inner Child is active in one's life. There is trust, spontaneity, and warmth. Many adult children can describe an Inner Child's voice, physical appearance, and likes and dislikes. Meditation and consistent writing with the opposite or non-dominant hand seem to reveal the greater presence of the Inner Child.

Family dysfunction drives the Inner Child into hiding, leaving states of fear that wander the adult's soul. While the Inner Child or True Self can be the spark of our creativity, we must also remember the child is a deeply hurt part of ourselves. Some of us believe the child within can sabotage our current relationships through the fear of abandonment and shame. Through recovery, we have learned that our Inner Child has an array of protective tools. The tools, however, can lead to self-harm and great emotional pain. We can sabotage ourselves as we seek help. This is a paradox of sorts. The Inner Child or True Self is our original wholeness who believed in people without effort. The Inner Child freely gave love and trust without effort. Yet, as a result of abuse, an angry Inner Child can fuel self-destructive behaviors that we seem powerless to stop at times.

An angry child within can exhibit feelings and behaviors of crippling fear and extreme dishonesty. There can be blistering rage. These feelings or behaviors were necessary to survive the unhealthy family. As adults, when we encounter situations that resemble our childhood experiences, we can be rageful. We can seem to lash out at people or co-workers for no cause. We have shocked people with rage, which comes from this hurt child within. We feel embarrassed by our rage, but we also feel powerless to change. We feel sabotaged. The good news is that this hurt child within will listen if we take the time to build trust and intimacy from within.

Tools and Techniques for Connecting with our Inner Child

By keeping the focus on ourselves, we will find freedom from our critical self as well as our addictive and destructive behaviors. The ACA program provides us with tools of recovery. This chapter outlines the steps we take and the tools we use to reparent ourselves and to connect with the child within. Connecting with our Inner Child brings greater integration within ourselves and moves us closer to our Higher Power. Connecting with the Inner Child also helps us remember. One of the rules of a dysfunctional family is "don't remember." In ACA, we seek a full remembrance or the most complete remembrance we can obtain of the growing up years. Our memory holds the key to living in the present with a full range of feelings, hope, and spirituality.

First we must be willing. With willingness, we can overcome self-doubt or the sense that we are not making progress. We apply the tools of recovery and make progress at our own pace. We remain free of stagnation by avoiding unwillingness or inaction.

With willingness we attend ACA meetings, work the Twelve Steps, and develop a support system. The support can include ACA members, a healthy socializing group, or family members supportive of our recovery. In ACA, we learn to seek out people who are honest with us and understand what we are trying to accomplish in recovery. Through our Loving Parent, we can feel confident that we can select supportive people. Supportive people tend to be engaged in recovery and are sincere about living differently than in the past. Supportive people are caring people who are intrigued about living. They can notice the wonder in small things or appreciate great accomplishments without jealousy. In addition to being sincere, such people generally talk about feelings and avoid judging others or putting others down. This is the support we seek and learn to feel comfortable with.

Tools for connecting with the Inner Child can be counseling, journaling, and guided meditation in addition to attending ACA meetings. Childhood pictures are a great tool to connect with the child that still dwells within us.

As mentioned, there is non-dominant handwriting in which we write out a question to our Inner Child with our dominant hand (the hand we use to sign our name). Then we write the response to the question by placing the pen in the opposite hand. We might write out: "Hello, Little Johnny or Little Marie. I would like to talk to you and to introduce myself. How have you been? I am here to listen to you if you would like to talk." Write down any response with the non-dominant hand. The thoughts may be random or incomplete sentences, but we write down what comes to mind without judging ourselves. We keep an open mind. We do not try to force solutions or results. We will get results if we are patient and consistent with the exercise.

After introducing ourselves to the child within, we can ask other questions. We write out the question with our dominant hand and write the reply with the other hand. We can talk to others about how they connected with their Inner Child, but we are mindful to be true to our own connection. We do not have to impress anyone or embellish any response. This exercise can literally speak for itself when practiced often.

Other tools for connecting with the Inner Child can involve drawing or painting pictures of our family. We can go to our old school house and sketch the playground, or we can visit a favorite spot and draw or doodle. Sketching our family may reveal insights as to how we felt growing up. We do not have to be professional artists to do this exercise. Stick figures can work just as well. Some pictures may help express what words cannot. The drawings can be done with our dominant or nondominant hand. There is no limit on what scenes can be drawn.

We can listen to music or dance as part of connecting with the Inner Child or True Self. Moving our bodies to music (or without music) can stir memories and feelings. Listening to various forms of music can help us tap into memories and feelings as well. Nursery rhymes, hymns, or songs our parents listened to will help us remember our childhood and the child within.

These activities tend to access areas of our subconscious that we have not visited for many years. Feelings and memories will emerge if we are consistent with these methods. For many of us we learned to tune out our true feelings because it was too painful to admit we were neglected, abused, or mistreated in various ways. We locked away events of our lives. As adults we learn to free ourselves from our self-imposed prisons. We give ourselves permission to feel and to be truly alive.

Some of us choose to do this work with a sponsor, counselor, or recovery partner. The results of Inner Child work and reparenting pay off in clarity about our childhood years. With time, we can feel more at peace inside, and we will have a better grasp of our feelings and our choices. We are on the way to becoming whole and healthy human beings. We can connect with a power greater than ourselves and find balance.

Identifying Our Inner Critical Parent

All adult children arrive at ACA with hypercritical messages in their minds. We can judge ourselves or others without mercy. These are the "old tapes" that can pilot our lives onto the jagged rocks of self-destruction. The old tapes can be personified as the inner Critical Parent. This is the critical voice who blames and belittles or who judges and undermines. Becoming aware of the Critical Parent is essential for the development of the Loving Parent.

Many of us do not become fully aware of these negative messages until we stop long enough to hear them. They are there. Each day these messages can create self-doubt, self-disgust, depression, or panic. This is the inner voice or feeling that tells us that we are not good enough, smart enough, or worthy enough for our job or our relationships. There is also the critical inner voice of blaming others.

This unchallenged Critical Parent is the barrier that keeps us from experiencing wholeness and happiness. We can identify this inner critic by keeping a notepad handy for several days. As we go through the day, we pay attention to our attitude about ourselves or others. We jot down negative thoughts, doubts, and fears as they arise. Judging others and comparing ourselves to others is the classic sign of an inner Critical Parent. Judging someone's clothing or how the person speaks is a sign of the Critical Parent. Judging ourselves harshly for mistakes is the Critical Parent. Comparing ourselves to others financially, physically, or intellectually is the Critical Parent. Assuming we are wrong when something happens that is not our fault is this inner critic. Blaming others or saying "I'm sorry" often is the Critical Parent. Gossiping is this inner critic.

After identifying the Critical Parent, we step up our efforts to delete many of the old messages or to turn down the volume on the negative tapes. By practicing affirmations, we begin to lessen some of the harshness that we have lived with before ACA. These affirmations can be spoken or written as part of the Tenth Step inventory. This is the daily inventory in which we look at our behavior and make amends for harms we have done to others, but we also look at what we have done right or what is positive in ourselves. We can write out affirmations such as: "My feelings are okay." "I am human." "I make mistakes, but I am not a mistake." "I don't have to be perfect." "It is okay to know who I am." We do these affirmations often because creating the Critical Parent took time. It took years of practice to be so critical or doubtful of ourselves. We cannot change such negativity in one week or one month, but we make a beginning with affirmations. We ask our Higher Power for help as well. After awhile, our Loving Parent awakens, and we are comfortable with affirmations and with believing them. We begin to have the choice of whether we will believe a negative thought, or instead believe a positive message from the program.

Eliminating the inner Critical Parent is not the goal. We seek to integrate this part of ourselves so that we won't go overboard trying to eliminate all negatives from our lives. Eliminating all discomforts or negatives is not practical. It is foolhardy at best. Learning to deal with some internal negativity with the support of an ACA group is healthy. But first, we use the full strength of the program to deal with the inner Critical Parent. We can tell the internal critic to be quiet as we learn to think differently about ourselves.

Some of us use a Twelve Step template to address our Critical Parent. In Step One, for instance, we recognize that we are powerless over this Critical Parent and its judgments. In Steps Two and Three, we ask our Higher Power for guidance. We ask for the strength to turn over the false power wielded by the Critical Parent. We trust that something greater than ourselves can help us release our old way of thinking about things. With Steps Four and Five, whenever we do something that distresses us, we can immediately wrap our arms around ourselves in a hug and say, "Well, we don't like how that went, so we will learn a lesson from it and do better next time." That is what a Loving Parent would do for his or her child within.

With Steps Six and Seven, we ask for the help we need from our Higher Power to integrate the Critical Parent into our lives. Integration is a sign that we recognize that the critical inner voice has some value and should not be totally eliminated. Our critical nature must be toned down, but we also recognize it guided us through dependent times. We cannot live life without judgment, but we seek judgment that takes the course of discernment and fairness instead of comparing ourselves to others. We ask for patience and guidance in tempering the inner critic into usefulness. Facing our own self-criticism with the help of a Higher Power prepares us to face criticism and challenge from others.

With Steps Eight and Nine, we make our amends for any behavior caused by acting under the influence of the Critical Parent. Finally with Steps Ten through Twelve we stay mindful and present. We inventory ourselves, we meditate, and we help others. We acknowledge our own behavior. We ask God, as we understand God, to continue providing us with willingness to love ourselves.

ACA Experience: Loving Parent and Inner Child

The following vignettes offer a variety of ACA experiences involving the Loving Parent and the Inner Child. These brief stories were voluntarily recorded during many years at ACA meetings, conventions, retreats, and by invitation. Since the founding of the adult child movement, the ACA fellowship has taken the lead in developing this new frontier of recovery. ACA members have some of the most comprehensive experience with reparenting themselves and with sketching out the existence of the Inner Child. These shares are the fellowship's first in-depth publishing on this topic. The stories represent honesty, open-mindedness, and willingness. The experiences reveal how ACA members are thoughtful in their approach to identifying the Loving Parent and Inner Child. The reader will see that the realm of Inner Child work, in particular, can be tender and humorous, or it can be volatile and unsettling in some cases.

What is a Loving Parent?

Loving Parent #1

When I got involved in ACA in the 1980s, the concept of a Loving Parent was real new. We used affirmations, the Steps, and journaling, which I now believe to be a form of reparenting. The affirmations and the feelings work set the groundwork for me to counter my critical inner voice. This was a Loving Parent of sorts. The affirmations reminded me that I can do things right. I can give myself a break. This confounded my negative thinking, which had run wild before ACA. I have a Loving Parent today who is compassionate and funny. My Loving Parent inside does not criticize me when I pray or do things for myself. Reparenting myself with gentleness and self-love is as natural as being critical once was.

Loving Parent #2

My Loving Parent is a gentle disciplinarian, the person inside of me who lets me know when I have had enough of something. A Loving Parent is the person who is able to define how much is enough. She says, "You've had enough now, and I will help you to stop doing this." It is the part of me that says, "Here is the reason why I'm stopping you. You don't need more."

When I realized that there will never be enough food, or money, or love to please me, I could just let that go. My Loving Parent helps me to define or name my emotions so that I know what they are. My Loving Parent helps me choose what to wear so I'm comfortable. My Loving Parent helps me to be comfortable.

Loving Parent #3

A Loving Parent is someone who guides you and who takes you by the hand. When you make a mistake, a Loving Parent hugs you and says, "It's all right. You don't have to do this. It's okay if you don't meet my expectations for you. It's okay to try and do the best you can. Here are some ways you can do that. Just do the best you can."

The ineffective parent would say, "Just do it." But do what? I never knew where to start because I never saw things done correctly. I never had the self-esteem to believe I could accomplish anything.

Loving Parent # 4

A Loving Parent is someone who stops and pays attention to the Inner Child, who sits with her, who makes time for her, who acknowledges her feelings when she is happy or sad. A Loving Parent respectfully touches the child and kisses the child, but does not demand that the child kiss back if she does not want to. A Loving Parent doesn't tell the Child she is stupid for the things she feels or thinks. My sponsor gave me some tools to use to talk with my Inner Child. I visualize this little child. I don't see a face, but I see this little child. I bring her onto my lap, hold her, and respect her. I even ask my angry child, "Why are you angry today?" That's what a Loving Parent is. I'm trying to be that for myself today.

What is an Inner Child?

Inner Child #1

I am still discovering what an Inner Child is. In the beginning, I thought the Inner Child might only be a collection of childhood memories, but something happened that makes me believe my Inner Child is a distinct entity. It involves writing. When I think only of childhood memories, not much happens. But when I start writing and start asking questions, things start happening. But I also have to listen. I have heard a little boy's voice in my mind when I do opposite-hand writing. This little boy seems to answer questions when I ask him how he is doing or if he would like to talk. The voice is consistent in tone and attitude each time we talk. He doesn't seem interested in memories, but he will answer questions about them if I ask. He likes to talk. I have lots of notes with my opposite-hand. Some of the things are simple. He likes his bicycle and making mud balls. Other things he says are shocking. I am still thinking over some of the things he has mentioned.

Inner Child #2

It's easier for me to define an Inner Child than an Inner Parent because I'm more in touch with my Inner Child's misbehaving. There is a part of me that does not want to obey the rules, that does not want to follow directions, and does not want to do her chores. At times she knows more than anybody else, and conversely knows nothing and is very frightened. She is afraid what she is doing is wrong, but she is unable to stop.

My Inner Child also loves to play, sidestep responsibility, sing, walk in the woods, talk with others, play with clothes, create, and play on the computer. My Inner Child has energy I don't always know how to channel, but I'm learning.

Inner Child #3

"Inner Child" is a technical term in the field of psychology, a definition of a personality, not a real person. To me the Inner Child is my dissociated self, the child that would have been were it not for the beatings. The Inner Child is the person who really wanted to go to the beach, excel at sports, and build model airplanes and ships, but he never learned because no one showed him how to do it. I grew up physically into an adult, but my Inner Child never learned to express himself.

My Inner Child is a person within me who is sick and who is afraid of me and all adults because he never got his expectations met; he never got the love, he never got the nurturing that a child should get. So the Inner Child is still seeking that affirmation. It's the child, the children of different ages within me saying, "I didn't get this at ten years old; I didn't get this at twelve years old; I didn't get this at sixteen years old. I'm mad. I'm angry and I don't know what to do about it, but I'm going to get my parents for it; I'm going to get everybody for it because my parents didn't give this to me."

Inside me the Child is still residing there, still waiting for something to bridge the gap, to integrate with the adult. Sometimes my adult hears the Child, and I say to the Child, "We can make it through. It may be difficult, but we'll get by this."

It took years for this to develop, and it's going to take many more years for me to overcome it. For me the answer is going to meetings. If a meeting folds, then I find another to attend. I can't let the world destroy me. It's important for me to attend ACA meetings so I can learn and my Inner Child can heal. I have learned to recognize my Inner Children. I have learned they have needs, and I am learning how I can satisfy those needs.

Inner Child #4

I feel very strongly about my lost innocence and the forfeited innocence of all children who are forced to survive by any means necessary. My little, adapted self protected my vulnerable children inside, so they are there waiting with so many stories to tell – joys that they could never express, horrors that were inconceivable, and all that had to be "forgotten" to win sufficient love and approval to sustain the life force on a daily basis.

Inner Child #5

I was unclear of what the Inner Child was when I heard about it from a counselor. I am from a place where this stuff seems far out. This was really odd at first, but I was open-minded and willing. One of the things that helped the most was that no one pushed me to do it. I did not feel pressure to conform or to impress someone. All I needed was willingness and a pencil.

How Does the Inner Child Connect with a Higher Power?

Inner Child Connecting with a Higher Power #1

I heard how the Inner Child or True Self is the way that we connect with our Higher Power, so I wrote out some questions for my Inner Child. I said: "Do you believe in a Higher Power?" He wrote back: "Yes. God is in the stars." I said: "Can you help me connect with God or let God in?" He wrote back: "It's not a big deal. Just take in air." I said: "Breathe?" He wrote: "Yes."

I asked him again: "Will you help me let in a Higher Power?" My Inner Child wrote: "God's already in."

Inner Child Connecting with a Higher Power #2

A wise person told me that the Laundry List represents a personality that cannot truly know a Higher Power. My Laundry-List "self" rejects God or can only know God through an intellectual understanding. Unless I become like a child I cannot know my Higher Power. The child within is my True Self and knows God, as I understand God.

Chapter Eight

Inner Child Connecting with a Higher Power #3

I talk to myself aloud. I do this everywhere, including at work. Just recently I've struck up a nightly conversation with God. I haven't done this in a long time. He helped me speak to my Inner Child about my feelings and my fears, when I really want to be numb.

It is a conscious, on-going conversation that I have with my Inner Child. That is the only way I can tangibly grasp my problems instead of denying them. This is the way I discuss my feelings, my problems, and my plans for resolving my problems as I work toward their resolution. Voicing these things is how I communicate with my Inner Child.

How Many Inner Children Do You Have?

Inner Child or Children #1

I've read about Multiple Personality Disorders (MPD). A Multiple Personality Disorder is the state of being where different personalities coexist in the same body. One persona may or may not recognize that another person or persons are there, too. Each person has a different personality, different penmanship, different everything. He may even be a different gender from the original person. I don't have MPD, but it gives me some idea of my Inner Child.

My form of dissociation is embodied in the concept of an Inner Child with various stages of stymied development at different ages. I have so many different children within me that I can't identify with only one Inner Child. I was abused before I had words I could use to save memories.

I didn't have the love and the attention I needed, and I was beaten severely. As a result I found it difficult when I started growing up to find my identity. I remember lying in bed many times as a child wondering, "Who am I? Did I come from another planet? Was I put on this earth as a test-model, a guinea pig?" I really felt I wasn't real, that I was just some experiment.

I can't remember anything that happened before I was five years old. I do not know if I was sexually abused, but my sister was definitely abused many times. I may have witnessed it. That may have been a trauma I could not cope with and compartmentalized, and then severed from the rest of my being until I had the ability to understand it later. I may have wondered why my sister was treated that way. I may have thought, "I need to help her, but I can't."

There seems to be more than one part of me demanding recognition. If there was only one personality within me I could handle it. When there are so many clamoring, it's hard to deal with them. They are all envious of one another. They all want to be taken care of, and they all have different needs.

Inner Child or Children #2

Although I came into recovery with only one or two childhood memories, I now have a very clear picture of the little children within me of various ages that got left behind. It's a long and difficult road requiring untiring patience and a lot of humility. For me it is a process of differentiating between the feelings that tell the stories of the true Inner Child, and the terror of the little girl who I became in order to survive.

I call my adapted self, Little Me. She is about six years old. She doesn't believe that Big Me will be there. She also thinks I am trying to eliminate her when I suggest there may be alternative solutions to the one she has used so successfully in the past. It makes her very sad. She has no other reason to exist as she sees it. She feels sad that I don't seem to recognize the wonderful care she has provided over almost thirty years. She is angry that I am often so ungrateful for her efforts.

I see my recovery as a process of developing an internal dialogue and an active negotiation with this little child. Often I picture her, hands on hips saying, "No, you can't come past" or "I don't believe you are going to be able to take care of me." Sometimes she is so frightened that she has knives. Recovery is taking her hand when she has had her say and going with her to the bundle on the floor. This bundle contains a little Baby Me who is battered. It is sometimes difficult to extricate the battered little baby girl from the protective grasp of the 6-year-old in me. After all, the conditions for her acceptance in the family were that she could never reveal the shameful feelings.

Winning her trust is taking time. With each new discovery the process must begin again. As the stories become revealed, the 6-year-old endeavors to silence the true voice in this untiring way. Sometimes she would rather die than to reveal the truth. Discovering her presence behind my suicidal impulse has been very liberating. My adapted self needs so much understanding and deserves so much gratitude. Without her I would have died from the utter emotional deprivation I suffered at the hands of my parents. My darling little girl. Thank you.

How Did You Meet Your Inner Child?

How I Met my Inner Child #1

When I was a child, I noticed that adults didn't seem to remember what it was like to be a child. I told myself I was never going to forget what it feels like to be a child. I don't remember everything at each age, but I'm far more aware than other adults seem to be. Perhaps it is because of my childhood vow to remember, so I would never mistreat a child the way I was mistreated. I'm not real clear on the idea of an Inner Child, but I'm aware of living life from the standpoint of a child. I'm also aware I feel as if I need to disguise my awareness.

How I Met my Inner Child #2

I got in touch with my Inner Child through meditation and writing with my non-dominant hand. I sat quietly and tried to coax this other personality to come out and share what he thinks or feels. Like pushing the planchette around a Ouija Board, it is unclear to me if I am deluding myself or if a dialogue is actually taking place. Regardless, I found it to be helpful. It certainly brought back memories more vivid than I would have chosen. I really relived some of those uncomfortable moments of my childhood. I found I could pinpoint where and when the emotional damage occurred.

How I Met my Inner Child #3

My therapist guided me through a meditation exercise where I went far, far down in the elevator. A door opened into a big hallway. I walked down the hallway and saw a light. I walked towards the light. I saw a door. I opened it and walked into a room. In the corner was a small child. I recognized it as being my Inner Child. I walked over to the child and introduced myself.

How I Met my Inner Child #4

I met my Inner Child through affirmations and guided meditations in counseling. I had to seek him out many times because he was covered up with thick layers of learned helplessness and rage. I was not sure he was even there, but I was willing to find out.

My Inner Child was very defeated but still holding out hope. When I look back, I can see how my family seemed to do all they could to ensure that I would be dependent upon them, and then they blamed me for not holding jobs and for mooching off them as an adult. I lived with my parents until I was 25 years old. I borrowed money from them and stole from them the whole time. I couldn't hold a job, or I worked sporadically. Not much changed until I got help and moved out. When I connected with my Inner Child in ACA, he thought he was lazy and no good. He seemed encased in a belief system that told him he could not do anything at all. I noticed a little chink in his protective armor when I reminded him that he was very bright. He had figured something out. He figured out how to survive a violent, alcoholic upbringing. That got his attention, but it was many months before he would talk to me.

That was years ago. My Inner Child now trusts me and believes in recovery. He is eager to try many things. He thinks he can do everything, so I have to help him understand what he can do and can't do for now. But he thinks he can do everything. This is cool.

What Happened When You Met Your Inner Child?
Nothing. I'm Still Blocked #1

I've really struggled with my Inner Child work. I've done meditation. I've done writing with my non-dominant hand. I remember hearing an ACA speaker at a convention years ago. When his therapist asked him about his childhood, he began to tell her about being on the high school football team. She stopped him and asked him again to tell her about his childhood. He broke down crying because he didn't remember anything that happened to him in his childhood. The same is true for me.

He Wanted To Kill Me #2

The second time I did a meditation of traveling deep, deep down into the earth in an elevator and approached my Inner Child, I saw an apparition of a child come out of me. It grabbed me and stabbed me repeatedly. I told my therapist it wanted to kill me. My psychoanalyst said: "This could mean your Inner Child wants you to change your life, to kill the life you had and replace it with the life you want to live. It's a beginning, not an end." That was my realization of the tremendous conflict between my Inner Child and me.

He Told Me What He Wants From Me #3

My Inner Child is about five. He's a very nice person. He's patient. He accepts neglect and abuse with some grace. When I asked him what he wants from me, he said he wants to be loved and protected. That's what I try to do now.

How Does Your Inner Child Sabotage You?

Inner Child Sabotage #1

Having an Inner Child is like having a subconscious experience. He seems to know what he wants and what he wants to do, right or wrong. He gets mad when I ignore him for a long time, and then little things start to go wrong. I notice this at work.

I work at a job that is not the career I want. Even when I put my heart and soul into my work and do the best job I can do, still little things go wrong. That reminds me that this is not the job I really want. It is as if my Inner Child says, "I'll let you masquerade as much as it takes to survive."

But it is really just a truce between my Inner Child and me. I feel my Inner Child wants what I want, but he wants it now. I have to tell him: "If I can't get that job now, I'll give you a deadline of when I will have it." Then I have to uphold my promise to him.

Inner Child Sabotage #2

I heard a lady share at an ACA meeting about a radio interview she had listened to. She mentioned an author, who said that everyone lives in a fourteen-room mansion. In this mansion they have a special place where they make love. They have the backyard where they take special care of the flowers and the lawn. There's the living room where they play with their favorite pets. In the basement they quietly build the bomb to blow it all up.

I've frequented that basement all too often in my life. I'm fully aware of my tendency to sabotage myself. I still catch myself in the act of lighting the fuse. It's getting to be less of a threat now, thanks to the tools I've discovered through the program.

When I catch myself inching toward those cellar steps, I get to a phone and call my sponsor or a friend, or I'll get to a meeting and share about what's going on, or write of my predicament relentlessly in my journal. My response to fears these days is one of action, not reaction. Now, don't get me wrong. I still find myself sabotaging, but a lot less often.

How Do I Build Trust with my Inner Child?

Trust #1

Building trust is about being worthy of trust. Like a flesh-and-blood real child, my Inner Child responds to me just as a real child would in similar circumstances. I have to work at the relationship. I have to make time in my life to talk with my Inner Child, to listen to what she needs, wants, and values. I need to get to the heart of the message and respond to the need behind the want or demand.

When she takes over my conscious thoughts with a pink luxury automobile, curls up in the fetal position, or punches me from inside for boundary violations, I have to stop, and hear what she is saying directly as well as what she isn't verbalizing. Generally she wants me to hug her, talk to her, play with her, address her fears, and be reasonable in my expectations of her.

I have to know my adult limitations and make only promises to her that I can keep. I need to follow through on my commitments to her. I have to meet her needs as well as my adult needs. If I don't give her the attention she needs or wants, she takes over completely and neither of us gets what we want.

In talking with her I have to firmly guide her toward healthy, rational choices and behavior using explanation and negotiation. I have to set and enforce reasonable boundaries with her. I stop myself from abusing her through neglect, actions, and words. I keep her safe from the abuse of others each and every time my boundaries are violated by standing up, making my truth known, and holding my ground.

Trusting others was never my issue; my issue was in trusting me. Without boundaries, I had no identity, no values, and no morality. I had to construct an identity by taking my opinions about what was right and wrong in the behavior of others, adopting that behavior, and acting "as if" I always believed or acted in this manner until it became automatic to me. Having built my identity, I then established and enforced my boundaries consistently and conscientiously. My Inner Child knows she can now depend on me to listen to her without fear.

How Do I Help my Inner Child Build Self-Esteem?
Inner Child Self-Esteem #1

I tell my Inner Child his feelings are right. I help him understand he is correctly reading situations, but that there are better ways to deal with setbacks. For example, there is cutting someone off on the freeway after they cut me off or sharing with my boss my true opinions about a recent directive.

I have given my Inner Child what he wanted in the various life stages. I try to be sincere with him, so he can trust me. If he trusts me, he won't sabotage me. I'm having trouble with the idea of encouraging my Inner Child's self-esteem when he is banging his knife and fork on the table demanding immediate gratification. I don't know how to maintain some semblance of being an adult and deal with this right now. Maybe I will be able to do this in time.

Inner Child Self-Esteem #2

I help my Inner Child build her self-esteem in a variety of ways. I affirm her identity every day by telling her, eye-ball to eye-ball in a mirror, "You are loved. You are lovable." I encourage, affirm, and reinforce her when she tries to learn or do something new. I show her how to do things before I ask her to do them by herself, or I take her to a class or hire an instructor to teach us if we don't know how to do something we want or need to do. I help her make a plan to get to a goal, create incremental objectives that lead to the goal, and then help her take the baby steps by cheering her on as she takes those steps. I reward her for trying and finishing. If she does not complete the goal, I tell her she did a great job of trying, and now we need to decide if we want to make a better plan with even smaller steps or if we want to do something different.

My Inner Child and I have an agreement that if someone crosses our boundary-lines, she gives me a tiny tap from inside to alert me to incoming salvos. It is then my adult job to respectfully confront the abuser and resolve the situation amicably if possible. If not, then it is my adult job to decide what to do about this situation that is both moral and legal. That may mean deciding if the fight is worth fighting at all. If not, we walk away with the full understanding there are some things that just are not worth dying for, that there is a time to stand and a time to walk away.

My Inner Child today feels safe enough to speak freely to me. We have a good relationship now that I honor her and she honors me. We have mutual respect for one another, for our strengths. We have forgiveness in our hearts for our weaknesses. We are both working to keep the relationship growing.

Chapter Eight

How I Validate My Inner Child
Validate #1

When I work with non-dominant handwriting exercises, the responses and comments of my Inner Child are sometimes so unexpected that it seems like a separate person is inside me. But in conversations with my Inner Child, she reminds me that we are one. When I harm my adult self I am harming my Inner Child. And when I nurture and protect my Inner Child I am healing my adult self.

Not long after meeting my Inner Child, she pointed out two of my frequent remarks that hurt her feelings. I've always criticized myself for "crying for no reason," and I've brushed aside compliments by saying "girls like me are a dime a dozen." I never paid any attention to either comment until my Inner Child asked me to stop. She informed me that she doesn't cry without reason, and that little girls like her are not just cheap and common. I stopped saying those things to be kind to my Inner Child, but my adult self has felt the benefits, too.

Validate #2

I just feel my feelings. I learned from my mother at an early age that it is all right to express what I feel. I try not to judge the way I feel because that invalidates my Inner Child. I have been sad, or maybe intense is a more accurate description, in recent times, so I've been crying. That is me. Lately I've been judging rather than accepting my crying, and that is wrong. I give myself the freedom to express my feelings. I feel good when I listen to a good song, read poetry, or watch a really good movie. Those are times when my feelings come up, and I am able to express them easily. My Inner Child expresses himself often, and that is the way I validate my Inner Child.

Validate #3

The best validation I can give my Inner Child is through my sense of humor. In my family humor was sarcasm. When I recognized that sarcasm is hurtful and is really anger thinly disguised by flippant or hurtful remarks, I began to come out of a very dark period of my life.

The humor I express today is gentle, relaxed, and playful. It is the reflection of the little girl who lives in me. Since I've been in the program I smile at people more. I speak to people more. This is the positive, loving humor that has always been there. It always will be there because my little girl inside will always be with me.

How I Negotiate With My Inner Child
Negotiate #1

For me a key word is balance. I know that a child part of me needs a caring parent. There needs to be a hierarchy within my own psyche or my own soul. If I stay in my child too much of the time, things don't get done. I behave irresponsibly. My adult is excessively responsible, so the negotiation for me is to listen to my Inner Child, but at the same time take care of adult business. Ultimately I have to integrate my Inner Children of different ages with my adult being in order to come out as a whole person. For now I just have to pay attention. That's how it works for me.

Negotiate #2

This program has helped me learn how to nurture my Inner Child. She was so frightened when I first got into recovery. Now she's squawking constantly and won't leave me alone. One day I could feel my chest heaving from heavy breathing, and I became so angry about this that I hit myself in the chest. Immediately I felt a big, old, hard lump. I thought, "Oh no!" I had been treating her like I was treated as a child. So I said to her, "I won't treat you badly anymore." Slowly I felt the lump disappear. My Inner Child had answered. I decided it was time to learn to take care of her.

Chapter Eight

How I Celebrate My Inner Child
Celebrate #1

I have a hard time identifying with the term "celebrate." It implies pure joy, something I just don't know well. I have a hard time participating in any celebration.

When I was six or seven I went to my friend's birthday party. I didn't see an empty chair at the huge table where twenty children sat, so I walked into another room. A lady wrapping presents in that room told me to go into the party, but I knew there was no room for me there, so I walked into the kitchen. The boy's mother was preparing food for the party, so I knew I couldn't bother her, either. Then I left and went home. That is a big pattern with me. There is a feeling that I don't belong or that the celebration is not for me.

When I play games on my computer or visit websites, that is how I begin to celebrate. The jokes I find and forward to all my friends is a kind of celebration. To me celebration is the sharing of joy. I try to find things I really enjoy, and I share them. This makes me happy.

Celebrate #2

I don't do a lot of celebrating. When I think of celebrating, I think of joy, frivolity, or silliness. I am not outwardly like that. My humor is intellectual or esoteric. It is more thoughtful than silly. It may be that being able to celebrate who my little girl is, is really more of an acknowledgement of her gifts, or her value in my life, or her value of having acquired the skills or the perseverance to get through a difficult childhood.

When I look back at pictures of me, especially those in adolescence, few capture a look of happiness on my face. I've always been an athlete. I've always been relatively graceful. In spite of that I felt terribly awkward. I felt I didn't belong there. That period of time is hard to celebrate. I also took some phenomenal risks then. I was a shy, fearful, sad young woman with a willingness to stick my neck out. Celebrating that ability or willingness is something I do when I make up my happiness and gratitude lists. When I look back on a period of time, I remember what made me smile or what made me feel good. I remember it by writing it down and reliving it by thinking it through. These are some of the ways I try to celebrate who I am, who I have been, and how I got here.

Integrating My Inner Child With My Adult

Integrate #1

Total integration of my Inner Child with my adult would be a continuous, shared decision-making between them throughout the day. When I make decisions that I later regret or don't follow through on, I think that is my Inner Child saying, "No, I don't agree with that decision you made."

I feel my Inner Child is totally integrated now. I've always felt connected to my Higher Power. I lived in an area when I was growing up where there were horse trails through the trees, fields, and grass behind people's homes. It was fun to walk around there on Saturday or Sunday. It was like a communion with God. That is a connection I've always felt. My Inner Child has an understanding of what God's will is. Me, I only know what God's will was after looking at the result of my decisions. I also get confused trying to figure out what is God's will and what is my Inner Child's will.

I'm the same person I was when I was six or seven years old, but it's the experiences I've had that make me an adult. Those experiences have shown me the way to use principles to make my decisions. The principles should determine the choices I make.

Integrate #2

Growing up I didn't trust how I felt. I learned not to feel. In program, therapy, and reading for my profession I learned to listen to the wisdom of my Inner Child. I learned to trust that I know more about myself than anyone could, short of my Higher Power. Listening to my Inner Child and acting on the information with confidence that I get from her has helped me bring together or develop a stronger soul or persona.

In the past, when I was afraid I either did not recognize my fear, or I told myself I had no reason to be afraid. Today when I feel uncomfortable or unsafe, I take action to make myself more comfortable or safer. I honor who I am. I pay attention to my intuition, the gut feelings I get. If I honor the information and act on it, it almost always comes out better for me in the end. This is, to me, the integration of self and spirituality.

What We Can Expect from Reparenting Ourselves

These shares represent an array of learning as we become a Loving Parent to ourselves while also exploring the world of the child within. This is the ACA Solution. These shares show the feelings and spiritual guidance that come from connecting with the Inner Child. These shares also raise the question of recognizing the Loving Parent and developing this inside parent for our own well being. The Critical Parent is developed and entrenched in most adult children, so it takes effort and focus to develop a Loving Parent who can connect with the Inner Child on a consistent and meaningful level. With a Loving Parent, we stop harming ourselves. We disrupt self-harming behavior more quickly.

With the Steps and by reparenting ourselves, we can further remove the "buttons" that have been pushed by others to manipulate us or to get a reaction out of us. Through a Loving Parent inside, we gain greater independence from codependence. We find the skills and support we need to become independent adults. Healthy adults understand they are responsible for themselves and their actions, but they can also rely on others for help and feedback. Healthy adults develop friendships and relationships with people they can trust. These people form the basis of our support system. These relationships may include members of our family of origin or they may not.

With reparenting, we integrate the Steps, Inner Child, and our Higher Power into our daily lives. The person within us that our Higher Power created will emerge safe at last to love and be loved. The Inner Child and service to others will keep us awake spiritually. Along with the Steps, they will underpin our spiritual experiences.

Our support system may involve many different people in different capacities. By working the Steps and coming out of isolation, we are learning to be more honest with ourselves and others. In nurturing healthy relationships, we see our ACA recovery seeping into other areas of our life. We begin to know what it feels like to have someone accept us for who we truly are. We discover that some of our co-workers or acquaintances seem more comfortable with us and become more interested in our lives. They become an increasingly significant part of our support system. We notice that others begin to seek us out to become part of their own support systems. We find out what we like and what we can live without. We lighten up.

Chapter Eight Exercises

Loving Parent Questions

1. What is a Loving Parent? What is an Inner Child?

2. If you can envision a Critical Parent inside, is it possible to envision a Loving Parent, who is there as well waiting to step forward? Are you willing to explore this possibility?

3. Can you see how you took care of yourself as a child and how you can now use that care to nurture a Loving Parent within?

4. If you were self-destructive as a child, how would a Loving Parent care for an abused or neglected child? Would you be willing to do these caring things for your Inner Child?

5. Name a way you can meet your Loving Parent.

6. What are five traits of a Loving Parent?

Inner Child Affirmations

1. I love my Inner Child unconditionally.

2. I will protect my Inner Child to the best of my ability.

3. I will take time to listen to my Inner Child and to follow through on promises.

4. I will integrate my Inner Child into my life through play, creativity, and spirituality.

5. I will take time to become my own Loving Parent.

Inner Child Questions

1. How does your Loving Parent communicate regularly with your Inner Child?

2. How might you establish trust with your Inner Child?

3. How do you let your Inner Child play regularly?

4. How do you integrate your Inner Child into your feelings and decisions?

5. How do you affirm your Inner Child or Inner Children?

6. How does your Inner Child help connect you with a Higher Power?

7. Do you love your Inner Child unconditionally?

8. How has your Inner Child sabotaged you from getting things done?

Affirmations to be Repeated Each Day

Affirmations with other program work are a powerful tool for addressing our critical nature toward ourselves and others. These affirmations represent basic truths that most of us did not receive as children, but we can claim as adults. Read these affirmations out loud for several weeks. You may also write down some of them and post them where you can read them. With affirmations, we begin to challenge the inner Critical Parent. We learn to give ourselves a break.

1. It is okay to know who I am.
2. It is okay to trust myself.
3. It is okay to say I am an adult child.
4. It is okay to know another way to live.
5. It is okay to say no without feeling guilty.
6. It is okay to give myself a break.
7. It is okay to cry when I watch a movie or hear a song.
8. My feelings are okay even if I am still learning how to distinguish them.
9. It is okay to not take care of others when I think.
10. It is okay to feel angry.
11. It is okay to have fun and celebrate.
12. It is okay to make mistakes and learn.
13. It is okay to not know everything.
14. It is okay to say "I don't know."
15. It is okay to ask someone to show me how to do things.

16. It is okay to dream and have hope.

17. It is okay to think about things differently than my family.

18. It is okay to explore and say, "I like this or I like that."

19. It is okay to detach with love.

20. It is okay to seek my own Higher Power.

21. It is okay to reparent myself with thoughtfulness.

22. It is okay to say I love myself.

23. It is okay to work an ACA program.

Meditation

Higher Power. Help me to be willing to recognize the Loving Parent inside of me. Help me integrate my Inner Child more actively into my daily life so that I remain awake spiritually. Grant me the courage to change the things I can. Grant me the wisdom of my Inner Child.

Chapter 9

Questions and Answers About ACA

*A*t this point in the ACA basic text, we have been introduced to many aspects of the ACA recovery journey. ACA recovery involves five basic elements: Twelve Steps, Twelve Traditions, The Laundry List (Problem), The Solution, and Sponsorship. We will read about ACA sponsorship and the Twelve Traditions in the chapters ahead.

These five elements are the core of the ACA program, but there are other aspects such as the Inner Child and reparenting that are equally important. Additionally, understanding "stuck" grief and post-traumatic stress disorder is vital. Discussed in Chapter Seven, grief usually presents itself as depression or lethargy. For some ACA members, the release of stuck grief can result in "crying episodes" without an apparent cause. This is not harmful. In our experience, the grief is stuck because it represents the cumulative loss and rejection that we have never been allowed to name and mention in a supportive setting. ACA offers a safe place where we can grieve our childhood losses without being judged.

This chapter offers a review of some of the recovery terms already introduced, while also defining a few terms which will be discussed in the remaining chapters. We answer common questions about ACA as well.

Chapter Nine

Introduction

How Do I Use This Book?

The ACA basic text is a meeting book, workbook, and group manual that allows its user to work an ACA program or to start an ACA meeting anywhere in the world. The book contains all the recovery and meeting material needed for a personal program of recovery. The first section of the book involves 15 chapters that outline the adult child problem, the Solution, and how to apply ACA in daily living. Section I includes an extensive chapter on working the ACA Twelve Steps. There are workbook exercises, focused questions, and meditation items in addition to fellowship vignettes taken directly from ACA meetings and events. Chapter Seven can be used by the individual to work the Twelve Steps or by an ACA group to conduct a Steps study meeting. To work the ACA Steps, we urge you to use a sponsor and to avoid working the program alone.

Section II involves information on the Twelve Traditions and the use of counseling in recovery. There is also a chapter on the newly formed concept of ACA Teen and a chapter on our international fellowship. The chapter on the Twelve Traditions involves extensive ACA experience in carrying the ACA message to those who still suffer. There are numerous stories on ACA's experience with fellowship unity, group autonomy, and our public relations policy. This chapter can be used by ACA groups for a Traditions study.

Section III involves a detailed Handbook Section on how to establish an ACA meeting, Intergroup, or Hospitals and Institutions meeting. All the materials needed to start a meeting, elect group officers, and handle group funds are here. There is also information on how to contact the ACA World Service Office.

What is ACA or ACoA?

Adult Children of Alcoholics is known as ACA or ACoA. They both identify the same fellowship. For this book we are using ACA, but ACoA is still acceptable and widely used. ACA is a

Twelve Step, Twelve Tradition program of men and women who grew up in alcoholic or otherwise dysfunctional homes. We are not allied with any other Twelve Step program. We are an autonomous program founded on the belief that family dysfunction is a disease that affected us as children and continues to affect us as adults. Our membership also includes adults from homes where alcohol or drugs were not present; however, abuse, neglect or unhealthy behavior was.

We meet regularly at ACA meetings sharing our experience and recovery in an atmosphere of mutual respect. Our meetings offer a safe environment for adult children to share their common experiences. We discover how alcoholism and other family dysfunction affected us in the past and how it influences us in the present. We take action by attending meetings and working the program with a sponsor or spiritual advisor. We do not practice therapy in our meetings, but many of our members use an informed counselor with good results. By practicing the Twelve Steps, focusing on the ACA Solution, and accepting a loving Higher Power of our understanding, we find freedom. Our lives improve consistently.

Why We First Came to ACA

Our decisions and answers to life did not work. The best that many of us could do before finding ACA resulted in failed relationships. There was isolation and self-hate obscured by a lack of communication or odd behavior. Or there was success and notoriety while we felt empty inside. Our lives had become unmanageable. We exhausted all the methods we thought were supposed to make us happy and successful. In trying to reach our desired ends, we exhausted our resources. We often lost our creativity, our flexibility, and our sense of humor. No matter what we did, the results no longer gave us the thrill, the joy, the sense of power, or the feeling of elation they once did. We were at a dead-end. Continuing the same existence was no longer an option. Nevertheless, we found it almost impossible to abandon the thought of being able to fix ourselves.

Even though we were whipped emotionally, we held out hope that a new relationship, a new job, or a move would be the cure, but it never was. We made the decision to seek help.

How We Work a Program of Recovery

Individuals recover at their own pace. We have learned by experience that those ACA members who make the greatest gains in the shortest amount of time are using the tools of recovery. Briefly, the ACA program involves going to meetings, actively practicing the Twelve Steps, and calling program people to discuss recovery. We read ACA literature and associate with recovering people. We define and enforce our boundaries; we build a personal support network and actively make contact with the child within or True Self. In addition to living the Twelve Steps, we practice reparenting ourselves with self-love.

Why We "Keep Coming Back"

At the end of an ACA meeting, the group members encourage one another to "keep coming back" to meetings. The group members usually say this phrase together. We keep coming back because ACA is a way of life that fulfills us emotionally and spiritually. Through recovery, we realize our childhood experiences have great spiritual value. We recognize that we can help ourselves and others. An adult child can help another adult child when few others can. We keep coming back so that we can have true choice in our lives and to strengthen our relationship with a Higher Power. We learn to reparent ourselves with love. We participate in life as an equal person.

ACA Recovery Concepts

What Is The Laundry List?

The Laundry List is a compilation of 14 traits that describes the effects of being raised in an alcoholic or other unhealthy family. The traits describe the general thinking and behavior of an adult child. Identification with some or all of the traits provides a starting point of recovery for each adult child looking for help. Written in 1978, The Laundry List serves as the basis for The Problem read at the beginning of most ACA meetings. Many of the traits are also known as common behaviors.

What is Codependence?

Codependence has many definitions. For the most part, codependence involves placing the needs and wishes of others before our own needs usually to the point that we deny ourselves physically and emotionally. We focus on others to avoid looking at our own behavior and fear. Symptoms include feeling like a victim, controlling behavior, passive-aggressiveness, lying, rage, apathy, and denying feelings. There can also be addiction to one or more elements that include drugs, food, sex, work, gambling, or other compulsions or obsessions.

9

What is Para-alcoholism?

Para-alcoholism involves the stored fear, abuse, and distorted thinking acquired by growing up in an alcoholic or other dysfunctional family. The stored fear and distorted thinking take on a "drug" form within. The para-alcoholic becomes dependent on the fear and distorted thinking for survival.

In the sequence of time, para-alcoholism precedes codependence since it was formed in childhood. As adults, para-alcoholics live out their dependence as codependents with chronic fear and distorted thinking carried over from childhood. We believe that the fear and confused thinking of the codependent is one of the mechanisms that passes on alcoholism and other family dysfunction even when alcohol is removed from the home. The fear and thinking are represented as chronic worry, verbal abuse, physical abuse, or shaming projections aimed at defenseless children. This is how an adult-child parent who does not drink can still pass on alcoholism or other family dysfunction to his or her children.

What is "Hitting Bottom?"

Bottoming out can vary from person to person; however, the general consensus reveals that the person usually has exhausted all resources, lacks self-love, and is practicing self-harm. There can be a crisis or chronic problems with finances and health. Addiction can also be present. There can be a strong sense of hopelessness or being without direction.

The person may be allowing others to neglect and abuse him. Or he may be abusing others. While a bottom is in progress, denial is rampant, and relatives or friends may have turned away. At the same time, some family members may still be enabling the person.

9

Other bottoms can include a different scenario. A person may be extremely successful and self-sufficient, but secretly believes he has no real friendships. Understanding feelings and spirituality can be confusing to this person. This person may be addicted to work or some other compulsive behavior. The person usually seeks an intellectual relationship with a Higher Power.

What is the False Self? Am I Being Phony?

No. The false self represents our addicted or codependent self, which helped us survive our dysfunctional family, but which now causes great torment or discontent in adulthood. This false self is not who we are. The false self does not work well in adult relationships or on the job. Through the false self, we can feel shameful and helpless to stop some of our controlling, perfectionistic, or addictive behaviors. The best example of the false self is the personality represented by The Laundry List. The Laundry List represents a fear-based person who cannot distinguish feelings and who is dominated by others or seeks to dominate others. Other examples of the false self are the dysfunctional family roles of family hero, scapegoat, lost child, and mascot.

What is the Inner Child? I Am Not Sure I Have an Inner Child.

The Inner Child is the free, curious, and loving being within each adult child. The Inner Child is a real being that believes and offers love naturally. The Inner Child is the true connection to our Higher Power. This is also the True Self.

What is the Inner Critical Parent Or Critical Inner Voice?

We read about the Critical Parent in Chapter Two and Chapter Eight. The critical inner voice is that part of us that judges others and ourselves harshly. It is the voice that tells us that we cannot recover or that no one understands us.

What is a Loving Parent? What Does It Mean to Become Your Own Loving Parent?

Most adult children arrive at ACA with a critical inner voice. Some of us call this voice a Critical Parent. By becoming our own Loving Parent, we begin to take better care of ourselves. By learning the true qualities of a Loving Parent, we recognize that the care we received from our biological parents was not healthy love. By reparenting ourselves, we accept that we have positive qualities. We stop the critical self-talk through affirmations and journaling. We learn to parent ourselves with a more loving voice inside. We realize we have something to offer to our ACA support group and to society.

Identifying

I Am Not Sure My Family Affected Me, But I Relate to The Laundry List a Lot.

This is common. The Laundry List represents the fear and distorted thinking which result from being raised in a dysfunctional family. We are not at fault for developing these survival traits, but we are responsible for our recovery. Recognizing the link between our adult lives and our childhood years is clouded by our loyalty to the dysfunctional family system. Even if we seemingly have rejected our dysfunctional family's lifestyle, we can still carry it with us wherever we go. ACA believes there is a direct link between our childhood and our decisions and thoughts as an adult. A clue that we are affected by family dysfunction can be found in our problematic relationships, perfectionism, addictiveness, dependence, or compulsive and controlling behavior.

My Parents Did Not Drink, But I Can Relate.

Alcohol or drugs do not have to be present in the family for dysfunction to exist. Many ACA members relate to ACA literature and meetings, but their parents did not drink or have an addiction. In addition to the alcoholic family, there are at least five more family types that create the shame, abandonment, or perfectionism that create an adult child. You are a member of ACA as long as you identify with The Laundry List traits and have a desire to recover from the effects of growing up in a dysfunctional home.

What Are Grandchildren of Alcoholics?

Grandchildren of alcoholics represent a growing number of adult children qualifying for ACA.[†] They qualify because their parents were affected by alcoholism and passed on the disease to their children. The parents may not have used alcohol, but they passed on the traits of alcoholism and other family dysfunction just the same. Most grandchildren of alcoholics identify profoundly with topics at ACA meetings and with The Laundry List traits without knowing why. Family stories they have heard usually omit or minimize drinking or drug abuse, thus making it hard to know what happened in the past. At the same time, there are grandchildren of alcoholics who grew up in homes where family alcoholism and addiction were mentioned openly. These grandchildren identify with ACA as well.

Grandchildren of alcoholics offer compelling proof of the generational nature of alcoholism and other family dysfunction. With grandchildren of alcoholics, the pathway of dysfunction can be traced from one generation to the next even when alcohol or other dysfunctional behavior appears removed.

How Can ACA Actually Help Me?

ACA works for people who want it, not people who need it. People who want ACA attend meetings and work the program. ACA helps those who become willing to ask for help and accept the help offered. ACA offers freedom from unhealthy relationships and behaviors that recreate the shame and abandonment of our childhood. ACA addresses the effects of growing up in a dysfunctional family. The effects can include fearing others, taking care of others to our own detriment, and feeling trapped in abusive relationships. We can feel guilty when we stand up for ourselves. There are also a variety of secondary addictions that can include addiction to food, sex, drugs, alcohol, gambling, spending, work, or relationships.

By attending meetings regularly and by talking about our lives, we gradually change our thinking and behavior. We stop trying to control or manipulate others. In ACA, we find people who understand our situation because they have lived as we have lived. They have experience in changing their lives for the better. At the same time, we learn to identify our problem and to address it with the Twelve Steps and fellowship support. We learn to give ourselves the love we did not receive from our family. We do this by taking action. The Solution states: "We use the Steps; we use the meetings; we use the telephone."

I Have a Lot of Experience in Another Twelve Step Fellowship. Is ACA for Me?

Many ACA members have worked other Twelve Step programs with good success for their most problematic addiction or behavior; however, these programs are not designed to address the effects of family dysfunction at the level found in ACA. These programs are life-savers, but many ACA members have spent years in other Twelve Step fellowships struggling with other compulsive behaviors not addressed specifically by their program. Without focused help, many of these recovering people will switch from one destructive behavior to another. They can blame themselves and believe they are not willing enough to change. For the most part, these behaviors are survival skills related to being raised in a dysfunctional family. ACA addresses switching from one destructive behavior to another in addition to addressing other effects of family dysfunction.

Should I Stop Attending My Other Twelve Step Meetings and Only Attend ACA?

Many ACA members only attend ACA. Other ACA members have concurrent memberships in ACA and other programs that can include Alcoholics Anonymous, Narcotics Anonymous, Overeaters Anonymous, Survivors of Incest Anonymous, Co-Dependents Anonymous, or other Twelve Step fellowships.

What About Other Fellowships that Seem to Address Adult Child Issues?

Another Twelve Step fellowship that attempts to offer adult child recovery focuses primarily on spousal drinking and being powerless over alcohol. ACA addresses the effects of alcoholism and other family dysfunction. We address how our childhood experiences can affect our adult relationships and behavior. Our solution of learning to reparent ourselves is specific to the adult child experience.

What Are The Membership Requirements for ACA?

The only requirement for membership is a desire to recover from the effects of growing up in an alcoholic or otherwise dysfunctional family.

If I Become an ACA Member, Does That Mean I Have to Shut Out My Family?

Working an ACA program does not mean that we will abandon our family. However, we will learn to focus on ourselves and to stop our efforts to fix or to rescue the family. That said, in some cases where there are threats and acts of harm, we must remove ourselves from the abusive situations.

Getting Started

What Do I Do First?

We suggest that you attend at least six ACA meetings and become familiar with an ACA group in your area. Ask the group secretary for ACA literature and read about ACA recovery. Next, decide if you would like someone to help you begin your program. Attending meetings is one thing, but deciding to ask someone to help you and then accepting the help are crucial steps in moving forward in the program.

What Do I Do in the Meeting?

ACA meetings usually last 60 to 90 minutes. When the meeting starts, group members read handouts that describe the ACA program. At some meetings, group members share their experience on ACA topics such as working the Steps, denial, choice, setting boundaries, or feelings. Other meetings can involve reading ACA literature and commenting on what is being read. At ACA meetings, we listen to others share their stories and learn to talk about our own stories and experiences. If the meeting involves reading ACA literature, we listen and talk about how the literature relates to our experiences.

What is Cross Talk?

At the beginning of most ACA meetings, group members are asked to avoid cross talking. The word "cross talk" means interrupting, referring to, or commenting on someone else's remarks made during the meeting. ACA members come from family backgrounds where feelings and perceptions were judged as wrong or defective. In ACA, each person may share his or her feelings and perceptions without judgment from others. In ACA, we create a safe place to open up and share. As part of creating that safety, we ask that group members avoid cross talking. If we disagree with someone, we accept what another person says as being true for him or her.

What if I Can't Attend Meetings Regularly? I Am Very Busy with Work and Things.

In our experience, adult children have spent countless hours rescuing others or care-taking for others. We always made time to do things that would ensure that our codependent relationship was there for us, so we could avoid being alone.

Others have spent a great amount of time avoiding others. We have isolated and run from ourselves and from life. We always took time to isolate.

We cannot use work or being busy as an excuse for avoiding meetings or program work. We cannot isolate and expect to recover. We find plenty of time for meetings once we begin to focus on ourselves instead of others. We make time for meetings because we are worth it.

What if I Am In An Area Where No ACA Meetings Exist?

We should always make an attempt to attend regular ACA meetings so that we can have face-to-face interactions with other recovering adult children. For ACA members who are geographically isolated, we can still work a program. There is mail, e-mail, and the telephone. Additionally, there are online ACA meetings and live chat rooms hosted on the Internet. We can use a long-distance sponsor to help us work a program no matter where we are. There are also ACA meetings held by telephone.

What Is a Sponsor? Do I Need a Sponsor to Work the ACA Program?

To make steady progress in ACA and to break out of isolation, we need a sponsor. A sponsor is someone who attends ACA meetings regularly and who has worked the ACA Twelve Steps. The person has made progress in recovering from the effects of growing up in a dysfunctional home. A sponsor does not give advice, lend money, or serve as a counselor. The sponsor is a recovering ACA member who shares his or her experience, strength, and clarity brought by ACA recovery. The sponsor can help you work your Steps and other aspects of the program. We choose a sponsor with which there is little chance of romantic entanglements.

How Do I Find a Sponsor?

We find ACA sponsors at ACA meetings, retreats, or other recovery events. We attend meetings and listen to others share their recovery. If we relate, we can ask the person if he or she is available for sponsorship. For more information, see the chapter on sponsorship.

What Are Feelings? I Have Read About Feelings and Hear About Feelings In ACA Meetings, But I Just Feel Numb. Is There Something Wrong with Me?

No. Having difficulty identifying feelings or being confused by the talk of feelings is common for many adult children. We learned to block or deny our feelings as children to protect ourselves from our unhealthy family. We block the feelings as adults with various addictions. We can also deny or disguise feelings with a variety of compulsive behaviors. We suggest that you review the feelings segment of Step Four in Chapter Seven. The segment offers a definition to 14 feeling words with a corresponding reaction in the body. Learning where feelings are located in our body is a key step in recognizing and talking about feelings.

What is Shame? What is Guilt?

In ACA, we believe that guilt usually involves a feeling of discomfort when we have done something dishonest, selfish, or illegal. Shame involves a belief that we are inferior, defective, or unwanted. Unlike guilt which is usually associated with an action, we can have a general feeling of shame without having to do anything to cause the feeling.

What is Denial? Are There Different Types of Denial?

Denial has many forms which involve denying facts and events that are true, down-playing the severity of abusive or neglectful behavior, blaming others, selective recall of events, and an unwillingness to talk about past events.

What is Dissociation?

Dissociation is a survival tool from childhood. Adult children can dissociate from themselves in a variety of ways that can be difficult to recognize until we get help. In addition to drugs, work, sex, or food, we dissociate in other ways that can include: compulsive cleaning, compulsive exercising, obsessive reading, fantasizing about sex or romance, telephone sex, pornography, compulsive masturbation, workaholism, or harmful thrill seeking. There is also compulsive spending and cluttering. Dissociation responds well to honesty about our behavior and a willingness to do program work.

What is Post-Traumatic Stress Disorder?

PTSD is a condition of the body and mind in which a person stores the memory of a violent attack or life-threatening event. The intense feelings of fear, despair, or potential loss become stored in the body and mind, creating post-traumatic stress. The condition can govern behavior and decisions on a subconscious level. In some cases the fear can be triggered by events similar to the original trauma.

PTSD symptoms can include hypervigilance or the constant monitoring of one's surroundings for potential threat of harm. Other symptoms can include an uneasiness that is associated with a certain place or event. There can also be sensations in the body that seem unexplainable but persistent under certain conditions. Rage is also a symptom.

PTSD was initially identified as a condition that affected war veterans or victims of traumatic events such as a natural disaster. It is a generally accepted fact that ACA members who lived through violent and unsafe homes developed PTSD. Our fellowship recognized PTSD as an adult child concern as early as 1984. Fellowship writing from that time shows the link. The knowledge of PTSD and its effects on the body continue to be broadened. There appear to be other forms not related to overt violence or trauma.

This All Seems Like Too Much. I Feel Overwhelmed.

If we feel overwhelmed at the prospect of recovery, we can step back and keep it simple. We realize that we did not become dependent in one day, so we will not recover in one day. ACA recovery is gradual, but noticeable, if we put in the effort. We also realize that others have recovered in ACA and will help us talk about our feelings and thoughts. When we feel overwhelmed, we remember the slogan: "First Things First." We simplify our program and focus on one thing at a time. We focus on the Steps, attending meetings, or choosing a sponsor to help us make progress. We remember to live in the moment and try to avoid projecting what will happen in the future. We avoid living in the past. We live one day at a time.

Working the Program

What Are the Twelve Steps?

ACA officially adopted the Twelve Steps from Alcoholics Anonymous in 1984. AA is the original Twelve Step program, which has brought relief and recovery to millions of suffering alcoholics. The Twelve

Steps are a proven method of recovery from addiction and unhealthy dependence upon others. The sequence of recovery usually begins with hitting a bottom and asking for help. After accepting help, we proceed with Step One. We admit that we are powerless over family dysfunction and that our lives have become unmanageable. The sequence continues in Step Two with coming to believe in a power greater than ourselves and so forth.

What Are the Twelve Traditions?

While the Twelve Steps address recovery for the individual, the Twelve Traditions promote group unity and stability. The Traditions guarantee that we will always have a meeting to attend and that the meeting will focus on recovery from the effects of family dysfunction. The Traditions allow our groups and service structure to remain focused on the primary purpose of carrying the ACA message to the adult child who still suffers. We have no other purpose. The Traditions give us our single requirement for ACA membership. The requirement is a desire to recover from the effects of alcoholism and other family dysfunction. With that, you are an ACA member when you say you are. The Traditions also give us fellowship unity, anonymity, and group autonomy. The ACA fellowship has no opinions on outside issues.

What is a Boundary?

There are different types of boundaries, but their purposes are to allow us to remain safe, respected, and free of harm. All boundaries remind us that the feelings, behaviors, and attitudes of others are separate from our own. The feelings and thoughts of others are not our responsibility. We can feel empathy for another person and show compassion, but we are separate from the other person.

One type of boundary is a statement or request that we communicate to someone. The statement is usually a request for a particular behavior to cease or to be modified. When we establish a boundary, we must be willing to follow through. We must honor our boundary even if others do not. For example, if we ask someone who is verbally abusive to stop the behavior in our presence, we must be willing to walk away from the person if he remains abusive. We do not negotiate our boundary with the person. We avoid haggling over why he does not honor it. We state our boundary clearly and honor it for ourselves.

What is Emotional Sobriety?

In ACA, we seek emotional sobriety by attending ACA meetings, working the Twelve Steps, and mentoring others. Emotional sobriety is measured by the freedom we gain by abstaining from acting out on The Laundry List traits. We cease self-harming behavior and make an effort to mature emotionally and spiritually. Emotional sobriety is evident in our willingness to seek and do God's will.

What is a Relapse?

An ACA relapse always involves a return to dependence on one of our childhood roles and a prolonged return to using the survival traits of The Laundry List. Momentary lapses into old roles or behaviors are not necessarily relapses unless we use these lapses to avoid program progress. The roles include family hero, scapegoat, lost child, or mascot. These are predictable roles developed by children in dysfunctional homes and used in adulthood with mostly negative results. Without help, these roles can endure a lifetime and be passed to the next generation.

What is a Spiritual Awakening?

A spiritual awakening is the result of working the ACA Twelve Steps and by actively participating in recovery. We remain spiritually awake by attending meetings and working the program. We pray and meditate regularly. We also help other adult children with their program. Spiritual experiences, which can lead to a spiritual awakening, can be sudden and dramatic. Other spiritual experiences can be subtle but equally powerful and enlightening.

What is an ACA "Birthday"?

ACA groups recognize fellowship involvement with recovery chips and medallions. The chips represent a person's first 30 days, 60 days, 90 days and so on in ACA. There are yearly medallions as well. For yearly birthdays, the group usually has a speaker who shares his or her story during the meeting. The medallions are handed out at the end of the meeting.

What is a Home Group or ACA Support Group?

An ACA support group or home group is a meeting we attend regularly. We become involved in keeping the meeting going so that we can recover and help others recover. We volunteer to chair meetings, sponsor others, and carry the ACA message in our area. We celebrate our annual ACA birthday with our ACA support group. We develop friendships and celebrate life with the support of our group.

What is Service Work? What Does "Giving Service" Mean?

Service work is a key aspect of the ACA recovery program. Service is our way of giving back to ACA what was freely given to us by the fellowship. When we help others we help ourselves, and we maintain emotional sobriety. We can give service in a variety of ways that include: sponsoring others, chairing meetings, mailing out ACA literature, establishing an ACA contact number, serving as the group secretary, serving as the Group Representative, starting a new group, taking ACA meetings into a treatment center or prison, and other ACA-specific activities.

What is the Difference Between Service Work and Being a People-Pleaser?

Service work comes from an attitude of giving back to ACA what was given to us. We want to help ourselves and others. People-pleasing comes with manipulation with some predetermined goal in mind. When we people-please, we usually are trying to manipulate outcomes or attitudes for our own self-interest.

What is the Thirteenth Step?

Some people attending ACA meetings have not grown beyond their victim or victimizer roles. They may attempt to meet their own needs by manipulating newcomers to ACA. This is known as the "13th Step" in most Twelve Step programs. When this happens, it can violate the safety of the meeting and drive away group members. An experienced ACA member should never take financial, emotional, or sexual advantage of anyone, including a new person in ACA.

The love and respect we offer to newcomers is a reflection of the love and respect we are learning to offer ourselves.

If we are struggling with this area of our lives, we are usually not willing or ready to surrender acting-out behavior. We may not know how. We may have tried and failed. Some of us are not sure how to face the internal pain and self-hate that drives our selfish behavior. Perpetrator or manipulative behavior is almost always driven by our avoidance to face our abuse and neglect from childhood. This is not an excuse for adult behavior that harms others and us. The perpetrator must be held accountable, but many perpetrators do not link past abuse with their acting-out behavior. If this is our situation as a 13th Stepper, we ask a Higher Power for the willingness to seek extra help and to get honest about the effects of our childhood experiences. We also must get honest about our behavior and its harmful effect on others. We cannot use our childhood abuse as an excuse to perpetrate against others. No matter what we have done, we can still work our program with the knowledge that a Higher Power is with us always. We can change if we have the capacity to be honest. We seek help with an attitude of earnestness and humility.

Other Common Questions

How Big is ACA?

ACA is a worldwide fellowship with meetings in North and South America, Europe, Asia, Pacific Islands, Middle East, and Australia. New groups are established each week somewhere in the world. The translation of ACA literature into other languages is ongoing.

Is ACA a Religious Program?

No. ACA is a spiritual program. We have no religious hierarchy, religious script, or instructional method of worship. While we are not religious, we do not shy away from spiritual matters. The disease of family dysfunction is a spiritual dilemma. The solution includes seeking a power greater than ourselves to bring true freedom. ACA members are free to choose the God of their understanding.

What is ACA Teen?

ACA Teen is a newly developed concept adopted by fellowship vote in 2005. ACA Teen is for any group of Children of Alcoholics who would like to adapt the ACA program for their own purposes. ACA Teen groups should honor the Twelve Steps and Twelve Traditions and be sponsored by an ACA group. For more information, see the Chapter on ACA Teen.

How Do I Start an ACA Meeting?

See the Handbook Section of this book for information on how to start an ACA meeting and how to contact the ACA World Service Office.

What is an H/I Meeting?

Hospitals and Institutions meetings are ACA meetings held in a treatment center, jail, prison, or other facility that houses adult children. Many members carry the ACA message into these facilities as part of their service work and personal program of recovery. At the same time, many ACA members began their program in one of these facilities.

What Are the Identity Papers?

The Identity Papers are three foundational articles of the ACA fellowship that detail the adult child dilemma, personality, and effects of growing up in an alcoholic home. The papers also outline a solution for healing in addition to presenting the basic focus and purpose of ACA. Written between 1984 and 1987, these papers are presented in Chapter Six and Chapter Ten.

9

End Notes

†ON PAGE 338: Grandchildren of Alcoholics: Another Generation of Co-Dependency, by Ann W. Smith, 1988, HCI Publications.

Chapter 10

The Importance of Service in ACA

$\mathcal{W}$e are presenting the third Identity Paper in its original form. For historical reasons, we are presenting the paper without modifications.

The Importance of Service in ACA
The Identity, Purpose and Relationship Committee
January 17, 1987

Last year, the delegates to the Annual Business Conference asked the Identity Committee to examine and define the roles of the Central Service Board and the Interim World Service Organization in our service structure and to propose the best method for forming a World Service Organization (WSO).

We recommend that any decision about the necessity or structure for a permanent WSO be deferred until more input can be received from the meetings and groups concerned with the development of world service.

As a preliminary to further development, we would like to examine the basic idea of service.

THE PURPOSE OF SERVICE

As the experience of service continues to evolve in ACA, we see the need to address the basic idea of service and to acknowledge the service we give to ourselves.

Chapter Ten

Service in ACA

The purpose of service in ACA is to support one another in becoming responsible for our own well-being. We lose our sense of personal responsibility when we are forced to separate from our feelings. Without emotional integrity, our actions become scattered and unfocused, and we are helpless in responding to our essential need for love and care.

Action Coming From Love

The essence of service in ACA is action coming from an attitude of love. But before we can serve one another, we must first be willing to love and serve ourselves. In seeking to understand their experience of pain, children in an alcoholic family will reverse the normal sequence of cause and effect and decide that they are the cause of the family's distress. They react to this decision by hating and punishing themselves for needing love and by retreating into emotional isolation. In being willing to again acknowledge and respond to our own needs, we regain our sense of emotional wholeness and reclaim the power which comes from taking responsibility for our own well-being.

Service Allows Us to Trust Ourselves

Our feelings of self-worth and adequacy start to grow as we successfully reparent ourselves, and we begin to trust our ability to love and serve others. We give service just by being present to support and encourage other members of the program as they make the transition from frightened adult children to whole human beings who are capable of acting with the spontaneity of a child and the wisdom of a mature adult. This central concept underlies and supports all forms of service.

Service Provides Our Program

By uniting in service, we create a program for living which provides a sane alternative to the insanity of family alcoholism.

PAIN, SHUTDOWN, & SURVIVAL

Perceptions are Learned

Children need to believe their perceptions of reality are accurate and can be trusted to guide their behavior and to keep them safe from harm. They become obedient to what they believe is true and follow what they hope is the best path for finding happiness, peace, and joy. Children look to authority to help them define what is real and to make sound decisions in relating to others. The support of responsible authority gives them confidence in developing their own ability to effectively live in the world.

Stinkin' Thinkin' is Learned

The tragedy for children in an alcoholic home is that they are robbed of a model for living that is based on a responsibility to sanity. At the core of alcoholic thinking is the insane belief that self-destructive behavior can lead to serenity and peace of mind. The abuse of alcohol becomes a model for destruction. The attitude of abuse that underlies all addictive behavior dominates the family, and children learn to accept this attitude in others and themselves. By practicing and supporting a pattern of self-annihilation, one generation conveys to the next a never-ending cycle of despair.

Insanity Begins

Insanity begins when children are compelled to deny the reality of pain and abuse. Once children have accepted the idea that alcoholism is not violent or dangerous, they have no basis for deciding what is real or for knowing how to respond to those around them. They no longer trust authority to guide them or to protect them from harm. They are paralyzed by indecision and grow to hate themselves for being confused and vulnerable and for needing to be safe and secure. They learn to survive by punishing themselves for being vulnerable and by denying their need for love.

Chapter Ten

We Learned to Abuse Ourselves

It is this sense of self-betrayal and self-abandonment that is the source of rage and despair in ACAs. Adult Children live in two realities attempting to meet the needs of a mature adult while seeing the world from the perspective of a frightened child. Neither aspect of the personality fully comprehends or understands the motives or actions of the other. The adult need for interdependence and self-expression seems to be in direct conflict with the child's need to be dependent and gently controlled.

The frustration of being forced to choose between two competing points of view builds into rage as each side of the personality struggles to be heard by the other. Rage turns into despair when we realize the legacy of insanity we inherited from our alcoholic home does not provide for the well-being of either the adult or the child.

Becoming Codependent

To withstand the intense pain of living with insanity and to have any sense of control we must deny our feelings and hide our vulnerability. Without the guidance of our emotions, we become dependent on others to direct our behavior. We move from an internal sense of direction based on our own perceptions of the truth to a dependence on alcoholic authority to interpret reality. We are caught in the trap of being obedient to a system of beliefs and behaviors that is actually the cause of our confusion and pain.

Underlying Terror

We continue in our obedience to an alcoholic view of the world because the expected consequence of disobedience is more terrifying. Disobeying the rigid beliefs of our childhood means to risk being overwhelmed by unpredictable chaos. We cling to the familiar pattern of unthinking reactions and see anything new as a source of confusion and a threat to our tenuous sense of control. We avoid the terror of abandonment by holding fast to our childhood beliefs, but pay the price of enduring the abuse which comes from following the family's distorted idea of reality.

Consequences of Codependency

The cost of our continued allegiance to alcoholism is the loss of our ability to love. We lose our capacity to give and receive love as a result of failing to resolve the violent conflicts that threatened to destroy our families. We internalize these conflicts and carry them into adulthood, constantly seeking to control the unmanageable chaos inside. We no longer feel able to provide for our own well-being or to contribute to the well-being of others. We develop a profound sense of inadequacy in giving and unworthiness in receiving affection and love since nothing we did as children seemed to have any effect in stopping the progressive deterioration of the family.

Our sense of failure increases until we believe our inadequacy extends to everything we do. We lose faith in our ability to love and care for ourselves and feel unworthy of receiving warmth and love from those around us. We accept our feelings of unworthiness as a definition of who we are and continue to let the insane perceptions of alcoholism distort our view of the world.

Powerless and Alienated

When children have been injured by alcoholism and cannot find relief from their pain, they are forced to deny their reality and to withdraw into isolation. The experience of being powerless to control the events that damage us as children leaves us with a deep feeling of alienation, not only from others, but from our own openness and vulnerability as well.

Chapter Ten

A Feeling and an Unfeeling Self

To protect ourselves from the disorienting effects of living with confusion and pain, we divide into a feeling and unfeeling self and isolate ourselves from our own vulnerability.[1] We alternate between the extremes of wanting to escape our isolation and the need to stay securely hidden in our familiar prison of pain. Our beliefs and behaviors become rigid and inflexible, and we swing from the depths of isolated depression to frantic attempts to find help in the outside world. We endlessly repeat the cycle of frustration, rage and despair, but the goal of the divided self remains the same as it was in childhood: to become whole once again and to find happiness, peace, and joy.

Challenging Authority

Freedom from insanity requires that we disobey the guidance of dysfunctional authority. The process of breaking away from alcoholic authority starts with the idea that disobedience is possible.

Defiance, a Natural Response to Abuse

Stanley Milgram, in his study of obedience to authority, writes that a single individual has little way of knowing that defiance is a natural and appropriate reaction to being abused. The horrified reactions of others are needed to define the abuse as painful and intolerable. With the support of those who have successfully resisted authority, a single individual can see that the expected consequence of disobedience does not necessarily occur and that the power of authority is weakened by each successful act of defiance. Milgram concludes that unity and mutual support are the strongest bulwarks against the effects of abuse by authority.[2]

---

[1] The fairy tale of "Sleeping Beauty" is used by M.K. Toomim to describe the process of protective self division.

[2] Milgram, S., "Obedience to Authority," New York: Harper & Row, Publishers, 1974, pp. 120–121.

RE-EMERGENCE OF THE UNITED SELF

Sharing the Truth

In the safety of our meetings, we learn the truth about alcoholism and find the courage to risk moving out of our prison of isolation and fear. We are united by the idea that we can break away from the pattern of insanity and violence we learned as children and that we no longer have to tolerate the attitude of abuse it represents. We see the power that comes from acknowledging the truth demonstrated by others in the program.

Experience, Strength, & Hope

Hearing the message of recovery and hope from someone else fans the dim spark of aliveness we keep buried inside. We become aware there is a sane model for living which can replace the model of insanity we learned in childhood. We realize that we can defy the authority of alcoholism and not be destroyed by that defiance.

Support & Security

Our meetings provide us with the mutual support we need to detach from insanity. Our program gives us a secure structure to hold us as we connect our energy to a system of beliefs and a way of life consistent with serenity and peace.

Why We Give Service

Between the time we have decided to disconnect from our alcoholic beliefs but have not yet reached the security of a spiritual awakening lies a "dark night of the soul" where we perceive there is no guiding force whatsoever. Our passage through this terrifying and often chaotic period of uncertainty and doubt is where we experience the power of our program and realize the importance of the service we give and receive.

Chapter Ten

Sharing Our Recovery is Service

In ACA we give service by reflecting for one another the progress we make in awakening the inner spirit of freedom and joy. We trust this process of reflection because of the history of recovery in other Twelve-Step programs and the growing evidence of recovery in ACA as well. The shared experience, strength and hope of those who have successfully negotiated portions of the journey towards spiritual reconnection serves to strengthen and encourage those who are just beginning the process.

Each individual's experience of recovery is an essential piece of the mirror which serves to redefine our self-image and increases our sense of self-worth. Our combined experience of spiritual transformation provides a complete model and picture for a return to sanity.

Reawakening the Inner Child

In ACA we carry the awakening of the spirit down to the deepest level where the inner child is paralyzed by fear. When we share even our smallest triumph or success in a meeting, we encourage one another to persist in the difficult process of recovery and offer support in times of despair. Our strengths are maximized and our deficits are overcome through sharing in the group. The need for loving reflection and consistent care that was tragically missing from our families is met by the love we receive from other members of our program. The burden of responsibility we feel when we attempt to reparent ourselves in isolation is eased by sharing the task with each other.

Forgiving Ourselves

As we learn to trust the process of recovery in ACA, we gain the confidence to end our emotional isolation and to heal the divided self. Healing the division between the feeling and unfeeling self begins with the willingness to accept our vulnerability and to forgive our self-hate.

Forgiving our self-hatred is how we acknowledge the reality of our past experience. Forgiveness does not imply support for the violence of alcoholism or for our continuation in the role of victim. It means to give validity to what has gone before. By accepting our vulnerability, we end the need for denial. Forgiveness opens the door for transforming the energy of self-hate and repression to that of self-expression and love.

Reclaiming Our Energy

By acknowledging the past, we reclaim all of the energy used in the self-protective process of denial and isolation. By releasing self-hate we give up the need to punish ourselves for being powerless over the destructive effects of living in an alcoholic home.

10

Making Healthier Choices

As we move out of emotional isolation, we regain the ability to recognize and express all of our feelings. With the guidance of our emotions, we are able to choose our actions and to make balanced decisions on how to live. We discover we have the freedom to choose healing, life-giving experiences and to avoid those that cause us pain.

Trusting in the Program

As we develop trust in our ability to care for the vulnerable inner self, we begin to see our childhood experience from a new perspective. When we realize that the authors of our childhood reality were themselves out of touch with the truth, we stop giving power to the beliefs which guide alcoholic behavior. We become willing to follow the principles of sanity found in the program and to trust the power of the loving authority they reflect.

We realize we can trust the program because the promised support is real. The encouragement we receive in ACA allows us to heal the separation between the adult and the child and become whole once again.

Chapter Ten

Our program provides for the needs of both the adult and the child. The child's need for concrete evidence of a loving Higher Power can be met by the presence and gentle touch of another human being. The adult's need for intimacy and self-expression can be satisfied by giving service in the fellowship. The uncertainty and doubt at the heart of self-hate can be removed by the reality of being loved.

Ending the Internal Conflict

The conflict between the two sides of the self is one of strategy and not of intent. Both the adult and the child long for the love and respect necessary to sustain the human spirit but disagree on how to attain their desire; the child by hopefully waiting in isolation and the adult by rushing into frustrated action. In ACA we learn both strategies lead only to despair.

Ending our inner conflict depends on both the adult and the child recognizing the need for unity in recovery. By acknowledging their need for each other, the adult and the child create the sense of wholeness needed to fully respond to the world.

Mutual acceptance allows the child to see that the ability to trust is damaged but not broken and can be restored by gently and slowly emerging from the protective prison of isolation. The adult becomes aware of the spirit of joy that inhabits every child and recognizes the need for openness and spontaneity in feeling completely alive.

Finding a Cooperative Solution

The best way to resolve a conflict between two people is to find a cooperative solution in which both get what they want and need.[3] The Steps and Traditions offer a simple program for living that allows the adult and the child to join together in ending the cycle of alcoholic insanity and in finding the happiness, peace, and joy they deserve.

---

[3] Tessina, T.B. and Smith, R.K. "How to be a Couple and Still Be Free," North Hollywood, California: Newcastle Publishing Co., Inc., 1980, pp. 73–112.

Benefits of Giving Service

The healing we receive by giving service in ACA removes our deep feelings of inferiority in giving and receiving love. Our sense of inadequacy begins to disappear when we see the value of the service we give. Our idea of who we are and what we deserve starts to change as we see our real worth reflected in the eyes of other adult children. Our feelings of unworthiness are transformed into positive self-esteem as we realize how important our experience of recovery is to others in the program. With our increased sense of self-worth, we are able to let others love us in return.

Service Ensures Unity and Strength

10

In giving service to each other, we show we are united by the common belief that we can transcend the crushing burden of demoralization that is the legacy of family alcoholism. By taking the action of responding to one another with love, we simultaneously allow ourselves to give and be given to in a way that heals the wounds of our childhood and meets our simple human requirements for attention, love, and respect.

Identity, Purpose, and Relationship Committee:

Chapter 11

ACA Sponsorship: Fellow Travelers

*T*he relationship between a sponsor and sponsee represents a spiritual connection between two people helping each other find life beyond the effects of growing up in a dysfunctional family. As fellow travelers on the road of recovery, the sponsor and sponsee find empathy. This is the mutual understanding that puts action into our identification with another adult child. With true empathy, we recognize our similarities. We recognize the difference between love and pity. With empathy, we are ready to help another person and to accept help. We understand what it means to be a friend.

Most of us choose a sponsor who has similar experiences or someone we can relate to from ACA meetings. We attend meetings and listen to those sharing their stories and experiences. Choosing a sponsor can be as simple as walking up to the person after a meeting and asking for help with the Twelve Steps.

If we are asked to be a sponsor, we try to say yes. We do not need to be intimidated or afraid that we will do something wrong. If we attend meetings regularly, we have something to offer another person.

Sponsorship is one of the program tools that helps us grow and learn more about ourselves and the Twelve Steps. Working the Twelve Steps with a sponsee dramatically improves our understanding of the principles of the Steps. By working the program with another, we are compelled to think about the

Chapter Eleven

Steps and how they fit together. We begin to understand their order and how they walk us toward a spiritual awakening. We see why an admission of powerlessness in Step One leads to surrender and seeking a Higher Power in Step Two. The decision we make in Step Three leads to willingness to begin a searching inventory in Step Four. The connection between the remaining Steps emerges for us as well. At some point, we realize we learned a lot by working the Steps for ourselves, but we learn even more by sponsoring someone in the program. Being a sponsor is a fulfilling journey that you will not want to miss.

For many, ACA sponsorship represents the first time we have tried to establish a relationship on equal footing with another person. This is an unfamiliar concept for us since we came from families in which healthy relationships and mutual respect were not practiced. In ACA, we need not fear sponsorship as a reenactment of the domination, neglect, or control we experienced as children. ACA sponsors offer respect and understanding instead of criticism and conditional love.

We learn to desire the equality and trust that come from being in a sponsor and sponsee relationship. This partnership is such a contrast to our relationships before we arrived at ACA. As adults, most of us seemed to have relationships in which we dominated people or worshipped people. Most of us were discreet about these two extremes. But when we think about it, we can agree that we have been near one end or the other of these two positions. There seemed to be no middle ground or equality in our relationships with another person. Many of us thought we were either superior or inferior. We seemed to never feel like we were good enough for our friends or others. In a sponsor and sponsee relationship, we have a chance to make a real connection with another person based on mutual respect and trust. We find friendship and intimacy with another person that brings self-respect. We are learning how to love one another.

Being A Sponsor – The Emotional and Spiritual Benefits

Sponsorship in ACA is one of the key actions that helps an ACA member maintain emotional sobriety while continuing to grow spiritually. ACA sponsors who actively help others with their program tend to face the challenges of life more easily. They have developed a support system in their ACA groups. They know how to ask for help and accept it. Sponsorship represents the third element of a key promise made in The Solution: "We progress from hurting, to healing, to helping."

While a sponsor can give much time toward helping others, the sponsor learns how to avoid the hero or rescuing roles learned in childhood. An ACA sponsor is someone who truly understands the effects of being raised in a dysfunctional family. A sponsor understands the importance of focus and reparenting one's self through the Twelve Steps. The sponsor knows the difference between discovery and recovery. Discovery can involve reading self-help books and educating ourselves about the disease of alcoholism and family recovery. However, recovery from the effects of family dysfunction involves attending ACA meetings regularly, working the Steps, and sponsoring others. Discovery is knowledge. It is not recovery. This understanding comes from working the ACA program of recovery instead of merely reading or talking about it.

In addition to having experience with the Steps, listening is perhaps one of the most important skills that a sponsor can develop. An ACA sponsor hones the skill of active listening and reflects back what is being said by the sponsee. That means a thoughtful sponsor helps a sponsee hear what he or she is saying. In these moments clarity emerges for the sponsee. In some interactions denial is exposed or personal progress is realized. Many times a sponsee is making more progress than he or she can see. Most adult children tend to look at what they think they are doing "wrong" instead of seeing progress. A sponsor can point that out.

11

In moments of self-doubt, the ACA sponsor holds up a mirror, which reminds the sponsee that he or she is doing a lot of things right and that things can work out. The sponsor suggests that doomsaying and predictions by the critical inner parent are not always inevitable.

Sponsorship is not one of the Twelve Steps, but its importance could be ranked in the same category. Through sponsorship, we pass on the gift of recovery which was given to each of us. Sponsorship is the vehicle by which we take the road less traveled to a true connection with others and a God of our understanding. Sponsors receive more than they give by helping another ACA member work the program.

ACA sponsorship has evolved from the many styles of sponsorship of the various Twelve Step programs. ACA uses the "fellow traveler" or co-sponsor method of sponsorship in most cases, but there are other variations of these methods. ACA sponsorship could be described as peer-to-peer help. The sponsor and sponsee are on equal footing, seeking answers and solutions together.

In ACA, we tend to avoid the teacher-student style of sponsorship since we rebel against authority and since we have difficulty asking for what we need in these situations. If our sponsor appears as a teacher, we tend to regress to a people-pleasing mode. Some of us can try to anticipate what our sponsor would want us to think or do. In the teacher-student style of sponsorship, we can recreate the abandonment of our family. We can fear displeasing the sponsor just as we feared displeasing our parents. We subconsciously think we have failed or displeased our parent when we make mistakes or struggle with ACA recovery. Under the teacher-student scenario, some us can see Step work as assignments to be dreaded. We can view the Steps as something to be perfected, instead of the healing path they lead us upon. Many of us coming over to ACA from other Twelve Step programs have had the experience of this model, and it did not tend to work well with us. We often felt belittled or unheard, but we remained silent. Many of us blame ourselves for not using sponsors effectively in other programs. But we find ACA sponsorship comfortable and desirable.

The fellow traveler method of ACA sponsorship seems to work best for us because it places us on equal footing with our sponsor. We can drop our people-pleasing or self-sufficient traits and ask for help. We do not have to feel intimidated. We do not have to think we are a burden by asking for someone's time. We also learn we can make mistakes and not have to know all the answers to be helped. We see sponsorship, whether we sponsor others or are being sponsored, as a chance to grow.

Being a sponsor for others is something we look forward to in ACA. We want to give back to the fellowship. We keep what we have by giving it away. This is a key to reparenting one's self and maintaining emotional sobriety. We also keep our word as a sponsor. We follow through. The sponsee keeps his or her word as well. The sponsee must be willing to do what it takes to recover in ACA. This is the two-way street of sponsorship – willingness and following through with focus.

General Information

Sponsorship in ACA – The Beginning of the Fellow Traveler Model

In 1989, the ACA Sponsorship Committee recommended the "fellow traveler" or co-sponsor approach based on fellowship input. The ACA model of sponsorship is a modification of the method used in Alcoholics Anonymous. The AA model is a proven method of helping AA members find and maintain sobriety. AA members learn to surrender destructive self-will, practice rigorous honesty, and seek God's will in this model. These results are desirable in ACA as well; however, the Sponsorship Committee did not believe the AA method adequately addressed the tendencies of the ACA personality, namely our over-reliance on others for direction and approval, and our tendency to try to manage someone else's life. Without a modification of the AA model, it was feared that an ACA sponsor would play lord over a sponsee more than willing to give up personal freedom and choice. So the fellow traveler model was developed to place the sponsor and sponsee on equal footing from the beginning.

The "ACA Sponsorship: Fellow Travelers" trifold states:

"We suggest the 'Fellow Traveler' approach which allows the sponsor/sponsee to share the same road at this time but urging the person being sponsored to soon choose their own way. The sponsor helps (the sponsee) see alternatives and explores the consequences of his/her actions. When asked for advice, the sponsor would be urged to respond, "I don't know what you should do. Here's what I did in a similar situation."

This 1989 trifold also states:

"The question on when to get a sponsor is best answered by the newcomer, but it's agreed that as soon as the newcomer commits to the program of recovery he/she should connect with a sponsor so that they can find direction and not wander rudderless from meeting to meeting."

Some sponsor and sponsee relationships last a lifetime, one day at a time. Others are temporary, while even others begin, and stop, and begin again. Whatever the rhythm of the relationship, the fellow traveler model of sponsorship calls each person in the relationship to practice the principles of the Steps in all their affairs. The principles include surrender, self-honesty, self-inventory, and a willingness to seek and do God's will.

ACA sponsors are not limited in their ability to help a variety of ACA members. For example, a sponsor with a history of verbal abuse may be asked to help a person who was subjected to physical abuse of hitting and battery. Even though the sponsor had no physical abuse growing up, he or she can relate to someone physically abused because emotional and physical abuse produce the same damage. The abuse creates obsessive fear, self-hate, and a sense of being lost.

If the sponsor does not have an experience that relates to the situation at hand, he or she relates this truth. It is okay to say "I don't know your exact circumstances, but I understand the loss. I understand the fear." The sponsor and sponsee talk about the situation and options. Occasionally, the sponsor will recommend that the sponsee talk with someone who has had a similar life experience.

This is the crux of understanding the fellow traveler model of ACA sponsorship. The sponsor and sponsee are more alike than different. Because of this great fact, we can help one another when few others can. We can help each other find the ACA solution through the Steps and through reparenting ourselves.

With a willingness to be a fellow traveler, the ACA sponsor remains ready to travel with the sponsee to find solutions that benefit the sponsee's recovery. At the same time, the person being sponsored becomes willing to listen and take action when another's experience can be helpful. The sponsee admits and accepts that family dysfunction occurred and is willing to take action to move forward into recovery.

As a sponsor, we do not need to fear that we will make mistakes or harm someone through sponsorship. Adult children are survivors, and they know how to protect themselves. In some cases, there are hurt feelings and miscommunication, but lasting harm is not likely. With the fellow traveler model of sponsorship, we are not taking responsibility for the other person. We are not the person's therapist, counselor, or life coach. We are traveling with the person as he or she participates in ACA recovery.

The trifold on ACA sponsorship recommends a list of recovery actions that a sponsee could be expected to do. The trifold suggests that the sponsor help the sponsee develop an action plan from this simple list. The list includes doing family-of-origin work (a family history), Step work, journaling, and some level of service work. The service work can begin with volunteering to chair an ACA meeting. By doing this, the person being sponsored learns about giving back to the group and to the fellowship.

11

Having a sponsor can be the difference between remaining stagnated or finding greater levels of choice and freedom. We cannot overstate the need for the assistance of an ACA sponsor to make real progress in ACA.

In some cases, a sponsor might recommend counseling. In ACA, we are revisiting traumatic events suffered in childhood, releasing powerful emotions, and opening the doors on the past. Our sponsors are not therapists or counselors, but they offer needed support to those revisiting abuse and trauma. A sponsor understands the need for counseling, but he or she also knows that counseling alone is not the sure path for the adult child. Counseling does not replace the need for meeting attendance and joining an ACA support group.

Another form of ACA sponsorship is the co-sponsorship model. This model works best for two ACA members with long-term recovery rather than newer members just beginning the program. In co-sponsoring one another, the two experienced members have a working knowledge of the Steps and Traditions and have completed family-of-origin work. They understand grief work and post-traumatic stress disorder and know how to address both. They have carried the message to others and served their group or Intergroup well. They sponsor one another with experience and respect.

In ACA, there is also short-term, temporary sponsorship until a person settles on a more permanent relationship with a sponsor. Temporary sponsors have been used by ACA members who have just been released from a treatment setting or prison. These new members use a temporary sponsor to learn about the ACA program, meeting locations, and other program information. Some temporary sponsors become more permanent sponsors for some new members.

Multiple Sponsors

If we have an addiction in addition to being an adult child, we may also have a sponsor in a program that addresses the addiction. For example, there could be an overeating ACA member with a sponsor in Overeaters Anonymous or a gambling-addicted ACA with a sponsor in Gamblers Anonymous. Many ACA members are recovering addicts in AA and NA as well. While ACA is a way of life that can meet all of our emotional and spiritual needs, it does not eliminate the need for or usefulness of these other programs.

An ACA Sponsorship Story on Learning From a Sponsee

I learned quickly that there was more to being a sponsor than just being in the program for a specific period of time. It takes kindness, caring, and an abundance of patience and nurturing, things I did not know existed. I learned them in ACA and other Twelve Step programs. I also learned my unhealthy attitudes and my negative feelings could be changed. The change would result in undreamed of good fortune.

I became an ACA sponsor after eighteen months in the program. It was a decision I mulled over for three months. I was not sure I was ready. I was not sure I had anything to give, and I was not sure that what I had to give was worth giving. I read a sponsorship trifold. I talked with my own sponsor. Then I took a long, searching look at myself as a candidate and made what I now consider my most healing decision.

Sponsoring others is my way of showing my gratitude for my program of recovery. To do it well, I try to maintain healthy boundaries between my sponsees and me in order not to take on their pain or try to fix them. This helps me show my sponsees the paths to take toward their recovery. By helping them, I am changing my unhealthy behaviors into positive ones. I try not to tell them what I think is best. I do, however, try to help them see that the decision they make is a good decision for them.

I applaud the intuitiveness they invariably exhibit, which they have been programmed to disregard before ACA. I believe that whatever they decide to do is a good move forward for them. Whether I would take those roads is irrelevant because, just as I am my own person, they are their own persons.

Chapter Eleven

When we talk, I learn as much as they do. When I listen to them, I have found they hear me. We all want to be seen and heard. We want to be acknowledged for our ideas, our hopes, and our fears. When no one cared enough to acknowledge us, much less validate us, we locked ourselves up in a place that smothered us until we had to savagely fight for our very survival. Being an ACA sponsor means aiding a sponsee in that fight until they can stand up to whatever comes at them. If they feel overwhelmed, I try to help them see the problem in its less intimidating, basic form. When they can't do it alone, they learn to reach out and get the necessary emotional support and information to see their problem can be solved, how to solve it, and then solve it. After learning to solve their problems, their lives are more peaceful. For some of us serenity is unnatural and frightening, so we have to learn to accept it.

When I speak with my sponsees, I remember their words and I learn. While the causes of our dysfunction are different, the effects are the same. In sponsoring others I sometimes find solutions to my own problems. Or I find solace in the fact I am not alone. As a sponsor I try to be a guide, not a teacher. I make it a point to praise the good work my sponsees do because validation is always important. I love seeing the miracles of their recovery as much as I love seeing my own. I make it a point to talk about those miracles, to remind my sponsees of the light awaiting them at the end of the recovery tunnel. Being a sponsor is a learning experience and a loving gift from God.

Sponsorship Overview

While the goal is to be in a one-on-one relationship with a sponsor, we offer an overview of ACA sponsorship experience that includes other methods as well.

Direct Sponsorship

Fellow Traveler – This is the traditional method of ACA sponsorship. A person who is willing to share experience, strength, and hope in helping the sponsee work his or her way through the Twelve Steps and to pick up the recovery tools for facing life on life's terms.

Temporary Sponsor – Serves as an interim sponsor for a short time until a permanent one is found.

Multiple Sponsors – More than one sponsor to serve various needs of the sponsee, as long as the sponsee isn't hiding out in the various relationships. We don't use multiple sponsors to avoid intimacy with one person or to "shop" for an opinion that we desire.

Co-Sponsors – Where two people are in agreement to sponsor each other. This model seems to work best for ACA members having significant time and experience in the program.

Long Distance Sponsors – This can work well for geographically isolated ACA members. There is mail, e-mail, telephone, tape recordings, and voice stream where distance or circumstances prevent person-to-person contact. Additionally, the Internet has made these long-distance relationships more meaningful. Some ACA members who are geographically isolated use online ACA meetings and live chat to work an ACA program. They use a private chat room or the telephone to do extensive Step work with a long-distance sponsor. In addition to the Steps, there can also be discussion and meaning found in the Twelve Traditions in this method of sponsorship.

Indirect Sponsorship

*ACA Meeting*s act as a sponsoring influence. The groups that sponsor a person indirectly usually emphasize the Twelve Steps, Twelve Traditions, sponsorship, other program tools, and offer a well-stocked literature table with a phone list. The meetings are friendly and focus on recovery.

Step Study Groups that meet regularly to work the Steps together can provide indirect sponsorship.

Service Boards or Committees should not be used as a replacement for traditional sponsoring, but these boards and committees can mentor healthy behavior and offer sponsorship influence.

Chapter Eleven

Frequently Asked Questions:

Why Do We Have Sponsors in ACA?

We cannot recover alone or in isolation. Without sponsorship we are usually relying primarily on self-will and self-reliance. Being sponsored gives us a chance to surrender our compulsive self-reliance and move forward. For the sponsor, it gives us a chance to transform our rescuing role into true friendship in which we give help and ask for help. This is what true friends do.

What Does a Sponsor Do For a Newcomer?

A sponsor provides guidance for the newcomer for building a foundation for recovery on his or her journey through the Twelve Steps. The sponsor shares his story with the person being sponsored. The sponsor helps the newcomer move beyond discovery into recovery. The sponsor helps the sponsee understand the characteristics of an adult child. He or she explains the many forms of denial. In addition to Step work, the sponsor encourages meeting attendance, journaling, meditation, and seeking a Higher Power.

The sponsor encourages the newcomer to speak the truth of the abuse suffered in childhood. He or she validates the progress the newcomer makes in recovery. The sponsor helps the newcomer identify, express, and understand feelings. He or she explains the importance of resolving stored grief.

The sponsor shares about the importance of connecting with the Inner Child and becoming one's own Loving Parent. The sponsor shares his or her spiritual program with the sponsee.

What Does a Sponsor Do for Oldtimers?

We can always benefit from sponsorship, no matter how many years we have in the program. Many oldtimers in ACA did not have sponsors because there were none or only few in the early days of ACA development. Many read the program information, founded ACA groups, and immersed themselves in service work.

They achieved recovery as best they could. As a result, some of our older members have realized they missed crucial parts of the sequence of ACA recovery. Many of these older members have shown humility by asking a newer member to help them with the Twelve Steps. Some older members have worked their Fourth and Fifth Steps (inventory Steps) for the first time through this method. It is never too late to work all phases of the ACA program, including the Twelve Steps.

What is an Effective Sponsor?

The effective sponsor watches for willingness from the person he or she is sponsoring. The effective sponsor pays attention to whether the sponsee completes Step work and attends meetings regularly. Some newcomers want to talk on the phone in great detail about their childhood experiences or relationship issues, but they remain unwilling to take action. They have many excuses, ailments, and rationalizations for failing to take action. None of it makes sense when compared to the insanity or dysfunction in their lives. When this occurs, the sponsor moves on to someone who is willing to go to meetings and work a program. This is not a cruel decision, nor is it abandonment. We risk becoming an enabler if we listen to someone languishing in the problem without a plan to move forward. We also deny our recovery experience from someone who really wants what we have to offer as a sponsor.

Effective ACA sponsors are in active recovery. They have worked the Twelve Steps and have an understanding of the sequence of recovery. The sequence begins with realizing an ACA bottom, confronting denial, and surrendering. There must be an admission of family dysfunction, followed by openmindedness on spiritual matters, followed by a self-inventory and admission of wrongs. Next the person asks for character defects to be removed and becomes willing to make amends, take a daily inventory, and carry the ACA message to others. Active sponsors know this sequence and look for ways to help others follow this path through the Steps.

A potential sponsor leads by example. He or she shows up at meetings regularly and provides humble leadership and service at the meetings. In program business he or she observes the Twelve Traditions. The sponsor honors commitments.

An effective ACA sponsor keeps the focus on himself or herself. The active sponsor knows his story and how to tell it with honesty and humility. In addition to Step work, the story can include childhood neglect, understanding grief, getting in touch with the Inner Child, and becoming one's own Loving Parent. The sponsor explains the connection between childhood abuse and neglect, and the effect that has on his or her adult life.

An ACA sponsor deals with problems in a timely manner as well. The sponsor admits strengths and limitations readily. The sponsor is considerate and respectful of others. He or she has achieved an observable level of serenity.

What a Sponsor Does Not Do

An ACA sponsor with an addiction must not be active in that addiction. We cannot sponsor others if we are drinking, drugging, or engaged in some other addictive behavior that would qualify as relapse.

A sponsor in ACA is not a parent, partner, guru, family member, authority figure, or Higher Power to the person being sponsored. The sponsor does not presume to have superior intellect, skills, or talent. The sponsor does not judge or label the sponsee. The sponsor does not invalidate the feelings or the insights of the person being sponsored.

He or she does not do for the sponsees what they can do for themselves. The sponsor does not give or lend money. He or she typically does not provide food, clothing, shelter, or jobs. However, in some cases, the sponsor can urge a sponsee to become employed to gain financial independence.

The sponsor does not abuse, threaten, or abandon sponsees. A sponsor does not become sexually involved with the person. Finally, the sponsor does not accept abuse from a sponsee. The sponsor protects his or her own boundaries.

Overcoming the Fear of Sponsorship

Abuse from authority figures in childhood has left us on guard as adults about authority figures. We tend to place people in the category of an authority figure when they may not be such a person. Some of us can be skeptical of sponsorship and sponsors. Our past experiences tell us that any leader, employer, or officer is inherently an authority figure and is to be distrusted. This is one of the reasons that the fellow traveler model of sponsorship was implemented in ACA. Sponsors in ACA lead by example instead of by rules and threats. We need not fear sponsorship. Some of the recovery work we do in ACA is far too intense to face alone. On our journey, we need the assistance of a trusted friend with knowledge of recovery.

A sponsor is definitely needed for the sponsee to get the most out of ACA. In dysfunctional and alcoholic families we learned to avoid telling the truth about the family to outsiders. We are honest with our sponsors, but there is no coercion here. We share with our sponsors only what we feel comfortable in sharing when we are ready. However, we make an attempt to challenge our denial. We break the family rule that tells us to keep secrets or to keep information hidden. Hiding information or keeping secrets can prolong our confusion and isolation.

How Do We Locate a Sponsor?

We go to different ACA meetings and listen to members sharing their experiences. In addition to meetings, we can look for a sponsor at conventions, retreats, and service activities. We find people who work a program, attend meetings, and have an understanding of ACA principles. We ask potential sponsors what they expect of their sponsees. As we listen to what we might be expected to do for our recovery, we remember how much effort we put into codependence and care-taking of others. Before recovery, some of us spent countless hours in resentment, losing sleep and cleaning up after someone in our codependent relationship. We usually worked long hours and paid all the bills. We rescued ungrateful people with our money or our time. We typically placed everyone else first. There were moments of exhaustion or near exhaustion. In some cases, our immune system was affected, and we became ill. No day was too long, and no amount of effort was too much. So as we listen to suggestions about attending meetings or working the Twelve Steps, we realize that recovery takes far less effort than the struggles of codependence.

As we talk with a potential sponsor, we get a sense of compatibility, but we avoid notions of perfectionism or the perfect match. Differences are not always a negative. We should not be too picky as long as the person is committed to ACA recovery and helping others.

Next, we can ask for the person's telephone number and call to talk about ACA. We see if we are comfortable talking with that person on the telephone. We might go through this process with two or three people. Eventually we ask one of them to be our sponsor. If we want to move at a slower pace, we might ask to meet that person at a restaurant to talk about expectations. We can talk about what sponsorship includes and what it does not include. It usually includes availability of time to do Step work and an exchange of mutual respect. In some cases, we might talk about a trial period to see if it works out. We can commit to a trial period of four to six weeks to see how it goes. At the end of the time period, we revisit the agreement.

Sometimes ACA sponsors are not readily available. When this happens we may have to seek out a sponsor through a long-distance method or by visiting other towns where ACA is more active.

What Will a Sponsor Expect From a Sponsee?

A sponsor will expect a sponsee to actively participate in his or her recovery. The sponsor will expect the person to be honest and respectful. He or she will expect the sponsee to follow through on commitments to attend ACA meetings. The person being sponsored will need to make regular contact with the sponsor. The sponsor will expect the sponsee to accept full responsibility for his or her program and behavior.

When Should I Get a Sponsor?

Newcomers are encouraged to get a sponsor immediately. Oldtimers without sponsors are also encouraged to get a new perspective on their process from a peer sponsor.

Should a Sponsor and Sponsee Be Members of the Same Sex?

The ACA Sponsorship Committee interviewed many members of the fellowship. They concluded that having a same-sex sponsor is preferable for heterosexual members to avoid romantic involvement. Newcomers are vulnerable to manipulation and seek to accommodate others. They can focus on others rather than the program. Even if there is no romantic involvement between a sponsor and sponsee, the potential for confusion is too great. It is best for men to sponsor men and women to sponsor women to avoid confusion.

Gays and lesbians need to consider similar issues. Dysfunctional behavior – whether gay or straight – can undermine the program for the sponsor and the sponsee. We avoid these situations by having same-sex sponsors for heterosexuals and being mindful of our orientation if we are gay, lesbian, or bisexual. This does not prohibit a gay man or woman from having a male or female sponsor, but there are issues to consider and to talk over.

Who Can Be an ACA Sponsor?

Anyone in the ACA fellowship actively working his or her own program may sponsor others in this program.

How Does Sponsorship Help the Sponsor?

By becoming involved in ACA and helping others, the sponsor realizes he or she is making a real connection to life and people. This is what the person has craved but missed in childhood and in attempts at relationships before finding ACA. By staying involved, the sponsor remembers where he or she came from. The person remembers the isolation, despair, and confusion and does not want to go back there. By staying involved, the sponsor can avoid an ACA relapse and a return to isolation or self-sufficient hell.

Involved sponsors also continue to grow spiritually and gain all the benefits of the ACA way of life. He or she remains connected to a Higher Power through the Inner Child. By staying in meetings and in fellowship with others, the sponsor recognizes and lives the promises of ACA. The person can reflect upon how far he or she has come.

When is a Person Ready to Be a Sponsor?

We are aware of members with many years in the program who have never done their family-of-origin work, grief work, or Inner Child work, meaning they have not grown emotionally. So while time in the program is a factor for selecting an informed sponsor, it should not be the only factor. At the very least, a potential sponsor will have worked the Twelve Steps and will be aware of The Laundry List traits. The sponsor will be aware of his or her dysfunctional family role. The potential sponsor will have identified with a Higher Power and Inner Child and addressed some of his or her wreckage of the past.

11

Does a Sponsor Need a Sponsor?

Most definitely. Sponsoring others does not exclude a person from having feelings and needing to ask for help and support. The healthiest ACA sponsors have sponsors and use them.

How Many People Should You Sponsor at One Time?

Most people who have achieved a level of recovery have a full, rich, and rewarding life, so their time is limited. Some ACA members sponsor one person at a time while others sponsor as many as half a dozen. The number is not always important. The main focus is how well we can help another person make progress in the program. Some sponsors can help only one person at a time make progress in the Steps while others can help several.

New sponsors might start with one sponsee before expanding their commitment. The sponsor may gradually add another sponsee as his or her time permits. We should not use work, play, or other activities to avoid sponsoring others. When we do this, we cheat ourselves out of the rewards of this important aspect of ACA recovery.

What Can I Do for My Sponsee If I Am Unavailable at Times?

If we are pressed for time but still want to sponsor others, we can make it work. We begin by being clear from the start that we are limited on time but that we want to be a sponsor. We also make a commitment to attend ACA meetings regularly ourselves. Effective sponsors need to attend meetings to be able to pass on the hope that ACA offers. We cannot give away what we do not have, so meeting attendance is critical for our own recovery and personal growth. If we travel a lot, we must make a commitment to attend meetings in the cities we travel to. We can also participate in online meetings and telephone meetings. We make a commitment to find ACA wherever we might travel.

We next help the sponsee develop a support network of ACA friends and contacts. This helps when the sponsor is not available. With the support plan, the sponsee may attend extra meetings, call group members, journal, or contact the sponsor by cell phone or e-mail. These options help the person being sponsored to seek support from others, in addition to seeking support from the sponsor. The sponsor and sponsee have face-to-face meetings when time allows. This type of relationship can work as long as the sponsor and sponsee are committed to making progress in the program. All the elements of a traditional sponsor and sponsee relationship can be accomplished by this arrangement as well. Step work, phone contact, meeting attendance, and service work can be accomplished even if a sponsor has limited time to give.

How Does a Sponsor or Sponsee End the Sponsorship?

There are a variety of reasons for ending a sponsee and sponsor relationship. We have already discussed moving on from a sponsee unwilling to take action. At the same time, a person being sponsored may move on from a sponsor unwilling to return calls or be available for program work.

Relapse into alcohol or drug use, disrespectful behavior, and illegal or immoral behavior are grounds to dissolve the partnership. That said, disagreements in general are not always a reason for dissolving the relationship. When either party decides he or she needs to move on, that person needs to honest, but tactful, about the decision.

We offer a fellowship story on how one sponsor and sponsee ended a relationship.

In another Twelve Step program, a meeting leader suggested to newcomers to attend three meetings a week and study the Steps in one of them. I did those things. When it was time to find a sponsor, I got up my courage, asked that meeting leader, and she agreed.

Two years later I wrote out my Fourth Step inventory. After I shared it with my sponsor she offered me refreshments. I realized that her regard for me had not changed, even though she knew all my shameful, guilt-producing behavior. I had no more secrets.

I have no words to express how light I felt. I truly thought I could walk on air.

Then one day my sponsor stopped attending meetings. I called to ask why. She said she attended an assertiveness training workshop and now had the tools to deal with her life. She no longer needed a program. She invited me to continue to call her, but I did not want to. It did not seem right if she was no longer coming to meetings.

I felt abandoned. If she loved me, she would come to meetings to see me, I thought. So I decided not to ask anyone else to be my sponsor. Someone else could just abandon me, too. I did not want to have to go through that feeling of being abandoned again. I did not know then that pain is built into all relationships. I gave up the good in fear of the pain.

So, while I still called people on the phone to "talk program" with them, I no longer had a regular sponsor. One program friend, in particular, became a co-sponsor. She calls me to talk, but then she insists that I share my current issues with her before she hangs up. We have never talked about a formal co-sponsorship, but that is how I view it. She is the one who will always listen to me.

As for my former sponsor, I saw her not long ago. I was taking an evening walk, saw her, and greeted her. She smiled, nodded, and passed me. I turned to say something further but stopped when she did not look back. I let her go.

There have been others down through the years who have been informal sponsors for me: people I called for help and people who read my face at meetings and would not let me go until we had come to some resolution for what was bothering me. All of their help has been invaluable in my recovery.

The following affirmations and exercises are for sponsors and sponsees. Read over the affirmations and attend an ACA meeting. Share about what you have learned.

11

Affirmations for Sponsees (These Can Also Apply to the Sponsor)

1. I can ask for help without feeling like I am a burden.

2. I am treating others with respect and expect others to treat me with respect.

3. I can be equal in a relationship with another person.

4. I am capable of selecting a healthy sponsor.

5. I have willingness to do whatever it takes to recover.

6. I am following the suggestions of my sponsor in my path of recovery.

Affirmations for Sponsors (These Can Also Apply to the Sponsee)

1. I have something to offer another person.

2. I can help someone with what I have learned in recovery.

3. I will share my experience instead of giving advice.

4. I will avoid "fixing" others or rescuing others.

5. I can help another ACA regardless of the type of abuse we experienced as children.

6. I am more alike than I am different from another person.

Sponsorship Writing Assignment – For the Sponsor

To be an effective ACA sponsor, you must understand the connection between The Laundry List traits and the ACA Steps, particularly Step One. The effects of family dysfunction mentioned in Step One are The Laundry List traits which include fearing authority figures, getting guilt feelings when we stand up for ourselves, and becoming an alcoholic or marrying one or both. There are other effects of family dysfunction, but The Laundry List traits are critical in understanding and working ACA's First Step.

ACA's First Step places the focus on the effects of alcoholism and family dysfunction and how we are powerless over these effects. Step One causes us to think about how our learned survival traits from childhood disrupt our adult lives. Our lives are unmanageable if we are honest about our hidden fears and secrets. We have no real choice until we address these Laundry List traits in ACA. Another program that attempts to help adult children places the emphasis on being powerless over alcohol in Step One. In ACA, we place the emphasis on the effects of alcoholism and family dysfunction in Step One. The ACA adapted Steps are designed specifically to help the adult child. They are designed to address trauma and neglect in addition to addressing the addictiveness of the adult child personality. The ACA Twelve Steps address shame, abandonment, fear, and a deep sense of being flawed, while also leading the Step worker to self-worth, self-forgiveness, and a true connection to a Higher Power through the Inner Child.

After understanding the powerlessness and unmanageability in Step One, the effective ACA sponsor must know the sequence of recovery to help another person with his or her recovery process. There are different views on the sequence of recovery so we have chosen the Twelve Steps for one method. The Twelve Steps show a progressive line of recovery that begins with hitting bottom and leads to a spiritual awakening or awareness.

11

Chapter Eleven

For this assignment, you are being asked to list the sequence of recovery contained within the Steps. After bottoming out, the person proceeds through the Steps if willingness has been achieved. The person admits powerlessness and unmanageability in Step One and becomes open to the possibility of a Higher Power in Step Two. Beginning with Step Three, finish out the sequence of the Steps as you understand it. For help, look at each Step and ask yourself what the Step is asking the person to do. For example, Step Three involves making a decision while Step Four involves a personal inventory. Complete the sequence of the Twelve Steps:

Step One – Hitting bottom and admitting powerlessness and unmanageability.

Step Two – Coming to believe. Becoming open to the presence of a Higher Power and restoration to sanity.

Step Three_____

Step Four_____

Step Five_____

Step Six_____

Step Seven_____

Step Eight_____

Step Nine_____

Step Ten_____

Step Eleven_____

Step Twelve_____

NOTE:
You may refer to Chapter Seven to learn more about the ACA Twelve Steps.

Suggestions for Hosting a Workshop on ACA Sponsorship

Many ACA groups contact the ACA World Service Office wanting to know how to improve sponsorship or get more people involved in sponsorship at the group level. The ACA Annual Business Conference has also addressed motions from groups wanting more information about sponsorship. The ACA trifold on sponsorship and this chapter are a great starting point toward that effort, but sponsorship begins with the individual and his or her attitude. We must understand that we have something to offer another person. We have lived through a dysfunctional upbringing, and we are practicing the principles of recovery. We are moving beyond mere survival to a real connection with ourselves, others, and a Higher Power. We can help an adult child when science, religion, and other avenues fall short. This is the great hidden fact about ACA. It is with this fact that we can build our sponsorship base and help the most people.

To put on a sponsorship workshop in your area, we offer some basic suggestions. In addition to this chapter, read the ACA pamphlets on sponsorship. Next, select presenters active in the ACA program. Ask them if they have worked the ACA Twelve Steps and if they participate in ACA recovery. Ask them if they have a sponsor or have used a sponsor. Workshop presenters should carry a clear ACA message as well.

In addition to selecting presenters, planning a workshop on ACA sponsorship includes selecting a date, time, and location of the workshop. A flyer should be distributed announcing the workshop. You should also prepare an agenda that outlines the events of the day. You may want to record the speakers and use the recordings as a resource for newcomers or to help new sponsors learn about sponsoring others.

You may also select a theme. For instance, you might announce an ACA sponsorship workshop that focuses on the sequence of the Twelve Steps; journaling and the Twelve Steps;

11

Chapter Eleven

the Inner Child and the Twelve Steps; long-distance sponsorship; group sponsorship; the fellow traveler model of sponsorship; working the Steps in a study group; or the principles of the Twelve Steps.

Another theme might be Step Five and how to hear a Fifth Step. Sponsors can share their experiences with listening to a Fifth Step and what to do when Step Five is completed by the sponsee. Many sponsors instruct the sponsee to immediately work Steps Six and Seven once they complete Step Five. The sponsee is instructed to go home and to meditate on willingness (Step Six) before humbly praying (Step Seven) to have shortcomings removed.

To determine interest in holding a sponsorship workshop, announce a business meeting for that purpose. You can usually set the workshop time and date at this meeting and begin contacting presenters.

11

Chapter 12

Relapse

*I*n ACA, we have stories of relapse and the importance of getting back to the program if relapse occurs. An ACA relapse always features a reenactment of our role while growing up in a dysfunctional family. We recreate the same fear, self-hate, and abandonment of our childhood. A relapse can take many forms, but all ACA relapses have this central feature.

An ACA relapse can bring a return of self-harming behavior. The behavior can include emotional eating, drug use, compulsive sexual relationships, or other harmful behaviors. We can become an aggressive authority figure and emotional persecutor while in relapse. The critical inner parent can return. We may also find ourselves in a controlling relationship without baseline honesty or trust. We can feel used.

Relapse in this program can be subtle, gradual, and insidious. While there are different forms of relapse, the setback has the common characteristics of willful control, manipulation, dishonesty, and turning away from a Higher Power. Sometimes a single act can be considered a relapse. At other times we consider ourselves in relapse when we have engaged in an unhealthy behavior for many months with no honest effort to change our behavior. Some warning signs of relapse can include: not talking about things that upset us; keeping secrets; failing to get a sponsor; attending meetings but failing to work the ACA Twelve Steps; working only the Steps of another Twelve Step program while attending ACA; withdrawing from the fellowship and isolating; replacing our old addiction with another equally destructive one; skipping meetings or quitting meetings; seducing a newcomer; substituting another Twelve Step group or enlightenment group for this one; or pronouncing ourselves cured.

By pronouncing ourselves cured, we wrongly conclude that ACA is a limited program that addresses only certain areas of our lives such as abuse. In reality, ACA is a way of life that can improve every aspect of our lives. We can rely upon ACA to fulfill us emotionally and spiritually if we work the program. By facing our pain and fears, we experience a spiritual awakening that transforms us. We continue to attend meetings year after year so that we can grow spiritually and pass on what was given to us. The reward is emotional sobriety and a personality change that moves us away from being a fear-based person to a God-centered person. With our personality change, we claim our true identity. We realize that God is real and available to us. In ACA, a common result of a spiritual awakening is knowing that a Spirit of the Universe exists.

Some of the stories in this chapter represent relapses that are connected to romantic relationships. However, there can be relapses associated with our workplace or with an interaction that is not of a romantic nature. We can have a workplace relapse through workaholism that causes us to neglect our program. We abandon ourselves by avoiding meetings and by avoiding meaningful interaction with others. We fail to take time off from work to relax or play as well. In another situation, we can be in relapse with our parents as we try to extract love or acknowledgement from people who can give neither. Some of us have held out hope that a parent will finally love us or show understanding, but it never seems to come. We avoid our program and focus on their needs to our detriment. We can recreate our self-abandonment or self-harm in these interactions. We must turn away from this biologically-based relationship and focus on the actual parent to be free. Many of us believe our Higher Power is the parent who never abandons us. If we find ourselves in relapse with a birth parent, we pray for the strength to focus on ourselves and the ACA program. We turn toward God.

That said, many ACA members work a faithful ACA program with noticeable change only to stumble when they get involved in a romantic relationship. This is no cause for alarm. When this occurs, we apply what we have learned in meetings and this book. We review our Step work, we journal, we talk to our sponsor and attend a meeting. We talk about what is happening in our lives. We give ourselves a break and realize that we are learning to live differently. There will be a learning curve. We accept that we may not always look pretty while learning to live differently, but we have the acceptance of our ACA support group. We know our recovery does not have to be perfect, but we must be sincere in working the program instead of applying half measures.

With relationships, we apply the program principles of surrender, honesty, and self-inventory. We ask our Higher Power for help. We don't stop attending meetings or working the program just because we might be struggling with a relationship. The solutions to our relationship challenges can be found in ACA meetings and the literature, not in the struggling relationship.

A relapse can provide the motivation for us to truly give the program a chance to work. When we feel powerless and our lives again become unmanageable, we consider returning to ACA. Many people who have relapsed have expressed fear in being judged if they return to ACA and tell their story. In relapse, we forget that our ACA family is different than our dysfunctional family. We will not be judged, but we could be encouraged to apply the program and the Twelve Steps more vigorously. The Steps work if we work them with openness and honesty. ACA is an example of the healthy family we did not have growing up. ACA gives us a second chance.

Our members share about their experiences with relapse and finding their way back to ACA meetings.

When I Think I'm Okay, I Know I'm in Trouble

Relapse for me is thinking I have no problems. Thinking I can control my life without help from God, my program, or my Steps are the warning signs. I often feel I know what to do when I really don't. I need my program and my Higher Power so I can make the right decisions in my life.

I heard a joke about the ways different Twelve Step people overcome their addictions. In AA, they go hunting and shoot the lion. In Overeaters Anonymous, they capture the lion, put it in a cage, take it out three times a day, and pet it. In ACA, we track down the lion, catch it, put it in a cage, and then move in with it.

I see relapse in ACA as believing there is no lion. By ignoring the lion, I believe I don't have to wake up in the cage, do the work necessary to tame the lion, and get out of the cage.

I Traded My Program for a Woman

After two years in the program I married a bright, beautiful, ambitious woman. She was so unlike my mother. As I spent more time with her, I spent less time at meetings. We moved to a small, garden suburb far away from where we worked. I maintained program friendships, but I was too enamored with her to leave her and attend meetings. I lost contact with many program people. The problems started in the last year of my marriage, but I didn't go to meetings when I was in pain. I didn't want to admit I was having problems with this "perfect" marriage.

I needed my life to be in chaos to recognize that I needed to come back to ACA. I was in the middle of my divorce. Because I owed thousands of dollars to creditors, I had to declare bankruptcy. I felt I had wasted three years of my life.

I attended six meetings a week when I returned. I found out so much more about myself in one year than in the first five, because this time I had to work to alleviate the pain. I volunteered for service. I decided I didn't have to share at every meeting, so I was able to listen more. If I wasn't comfortable in a particular meeting,

I found another one so I had no excuses not to go. I found supportive people I liked. I stopped feeling I had failed in my marriage when I realized that I had simply made an error in judgment that I will not repeat.

Another kind of program relapse for me is not stopping myself before I act inappropriately. I now catch myself before I act without discretion or, at least, when I'm in the middle of the action. When I'm feeling threatened now, I step back, look at the situation objectively, and then decide how to handle the problem. I still don't always make the best decisions, but I do see the disaster coming in time to avoid much of the resulting damage. I don't create a drama. The more I catch myself, the more I become aware of my behavior. The veil of denial is lifted, and I am learning about my assets and deficits as well as responding appropriately in situations. I'm glad I am not repeating the dysfunctional cycle, changing what I can in me. Lately, I often walk away from situations that are likely to bring out my worst behavior.

God, of course, is helping me change the things I can when I turn my will and my life over to God. Many times when I let go of difficult or volatile situations, I don't have emotional slips. Where the result of my behavior used to be disaster, it is now quite pleasant. I used to expect a warning followed by a painful situation. I believed that when things got bad, they were only going to get worse. I even caused situations to get worse. I don't sabotage myself in that way anymore.

During the first two years in this program I learned about the characteristics of adult children and the ways to overcome my dysfunctional behavior. I recognized that my father is an alcoholic. I learned about family dynamics and the relationship of alcohol in dysfunctional family systems. I understood the rudiments of how and why other people act as they do. Now I'm working on me and putting the focus on my own behavior.

It was difficult for me to learn these simple concepts about living, because they challenged the dysfunctional tenets I was taught as a child and on which I built my life. In ACA I have laid a solid foundation on firm ground, and I am constructing a happier, healthier life.

12

Chapter Twelve

What I Least Want to Divulge

Relapse in ACA, I thought, is only an illusion, because there's really no going backwards, just very sloppy progress at times. Then I remembered my first attempt to date after a year in the program. My life was working. I had done many anger and Inner Child workshops, and I felt so good I decided that it was time for me to try relationships again. I immediately became involved with an active sexaholic.

I didn't stop going to meetings, I just stopped being rigorously honest in them. I became selective about what I would share, because the people in the meeting knew my partner. Even in therapy I didn't want to talk about my imperfect relationship because it carried so much shame for me. I could be having problems in all other areas of my life and talk about that freely, but a relationship problem was a profound failure in my mind. When I talked about it, a throng of people gave me their opinions as to how I should proceed, so I stopped talking.

We're only as sick as our secrets, however, and I started having many secrets. Like keeping house, ultimately the work got done, but I stayed in a messy house for a very long time instead of cleaning it regularly.

None of the relationships I've had were mistakes, and none will be in the future. I simply need to work out my issues. I can't do it alone. I do it by trying, failing sometimes, and learning from my mistakes. Success is getting up one more time than I fall down.

I have learned why having an unsuccessful relationship is shameful to me. I still hear my mother's voice in my mind telling me every family failure was my fault. I internalized and accepted that shame, and I feel responsible for the failures in my relationships.

In my marriage it's tempting to harbor my secrets, too. It would be easy to fall into the pattern of deciding what I will and won't share in meetings since groups of people are still threatening to me. I have decided, however, to ask myself, "What's the one thing I really don't want to talk about?" I use that question as a tool to hone in on the thing I want to keep as a secret because it tells me where my sickness is. That is what I share about.

I believe my recovery will continue as long as I work on it. I can make my progress easier or harder depending on the choices I make, but my progress is not going to stop. I'm moving forward, regardless, and my choices will determine how comfortable I'll be.

Standing in the Heart of God

Unlike many programs, ACA seems to have a continuous stream of people coming in and leaving. In other Twelve Step programs, relapse too often results in ultimate death. Here, however, people learn some principles they practice until they get comfortable, then they leave believing they have what they need to succeed. When their lives deteriorate, they return.

My mother left my father and dropped me off with my grandmother when I was one year old. Seven years later she reclaimed me, we moved to another country, and she abandoned me. I became a latchkey child. I had a key to let myself into an empty house, and I stayed alone for hours. From this I learned I was supposed to be abandoned and that abandoning others is acceptable behavior, too. This message had tremendous influence on my life.

I learned to accept being alone. That was unchangeable. People were going to leave me. The rule in my family was, "Don't get close to anything or anyone because it is all going to be taken away." My grandmother, who was chased out of her homeland by enemy soldiers, learned that lesson and passed her fear on to her children. My mother passed it on to me. I wanted to die when I was growing up, so I used drugs and alcohol to stop feeling that all-pervasive fear. I needed to anesthetize myself daily.

I didn't want to go to ACA. I came here because I was suicidal. I had lost everything in my life, and a therapist told me to go to Adult Children of Alcoholics. I was absolutely astounded when I heard "The Problem" statement read at the beginning of my meeting, and I couldn't believe other people lived the way I did. Others had come from households like mine. Their lives were in constant upheaval. They had problems in their relationships, and they isolated. "The Problem" exactly delineated my characteristics one after the other. I really got excited, because I wasn't alone for the first time in my life. People told me to work the Twelve Steps. I worked my program enthusiastically. I reached out. I went to weekend retreats. I got a sponsor, and I began working the Steps. In nine months, I was so thoroughly involved in recovery I felt great, empowered, and healthy. Then I got into a relationship.

I had become sober, and I was taking care of myself. It was the best relationship I had ever had in my life. I believed I loved her, and she loved me. It was a relationship, however, that was doomed. The more she put her arms around me and held me, the less I needed to be nurtured. I no longer needed "the fix," because I knew it was there for me. I felt good. I had everything I wanted. I had someone to share my life with, somebody to hold me.

Unfortunately, I ignored my Inner Child. I was not considering how my Inner Child was reacting to this relationship or what my Inner Child wanted. I was dragging my Inner Child everywhere, just as my parents dragged me around. I began missing meetings because I had all these feelings surfacing. I thought I was out of control if I had to express my feelings. So I stopped sponsoring others and attending retreats. While I still went to other Twelve Step meetings, I used them to avoid dealing with my feelings about my family's dysfunction and isolation. I could easily discuss methods and techniques I used to avoid drinking. I just couldn't give voice to all the feelings inside me.

Knowing that this is the program that saved my life, I pulled away from it nonetheless. I got sober and gave up drugs, but I was dying. The path for me now is to reach the child inside of me. I was doing a great deal of work, but I decided that what would fix me was a relationship. I had a total relapse in ACA because I made the relationship more important than the program.

To work a good program, I was told, the Higher Power comes first, the program comes second, and everything else comes third. If a person adheres to these principles in this order of priority, everything else will work out.

My relationship became too important, and soon that relationship fell apart. I thank God for the nine months I was really involved with this program because program precepts automatically engaged for me when I needed them. I knew I had to get back here. I knew my relationship was stopping me from feeling. When the relationship was dissolved, it was as if Pandora's box was opening. I knew I had to get back here and get in touch with my Inner Child again. Returning to ACA, I worked on anger, on being a victim, and on interacting with my Inner Child. I learned to be a loving parent. No longer did I take my Inner Child into unsafe places. I also took a self-defense course so I can protect my Inner Child. I became stronger as a result of the efforts I made to protect my Inner Child and because of the strength he gives to me when we now work together. We are both flourishing.

For me, recovery is about spirituality. I've never been able to get into religion, but the spiritual part of this program has helped me. God got me here, God brought me back after my relapse, and God kept me sober. When I tried to find God and couldn't, somebody asked, "Why don't you live with God in your heart?" It seemed like a good idea, until I thought that if God resided in my heart he'd be about two inches tall. Instead, I decided to live in the heart of God. I can't tell you how big the heart of God is, but I'm standing in it today, and so are you.

12

Chapter 13

Relationships:
Applying What We Have Learned

*I*n ACA we become willing to apply what we learn in the program to our daily lives and to relationships. We must be willing to apply the principles of the Steps and to reparent ourselves if we want to change.

Moving away from codependent behavior and toward healthy relationships is one of the results of working the ACA program. We are not saying relationships become workable overnight, but they also are not as impossible as we once thought. For us, relationships can be a measuring stick for how well we have applied the ACA program in our lives.

Because of ACA, we have learned there are many kinds of relationships other than romantic involvement. This was a surprise to many of us who never had friends or who tended to sexualize relationships that ended in pain and loneliness. In ACA, we learn there are friendships, business relationships, and casual acquaintances in addition to romance. We also learn that it is okay to be alone. Learning to be alone in recovery is different than the isolation we practiced before recovery.

There are also unique relationships that are fulfilling and open up to us because of our ACA involvement. Some of us have become a big brother or big sister to a child from a single-parent home. This is a rewarding relationship for those of us who never had children for fear of harming or neglecting a child. In ACA we learn to trust ourselves and to contribute to a child's life.

Another unique relationship can include being paired with a new employee at work in a mentoring role. In this relationship, we are teamed up with a new employee to teach the person a new job or skill. We can use our listening skills and sense of patience learned in ACA to make this relationship enjoyable and meaningful. By addressing our control and perfectionism in ACA, we let others make mistakes and learn from them.

We have learned that not every relationship needs to lead to romantic or sexual involvement. If we have addressed our area of abandonment and shame thus far, we no longer see people as a potential source to medicate our fear of abandonment. We no longer use people to divert us from our own feelings by focusing our attention on someone else. We can finally face down the 12th Trait of the Laundry List. We no longer fear abandonment so much that we remain in unloving relationships.

Through ACA, we can begin to see people as individuals we would like to know rather than possess. This is freedom from codependence. For some of us we become a true friend to someone else for the first time in our life. This happens a lot in ACA. Many of us did not know how to be a friend to another person before working the ACA program. Through ACA, we have been given the gift of being called "friend." We have done the work. We know what it means to be a true friend.

Romantic relationships can bring great fear to adult children. Even some of us who have practiced an ACA program for years can struggle with intimate relationships. For the most part, if we are struggling with relationships we could have unfinished business in addressing our fear of abandonment. This fear is usually coupled with a fear of feeling our feelings. We must get past this fear that we cannot survive our feelings. We can. This is ACA. It is different than when we were children and were either forced to stuff our feelings, or we were traumatized and left alone to lie in pain.

Through recovery we learn to think about a relationship before entering one. This is new for us. Before finding ACA, we tended to jump into a relationship without thinking. We were impulsive and perhaps seeking excitement. When problems arose, we felt trapped or too embarrassed to leave. We worried what others might think, or we stubbornly stayed believing we could make the relationship work. But nothing changed. With ACA, we have a chance to do things differently. We have the gift of choice. We can think before we act.

Since relationships can be challenging, we ask new people to wait at least a year before attempting a more intimate relationship. The reason seems obvious. We are people who are vulnerable when we get here. We want to please others so we can easily focus on another rather than the ACA program. There is no true recovery in focusing on another at the expense of the Twelve Steps or attending meetings regularly.

Most of us know what an unhealthy relationship involves. It can be summed up in a few words: attempted control of another.

A healthy relationship involves talking about feelings, mutual respect, and a commitment to trust and honesty. There are many other elements to a successful and intimate relationship, but these are a good start. Not surprisingly, these are the tools and principles included in the ACA program: feelings, respect, trust, and honesty.

We learned about feelings and talking about feelings in great detail in Step Four. We learned that feelings can be our spiritual connection to the God of our understanding in addition to our connection with another. Feelings are how we let others know that we are angry, lonely, compassionate, or joyful. We also learned that the feelings of others are different than our own. We learned that others' feelings are not our feelings, but we can empathize with someone who is feeling fearful or alone. This is a critical aspect of romantic or intimate relationships. We can love someone and empathize with the person's feelings, but each person is responsible for his or her own feelings in the relationship. When we understand this, we can support our spouse or partner without trying to fix them. We avoid trying to talk them out of their feelings. We can listen to them instead of giving suggestions on what to do. Feelings pass. We learn that listening is sometimes the best support we can give our lover or partner. We let them feel their feelings and ask for the same when we have feelings.

We learned about respect at our first ACA meeting. We learned that we were respected and accepted for who we were. There were no pledges to sign or promises to make in ACA. We did not have to people-please or placate anyone in the meetings. We were respected for having survived our family of origin and reaching out for help. At our first meeting, we were offered unconditional acceptance and respect. We realized we could focus on ourselves and respect ourselves as well.

Another aspect of respect is asking for what we need, so that we can respect others and avoid passive-aggressive behaviors in our relationship. We can ask for what we need in a relationship instead of expecting someone else to read our minds. In ACA, we learn the difference between asking for what we need and making unrealistic demands on another. We figure out what we can live with and live without. This helps us understand what we truly need, instead of what we think we want. We respect others by telling them what we like and dislike. We listen to others do the same.

Gradually we learn to trust others, but trust begins with ourselves. We cannot trust another until we trust ourselves. We got our first inkling of trust from our ACA support group. This is perhaps the first group of people who truly accepted us and allowed us to recognize trust. We can talk openly in ACA about our lives without being judged.

That said, our groups are not perfect. Fellow ACA members have let us down, but for the most part, we know we can trust our group to listen to us and support us when we do not feel good about ourselves. They also share the good times with us. Our group members celebrate our growth and recovery with us.

With this kind of trust, we feel more confident in risking our feelings and hopes with another person. We know that we have a place to talk about our relationships and lives when things get clouded. We are not alone anymore. With trust, we let go of control in our relationships. We can trust another person to be who they are without having to monitor their thoughts and actions. With trust, we lay down a hypervigilant watch for signs of abandonment. We have exposed our false belief that we are not good enough. With the help of our home group, we have faced our fear that abandonment is inevitable.

Because we have an ACA group to rely on, we know we are going to be okay no matter what our significant other is doing or not doing. We know that we can focus on ourselves. We have friends we can trust. We learn that we do not have to depend upon a romantic relationship to supply all of our needs.

In addition to feelings, respect, and trust, honesty is a baseline element of any loving relationship. We cannot have an intimate relationship without honesty. We learned about the value of honesty beginning in Step One. We admitted that we are powerless over the effects of growing up in a dysfunctional home. We talked honestly about what happened in our families. We broke the "don't talk" and the "don't remember" rules. We got honest about our family secrets. This was not easy since we were raised with a strong emphasis on keeping secrets or not challenging authority figures who defined our reality. But we must have honesty in our relationships. This is a deal breaker for us. If someone is chronically dishonest with us, we must consider terminating the relationship. Because of ACA we are giving more of our true selves in a relationship, and we learn that we can ask for more.

We could write many more pages on relationships, but many of the answers are in front of us. With feelings, respect, trust, and honesty we no longer confuse love and pity. As our Promises state: "We will choose to love people who can love and be responsible for themselves."[1]

---

[1]ACA Promise Number Eight.

Our Relationship With Our Family

In addition to learning about the various types of relationships, we also realize that our existing relationships change as we begin to grow spiritually and emotionally in recovery. The changes we are making in our lives are not always accepted or understood by those closest to us. ACA is an anonymous program so we do not have to tell anyone that we are a member of the program. However, some of us will tell a brother or sister about the involvement. Some family members are supportive of our decision to join ACA. Others are confused or suspicious of the program. A few ACA members have been abandoned by their families when they begin the recovery process. They have been accused of being disloyal to the family. This is only natural since the ACA member is confronting denial and family secrets. The member is breaking his or her loyalty to the dysfunctional family system.

If the family withdraws support, this might feel new, but in reality the abandonment has always been there. We must realize that the family is actually withdrawing codependence instead of loving support. This is a critical distinction. We are not losing anything except codependence. We replace the codependence by focusing on ourselves and attending meetings.

Nonetheless, we can feel fearful or disappointed by our family's reaction. We can also see their pain, and we want to help. Through ACA, we realize we are powerless over another person. We know we cannot change anyone but ourselves. We cannot give ACA to someone who does not want it.

Not all families abandon the ACA member in recovery. Many families are supportive. A brother or sister, and sometimes a parent, will join ACA and find a new way of life. At the same time, some family members who have shunned an ACA member will have a change of heart. They open up a line of communication even though they might never enter the doors of ACA.

The following shares represent our relationship with our family or significant others once we find recovery. The shares reflect noticeable change and personal growth.

A couple of shares show how people enter recovery while a significant other may not be working a program. The relationship becomes more difficult because only one person is headed toward change.

My Family Thinks I'm a Little Crazy

Although I was the youngest child I've always been the one to take care of everyone in the family. I've never been able to speak up for myself or say "no" to anybody. I designated myself as the person who would solve every problem because it was easier than solving my own problems.

I have difficulty dealing with my family today. They ask me to do something now, and I politely refuse to accommodate them. I feel uncomfortable denying them. They often stare at me as if I had no right to refuse them. They expect me to do everything they ask me to do.

My sister and I don't communicate any longer since she doesn't understand who I am. She says I'm not the "normal" person I used to be. They assume the death of my other sister has seriously affected my behavior. They truly feel I'm the crazy one now.

None of my family can understand why I'm changing and working a program of recovery. I feel like I'm an infant learning how to walk, taking very small steps.

His Family Knew He Was Changing

When I found ACA I wanted to tell my family, but I knew they might not understand. I remained quiet. As I recovered and stepped out of my role as the family mascot and screw-up, my family began to notice. I did not see my family a lot because I lived in another city, but they noticed a change in me at holidays. I had quit drinking and drugging so they noticed.

When I finally told them about ACA their response surprised me. One sister began talking about our father's alcoholism in a new light. Another sister smiled and said she loved me. She encouraged me to keep going in recovery. My mother never understood, but she was happy that I was staying out of jail and working steady. My alcoholic father was dead so there was no issue with him. I eventually forgave him after much anger work and prayer. He had a disease called alcoholism, but what he did to his family was not right.

Twenty years has passed since I started my ACA journey. My family has not changed that much, but I have. I still have a sister who is the lost child, and I have another sister who is the hero, knocking herself out for dinners and get-togethers. She is 60 years old. I gave her a recovery book to read years ago. I have nephews and nieces who are active in codependence and addiction. But I also have a nephew who is open to what I am talking about in ACA.

I am not overly concerned with my family. I don't view them as gloomy or lost. I see their pain and their loss, but I know I can't fix them. God will take care of them. I remember someone telling me once that I can love someone where they are at. I never knew what that meant until recently.

Will She Stay if She's Not As Needy?

We need to move soon. I have been comparing my family's resistance to the coming move with my wife's reactions to the changes I am making in recovery.

As I got healthier in recovery, my wife felt threatened and became anxious because she was unsure of the outcome. This is a typical reaction of a spouse in a codependent relationship. As I became more independent my wife perceived me as less needy and, therefore, less needful of her. Her great fear was that she would ultimately become expendable. She did not understand how people could have a relationship that was not based on need. Neither did I. It was beyond our experience.

Recovery was so threatening because we each believed we would not have a role to play in our marriage if the other person grew stronger. I was surprised to see that belief in her, and then I recognized it in myself as well. As we became healthier we asked counselors and people in support groups to tell us if we were making progress.

My wife got healthier, too. She looked more beautiful, more capable, and more independent, and then I started feeling anxious. I thought I had to grow as fast as she did so I would not become useless to her and then eventually be abandoned.

Knowing we both feel anxious and threatened by change, I will use this information to make our move less stressful. Keeping the kids in school for as long as possible will help provide stability for them. If our lives remain stable in the period leading up to the move, then the actual moving process will be more pleasant for all of us.

I Changed My Focus to Change My Life

Before I came to this program I was barely surviving. I felt depressed, powerless, and alone. No longer willing or able to suppress my feelings, they came up effusively and erratically. I spent weeks crying, even sobbing, from the pain, the confusion, and the hurt about unfinished childhood experiences.

When I came to this program I was ready for a change. I am changing what I can. My feelings changed when I accepted my feelings, my past, and my post-traumatic stress. I did not accept that process easily. I had to convince myself my feelings were legitimate.

I needed to acknowledge and accept that I was an abused child. Once I did the in-depth family-of-origin work thoroughly, I felt stronger. I moved forward in recovery more easily when I didn't have to spend so much energy feeling old feelings or repressing memories of the past. Only then was I able to turn my attention and energy into discovering who I am.

I still get flashbacks. I relive the childhood visions when they come. I confront the very real, very scary parts as though I am actually back there in time. After I cry, I feel and express my anger. To stop my need to relive each traumatic event endlessly, I expose the perpetrator aloud at meetings; I bash them symbolically in the guise of a cushion or punching bag. In these ways I validate myself. With the support of my meeting I no longer feel alone.

I am now making huge changes in my life by taking small steps. I have the same job I had, but now it is very satisfying because I'm using my full potential. My job hasn't changed, but I have. The same

13

is true with my imperfect marriage. My husband and I have more intimacy, more honesty, and more interaction. Our marriage is becoming authentic. If we ultimately get a divorce, it will be a real divorce for irreconcilable differences, not for undefined identities, values, or boundaries. At this moment my marriage is a relatively minor issue. Divorce would be disruptive and not the right thing to do to myself at this time. I just have too many other things to do.

I'm growing a garden so I have beautiful flowers around me and delicious fresh fruit and vegetables to eat. I take the time to plan for my own comfort and take care of my needs. I exercise daily. I take long hikes. Even when I'm very busy and find it hard to legitimize taking time for myself, I take it. I know if I don't, I will lose the recovery I enjoy today. Taking care of myself is the right thing for me to do. It is the only way I can live today.

He Held on to His Truth

Change has been difficult in my life, but absolutely essential. When I started coming to this program I started being truthful with myself for the first time. I was learning how to honor my relationships.

I found when I was honest with friends and family, it often upset them. Some of my friends moved a step or two with me, and others simply would not budge. I had to let those friends go. My best friend said he thought ACA was a Twelve Step cult when he ended our friendship. Even though I was new in recovery, I recognized this as his defense mechanism. When I was sharing insights in my recovery, he couldn't accept any of it because it was far too threatening. He had to keep himself safe by denying the validity of what I was telling him.

I also had to stay away from my parents for quite a while, because I just couldn't hold my truth and be in their presence at the same time. I needed to be around people in recovery.

At the same time there were despicable things I had done that I was too afraid to admit to anyone including myself. I came to meetings and shared this ugly side of myself. People in recovery would genuinely embrace me for having shared so honestly. Their acceptance was quite a contrast from what I expected.

13

It's been very scary to let go of my old predictable behaviors and embrace new behaviors with unknown consequences. I feel off-balance as if I'm stumbling or falling. When I do reach out for the unknown I inevitably grab hold of something new, something different, something better.

I write in my journal daily. I occasionally have an insight or two that comes to life when I share it. In doing my family-of-origin work, I recognized that my behavior in the past has caused me a great deal of pain.

I attend my meetings once or twice a week to provide me with the comfort, support, and the stability I need to participate in the change process. Having a safe place allows me to slowly take the little steps, admit the truths, and have the insights.

Change in Me Sometimes Makes Others Uncomfortable

Change makes me feel unsafe, abandoned, and alone. I have never found a way to make change less scary. I am not a person who welcomes change. I learned to be safe as a child by following all the rules. I like rules. I like regulations. They make me feel safe. It's much more difficult for me to grow and recognize when people are stepping across my boundaries.

My family, my friends, and my boyfriend all had difficulty accepting changes in me. When I had made a change, my boyfriend would throw his arms up in the air and say, "I just don't know if I can put up with this!" The implied threat was that he would leave me if I continued in my recovery. He isn't alone in these feelings. The more I change, the more I get these little hints from people around me to go back to my prior behavior, because that's when they felt safe with me.

I thought the dysfunctional people who were continually disrupting my life would finally become aware of their bad behavior, change their behavior, and follow my rules. They didn't. They continued drinking, using drugs, or practicing other addictions. I continued trying to control other people. No one was changing.

I still interact with many family members who are unaware they are dysfunctional. They just think I'm sick, but I'm quite sure they are also dysfunctional. I am able to interact with them today by not participating in their current drama. That doesn't mean I don't ever get involved, but the minute I recognize the drama, which becomes easier and easier to do, I disengage and let them do whatever they need to do to get comfortable.

My hardest lesson to learn is that I am the one who needs to change her behavior. One of the gifts of the program is my understanding and recognition that reactions or over-reactions by family and friends to my change are not personal. Their reaction is not about me, but about their fear of their lives changing. My recovery is easier because of this insight.

In recovery, I feel the fear and take the difficult walk through the fear. I use the Twelve Steps, the meetings, and the telephone.

My Parents were not Monsters, Just Alcoholics

I came to ACA with the deep, dark secret that I hated my parents. I knew there was something terribly wrong with me. People are supposed to love their parents. My father, however, was an alcoholic, and my mother raged incessantly. Both were violent. They frightened me, and I hated them for it.

My parents' illness affected my siblings and me profoundly. I believed if I had been a better daughter and a better person, my parents would not have acted the way they acted. Knowing that my behavior as a child had no effect on how my parents chose to live their lives is a wonderful gift.

I thought my parents, my husband, and my children were keeping me in bondage, locked up, and unable to live my life freely. I have learned in this program that I am the only person limiting my freedom because of my fears.

In ACA I've started coming out of denial. I discovered others who had parents like mine. By exposing many of my family's secrets in meetings I have changed the impact of my childhood on my life today. Merely stating aloud, "My father was an alcoholic," relieved me of the overwhelming stress of keeping the secret hidden. I know now that the things my parents did which hurt me so much were not done to hurt me. My parents' behavior and their choices weren't about me. I've come to understand my parents were not monsters, just alcoholics.

I've been able to release many of my fears by using the Twelve Steps as the method and the meetings as a supportive forum. When I expose my fears to the light of day by telling others, the fears don't seem as bad or evil as they were when hidden within that dark place inside of me.

Confronting my fear was not easy, but it has changed my life dramatically. I certainly could never have made this change in myself, by myself. I thank ACA for being here and supporting me through this.

I Wondered If I Contributed to the Dysfunction

I came to the program because I felt unhappy, abandoned, and generally miserable. Aspects of "The Problem" fit my life so well, particularly the parts on responsibility and choosing unhealthy relationships, even though neither one of my parents was alcoholic.

As a child I was abandoned quite often, though I wasn't aware of it at the time. I was expected to entertain myself, to make friends, and to work hard to make others comfortable. I didn't have many childhood friends. I had no instruction and few experiences in choosing friends.

I had no modeling for having, stipulating, or enforcing boundaries. I would allow children, family members, and others to use me to their advantage. I would do many things for others and then receive nothing in return.

Because of this program I've become aware of what I was doing. I was the giver in my relationships, because I wanted to be involved. I wanted my partners to reciprocate. I expected more than they were willing or able to give. When I would invest so much into my family or friends and they didn't respond with as much enthusiasm, I felt abandoned.

I began to wonder how I was contributing to this. My conclusion is that I am responsible for focusing my attention on people who were not in a position to respond appropriately, or they weren't who I thought they were.

This program has helped me become more aware of my shortcomings so that I've made changes in my behavior. I am more aware of how I overstep my boundaries, and how I try to force things to work the way I want them to work. I've stopped "fixing" my relationships and initiating all the family celebrations, even though I feel uncomfortable and guilty for abandoning family and friends. I'm learning to reallocate my misused energy more appropriately.

I am still uncomfortable with different family members who encourage me to please them as I had done in the past and do for them what they are unwilling to do for themselves. They prefer that I do all the work so they reap the benefits. These one-sided relationships just weren't working out well for me.

I am learning a better way to take care of my own needs, and I am more content because of it. I have a lot to offer people who will take responsibility for half of the relationship. I am no longer doing things to please others or to get love, appreciation, or respect. If I do things that happen to benefit or please others, I do them for self-education, self-love, self-appreciation, or self-respect.

My blinders are off. My denial is gone. I don't get excited about something that isn't there, something that's only a fantasy of what I would like. Instead I see what is really there.

13

Chapter 14

Taking Our Program to Work

*A*CA is a proven program that can help us in every area of our lives if we apply it. We can take our program with us wherever we go. Working our program outside the meeting rooms of ACA has produced dramatic changes in our lives. In addition to seeing changes in our closest relationships, we can see a change in our attitude and in our relationships at work. We seem to feel more confident in what we do for a living, or we learn to give ourselves a break when we make a mistake. We learn to resolve situations that may have been simmering for months or even years. We become actors rather than reactors, and for some of us, our rediscovered inner strength prompts us to leave a dissatisfying job.

We gradually integrate our program at work. We make small changes, such as not always volunteering for overtime. We make a conscious decision to step back from our role as people-pleasers and let others volunteer for extra work. We may gently set a boundary with a fellow employee who takes things from our desk without asking. We learn to say, "Can you ask before taking things from my desk?"

Taking our program to work doesn't mean we analyze others or invite them to ACA meetings. We avoid preaching about ACA. We do not invade boundaries with our ACA program, but we stand ready to apply the principles of honesty, humility, and forgiveness in our lives outside ACA meetings. We usually don't break our anonymity at work; however, there are occasions when we can share about our program with a co-worker if our motives are clear. We usually talk to our sponsor or another ACA member before breaking our anonymity.

It is essential that we practice ACA in every area of our lives to continue to grow emotionally and spiritually. We cannot act one way in an ACA meeting and another way outside the meetings. We cannot let the behavior of a co-worker or any other person divert us from our program. We are stepping away from the days of giving away our power to others and wandering through life in an unfocused manner. By practicing ACA outside of meetings, we can avoid recreating our family of origin at work. We can avoid being a victim, a hero, or the invisible employee who is rarely noticed and passed over for pay raises. Without working our program, we can easily take the patterns and roles we learned at home and apply them in the workplace. We risk taking our parental programming and our false attitudes about ourselves into our working life.

Even if we don't work full-time, looking at ACA traits in the workplace can help improve our interaction in other groups or social settings. We may work part-time or have a position in a volunteer, charitable, or worship group. We may be retired and be part of a recreational group. The personality types that can be difficult for us will likely show up whenever and wherever we interact with others on a regular basis. This chapter on ACA experience in the workplace will help us focus on our program and improve our behavior in relationships wherever we go.

What is the Workplace Laundry List?

The workplace laundry list is a list of 24 statements that describe many of our thoughts and interactions at work.[1] The list is a creative adaptation of The Laundry List (Problem), which is a detailed look at the 14 traits of an adult child. The workplace

---

[1] The ACA annual convention held in southern California has offered panel discussions on "ACA in the Workplace." A literature search discovered an item in the ACA WSO files titled "A Laundry List for the Workplace," but no source was identified. At the 2005 convention, a Twelve Step meeting was held which focused on "ACA in the Workplace." The meeting leader developed a new handout, "Working at the Laundromat: A Laundry List for ACAs in the Workplace."

list shows how we can attempt to recreate our dysfunctional family roles at work or in some social settings. While working the Steps and attending meetings improves much of this behavior, the workplace laundry list further focuses our efforts to improve ourselves outside of meetings. Many ACAs have used this list to identify and change their ineffective behaviors. The "qualifier" mentioned in these statements is the person who infected us with the disease of alcoholism or other dysfunction.

Working at the Laundromat – A Checklist for ACAs in the Workplace

1.   We confuse our boss or supervisor with our alcoholic parent(s) or qualifier and have similar relationship patterns, behaviors, and reactions that are carry-overs from childhood.

2.   We confuse our co-workers with our siblings or our alcoholic parent(s) and repeat childhood reactions in those working relationships.

3.   We expect lavish praise and acknowledgment from our boss for our efforts on the job.

4.   Authority figures scare us and we feel afraid when we need to talk to them.

5.   We get a negative "gut reaction" when dealing with someone who has the physical characteristics or mannerisms of our alcoholic qualifier.

6.   We have felt isolated and different from everyone around us, but we don't really know why.

7.   We lose our temper when things upset us rather than dealing with problems productively.

8.   We busy ourselves with our co-workers' jobs, often telling them how to do their work.

9. We can get hurt feelings when co-workers do things socially together without asking us, even though we have not made an effort to get to know them and join in the social life.

10. We are afraid to make the first move to get to know a co-worker better, thinking they will not like us or approve of us.

11. We usually do not know how to ask for what we want or need on the job, even for little things.

12. We do not know how to speak up for ourselves when someone has said or done something inappropriate. We try desperately to avoid face-to-face confrontations.

13. We are sensitive and can get extremely upset with any form of criticism of our work.

14. We want to be in charge of every project or activity, feeling more comfortable when we are in control of every detail, rather than letting others be responsible.

15. We may be the workplace "clown" to cover up our insecurities or to get attention from others.

16. We are people-pleasers and may take on extra work, or our co-workers' tasks, in order to be liked and receive approval from others.

17. We do not know how to be assertive in getting our needs met or expressing a concern. We may have to repeatedly rehearse our comments before delivering them.

18. We have felt that we do not deserve a raise, promotion, better workspace, or a better job.

19. We do not know how to set boundaries, and we let others interrupt us. We can accept more work without knowing how to say "no" appropriately.

20. We are perfectionists about our own work and expect others to be the same and have the same work ethics and values.

21. We become workaholics because it gives us a feeling of self-worth we did not get as a child.

22. We may jump from job to job, looking for the perfect position as the substitute for the secure and nurturing home environment we did not have.

23. We get upset when people do things that affect us or our work without asking us first.

24. We have a high tolerance for workplace dysfunction and tend to stick it out in an unhappy job because we lack the self-esteem to leave.

Identifying with The Laundry List (Problem)

Many of us express a profound "that's me!" when reading this description of workplace behavior of some adult children. This reaction is similar to the reaction we got when we heard The Laundry List (Problem) read at our first meeting. After awhile, the characteristics we seem to have in common begin to relate to several areas of our life and not just the main one that may have led us to an ACA meeting in the first place.

Some behaviors listed in The Laundry List (Problem) may be easy to spot at work: "We became isolated and afraid of people and authority figures," or "We are frightened by angry people and any personal criticism." Other traits may be more subtle to uncover because we are so accustomed to living our lives from an ingrained point of view. Without focus at work, we can overlook these traits: "We get guilt feelings when we stand up for ourselves," "We judge ourselves harshly and have a very low sense of self-esteem," and "We are reactors, rather than actors."

My first recollection of an incident that I can now attribute to an ACA reaction in the workplace was with my boss, who was the CEO of the company. He always treated me very kindly and had a grandfatherly manner with me. I had just finished an important, very lengthy document for my company. I was so proud and glad to be finished with it. I hand carried it into my boss's office and put it into his "IN" basket while he was sitting at his desk. "Here's the document," I said proudly. He responded with one word "Good," and turned back to the work on his desk. I felt hurt and rejected. Why didn't he tell me what a good job I had done and stop what he was doing to thumb through the document? I was anguished and started crying back at my desk. I hid my feelings from everyone in the office. I knew I shouldn't be so upset, but I was. Now I recognize that the situation had instantly taken me back to my childhood. I was bringing work home from school with a good grade, wanting attention and praise from my alcoholic father, but I was ignored or he was simply unavailable. I was totally unaware that I was having an ACA reaction at the time.

ACAs can feel different from everyone else in the workplace. There is a noticeable feeling of not fitting in. We may be highly competent in our work but live with an unspoken fear that we will be exposed as being incompetent or unprepared. We can play scenarios in our heads about the possibility of being shamed or belittled by a co-worker. We can become hypervigilant about being exposed. We fear someone might say, "You don't know what you are doing, do you?" or, "Can't you figure that out?"

Manipulation was essential for my survival in the workplace. As a result of believing my father's messages that I was stupid, I was too embarrassed to let someone know I needed help or didn't know how to do something. To get help, I would manipulate my co-workers by playing a role, such as being overly nice, being the victim, or volunteering to do something for them. After all, asking for help was not an option because it cemented my father's opinion. One day, I called another branch of our company with a question. When my supervisor found out, he said not to call another branch because it made me look stupid and consequently reflected negatively on him. In my mind, I instantly turned 12 years old, lowered my head and thought dad must have been right. Now after 18 years in the program, I've learned there is no need for manipulation, and I've changed my way of thinking. I can ask for something directly because I have higher self esteem and don't worry about appearing stupid. Sometimes I fall back into old habits and behaviors, but now I have the tools to get myself right back on track.

As adult children, we may be more sensitive to the difficult people in the workplace. Our co-workers seem to be able to shrug off unpleasant people, unfounded criticism, and the so-called "bad boss." We can feel powerless and may go home thinking "Why do others treat me the way they do at work?" Or we may feel revengeful: "I'll get back at them!"

At the same time, there are genuine "problem employees" who everyone recognizes. Most of these difficult employees are adult children playing out their scapegoat role from childhood. Literature about adult children of alcoholics includes a description of four roles that children can take on in an alcoholic or dysfunctional family: hero, scapegoat, lost child, and mascot/clown.[2] These roles can easily be transferred to the workplace.

The scapegoat child grows up accepting blame where none is due or attracts blame and acts out with negativity. In the workplace, the scapegoat or problem employee may attract blame with negative behavior and then complain about being picked on or treated unfairly. Operating from a sense of resentment, the scapegoat easily stirs up trouble at work. The ultimate result can be a showdown with an explosion of anger at the boss or a co-worker. Some scapegoat or problem employees quit their jobs, believing they have been treated unfairly. Many of these problem employees are within the ACA family and can change with willingness and effort.

14

---

[2] Roles developed by Sharon Wegscheider.

The hero child usually grows up to be the perfectionist workaholic who is independent and overly-responsible but who still has feelings of low self-worth. The lost child is often a good observer and listener and does not demand much of others. As an employee, the lost child does not want to draw attention and may be depressed and unable to establish close relationships. This is the invisible employee who no one knows much about.

The mascot or clown child has a good sense of humor and is easily identified as the workplace clown. He or she is able to entertain and amuse co-workers. The mascot or clown worker seeks attention and makes friends easily, but underneath has feelings of unworthiness.

We learned these roles as children to protect ourselves. Most of our behaviors started as defense mechanisms that helped us survive an alcoholic, dysfunctional, or abusive experience. These roles transfer into adulthood with an uncanny accuracy. We look to the ACA solution to change our workplace behavior.

Identifying with The Solution

Many parts of the ACA Solution help us handle workplace issues in ways that work better for us. Some of these items from The Solution are:

- we risk moving out of isolation
- you will become an adult who is imprisoned no longer by childhood reactions
- you will become your own loving parent
- we learn to reparent ourselves with gentleness, humor, love, and respect
- you will learn how to keep the focus on yourself in the present
- we become free to make healthful decisions as actors, not reactors

Working our program on a daily basis helps us to spot situations where our tendencies are motivating our behavior and thinking in ways that are not in our best interest. That "ah-ha" moment when we recognize that our past is affecting us in the present is a first big step toward a new way of thinking and behaving at work.

Isolation. That's the big ACA problem I encounter in the workplace. That's why, both consciously and unconsciously, I've arranged my life to be self-employed. In doing so, I have completely isolated myself. Sometimes the loneliness borders on unbearable. But by recognizing through ACA that I tend to isolate, I've taken steps to forge other non-work relationships. It's hard at times, but I'm not quite as isolated as I used to be. I find that when I am in the traditional workplace for meetings, I recognize my desire to pull away and, instead, step into what I fear. More and more, I believe in myself in situations that used to make me dive for emotional cover. That's a huge accomplishment, and I know that in the future, I'll be even more whole and present.

As we apply ACA principles in the workplace, we learn when to take action or when we can accept something we cannot change. In any given situation, we can think about what we will do instead of reacting to another's behavior. As we consider our options, we can ask ourselves some questions: Am I recreating my family role in the workplace? Am I moving out of isolation at work and making friends? How can I reparent myself in this situation? Can I accept my co-workers, knowing I have no control over them?

Finding the answers to these questions can be difficult. The "wisdom to know the difference" is sometimes a gut feeling, sometimes a hunch, and sometimes the result of focused soul searching. Sometimes it is just a leap of faith, trusting in our Higher Power to take care of us in the current situation. Some of us use an adaptation of the Serenity Prayer that can be helpful in dealing with workplace challenges.

14

God grant me the serenity to accept the people I cannot change,
the courage to change the one I can,
and the wisdom to know that one is me.

Relying on the ACA Program

Usually our ACA group is our best resource to help us deal with workplace relationships. Where else can we go and talk about something that is bothering us and have total acceptance? We can share even the smallest work incident and how it affects us. We can share our successes and failures in a supportive atmosphere. There may be no other place where we can really share what is in our hearts and minds without judgment. When we share our story at an ACA meeting, we can see the nodding, smiles, and laughter from those identifying with us. Many of us have chosen an ACA sponsor to help us with our program. Having someone to call outside of meetings can be helpful, especially if we have something to share at the end of the workday.

When we start using our program at work, we begin to understand that there is a difference between our parents and a boss or co-worker who we dislike at times or find easy to criticize. We do not have to use our family roles and old behaviors on the job. We can retire these roles and pick up the tools of the ACA program. When we retire our family role, we begin to see the spiritual nature of our work. Our perception of our work changes in addition to our attitude about it.

If we feel we are being criticized at work, we can stop and do some positive self-talk: "My boss is not my parent who I could never please. I don't like my boss's attitude sometimes, but I can do things differently than when I was a child. I can talk to someone. I can use the phone. I can use the meetings. I can ask my Higher Power for help."

A helpful tactic is to change our perspective. If our current issue is dealing with people and their personalities, we need to remember that they are not our family members. When we stop mentally putting a family member's face on our co-workers, what they say or do will affect us less. If we are having a strong reaction to someone in the workplace, we learn to ask ourselves: "Am I projecting a family situation into this moment? Am I having an ACA reaction?"

I used to always have confrontations when communicating with a co-worker face to face. I ended up communicating with this individual only by voice mail. The owners of the company finally decided to intervene and arranged a face-to-face meeting with all of us. It occurred to me while we were discussing the personality conflict that I was reacting to my co-worker's physical demeanor, which subconsciously reminded me of my brutal alcoholic stepfather. From the day I recognized this, we have not had another confrontation.

For some of us, it is the work itself that is the problem and not the people. We may have chosen a job that doesn't make the most of our talents and abilities because we have been programmed from childhood to have a low opinion of ourselves. We may be in an organization that has a culture of not respecting the employees. It may take a while, but as we work our program, we can develop the strength and courage to move on and find another job that allows us to feel good about ourselves. This is the hard part of "becoming our own loving parent" in the workplace. As much as we would wish it, no one is going to suddenly appear and magically whisk us out of that poor work environment. We come to realize that we will have to do it ourselves, sometimes in small steps that ultimately lead up to a giant leap. By using our program and the support of our fellowship, we learn that we can affect changes in our working lives.

Working in a creative field, where rejection is the norm, I've had plenty of opportunities to re-feel the terror of abandonment. In my mind, rejection represents abandonment by my alcoholic mother. But over the years, by first working in a step-study group and then attending weekly meetings, I've learned to recognize that fear. It still gets me, but not as often. And even when I am in the grip now,

I have the group to turn to for support and new management skills. I still have a long ways to go. The difference is that I can recognize and respond to what's going on.

Using Your Toolbag at Work

We have an ACA toolbag. Sometimes we may fortify ourselves mentally with all our tools before we begin our workday. Sometimes we may forget to mentally strap on our toolbag before we go to work. That is okay, too. We learn that we are not perfect, another important step in our personal growth. We must accept that there is a learning period in ACA. We can work a stellar ACA program by going to meetings, working the Steps, and helping others, but we must be patient with ourselves as we apply the program and change behavior. If we try something and it does not show immediate results, we must be willing to try it again. We must try something more than once. The tools and principles of ACA work if we are willing to work them.

The following tools have been gathered from workshops, panel discussions, and group sharing. In addition to attending ACA meetings regularly, applying these workplace tools can help you make meaningful change and progress.

Some Tools to Use

- Make a decision to use ACA principles in the workplace.
- Circle the number of workplace laundry list items you identify with and make a decision to work on one of the items each day.
- Establish a telephone or e-mail pal and share your need for support. We know of two ACA members who support each other by e-mail during the work day. Reading a message such as "Hang in there. I'm with you" can mean a lot when you are changing your behavior at work.

- Break out of isolation at work. Sometimes you are not the only one having problems with a difficult person or situation at work. Share your thoughts with others, and they will often share their views with you. Avoid engaging in workplace gossip or repeating claims that you cannot prove to be true.

- At the end of the day, make contact with someone in ACA. When they ask, "How are you?" begin talking about your day at work. Describe which workplace trait you are trying to change. Avoid focusing on a co-worker's behavior. Talk about your behavior and what you are doing to change.

- Remember HALTS. Do not get too hungry, angry, lonely, tired, or serious. When you get overly tired, it is easy to over-react to a situation. Exercise, get enough sleep, write in a journal, and aim for a balanced lifestyle.

- Take a risk, and try to make new friends and acquaintances. Ask someone to go to lunch with you, or join others at lunch if the opportunity arises.

- Keep a journal on the progress you have made in addressing the workplace laundry list.

- Carry an ACA token in your pocket or carry the Serenity Prayer with you in your pocket or purse. Say the Serenity Prayer as often as needed.

- Seek counseling if necessary. Many in ACA have found this very helpful in addition to their group work or Twelve Step study work.

This chapter reveals the experience of ACA members taking their program to work and into other relationships. When we work ACA principles outside the meetings our lives improve dramatically. We learn to truly connect to life and to contribute to society in a manner that is fulfilling to ourselves. We find the spiritual meaning in our work.

Chapter 15

Beyond Survival:
Practicing Self-Love

*A*s we end this section of the ACA basic text, we realize we have learned many things helpful and spiritual. We have a better understanding of what happened to us as children and why we reacted to life the way we did. We can reflect on the fact that we have faced our darkest moments and emerged with a firm grip on reality. By reading and studying this book, we realize there is a way out of family dysfunction. We know we are survivors, but we realize we can move beyond mere survival. We can live with self-love and the confidence that we can survive our feelings. We know we can ask for help and accept it. We also realize we can bring our True Self rather than a codependent self to relationships. We have something to offer.

By moving beyond survival, we realize that lost dreams or wishes can reemerge. The return of dreams is a signal that we are continuing our separation-from-family work. We learned in Chapter Two that we had internalized many aspects of our parents' thinking and behaving. We had no real identity or dreams separate from them. Even if we had moved far away, our parents and their dysfunction still lived inside us. By working the ACA program we began the process of externalizing our parents so to speak. We are moving them out of our thinking and behaving so we can find our own identity. Through ACA, we get to say who we are instead of a dysfunctional relative saying who we are not.

Dreams, hopes, and desires represent a key step in separating from the family. We separate from our unhealthy family on two levels. We can physically separate by moving away from them, setting healthy boundaries, or by limiting contact. There is an internal separation that must occur as well for us to live our own lives beyond survival. Without this internal separation, we can continue to struggle with the critical inner parent. We can be vulnerable to the chaos that still goes on in our families. With help, we can throw off or expel our internalized dependence. Forming our own dreams and healthy relationships is a sign of internal separation. Other signs include a willingness to reparent ourselves with ACA principles. Through reparenting we go inside ourselves and take an inventory of what must go and what can stay.

Separation does not mean we are abandoning our family. It means we will have a separate identity. We will know where our feelings end and their feelings begin. We give up our mistaken childhood belief that we can fix or heal our family. Through ACA, we arrive at a place of neutrality with our family. We are no longer affected by their dysfunctional behavior. We do not feel compelled to join their crises or endless arguments. We can love them while leaving them to their own choices and decisions.

With the new freedom we find in ACA, many of us remember dreams from our childhood or teen years. We thought we had forgotten these dreams, but our Inner Child remembers.

Some of us wanted to be a pilot, a teacher, or a professional dancer. Others wanted to be a fashion designer or runway model. For others, there was the fascination of being a forest ranger or private investigator. Some of us wanted to be a novelist. Other adult children wanted to travel to far away places or sail the ocean with only a compass to guide them. We had many wishes that we thought we had forgotten, but they are there. They are worth revisiting.

Beyond Survival: Practicing Self-Love

Through ACA, some of us realize we had career dreams that were not ours. They were dreams that were merely an extension of our family's control. These dreams matched our parents' wishes. We may have become professionals in a given field when our hearts were in the fine arts profession or another interest. Many of us did well in our professions and found a measure of contentment; however, we occasionally remember what we gave up to please our family. We can now pursue a new chapter in our lives if we choose to do so.

While some of us will revisit our dreams, there are others who are confused by such talk. We do not relate to dreams because we never truly developed them as children. We were too focused on survival. We learned to keep our thoughts and desires close to our hearts. We knew from experience that we could be criticized or discouraged from going after something we liked. In ACA, we realize that most of our thoughts and actions were aimed at pleasing the adults in our lives. Through recovery, we realize we get to form a dream perhaps for the first time. This is new and exciting. We are thrilled that we actually get to choose something that we like to do without thinking about how we will be judged.

This is the path for those willing to embrace the ACA way of life and the freedom it offers. This can be exhilarating, yet frightening, for some. To be given a chance to craft our own identity seems daunting, but we can do it. Through ACA, we no longer fear success or failure. We move beyond mere survival. We surrender, which means we are willing to do whatever it takes to recover and dream. This is the sure path that many ACA members have taken into a new way of life with feelings, trust, and spiritual awareness. Our lives won't be perfect or free of challenges, but we embrace recovery. Adding dreams to our lives is a key spiritual element in maintaining emotional sobriety.

Having said all of this, we know some ACA members will struggle with making progress in ACA. This is only natural since we are attempting something that takes effort, courage, and a willingness to let a Higher Power into our lives. Rebuilding,

15

or building, our lives takes time. It takes patience and steady focus. ACA members who struggle with the program usually have neglected honest Step work. Their meeting attendance may be inconsistent. They may focus on service work or counseling at the expense of an honest admission of Step One powerlessness and unmanageability. These ACA members find it difficult to ask for help or accept it once it is offered. There are other ACA members who seem to nibble at the edges of ACA without embracing the program. They seem to have settled for a half-serving of recovery. They may have attended ACA for years without committing to a home group or passing on their recovery by sponsoring someone new. They cannot seem to give back what was freely given to them, so they remain hungry. These members seem to work their own program which has little resemblance to the ACA program. They survive, but they are usually unhappy or feel "stuck."

For whatever reason, some of us may find ourselves penniless or feeling hopeless after years in the program. Some of us can inwardly blame ourselves for not doing better. When this happens, we begin to judge our insides by the outsides of others who seem to have it all together. We look at how well others seem to be doing and find fault in ourselves. Even if we have made progress in ACA and had moments of joy, some of us can find ourselves struggling on a daily basis. We do not feel good about ourselves, but we are going through the motions of acting okay. We may be speaking program lingo, but we are not talking about what truly bothers us. We may have employment problems, relationship troubles, or health complications. Most adult children do. We find ourselves talking less in meetings or feeling different.

When this occurs, we usually have been living in the survival mode without wanting to admit it. We forget that there is another way to live beyond survival. When we think about it, we realize we do not trust ACA or a Higher Power to truly be there for us. We have no dreams or wishes that we can call our own. We may have stopped being loyal to our dysfunctional family, but we have not taken the crucial step of walking toward our own dreams or desires. Many of us are still projecting our abandoning parents onto others or ACA. We may have changed some of our most damaging thoughts and behaviors, but we still rely on some of the worst ones.

Under these conditions, we may tire of working the program. It seems like too much, and we have heard it all before. We may still attend meetings, but we cannot seem to hear what we need to hear. We can secretly become critical of others and ourselves. Without knowing it, we may be nearing a crossroads in our program. We feel alone and perhaps misunderstood. If we can recognize what we are doing, we pray and pray hard. We ask our Higher Power to show up in our lives. We must remember that a loving God has not brought us this far to drop us now. The ACA way of life works. We can ask for help and trust ourselves to be okay.

If we have learned anything in ACA, we have learned that we can live beyond mere survival. We do not have to live alone with our thoughts or vulnerabilities as we did as children.

It is regretful to say that some ACA members have died by failing to reach out for help after finding the ACA program. These adult children are perhaps the most troubling to think about. We may have attended meetings with a person who seemingly worked a meaningful ACA program only to take his own life. Sometimes there might have been a warning. At other times there was not. We are naturally disturbed by these events. We may even be angry with God for allowing such a thing to occur. "Doesn't God hear all prayers?" we might ask. "Why that person and not me?"

There are many reasons why these things occur. We do not claim to know why people would choose to stop living. Some of us have thought about it ourselves at times, but we made the decision to live. We chose life and found life through ACA principles and fellowship.

15

Chapter Fifteen

Self-Love

It has been said that you cannot give away what you do not have. It has also been said that you cannot love another person until you learn to love yourself. We believe these declarations of wisdom are the basis for an ACA axiom: You cannot love another person until you love yourself and claim that love with belief and consistent action. We have seen many people speak words of self-love and affirmation while practicing something else. Self-love is never harmful or selfish.

The life beyond survival is the life of self-love, but lack of self-love was our dilemma. How can an adult child who is taught from the earliest years to abandon himself truly love from the inside out? We have an answer grounded in ACA experience: The love is there and God given. The love has always been there. We need a power to reawaken this love from within. The main focus of this book is to help you find a power greater than yourself to transport you from mere survival to self-love. We believe that loving one's self is the only way we can truly recognize God because God is love. Learning to love ourselves and connect with our Higher Power addresses our original cause of self-hate or self-abandonment. Since childhood we have carried a wound created by our primary relationship with our parents or family. We were ruptured emotionally and spiritually as children. To survive, we lived by The Laundry List traits which reject self-love and God. Driven by fear and para-alcoholism, we sought an unending number of relationships, schemes, and addictions in an effort to connect with someone who would fix us or let us fix them. We tried hard, but it never worked. We cannot find love or the Higher Power in someone else. It must begin with us.

We are protected by a Higher Power as we make this inward journey. We will not be abandoned or judged even if we think we cannot do it right. A loving Higher Power waits for us to accept that we are lovable regardless of what we think or do. This is grace.

We began this journey to self-love in Chapter One. By reading this chapter, we realized that we lived by a set of survival traits known as The Laundry List. This list describes a false self that can only accomplish self-hate and self-harm. There is no self-acceptance in the false self.

In Chapter Two, we learned more about survival. We learned about four modes of thinking that condemned us to control, all-or-nothing thinking, and perfectionism. These modes of thinking found a voice in the critical inner parent or the fourth feature of our thinking. Before ACA, most of us lived in self-doubt or self-condemnation, listening to this inner critic without realizing it. In Chapter Three, we learned that adult children of all dysfunctional family types find themselves with a common form of self-hate or self-abandonment.

In Chapter Four, we were introduced to hitting a bottom. We learned we could change if we could admit that we had bottomed out and became willing to work the ACA program. But first we had to become willing to accept help. In Chapter Five, we learned that a Higher Power was not a God made up of the attributes of our parents. We were asked to keep an open mind about a Higher Power. We learned that ACA is a spiritual and not religious program.

In Chapter Seven, we embraced the healing power of the Twelve Steps. We learned about the principles of the Steps. We learned about powerlessness, willingness, surrender, and self-forgiveness. We were told that life was more than survival, but we had to release control and fear. The ACA Steps gave us a foundation to gain a full remembrance of our past and to focus on ourselves. We learned we could be free from self-harm and self-abandonment. We were introduced to a spiritual awakening that lets us know God is more than a theory. Our Higher Power is real to us.

In Chapter Eight, we opened a channel to the Inner Child and learned about the true connection to God as we understand God. We also were introduced to the notion of becoming our own Loving Parent. Some of us struggled with this concept

15

until we realized that we had lived our lives with a critical inner parent, so why not begin a relationship with a Loving Parent from within?

With the Twelve Steps and a Loving Parent inside we took a giant leap away from a life of mere survival and toward a life of self-love. But what is self-love and why is it so important to adult children?

Self-love is an indispensable spiritual element of the ACA program. Self-love enables the adult child to back-fill the love or nurturing we did not get as children. By loving ourselves, we stop the negative self-talk. We confront the negative inner parent. We pay attention to our feelings, and we remove ourselves from abusive or neglectful situations as well. We realize we can walk away from the craziness that once confused us and trapped us. Self-love gives us a new pair of glasses. We can recognize abuse and when we are settling for unfulfilling relationships. Unhealthy behavior is no longer "normal" to us. We recognize it and choose another path. We have stopped willingly harming ourselves.

We have learned there can be many levels of self-love. On one level, self-love is a simple matter of reminding ourselves that we have worth. On another level, we rely on self-love to remind us that God, as we understand God, loves us always. This True Parent loves us as we stumble, right ourselves, stumble again, and right ourselves again. The True Parent loves us as we learn to love ourselves. Self-love helps us find our true place in the world. We stop doubting ourselves. We step back from fear and embrace life.

We cannot address the issue of self-love without examining some of the confusion surrounding this important spiritual principle. On one side, there are those who argue that self-love always leads to the slippery slope of narcissism. In this line of thinking, self-love is cast as self-absorption. These critics usually cannot define self-love because they are too absorbed in saying what it is not. They liken self-love to Narcissus, the character of Greek mythology who "fell in love" with his own image.

Transfixed by the pool, gazing at himself, Narcissus dies emotionally and physically due to his inability to connect with another person or God. This is not self-love.

Narcissism and self-love often get linked together, but these two concepts could not be more different. One is self-absorption while the other is self-awareness. The person who practices true self-love cannot be narcissistic. The practicing narcissist can never know self-love.

There are some sincere, religious folks who think that self-love diminishes the authority of God. They believe it elevates the human side of the person while lowering the Almighty. These well-meaning folks stand ready to correct any talk of self-love or self-worth. They fear that selfishness or unclean motives can rule the person and society. This attitude is akin to defining self-love wrongly as narcissism.

At the other end of the argument is the sexually open crowd who believe that self-love is a masturbatory practice that can solve world wars. The more "self-love," the better, they say. This is not self-love.

We also have seen thoughtful people who confuse self-love and self-esteem. This confusion represents a segment of the self-esteem movement that seems to place too much emphasis on affirmations and positive self-talk while attempting to neutralize anything negative in a person's life. Under this model of self-esteem, the person experiencing failure or challenge is encouraged to minimize any uncomfortable feelings associated with an event. This is all noble and kind, but a key element of building true self-esteem is left out in some cases. Feelings of discomfort, which can come with failing or being challenged, are not always supported in a patient manner. Learning to experience painful feelings is just as important to building self-esteem as being encouraged to believe in one's self. In some situations, a person is talked out of the discomfort through affirmations and encouragement. The affirmations sound good and loving, but they lose their weight when overused. At some point, the encouragement has the opposite effect and undercuts

15

a person's motivation to try harder after doing poorly on a task. Well-meaning friends attempt to "fix" the person with affirmations when they should just listen. The value of sitting with uncomfortable feelings can be lost or unwittingly pushed aside by supportive friends. Consequently, you can be left with a person who can talk about self-love or self-esteem but has difficulty facing true adversity. The person may not know how to ask for help or accept it. This type of self-esteem building is a form of enabling with window dressing in our view.

We have nothing against self-esteem that balances affirmation with meaningful challenges and the ability to listen to people rather than attempting to fix them with diluted praise. Affirmations are an important part of ACA recovery, but they must be balanced with active listening. We must not use affirmations in an attempt to "fix" someone or ourselves.

Self-love as we understand it does not eliminate pain or the need to try harder in some circumstances. ACA recovery is challenging, but the rewards are immense. We must put forth effort and feel the uncomfortable feelings that might come. At the same time, the goal is self-love and knowing that we are good enough just the way we are. This is an ACA paradox. We do not have to earn self-love, but there is effort in the process of claiming it.

Self-love as we know it offers more than mere self-esteem. There is much more. There is self-love that is expressed as unconditional love. In this realm, self-love illuminates our perceptions, and we view ourselves and others in a new dimension. We recognize a spectrum that transcends language and trauma. We recognize the light in ourselves and others. We realize that everyone has a heart beat. Everyone counts and has spiritual gifts.

We believe that self-love is essential for the adult child who is subjected to a love deficit that approaches holocaust dimensions. This love deficit condemns us to an existence of addiction, para-alcoholism, codependence, or seeking some other outward source to heal an inward feeling of being unwanted or defective. If any group of people should qualify for self-love, even in small amounts, it should be the adult child. We have been threatened, cursed, kicked, molested, and unseen in childhood. Before finding ACA, we lived lives of isolation and acquired shame. If God, as we understand God, created the concept of self-love, it must have been done for the hurting children of the world. We are God's children.

The key to gaining self-love is similar to obtaining other measures of spiritual growth in ACA. We encourage adult children to be patient and gentle with themselves as they travel inward. Self-love is typically a result of working the Twelve Steps, going to meetings, and changing destructive behavior. The realization of self-love seems to come after we have done the recovery work and then reflected upon our changed thoughts. We know we are on the path of self-love when we avoid acting on that one self-destructive behavior that guarantees isolation in our lives.

With self-love, new possibilities arise in every aspect of our recovery program. Since it strengthens our connection to God through the True Self, we begin to see the greater meaning of ACA. We see that ACA is not a selfish program. We see ACA's great potential for helping suffering adult children. We have come to believe in ACA and its message on a deeper level.

Additionally, self-love brings deeper meaning to the Twelve Steps, Twelve Traditions, and to sponsorship. With self-love we act on our belief that we have something to offer our ACA support group and others. We are motivated to get out of ourselves and to be of service to others. We balance our journey inward to self-love with an outward commitment to become involved in society in a productive manner. We give back what has been given to us freely in ACA. We go outward to help others by going inward to help ourselves.

With self-love, we can also consider the usefulness or value of all things. For instance, we can see the value of mistakes. Our Step work thus far has revealed that we are not mistakes, although we make mistakes. We learned this in Step Six as we worked on the removal of ineffective behaviors. With self-love and patience, we can find the value in our mistakes. We learn from our mistakes rather than condemning ourselves for them.

With self-love, we can also see the value of healthy shame. Healthy shame is a new concept for us since most of us have been toxically shamed through incest, cursings, and hateful behavior. Others have been shamed by perfectionistic goals that we could never reach. We were judged as failures for not being perfect or for not trying hard enough. Unhealthy shame is near the core of the adult child wound. We feel deeply flawed as a person due to this type of shame. Dealing with toxic shame takes courage, patience, and a Higher Power.

Healthy shame is another matter. Healthy shame exists when we recognize a wrong we have done, and we want to make it right with ourselves and with the person we have harmed. For example, when we gossip about someone, spreading rumors or passing on hurtful information, we should feel healthy shame. We have willfully harmed someone by passing along sensitive information, even if the information was true. We should feel healthy shame because we know what it was like as children and teens to be gossiped about. We know how painful it is to be labeled or to be called names. We should never want to harm another person in this manner, but we can with gossip and rumors.

In addition to Step work, an effective way to cultivate self-love involves journaling and "mirror work." Wise sponsors or counselors will often encourage an adult child to begin each day by staring at one's self in the mirror while repeating a simple affirmation such as: "I love myself," or "I love you."

Unlike Narcissus who is self-absorbed by his image, the adult child can feel revolted or uncomfortable by gazing at his own image. Indeed, many adult children say they feel great discomfort or embarrassment while repeating an affirmation while looking into a mirror. The critical inner voice can use these moments to shame us.

Looking into one's own eyes seems to be extremely difficult for many adult children. The reasons are not hard to determine. We learned a lot about who we were through eye contact with our parents. If the adults in our lives used harsh facial expressions to shame us or discipline us, we learned to avoid eye contact with them and then with ourselves. We learned to avoid looks of disappointment, disgust, or anger that usually came with some kind of shaming statement. We have seen adult children come to our fellowship who have removed all mirrors from their homes and who have avoided eye contact for years. It has been said, "the eyes are the windows to the soul." We agree. For those who do the mirror work consistently, it pays off remarkably well in self-acceptance.

Additionally, mirror work can expose any unfinished business we have with body shame. Body shame is not reserved for our weight or shape. Because of our upbringing, many of us are uncomfortable with our foreheads, eyes, and noses. Our facial features have been shamed or belittled by our family or others. Even some strikingly handsome adult children cannot see their natural good looks due to the love deficit and shame within.

Meanwhile, other adult children are ashamed to hear their own voices because of critical parenting or neglect. Voice-shame is common among us because we were not allowed to develop a voice or identity as children. For some of us, hearing our own voice as we share in an ACA meeting can create extreme self-consciousness. We can feel our heart racing and our breathing becoming more difficult as we talk. For many of us, talking in an ACA meeting is the first time we have expressed our views and thoughts to another person. Talking openly without cross talk is new and frightening, but it represents a true step toward finding our voice in ACA. We realize we do not have to sound refined or smooth. We can speak and be heard.

With our traumatic and neglectful upbringing, we see mirror work as an effective tool for realizing self-acceptance. The acceptance can lead to claiming and practicing self-love in

15

all our affairs. We do not see much danger of an adult child loving himself or herself too much. We do not fear that adult children will wander into narcissism. We usually do not linger at mirrors.

We do caution our members about false self-love. This can exist when a person proclaims loving one's self while continuing to act out with destructive behaviors. In this scenario, the person has learned the lingo of self-love but fails to take honest steps to move away from self-hating behavior. Even this kind of self-deception responds well to honesty and a willingness to do the work to change.

At the same time, we can all have moments when we drift into an attitude of survival no matter how hard we try to avoid it. We would not be normal if we did not. And certainly moments of survival behavior will not cause us to do something drastic to ourselves. Through ACA, we realize that we have come too far and worked too hard to live with tension or hypervigilance. We can love ourselves and trust God as we understand God to show us the way. We can find serenity in ACA. We realize we can trust ourselves, ACA, and God.

The ACA Promises

The ACA Promises represent some of the rewards that we can expect from ACA and self-love. Within the Twelve Promises is the work of making healthier choices, setting boundaries, and discovering our real identities. There is also intimacy and feeling peaceful. We learn to not fear success. The Promises represent a balance of action, feeling, and being. This is the spiritual material that self-love is made from.

If we have been sincere about our recovery to this point we will have experienced many of these Promises already. For example, many of us began discovering our real identities at our first ACA meeting. This is the first Promise. We have learned to fear people less and how to set boundaries as Promises three and nine state. There is no time line on when we will experience an ACA Promise. The Promises are true. The Promises are:

1. We will discover our real identities by loving and accepting ourselves.

2. Our self-esteem will increase as we give ourselves approval on a daily basis.

3. Fear of authority figures and the need to "people-please" will leave us.

4. Our ability to share intimacy will grow inside us.

5. As we face our abandonment issues, we will be attracted by strengths and become more tolerant of weaknesses.

6. We will enjoy feeling stable, peaceful, and financially secure.

7. We will learn how to play and have fun in our lives.

8. We will choose to love people who can love and be responsible for themselves.

9. Healthy boundaries and limits will become easier for us to set.

10. Fear of failure and success will leave us, as we intuitively make healthier choices.

11. With help from our ACA support group, we will slowly release our dysfunctional behaviors.

12. Gradually, with our Higher Power's help, we will learn to expect the best and get it.

15

Mirror Exercises

For these exercises, find a quiet place with a full-length mirror or a mirror large enough to show your face and shoulders.

The First Exercise is known as silent mirror work. In this exercise, the person stares at his or her image in the mirror and remains silent while noticing any feelings or thoughts. The person looks at his or her hair, forehead, lips, throat, chin, and so on. With a notepad nearby, the person writes down any feelings, thoughts, or words that might arise. Also notice posture, breathing, and the location of your hands. The way that we look at ourselves and carry ourselves tells us a lot about how we view ourselves.

The final part of the exercise involves looking into one's own eyes for 60 seconds or more and then writing down any thoughts or feelings that arise as well.

Repeat the silent mirror exercise for at least seven days and share your writing with a sponsor or ACA friend.

The Second Exercise involves looking into your eyes in a mirror and repeating an affirmation. The affirmation can be: "I love you, —————— (your name). I am a human being. I am a good person. I am a decent person. I am here for me." There are other affirmations. You can add your own. Do this exercise for seven days and write down any thoughts or feelings that arise. Share your thoughts and feelings with your sponsor or ACA group. You can also tape the affirmations to the mirror and read them in between exercises.

You might also combine the two exercises and look into the mirror before repeating an affirmation. Write down thoughts, feelings, or words that come to mind as you work this exercise for several days.

SECTION II

Chapter 16

ACA and Therapy

$\mathcal{W}$e begin Section II of the ACA basic text with our fellowship experience on the use of therapy in recovery. The ACA program is a recognized resource among psychiatrists, therapists, and counselors. These helping professionals refer clients to our meetings regularly. We appreciate the good word and their confidence in our program. While therapy is not a replacement for the ACA program, many of our members have benefited from counselors who are familiar with ACA or Twelve Step work.

In ACA, we do not practice therapy, but therapy with an informed counselor can be the gateway to unparalleled levels of recovery. Therapy is not a substitute for ACA recovery, which involves focused Step work with a sponsor. Many ACA members have experienced remarkable recovery without counseling. The decision to ask for extra help is up to each individual. ACA is a stand-alone program that offers a proven solution to the disease of family dysfunction.

In the beginning, many of us can use basic, adult child counseling. The counseling makes us aware of dysfunctional family roles and the unspoken messages that drive us to doubt ourselves. Children growing up in dysfunctional families develop predictable roles. The roles can include hero child, scapegoat child, lost child, invisible child, and mascot or clown. The roles can overlap and can change as the child becomes older. Good counseling can help us realize our denial about what happened in our unhealthy homes. Denial and a lack of clarity are the armor that protects sick families from scrutiny. Effective counseling combined with ACA involvement can take years off the time it takes to be free of our old way of life through other methods.

In some cases, adult children will need treatment in a clinical setting to address their adult child condition. Treatment can be beneficial in breaking through the fog that obscures the effects of being raised in an unhealthy family. Many adult children enter a treatment facility voluntarily to be treated for an addiction or other problems. Once there, they often find out they suffer from the effects of being raised in an alcoholic or dysfunctional home. Many realize that their addiction to drugs, work, sex, or food is a symptom of being raised in an abusive or neglectful family. Once the addiction is addressed, the effects of being raised in a dysfunctional family usually become clearer.

Most treatment settings involve an extended stay of two weeks to four weeks. In addition to education about addiction, the treatment usually involves group work and an introduction to the Twelve Steps. Finding a facility that addresses the adult child condition in a focused manner can be challenging, but it is worth it. We have included questions in this chapter to help the adult child be an advocate for himself or herself in finding help.

The knowledge gained in treatment or counseling can bring greater meaning to recovery in ACA. If we have been stuck or blocked in our program, the extra help usually moves us forward in ACA. The benefits of counseling or treatment can improve our lives.

Grandchildren of Alcoholics

In addition to adult children of alcoholics, there also are grandchildren of alcoholics. Grandchildren of alcoholics represent a growing number of adult children qualifying for ACA.[†] They qualify because their parents were affected by alcoholism and passed on the disease to their children. The parents may not have used alcohol, but they passed on the traits of alcoholism and other family dysfunction just the same. In addition to the ACA program, grandchildren of alcoholics can use counseling to understand the link that transferred dysfunction from their grandparents, to their parents, and to themselves.

Many grandchildren of alcoholics identify profoundly with The Laundry List traits without knowing why. They identify strongly with fearing authority figures, judging themselves harshly, and staying in problematic relationships when others would leave. Family stories they have heard usually omit drinking or drug abuse among relatives. This lack of information makes it difficult to know what happened in the past. Without counseling, grandchildren of alcoholics can struggle with relationships and feeling connected to life.

At the same time, some grandchildren are from homes in which the parents talk openly about alcoholism among grandparents and relatives. They talk about drunk uncles or pill-taking aunts while feeling proud about shielding their own family from such dysfunction. These parents made a decision to be different than the rest of the alcoholic relatives. They removed drinking or some other dysfunction within the family, but their children turn out to be addictive or codependent. The parents are baffled and do not realize their part in passing on addiction even when they removed alcohol or drugs from the home. There is a link.

In our view, the link between the grandparent and the grandchild involves para-alcoholism. Para-alcoholism is an early term for codependence. It describes what goes on inside the codependent or nondrinking parent. For the most part, para-alcoholism is made up of the stored fear and distorted beliefs of nondrinking parents raised in alcoholic homes. These parents are not drinkers, but their fear and emotional pain take on an "alcoholic form." This para-alcoholism affects the children much in the same manner as alcoholism. When we apply this scenario to grandchildren of alcoholics, we can see para-alcoholism at work. The grandparent's alcoholism is passed through nondrinking parents to the grandchildren through para-alcoholism.

16

Most grandchildren of alcoholics grow up hearing "we are a good family." Yet, these grandchildren of alcoholics sense something is wrong or unsaid within the family. Many grandchildren of alcoholics are not necessarily in denial about family alcoholism or other dysfunction. They lack information about family history. This lack of information is a hallmark for some parents who had alcoholic parents but who remain quiet about family alcoholism to their own children. There are usually fragments of information about alcoholism or another dysfunctional behavior in the family stories. However, the connection between the sparse information and the grandchildren is not usually made until help is sought.

Grandchildren of alcoholics can wonder if they are making up problems, but their emotional eating, drug addiction, sex addiction, or perfectionism is obvious. Their confusion is confounded since there appears to be no cause in the direction of the family. Grandchildren of alcoholics usually believe that something is wrong but lack the information to identify the cause.

Grandchildren of alcoholics offer compelling proof of the generational nature of alcoholism and other family dysfunction. With grandchildren of alcoholics, the pathway of dysfunction can be traced from one generation to the next even when alcohol is removed.

Informed Counseling is a Must for Clarity and Progress

Adult Children of Alcoholics is an important source of help for adult children. We do not have all of the answers, but our fellowship has helped thousands of distressed adults find a better way of life. The fellowship continues to grow, with groups being established across the world. ACA works.

Before ACA was established, adult children seeking help were diagnosed with a variety of psychiatric labels that left out the true impact of being raised in a dysfunctional family. At the same time, there was psychoanalysis that seemed to over-analyze childhood development. Or childhood development was presented in clinical terms not useful to the general public. This style of therapy seemed to rely too heavily on the intellect or behavior modification to be truly effective for adult children.

In earlier times, a few psychiatric methods identified childhood trauma and neglect as being problematic in adult life. Yet, the individual getting help with this method lacked an ACA support group to move from therapy toward sustained recovery. Consequently, some clients remained in therapy almost indefinitely.

An intriguing method of help known as Transactional Analysis burst upon the scene in the 1960s, with buzz words such as scripts, games, and "nigysob" ("Now I got you, S.O.B."). Transactional Analysis identified the ego states of the parent, adult, and child within each individual.

In preceding generations, there were often passionate attempts to help adult children. Yet, there was a general lack of understanding about the ongoing effects of alcoholism and other dysfunction on the family. If understanding was gained, there seemed to be a lack of a support group to continue the progress that was made in therapy. Untreated adult children used addiction, denial, or dissociation to survive. They blamed their children or themselves for lives that were predetermined by family dysfunction.

Many adult children got help for their addictions in AA, Narcotics Anonymous and other Twelve Step fellowships but were usually discouraged from looking at the effects of family dysfunction on their adult lives. These are helpful and life-saving programs, but they are not designed to look at childhood trauma or neglect to the degree that ACA does.

As recovering adult children today, we have a chance that those before us did not have. We have ACA and a fellowship of recovering adult children to support us. We have regular meetings, literature, and fellowship. We can talk about the trauma and neglect of our homes without being shamed into silence. We can also take responsibility for our lives and we can take action to live a better life. We have a proven spiritual path.

16

Since the beginning of the adult child movement, helping professionals have become more aware of the effects of family dysfunction. Counseling methods have been modified with good results to successfully treat adult children. Scholarly research has verified the medical and behavioral clues of being raised in an unhealthy family.

Consequently, better counseling methods are available. The methods help bring clarity to the effects of family dysfunction on a person's life. The methods are effective enough to help those who may have lived through the times before the establishment of ACA. It is never too late to recover.

Even though recovery options are improved, we still must be selective in asking for help. We know of ACA members who have spent years in therapy that never addressed the impact of alcoholism or other dysfunction in their lives. Without quality therapy, the effects of growing up in a dysfunctional family can be missed or dismissed as a significant cause of current difficulties. Without focus, we will not comprehend the true impact of family dysfunction. Additionally, we will struggle with understanding dissociation and its many forms. Grief work and the remembrance of loss can be delayed indefinitely. We can struggle with understanding the importance of reparenting ourselves.

Counseling without an ACA focus can miss the mark and focus on behavior modification only or perhaps on one aspect of the ACA personality. For instance, many of us have angry or rageful behavior that is symptomatic of hidden fear. Counseling unaware of the ACA personality would tend to treat this as a choice in which the person learns to manage or control the anger. This technique can be helpful in curbing angry outbursts, but most adult children will switch to a new behavior that is just as troubling. This switch can trigger new levels of despair for the adult child.

If a counselor is unwilling to help us address the effects of family dysfunction and to be supportive of our ACA program, we move on. We avoid wasting time and money that could be better spent with focused therapy that supports our program.

ACA is unique in the fact that our fellowship encourages informed counseling along with Twelve Step work, meeting attendance, and sponsorship. ACA is not allied with any form, discipline, or technique of therapy. However, we make the distinction between informed counseling and general counseling without an ACA focus.

Informed counseling understands the long-term effects of a dysfunctional family. The counselor understands the importance of reviewing the family history and helping the adult child connect the events of childhood to current behaviors and thoughts. An informed counselor knows how to address the complex denial system developed by most adult children. The effective counselor knows that most adult children do not evolve into greater complexities. Adult children operate from basic defenses learned as children. Effective therapists know that most adult children appear resilient or complex but operate from a basic feeling of being defective. Through experience, the counselor knows that adult children develop basic survival skills in childhood that do not work well for adult life.

The experienced counselor keeps it simple and knows that most adult children are deeply frightened no matter what they might say otherwise.

Effective counseling methods for adult children should include the Inner Child, which was affected most by the family dysfunction. This is a child harmed by shame and parental manipulation. The symptoms of addiction or codependence shield the Inner Child and make it difficult to diagnose what has happened in the person's life.

Informed counseling also understands the principles of the Twelve Steps and the sequence of recovery for adult children. The sequence usually begins with hitting a bottom and reaching out for help or accepting help. Hitting bottom is followed by facing our denial and our powerlessness over the effects of growing up in a dysfunctional family. Denial for an adult child has a variety of definitions that include blaming others and minimizing memories. There is also an outright rejection of facts. Some aspects of adult

16

child denial involve recalling abusive or neglectful behavior as normal. We can also be in denial about drug addiction or substituting one drug for another, thinking we are in control of our addiction. We can substitute or switch destructive behaviors as well.

After hitting bottom and admitting our powerlessness over the effects of family dysfunction, the sequence of recovery continues with the adult child being open to spiritual matters. This is followed by a self-examination of behavior, removal of ineffective behaviors, and making amends to those we have harmed. By attending ACA meetings and working the Steps, we inventory our thinking and behavior on a daily basis. We meditate and seek direction from a Higher Power. We ask for the power to carry out God's will in our lives. We attempt to carry the message of recovery to others. This is the sequence of the Twelve Steps. This sequence has worked for thousands of adult children, willing to admit their powerlessness over the effects of family dysfunction and to apply that willingness to the remainder of the program. ACA sees recovery as a life-long journey instead of a singular event. We do this with the help of a Higher Power and an ACA support group.

Willingness and Accepting Help

One of the key ingredients for successful therapy involves willingness. We must be willing to be honest and to talk about what happened in our childhood. We must be willing to follow through on suggestions and assignments by the counselor. If we enter therapy with this attitude, we make greater progress toward finding true freedom.

Occasionally, adult children will enter counseling without a commitment to willingness or to accepting the help that is offered. The counselor must challenge the client to confront his or her behavior and to fully participate in therapy. The client – the adult child – must be willing to take direction from the therapist. The best therapist in the world cannot help an unwilling or uncommitted client. We must surrender the notion that we can reason out a solution alone or avoid discomfort. We need help, and we must accept it to make progress. Being willing to go to a counselor is only the first step in getting help. Once there we must be willing to accept the help offered. Making a decision to accept help is a crucial first step in beginning an ACA program.

Our experience shows that counseling alone tends to bring a good, short-term effect. Yet, the results can wane without ACA participation. Old behavior and thinking can creep back without continued effort in ACA. Counseling coupled with ACA participation can bring lasting peace. We can begin to recognize the serenity to be found in ACA.

ACA is deeply grateful to thoughtful counselors who have recommended clients to our fellowship. Many counselors have taken the time to understand our program, and it shows in their work with clients. A few therapists have benefited from ACA recovery themselves on a personal level.

For some ACA members, a qualified and caring therapist can be the difference between finding wholeness or living in unrecognized dissociation. Counseling can occur at different times. Some newcomers arrive at ACA through a therapist's referral. Some adult children have attended meetings for awhile before seeking counseling. The decision to seek counseling is a personal choice. Most adult children seek counseling during a personal crisis or when they feel blocked in making progress in recovery. ACA members with many years in the program have sought help for their abusive anger, anxiety, or problematic relationships. We must remember that we can be victimizers in addition to being a victim. If we find ourselves switching over to victimizing ourselves or others, we might need extra help.

In ACA, we do not recommend a particular style or method of counseling; however, in choosing a knowledgeable counselor, you have the right to ask the therapist if he or she is familiar with ACA or the Twelve Steps. Many counselors are knowledgeable of the Twelve Step process while others show

16

a willingness to learn. We recommend visiting with at least three counselors before making a decision. Many therapists will answer your questions on the telephone so this saves time and money.

Some ACA members find a knowledgeable counselor through a referral center or through a telephone listing. Others are referred by ACA members who are aware of a good and knowledgeable counselor. There are questions at the end of this section that will help you find a qualified counselor. However, the use of a counselor does not eliminate the need to have an ACA sponsor.

More About Para-alcoholism

Para-alcoholism is a foundational term for the ACA fellowship. The term is an integral part of The Laundry List traits. Trait 13 and Trait 14 specifically detail para-alcoholism (See the complete Laundry List in the Introduction section of this book).

Trait 13: Alcoholism is a family disease; and we became para-alcoholics and took on the characteristics of that disease even though we did not pick up the drink.

Trait 14: Para-alcoholics (codependents) are reactors rather than actors.

We use this term with codependence to restate the nature of an inside source of emotions that drive the codependent much in the same manner that drugs drive the addict. In our view, para-alcoholism underpins codependence and describes the inner drive of the codependent. Good counseling combined with the Twelve Steps can help us identify feelings, including the feelings we use as inner "drugs." The alcoholic has para-alcoholic fear and pain as well. The recovering alcoholic or addict must address stored fear and pain once the chemical dependency is dealt with.

As discussed in Chapter Two, we believe that some of our stored feelings become a "drug," driving us from the inside to harm ourselves or others. This is the para-alcoholic nature of codependence. As codependents we seek to control others or live through others without truly realizing that we are driven on the inside by fear and emotional pain born in childhood. As children, we developed the ability to dose ourselves with fear, doubt, or anxiety to match what we saw in our parents. We did this to survive. As adults, many of us sought out fear or emotional pain to match our feelings from childhood. In addition to fear, some of us became addicted to excitement, which is Trait 8 of The Laundry List characteristics.

We might question the use of fear or emotional pain as a drug. "Why would anyone choose to seek fear?" we might ask. "What would be the benefit of emotional pain?" Many of us can see how alcohol and drugs are used for relief, but what could be gained by creating fear or anxiety in our lives? For the adult child, the pay-off involves finding familiarity. Since we have known primarily fear and emotional pain as children, we can seek this out to feel "normal" as adults. We seek the familiar even though we know we are harming or neglecting ourselves in the process. To see the effects of inner drugs, we can inventory our relationships and find a pattern of emotional pain or fear-based decisions. Before we found ACA, most of us blamed ourselves for "bad choices" when in reality we had no true choice. Overpowering feelings ruled our lives through compulsions and obsessions.

We are not at fault for using feelings as inner drugs. We could not have turned out differently since we were raised by dysfunctional people. We are not at fault for our response to family dysfunction, but we are responsible for our recovery.

This is not pop psychology or an unreasoned assessment of what goes on inside each adult child. This is the bedrock experience for the person growing up in a dysfunctional home.[†] If there are still questions about the ability of the body to use fear as a drug, we can look to science for help. Medical research

16

tells us that the body can develop its own drugs for pain and trauma. Our bodies have the ability to release "pain medicine" for an injury to an arm or leg. The body medicates itself with endorphins from within. Another example of the body producing drugs from within involves laughter. Many people believe that the elements released in the body by laughter quicken the healing process for those who are ill. It has been said: "Laughter is the best medicine."

With this knowledge of the body, we believe that fear and other emotions can act as a drug. These "emotion-drugs" release chemicals in our bodies that we are powerless to stop until we get help. We seek these inside drugs because they are familiar, not because they make sense. Some of us have jokingly said: "My drug of choice is fear." Or "I must be addicted to chaos." To the outsider we seem odd or stubborn, but to another adult child, we are recognized as struggling with para-alcoholism.

Some of us need ACA and counseling to understand the para-alcoholism of the body. For the solution, we turn to ACA's First Step to find a way out. When we admit we are powerless over the effects of family dysfunction, we take our first step away from the obsessions and compulsions that drive us. This is an ACA truth.

In addition to these inside drugs, we address our addiction to alcohol, drugs and prescription medication from the outside. We can do this in ACA with the aid of counseling. Our experience shows that we cannot work an effective program as long as we use alcohol or other drugs. We must be honest about our use of mood-altering chemicals. Some of us have thought our drinking pattern was not alcoholic because it did not match our parent's pattern, but alcoholism is not a matter of degree. Alcoholism is a progressive disease of the body, mind, and spirit as well. We can see the progression if we are honest. Meanwhile, some of us have fooled doctors to get prescription medication and increase our tolerance for pills through addiction. We must remember that alcohol and drugs are part of the problem, not the solution.

For many of us, this talk of inside drugs and outside drugs appears complex, so we remember to keep it simple. "First Things First" is a good motto to follow in our experience. We learn about ourselves and the effects of family dysfunction one day at a time. We can work on one thing at a time and let the rest go until we are ready. We remember that we never get more than we can handle in one day. We truly live one day at a time in ACA. We live. We learn. We apply what we have learned.

Dissociation

With good counseling, we also learn to recognize the dissociation that blocks true intimacy with other people. As ACAs, we can dissociate from ourselves in a variety of ways that are difficult to recognize until we get help. In addition to drugs, work, sex, or food, we dissociate in other manners that block a true connection with ourselves or a Higher Power. Other examples of dissociation can include: compulsive cleaning, compulsive exercising, obsessive reading, fantasizing about sex or romance, telephone sex, pornography, compulsive masturbation, workaholism, and harmful thrill seeking. There is also compulsive spending and cluttering. Many of us leave clutter about our houses to cover up things we do not want to look at in our lives. There are other reasons for clutter, but dissociation is one of them in our experience.

Before finding ACA, we have struggled with dissociation many times in a losing battle. We have acted out impulsively with drugs, sex, or another form of behavior that leaves us feeling empty. Dissociation is the false self. It is not who we are. No matter what we have done, the dissociation is not who we are. Through the ACA program and counseling, we gather the courage to face the false self with a combination of grit and surrender. We also maintain close contact with recovering adult children during these times.

16

PTSD – Post-Traumatic Stress Disorder

PTSD is a condition of the body and mind in which a person stores the memory of a violent attack or life-threatening event. The intense feelings of fear, despair, or potential loss become stored in the body and mind, creating post-traumatic stress. The condition can govern behavior and decisions on a subconscious level. In some cases the original fear can be triggered by events similar to the original trauma.

PTSD symptoms can include hypervigilance or the constant monitoring of one's surroundings for potential threat of harm. Other symptoms can include an uneasiness that is associated with a certain place or event. There can also be sensations in the body that seem unexplainable but persistent under certain conditions.

In some cases an odor, sound, or story can trigger a PTSD remembrance. For example, a person who has been slapped or screamed at as a child usually has post-traumatic stress disorder. As an adult, the PTSD can be triggered if someone threatens or slaps the person. The person can regress to a child-like state of feeling shaky inside and feeling physically small. Or the person can shut down emotionally and feel numb inside. The PTSD can also be triggered when the person is a bystander and happens to hear screaming or slapping but is not involved in the altercation.

Another example of PTSD can involve more subtle features. For instance, an incest survivor might have his or her PTSD triggered by the facial features, noises, or gestures of someone else. There may not be a great upwelling of discomfort, but something is triggered inside. A movie scene or song can trigger a PTSD reaction as well.

PTSD was initially identified as a condition that affected war veterans or victims of traumatic events such as a natural disaster. It is a generally accepted fact that ACA members who lived through violent and unsafe homes developed PTSD. Our fellowship made the connection between PTSD and adult children as early as 1984. Fellowship writing from that time

16

shows the link. The knowledge of PTSD and its effects on the body continue to be broadened. There appear to be other forms not related to overt violence or trauma.

Recovering Memories

The ACA program has helped many adult children recall past memories or incidents. Many of these painful or frightening memories lose their power when shared in an ACA group or with a qualified professional. For many of us the memories are clear and are recovered with easy recall. For others, we may be unable to fully recall our abuse, but we have a sense that something happened. We have acting-out behaviors that seem consistent with abuse, but we are not sure if it occurred. There may be somatic behaviors or a vague uneasiness in certain situations. In other cases, there are flashes of images or bits of a story that make one wonder about what might have happened.

Occasionally, a brother or sister will corroborate abuse committed against us that we cannot remember. In some cases, hospital or social service records confirm abuse we do not remember.

While we do not want to place doubt in anyone's mind as they attempt to review the past, we do ask that our members use caution and common sense in recalling some memories or partial memories. Reputable research shows that most memories of trauma and abuse are accurate, but there should be no rush to recall the memories. There should be no pressure as well. We want to be fair to ourselves and others, but we also want to be diligent in seeking out what happened to us as children. Our memories hold the key to healing if we are willing and if we are committed to change.

Most memories will emerge on their own, and there will be no mystery. Even unclear remembrances handled properly can lead to healing and great insight. That said, we do urge some caution in choosing a qualified therapist for recovery work. Here are a few traits that a good therapist will have.

16

A Good Therapist

Should Not:

- Should not ask leading questions about abuse and typically does not push you to remember.

- Should not say: "I can tell you were sexually abused," or "I think you were abused, but you are blocking the memory."

- Should not say: "If you think something happened, it probably happened."

Should:

- Should ask you about trauma and abuse, including child sexual abuse, if there are clear indicators of family history, acting-out behavior, records, or other discernible factors.

- Should build trust and safety before attempting to review some memories or incidents of suspected abuse. Traumatic memories are processed as they come up naturally in a safe setting.

- Should listen and occasionally relate some of his or her story but maintain professional decorum and boundaries.

Questions to Ask a Counselor or Therapist

1. Are you familiar with the Twelve Steps?

2. Are you familiar with the ACA Twelve Steps? (Many therapists are familiar with the AA Steps but not the ACA Steps. Ask a follow up question to be sure the counselor is aware of the ACA Steps or is willing to learn about them.)

3. Do you believe that alcoholism or other family dysfunction can affect a person as an adult?

4. Do you understand the sequence of Twelve Step recovery (hitting bottom, facing denial, admission of powerlessness, self-inventory, amends, seeking a spiritual solution)?

5. Are you willing to learn about ACA or the Twelve Steps? (If the therapist is not familiar with ACA but is willing to learn about the program, he or she still might work out as a good therapist. At the minimum, the person needs to be familiar with some form of the Twelve Steps of AA, Narcotics Anonymous, Overeaters Anonymous, or Co-Dependents Anonymous and be willing to learn more.)

Therapy Affirmations

1. I have the right to get therapeutic help.

2. I have the right and the responsibility to interview therapists for free before I enter counseling. (This usually can be handled on the telephone.)

3. I have the right and responsibility to find a therapist I feel I can trust to treat me respectfully.

4. I have the right and responsibility to find a therapist who is knowledgeable about and supportive of my ACA recovery program.

5. I can hire a therapist to help me grow emotionally and spiritually.

6. I have the right and responsibility to terminate the therapy if I am not making progress toward recovery.

7. If I feel unsafe in therapy, I will share that with my therapist to find a solution instead of sabotaging the process or running away.

A Therapist's Rights and Affirmations

1. My counselor or therapist has a right to ask questions about sabotaging, evasive, or passive-aggressive behavior on my part.

2. My therapist has a right to expect willingness and honesty from me.

3. My therapist can suggest that I attend ACA meetings.

Past Experience with Therapy or Treatment

1. Most adult children have heard a few things said about therapy and counseling as they grew up. What do you remember hearing? Does this make you fearful of getting extra help?

2. Have you had drug and alcohol counseling that did not address your abuse, neglect, or other unhealthy experiences from the home?

3. Have you hired a therapist who did not identify the significance of alcoholism or dysfunction in your home? Did the counselor focus on something else and minimize your childhood experiences?

4. Why is it important to find a therapist supportive of ACA?

16

End Notes

[†] ON PAGE 448: Grandchildren of Alcoholics: Another Generation of Co-Dependency, by Ann W. Smith, 1988, HCI Publications.

[†] ON PAGE 457: Post-Traumatic Stress and The Loss of Ontological Security: Overcoming Trauma-Induced Neophobia in Adult Children of Alcoholics: 1987 – Martin R. Smith, M.Ed.

Chapter 17

ACA's Global Reach: Our International Fellowship

*T*his chapter offers a sample of stories from members of our international fellowship. The ACA fellowship has cross-cultural appeal and can be found in more than a dozen countries outside North America and South America. Currently there are ACA groups and meetings in Turkey, Denmark, Finland, Italy, Japan, Hungary, France, Germany, Sweden, Belgium, Russia, England, and Australia in addition to other countries.

The following stories represent a sample of ACA recovery around the world.

ACA in Finland

Adult Children of Alcoholics groups (Alkoholistien aikuiset lapset) have existed in Finland since 1987. The organization and expansion of Finnish groups has survived growing pains and a formal separation from Al-Anon. The final separation from Al-Anon took place in 1999. Each group was given the right to decide if the group wanted to continue to be affiliated with Al-Anon or to belong to the independently established Adult Children of Alcoholics Peer Group. AAL Keskuspalvelu, the Central Service Organization, was officially founded on September 1, 1999. (Submitted by the Finnish fellowship.)

An ACA trifold carried the message in Finland.

My name is A-P, and I'm a 30-year-old adult child of an alcoholic. My father is an alcoholic who still drinks.

I live in Finland, and I'm the oldest child in our family. I have also a brother and sister. In my childhood I have seen lots of drinking, although my father drank mainly at weekends. I guess that my mother has learned how to control the amount of liquor so that the drinking is finished by Sunday morning. My mother has always been the one who takes care of the things in our family. She has drunk with my father occasionally, but compared to my father she didn't drink so holistically. Although nowadays I see that her drinking wasn't normal either. She always drank to get drunk and sometimes even passed out.

It's common in Finland that people use lots of alcohol on weekends. You could say it's a popular entertainment here. Our family wasn't an exception. Every weekend, when I was a child, my father would buy a bottle of liquor or two. Sometimes we'd go to our summer cottage or to visit friends. Adults would drink, and we children would play on our own. Sometimes that was really fun when all the adults were happy and playful. Other times there would be arguing or even fighting, which was really scary.

My father wasn't actually violent, but he tried to control us, the children, with aggression and fear. I've been told that my grandfather used to beat up my father and his mother. So I guess that my father couldn't help being aggressive being raised in that kind of home. But he didn't beat us or our mother. He used to shout loudly from the sofa where he was lying down and nursing a hangover. He would tell us to shut up while we played. Of course we couldn't be quiet very long, and then he would jump up and come with his feet stomping aggressively against the floor. He would give us a scary look and pull our hair. When we heard the stomping we'd try to run and hide under the table or somewhere.

I think that the biggest thing that has affected my adult life was the abandonment. Although my father, and occasionally my mother, was usually physically present, inside I felt that I didn't have parents when they were drunk. They couldn't help me with my things or

17

weren't interested about my needs as a child. They weren't really present. Subconsciously, I thought my father was a different person when he was drunk. The sober father was totally different.

One weekend we were at our summer cottage by the sea, and I fell from the roof of some old shelter and broke my hand. I cried and ran to the cottage with my broken hand. My mother was angry and said: "Why did you climb there; we can't help you because we've had some drinks and can't drive the car." Finally they called my grandparents to take me to the hospital. Although my mother came with me to the hospital, I had a strong experience that my parents could not take care of me when they were drunk. This equaled abandonment. I was 12 years old.

Having been mentally abandoned for hundreds of times in my childhood, I developed a great fear of abandonment. But I was unaware of this. When I grew up and girls started to have interest in me, I only rarely dated them. I didn't know that then, but I tried to protect myself from getting abandoned. I just thought that for some reason I couldn't find a girl that would be good enough for me to fall in love with or who would fall in love with me. If I met somebody interesting, I would discover something that I didn't like about her for an excuse to dismiss her.

Another thing about my family involved the shame. I learned to hide the abnormal drinking of my father from the outer world. The mechanism for this pattern was developing a feeling of shame about my family. Without consciously thinking about it, I did not want to bring home friends who were from "good homes." I thought that my family was not good enough. That same mechanism expanded to include myself. I was part of the family. My self-worth was very low.

So, when I met somebody that liked me, I ran, thinking she wasn't good enough. And when I met somebody that I liked, I thought I wasn't good enough for her! With this pattern, I managed to be single until I was 26 years old. Before that, my longest relationship was about three months.

17

Chapter Seventeen

I finally met a girl that I thought was perfect for me. She dressed in leather gloves, was intelligent and somehow extreme like me. We both liked motorcycles and, not knowing it, based our values in superficial things. It was more important to look and act cool, have a certain status and work title, than to have inner peace and happiness.

We met in a bar, both very drunk. After a month of dating (actually we were always together) we decided to go to a bar again to have some good times. After that evening I found out that she was an alcoholic. She couldn't stop drinking for a week.

So this began my first codependent relationship with a woman. I tried to rescue her from alcoholism, and in the process I lost all my power.

After three months I gave up and was willing to seek outside help for the relationship. At that time we were already living together. We saw some professionals, but they weren't helpful. I lost all my hope by seeing that even professional people were unable to help an alcoholic. We soon went to our first Alcoholics Anonymous meeting. AA isn't very visible in Finland, so I didn't know anything about it.

In AA I finally saw some hope. There were people – alcoholics – who had been sober for years. And the most important thing was that I could identify with AA.

I read the AA Big Book with my girlfriend, and she managed to remain sober for four months before relapsing. At that time we were already mentally exhausted. I had this feeling of anxiety in my stomach 24 hours a day. It felt like I had swallowed a hot rock. In the end the feeling wouldn't stop even when I was in a boxing ring. Before finding recovery, the hard physical exercise and the adrenaline from boxing would always empty my mind. Boxing was a place I could always escape the world. Now even that did not help.

I woke up each day remembering that my girlfriend was an alcoholic and thinking I needed to take care of her. The thought burned in my stomach all the day and until bed time.

From the AA meetings, where I went to support my girl, I got this trifold about ACA. After keeping it three weeks in a pocket, unread, I finally read it. Tears came to my eyes when I read the list of characteristics of an adult child. My defense mechanism of

17

denial was broken by the traits. I realized that I also had some serious problems with my emotional life. I was in a codependent relationship with an alcoholic. I wanted to end it, but I couldn't. I felt I was responsible for another person's life.

After that experience I started to participate in ACA meetings regularly. ACA was the place I could get rid of that anxiety I always felt. Sharing my experiences with others for three months and taking the first three Steps, I finally moved away from my girlfriend's apartment. That happened while she had relapsed again. I cried the whole week for my girlfriend's sake and for my own sake. I felt the sorrow I hadn't had courage to feel in my whole life. The feelings were so strong and physical that I feared something would break in me as I cried. Only the thought of a Higher Power could give me courage to go through it.

Half a year later I finally got a sponsor. With him I went through the Steps as they are explained in AA's Big Book. We went through the first seven Steps in one four-hour session. In that session, my sponsor opened up his life to me, and we went through the resentment list and the list of fears. I shared all the secrets I had and the things I had felt shame over. After that I felt great relief.

About one month later I felt a very strong experience. This happened one winter evening while I was walking. I felt a great feeling of love, and somehow I knew that something had opened to me. I thought that no one could understand this experience, so I decided that I wouldn't talk about it to anyone. Next week after the meeting, my sponsor suddenly came to me and said: "Have you had a spiritual awakening as a result of these Steps?" I was amazed! How could he know? I just mumbled something and later that evening thought about it in my home. Of course, the experience was a result of working the Twelve Steps. That never occurred to my mind, but now it seemed obvious. It was right there in the Twelfth Step.

Now, four years after my first ACA meeting, as I write this story I can still remember those feelings I had at my first meetings. I realize the grief I felt at times. Tears of gratitude form in my eyes when I think about how lucky I am. I'm grateful that I've had this opportunity to go through those times and those feelings. They were the gateway to a rich and full life I have today.

This path of self-discovery has led me to places I never dreamt possible. I can honestly say that my childhood and my experiences have become my most valuable property. Today I'm not only a member of ACA, but a sober member of ACA. The family dysfunction, which has gone through generations in my family, stops with me.

ACA in Canada

Raised in a violent alcoholic home, this adult child tried to live as if his abuse and neglect had not occurred.

My name is M., and I am a member of the French-speaking ACA community in Canada.

I am the youngest of a family of two children. As far as I can return in my youth, my memories always contain some scene of violence between my parents. It seems to me that those were mostly verbal in the early period. Later, as I reached the age of 12, I was the witness of extreme manifestations of anger where screams, gunshots, and blood intermingled in our house. As a survival mechanism, I learned quickly that it was critical to be in tune with the mood of my unpredictable father to escape harm. In fact, I gripped this survival attitude so tightly that it became my lifestyle. Monitoring another's behavior so I could feel safe became a part of my inner life as an adult.

As a child growing up in an alcoholic home, I kept my ears open to the slightest gestures or deeds. In this way, I was hoping I could guess my father's state of mind. This anticipation would extend to the point where I could recognize the sound of my father's car motor blocks away. I could tell his mood as he climbed the stairs to our home. What a relief to hear him enter the house, animated by a joyous drunkenness. On these nights, I could then expect to sleep quietly.

This disease of family dysfunction affects everyone in the family. My mother, exhausted, would eventually decease from a generalized cancer. As I turned 13 years old, and as the family broke up, I was sent to my maternal grandmother to stay. Then, I was sent to several foster houses. I ended up on the labor market near my 16th birthday.

In these foster houses, I silently wished to be placed in a different house away from my brother. I wanted to forget about the family violence and have a chance to make myself a completely new life.

Feeling abandoned and alone, I found it most difficult to get into friendship or relationship with others. I had the impression that I didn't have anything in common with them. I believed I was too different. I then tried to adapt myself to the people around me, forgetting my past family experience. I tried to go forward as if the abuse or neglect had not occurred during my childhood. Naturally, I repeated the very same behavior that I knew most. I organized my life in accordance with the mood of others so I could feel safe or less unsure about myself. Yet, when the relationships became more intimate, I experienced an enormous sense of anxiety. It was like if my past had turned to be an open wound, which was best not to touch. I couldn't understand why I felt so vulnerable when I interacted with others.

For quite a long time, I believed that I was suffering from a social phobia. Fortunately, I very soon experienced a strong thirst for knowledge. I was in search for an explanation to my existential suffering which only spirituality seemed to have the power to address. Nevertheless, besides this spiritual inquiry, I believed that more specific efforts or help were necessary. I then undertook all sorts of endeavors for recovery. On my way, I then learned about the existence of Adult Children of Alcoholics. I immediately felt that ACA was the movement which was most directly connected to my life experience. I could recognize myself in The Laundry List (Problem). Reading the characteristics of a dysfunctional family did provide me, for the first time, a sentiment that I was understood and I was not alone.

I was so much in pain due to my lack of knowledge concerning my family situation. I quickly realized that ACA had emotional and spiritual recovery tools which I could use to understand and heal my anxiety. The recovery tools, the Steps, and attending meetings opened a whole new way of life for me.

What a wonder to be able to speak directly from the bottom of my heart in meetings and to relate to others. I was convinced that everything I was saying couldn't possibly make sense. Yet, curiously, all of what the other members were saying appeared to me strangely familiar *and pertinent. This is the strength and special nature of ACA. I felt totally different, but I found out that there are people like me. We can find a new way of life.*

On my journey of recovery, I continue to find out more about what happened to me in my childhood and how it affects me today in my life. I tried to live like the past never occurred, but it did not work. I can see I recreated my family in my relationships with others. ACA recovery and information are opening up new ideas for me. I found out about post-traumatic stress disorder from a doctor, who is convinced that I was not really affected with a social phobia as I thought.

At this time, I did not realize the value of this diagnostic insight. It wasn't until I read the Identity Papers that I really understood the link between this diagnosis and my family past experience. This brochure did truly open my eyes on my condition as an adult child. For me, this document describes very well the process which is presented by The Problem and The Solution. By being involved in the ACA meetings and working a program, I understand better what is going on in my life.

I understand that the difficulties that I have in confronting an anxious situation is mostly related to the dynamic from my alcoholic family. The work on the Twelve Steps and Twelve Traditions helped me to know better my needs as a para-alcoholic (codependent) person.

I have also learned that my concern for anticipation is named hypervigilance and is a typical response of post-traumatic stress. Actually, when the Traditions are well applied, they provide me with a model to harmoniously function in a group. I always learn a lot in a group where the members are capable to exchange in respect toward each other in accordance with ACA's Traditions.

It is like learning to live in a more functional family. I have learned to give up the influence from my father who happens to have been an adult child, too. By working an ACA program, I have identified my repressed feeling and learned to stay away from another person's harmful influence. I am working on a reunion of the self (adult child). I can see now that my feelings of low self-worth are linked to my violent and unsafe childhood. Thanks to the structuring approach of the ACA lifestyle, I can now look at this with honesty and with hope that I am not alone or defective. I also have learned that I don't have to organize my life around others to be loved or accepted or to feel safe.

Although nothing can be changed from my youth, I can take responsibility toward myself. I can view my own deficiencies and try to find the proper tools to change my behavior. In this way, I have obtained many means by which I can get in better relationship with others.

ACA and the Twelve Steps are not only complementary to my spiritual path, they are even a source of spiritual motivation. I like to use a metaphor to describe my recovery work. Every effort that I make is comparable to cleaning a stained-glass window. With each cleansing, the light shines in a little better from all angles. More detail is revealed. Eventually, and at some distance, I happen to perceive that the whole thing begins to make sense. The colors radiate.

17

Chapter 18

ACA Teen

As ACA moves forward, we are seeing more young people in our meetings who are children of alcoholics (COAs) and other dysfunctional families. Our groups are welcoming these young people with the knowledge that they are minors still under the legal supervision of their parents or guardian relative. We are not taking over the parental role, nor are we embarking on a crusade against abusive parents with this topic on ACA Teens.

We are a fellowship of adult children, but we want to do all we can to help children of dysfunctional families if they pass our way. Our primary purpose is to help adult children of alcoholic or dysfunctional families. We believe, when the time is right, that teen leadership will form meetings for abused and neglected young people wanting what ACA has to offer. The formation of teen programs has occurred in other Twelve Step fellowships. ACA's Steps and Traditions can be adapted easily for this purpose.

We must remember that ACA was founded by a group of Alateens, wanting to hold a meeting where they could talk openly about the hurt, rejection, and confusion in their homes. Because of our roots, ACA meetings attract teenagers growing up in situations similar to our own. Children of alcoholics identify with ACA literature and our meeting discussions.

We write this chapter at the direction of the 2005 Annual Business Conference, which supported the concept of an ACA Teen fellowship. There are an estimated 11 million children of alcoholics under 18 years old still living in families with alcohol and addiction as a significant factor.[1] If you are a child of an alcoholic or another dysfunctional family type, welcome to ACA.

From One Teen to Another

Adults don't understand. Or they forgot. Maybe it is too painful to remember. Issues from their childhood are buried in a hidden place they cannot easily find. The adults say they don't mean to hurt us. They don't know exactly why they act like they do, but they do it anyway. They try to control us, and they punish us. They over react to little things then miss the bigger issues. They constantly argue with one another without realizing we are listening. They miss our feelings, our needs, and our questions. They tell us that we are not good enough, then complain that we have low self-esteem.

Many adults can have no fun. Others can't be serious enough to listen. Inconsistency and chaos is the rule. Many of our parents have difficulties at work and with their friends. As their children, we see and live these problems with them. They criticize themselves or us without mercy. Sometimes they want to live our lives instead of living their own. At times we become the parent. We take care of our brothers and sisters, and we take care of our parents too. Often we think their arguments are our fault. They tell us they want us to have a better life than they had. But we grow up feeling guilty about what they give us. They tell us we are lazy and ungrateful and blame our school or friends for our behavior.

We see, we think, and we feel; we also choose, and we dream. But our human freedoms are often denied. We are told what to see through the eyes of our parents who are adult

[1] National Association for Children of Alcoholics

children of dysfunction. We're taught that our views are wrong even though the truth is right before us. We are taught to fear our thoughts and then we are ridiculed for not thinking. Our choices are shamed; our dreams are ridiculed and belittled. We know how to act out and get attention. We seem invisible, but we react with the passion of youth, and we struggle mightily to survive as we seek our own identity. The family chaos will not allow us to be truly seen.

Our emerging strengths are both a benefit and a problem. As we grow, feelings surge forth with a force we've never known. Our loves are great and our disappointments crushing. The exhilaration of life takes our breath away, just like the nights spent cringing in terror at home. In this world of denial and confusion we find our way. We experience pain and abandonment, then cry out for connection the only ways we know, ways that sometimes hurt ourselves or others. We swing between extremes. We love our parents and hate what they do. We need them so much, but we want to leave them. We want to be like them, but we promise to never be like them. We live in a land of black and white where there is no gray. Our needs are complex and compelling. We are teen children of alcoholic, addicted, or dysfunctional homes.

Yet, we have hope. Deep in the darkness we seek a light of truth and our rightful freedoms. We review our chaotic life. We look at our parents' alcoholism or dysfunction and label it as such. We say, "My parent is an alcoholic" and feel relief. We understand that we didn't cause this behavior, and we can't cure it. We release our need to control others and begin focusing on ourselves. We find identity and hope with our friends in ACA. We take responsibility for learning, understanding, and talking about the truth inside each of us. Our feelings become known. We make healthy choices as we learn to love ourselves and parent ourselves. We can talk about what happened. We have courage inside that we are discovering. We celebrate a newfound peace and serenity. We are ready to embrace the promise of our new lives in ACA Teen.

18

Hope for ACA Teens

As adult children in ACA we say: "Take hope teens from addicted and other types of dysfunctional homes. There is hope today. Right now."

If you can handle the trials of your home and have made it this far, perhaps you can go a little further. Begin to put yourself first because you deserve it. Get to a safe place. Find someone that you can trust. Learn more about ACA. There is recovery from the hurt and pain of your alcoholic family. You can find your true freedoms. You have inner strength. You can talk. It is not your fault what is happening in the family. If you are acting destructively, think about options. Think about another way to respond.

Get to a Safe Place

For many teens life can become a prison where there is no safety. Abuse is rampant within alcoholic and dysfunctional families. The home is not safe. At the same time, some parents seem normal in public, but at home they are different people. They are unhealthy in ways that confuse the children and leave them feeling conflicted inside.

Domineering or neglectful adults create unsafe circumstances in different ways, but the end result is always danger for the teen. The danger may be emotional, spiritual, physical, or sexual. It manifests itself in many different ways, and even when not apparent, the threat of hurt is always there. Being alert in this constantly dangerous world is exhausting. It is important to have a safe place where it is okay to relax and rest. A first step in recovery for the ACA Teen is often simply finding this safe place.

To find a safe place, look to all available information sources. Get educated. Most children of alcoholics do not understand alcoholism or dysfunction even though they are living in it. An amazing number of children of alcoholics do not consider their parent a problem drinker even though the evidence is clear. In addition to the drinking or pill taking, there may be cursing, shouting, and threats. In some cases, children are left alone for days, but alcoholism is over-looked as the cause. The parents also can miss work, have hangovers, or have numerous failed relationships. There are often money problems due to drinking and drugging.

Go to your school counselor and talk about what is happening. You are not betraying your parents. If they are violent, neglectful, or letting themselves go, they need help. But you need help first. You come first.

Get a telephone book and call a referral service dealing with alcohol or drug addiction in the home. Check the Internet for youth services and reputable assistance agencies. If you are forced to live on the street, there are places that offer refuge from the chaotic existence of the street. If you are a runaway, stop running and start living. Having a safe place can be an important element in your teen recovery plan. Do not be afraid to talk about what is happening.

Find Someone You Can Trust

In ACA, we attend regularly scheduled meetings and talk about the Twelve Steps and other topics of recovery that include feelings, boundaries, and our future. ACA has sponsors who help new members work the Twelve Steps. These are trusted friends that help guide a new person through the healing steps of recovery.

For the ACA Teen, finding a trusted person may be difficult. Trust is rare in dysfunctional families so recognizing trust can be difficult for teens. Learning how to trust is often just as difficult as finding someone to trust. You can use your listening and observing skills here. All ACA Teens are good listeners and observers, no matter what adults might say. You know you listen, but you don't tell the adults. So use your listening and observing skills to find someone you trust. Listen for people who don't put other people down and who don't use alcohol or

18

drugs. This might be someone you can trust. Avoid people who make fun of others or who pressure you to think like them. You are your own person. You have choices.

When you find someone you think you can trust, share one or two things about yourself and see how the person handles it. Don't unload everything at once. If the person handles one or two things, you can tell him or her more.

You can also use the hypervigilance learned in your chaotic home as you search for a safe person. Hypervigilance is your listening and observation skills with the volume turned up. Trust your instinct if you feel a person seems dangerous or behaves strangely. You can walk away. You have a choice. You can take care of yourself first by being in a safe place and with someone who can be trusted not to drink, use drugs, or cause further harm.

Learn more about ACA

Answers for many ACA Teen questions can be found in the ACA program, The Laundry List (Problem), and other ACA literature. This literature can work for you since it is written by adults who grew up in homes just like yours. Locate an ACA meeting and attend. Seek out ACA materials on the Internet at www.adultchildren.org. This website also has literature and cool things to read.

You can also attend an online ACA meeting. There are many. You will meet teens like you who are already attending online meetings. You may also find ACA dances and events in your area.

Learning how adult children can recover is very helpful to current teens in alcoholic or other dysfunctional families. In the ACA program, there are people who understand. They know what it is like to be frightened, confused, or having to act perfect all the time as teenagers. They know what it is like to be called a "screw-up" or to be left home alone to take care of brothers and sisters. ACA members know how to listen.

Start Your Program by Working the Twelve Steps of ACA

The Twelve Steps of ACA can bring miracles into your life. This has been our experience as ACA members. The principles of the Steps can free you of self-blame, confusion, and impulsiveness. You can find a place where you belong. Discovering that you are not alone is an incredible feeling. For the first time there is the hope that all is not lost. The Steps can offer a way out. Your future can be as bright as you have dreamed about it being, no matter what you have heard before. If you have not thought of a dream yet, you can begin now. Dreams are born in ACA.

Elsewhere in this book are chapters devoted to working the Twelve Steps as an adult child, finding a sponsor, understanding ACA Traditions, and other program guidelines and suggestions. We urge you to explore these chapters and use the tools offered there. Embark on the wondrous journey of recovery in ACA. Read Chapter One and the questions at the end of the chapter. Also read The Laundry List (Problem). How many traits can you identify with?

If you are in a treatment facility, read this book and begin your program from where you are. Read Step One, and ask someone to help you work this Step. The Step asks you to admit that you are powerless over the effects of family dysfunction. Many of these effects are listed in The Laundry List (Problem) in Chapter One. Attend an ACA meeting when you are released from the facility. If you are in a long-term facility, ask for meeting support from an outside ACA meeting. Contact the ACA World Service Office for meeting information.

18

Create Your Own Wallet Card

Your ACA Teen Plan for Finding Safety or for an Emergency Situation.

1. If danger arises, call a friend and talk. (Put the number in your cell phone or wallet).

2. Talk to a school counselor.

3. Go to a friend's house. Let one of your parents know you are safe, but be careful about giving the location if your parents are violent or explosive in personality.

4. Remember that your parent's behavior is not your fault.

5. Stop taking drugs or drinking alcohol if you are doing so. Avoid friends who drink alcohol or take drugs.

6. Stop your self-destructive behavior if you are acting in such a manner.

7. Start reading about ACA. Attend an ACA meeting.

8. Remember you have inner courage. You are not alone.

18

For ACA Group Members:

What if a Child of an Alcoholic Shows up at My Meeting?

Some ACA members have asked for guidance on what to do when a child of an alcoholic – a minor – shows up at their meeting. For a solution, we can look at our fellowship experience. For the most part, our groups are handling this situation with the compassion and care that is typical of the ACA fellowship.

Group members are keeping it simple. They welcome these young people into ACA meetings. They share their story and recovery with the young person.

We treat children of alcoholics as equals. We do not talk down to these young people nor do we place them on a protective pedestal. We were once children of alcoholics so we can relate to them and share our ACA story with them. We can also ask them to pick up the tools of recovery and to work a program. They can appear fragile, but they are also survivors. We recognize this in ourselves.

While we gladly welcome teenagers into our meetings, there are special considerations that we must note. We must realize that these young people are vulnerable, and we must never take advantage of this vulnerability. Our behavior with young people must be above reproach. We are not their buddies, saviors, or replacement parents. We are not the brother or sister that they never had. We naturally avoid any inappropriate intimacies for legal and ethical reasons. If we believe we cannot honor these boundaries, then it is best to leave this type of work to another person.

The stories that we hear from these young people can be horrific and can trigger some of our own memories of childhood abuse. We want to act. We want to help. There are things we can do; however, we cannot wage a campaign against erring parents or caregivers. We have given up our rescuing roles and taking out our anger on others who are still spiritually ill and who may be doing the best they can. If we take a position of hostility against alcoholism or any dysfunction, we could ruin a chance to be helpful in the future.

If an extreme act of abuse is known, the appropriate authorities should be contacted. These acts should show clear and compelling evidence of battering or sexual abuse. A child of an alcoholic simply sharing in a meeting about such abuse is often not enough evidence. We must be careful here and not place ACA in the position of intervening when matters are best left to professionals.

18

Our singleness of purpose in ACA is to carry the message of hope to adult children. As a fellowship, we do not get involved in matters of policing or reporting dysfunction in the home. To do so would violate our Twelve Traditions, which outline our singleness of purpose.

In severe situations, we can suggest that the parents get help. Some parents are open to change, but they do not know about ACA. If we sense that parents are open to seeking help, we can give them information about ACA. But we do not force solutions or wear out our welcome in these matters. We do not take on the role of rescuer or therapist for the family. We can provide information and share our story, but the family must be willing to take action. We take this action as an individual and not as a representative of ACA. We typically do not act alone in these situations. We can ask a fellow ACA member for support.

The person you help may help others down the road. Your listening and your experience as a recovering adult child matters to a child of an alcoholic. There is a common element for many of us who overcame incredible odds as children and teens. That element involved having one caring adult in our lives. This was a safe adult who took time to listen to us and to accept us. We can do this for children of alcoholics.

Relating To a Child of an Alcoholic: Listen, Share, Listen

Since we are adult children of alcoholics, we have much to offer a child of an alcoholic. As survivors of abuse, neglect, or unhealthy parenting, we understand the maltreatment young people endure in alcoholic or dysfunctional homes. We have lived through such treatment before finding the Adult Children of Alcoholics fellowship. We can share our childhood experiences and recovery with a child of an alcoholic. We can help when few others can. We have been given the gift of identification.

As teenagers, many of us believed we caused our parents' drinking or dysfunction. We believed we were not good enough, smart enough, or perfect enough so our parents drank. We thought we deserved what our parents did to us. We have been cursed, slapped, and belittled. Sometimes our behavior called for discipline, but we usually got abuse instead of caring discipline. We carried our feelings of being defective or "being bad" into adulthood. For other ACA members, the neglect or unhealthy parenting was subtler, but it was there. The evidence is in our addictions and compulsive behaviors. These are the things we can share with a child of an alcoholic seeking help in ACA. We keep it simple. We do not glorify our story or blame our parents, but we also do not minimize what happened. When we talk to a child of an alcoholic, we also listen to them. We listen, share, and listen.

We can talk about our experience with the First Step of ACA, and we can explain why we call ourselves adult children. We call ourselves adult children because we are grown up, but we can react with the fear or anger of our teen years when we are dealing with other people. We thought we were simply immature until we found ACA. We now know that when we are angry with someone or fearful of someone, it is usually a reaction from our childhood. We can say that we are learning to change this in ACA. We have learned that we have choices and that we can help create workable relationships. These are experiences we can think about as we share our recovery with the child of an alcoholic.

Some children of alcoholics are curious about the Twelve Steps. The topic of a Higher Power might come up. If it does, we keep it simple. We share about our experience with Step Two and then we listen.

As adult children, we know that many children of dysfunctional parents attend school during the day only to return home each night to neglectful or unavailable parents. We know the roles

18

the children engage in at school. The roles include class clown, troublemaker, and honor student. There is also the invisible child. To build identification with a child of an alcoholic, we can share about the role we played in junior high school or high school.

There is not always violence or outright threat in the dysfunctional home. Many children of alcoholics have addicted parents who are functional on the job but who place too much responsibility on children in the home. The child is confused. Some parents turn over their parental roles and allow their children to prepare meals, drive the car, and take care of other parental duties. The child of the alcoholic or dysfunctional parent often becomes the "parent" and misses out on being a child. We know this because we have lived it.

Many of these parents drag their children into arguments, making them take sides with one parent or the other. In addition to creating shame and fear within the child, this is also a form of parental abandonment. It forces the child to choose between parents, which is a position a child should never be placed in.

To live in fear and learn to deny feelings are common responses to these types of homes. Many children of alcoholics live in fear of being embarrassed by a drunken parent at school events or other gatherings. While many children of alcoholics appear mature and stable beyond their years, they are actually never sure if they are loved. They live in fear of a vengeful parent withdrawing love when the parent changes moods or the child makes an error. Other children of addictive or dysfunctional homes immerse themselves in schoolwork or find excuses to stay away from home. These children can use sports, school trips, or other activities to avoid home. Many of these children sleep with their clothes on, ready to flee their homes when predictable, parental arguments escalate to violence. We know this. We have lived it.

Other dysfunctional homes appear calmer but lack love and acceptance. These homes are no less frightening or suffocating. On the contrary, many of these perfect homes are deadly to a child's spirit. The damage comes in the form of perfectionism, rigidity, and overly controlling parents. These are parents who often mean well but who miss the mark in nurturing their children. When the child has done something well, these parents will pick out one thing the child has not done right. The parents believe they are challenging the child to greater heights, but the child feels failure.

Even though numerous books have been written about the effect of addiction upon the family, the legacy of denial continues in many homes. There have been mentionable strides in combating the disease of addiction, but the "elephant" is still in the living room. This is the great beast of addiction that each family member tiptoes around without identifying it as the real problem in the home. In addition to breaking all the furniture in the house, the elephant of dysfunction breaks the hearts of the children.

These are the things we can know about ourselves and the teenager we are attempting to help. We remember that we are helping ourselves as well. We remember to treat teens as equals. We let them talk. We can ask them to work a program.

The Future of ACA Teen

18

The future of ACA Teen is bright. The Annual Business Conference of ACA has discussed this issue and voted to recognize the ACA Teen fellowship concept. The ACA WSO Board of Trustees stands ready to support those interested in establishing ACA Teen meetings and groups. We believe the leadership must come from the teens themselves for it to work.

Chapter 19

The Twelve Traditions of ACA

*A*dult Children of Alcoholics has the Twelve Steps of ACA, so why do we also need Twelve Traditions? It is commonly believed that the Twelve Steps provide direction for the individual member, while the Twelve Traditions provide comparable guidance to ACA groups and the service structure. The ACA Traditions outline fellowship unity, group autonomy, and the ultimate authority of ACA – a loving God – as expressed in our group conscience. The Traditions offer wisdom on being self-supporting as a fellowship and on avoiding promotion when attracting new members. There is also guidance on the use of special workers who help make Twelfth Step work possible. The ACA Traditions frame our leadership style in the language of being a trusted servant. We avoid a style of governance or authority over another. When asked to serve, we lead by example rather than by directive.

The Twelve Traditions guarantee simplicity in our primary purpose and in membership requirements for ACA. There is only one requirement for ACA membership – desire. The primary purpose is to carry the ACA message to other adult children. Anonymity coming from love underlines all of the Traditions and our group conduct. With the Twelve Traditions, we sustain ACA groups that allow the ACA Solution of reparenting one's self to emerge and thrive.

The ACA Twelve Traditions were adapted from the Twelve Traditions of Alcoholics Anonymous. Our groups, Intergroups, and World Service Organization have built on a framework that has worked so well for AA. While we have cited some AA experience in this writing, this chapter contains a detailed picture of ACA's proven experience with the Traditions.

We have learned from our own experience that the Twelve Traditions are nonnegotiable. The principles of each Tradition fully complement one another and are not in conflict with one another. For example, the principle of unity in Tradition One resonates with each principle in the following eleven Traditions.

Group decisions that follow the Traditions and their intent have a signature that we learn to recognize as a group conscience. By adhering to the Traditions, we begin to see God's footprint in our group decisions. We begin to understand how we feel about what we are doing for ACA through the group and service structure.

Chapter Design

In this chapter, the Twelve Traditions are explored in detail. Each Tradition is introduced by individuals sharing their personal experience with the Tradition. These shares were voluntarily recorded at ACA meetings, conventions, retreats, and by invitation. The shares are followed by a Tradition Insight which highlights the spiritual principles and function of the Tradition. The insights are followed by questions and a meditative thought.

19

The Twelve Traditions are reprinted and adapted from the original Twelve Traditions of Alcoholics Anonymous, and are used with the permission of Alcoholics Anonymous World Services, Inc.

TRADITION ONE

Our common welfare should come first; personal recovery depends on ACA unity.

When I came into the program I heard people say, 'Do it my way, or I'll quit.' This was my lifelong attitude as well. I did get angry and quit, and not just once. Each time I came back to ACA, the original group was still there, still pulling together and still moving forward. They were unified in their likenesses. I had run away because of our differences.

My ego kept me a prisoner of my sickness. I wanted to overpower these people and make them do things my way, even though I knew my way did not work. I wanted to do to them what had been done to me. I soon discovered that bullying others into submission does not work here.

When I understood that the unity of my program was essential to my recovery, I took my first real step away from the survival behavior I learned as a child. Now I contribute to the common welfare of the group by encouraging the group to work together and move ahead. Even as I wander back and forth on my recovery path, my ACA group remains stable.

ACA is my lifesaver. It is the basic recovery source in my life. I depend on the program to be there for me when I need it. *To ensure that ACA survives and remains available to me, I do everything in my power so it will be there for me. The common welfare of ACA is, therefore, of primary concern for me as well as for each member of the ACA fellowship. In ACA I have seen members resolve problems amicably. In one situation, the group voted to change a rule that required a certain amount of recovery time to serve in a group office. The group wanted to appoint a person who did not have the required time. A group conscience vote was taken, and the rule was changed for this situation. The group figured that the value of the change outweighed the application of the rule on recovery time. The next situation might be different, but on this night the rule was suspended. This was done in a calm, easy-going manner with very little discord.*

19

It was so smooth, in fact, that some of the members were shocked to see the rule-exception adopted so quickly and smoothly. When a program issue arises, I simply express my opinions and then vote with an attitude of acceptance of the outcome. I don't try to control the outcome. This is how unity is maintained in ACA.

Tradition One Insight

ACA's journey to find its identity as a fellowship has created a proven unity that underpins our primary purpose of carrying the ACA message to suffering adult children. ACA unity is based on our similarities rather than our differences. Adult children come from many different family types. We have different viewpoints, but we are the same at the core. We are a group of trauma survivors who can depend upon each other as we heal and recover. Our groups have been tested by a fire that has forged our future as a viable fellowship. Through unity, the groups have emerged with a maturity that has withstood growing pains and the evolution of the program. We are a fellowship of adult children from alcoholic and other dysfunctional families.

At first glance, the First Tradition seems to put a meeting's common welfare above individual recovery. When we think about this possibility, we must ask: "Can we even have personal recovery without ACA unity?" Our First Tradition frankly says "No." ACA members working the Twelve Steps recognize the need to place the group's survival ahead of their own selfish needs or their fear-based urge to control others. In ACA, we learn to keep our groups safe and inviting for our members.

Do established meetings placing the common welfare of the group first have problems or conflicts? Sure. But at such healthy meetings, problems become opportunities to further one's recovery. The groups' members have learned to trust one another and to disagree without being disagreeable. The group members trust the collective decision-making process known as a group conscience.

ACA meetings include business sessions that typically precede or follow a regular ACA meeting. At the typical ACA business meeting, reports are given on group finances and the general operations of the group. Groups carrying the ACA message into prisons or treatment centers may discuss the needs and development of these meetings as well. These meetings are known as Hospitals and Institutions meetings. ACA group members with recovery experience volunteer to conduct a meeting in these facilities or help out with meetings conducted in the facilities.

An ACA business meeting also addresses a group's problems and solutions. These discussions typically are called a group conscience. At a group conscience, each group member is allowed to share his or her point of view on the issue at hand. Each member is equal and has an opportunity to share his or her thoughts and solutions. The group conscience is similar to a healthy family seeking a resolution everyone is content with, or at least which everyone can take ownership in.

How about what some members would consider an unhealthy ACA meeting? First of all, a meeting is not unhealthy just because one or two people say so. Unhealthy ACA meetings typically don't survive, but those that struggle usually share some common traits. Problems at unhealthy or struggling meetings tend to fall into three categories: interpersonal squabbling between ACA members; suspicion about the handling of group donations; and older members gripping the group with self-righteous control. There are other scenarios that can give a group the label of being unhealthy or "sick," but these seem to dominate.

Listening to members complain about the meeting or group, one gets the sense of the meeting being dominated by a small group of individuals. Occasionally, one individual can appear to dominate a group. When this happens, group unity and the sense that all group members are equal suffers. The group's future and its ability to attract new members to sustain itself can hang in the balance. If it can be clearly determined that the group is controlled by a few members, the remaining members

19

of the group must summon the courage to speak up. However, no one should be a single spokesperson. Those believing the group is not adhering to ACA principles must talk about their thoughts with one another and with a sponsor or friend. There should also be prayer and thoughtfulness about what should be done. Decisions about what to do should be measured by the principles of unity and the most loving path to take. There should be no harsh talk. There should be no gossip that could be followed by an ambush at a business meeting.

Without thoughtful action, some of these ACA groups can die. The group withers because group members cannot apply the principles of the Twelve Steps or Twelve Traditions in their lives long enough to place the group first.

In other cases, the group changes direction and finds new strength. Group members call a business meeting to discuss unity in addition to the problem at hand. If the members are humble and value their ACA group, a Higher Power will enter the discussion and show the path for cooperation and group survival. We have seen this happen many times in the history of ACA groups seeking unity over personal gain.

Group members who once believed they could not tolerate one another discover their differences are not that important when the survival of the group is on the line. They realize the group suffers when ACA members fail to cooperate for a common purpose. When the group suffers, so does the individual who cannot recover alone.

ACA members not getting along or failing to place ACA first can trigger relapse for some ACA members. Resentments fester, and members in the conflict are tempted to pick up the destructive tools of manipulation, gossip, and dishonesty. ACA members can fight dirty when they believe they are threatened, whether the potential for harm is real or not. We learned how to fight by stealth or with verbal razors from the best – our family.

An ACA relapse can bring a return to our dysfunctional family role. When a member walks away from ACA over a dispute or resentment, he or she can face adult child addictiveness.

An ACA member in relapse can binge on food, drugs, sex, gambling, spending, or some other compulsive or obsessive activity. Some ACA relapses involve extreme isolation and a refusal to communicate with anyone. The common behaviors of fearing authority figures, judging oneself without mercy, and tolerating abuse can return during relapse. We may have changed some of our most harmful behaviors, but some of us can switch to another harmful behavior or compulsion during an ACA relapse. Our survival traits learned as children can return with greater fierceness and emotional pain than before recovery.

Does the First Tradition mean ACA members should give up their identity or personal recovery to gain unity? Do we all have to think alike and act alike for the common good? To the contrary, group members will usually find their individuality honored and celebrated in ACA. They find the greatest support for their program and identity while attending meetings that work in unity. Those of us with dysfunctional childhoods may not have had a healthy experience in dealing with problems and resolution. Many ACA members have learned to form opinions, and to argue constructively in an ACA group business meeting, perhaps for the first time in their lives. We may have been told to stay quiet or were scolded as children for talking. In ACA, however, we are asked to speak up and express our views. We are encouraged to find our true voice and identity. We are asked to add our views and our voice to ACA unity.

Writing / Sharing

1. How do you feel when group members respectfully state their opinions, negotiate with one another, resolve their differences, and agree calmly to disagree respectfully?

2. When you feel yourself getting pulled into an "all or nothing" fight over a program issue, what can you do to change your behavior?

3. What is your group doing right? On a scale of one to ten, how much unity is in your group?

4. How could your group, Intergroup, or ACA committee improve?

5. What is the spiritual principle in Tradition One?

Illustrating Tradition One

Make a wall poster or computer graphic depicting this Tradition.

Meditation

Higher Power. I am your trusted servant seeking to support my ACA group and its primary purpose. Please remind me that the life of my program and my own recovery depends upon my willingness to put the group's welfare above my own will. Help me recognize unity.

TRADITION TWO

For our group purpose there is but one ultimate authority – a loving God as expressed in our group conscience. Our leaders are but trusted servants; they do not govern.

With a lifetime of clinging to structure so I wouldn't make a mistake, this seeming lack of leadership threw me into emotional chaos. I was used to being given absolute orders, and that seemed preferable to not getting any direction at all. Who would I turn to for absolute answers when no one had them? How could everyone be right when opinions varied so much? How could the group resolve anything when no one put his foot down and made the decision for the group's own good? How could I possibly believe, coming from a self-serving background, that anything could or would be resolved through group conscience and be good for everyone?

I learned to trust the wisdom of Tradition Two by watching it work. Time after time I saw the impossible happen when group honesty prevailed. Time and time again I saw unity reestablished when the oldtimers led by example, not by mandate, through group crises.

My mistake was in needing to understand this paradox. I couldn't do spiritual thinking with a dysfunctional mindset. I simply had to accept the truth of this principle, whether I believed it or not.

The group's decision is a reflection of our Loving God and His will for us. *No one is in charge in our ACA groups. We really are but trusted servants with no authority to govern the group. Where questions arise, we ask for a group conscience for the answer. Our group depends on participation. When an issue arises that could affect ACA, the group is called on for a group conscience decision, to determine the way the problem should be handled. A "loving God" is a God who cares about the group and endorses the recovery of its members. As a group we want, and expect, the cooperation of our Higher Power in our group decisions. When the members decide on an issue, our Loving God is expressed in that decision by the group members.*

19

A group conscience is an acceptance that we reflect the will of God in our discussions or votes. The results are considered to be an answer on action or no action for the group. The answer or direction comes from God through our members. When we make decisions, we "suit up, show up, listen, participate, and let go of the results." Too often we try to force our own will into a decision that will ultimately be settled by the group's vote. A group conscience is simply the vote of the group that supersedes any individual's opinion. The discussion takes place followed by a group conscience vote. In that vote a collective wisdom emerges. The collective wisdom is better than an individual opinion, because it is much more likely to be impartial. When a group decision is made, I support it whether I agree with it or not. The group conscience is considered to be the expression of the will of God as we understand God. When presented with an issue, the group conscience is really just the way issues are considered.

Tradition Two Insight

Many new members of ACA wonder who is in charge of meetings and groups. It is only natural since we have a history of fearing authority figures or being authority figures. We can be hypervigilant about identifying the authority figures in any group so we can survive as we did in childhood. By identifying what we believe to be the authority figures, we reason we can adapt as we did as children in a dysfunctional home. But ACA is different than other groups or organizations. We don't have rules that delegate powers or a structured chain of command. ACA is different than our families.

For those of us who are new, it is easy to make wrong conclusions about ACA's benign organizational structure. If there are numerous newcomers at a meeting, it is easy for them to assume that older members know everything and are in charge. If it is not the older members, then we conclude it must be the chairperson of the meeting. But the chairperson changes frequently. Maybe the secretary is the one in charge since he or she unlocks the meeting door, orders literature, and takes minutes

19

at the business meeting. But the secretary takes direction from the group conscience. "Who runs ACA anyway?" some newer members have asked.

Fortunately, our Second Tradition reminds us that our real authority in ACA meetings and service work is "a loving God as expressed in our group conscience." We will discuss more about that group conscience, but for the moment, just note that our leaders – chairpersons, secretaries, group representatives, and the like – are not in charge. No one is in charge of ACA. We do elect trusted servants directly responsible to those they serve. They have no power. They serve the fellowship from the motives of compassion, love, and humility.

For those who might flirt with the notion of being in charge, ACA gives them a chance to learn the meaning of ACA service. By watching other trusted servants in ACA, these members soon learn the value of serving rather than taking. Hold-over notions of being in charge evaporate. Only God as expressed in the group conscience is in charge.

New ACA meetings are often established by one determined individual, who then assumes the tasks of the meeting secretary, treasurer, group leader, and general "jack-of-all-trades" for the meeting. In many cases, such leadership is necessary when a new meeting is just forming. When this person does a good job, the meeting soon starts to grow. Others usually affirm the person's position of leadership simply because the founder of the meeting usually understands group operations and has the meeting key. This is where a good leader begins the transition to being a trusted servant by remembering the Second Tradition and the Higher Power as the ultimate authority in ACA. The trusted servant looks for ways to get newer members involved in group service. He or she politely asks for help in setting up the meeting room, carrying the meeting room key, and ordering literature or making refreshments for the meeting. All of these duties are chances to get members involved in their group and to take ownership in the group.

19

The leader or founder of a new group also encourages others to take on service positions for the meeting. A business meeting is called to discuss these positions of secretary, treasurer, or group representative. The wise trusted leader knows to avoid keeping a tight hold on the reigns of the meeting or group. He or she knows that involvement in the meetings leads to meaningful change for the individual.

Since the group founder has done a good job, the group will probably elect the person to continue one of the leadership roles. In that moment, the group founder moves from being a leader by necessity to a trusted servant by election of the group members. This transition from founder to an elected trusted servant is subtle but critical for the group's growth and future. By taking an active role in the group, its members have assumed responsibility for their meeting. They share the responsibilities, but they also share the rewards of helping others.

Meanwhile, the group has also experienced a healthy group conscience. All the leaders can follow this example of being a trusted servant within the Twelve Step format. In subsequent business meetings, the original leader will probably choose to step down and let others take full leadership of the meeting.

Conversely, some new leaders try to govern their meeting with a tight fist. They think they know what is right for ACA and the group; there is no room for discussion at business meetings or settings involving ACA matters. These control-seeking members can be disruptive and divisive. They seem to act like "tradition lawyers" and are willing to split hairs over business meeting rules, meeting agendas, and voting procedures. Their short-sighted behavior, if left unchecked, can literally kill the group. Business meeting disputes spill into regular meetings and feelings are hurt and resentments fester. Members stop attending the group or feel unsafe to support the group. The group suffers until someone asks a loving God to enter a group business meeting and their regular meetings.

Group members may rise up and call a special meeting to discuss the group's direction. If circumstances have deteriorated enough, the original founder or trusted servant may be voted out of office. As a result, the disenchanted "leader" may leave the meeting, feeling abandoned by the group. But the meeting will continue as long as it follows the Steps and Traditions of ACA.

AA identifies controlling group members as "bleeding deacons." They may have meant well in starting an ACA group, but they failed to work the ACA program. Some of these members have turned into authority figures who harm the group's ability to help others. The good news is that these "bleeding deacons" can learn from their experience. By applying the ACA program, they can become trusted servants and ultimately become elder statesmen. Such is the strength of the program, and of the Second Tradition, when we allow a Higher Power to guide our behavior.

In conclusion, no one has authority over another in ACA, but we do have elected leaders who serve those who elect them. They do not govern, but they lead by example. Our group conscience is a spiritual method by which a Higher Power is expressed in our discussions and our decisions. Most of our decisions are based on what is best for the most, instead of what is best for the few. Through humility, we surrender our egos and place the group first in our decisions on ACA matters. Humility does not mean we are a doormat or that we have no opinion. It means that we are willing to stay focused on ACA principles. We open the door to listen to direction from our Higher Power. We bring our Twelve Step experience to these discussions. We apply surrender, hope, willingness, forgiveness, and other Step principles in our group business meetings and group discussions. We learn discernment and see that some ideas appear good and appealing; however, they can divert us from seeking the best for ACA. We can expect the best from our decisions and get it.

19

Writing / Sharing

1. What is a "loving God"?
2. Explain the concept of group conscience.
3. Explain the process to arrive at a group conscience decision.
4. Why is the collective wisdom of a group better than the opinion of one person?
5. Describe one successful experience you have had in making a group decision in this program.
6. What is the spiritual principle in Tradition Two?

Illustrating Tradition Two

Make a wall poster or computer graphic depicting this Tradition.

Meditation

Higher Power. I understand that you make your voice heard in a group conscience. I ask you to remind me that the life of my program and, therefore, my own recovery depends upon my willingness to put the group's welfare above my own will. Where I disagree with the common view of my fellows in service, allow me to state my case honestly and respectfully. Allow me to listen to and consider the views of others. May I state my view and support all group decisions, including the ones I might disagree with. Your will, not mine, be done.

19

TRADITION THREE

The only requirement for membership in ACA is a desire to recover from the effects of growing up in an alcoholic or otherwise dysfunctional family.

I attended meetings for six weeks without really knowing why I came. I had never heard anyone say such intimate things about themselves out loud. I didn't know my family was dysfunctional or that I had been abused emotionally and sexually. I assumed I deserved what I got.

For two years I changed my label frequently when I introduced myself at the beginning of the meeting. After that I quit using a label at all. I allowed others the same latitude. I came into this program with a hidden agenda and severe control issues, and I immediately sought to perpetuate my sickness by eliminating everything and everyone that made me uneasy. As insane as this felt, the people at the meeting let me go through my healing process. The fact that I was attending meetings at all and kept coming back to them was far more significant than anything I could say or do. In acting out, I was screaming when I could not voice my pain. I thank God for the tolerance I was given.

When I started ACA, I would have liked to have excluded some members who seemed scary or different. For example, I disliked gays. I didn't know any gay people, but that didn't stop me from not liking them. No. ACA should not allow them to be part of our regular ACA meetings. I also recall one rather gruff guy, who talked rough and irritated me with his hugs after the meeting. This guy had to go as well in my narrow thinking early on. These members were not the only ones who I selfishly deemed excludable. After all, we should only have respectable dysfunctional people at the meetings, or at least such was the opinion of me as a newcomer.

Fortunately, there were others at those meetings with more wisdom than I, for none of these persons were excluded. And over time, they became my friends, as well as my teachers. I found gays at the meetings to be generally likable people, struggling with issues much like mine.

I discovered that, other than their sexual orientation, we had much in common. And Ed, the rough hugger, I don't know if his violent language ever did lessen, or if I just got more used to it, but I came to realize he too was working on childhood issues much like mine. Over the years, he would also host many ACA parties at his house, parties which I remember as a lot of fun. I can't say we ever became close friends, but I did come to trust him implicitly, and in the process, overcame my fear of Ed and others who might speak like him. I don't know where I filed my rules on exclusion. They just don't seem that important anymore.

I had a desire to learn more about ACA before I developed a desire to recover from the effects of growing up in a dysfunctional home. *I had to get information in counseling and meetings to help me debrief what happened to me. Before I found ACA, I thought I was a no-good person, who needed to act right or smarter or something. The thought of developing a desire to recover from my childhood neglect and abuse would have never occurred to me without ACA. I would have remained lost in self-condemnation. There would have been no self-acceptance, no self-forgiveness, and no desire to become my own Loving Parent and a member of ACA. My desire to learn about ACA and my family of origin was good enough to get started. I developed a desire to recover from the effects of a dysfunctional home by attending meetings and working the Twelve Steps. I found out what happened to me with meaning and detail that I could understand. I have a desire to recover from my abandonment and shame. I am a member of ACA.*

Tradition Three Insight

In the early days of Alcoholics Anonymous, the fellowship looked for appropriate requirements for membership. The budding AA fellowship and its struggling groups feared that certain alcoholics would certainly sink marginal groups while bringing unwanted scrutiny to others. After much stumbling, AA came to realize that membership requirements could not be applied if AA was to become the inclusive, spiritual program that we know of today. Indeed, if the suggested membership requirements received from the AA groups had been implemented, the founders of AA would not have been allowed to join. AA settled upon a single requirement for membership: a desire to stay sober.

This brings us to ACA's Third Tradition. What membership requirements do we impose on those considering ACA membership? Following AA's lead, our Third Tradition reminds us to avoid creating a long list of requirements on ACA membership. Anyone having the desire to recover from the effects of growing up in a dysfunctional home qualifies, regardless of whether alcohol was a factor in the home. That is it. There are no screening committees, questionnaires, or waiting periods to join. You are an ACA member when you say you are.

In ACA, we welcome society's misfits into our meetings, as we have discovered that we are all misfits or have felt like such to varying degrees. Adult children who are codependents, addicts, debtors, overeaters, sexually compulsive, alcoholics, and gamblers are members if they have a desire to recover from the effects of a dysfunctional family. We cannot turn away anyone seeking help from the isolation and madness of the effects of a dysfunctional upbringing. With the simple requirement, ACA has a diverse fellowship with a variety of individual experiences. We are a fellowship of great width and depth.

Our single requirement for ACA membership gave rise to ACA's spirit of inclusion. Our membership includes adult children from homes without alcoholism being a factor. Soon after ACA was founded, adult children from homes with other forms of dysfunction began showing up and identifying with the ACA message. The Laundry List traits described their behavior and thinking in the same manner as adult children from alcoholic or addicted homes. These adult children attended ACA meetings and embraced recovery. They claimed the Inner Child and Loving Parent just like the ACA member from an alcoholic home. We see no difference in these members. Their voice is the voice of ACA.

In ACA, developing a desire to recover from the effects of growing up in a dysfunctional family can be one of our greatest tools of recovery. We need a sincere desire to sustain us. The effects of family dysfunction did not occur overnight, so recovery will not occur overnight. We will need desire and willingness to work our program consistently. Desire coupled with willingness is a strong formula for change.

Writing / Sharing

1. Using "The Laundry List" or "The Problem," check off the characteristics that apply to you. Are these the effects of growing up in a dysfunctional home?

2. Select three characteristics you have from growing up in an alcoholic or dysfunctional home. Explain how these traits are exhibited in your daily life.

3. Why do you want to change your life now? What happened that has brought you to ACA?

4. What is the spiritual principle in Tradition Three?

5. What is the only requirement for ACA membership?

6. How does willingness strengthen the only requirement for membership?

Illustrating Tradition Three

Make a wall poster or computer graphic depicting this Tradition.

Meditation

Higher Power. Help me recognize my desire to recover from the effects of growing up in a dysfunctional home. Give me willingness to attend meetings to recover from these effects. I participate in ACA because I want to change and help others. Thank you for leading me to these rooms where I belong. Thank you for giving me the courage to walk into an ACA meeting and stay and find my place. I am finally home. I finally know where I fit.

19

TRADITION FOUR

Each group is autonomous except in matters affecting other groups or ACA as a whole. We cooperate with all other Twelve Step programs.

Autonomy means that ACA groups can conduct themselves as they see fit as long as their actions follow the Twelve Traditions and their actions don't cause other groups, or ACA as a whole, to be adversely affected. A group represents ACA by its very nature and is often the only image the general public will see of ACA. It is important that we conduct ourselves and our meetings with common sense. We need to be a good neighbor. The group members are responsible to keep the meeting safe, recovery oriented, and to carry the ACA message. Group members are cooperative with their building landlords and keep the meeting place clean and presentable. They care about ACA and what it stands for.

In addition to honoring the Twelve Traditions and group upkeep, the group's responsibility is to meet its expenses and reserve an amount of money so that the group can continue to meet its expenses for several months if donations decline. ACA groups cooperate with one another for the common good of ACA.

When I first saw the Fourth Tradition and the freedom it gave the group, I thought, 'This won't work.' Where are the rules and authority and enforcement guidelines? As I listened and watched group members applying the principles of the program, I realized my fears were unfounded. I saw my fellow ACAs being respectful of the group and wanting to do all they could to help other adult children. They guarded the group autonomy fiercely, but they also guarded ACA's unity and image with just as much dedication. After awhile, I could see that the group members truly cared about ACA. They were thoughtful about their actions. We took care of our own business, but we were mindful of other groups. We thought about how our actions might affect the fellowship as a whole.

19

It's funny, but the Fourth Tradition almost began to look like one of the Twelve Steps to me. I began caring more about myself because I was part of something that others care enough about to keep it alive. I work the Steps, but this Tradition taught me a lot about caring for myself.

Tradition Four Insight

ACA, like most other organizations, has a structure which begins with individuals forming ACA groups. The groups form Intergroups to help organize meeting activities in their geographical area and to carry the ACA message into treatment centers and other facilities. Intergroups help the groups explore ideas of carrying the message within a given community. Intergroups may occasionally establish a local helpline or contact person, who answers inquiries about ACA. Regions are formed by several Intergroups in a geographical area. There is also the World Service Organization which provides support to the Intergroups and Regions around the world. WSO also provides support to areas where there is no Intergroup.

So what controls do the Intergroups hold over the meetings, and what controls does the WSO hold over meetings, Intergroups, or Regions? None. Each ACA group is autonomous, but the groups routinely seek guidance from Intergroups, Regions, and WSO for group affairs. There is no governance or enforcement of rules in ACA. Intergroups and WSO serve as a resource for the groups, and the groups, in turn, are encouraged to provide willing trusted servants to do the good work of ACA at the Intergroup, Regional, and WSO levels.

One of the few times the WSO or Intergroups might become directly involved would be in matters "affecting other groups or ACA as a whole." While WSO and Intergroups can and do provide guidance to ACA meetings, when asked, they ultimately must step back and let meetings decide for themselves how to run their particular meeting.

Being autonomous does not mean that ACA groups are alone or operate in a vacuum. As stated, ACA groups seek input from the service structure when questions or challenges arise in ACA meetings. For example, the WSO periodically is asked whether certain reading materials can be used in meetings. The answer is always, per our Fourth Tradition, that each meeting is free to select the material for use in their meeting. WSO and Intergroups do not approve or disapprove material selection for meetings. There are suggested guidelines in the ACA Literature Policy trifold. The trifold asks groups to pick materials or books that focus on the Twelve Step process and Twelve Traditions. The groups are asked to avoid books which might promote a particular author or move the group toward a therapy-session setting. While groups are autonomous, it is a standard for ACA groups to use The Laundry List (Problem), The Solution, the Twelve Steps, and Twelve Traditions as the foundation of their traditional meeting format. The use of these standard readings, and nonaffiliation with outside entities, are required for a group to be considered an ACA group.

Another common question is how does a meeting resolve a conflict between its group members? Or how do we handle members who might be disruptive in meetings? Again, the WSO or Intergroup does not intervene in these situations, but can offer suggestions on how past situations have been handled. Typically, the group would contact the Intergroup on these matters first. However, any group can contact the WSO with questions or to seek experience, strength, and hope.

With all this talk of group autonomy, a question arises: Can allowing such autonomy really work? Couldn't a meeting make some really bad decisions? Yes. Indeed, many ACA meetings over the years have made poor decisions – ones that subsequently caused them much grief. But like a family, we learn through such decisions, generally coming out much wiser from the

19

experience. Groups that remain close to the Twelve Steps and Twelve Traditions tend to ride out difficult times more smoothly. They tend to survive. Through experience, ACA groups have gained a measure of toughness and durability while still offering warmth and acceptance to its members.

The wisdom of the Fourth Tradition allows every ACA group the right to make its own decisions. Within the guidance of the Traditions, the groups run their own meetings and choose the method for carrying the ACA message within their community. The groups are given freedom to make mistakes. In other words, every group has the unabashed right to be wrong. And when wrong, their decision then becomes part of the growth process, both for the meeting and, more especially, for the meeting members.

These are the groups that gain wisdom and some tenacity by learning from their mistakes. The group survives and can flourish if the members are willing to focus on ACA principles and invite a loving God into their decision-making processes. Placing ACA first and cooperating with one another is essential for healthy group autonomy.

Cooperation brings us to the second part of the Fourth Tradition: "We cooperate with all other Twelve Step programs." There are many different Twelve Step programs based on AA's original Steps and Traditions. Sometimes comparisons are made among the members of the various programs. "My program is better than your program," has been heard but adds little in the effort to truly help others. After years of listening to members of many Twelve Step programs, we have come to realize that all these programs have a purpose to help others seeking a better way of life. ACA is an autonomous program that helps thousands of adult children in ways that no other program can. We are an experienced fellowship that is equal to other Twelve Step programs. We are not superior or inferior.

Writing / Sharing

1. Define "autonomous" as it relates to ACA meetings/ groups.

2. If each ACA group is autonomous, then how do they have a consistency in meeting format and message?

3. What is an Intergroup? What is the World Service Organization?

4. In what ways should ACA cooperate with another ACA group or Twelve Step program?

5. What is the spiritual principle in Tradition Four?

Illustrating Tradition Four

Make a wall poster or computer graphic depicting this Tradition.

Meditation

Higher Power. Help my home group remain focused on the Twelve Step process of recovery while still having its own personality and flavor. When the actions and decisions of my group might affect ACA as a whole, may we find the spirit of cooperation and a willingness to seek help from the ACA service structure. My group is autonomous, but it is not alone.

19

TRADITION FIVE

Each group has but one primary purpose – to carry its message to the adult child who still suffers.

I am so glad that ACA does one thing and one thing well. We don't debate politics or fuss over causes, no matter how worthy or unworthy. I know what to expect every time I attend an ACA meeting or event. I know we are going to read about or discuss recovery from the disease of family dysfunction. We are not going to get diverted into fixing one another or practicing therapy, either. Sports talk is nice, too, but it is not part of the ACA message of hope.

ACA groups also carry the ACA message into prisons and treatment centers. This is rewarding service work. Through the Twelfth Step, we tell our stories and carry the message to future group members.

In ACA, it seems to me that we focus on learning to love ourselves and to contribute to the world. That's our primary purpose. We carry the message to other adult children wanting a new way of life. By doing this, I stay emotionally sober and help myself in the process. I give it away to keep it – recovery.

My primary purpose is to remember what it was like before ACA so I can reach out to the newcomer. While I can remember partly what it was like, reaching out to the newcomer can make my past experience more vivid and remind me why I continue to attend meetings and to help others. I give hope and get hope. This is my only purpose, our only purpose.

It is so easy to drift away from the memories and become preoccupied with things that come with recovery – jobs, relationships, and good-times. I can become so busy with what I have to do that I forget what I have done. When this happens, all gratitude is gone, and I'm as needy as the newcomer. Given the life of survival I've led, it is a comfortable role for me, but this isn't recovery.

Early on in the program, I asked, 'How will I know when I understand this program?' I was told, 'When the world stops revolving around you, and you can look outward instead of inward, then you have achieved enlightenment.' This Tradition paraphrases that statement.

19

The primary responsibility of an ACA group, or a meeting, is to carry the message to newcomers, but another very important purpose is to assist all members in maintaining their recovery, as well. If a meeting has no newcomers would we cancel the meeting and go home? No. The meeting would continue because the group carries the ACA message to all of us, including members with many years in the program.

Greeting newcomers is one way our group carries the message. Another is to encourage newcomers to ask questions. We also offer our phone numbers, or e-mail addresses, so that newcomers can get help between meetings.

In the meeting, we welcome newcomers, we share our experience, strength, and hope by sharing, and we provide literature for their information.

In addition to the meetings, we chat after the meeting with others. We go for coffee at a nearby coffee shop, and we introduce ourselves. This is carrying the message as well, outside the walls of the meeting.

Tradition Five Insight

The AA program learned early on that the fellowship should do one thing well instead of doing many things poorly. ACA has adopted a similar attitude. While we encourage diversity in our fellowship and taking reasonable risks for personal growth, the fellowship focus remains constant. We carry the message to others and avoid distractions that could divert our groups from this singleness of purpose. Each group decision must ultimately answer this question: "Does the decision we are about to make contribute to carrying the ACA message?"

By adhering to our primary purpose of carrying the message to those who still suffer, ACA avoids getting involved in outside causes. Some of the causes seem notable, while others are obviously political or controversial. We have learned that even noble causes can divert ACA from its singleness of purpose. Good causes can come with affiliations or expectations that ACA avoids. We are an autonomous fellowship who answers to its membership and no one else. We are guided by the fellowship voice and a Higher Power.

The message we carry in ACA meetings, treatment centers, and to professional groups is a clear message free of affiliation with outside issues. We don't mix the ACA message with other causes or philosophies, no matter how noble. To do so would cloud the ACA message of recovery. The message we carry is that ACA works for those who are willing to surrender, ask for help, and accept it. Recovery cannot begin until the adult child admits that he or she is powerless over the effects of family dysfunction. The admission of powerlessness is followed by an acknowledgment of an unmanageable life. With ACA, there is hope for another way of life that moves us away from isolation and toward others and God.

Each of us comes to ACA with many talents. As we grow in our recovery, we discover even more talents within us. We also discover that we share many common experiences with others growing up in dysfunctional households. Through attending ACA meetings, we find we are not alone. With our common experiences, we find that we can help one another in ways that others cannot because we carry with us empathy and an understanding of the disease of family dysfunction. With our experiences as children and adults, we can reach a suffering adult child when few others can. We are not bragging, but we know what we are talking about because we have lived it We have survived family dysfunction, and we have found a sure way to move beyond mere survival. A bewildered or confused adult child, who is suspicious of most people, will trust another adult child in a matter of moments upon hearing a piece of the person's story. We have the gift of identification. By carrying the message, we embrace the power of identification. We don't have to promote ACA. Our stories and sincerity attract people to ACA and to a better way of life.

19

When first entering the ACA program, most are surprised to discover others with childhood experiences similar to their own. Listening to the stories of others, we realize we have much in common. Soon newcomers begin sharing their own stories as well. The new person discovers that his or her personal experience is similar to the experience of others. The person finds a common bond, something many hadn't found with others before coming to ACA. With this common bond, we learn to work together so that the group and ACA survives. We learn that we cannot recover alone or in isolation.

Our Fifth Tradition reminds us of the single-minded purpose of our program – carrying the message to others looking for a way out of confusion or despair. When carrying the ACA message, we stick to our story and to the principles of recovery. We don't proselytize, bully, evangelize, or manipulate the person we are attempting to help. We also don't accept abuse or stay in the presence of someone who obviously does not want to hear the message of recovery. While we don't preach, we also do not shy away from sharing briefly about the spiritual aspect of the ACA program. However, this topic usually comes up after we have created identification with someone with a few stories about our growing up years in a dysfunctional home. As a simple guide to help build identification while carrying the message, we use the common behaviors or The Laundry List (Problem). With the common behaviors, we tell pieces of our story that soon has the listener wanting to hear more, or in some cases, interrupting to tell some of his or her story. In addition to creating identification and carrying a clear ACA message, we encourage the listener to attend a meeting that night or as soon as possible. This is where the Twelfth Step intersects with the Fifth Tradition and produces the ACA message, which can be irresistible for the person wanting help.

At the same time, if the person is unreceptive to ACA ideas, we move on. ACA works best for people who want it, instead of people who need it.

Writing / Sharing

1. What is the ACA message?

2. How does the primary purpose of carrying the message to others contribute to group unity and to consistency in ACA meetings?

3. How does the primary purpose help the group avoid controversy with outside issues?

4. What can your group do to carry the message? Suggestions: distribute local meeting directories in the community; put on fund-raising events[1] and donate proceeds to Intergroup and WSO; host recovery workshops or holiday marathon meetings; organize fun events and invite friends and relatives; or take an ACA meeting to a local hospital or institution.

5. What is the spiritual principle in Tradition Five?

Illustrating Tradition Five

Make a wall poster or computer graphic depicting this Tradition.

Meditation

Higher Power. Help me remember that ACA has one primary purpose, which centers the fellowship and which simplifies most discussions. Help me remember to ask myself a simple question when I am doing the business of ACA. 'Does what we are about to do support the primary purpose of carrying the ACA message to another adult child needing help?'

19

---

[1] Fund-raising events can be dances or conventions for ACA members and friends.

Chapter Nineteen

TRADITION SIX

An ACA group ought never endorse, finance, or lend the ACA name to any related facility or outside enterprise, lest problems of money, property, and prestige divert us from our primary purpose.

This Tradition has taught me a lot about my rescuing traits and wanting everyone everywhere to get ACA recovery. *I toyed with the idea that ACA was a cure for every kind of mental illness and some forms of cancer, in addition to codependence, addiction, and compulsion. It is true that ACA has a great reach and brings healing and hope for a wide variety of dysfunctional behavior. But we can't do everything for everyone. We can't help people who don't want help, and we can't entangle the ACA name with organizations or plans that would divert us from our primary purpose.*

We can't chase after prestige as a fellowship either. We seemed to have some prestige in the 1980s, with talk shows focusing on ACA and writers selling books about adult children. But where is that now? In the end, ACA must tell its own story without lending our name to authors or any other outside entity. When we do that, we can stay focused as a fellowship, and offer ACA to the world and to those who want what we have to offer.

There are lots of ways we could be diverted from our primary purpose of carrying the message. *Experience has shown that if ACA should become affiliated with outside activities, harm could be done. The simple saying I have heard is: 'ACA has no opinions on outside issues'.*

We favor no particular political party, endorse no one church, and are not embroiled in any of the hot news stories of the day. We simply carry the message of recovery.

Specifically, we do not, as a fellowship, endorse any outside group, business, or entity by stating they are acceptable or good or bad. We have no opinion on these outside entities. We are silent on them.

ACA does not finance; we don't give or lend money to an individual or an ACA group. We don't lend the ACA name to any cause or purpose no matter how noble or well-deserving. We don't endorse or lend the ACA name to any therapist, doctor, hospital, treatment program, medical group, or agency. We don't lend ACA support to any legislation, educational effort for domestic abuse, or any business organization, no matter how noble or good. We are not for or against these causes. We have one primary purpose as stated in Tradition Five.

Tradition Six Insight

ACA is an awesome program, right? Wouldn't it be great to expand ACA to have some ACA Counseling Centers? Perhaps we could have some hospitals for persons recovering from abusive relationships? We could even form some political action groups to force our legislators to enact laws to resolve such relationship problems. While we are at it, why not just save the world?

We are not trivializing the ACA program or these causes with outlandish ideas. ACA is a mature program on the front line of life, offering sure hope to some of the world's most injured people. We don't balk at stating that ACA has been tested. We have been the last hope for many adult children, but we cannot do all things for all people. We are a fellowship of recovering adult children. This is our focus.

The problems of the world are easy to see, and we are often eager to attempt to fix them. But few of us would know how to manage a worldwide effort to end abuse, neglect, or other forms of terrible dysfunction. We would soon be so busy trying to manage all the programs of such an effort that we would be diverted from our primary purpose. Shortly overwhelmed, we would eventually have to save ourselves if it was not too late. Our Sixth Tradition cautions us against such grandiose plans.

Does that mean we cannot become involved with other organizations? Well, yes and no. As individuals, many of us can and do offer much to many non-ACA programs. We volunteer

19

our time and contribute to the outside group as individuals. The problem arises when we try to identify such programs with our ACA group. There are many fine community groups, treatment programs, or therapists who would like to link their programs or practices to the ACA program, but we must decline their offers. To accept could eventually lead us into controversy or link us to groups outside of ACA. To be associated with such groups in the public eye can confuse those seeking our help. We could turn people away by appearing to endorse or affiliate with an outside entity.

For example, an ACA group may receive an offer from a treatment center to jointly sponsor a community outreach program about dysfunctional families. The center believes in the ACA program and its fine work. With good intentions, the recovery center wants to finance the event and provide the site. In return, ACA gets its name in the newspaper or on television along with the recovery center. Is this a good idea? It is tempting to accept such an offer. We would like the publicity and a chance to reach adult children with our message. However, our Sixth Tradition reminds us of the pitfalls in such joint efforts. In the public eye, we would be linked to the recovery center and in violation of Tradition Six. ACA is not a recovery center program. It is an autonomous Twelve Step program grounded in spiritual principles. It would be better to let the recovery center sponsor its own event, while ACA would remain autonomous and carry the message to clients in the center.

Additionally, Tradition Six reminds ACA groups and service committees to avoid owning property or assets of great value. To own property sets up the group for discussions on asset ownership that are not relevant to ACA recovery. ACA clubhouses, overseen by a board of directors separate from ACA, are one way that groups have found a consistent meeting place while keeping discussions of land and assets separate from the meetings. Other ACA groups avoid the issue of property by renting meeting space from a variety of facilities without affiliating with the facility.

Tradition Six keeps ACA free of outside influences and reminds us not to lend the ACA name to any related facility or outside enterprise. By following this Tradition we also avoid money and prestige issues that would hinder our primary purpose.

Writing / Sharing

1.   What does "endorse" mean?

2.   What does "finance" mean?

3.   What does "lend the ACA name" mean?

4.   What is a "related facility?"

5.   What is an "outside enterprise?"

6.   What is the spiritual principle in Tradition Six?

Illustrating Tradition Six

Make a wall poster or computer graphic depicting this Tradition.

Meditation

Higher Power. Grant me the wisdom to know when a group project will carry the message of recovery to those who still suffer, or will direct group energy away from carrying the message. Guide us away from discussions about property, prestige, or endorsing causes that are not ACA. Give me the courage to speak clearly and thoughtfully for what I believe honors Tradition Six.

19

TRADITION SEVEN

Every ACA group ought to be fully self-supporting, declining outside contributions.

When I first arrived in ACA, I had financial problems. Many nights I had to choose between putting money in the basket and buying bread for my lunch the following day. I was angry about having to make that decision, since everyone around me obviously had much more. I kept hearing how imperative it was that I feel a part of the group. Eventually, I realized that my meager group donation was all I could share to make myself part of the group. I was much too distrustful of people to give more of myself.

Now I contend with the overwhelming desire to make up for those lean times. I have to stifle the urge to give more than my share. In the beginning I wanted to be relieved of sharing; I wanted someone to take care of me. I want to take care of the newcomers now, but to do so would rob them of their chance at belonging and ultimately recovering.

Our primary purpose is not to accumulate money. I get agitated when discussing these issues takes up time in my recovery group. Having too much money is always a bigger problem than having too little for individuals as well as groups. I was taught early on in ACA not to accumulate money beyond my need, because the disbursement, or the options of disbursement, became more powerful than my recovery.

The question sometimes arises in my meetings, 'What should we do with our money?' My answer is, 'It is given for Twelve Step work, so let it go for Twelve Step work.'

Self-supporting means that we, the members of ACA, contribute to our own support, and we rely on no other person, agency, or outside influence for financial assistance.

Fully self-supporting means that we, the members of ACA, support all of ACA, including rent, refreshments, literature, Intergroup and World Services, and any other miscellaneous expenses we incur.

The Seventh Tradition contributions are the collective offerings of our members to support ourselves, independent of any, and all, outside contributors. *We refuse outside contributions, so that we will be free of any outside pressures, influences, or control that could contaminate our ACA goals. We are independent of non-ACA contributors.*

A group is to pay for its basic meeting expenses and keep a prudent reserve to pay meeting expenses during difficult times. When that is taken care of, a percentage of what is left is sent to World Service Organization and to your Intergroup. The service boards, Intergroup, and WSO use these group contributions to support ACA literature development, coordinate treatment center meetings, and support other ACA efforts here and abroad.

Using Seventh Tradition contributions for a pizza party would be a misuse of the contributions intended for ACA's operating expenses. Group celebrations should be funded by the function's participants.

ACA groups decline outside contributions to keep the control of our ACA program in our own hands. Accepting outside contributions could lead to interference, even though some donors mean well. We must pay our own way to keep free of entanglement.

Tradition Seven Insight

Most adult children fall into three main categories when it comes to handling and spending money. Some are financial wizards, spending much of their time chasing stock trends. Others may struggle between paychecks, wishing they could earn more money, while sinking deeper into debt. At the same time, some adult children live within their means and know when enough is enough. They tend to delay gratification and can avoid seeking outside financial help to bail them out. When things sour financially for them, their lives tend to work out. They have resources and options by living modestly. The money or resources show up, and they move on.

This is one of the principles of the ACA program. We don't have a lot of money, but membership donations show up when there is a need. Group members respond and believe in what their group is doing for ACA and its members. In ACA, we don't hoard excessive amounts of money. But we do need cash

19

to pay the rent, order literature, and fund helplines and ACA events. Our members give donations because they know they are helping themselves by giving the right way. Before ACA, many of us gave our bodies, minds, or souls for the wrong reasons. In ACA, we learn to give for the right reason, and we learn the right amount to give. We give our fair share and let others give their fair share, so we all take ownership in ACA.

There is a story in AA history that illustrates the need for members to support their groups and service structure for their own good. The year was 1948 and a well-meaning person left the AA fellowship $10,000 in a will with no strings attached. Since AA was struggling with keeping open its small office and answering a constant stream of mail, the fellowship could have used the money. The story continues with AA trustees struggling with the possible consequences of accepting this large sum of money. During the discussion, the trustees realized that the gift could possibly open the door to future donations that would one day bring great wealth and great potential harm to the fellowship. For AA trustees knew that large sums of money held by AA groups or service boards inevitably turned into squabbles over how to spend the money. Taking the $10,000 would be like taking the first drink, AA trustees reasoned. And once the word was out that AA accepted large donations, surely others would follow. With donations flowing in and wealth apparent, AA members would reason that AA no longer needed donations. And therein lay the problem. AA realized that its members must pay their own way to keep their program for themselves. To allow outside entities to contribute, or to allow individual members to give more than his or her fair share, could diminish the key spiritual principle of everyone giving back what was freely given.

History shows that AA refused the $10,000 gift and established the principle of fellowship "poverty." AA was to remain poor to keep the fellowship free of excessive riches. The decision also limited arguments over money and the handling of money. However, it is understood in AA that groups and World Services need money to reach out to the suffering alcoholic. Individual AA members and their groups are asked to help support that effort, and they respond with gratitude. The money shows up. AA members own their fellowship by giving their time and by giving in the meeting basket.

ACA is in a similar situation. Our groups and services depend on individual and group donations. The principle of being fully self-supporting through our own contributions has been established at the group level and throughout the ACA service structure. No ACA member should be pressured to give money or be made to feel less-than for not being able to contribute. At the same time, ACA members with financial resources are asked to contribute their fair share. We know of ACA members who spent lavishly and courted great debt before finding the program, only to become tight-fisted once finding ACA. They seem unable to contribute with good spirit to the fellowship that has given them new life and, in some cases, better wage-earning potential. We would ask these members to consider the spiritual meaning of giving. This is the giving that helps an ACA group carry the ACA message to its greatest potential. We are not talking about large sums of money, but it does take money to carry the message effectively. This is where spirituality and money mix. It mixes with giving by the individual for the right reason and for the right amount for that person.

Tradition Seven instructs the ACA groups to be fully self-supporting and to decline outside contributions. The Tradition also reminds us of the spiritual principle of giving, and of giving with a willingness to help another. Some members give their time in sponsorship, while others give their talents in the service structure. We all try to support our group and the service structure as best as we can. Tradition Seven teaches us how to give and how to handle money in a spiritual manner.

Tradition Seven also reminds us of our need to pay our own way as a group or fellowship. While it is noble to turn away large gifts from an outside source, we cannot expect others to pay our own way at the group level. Refusing outside contributions means that we pay rent or attempt to pay rent for meeting space. Some churches and hospitals choose to offer such a meeting room free of charge. They view ACA as a positive addition to the community. To honor our Seventh Tradition, the ACA meeting should still make some payment for use of the room. We want to pay our own way to honor the Seventh Tradition and to show support of something we believe in. We want to be fully self-supporting so that ACA remains alive. We want ACA to be free of entanglement and to be available when someone reaches out for help.

Writing / Sharing

1. What does it mean to be "self-supporting"?

2. If you cannot contribute to ACA with money, how else can you contribute?

3. What is a prudent reserve?

4. What is the importance of supporting ACA service boards and committees?

5. What is the spiritual principle in Tradition Seven?

Illustrating Tradition Seven

Make a wall poster or computer graphic depicting this Tradition.

Meditation

Higher Power. I am here to do your will. Help me give for the right reason with the right amount. Help me remember that I have a different life today because of ACA. May I be willing to give back what was freely given to me. May I claim spiritual ownership in this fellowship.

TRADITION EIGHT

Adult Children of Alcoholics should remain forever non-professional, but our service centers may employ special workers.

In my role in the Intergroup structure, I am responsible for organizational information. At the same time I receive many calls from newcomers wanting to know about my ACA experience. In the beginning I tried to give out meeting information and share my recovery as well. I found myself taking care of the callers instead of getting them to meetings. They kept calling me instead of doing the recovery work themselves. I continue to struggle with this, even when I know I need to supply the callers only with meeting information.

People coming to ACA from therapy often assume I am a therapist, counselor, or some program authority figure. They cannot comprehend a program without governance. It is easier to get them into the program and let them experience the way the program works for themselves, rather than attempting to explain the inexplicable.

In the early days of my recovery, I needed some professional help; even others at my meetings were saying I needed help beyond that of the ACA meetings. When I gave in and sought out a counselor, I specified that I needed someone familiar with the ACA program. I got a great counselor with those qualifications who helped me immensely. The counseling helped, but was this in violation of the Eighth Tradition?

I know a special worker who does a great job for ACA and expects nothing in return. We should probably pay him for his work, but we have no funds at this time. This is not a group secretary, treasurer, or other trusted servant job that I am speaking of. It is a manual job that requires daily attention so that the ACA message can be carried.

This person is also a solid group member, who helps others without thought of money or recognition. This person understands ACA, and we are fortunate to have him in the position he is in. He also knows the difference between doing his ACA job and carrying the message for ACA just like the next member.

19

Tradition Eight Insight

ACA actively encourages its members to seek therapeutic help from a paid professional, but ACA sponsorship and Twelfth Step work are free. Always. No one should ever be paid for sponsoring another adult child. No one is paid for carrying the ACA message into treatment centers, prisons, or other facilities that might house adult children. Accepting money for Twelfth Step work or service work does not succeed because the exchange of the ACA gift of hope cannot be sold or purchased. ACA hope must be given and received without strings attached. Money fouls this spiritual transaction. Always.

But what about the ACA member who works for the treatment center, or who becomes an employee of an agency that provides services to adults affected by addiction or family dysfunction? What about the ACA member who becomes a counselor and accepts clients from ACA? Aren't these people making money off of ACA's good name? Aren't they selling sponsorship or something?

Some would answer yes to these questions. Yet, the clear line between professionalism and nonprofessionalism emerges when we look at ACA experience on these issues.

First, there is no professional class in ACA even though some members might hold an advanced degree or have a prominent position in society. Each ACA member is equal to the next and has an equal voice regardless of job status or career track. We are all adult children who relate to one another at the level of empathy instead of the level of employment or lack of employment. Some ACA members struggle with holding a job, but they still have something to offer ACA. They can still contribute.

Many ACA members are professionals with expertise in finance, office systems, or computer networking. They donate their time and expertise to ACA service because they want to give back to the fellowship that brought them sanity. The fellowship benefits from their service work, which is but one part of a greater effort by the entire fellowship. There is no professionalism here. These are professionals doing the good work of ACA alongside fellow ACA members from all levels of social standing, education, and recovery. All ACA members have a talent or passion that can benefit ACA's well being.

Other forms of service work such as group secretary, group representative, Intergroup representative, or WSO trustee are volunteer positions without pay. Members elected to these positions accept them with an attitude of giving service rather than receiving anything of monetary value. These trusted servants often pay their own way to meetings and conferences on behalf of ACA.

Looking at ACA sponsorship and one recovering ACA helping another, one finds no professionalism here as well. The exchange of recovery and support between ACA members working the program together is free. The fellow traveler model of ACA sponsorship allows each person to help the other. The sponsor helps the sponsee, and the sponsee can help the sponsor in working the program. As stated before, money would foul this exchange of love and support for another.

In the past, as we worked out our experience with the ACA Traditions, there were questions about ACA members working for Intergroups and other ACA service boards. Some Intergroups had offices to maintain, telephones to answer, office floors to clean, and literature to ship. In the beginning, ACA tried to use volunteers to handle these endless tasks, but volunteers can only be asked to do so much. Usually these duties would fall to a few volunteers who faithfully did this work for many years without pay. The fellowship benefited from their service work, which was done without thought of recognition or wages. They did their volunteer work for free and for the love of ACA.

A few special workers were hired to run ACA offices and answer telephones. Common sense revealed that they were not professionals benefiting from ACA's name and should be paid comparable wages for their work. Their office work helped ACA carry its message by helping adult children locate meetings or by putting an ACA member in touch with someone needing

19

to talk. These special workers are often ACA members with fellowship knowledge that allows them to bring an insightful touch to ACA work.

The issue of professionalism or someone attempting to earn money off of ACA's name tends to surface in two main areas. In the early days of our fellowship, there were many ACA members wanting to publish books and articles telling their stories for a fee. Some ACA members published books and made money, but most of these folks seem to have moved on since the market is now flooded with every kind of Twelve Step book imaginable. The issue here was more about breaking anonymity rather than making money off of ACA's name.

Those crossing the line of professionalism tend to involve a therapist who conducts group sessions for adult children, calling the session an ACA meeting and charging the clients for the sessions. While the professional may liken the sessions to an ACA meeting, it should not be labeled as an ACA meeting or group. To do so clearly violates ACA's Tradition of remaining nonprofessional, not to mention violating other Traditions.

Through ACA experience, we have learned that ACA and professionalism will not mix. However, ACA members are encouraged to hire a knowledgeable professional for counseling work. This is recovery work done outside the fellowship, but which contributes to a person's recovery.

We know that sponsorship, Twelfth Step work, and special workers do not fall under the category of professionalism. Sponsorship and Twelfth Step work are free, but the special worker should be paid for his or her good work. All aspects of recovery in general are free. Donations to the meeting basket are voluntary.

Tradition Eight addresses a wide range of issues. The heart of the matter is that the demand for ACA meetings and ACA support is far greater than the number of groups and volunteers we have available to meet the demand. But our members meet that call each day, each week, and each month. We do all we can to make ACA available to the greatest number of people.

We give our time and our own money because we believe in helping one another.

Writing / Sharing

1.   Why must the ACA message remain free?

2.   What might happen if we pay individuals to carry the ACA message for us?

3.   What is the spiritual principle in Tradition Eight?

Illustrating Tradition Eight

Make a wall poster or computer graphic depicting this Tradition.

Meditation

Higher Power. Remind me that the direction of our program comes from the ACA members and the groups. Remind me that we must make our own decisions. Guide us when we discuss the need to hire special workers that will help us fulfill ACA's primary purpose. Grant us the wisdom to make the best decisions for our groups, service structure, and our fellowship as a whole.

19

TRADITION NINE

ACA, as such, ought never be organized, but we may create service boards or committees directly responsible to those they serve.

In addition to Tradition Two, a loving God as the ultimate authority, Tradition Nine helped me believe that ACA truly was different than other organizations I had encountered. Before I got to ACA, there was always some person on my job or in the group who seemed to be an organizer. He knew the rules and wielded power over others with authority. For awhile, after arriving in ACA, I kept thinking there has got to be an authority figure around here somewhere. He'll show up and get us organized, so we will know how to conduct ourselves. That has not happened, thanks to Tradition Nine and its warning about being too organized.

It took me awhile to understand what 'ought never be organized' meant. I realized that 'ought never be organized' did not mean that we lack organization and dissolve into chaos. It means that we have service boards and committees, but there is no central governing force in ACA. No one has authority over another person even though we have chairmen who lead meetings and trustees who serve on the WSO board. They are trusted servants who serve the fellowship. They have no power. Neither do I. Tradition Nine helps us find that balance between nongovernance and forming the committees and groups we need to serve ACA.

In my opinion, Tradition Nine is perfect for adult children, who ask for rules and structure, and then decry any rules that might be applied. Tradition Nine says there will be no organization, as such, but there will be service boards and committees with bylaws, motions, and voting rules. Tradition Nine says no one has power over another. But there are trusted servants elected to do the business of ACA. Tradition Nine and Tradition Four (group autonomy) say my group can do what it wants as long as it does not affect ACA as a whole. I know this all sounds contradictory, but it makes sense to me. I have learned to trust ACA and its lack of formal organization.

Tradition Nine keeps me and my ACA group from over-controlling the fellowship with a rule book or a policy manual. It would never work for us anyway. I guess the issue is trust. I need to remember that ACA is different than my family of origin. I don't need to make people honor their words or actions with rigid organization. I need to trust them to keep their word. I need to keep mine as well.

Tradition Nine Insight

How is any organization expected to function without being organized or structured by rules? Who ever heard of a successful company without some organization? Don't we need some form of governing board keeping the meetings in order? Yet, here is our Ninth Tradition reminding us NOT to be organized. How is ACA supposed to function?

ACA is an exception from the normal rules of how to run a business or organization. Other organizations have governing boards which assert their power onto the rest of the organization. The governing boards put out the directives needed to keep everyone else in line. As a Twelve Step organization, ACA does not have any such directives because experience shows they don't work for adult children. Too many rules, or any rules, would ruin ACA and its effectiveness in helping adult children.

When an Intergroup or the WSO is asked for direction on a certain matter, these committees typically answer with "We suggest ..." or "Our experience shows ..." There are no directives. No one can tell ACA groups how to run their meetings. There is no authoritative governance in ACA.

But what about an ACA group facing someone who regularly interrupts the meeting or who makes it unsafe with such behavior? Can't the group organize a committee to keep the meetings safe? Can't the Intergroup be asked to organize a subcommittee dedicated to group safety?

While a committee on group safety might sound like a reasonable idea, the truth is such a committee would lead to unnecessary organization. A safety committee would take away from the power

19

of group members to handle their own affairs. The committee would place group safety in the hands of a few people, when safety is the responsibility of each ACA member.

A committee on group safety would invariably lead to a set of rules that groups could use to expel troublesome ACA members. Bad idea. Our experience shows that we cannot organize committees or create rules to expel anyone unless we want to ignore Traditions Nine or Three. Within ACA we simply don't have that kind of power. The Ninth Tradition reminds us to avoid trying to create such power with rules.

We must remember that disruptive members are not the norm in ACA. Groups only occasionally encounter such individuals who usually change their behavior or move on from ACA. Our groups have demonstrated maturity, compassion, and assertiveness in handling these situations throughout the years.

There are actions the group can take to remain safe without organizing a committee or expelling the errant member. Often, when dealing with a problem person, two or three ACA members with demonstrated recovery will talk to the person after the meeting. In some cases, this can become an opportunity to do a Twelfth Step in the fashion that a sponsor might do it. With such extra effort, disrupters are often enlightened to change their behavior and join the group. If the disruptive behavior continues, then the ACA members can ask the person to take a break from meetings until he or she is willing to work the program. The group can ask the person to seek counseling help as well.

Each situation is somewhat different. Some disruptive members may refuse a request by experienced group members to step aside and talk it out. The person's behavior is a menace to the meeting while the meeting is in progress. This is the person who continually disrupts others' sharing, even after multiple group consciences asking him to stop. It is clear he or she has no intention to abide by the rules or meeting decorum. Such a person could be asked through another group conscience to leave the meeting until he or she has a change of heart regarding disruptive behavior. The person has a choice. In this scenario, the disruptive member decides his or her membership status in ACA, instead of the group banning the person from meetings. If he chooses, he removes himself from the fellowship by his unwillingness to change disruptive behavior.

In a more serious example, the group might be confronted by an individual who continually makes threats against other ACA members. Or a non-member could show up and threaten the group or an individual member. For example at one meeting, an abusive husband arrived at the door for the purpose of accosting his estranged wife. The wife was hiding from him at the time, but he knew about her attendance at ACA meetings. When he refused to leave the meeting voluntarily, the meeting secretary called the police. The man was detained until the wife was able to leave the premises without harm. Such instances are extremely rare. Most ACA meetings will run a lifetime without having to ask anyone to leave.

Many of us arrive at ACA wounded and angry. We hurt, so we want to hurt others. However, no one has the right to harm anyone in ACA. We must avoid our misguided attempt to recreate our dysfunctional family system through the ACA group. Angry or disruptive members are usually acting out their family role, unknowingly reconstructing their dysfunctional family setting. Some of us can relate to this claim. We realized that our disruptive behavior allowed us to blame the group. We could avoid working on ourselves by blaming group members for imagined wrongs and slights. The tolerance we found in ACA allowed many of us to change.

Experience shows that our groups have met these situations without forming special committees. The groups have used common sense and assertiveness to handle each situation.

While we have talked much about the lack of organizational rules in ACA, we must note that our meetings and service committees are not without structure. Our meetings and service

19

committees have procedures to conduct meetings in an orderly fashion. Yet, there is no organizational system of rules that gives anyone power over another.

With service grounded in love, ACA creates service boards and committees directly responsible to those they serve. The committees have bylaws and procedures but, as such, are not organized into a governing body.

Service committees develop ACA literature, organize Hospitals and Institutions meetings, and sustain helplines for adult children seeking help. ACA members accepting the call of service work provide the energy we need to do the good work of ACA around the globe. There could easily be 300 million adult children in the world, so the work ahead remains steady. But we make progress each day.

One of the guiding principles that holds ACA together without rigid organization is the same principle we use when dealing with a problematic group member. The principle is trust. When dealing with a problematic person, we trust our decision as a group to work. We stand ready to wait out the results with group unity.

With trust, we also avoid the tendency to manage or control our trusted servants who are trying to do the best they can on behalf of the fellowship. We trust our trusted servants to do the right thing, whether they serve at the group, Intergroup, or WSO level. We trust them to fulfill the duties they were elected to do. We avoid strapping them with unreasonable rules and regulations. ACA has a defined service structure, but it is not mired in over-built structure or unneeded protocol.

This trust is grounded in our Identity Paper on Service. In ACA, we give service with an attitude of love that helps ourselves and those we serve.[2] When there is service coming from love, governance or weighty organization is unnecessary.

Trust does not mean that we are in denial about what happens around us. It does not mean that we allow our trusted servants to avoid fulfilling their responsibilities. Instead, trust means we realize that ACA is different than our family of origin or outside

[2] 1987 Identity Paper: "The Importance of Service in ACA."

organizations. Our families could not be trusted to keep their word or follow through on promises. ACA members can be trusted to keep their word or at least be given a chance to do so.

Writing / Sharing

1. Who is the ultimate authority in ACA?

2. What is the purpose of a group business meeting? Intergroup? World Service Organization?

3. Why is trust important throughout the ACA service structure?

4. Why should ACA never be too organized?

5. What actions are appropriate in dealing with a disruptive or otherwise unsafe person at an ACA meeting?

6. What is the spiritual principle in Tradition Nine?

Illustrating Tradition Nine

Make a wall poster or computer graphic depicting this Tradition.

Meditation

Higher Power. May I remember that ACA and its meeting and service structure are different than my family of origin. May I be patient and avoid reaching for the easiest way out when I am confronted with a difficult situation. Help me and my ACA group ask for help in keeping our meetings safe and recovery-oriented. Also help us celebrate the things that we do right.

19

TRADITION TEN

Adult Children of Alcoholics has no opinion on outside issues; hence the ACA name ought never be drawn into public controversy.

The image of ACA needs to remain clear. We have one purpose only: to carry the message to ourselves, to the one who still suffers, and to those still to come. *This keeps our 'reason for being' clear to the outsiders who become newcomers. They know exactly why they came to ACA. It was not for money, jobs, places to live, therapy, or religion, but to be whole so they can provide these things for themselves.*

Outside issues are any matters that do not link themselves directly to the principles of the ACA program. *In meetings we share about any issues affecting our recovery. If others share about outside issues of politics, or state opinions not shared by others in the group, they are only expressing personal opinions. People do have squabbles and do quarrel. Tradition Ten is about ACA as a whole having no opinion on outside issues. The individual has his or her own opinion, but that is not ACA's opinion. We must keep this clear when we speak at meetings or are asked to speak elsewhere.*

Some months ago, one of the members at my ACA meeting became upset with the U.S. Government when it went to war with another country. *At the ACA meeting, the person's sharing consisted of how horrible our government officials were in making this choice. He stated how we needed to band together to stop such government action. After his tirade went on several minutes, several group members stood up to leave the meeting.*

Luckily, an ACA oldtimer interrupted the person's tirade and reminded everyone (and mostly the speaker) that ACA had no opinion on outside issues. He then asked for a group conscience, which asked the person speaking to limit his sharing to his own experience, strength, and hope. The speaker elected to be quiet. The group regained its focus on ACA recovery and avoided getting into an outside issue on a debate about war.

19

Tradition Ten Insight

ACA members are a lot alike, but each member is free to believe and to think as he or she wishes. Even though our experiences as adult children are similar, and we work the Twelve Steps to recover, each person is an individual. Each person has ideas and dreams of his or her own. However, stating those ideas as ACA opinion or saying that ACA supports this or that cause goes contrary to Tradition Ten. As a fellowship, we have no opinion on outside issues. We exist for one purpose: To carry the message to those still suffering from the effects of growing up in a dysfunctional family. We avoid public controversy, and some group controversy, by focusing on what we do best.

As we move from isolation into ACA recovery, some of us become more involved in issues that matter to us, including those of political and social natures. We also find ourselves becoming more confident in sharing our opinions with others. However, within the ACA meeting, we also realize that discussions need to remain focused on our individual experiences with ACA recovery. This is a focus of our Tenth Tradition, reminding us to keep personal ideologies apart from the ACA meetings. Our members attend ACA meetings to share their recovery experience and to hear the program experience of others. They rightfully expect to hear discussions on ACA recovery topics.

Have you heard the story about the Washingtonian Society, a group started shortly before the Civil War? It was begun by alcoholics as a program to help them stay sober, much as AA does today. However, as they grew, the Washingtonians found their meetings becoming embroiled in political causes. The abolition of slavery was becoming a hot topic, causing much squabbling in the meetings. Soon various politicians were finding the Washingtonian Society to be a useful tool to further their political causes. After the Civil War, temperance crusaders joined the group to fight against demon alcohol. Then, it became necessary to push for passage of laws banning all liquor.

19

Unfortunately, as the Washingtonians got mired in these issues, their ability to help alcoholics was all but lost. The society eventually stalled and disbanded.

When historians surveyed the wreck of this once promising fellowship, it was easy to see that the Washingtonians lost their focus of helping suffering alcoholics. They tried to be too many things for too many causes. Many of the causes were worthy, but for the Washingtonians to take a position as a group set up the fellowship for internal disagreement and public criticism. Both happened, and both contributed to the Washingtonian demise.

This experience is one of the reasons that ACA, as a whole, avoids discussion on outside issues. ACA groups and our service structure honor Tradition Ten and create a safe and consistent place to discuss ACA recovery. We leave legislation, education, and raising public awareness about family systems, abuse, or neglect to those involved in such endeavors. These are good causes, but they are outside ACA's reach and purpose. Our individual members are free to take on these issues, but as a fellowship we decline. In the discussion of Tradition Eleven, we will further see how ACA interfaces with the general public and how our fellowship avoids public controversy through the principle of anonymity.

Writing / Sharing

1.   Define "outside issues."

2.   Why shouldn't ACA take a position on an issue that would bring about improvements for society in general?

3.   What is the spiritual principle in Tradition Ten?

Illustrating Tradition Ten

Make a wall poster or computer graphic depicting this Tradition.

Meditation

Higher Power. Help me to honor ACA's primary purpose, and focus my sharing in meetings on topics of recovery. Help me remember that ACA is a spiritual program and not a political, religious, or other type of program.

19

TRADITION ELEVEN

Our public relations policy is based on attraction rather than promotion; we maintain personal anonymity at the level of press, radio, TV, films, and other public media.

I can appreciate that we don't advertise ACA or run television spots promoting the program as a miracle cure for the ages; however, we must do our best to get out the word about who we are and what we have to offer. *Adult children are still being misdiagnosed. They are still being overlooked and sent to the wrong places to get help. Some of these adult children will die or go insane without finding us. As much as counseling has improved, it still seems to be overlooking ACA and its decades of experience in holding meetings and changing people's lives. This is not their fault. It is our job to tell people and counselors about ACA within the Traditions.*

ACA is the real deal. We are a program that offers a proven solution. I have been to other places looking for help. I can tell there is nothing like ACA and our literature and our understanding of one another. This is our attractiveness.

I don't break my anonymity at the level of press, radio, television, films, or online. *However, I have broken my anonymity on the job with a co-worker. I did this when I thought the moment called for it. I prayed about it and checked my motives. I asked myself if I wanted to look good to this person by telling her I was in ACA. Or did I want to help her? I wanted to help, so I showed her The Laundry List (Problem) and she cried. She could not believe that someone could write such a list of traits that described her thinking and desperation. She realized she was not alone anymore.*

I always try to keep it simple whether I am carrying the ACA message at my home group or if I am leading a meeting at the treatment center. *I don't have to sell ACA to anyone with a pitch or a dance. I simply tell people what it was like, what happened and how ACA has helped me find a better way of life. I always get*

19

questions from people interested in the program. I ask them to attend meetings. That's the goal. Get them to a meeting, and let the group carry the message as well.

To build identity, I will share about the common behaviors, and I will talk about my powerlessness and unmanageability in Step One. Upon occasion I might briefly touch on the Higher Power in Step Two, but rarely do I talk at length about God in Step Three. That's later. That's for the meetings.

This is attraction rather than promotion for me. I am telling my story and giving out information about the meetings and the Steps. I don't try to sell ACA. That would be promotion.

I recall an ACA meeting I attended years ago. It was at a public beach; we all sat around a large fire pit as we shared our experience, strength, and hope. *One evening, a reporter saw us and asked to film our meeting. I suspect he saw it as a great opportunity for that " feel good" news segment with which to close the evening newscast. Many in the circle were excited about the possibility of being on television. However, after some rather animated discussion within the group, we realized it would have violated the Eleventh Tradition and the need for personal anonymity. We thus turned down the offer. Some weren't happy with the decision (especially the reporter), but it was the correct decision, nonetheless.*

Tradition Eleven Insight

Many baffled or dejected people who find ACA are amazed at our program and what it has to offer. Even adult children with years of recovery in other Twelve Step programs find our program and new meaning in their lives. They are astonished at the level of identification and understanding found in ACA and not found elsewhere. Newer ACA members have said: "I had no idea that something like this existed. I can identify with so much. I never knew something like this could be available."

For every person who finds ACA through a flyer, a counselor, or other source, there are perhaps 1,000 who could use it but never make it to our doors. There are many reasons. Some are not ready to seek recovery, while others do not believe they have a problem and ignore suggestions to get help. Others are referred elsewhere where they may or may not find the help they need. Thousands visit the ACA websites, nibble at the fellowship literature, but move on for reasons of their own. ACA is not for everyone.

Finally, there are heartbreaking cases of adult children who are ready for ACA, but who cannot find us, or are without an ACA meeting in their area. This is no one's fault. As a fellowship, we are doing the best that we can to reach the most people. In addition to holding meetings and events, ACA members post informational flyers, list their group in the newspaper and hold meetings in facilities where adult children are being treated. But the need for ACA is sometimes greater than our resources. We are making progress. We claim progress and not perfection.

As we carry our message to the public, we must remember that ACA is a viable and proven program that lines up nicely with decades of clinical and medical research on the disease of family dysfunction. No other fellowship addresses the body, mind, and spirit in the manner of ACA understanding. We don't brag about our fellowship. Yet, we are a program that works for some of the most complex human conditions of the 21st century. We have a proven solution that brings sure relief and real change. ACA is a way of life that fulfills a person emotionally and spiritually. As a fellowship, too, we can ask for what we need and get it. We can give respect and receive respect from helping professionals who would consider referring our program.

When carrying the message to the public, we avoid using grand pronouncements or gimmicks. It would be tempting to find an important personality to promote ACA or to appear on national television, touting the ACA solution. But is this really okay? It might be great publicity for the individual, but what would it mean for ACA and the principle of anonymity in Tradition Eleven? We have to adhere to personal anonymity at the level of press, radio, and other media to avoid entangling the ACA message with individual personalities. At the same time, we must meet the need to inform the public about our program.

In ACA, we have learned that the spiritual principle of anonymity means much more than merely identifying by our first name only at meetings. Anonymity means that we are willing to surrender our notions of personal ambition. Whether we would admit it or not, appearing in the media using our full name sets us apart from other ACA members. By doing so, we begin to feel different and the feeling of isolation creeps in. We also get the feeling that we are required to perform or say the right thing, which is a version of our people-pleasing trait. We can set ourselves up for an ACA relapse by placing ourselves in the public eye.

Some ACA members disagree with the anonymity of Tradition Eleven, claiming that it is a method to hide family secrets. This is a faulty assumption. Maintaining our anonymity at the level of press, radio, film, television, and other media cannot be compared to keeping family secrets. ACA members are free to reveal their stories at meetings and among anyone else they feel comfortable sharing with. We urge prudence here of course.

Technically, we could also use our first and last names at meetings and events, because ACA meetings do not rise to the level of press, radio, film, or other media. We typically use only our first names to show the newcomer that his or her identity is safe in the meetings. We offer this anonymity to our members. We also avoid breaking the anonymity of a fellow ACA member by telling his or her story to another person. We may have good intentions for telling the details of someone else's story to others, but we try to avoid this. As the saying goes: "What is said at ACA meetings stays at ACA meetings."

19

So what is the middle ground on carrying the ACA message? How do we get out the good word to the public about ACA? Borrowing from previous experience, ACA has discovered that attraction, rather than promotion or personal publicity, is the sure course. We have already mentioned personal publicity, so here is one definition of promotion: Promotion is soliciting support even where the person has no direct involvement. For example: "Vote for my candidate" or "Send money to my charity." These are promotional acts. Another way organizations promote themselves is through enticing others with various promises to use the organization's services or products. They say: "Join my weight reduction program and quickly lose those 60 pounds."

Attraction is different. Attraction is making information available about ACA without strings. There are no pitches and no grand promises. This means that ACA members let others know about the program without promoting ACA or breaking personal anonymity.

Sharing how ACA has helped us as individuals can result in the attraction of new members. This is where telling our story in Step Twelve converges with attracting others to the program in Tradition Eleven. We may share our story at a Hospitals and Institutions meeting or on a panel at a professional workshop. We may also work Step Twelve while volunteering for an ACA helpline or placing informational flyers about town.

Flyer campaigns and Hospitals and Institutions meetings are usually coordinated by an ACA group or Intergroup. Upon occasion, Intergroups and groups also supply information about ACA to hospitals, therapists, social workers, and clergy. In areas without active Intergroups, the group can place a meeting notice in the local newspaper that lists Twelve Step meetings. In the same manner, the WSO has an outreach function to reach hospitals and therapists around the world. The WSO also maintains two web sites, www.adultchildren.org and www.acawso.org, with forums and ACA related information available to the world at large. This is informational, and thus not promotion.

When we carry the ACA message to those who still suffer, we keep it simple. We share our personal experience about growing up in a dysfunctional home. We share honestly and openly about how we were raised and how we found the ACA program. We may share about The Laundry List (Problem) traits and the Twelve Steps as well, depending on the setting. We don't shy away from our growing-up experiences, but we balance that sharing with recovery experiences as well.

Our best public relations policy is twofold. We survive and grow as a fellowship by carrying the message to others in a manner that creates attraction rather than promotion. We also flourish through the good word of others who know about our program and recommend us.

Writing / Sharing

1. Explain the differences between attraction and promotion.

2. Why do we choose attraction as our public relations policy rather than promotion?

3. Why is it important to maintain your anonymity with the media?

4. What has happened or what might happen when someone breaks his anonymity with the media?

5. How would you explain anonymity to a newcomer or sponsee?

6. What is the spiritual principle in Tradition Eleven?

19

Illustrating Tradition Eleven

Make a wall poster or computer graphic depicting this Tradition.

Meditation

Higher Power. I ask you to guide me in maintaining my anonymity at the level of all media because no one speaks for ACA or gives the appearance of speaking for ACA. We attract others to ACA by our good works and the good word of others. Help me discern when I might break my anonymity for a suffering adult child looking for a way out of confusion. This person might be a co-worker or a family member. Help me know when to share some of my story, or when to remain quiet and maintain my anonymity. May I avoid speaking out of turn, or using my ego to share with people who may not be interested in ACA. At the same time, give me courage to share this program when the moment is right.

TRADITION TWELVE

Anonymity is the spiritual foundation of all our Traditions, ever reminding us to place principles before personalities.

We don't use anonymity to hide our worst secrets. That is not the purpose of ACA anonymity. In ACA, I learned to share my story openly in meetings and with a sponsor. We use only our first names at meetings and retreats, so that we protect our anonymity within the community. This does not mean that I am ashamed of my program. I break my anonymity when I think it is appropriate, but not at the level of the media. I have shared with people who express an interest in what I am doing to change my life.

Anonymity means so many marvelous and spiritual things. It is so much more than merely using my first name only at meetings.

Anonymity reminds me to place ACA principles before personalities. To me, some of the principles are surrender, hope, acceptance, courage, forgiveness, and humility from the Steps and unity, compassion, autonomy, and inclusiveness from the Traditions. These principles are underlined by anonymity. My relationship with others in meetings, and even in the work place, go smoother when I keep my personality focused but compassionate through Tradition Twelve principles. I am able to let these principles rise above my wants and personal motives.

I consciously review these principles during the business meeting or a group conscience discussion. They are a measuring stick that help me gauge what I will say. I often ask myself a question before I speak, especially if my Inner Child is getting restless and wants to blurt out something. I ask: 'Will what I say promote unity and clarity, or am I using my personality to control or manipulate others? Do I want to do the most good for the most people, or do I want to help only a few or just myself?'

When I can ask myself these questions, I feel better about what I am doing. I can listen to others without discounting what they say, but I can also state my own opinion.

19

The Twelfth Tradition is so cool. I never thought it was possible for people to talk about topics and disagree without someone being shamed or hit. Whether adult children know it or not, they are practicing anonymity each time they hold ACA meetings or discuss ACA business. Each time we make an effort to respect one another, or each time we make an effort to place ACA first, we are sending our attacking, shaming, and Critical Parent into anonymity. In my view, my Critical Inner Parent has broken his anonymity long enough. He goes into an anonymity time-out. My Loving Parent gets to be less anonymous from now on.

I was anonymous in my family of origin, but it was an anonymity that actually meant I did not count. I was invisible without an identity. This was unspiritual anonymity. The anonymity that we speak of in ACA is spiritual, and it allows me to find, build, and state my anonymity with humility. Through anonymity and recovery, I can actually find out who I am and then not have to be held up as special. It's a paradox. I found out that I am someone in ACA, but I am not more important than the next person. This is anonymity to me.

Tradition Twelve Insight

Anonymity underlined by humility is the bedrock of ACA principles. Anonymity is a spiritual principle that anchors not only the Twelve Traditions, but also the Twelve Steps. Each of the Twelve Steps has an inherent element of anonymity, which diminishes our egos and places God in the center of our lives.

Anonymity is the spiritual thread that links each of the Twelve Traditions together.

We practice anonymity in Tradition One when we place unity and the survival of the group ahead of our own selfish desires and wants. In Tradition Two, we practice anonymity by asking a loving God to enter our group conscience decisions. The Higher Power anonymously shows us the path to take on a given ACA action. In Tradition Three, anonymity is in our desire for personal change. We are asking the false self to step

19

aside into anonymity and to allow the True Self to emerge. We desire to replace our codependence by reparenting ourselves with respect and gentleness.

There is also anonymity in group autonomy in Tradition Four. Each ACA group is anonymous to its community, yet the group provides a haven for suffering adult children. The group seeks no recognition and anonymously helps anyone with a desire to get better. In Tradition Five, we focus on our primary purpose. We carry the ACA message with anonymity and a sincere desire to help others. We practice anonymity in carrying the message, by making the message the focus, rather than making our personality the focus.

In Tradition Six, we practice anonymity by declining to link the ACA name to any related facility or outside enterprise. ACA meetings remain anonymous by not placing the ACA name on signs or clubhouse marquees.

In Tradition Seven, we are self-supporting, which means we don't rush about trying to use our personalities or the ACA name to drum up outside money. We pay our own way in anonymity. We do this by dropping money into the ACA meeting basket without thought of being recognized.

In Traditions Eight and Nine, anonymity ensures that our Twelfth Step work and service work are nonprofessional and always free. ACA members who serve on service boards and committees do so for free and without thought of recognition.

Anonymity speaks again in Tradition Ten when we are reminded that ACA has no opinion on outside issues. While the individual has opinions and thoughts on outside issues, the fellowship, as a whole, remains silent. We remain anonymous as a fellowship. We ask our membership to not entangle ACA in political or social issues.

Traditions Eleven and Twelve directly address anonymity and its spiritual application and meaning. No one speaks for ACA at the level of press, radio, film, television, or other public media. We maintain our personal anonymity. We also choose the path of anonymity when we place ACA principles before personalities.

19

When woven together by anonymity, the spiritual principles of the Traditions create a vibrant tapestry of ACA wisdom that cannot be easily torn. In this spiritual fabric, we see that anonymity is the spiritual foundation of all our Traditions.

But what is anonymity more specifically? For some ACA members, anonymity is merely stating their first name at ACA meetings to protect their identity. Many ACA members fear repercussions from family members. They fear that family members might find out the person is attending ACA and identifying the parents as dysfunctional. Dysfunctional parents still in denial can act poorly if they find out that a grown child has identified with ACA. Anonymity serves these ACA members well.

There is also an historical meaning of anonymity that fits ACA in a way that is specific to our Twelve Step fellowship and no other. The meaning applies to the Alateens, who founded the first ACA-like meetings. Some of the Alateens had stepped up to Al-Anon and were attending meetings with a dysfunctional parent. Some of these Alateens believed they could not share fully in front of their parents about what was going on in the home. Others felt uncomfortable sharing in front of adults focused primarily on adult issues. These young people needed a meeting where they could have anonymity. They wanted to share on pertinent topics that did not revolve around spousal drinking, which was the focus of Al-Anon. In response, they started two meetings – Hope For Adult Children of Alcoholics and Generations. They created anonymity so they could truly break the "don't talk" rule of a dysfunctional home.

Anonymity also means that we do not talk about someone else's story or sharing that occurs during our ACA meetings or events. What is said at meetings stays at meetings. If we do not have permission, we avoid sharing another's story even under good intentions. At the same time, gossip or the sharing of another's story under poor motives has no place in ACA. We protect personal anonymity at all costs to keep our meetings safe. By keeping ACA safe, we strengthen our group unity, and we attract new members who are an important life source for the fellowship.

ACA anonymity means that we know who we are. We do not need recognition or accolades for the service we give to ACA. We don't need recognition or distinction but we do not avoid it either. If someone wants to praise us or honor us, we allow it. We celebrate it. We have earned it. However, we are just as comfortable and focused on service to others without the need to be honored or set apart. Through anonymity, we understand that we have a great gift. We know that we can help other adult children when few others can.

With the promise of ACA anonymity, we begin to feel more comfortable with telling our story in meetings. We also discern how much to tell people who are not in recovery. Some ACA members, feeling excited at having found ACA and its gifts, have made the mistake of telling too much of their experiences to family members or friends. They feel hurt or betrayed when the person gossips about them or minimizes their recovery work. By listening to others or our sponsor, we learn when it is appropriate to "break" our anonymity with family or friends. We are not compelled to tell anyone of our involvement in ACA. However, we learn what to tell and not tell, if the moment arises for us to open up about our lives.

There is a second part of Tradition Twelve, which gives us specific direction in practicing the spiritual foundation that anonymity brings. The Tradition reminds us to place principles before personalities.

ACA is program of people, and therefore a program of diverse personalities. Our membership is made up of people in varying degrees of codependence, addiction, and PTSD recovery. Some of our members are new and still hurting from growing up in a dysfunctional home. Others have worked through some of the effects of being raised in a dysfunctional setting. There will be conflicts, hurt feelings, and differences of opinion in ACA. There will be people storming out of business meetings, thinking they have been poorly treated in the meeting. Some have been

19

mistreated, and some have not. There will be trusted servants believing they have been shunned and unappreciated by the group. There will be game players, not yet committed to ACA recovery, who manipulate others and unwittingly disrupt another's recovery through selfishness. There will be romantic relationships that sour and occasionally spill into meetings. Some group members may unwisely take sides.

However, anonymity is there ever reminding us to place principles before personalities. And it works. Each one of the scenarios mentioned above has been met with Tradition Twelve anonymity. Held up against anonymity, our perceived wrongs, gossip, and pettiness hold no light. When we place principles before personalities, we change as people, and we honor ACA. Anonymity ensures that everyone gets collective credit for ACA's success.

Writing / Sharing

1.   How does placing principles before personalities in Tradition Twelve relate to promoting unity in Tradition One?

2.   Identify and list the spiritual principles of each Tradition.

Illustrating Tradition Twelve

Make a wall poster or computer graphic depicting this Tradition.

Meditation

Higher Power. Help me see the connecting thread that anonymity brings to the ACA program. Give me the willingness that I need to practice ACA principles instead of a false self personality.

SECTION III

Handbook For Adult Children

$\mathcal{T}$he Handbook Section of the ACA basic text offers detailed information on starting an ACA group, Intergroup, and Regional Service Committee, in addition to other information about maintaining groups or meetings. If you are reading this book in an area where no ACA meeting exists, we encourage you to contact our World Service Organization at our Website addresses at www.adultchildren.org and www.acawso.org.

By contacting the WSO, you will connect with other recovering adult children from around the world. ACA is a worldwide fellowship founded in 1978 in the United States. ACA is now available in numerous countries. This book represents the experience, strength, and hope of the ACA fellowship. You are not alone. We do recover from the effects of growing up in a dysfunctional family.

This section begins with details on how to start an ACA meeting or group. The section contains a meeting format, Twelve Steps, Twelve Traditions, The Laundry List, The Solution, a description of meeting types, and how to conduct a business meeting. The Laundry List is a list of 14 traits of an adult child of an alcoholic. The list has been adapted and is read as The Problem at the beginning of most ACA meetings.

In addition to helping you start a new meeting, this information should help you understand how to address group challenges and how to maintain the group. There is also a segment on sharing or talking in meetings. After finding a suitable location for the new meeting, register the meeting with ACA World Services as soon as possible. Contact your local newspaper, and list the new ACA group among other Twelve Step groups. You can obtain information about registering the meeting through the ACA websites.

ACA is an independent Twelve Step program founded on the principles of the Steps and the Twelve Traditions. Additionally, ACA focuses on nurturing the Loving Parent within and seeking a Higher Power. In ACA, we believe connecting with our feelings and Inner Child are just as important as working the Twelve Steps and sponsorship. We confront our inner Critical Parent and allow our Loving Parent to emerge. With our Loving Parent guiding us, we remove ourselves from codependent relationships and stop harming ourselves. We seek help for our addictions if we are acting out with drugs, sex, food, spending, gambling, or another compulsive behavior. We learn that we can recover from trauma and neglect.

Welcome to ACA and the journey.

HOW TO START AN ACA MEETING

Starting an ACA Meeting Involves Six Basic Steps:

1. **Locate a suitable meeting site:** A group needs a safe place to meet. For many this is a location free of unnecessary noise, distracting surroundings, or physical dangers. Check with local Alano clubs, churches, schools, or civic organizations that have meeting spaces. Members of other Twelve Step groups may also know of possible meeting locations. Some meetings have successfully started in the home of one group member, but usually found the need to move into a neutral space within a few months.

2. **Obtain meeting materials:** This section of the ACA text contains many of the readings you will need to start your new meeting. You can order a New Meeting Packet from our website at www.adultchildren.org. Free ACA literature is also available for download from our website.

3. **Register the meeting with the WSO:** Complete and mail a Meeting Registration Form to the World Service Office at P.O. Box 3216, Torrance, California, USA, 90510. You can also register your meeting on our website at www.adultchildren.org. Registering your new meeting will ensure the information is posted on our website. You can find a Meeting Registration Form on the website or by writing to the WSO.

4. **Inform potential ACA members about the meeting:** Get the word out about your new meeting. Tell your friends. Go to a few Twelve Step meetings like AA, NA, or CA and talk with others before and after the meetings. Avoid announcing your new meeting during the AA, NA, or CA meeting because this would violate the group's Traditions. You can also make a flyer announcing your new meeting and

HB

leave copies at other Twelve Step meetings. You can post your flyer at some referral centers or business offices that help people seeking recovery, but ask first. Contact your local newspaper and have your meeting listed among other Twelve Step meetings. This should be a simple announcement about the time, place, and focus of the meetings. Promotion is not necessary.

5. **Start your ACA meeting:** Begin the new meeting with a focus on ACA recovery and ACA literature. Most new groups do best by having a discussion format that focuses on the ACA Twelve Steps, ACA booklets, trifolds, or chapters from this book.

6. **First group business meeting:** Hold your first group business meeting as soon as possible to elect a secretary and to determine the meeting format. For help, see the information on business meetings and group officers in this section.

Don't Give Up

Starting a new meeting requires determination and work, but the reward of watching others find the ACA way of life is worth it. In addition to offering hope, ACA restores the person. By helping others, we help ourselves.

Most ACA meetings take about a year to become established. Don't give up. Stick with it. Keep passing out flyers, and keep talking about ACA and how it focuses on one's self and the family system through the Twelve Steps. One group member we know recalled being the only person at a new meeting for six months. He opened the ACA meeting and read the format, The Steps, The Problem, The Solution, and other literature. One night a second person showed up and then another. The group continued to grow. Other new meetings start off with a group of enthusiastic people. These meetings attract others

HB

through Step studies, a speaker's meeting or Twelve Traditions meetings. Good luck on starting a new ACA group in your area. Keep coming back. It works.

Meetings

ACA meetings are 60 minutes to 90 minutes in duration. There are some two-hour meetings with a break at one hour. The ACA meeting might focus on reading and discussing ACA literature or a recovery-related topic. Members are asked to avoid intellectualizing the topics. We talk about our feelings and our life experiences and how the literature, Step work, or other ACA recovery works in our lives. We share about personal change, working the Steps, and connecting with our Inner Child and Higher Power. We talk openly about our lives and our hope.

ACA meetings are fully self-supporting and do not affiliate with any outside entity. ACA is an autonomous Twelve Step fellowship. ACA meetings are not Al-Anon ACoA meetings.

A chairperson or group secretary usually arrives at the ACA meeting early and sets up the meeting. Chairs are arranged and refreshments may be made available. The chairperson hands out the opening reading materials as others arrive. Reading is voluntary, so no one is pressured to read or speak at the meeting. However, we watch for newer members showing up and ask them to help out with the reading to get them involved in the group. The items that are generally read at the opening of the meeting are: The Laundry List (Problem), The Solution, the Twelve Steps, the Twelve Traditions, and the ACA Promises. These five pieces of foundational literature are presented in this section.

HB

Sample Meeting Format

Hello, my name is _____. I am an adult child. Welcome to the _____ Meeting of Adult Children of Alcoholics. We meet to share the experiences we had as children growing up in an alcoholic or dysfunctional home. That experience infected us then, and it affects us today. By practicing the Twelve Steps and by attending meetings regularly, we find freedom from the effects of alcoholism or other family dysfunction. As ACA members, we identify with The Laundry List traits. We learn to live in The Solution of reparenting ourselves, one day at a time.

Will you please join me in a moment of silence followed by the Serenity Prayer to open the meeting?

(silence) God, grant me the serenity to accept the things I cannot change, the courage to change the things I can, and the wisdom to know the difference.

We will now read the group's readings.

- I've asked _____ to read The Problem (or The Laundry List).
- I've asked _____ to read The Solution.
- I've asked _____ to read the Twelve Steps.
- I've asked _____ to read the Twelve Traditions (Some groups read Traditions at the end of the meeting).

You may have related to our readings even if there was no apparent alcoholism or addiction in your home. This is common because dysfunction can occur in a family without the presence of addiction. We welcome you.

If you are attending an ACA meeting for the first time, will you please introduce yourself by your first name? This is not to embarrass you, but so we can get to know you better. (The chairperson can lead the applause after the person has stated his or her name.) We are glad you are here. Keep coming back.

May we go around the room and introduce ourselves by our first names?

The ACA program is not easy, but if you can handle what comes up at six consecutive meetings you will start to come out of denial. Confronting your denial about family addiction or dysfunction will give you freedom from the past. Your life will change. You will make friends and truly learn how to live with greater choice and personal freedom. You will learn to focus on yourself and let others be responsible for their own lives.

If you would like to be a member of this group, please talk to the chairperson or secretary after the meeting. There is only one requirement for ACA membership: the desire to recover from the effects of family dysfunction.

The group has a phone list that I will pass around for updates or additions. This is a voluntary phone list for the group. Add your name to the list and make any corrections as needed. Copies of the phone list are available at the literature table.

I am also passing around a calendar. If you would like to serve as a chairperson for the meeting, place your name on the date that you would like to chair the meeting. We ask that you be active in the program to chair meetings.

(If this is a two-hour meeting, announce when the break will occur and describe what each hour of the meeting will involve, i.e., literature discussion, topic discussion, speaker meeting, or other.)

In the beginning, many of us could not recognize or accept that some of our attitudes or behaviors result from being raised in an alcoholic or other dysfunctional family. We behave as adult children, which means we bring self-doubt and fear learned in childhood to our adult interactions. By attending six meetings in a row and attending regularly thereafter, we come to know and begin to act as our True Selves.

We encourage each member to share openly about his or her experiences as time allows. This is a safe place to share your adult and childhood experiences without being judged. To allow everyone a chance to share during the meeting, we ask each person to limit their sharing to five minutes.

HB

What you hear at this meeting should remain at the meeting. We do not talk about another person's story or experiences to other people. Please respect the anonymity of those who have shared here tonight.

Before we begin the meeting, I would like to mention that we do not "cross talk" in the meeting. Cross talk means interrupting, referring to, or commenting on what another person has said during the meeting.

We do not cross talk because adult children come from family backgrounds where feelings and perceptions were judged as wrong or defective. In ACA, each person may share feelings and perceptions without fear of judgment. We accept without comment what others say because it is true for them. We work toward taking more responsibility in our lives rather than giving advice to others.

Fixing Others: Learning to Listen

In ACA, we do not touch, hug, or attempt to comfort others when they become emotional during an ACA meeting. If someone begins to cry during a meeting, we allow the person to feel his or her feelings without interruption.

To touch or hug the person is known as "fixing." As children we tried to fix our parents or to control them with our behavior. In ACA, we are learning to take care of ourselves. We support others by accepting them into our meetings and listening to them. We allow them to feel their feelings in peace.

ACA is Not Therapy

While many ACA members make fine use of therapists and counselors, our meetings are not therapy sessions. We don't discuss therapeutic techniques. While we might share about our counseling work, the focus of an ACA meeting is the Twelve Steps and Twelve Traditions. Therapy is not a replacement for ACA meetings or working a program.

Tonight's meeting is a _____ (Step study, Tradition study, speaker meeting, discussion meeting, literature study, or other).

Who would like to begin tonight's reading or sharing?

(Individuals share or talk on the topic or reading for the duration of the meeting.)

Meeting Closing

(Begin passing the basket.) It is time for our Seventh Tradition, which states that "Every ACA group ought to be fully self-supporting, declining outside contributions." Newcomers are encouraged to buy literature and need not contribute at their first meeting. Now it's time for the secretary's announcements.

That's all the time we have. Thank you for joining us and keep coming back. If you were not called on to share tonight, please speak to someone after the meeting if you need to talk.

It is time to read the Twelve Promises of ACA.

(After reading The Promises, ask group members to stand and form a circle by holding hands. Ask a group member to lead the closing prayer of his or her choice.)

Keep coming back. It works!

HB

Meeting Types

Closed Meeting/Open Meeting: Many ACA groups hold closed meetings, which means the meeting is reserved for those identifying as an adult child. Guests are asked to attend an open meeting, which is open to friends and relatives of the adult child. For some ACA members, closed meetings offer a sense of safety and stronger identification among those sharing or speaking at the meeting.

Step Study: ACA groups that thrive and grow typically focus on reading and studying the ACA Twelve Steps. The ACA basic text you are reading offers an extended study of the Twelve Steps in Chapter Seven. Additionally, ACA offers a Twelve Step Workbook, which further details how to work the Twelve Steps. Chapter Seven or the Workbook can be read and discussed in ACA meetings. Typically, an ACA group will begin with Step One and read a portion of the Step at each meeting. By this method, the Steps are read and studied during many weeks.

ACA Twelve Traditions Study: Our experience shows that ACA groups are strengthened when their members read and discuss the Twelve Traditions. ACA groups usually study one Tradition a month with the number of the Tradition corresponding to the number of a given month. For example, Tradition One would be read and discussed during one meeting in January. Tradition Two would be discussed in February and so on. The Twelve Traditions can be found in Chapter Nineteen.

Newcomer/Beginner Introductory Meeting: Many newcomers have expressed confusion over what they should be doing in the ACA program. Many have suggested that the group offer an introductory meeting to newcomers. While we don't want to separate newer members from the main meeting, some ACA groups ask newcomers if they would like an introductory meeting in another room. If so, the new person will accompany two group members to another room to learn about the basics of the ACA program.

HB

ACA members explaining the program to a newcomer should use a copy of The Laundry List (Problem) and the ACA First Step. It is not necessary to cover all Twelve Steps during an introductory meeting, but emphasize working the Steps with a sponsor. Most newcomers need to know about the disease of family dysfunction and the effects of growing up in a dysfunctional home. The Six Suggestions of Recovery are also a topic of discussion.

Writing Meeting: Each member of the meeting writes for twenty minutes on a given topic or one of the Twelve Steps. What was written is then read aloud and shared with the group.

Small Groups: After opening the meeting together as a large group, the meeting is divided into smaller discussion groups to allow everyone the chance to share. The smaller groups may rejoin one another at a specific time to close the meeting together; or each small group may end its meeting when the meeting time ends.

Speaker Meeting: The chairperson shares for 10 minutes on a recovery topic. Then one or two ACA speakers share for a total of 20 minutes. This is followed by open sharing among the group members.

Birthday Meeting: Usually occurs once a month. In addition to handing out monthly recovery chips, ACA groups give away yearly medallions that represent a person's length of time attending ACA meetings. The group usually has a speaker who shares his or her story during the meeting. The medallions are handed out at the end of the meeting. Some groups serve a birthday cake or refreshments at this monthly meeting.

Panel Discussion: Three or more speakers form a panel, and each shares for 10 to 15 minutes for the first half of the meeting. The remainder of the meeting is allocated to open sharing or question and answers.

HB

Sample Reading – Step Study Meetings

Note: If a Step study is the format of the meeting, the chairperson should read this section when announcing to the group the type of meeting that is occurring. This section can be read after the group has finished opening readings and is ready to begin the meeting sharing. The chairperson then reads:

The focus of this meeting is recovery, through the study, application, and practice of the Twelve Steps of ACA.

As children, we developed behaviors to survive our dysfunctional family. We carried these behaviors, attitudes, and feelings with us into adulthood. They are the source of our pain, unhappiness, and isolation.

If we wish to change our lives, we must learn a new way of life. The Twelve Steps are the tools that teach us how to live with a greater awareness. Through a process of awareness, acceptance, and action, we will begin to recover from the effects of family dysfunction.

In Steps One through Three, we will become aware that we are powerless over the effects of the disease of family dysfunction — that our lives are unmanageable. We will come to an acceptance of the fact that only a Power greater than ourselves can restore us to sanity. We make a decision to turn our will and our lives over to the care and guidance of a God of our understanding. We see this God as a loving parent who cares for us.

In Steps Four and Five we will continue the process of self-discovery and self-awareness by making a written inventory of attitudes and behaviors. We also see the generational nature of this behavior and how it was transmitted to us by our dysfunctional parents or relatives. With ACA, we learn to forgive ourselves and our parents. We change our behavior. In Step Five we tell our story with clarity and humility to our sponsor. We will learn to trust ourselves and break down the walls of isolation we have hidden behind.

HB

In Steps Six and Seven we will become willing to have God remove our defects of character. We also learn to integrate our Laundry List survival traits. We transform them into spiritual assets when possible.

In Steps Eight and Nine we will become willing to make amends for our inappropriate behaviors. We take responsibility for our actions and feelings. We also learn to be gentle with ourselves and to protect our Inner Child during this process. We balance taking responsibility for our inappropriate behavior with being aware that we also are protecting a wounded child within. We do not balk at making difficult amends, but we lovingly reparent ourselves during this process as well.

In Steps Ten through Twelve, having now begun the process of recovery, we will learn how to make the Steps a part of our daily lives. We will continue to take personal inventory, learning more about ourselves as we grow. We will seek to improve our contact with our Higher Power through prayer and meditation. We seek to learn God's will for us, and we ask for the power to carry that out. Finally, in Step Twelve, having experienced a spiritual awakening, we learn to practice these principles in all our affairs and to carry the message to those who still suffer. If we wish to keep what we have gained, we must learn to give it away, wherever and whenever we can. We must get out of ourselves. We insist on enjoying life and being a part of life. Each week we will focus on one of the Twelve Steps. By discussing the Steps, we develop an awareness of how to practice the Steps in our daily lives. Tonight's Step is _____.

Welcoming Newcomers

Note: Some groups have incorporated a newcomer introductory element into their meeting formats. Adding a newcomer introduction to your meeting format will lengthen the amount of time it takes to read the format at the beginning of the meeting. We are not suggesting that you incorporate all of this information into the format. We offer this information as a general guide on how to orient newcomers into ACA.

HB

Many newcomers have expressed confusion over what they should be doing in the ACA program. While ACA groups do a good job of welcoming new members, handing out literature and telephone numbers, we are being asked by the newcomers to give more direction. Many have suggested that the group offer an introductory meeting to newcomers. We believe this can be done without separating new members from the regular meeting for long periods of time. We try to avoid a meeting that is made up of new members only. However, an introductory meeting or two can work as long as it is understood that the new person needs to be in regular meetings as soon as possible.

At the beginning of the meeting, some ACA groups ask if anyone is attending his or her first meeting. The chairperson then asks if the person would like an introductory meeting in which one or two group members explain some of the elements of ACA: identifying with The Laundry List (Problem), getting a sponsor, and working the Twelve Steps. The meeting chairperson would say:

"Is there anyone here for his or her first meeting? Would you like to have an introductory meeting to learn more about ACA? You are welcome to remain in this meeting and talk to someone about ACA after the meeting. Or you can go with a couple of ACA members to another room to talk about the ACA program. We are glad you are here."

ACA members explaining the program to a newcomer should use a copy of The Laundry List (Problem) and the ACA First Step. We keep it simple, remembering how we felt at our first meeting. It is not necessary to cover all the Twelve Steps during an introductory meeting, but emphasize working the Steps with a sponsor. Most newcomers need to know about the disease of family dysfunction and the effects of growing up in a dysfunctional home. This is covered in The Laundry List (Problem). They also need to know about Step One, which address the effects of growing up in a dysfunctional family and which ties into The Laundry List (Problem). These two elements – Laundry List and Step One – are usually sufficient to orient the person to the program. If the person would like an additional introductory meeting, please accommodate the person. We can also mention the six suggestions.

The Six Suggestions for Ongoing Recovery

While ACA members avoid giving advice, we can share our recovery experience. These six suggestions of ACA recovery represent the basics whether we are a newcomer or a member with years in the program. These suggestions work in the first year of recovery or the 20th year. We find them helpful in getting the newcomer to focus on himself or herself.

1. Stop acting out with food, sex, relationships, gambling, spending, or alcohol/drugs.
2. Go to meetings regularly and break the "don't talk" rule.
3. Get a sponsor and work the ACA Twelve Steps.
4. Get the ACA "big book." Give yourself a break and read it.
5. Get telephone numbers. Don't isolate.
6. Get a Higher Power.

Newcomers and "13th Stepping"

Newcomers can be particularly vulnerable to emotional, financial, and sexual abuses. Some people attending ACA meetings have not grown beyond their victim or victimizer scripts and may attempt to meet their own needs through manipulation of newcomers. This is known as the "13th Step" in most Twelve Step programs. This violates the safety of the meeting and can drive away some newcomers. The love and respect we offer to newcomers is a reflection of the love and respect we are learning to offer ourselves.

We learn to respect ourselves and to honor ACA when we avoid acting out with someone new. If we are struggling with this area of our lives, we are usually not applying the program,

HB

or we are not willing to face our internal pain. Perpetrator or manipulative behavior is almost always driven by our avoidance of facing past harm and neglect. If this is the case, we ask a Higher Power for the willingness to change. We ask a sponsor to help us work the program.

Sharing in Meetings

Here, we offer some general guidelines on sharing at ACA meetings. Most people arrive at ACA meetings not knowing how to share or talk in meetings. In the beginning, we encourage ACA members to share whatever comes up. There is no wrong way to share at an ACA meeting, as long as we are not abusing others verbally or cross talking. ACA members listen with respect and empathy as we share. After awhile our sharing begins to take on a general form of recalling our childhood experiences and how we use the Steps and meetings to address those experiences. We talk of transforming The Laundry List traits into usable tools for our personal growth. We also talk of spiritual growth, living in the moment, and having fun. We learn how to play and enjoy life in ACA.

Suggestions for ACA Speakers and Lead Shares

Occasionally, ACA members are asked to speak at an ACA meeting or to start off group sharing with extended remarks on a given recovery topic.

When asked to speak at a group, convention, or other ACA event, we are expected to share our life story before finding recovery and what has happened since finding recovery. The key to speaking at an ACA meeting involves balancing your remarks with an equal amount of family dysfunctional history, living codependently or addictively as an adult, and living life in recovery with the Twelve Steps, sponsorship, and ACA meeting attendance. Each part is important. By telling all of our story in a balanced manner, we build identification, demonstrate honesty, and offer an example of how the ACA program works in our lives. We tell our story with enough

HB

detail to break through the denial of dysfunctional living. We break the "don't talk" rule and get honest about our parents' behavior and our own behavior. We do not belittle or shame ourselves when telling our stories, but we must be honest about what happened. We seek identification with other ACA members instead of seeking sympathy or self-pity when telling our story. When we are honest, we find empathy and acceptance among other group members.

The same principles of sharing hold true if we are asked to share briefly as the lead share at the beginning of an ACA meeting. The lead share (first speaker) will talk for 10 to 15 minutes on the topic of the meeting. The person offers his or her experience and recovery on the topic.

In addition to working the Twelve Steps, we suggest that ACA speakers place some emphasis on attending meetings, getting a sponsor, using the telephone, seeking a Higher Power, giving service, and fellowshipping with others outside of regular meetings. Some ACA speakers will read each of the Twelve Steps, sharing his or her experience with the Step. If you have not worked all of the Steps, you can share on the Steps you have completed and other aspects of recovery. If you have not worked any of the Twelve Steps, we urge you to make a beginning so that your story is balanced with recovery.

(See segment on Hospitals and Institution Meetings and Prison Meetings for sharing or talking in these meetings.)

Cross Talk

Some groups incorporate a definition of cross talk into their meeting format. This definition is usually read just before the group begins a discussion on the meeting topic. The term "cross talk" means interrupting, referring to, commenting on, or using the contents of what another person has said during the meeting. Cross talk also refers to any type of dialog that occurs as the meeting is in process as well. Members talking to one another or discussing what someone has just said is cross talk.

HB

Many ACA members come from family backgrounds where feelings and perceptions were judged as wrong or defective. In ACA, each person may share his or her feelings and perceptions without fear of judgment or interruption. In ACA, we create a safe place to open up and share. As part of creating that safety, cross talk is not permitted.

We respect these boundaries for two reasons: First, when we were growing up no one listened to us; they told us that our feelings were wrong. Second, as adults we are accustomed to taking care of other people and not taking responsibility for our lives. In ACA, we speak about our own experiences and feelings; we accept without comment what others say because it is true for them. We also work toward taking more responsibility in our lives rather than giving advice to others. Here are various forms of cross talk:

Interrupting

Each member of ACA should be able to share, free from interruption. When someone is sharing, all others should refrain from speaking, including side conversations with a neighbor. Gestures, noise, or movement could also be considered interruption if it were grossly distracting.

Referring to

In ACA we keep the focus on our lives and our feelings. We do not make reference to the shares of others except as a transition into our own sharing. A very general "what's been brought up for me is…" or the occasional "thank you for sharing" is fine, but please do not make more detailed references to another person's share.

Commenting on

In ACA we accept what each person shares as true for them. We go to great lengths to avoid creating the climate of shame that enforced the three primary rules of a dysfunctional family: don't talk, don't trust, don't feel. In ACA, we simply do not make comments either positive or negative about another person's share before, during, or after a meeting. In like manner, we never speak about the contents of another person's share. Everything that is shared in an ACA meeting is considered privileged and confidential and must be treated with the utmost of respect. Unsolicited advice can be a form of commentary and should be avoided.

Fixing Others

In ACA, we do not touch, hug, or attempt to comfort others when they become emotional during an ACA meeting. If someone begins to cry or weep during a meeting, we allow them to feel their feelings. We support them by refraining from touching them or interrupting their tears with something we might say. To touch or hug the person is known as "fixing." As children we tried to fix our parents or to control them with our behavior. In ACA, we are learning to take care of ourselves and not attempt to fix others. We support others by accepting them into our meetings and listening to them while they face their pain. We learn to listen, which is often the greatest support of all.

Cross Talk and Group Conscience

The guidelines listed above are what keep ACA safe, allowing us to heal from our past. Most adult children want to cooperate with meeting rules and guidelines. Many new members may not understand the cross talk rule or other meeting guidelines for several meetings. Under these circumstances, we can quietly explain the rules after the meeting.

However, any group member who believes he or she has been cross talked can ask the chairman of the meeting to restate the cross talk rule. This can be done during the meeting when the cross talk has occurred. If the chairperson is asked to restate the cross talk rule by someone in the meeting, the chairperson has a choice to restate the rule or to talk with the cross talking person after the meeting.

HB

If the cross talk is more serious or a nuisance, the chairperson or the person who has been cross talked can ask for an immediate group conscience vote. Under this scenario the person or chairperson would stop the meeting and say: "I would like to have a group conscience vote at this time. Would the group members like the cross talk to discontinue?"

A group vote can strengthen the group's resolve to stop cross talk. Each cross talk situation can be different. We want to balance keeping our groups safe from cross talk with our own responsibility to educate new members about group decorum. In most cases, a gentle reminder works.

More Information on Sharing at ACA Meetings

Sharing or talking at ACA meetings can be intimidating for some while it is confusing to others. At the same time, some adult children seem to talk freely at ACA meetings without making progress toward recovery. Our recovery is gauged by the changes we make in our lives and the progress we make in working the ACA Twelve Steps. Some ACA members may be using their talking skills to avoid focused Twelve Step work or reparenting work. These ACA members are knowledgeable about ACA dynamics. But they tend to avoid Step work and miss out on the benefits of the program. We do not say this to discourage anyone from sharing or talking in meetings; however, real change comes with working the Steps, using a sponsor, and associating with other recovering adult children. We must also be consistent in meeting attendance.

Other adult children can be timid about sharing in meetings. They believe they are being disloyal to the family. This is not the case. There is a difference between being disloyal and seeking help by talking about our lives in an ACA meeting. For some of us this is the first time we have challenged authority. Our dysfunctional family is an authority of sorts. We challenge the family secrets and rules by talking about our childhood and teen years.

HB

It is important that we balance our sharing. We share details about our family history and living as codependent adults. We constantly sought love and affirmation from people who could not give it. We also share details about living in the moment through the Twelve Steps, self-acceptance, and hope for the future. We can talk about our past and balance that with what is happening now.

In the beginning, some of us lack Twelve Step knowledge unless we have been active in another Twelve Step fellowship. When we are new, we listen to other group members sharing about a particular Step or recovery topic. By listening, we learn about how we are powerless over the effects of family dysfunction in Step One. We hear others share about a Higher Power in Step Two and doing a personal inventory in Step Four. In the latter Steps, we learn about ineffectual behaviors, making an amends list, daily inventory, and having a spiritual awakening. We also hear about focusing on ourselves and living one day at a time. Group members share about using the telephone and a sponsor to ask for help.

When we arrive here, we usually have an "abuse-logue" or codependent story, but little recovery. This is common. We start from where we are.

Our "abuse-logue" is a similar concept of the "drunk-a-logue," which is the qualifying portion of an AA story. During this portion of the story, the AA member will "qualify" as an AA member by detailing his or her drinking history. In ACA, we qualify as well by detailing our dysfunctional family history and the traits we developed to survive. It is important that we share the details of our family roles, inner messages, and feelings of fear and loss. Knowing our family history and labeling it properly without denial is critical to staying focused on recovery. We learn this detail and find our loss by talking about it.

As we listen to others and as we work the Steps, our story becomes more balanced between what happened in the past and what we are doing in the moment to change. We begin to have

HB

more than stories of abuse or neglect to talk about. When sharing in meetings, we mix reflections of our past with the changes that are occurring in our daily lives. We realize we are growing emotionally and spiritually. We are changing. We are beginning to see that we have choices.

One's sharing or talking in ACA meetings can evolve through various stages. The following phases are a guide to assist group members on the path to learning their story. Simply recounting our abuse or neglect history without feelings and without balance is not our true story. We must take time to learn the effects of growing up in a dysfunctional home and then reflect upon how ACA can help us change. It is then that we find our loss and our purpose in life.

The time lines of these phases are flexible. Some members may be in a certain phase for a longer or shorter amount of time.

Phases of Sharing: Growing and Becoming Involved in ACA Meetings

We cannot overstate the critical need to attend ACA meetings regularly and to share or talk about our personal growth by working the program. Regular attendance at ACA meetings allows us to sound out our progress in recovery. We learn to share our personal growth with friends who affirm us and celebrate with us. This is a major difference from our family-of-origin, which withheld praise or true affirmation.

Learning to share or talk in an ACA meeting can happen in various phases. Consistent attendance at meetings can come in phases as well; however, experience shows that irregular meeting attendance hinders recovery.

The phases mentioned here will not fit everyone in the same manner. We offer these phases as a loose guide to what we might be sharing in meetings at six weeks, six years, or 15 years. These phases are suggested only. Some ACA members will get involved in meetings, choose a sponsor, and begin working the Twelve Steps in the first year. Others will be involved in therapy for a year before committing to regular meeting attendance or sharing in meetings. Still others will drift in and out of ACA until they are ready to focus on themselves. Here are some basic phases of sharing and fellowship involvement.

Newcomer Sharing (1–6 weeks): Newcomers to ACA are often unclear about how to share or speak during an ACA meeting. The new person can also feel intimidated or confused by meeting topics. Each meeting offers new terms that include: Twelve Steps, cross talk, Laundry List, affirmations, shame, Inner Child, sponsor, Intergroup, and so on. With time, most of these terms are explained, but the new person can ask for explanations at the end of the meeting as well.

In our early ACA days, our codependent or self-abuse story is all we seem to have to share about. We come to ACA because we are in great confusion or pain. At the same time, many of us are inwardly numb from years of suppressing our feelings and thoughts. Talk of feelings or trauma in meetings seems to pass over our heads. We relate to the meetings nonetheless.

Some of us find hope at our first meeting and are eager to make a start on the program. Others are still in denial but continue to attend meetings because of the honesty and acceptance. Still others do not know what to do or if life is worth living; nothing seems to make sense. Some of us remember little of what is read or said during our first meeting. During this phase of early recovery, we listen. We begin to consider talking about what happened to us. Newcomers should speak about whatever is on their minds. For example, we might say:

My name is _____. I'm here because _____.
This is my story _____. I'm feeling _____.
I hope to get _____ from coming here.

Early Sharing (6 weeks – 1 year): During this phase, we learn to describe hitting a bottom or the crisis that brought us to ACA. Learning to recognize your bottom and share about it is a critical part of recovery. Bottoming out can range from

HB

being drug addicted and homeless, to having a life of luxury and standing but still void of feelings and intimacy. There are camouflaged bottoms as well. Many times our lives seem manageable and in order, but we sense that something is not right with us. This is a subtle bottom that we label as the blues, depression, or something else. It has the same traits of isolation, unhappiness, and moments of despair that most bottoms have. Read the Chapter on Hitting Bottom to learn more about this phase of recovery.

We also become aware of denial and its various forms during the first year of sharing or talking in meetings. ACA denial can involve blaming, minimizing, and rejection of facts. We also are in denial when we sanitize an episode of our lives by downplaying certain facts of a painful incident. In ACA, we face our denial about our parents' addiction or other dysfunction. We face our own behavior as well. The best way to face the denial is to read ACA literature and detail how you were treated as a child. We name what happened to us and claim what happened to us. As we attend ACA meetings regularly, we become aware of the hurt, blame, and shame. We talk about these experiences and feelings out loud to the people at the meetings. During the first year in recovery, we also can ask someone to sponsor us and begin to talk about what happened. We begin to work the Steps and attend ACA meetings on a regular basis. We learn about the Inner Child and inner Critical Parent. We begin our search for a Higher Power as well.

During the first year, we find an ACA support group where we feel comfortable attending meetings. This is known as a "home group" by many ACA members. We begin to help out with group duties of chairing meetings, ordering literature, or making refreshments. We notice other newcomers and begin to welcome them to ACA as we were welcomed.

Cleaning Up the Wreckage of the Past Sharing (1 year to 3 years): During this phase, we come to believe that ACA is a safe place. We are familiar with attending meetings, working the Steps, and giving service. Many of us have completed a personal inventory in Steps Four and Five and have begun the process of cleaning up the wreckage of the past. We also have begun to confront the inner Critical Parent. We become more gentle with ourselves by comparing the messages of the Critical Parent with what a Loving Parent would say to us.

We also learn during this phase that ACA recovery is not a linear progression upward. We see that recovery can have peaks and valleys. There are spikes of joy and hope followed by a dip into self-doubt or blame. Some of us deal with fear, self-harm, or worry. In meetings we share about the chaos of our lives, but we notice progress all the same. Many times we have attended a meeting and listened to ACA members sharing about the topic we were facing that day. If we are working a certain Step, we seem to find ourselves in meetings where that very Step is discussed. We get help and encouragement from ACA meetings.

During this phase, we talk about learning to use the phone, the Steps, and the meetings to begin the process of reparenting ourselves. We share about attempting to help others even though we may be hurting. We talk of walking though pain or fear with the help of a Higher Power. We learn to ask for help. We make a commitment to break the isolation of our lives and to let other people into our lives.

Putting Our Life in Order Sharing (2 years to 6 years): This phase is similar to the previous phase; however, we struggle less with fear and self-doubt. We are more adept at using the tools of recovery. We recognize our denial sooner, and we have faith that our feelings will not destroy us. Turning over control and resentment can become easier. We talk of retiring survival traits and feeling more comfortable with who we truly are. We attend meetings regularly and talk about life's challenges as they arise. We talk about feelings of insecurity, anger, and self-pity that might arise. We also talk about self-acceptance and hope. We talk about having fun and relationships. We learn we can survive our feelings and our codependent urges. We are committed to reparenting ourselves and connecting with the Inner Child. We are helping out with the group and sponsoring others through

HB

the Twelve Steps. We are living life one day at a time, with a growing sense of self-forgiveness and wholeness. There can be rough days, but we have come to believe that we have self-worth. We begin to have a greater understanding of grief and loss.

Self-Sponsorship Sharing: Irregular Meeting Attendance (Can occur anytime): Some of us find the ACA program and become active in meetings only to drift away. We become inconsistent in meeting attendance. Most of us who do this are not committed to meetings or working the Twelve Steps with a sponsor. Some of us "sponsor" ourselves, which is risky. We use fear of authority figures or self-sufficiency to avoid asking someone to help us work the ACA program. We reject the ACA axiom which states that adult children cannot recover alone. When we "sponsor" ourselves, we are subject to isolation, intellectualization, or denial.

Those of us who have uneven meeting attendance may have attended meetings regularly in the past. We found relief only to drift away once our lives improved. We forgot that the disease of family dysfunction is progressive and incurable. We forgot we could relapse into codependent behavior. Without an active ACA program, we could resume the traits of stuffing our feelings, confusing love with pity, and accepting high levels of abuse as normal. Some of us returned to our old ways of thinking and acting without giving ACA a chance. We returned to moments of rage and self-condemnation. We became a controlling authority figure again. Or we became a victim to manipulate others.

In this phase of our recovery, we are usually unwilling to release control or to admit our powerlessness over the effects of growing up in a dysfunctional home. We either disbelieve in ourselves, or we are afraid to move forward. Both of these obstacles can be overcome. When we think about it, we are actually more afraid of success than failure.

During this inconsistent phase, many of us still respect ACA. We enjoy the meetings when we attend. But we cannot seem to work the Steps or let someone help us with our lives. We are stuck. We attend meetings on an irregular basis and feel frustrated that we are not making progress toward true happiness. We may have stopped some of our more destructive behaviors. But we find that we have switched to other compulsions or unhealthy acts. We still judge ourselves harshly or project blame onto others.

Our experience shows that this phase can serve as a starting point for new personal growth if we are willing. That is the key. We don't have to believe the Twelve Steps will work. We only have to be willing to work them with someone who is knowledgeable. We confront our denial and make a start to a new way of life in ACA.

Oldtimer Sharing and Giving Service (6 years and up): We remain active in ACA meetings, and we understand that giving service is love for ourselves and others. We sponsor others and greet newcomers at meetings. We take care of ourselves as well. Although we have time in the program, we ask for help. We share in meetings about working the Steps, sponsoring others, and reparenting ourselves with self-love. We also share about learning to say "no." And we learn to say "I don't know." We support the Twelve Steps and Twelve Traditions. At a group business meeting, we state our opinion and support the group decision whether we agree or not.

We share about life on life's terms. We share our successes and let others celebrate with us. We talk about our feelings and insecurities as well. We talk about our spiritual awakening and the true connection to God through the Inner Child. We have come to believe. We know how to have fun.

Avoiding the Pedestal (always): Our primary founder, Tony A., stepped away from ACA for awhile because he felt like he was being placed on a pedestal (Interview 1992). Most adult children are looking for a hero or for someone to believe in when they find ACA. It is only natural. We had no real role models as children. Most of us had no one we could trust before arriving here. We attend meetings and listen to people who seem to have it all together. We are impressed.

HB

Most "oldtimers" have lived the ACA program and have much to share. They humbly work the program without thought of standing out among other members. They know Step work, facing feelings, and grief work. Their spirituality is obvious. These older members know joy. They freely give their time and share their experience, strength, and hope when asked. But they remain ACA members just like the next person. They are fallible and struggle with life at times. Their response to life's challenges may be quicker or more thoughtful, but they live life just like the newcomer.

Occasionally, the older member finds himself or herself on a pedestal. Some can get down with grace while others struggle with letting go. Some have been placed there while others have climbed up there. This does not mean that our older members do not have wisdom, discernment, or intuitiveness. Their recovery is solid and their experience proven. We need these trusted servants to help steady our program and to remind us when we stray too far from ACA's singleness of purpose. But we avoid placing people on a pedestal in ACA. To do so is not fair to that person and not fair to ourselves. When we place someone on a pedestal, we take the focus off ourselves. We miss the chance to truly find intimacy with others. We listen to our older members with respect, but we let them remain human. We remain human as well.

Safety in Meetings

Our experience shows that ACA meetings are safe, affirming, and orderly. In rare instances, however, ACA groups have had to address the problematic behavior of a group member. This is not uncommon among the various Twelve Step programs. ACA wisdom offers a wealth of common-sense actions, so that a group can maintain its safety while also not over reaching with exclusionary rules. In addition to these suggestions below, please review Chapter Nineteen – Twelve Traditions – to learn more about how ACA groups handle disruptive or bothersome situations. It is important to remember that all group members

HB

are responsible for group safety and order. Actions that address disruptive behavior should be taken by the group and with group support. Do not act alone in these situations. Ideas to address disruptive behavior in your group are:

1. Keep Tradition One in mind in all decisions your group would make about a disruptive person. The Tradition states: "Our common welfare should come first; personal recovery depends upon ACA unity".

2. Two or more group members can ask the disruptive person to leave the meeting and return when he or she is willing to work on recovery. Ask the person to talk to a sponsor or consider getting a sponsor.

3. If the problematic behavior persists, ask the person to take a one or two week break from the meeting.

4. If the person is disruptive and will not leave the meeting, escort him or her from the meeting if the person is not violent. Escorting is done by a group of meeting members instead of one member acting alone.

5. If the disruptive person becomes violent or threatening, shut down the meeting immediately and have all members depart for the common welfare.

6. Call the police if there is clear and present danger to lives, health, or property.

HB

The ACA Twelve Steps

1. We admitted we were powerless over the effects of alcoholism or other family dysfunction, that our lives had become unmanageable.

2. Came to believe that a Power greater than ourselves could restore us to sanity.

3. Made a decision to turn our will and our lives over to the care of God as we understand God.

4. Made a searching and fearless moral inventory of ourselves.

5. Admitted to God, to ourselves, and to another human being the exact nature of our wrongs.

6. Were entirely ready to have God remove all these defects of character.

7. Humbly asked God to remove our shortcomings.

8. Made a list of all persons we had harmed and became willing to make amends to them all.

9. Made direct amends to such people wherever possible, except when to do so would injure them or others.

10. Continued to take personal inventory and, when we were wrong, promptly admitted it.

11. Sought through prayer and meditation to improve our conscious contact with God, as we understand God, praying only for knowledge of God's will for us and the power to carry that out.

12. Having had a spiritual awakening as the result of these steps, we tried to carry this message to others who still suffer, and to practice these principles in all our affairs.

The Twelve Steps are reprinted and adapted from the original Twelve Steps of Alcoholics Anonymous, and are used with the permission of Alcoholics Anonymous World Services, Inc.

The "Laundry List"

These are characteristics we seem to have in common due to being brought up in an alcoholic household.

1. We became isolated and afraid of people and authority figures.

2. We became approval seekers and lost our identity in the process.

3. We are frightened by angry people and any personal criticism.

4. We either become alcoholics, marry them, or both, or find another compulsive personality such as a workaholic to fulfill our sick abandonment needs.

5. We live life from the viewpoint of victims and are attracted by that weakness in our love and friendship relationships.

6. We have an overdeveloped sense of responsibility and it is easier for us to be concerned with others rather than ourselves; this enables us not to look too closely at our own faults, etc.

7. We get guilt feelings when we stand up for ourselves instead of giving in to others.

8. We became addicted to excitement.

9. We confuse love and pity and tend to "love" people we can "pity" and "rescue."

10. We have "stuffed" our feelings from our traumatic childhoods and have lost the ability to feel or express our feelings because it hurts so much (denial).

HB

11. We judge ourselves harshly and have a very low sense of self-esteem.

12. We are dependent personalities who are terrified of abandonment and will do anything to hold on to a relationship in order not to experience painful abandonment feelings, which we received from living with sick people who were never there emotionally for us.

13. Alcoholism is a family disease, and we became para-alcoholics (codependent)[1] and took on the characteristics of that disease even though we did not pick up the drink.

14. Para-alcoholics are reactors rather than actors.

Tony A., 1978

---

[1] Added by Handbook Committee. Not part of original list.

The Problem

Adapted from The Laundry List

Many of us found that we had several characteristics in common as a result of being brought up in an alcoholic or dysfunctional household. We had come to feel isolated and uneasy with other people, especially authority figures. To protect ourselves, we became people-pleasers, even though we lost our own identities in the process. All the same we would mistake any personal criticism as a threat. We either became alcoholics (or practiced other addictive behavior) ourselves, or married them, or both. Failing that, we found other compulsive personalities, such as a workaholic, to fulfill our sick need for abandonment.

We lived life from the standpoint of victims. Having an overdeveloped sense of responsibility, we preferred to be concerned with others rather than ourselves. We got guilt feelings when we stood up for ourselves rather than giving in to others. Thus, we became reactors, rather than actors, letting others take the initiative. We were dependent personalities, terrified of abandonment, willing to do almost anything to hold on to a relationship in order not to be abandoned emotionally. Yet we kept choosing insecure relationships because they matched our childhood relationship with alcoholic or dysfunctional parents.

These symptoms of the family disease of alcoholism or other dysfunction made us "co-victims," those who take on the characteristics of the disease without necessarily ever taking a drink. We learned to keep our feelings down as children and kept them buried as adults. As a result of this conditioning, we confused love with pity, tending to love those we could rescue. Even more self-defeating, we became addicted to excitement in all our affairs, preferring constant upset to workable relationships. This is a description, not an indictment.

HB

The Solution

The Solution is to become your own loving parent. As ACA becomes a safe place for you, you will find freedom to express all the hurts and fears you have kept inside and to free yourself from the shame and blame that are carryovers from the past. You will become an adult who is imprisoned no longer by childhood reactions. You will recover the child within you, learning to accept and love yourself.

The healing begins when we risk moving out of isolation. Feelings and buried memories will return. By gradually releasing the burden of unexpressed grief, we slowly move out of the past. We learn to reparent ourselves with gentleness, humor, love, and respect. This process allows us to see our biological parents as the instruments of our existence. Our actual parent is a Higher Power whom some of us choose to call God. Although we had alcoholic or dysfunctional parents, our Higher Power gave us the Twelve Steps of Recovery.

This is the action and work that heals us: we use the Steps; we use the meetings; we use the telephone. We share our experience, strength, and hope with each other. We learn to restructure our sick thinking one day at a time. When we release our parents from responsibility for our actions today, we become free to make healthful decisions as actors, not reactors. We progress from hurting, to healing, to helping. We awaken to a sense of wholeness we never knew was possible. By attending these meetings on a regular basis, you will come to see parental alcoholism or family dysfunction for what it is: a disease that infected you as a child and continues to affect you as an adult.

You will learn to keep the focus on yourself in the here and now. You will take responsibility for your own life and supply your own parenting. You will not do this alone. Look around you and you will see others who know how you feel. We will love and encourage you no matter what. We ask you to accept us just as we accept you. This is a spiritual program based on action coming from love. We are sure that as the love grows inside you, you will see beautiful changes in all your relationships, especially with God, yourself, and your parents.

HB

The ACA Promises

1.   We will discover our real identities by loving and accepting ourselves.

2.   Our self-esteem will increase as we give ourselves approval on a daily basis.

3.   Fear of authority figures and the need to "people-please" will leave us.

4.   Our ability to share intimacy will grow inside us.

5.   As we face our abandonment issues, we will be attracted by strengths and become more tolerant of weaknesses.

6.   We will enjoy feeling stable, peaceful, and financially secure.

7.   We will learn how to play and have fun in our lives.

8.   We will choose to love people who can love and be responsible for themselves.

9.   Healthy boundaries and limits will become easier for us to set.

10.   Fears of failure and success will leave us, as we intuitively make healthier choices.

11.   With help from our ACA support group, we will slowly release our dysfunctional behaviors.

12.   Gradually, with our Higher Power's help, we will learn to expect the best and get it.

The ACA Twelve Traditions

1. Our common welfare should come first; personal recovery depends on ACA unity.

2. For our group purpose there is but one ultimate authority – a loving God as expressed in our group conscience. Our leaders are but trusted servants, they do not govern.

3. The only requirement for membership in ACA is a desire to recover from the effects of growing up in an alcoholic or otherwise dysfunctional family.

4. Each group is autonomous except in matters affecting other groups or ACA as a whole. We cooperate with all other Twelve-Step programs.

5. Each group has but one primary purpose – to carry its message to the adult child who still suffers.

6. An ACA group ought never endorse, finance, or lend the ACA name to any related facility or outside enterprise, lest problems of money, property, and prestige divert us from our primary purpose.

7. Every ACA group ought to be fully self-supporting, declining outside contributions.

8. Adult Children of Alcoholics should remain forever non-professional, but our service centers may employ special workers.

9. ACA, as such, ought never be organized, but we may create service boards or committees directly responsible to those they serve.

10. Adult Children of Alcoholics has no opinion on outside issues; hence the ACA name ought never be drawn into public controversy.

11. Our public relations policy is based on attraction rather than promotion; we maintain personal anonymity at the level of press, radio, TV, films, and other public media.

12. Anonymity is the spiritual foundation of all our Traditions, ever reminding us to place principles before personalities.

HB

The Twelve Steps Of Alcoholics Anonymous

1. We admitted we were powerless over alcohol — that our lives had become unmanageable.
2. Came to believe that a Power greater than ourselves could restore us to sanity.
3. Made a decision to turn our will and our lives over to the care of God as we understood Him.
4. Made a searching and fearless moral inventory of ourselves.
5. Admitted to God, to ourselves, and to another human being the exact nature of our wrongs.
6. Were entirely ready to have God remove all these defects of character.
7. Humbly asked Him to remove our shortcomings.
8. Made a list of all persons we had harmed and became willing to make amends to them all.
9. Made direct amends to such people wherever possible, except when to do so would injure them or others.
10. Continued to take personal inventory and when we were wrong promptly admitted it.
11. Sought through prayer and meditation to improve our conscious contact with God, as we understood Him, praying only for knowledge of His will for us and the power to carry that out.
12. Having had a spiritual awakening as the result of these steps, we tried to carry this message to alcoholics, and to practice these principles in all our affairs.

The Twelve Traditions Of Alcoholics Anonymous

1. Our common welfare should come first; personal recovery depends upon A.A. unity.
2. For our group purpose there is but one ultimate authority – a loving God as He may express Himself in our group conscience. Our leaders are but trusted servants; they do not govern.
3. The only requirement for A.A. membership is a desire to stop drinking.
4. Each group should be autonomous except in matters affecting other groups or A.A. as a whole.
5. Each group has but one primary purpose – to carry its message to the alcoholic who still suffers.
6. An A.A. group ought never endorse, finance or lend the A.A. name to any related facility or outside enterprise, lest problems of money, property and prestige divert us from our primary purpose.
7. Every A.A. group ought to be fully self-supporting, declining outside contributions.
8. Alcoholics Anonymous should remain forever nonprofessional, but our service centers may employ special workers.
9. A.A., as such, ought never be organized; but we may create service boards or committees directly responsible to those they serve.
10. Alcoholics Anonymous has no opinion on outside issues; hence the A.A. name ought never be drawn into public controversy.
11. Our public relations policy is based on attraction rather than promotion; we need always maintain personal anonymity at the level of press, radio and films.
12. Anonymity is the spiritual foundation of all our Traditions, ever reminding us to place principles before personalities.

HB

The Twelve Traditions and Twelve Steps are reprinted and adapted with permission of Alcoholics Anonymous World Services, Inc.

Group Organization and Procedures

Conducting an ACA Business Meeting

When to Hold a Business Meeting

We have found that most individuals who attend an ACA recovery meeting do so to benefit from the experience, strength, and hope shared at the meeting. We dedicate our regular meetings to topics of recovery and program study. We attempt to hold group business meetings before or after the regular ACA meeting to avoid disrupting the meeting. Yet, there are times when certain business must be conducted during the regular meeting.

Some group business needs to be considered by all members who regularly attend an ACA meeting. If only a quick vote needs to be taken on an issue, this could be done during the announcements at the beginning or conclusion of a regular ACA meeting. If this is done, we must remember to keep the discussion short and to vote quickly since we are taking up time from a regular ACA meeting. The topics can be group elections, changing the meeting format, time of the meeting, meeting location, and safety and security of members. Longer discussions on business items need to be handled in a regular business meeting before or after the regular meeting. If a business meeting is needed to handle items of lengthy discussion, the group usually announces the business meeting one week in advance so that a representative number of group members can attend.

Scheduling a Business Meeting

It is suggested that ACA meetings hold a regular business meeting monthly or quarterly.

Allow Everyone to Express Views

Keep in mind the right of everyone to express an opinion. Participating in a business meeting allows us to practice learned

HB

recovery tools. The minority opinion is important. There should be an emphasis on obtaining a group conscience of all the participants on all issues, particularly when there is disagreement. A group conscience is the method by which we invite a loving God into our group decisions and discussions. The group comes to an agreement on a given business item after each person has expressed his or her views. An agreement or course of action may not appear after the first round of discussion. If so, the chairperson of the business meeting asks for more discussion among the group members until a consensus is reached.

Some groups will use a combination of the consensus discussion approach and entertaining formal motions. A motion is a statement made by an individual attending the business meeting. The motion calls for an action to be taken by the group. The person might say: "I make a motion to change the meeting time from 6 p.m. to 7 p.m." If a motion is made and seconded by the group members, there is usually discussion and then a vote is taken. General motions are usually passed by a simple majority. More serious motions such as removing someone from office or changing the meeting time can require a two-thirds majority.

Group Voting and Substantial Unanimity – Twelfth Concept

Most ACA groups conduct business meetings with some form of rules of order or general consent. ACA groups are cautioned to avoid too much formality in conducting business meetings. Typically, a chairperson leads the business meeting, recognizes motions, and oversees discussion on the motions. Each person at the business meeting usually shares once on the motion before the chairperson asks if the group is ready to vote on the motion.

Some groups are more informal. They do not make motions or vote formally. Instead, the group discusses a topic or issue until a general consensus is reached by the group. In this form of business meeting, the chairperson of the meeting would listen to the discussion among the group and sense when a consensus is reached. The chairperson would then state that consensus to

HB

see if there is agreement with those attending the business meeting. The chairperson might say: "I sense that the group has decided to change the meeting time from 6 p.m. to 7 p.m." If the group agrees then consensus is reached; the decision is made. In determining a consensus, the chairperson states the consensus in an impartial manner and remains open to the will of the business meeting participants.

There is a principle from our Twelve Concepts for ACA World Service known as "substantial unanimity." The Twelfth Concept states: "that all important decisions be reached by discussion vote and whenever possible, by substantial unanimity." Substantial unanimity applies to the most important business of meetings, Intergroups, and Regions,[2] in addition to the Annual Business Conference. Substantial unanimity means that decisions reached by ACA meetings or service bodies need to reflect the clear will of the group. Each group and service committee must decide the "important decisions" that require substantial unanimity. Substantial unanimity is always greater than a simple majority and should exceed a two-thirds majority of those voting on the ACA business at hand. If agreement cannot be reached, it is best to postpone action on the motion or topic.

The election of service committee members typically is settled by a simple majority vote, which is acceptable and well below substantial unanimity standard. There are other examples of ACA business being settled by a simple majority. But we are always mindful of the need for substantial unanimity on business of greater importance.

Sharing at Business Meetings

Because our program focus is on recovery, ACA members occasionally attend business meetings to share their feelings without addressing the issues for discussion. While feelings are an important part of our recovery, we have found that it is best to share on the business at hand because of the limited time that most business

---

[2] See section on Intergroups and Regional committees for definitions of these committees.

meetings operate under. At business meetings, we ask questions, listen, and think about our response before speaking.

That said, ACA business meetings are not without emotion. Some ACA members speak with feelings and compassion while staying on the topic and without acting inappropriately in the meeting.

We ask that children not be brought to a business meeting so that disruptions can be avoided. This is true for our Inner Children because they, too, need attention and are equally disruptive in meetings. If a person is at a business meeting and realizes he or she has not negotiated a settlement to keep the Inner Child from misbehaving at the meeting, then that person needs to excuse himself or herself from the meeting to negotiate or renegotiate with the Inner Child. By taking care of our Inner Child, we are better able to participate in group business.

The chairperson of the business meeting can ask individuals who act out to leave unless they can conduct themselves in accordance with the rules of order, discuss only the business at hand, and accept the group conscience processes, deliberations, and decisions gracefully.

ACA Group or Meeting Officers

A)   Secretary

1.   The group secretary updates meeting information with its Intergroup and WSO for changes in meeting location and times, secretary or treasurer, or addresses and phone numbers. Meeting information should be updated annually. Notify the facility in which you meet when you are turning over the key to a new secretary. Provide their name, address, and phone number.

2.   The secretary opens and closes the meetings unless this is delegated to another trusted servant.

HB

Handbook For Adult Children

3. The secretary safeguards the meeting facility key. The secretary or meeting chairperson asks for volunteers to clean up the room when the meeting is over.

4. The secretary arranges for meeting leaders and speakers. We try to select speakers with an ACA message that reflects the Twelve Steps, the Inner Child and reparenting one's self with ACA principles.

5. The secretary and group members welcome newcomers at meetings.

6. The secretary and group chairperson are responsible for the unity and safety of the meeting; however, the secretary can ask for help in reminding members of the "no cross talk" rule and the limit on the amount of time that one is allowed to share.

7. The secretary announces when birthday meetings will be held and coordinates medallions, cards, refreshments, and a cake or treats.

8. The secretary presents his or her report and announcements at meetings.

9. The secretary announces service opportunities becoming available. The opportunities include: chairing meetings, serving as an Intergroup Representative, serving as group treasurer, helping with group duties, and carrying ACA meetings into treatment centers, psychiatric units, or prisons. It is recommended that group members have six months of recovery before taking on a meeting within a facility.

10. Former group secretaries are encouraged to continue their Twelve Step work by carrying the message to those who still suffer and giving back

to ACA what ACA has given them. Some secretaries become an Intergroup Representative for the meeting.

11. The outgoing group secretary helps the incoming secretary to update the new meeting information with the Intergroup, World Service Organization, and the meeting facility.

B) **Treasurer**
(if this office is vacant, the group secretary assumes these responsibilities). The group or meeting treasurer:

1. Collects and records 7th Tradition donations.

2. Pays meeting expenses (rent, Post Office box, etc.).

3. Reimburses members who present receipts for refreshments, literature, copies, recovery chips, etc.

4. Keeps a prudent reserve (usually two month's meeting expenses).

5. Sends 60 percent of remaining group funds to Intergroup and 40 percent to World Service Organization each month.

6. Suggests, when the 7th Tradition donation is taken, that the standard dollar donation of the 1950s does not cover the cost of carrying the message today. Two dollars is more appropriate.

7. Offers a monthly financial report to the group, detailing donations, expenses, and fund balance.

8. Should have one year or more in the ACA recovery program and have an exemplary record of honesty.

HB

C)   **Intergroup Representative**
     (if this office is vacant, the secretary assumes these responsibilities). The Intergroup Representative:

1.   Attends and participates at Intergroup and or World Service Organization (teleconference) meeting each month.

2.   Communicates information and activity announcements from the Intergroup and WSO to his or her meeting. This information is usually reported weekly.

3.   Makes concerns and questions of meetings known to Intergroup and World Service Organization. Also conveys experience, strength, and hope from Intergroup and WSO.

4.   Gets involved with the Intergroup and WSO Committees: WSO Office, Literature development, *ComLine* Newsletter, Treasurer, Website support, and Special Events.

D)   **Literature Chairperson**
     (if this office is vacant, the secretary assumes these responsibilities). The group or meeting literature person:

1.   Orders literature from Intergroup or WSO.

2.   Makes additional copies of depleted table literature.

3.   Displays literature at each meeting.

4.   Works with secretary to determine what literature should be stocked. May help group secretary with other duties.

HB

E) Other Possible Service Positions

Positions such as Public Information volunteer or Hospitals and Institutions coordinator are typically filled by group members who have a working knowledge of the Steps and Traditions.

There are also positions for newcomers that include meeting greeter, set up/clean up people, and meeting timer to ensure that each person can share at meetings. Newcomers should also be encouraged to chair meetings once they have demonstrated an understanding of meeting guidelines.

The Suggested Commitment to Service

I perform service so that my program will be available for myself, and through those efforts, others may benefit. I will perform service and practice my recovery by:

1. Affirming that the true power of our program rests in the membership of the meetings and is expressed through our Higher Power and through group conscience.

2. Confirming that our process is one of inclusion and not exclusion; showing special sensitivity to the viewpoint of the minority in the process of formulating the group conscience so that any decision is reflective of the spirit of the group and not merely the vote of the majority.

3. Placing principles before personalities.

4. Keeping myself fit for service by working my recovery as a member of the program.

5. Striving to facilitate the sharing of experience, strength, and hope at all levels: meetings, Intergroups, Regional committees, service boards, and World Services.

HB

6. Accepting the different forms and levels of service and allowing those around me to each function according to their own abilities.

7. Remaining willing to forgive myself and others for not performing perfectly.

8. Being willing to surrender the position in which I serve in the interest of unity and to provide the opportunity for others to serve; to avoid problems of money, property, and prestige; and to avoid losing my own recovery through the use of service to act out my old behavior, especially in taking care of others, controlling, rescuing, being a victim, etc.

9. Remembering I am a trusted servant; I do not govern.

Registering Your ACA Group or Meeting with WSO

An ACA group is any group of Adult Children of Alcoholics and other dysfunctional families that is based on the Twelve Steps, Twelve Traditions, The Laundry List (Problem), and The Solution, and has no other affiliation with an outside entity. Some groups are listed as ACA or ACoA, but they are the same program as long as they use ACA literature and have no affiliation with an outside entity.

Al-Anon meetings with an adult child focus are not ACA groups. Some Al-Anon meetings are known as ACAP or Al-Anon ACoA, but they do not use ACA literature. We cooperate with Al-Anon and all Twelve Step programs, but ACA meetings use ACA literature that includes The Laundry List and The Solution in addition to the Steps and Traditions. You can order or download ACA literature on the Adult Children of Alcoholics website.

When an ACA meeting is formed, a registration form should be filled out and sent to WSO so the meeting can be listed among other ACA meetings in your area. In addition to putting you in contact with WSO, the registration also links your group to ACA members and groups across the world. Your group will benefit from the experience, strength, and hope of ACA members in many different cities, provinces, villages, towns, and metropolitan areas. Registering your group helps the WSO refer newcomers and travelers to your meeting.

An updated registration form should be sent to WSO when group changes are made involving the group's meeting time or place and the election of new officers. WSO needs your help in keeping our web-page files current. The registration form should also be sent to your Intergroup or Region if these service committees exist in your area.

Registration of your group also allows your meeting to receive information from the ACA service structure, i.e., Intergroups, service committees, and WSO. Likewise, the registration gives you a channel to make your group conscience known to the ACA service structure. Registration confirms that your group is a Twelve Steps and Twelve Traditions meeting. By following the Steps and Traditions our meetings have a consistency in message and purpose.

Typically, the WSO attempts to update the worldwide meeting list once a year. Newly elected secretaries should file their contact information with WSO so the group can receive ACA correspondence and news of fellowship developments. If a meeting has not filed a current registration, or it cannot be confirmed by telephone, mail, or a visit to the location, the meeting is considered to be dissolved and will be dropped from the meeting directory.

HB

How to Start an ACA Intergroup or Regional Service Committee

In areas where many ACA meetings exist, an Intergroup is generally formed to provide a forum for conducting ACA business within a given geographical area. The individual groups continue to conduct their own group business; however, the groups can select a meeting representative to represent the group at an Intergroup meeting. The Intergroup, therefore, is composed of members from the various ACA groups. The Intergroup helps coordinate helpline functions, public information efforts, hospitals and institutions meetings, and ACA events in a given area. An ACA Regional Service Committee serves a similar function by helping coordinate ACA functions and fellowship business among Intergroups in a geographical area.

When an Intergroup is formed, each ACA group elects an Intergroup representative, who attends a monthly or quarterly Intergroup meeting. If there is no Intergroup in your area, your group can elect a Group Service Representative, who can attend the Annual Business Conference. A Regional Service Committee serves as a coordinating point for several Intergroups in a geographical area. Intergroup Representatives attend Regional Service Committee meetings as well. Here is how to establish an Intergroup or Regional Service Committee directly responsible to those they serve.

1. Contact ACA WSO for information on starting an Intergroup or Region. Also review material in this section on starting an ACA meeting. These suggestions may be helpful in forming ideas for election of officers and how to conduct a business meeting.

2. Think about your reasons to start a new service committee. Are you starting the Intergroup or Region to help yourself and others? Are you starting the committee to reach out to adult children and to promote ACA's growth and unity?

3. List the needs of your geographical area. Does your area need an ACA helpline or part-time special worker? Do you need to coordinate hospitals and institutions meetings? Are the activities within your area coordinated so that the events are

announced in a timely manner? Is there interest in a public information committee?

4. Locate and arrange for meeting space and announce an organizational meeting for the Intergroup or Regional Service Committee.

5. Invite interested adult children to attend this introductory meeting providing them with the time, day, and place; exchange contact information. If possible, invite members from an established Intergroup or Region to your first meeting.

6. To create an agenda for the first meeting, get input from those who might attend the meetings.

7. Ask for help to run the meeting and set up the room. Ask someone to chair the meeting.

8. Prepare a flyer announcing the meeting time and location. Also describe the purpose of the organizational meeting. Post the flyer at interested ACA groups or hand them out to ACA members. Maintain an attitude of inclusiveness and enthusiasm. Ask ACA members if they are interested in helping ACA reach suffering adult children throughout your area.

9. When the meeting day arrives, convene the meeting. Distribute the agendas and circulate a sign-in roster for telephone numbers and e-mail addresses. This will facilitate correspondence between meetings. Also pass out copies of the segment from this book on how to conduct an ACA business meeting.

10. Introduce yourself and those helping organize the new Intergroup or Regional committee. Explain the reason for the meeting and the goals you hope to accomplish.

HB

11. Elect a temporary secretary to take minutes and a meeting leader to present the agenda.

12. If appropriate, elect officers to establish the new service committee. (Officers would be a chairperson, secretary, and general committee members. A treasurer might be elected if there are group funds or the potential of group funds to be donated.) If more discussion is needed on the need for the new committee, delay the election of officers until the end of the meeting or until the next organizational meeting.

13. Prioritize any identified needs as urgent, important, low priority, or short-term solutions (In the beginning, keep it simple. Most new Intergroups focus on establishing an area helpline, organizing area events, or organizing volunteers for hospitals and institutions meetings. See the guidelines for a hospitals or prison meeting.)

14. Using a prioritized list, brainstorm possible solutions.

15. Select reasonable solutions, and ask for volunteers to work on implementing the solution.

16. If appropriate, elect officers to establish the new subcommittees. The subcommittees could be public information, helpline, hospitals and institutions, or activities.

17. Agree on a time and place for the next meeting. Adjourn the meeting.

HB

Issues for Meetings

Each ACA meeting is autonomous in keeping with the Traditions. We use the Traditions to provide guidance to the group in the same way the Steps provide guidance to the individual. The following topics address frequently asked questions about meetings.

Anonymity

For purposes of recovery, it is generally accepted that ACA is "an anonymous" program, meaning members of the fellowship or visitors should not divulge the names of those who attend a meeting or the content of the sharing to anyone. If someone chooses to use his/her first and last name or hand out an address or phone number, that is that person's choice.

ACA anonymity has its foundation in AA history when to be an alcoholic could mean death by liver disease or progressive dementia. In 1935 when AA began, just after the Great Depression, alcoholics and their families were shamed, ostracized, and condemned. Program affiliation could and did result in the loss of jobs, residences, friends, and family associations. AA was founded by Bill Wilson and Dr. Robert Holbrook Smith.

While the social climate today is far more accepting of alcoholism as noted by an occasional bumper sticker, "Protected by Smith and Wilson," for ACA there is another reason to protect our anonymity. In recovery, we express pent up feelings and relive the trauma of unexpressed childhood fear, anger, outrage and shame. This is the first step in the process of closure that allows for emotional maturation. Sharing may, therefore, include references to what we may have done or others may have done regarding a particular incident of our life. We protect another's anonymity by not repeating what is said in ACA meetings. We don't identify who attends ACA meetings when we are outside the meetings.

HB

There are times when ACA members must use their full names. When a member is doing service involving banking or legal contracts and liabilities as part of his or her group or Intergroup, the person may need to use the first and last name and include contact information. Trusted Servants on service boards where governmental jurisdiction is required for members to assemble legally are often required to supply their personal information (full name, address, phone, etc.) in writing, and this information must be made available on demand to any member of the organization who requests it.

Meetings or service boards need to have the names, residence addresses, and phone numbers of anyone empowered to handle their money or incur group debt. This helps the group and fellowship recover funds that might be taken dishonestly. There are also occasional stories of debts incurred by trustees of the group. When asked why this information was not taken, the response is too often, "We didn't want to ask the person to break his anonymity." Anonymity is a necessary convention of recovery; it does not absolve the group from taking responsible precautions in matters of program business.

Autonomy

Each ACA meeting is autonomous in keeping with Tradition Four. Autonomy means each group is free to conduct its own business as long as the group works within the parameters of the ACA Twelve Steps and Twelve Traditions and has no other affiliation with an outside entity. Autonomy does not mean that an ACA group is isolated and beyond the scope of the fellowship at large. We do not use autonomy to justify changing ACA or its message to fit our own personal desires.

Autonomy does not give a meeting the right to give up the precepts of the Steps or the Traditions. ACA groups are autonomous as long as the group's behavior does not affect ACA as a whole. ACA groups attempt to present a comprehensive

HB

and consistent ACA message. That message includes five basic components. The components are a dedication to The Problem, The Solution, and Sponsorship, in addition to the Twelve Steps and Twelve Traditions.

Autonomy gives an ACA meeting the opportunity to develop its own personality while offering a message of identity and hope. Autonomy allows us to make prudent, sober, and adult decisions about matters affecting our program and our recovery.

ACA Group Funds – Seventh Tradition

Every meeting should have a trusted servant, a treasurer, to maintain a record of all income received by the meeting and keep all receipts for disbursements by the meeting. The group treasurer should make a monthly report to the group and calculate the amount of the Seventh Tradition donations being sent to their Intergroup and the World Service Organization. This is sent monthly or quarterly.

The fund flow model of ACA is based on a 60/40 disbursement. After the group meets its monthly expenses and sets aside money for a prudent reserve, 60 percent of what is left over is usually sent to the local Intergroup and 40 percent is sent to WSO. A prudent reserve usually is the amount that equals two month's worth of meeting expenses. The meeting expenses would include rent, utilities, and other group expenses.

The most effective and efficient way to protect the finances of a meeting is to have a bank checking account that requires two signatures on each check.

Accountability

Accountability and responsibility go together in ACA. A group's financial report should be on hand and current. This is the treasurer's responsibility. Some group treasurers or secretaries offer a monthly report. This is recommended. Most ACA groups handle their funds with good conduct; however, there have been isolated events of stolen or "lost" money. Requiring a monthly report is one way of keeping track of fellowship funds.

HB

Some ACA meetings have established simple guidelines for financial protection. It is a sound procedure, when selecting a trusted servant, to ask for the person's full name, address, and telephone number. It is advisable to make every effort to contact the trusted servant responsible for the treasury if he or she has not attended two consecutive business meetings. We do not overreact and wrongly accuse someone of improper conduct; however, we are mindful of the group treasury and the need to protect fellowship funds.

Guidelines should be established for handling meeting funds when the treasurer is unable to attend meetings regularly. At the minimum, the treasurer must attend business meetings regularly and should attend regular ACA meetings. Groups need a treasurer who is active and who is available to keep the members updated on group funds.

Seventh Tradition funds are every member's responsibility. When ACA funds have been mishandled, ACA groups have taken a variety of actions that show our fellowship maturity and common sense. All efforts should be made to obtain the return of the funds. The treasurer or person responsible for the missing money should be contacted and asked to give back the money. If the person is willing, he may admit his behavior and ask to be allowed to pay the money back. In this case, the group sets up a simple but clear method of repaying the money. This method usually works best with lesser sums of money. It must be made clear that the person must be responsible and follow through on returning the money in a timely manner without delays or excuses. All such decisions are usually handled at a group conscience where financial records and statements can be looked over to determine the facts of the matter.

In matters of larger sums of money being stolen or group checks being written for personal use, the group must decide on whether to seek legal action or to allow the person to pay back the money. A group conscience should be taken to determine the best course or action. We must consider all the facts. We balance our decision to protect group funds with

HB

our compassion for the errant ACA member, who may be suffering from failing to work an ACA program. We can balance giving a member a second chance with our responsibility to recover lost or stolen funds.

It is rare that the local law enforcement authorities are contacted or that other legal action is pursued, but these are options for consideration.

Service Structure Support

The Ninth Tradition states, "ACA, as such, ought never be organized, but we may create service boards or committees directly responsible to those they serve." The ACA meetings have created Intergroups, Regions, and the World Service Organization to help carry the message with consistency and compassion to those not yet aware of our program. The support and manpower for the ACA service structure comes from the ACA groups. We cannot effectively carry the message without group guidance or without group volunteers.

The service boards and committees serve the groups. The groups have final authority over the service structure; however, the groups trust their trusted servants to do the good work of ACA without strapping them with weighty rules and regulations.

Literature in Meetings

Contact ACA WSO for the current list of ACA books, booklets, and trifolds. Some of ACA's literature has been standardized and accepted at the Annual Business Conferences. Responding to fellowship requests, WSO is in the process of publishing literature to provide a source of unity and consistency of the ACA message. ACA WSO approved literature carries the ACA logo and copyright. Literature developed by committees using a group conscience process may be submitted to the WSO Literature Committee for review and possible consideration for publication.

HB

Selection of Non-Program Literature

ACA members may use various books and literature in their meetings as long as the material meets the requirements of the ACA literature policy. Typically, literature used in ACA meetings should adhere to the Twelve Steps and Twelve Traditions and not be in contradiction with The Laundry List (Problem), The Solution, and Sponsorship. The non-ACA literature also should not promote an atmosphere of therapy in the meeting or promote a given author. Each group is asked to be extremely careful in selecting outside materials. For guidance on selecting literature, ask the following questions:

- Tradition 1: Does the outside literature support the growth of ACA and promote unity and continuity of our message?

- Tradition 4: Will the decision to use such material affect other groups in the local area or our fellowship as a whole?

- Tradition 5: Would the decision of the group to use an outside book or writing identify the group in a different way and define our recovery outside the Twelve Steps? Would we lose the focus of our primary purpose of carrying a clear ACA message?

- Tradition 6: Is the use of outside literature an endorsement of a particular author? Would the meeting be a "book study" that would make the work of a particular author the focus of the meeting rather than an ACA recovery meeting?

- Tradition 8: Does using such literature border on, or move the meeting toward, a therapy session and away from the Twelve Step recovery program?

- Tradition 10: Would such use violate any copyrights of others?

HB

After considering these questions, each meeting ought to announce that the literature is not approved or endorsed by the ACA fellowship. Each group needs to evaluate what effect the use of outside literature might have on the newcomer seeking recovery in ACA.

Outside Literature and Meeting Announcements

Meeting material which is not ACA WSO approved should be kept separate from ACA books, flyers, and other meeting material. It is suggested that the materials relating to outside facilities, publishers, treatment centers, or other enterprises be posted separately from Twelve Step recovery materials. During the ACA meeting, members should not announce outside activities that include therapist work, recovery events, workshops, and other activities that are not part of the ACA fellowship.

Carrying the Message

Attraction versus Promotion

Ours is a program of attraction, not promotion. There is a difference between making information available and promoting the program.

Attraction means we put information out where individuals seeking it have possible access to it. This may include flyers, brochures, booklets, audio or video presentations, speakers, panels of speakers, web pages, and information booths. The tone of these activities must remain close to supplying information instead of being promotional.

We are not limited to supplying ACA information at Twelve Step events. Meeting directories and literature may be dropped off or sent to schools, medical facilities, therapists' offices, libraries, and any other institution or hospital willing to accept it. We ask for permission before placing meetings flyers or leaving ACA material at these places.

HB

Promotion is different than giving out information about an ACA meeting or event. Promotion involves making promises of results. It has the tone of a sales pitch or a guarantee that cannot be delivered. While miracles and astounding recovery occur in ACA, we don't make promises or grand speeches about ACA in public or at ACA meetings. We can only say how ACA has improved our own lives. We can only extend an invitation to attend a meeting.

Hospitals and Institutions Meeting or Prison Meeting

The disease of family dysfunction is a progressive disease that forces some adult children to seek help in a treatment setting or psychiatric hospital. Other adult children are sentenced to prison for crimes they have committed while acting out with addiction or codependence. These adult children often form an ACA meeting in their facility. ACA members from the outside attend the meetings, carrying the message to the adult child wherever and whenever they are asked.

Adult children in these facilities are grateful for the outside support. Many attend ACA meetings once they are released. They become group members, carrying the message of hope that was carried to them.

It is recommended that ACA members carrying the message into one of these facilities have a clear understanding of the ACA program. The suggestions for how to share or talk in an ACA meeting apply here as well. We identify as an adult child and explain our recovery and the ACA program with clarity and honesty. Please read the segment on sharing in an ACA meeting.

We also abide by all facility rules and guidelines. We do not fraternize with adult children in these settings. We are there to carry the ACA message of recovery.

For prison meetings, we do not give out our contact information, pass notes or letters for inmates, or correspond with an inmate.

We do not become romantically involved with adult children in these settings; we maintain our focus on Step work or other ACA recovery work.

If we will honor these guidelines and practice the principles of the program, we will help ourselves and the adult child within these facilities. We will be living the Twelfth Step.

Twelve Concepts for ACA World Service

The Twelve Concepts keep our world services and groups focused on carrying a consistent ACA message while maintaining a service structure responsible to the fellowship voice. The Concepts help trusted servants discern the will of ACA and carry out the responsibilities granted by the fellowship. We bring humility and gratitude to this fellowship work. At times, we act on behalf of the fellowship, knowing our duties are on loan from the fellowship as a whole.

Ultimately, service work demands that we relinquish our individual will and accept God's will to do God's work. The Concepts make it possible for us to operate most efficiently and effectively while we strive to achieve a more perfect union with our Higher Power.

Concept I

The final responsibility and the ultimate authority for ACA World Services should always reside in the collective conscience of our whole fellowship.

Concept II

Authority for the active maintenance of our world services is hereby delegated to the actual voice, the effective conscience for our whole fellowship.

HB

(The Twelve Concepts are adapted from the Twelve Concepts of Alcoholics Anonymous)

Handbook For Adult Children

Concept III

As a means of creating and maintaining a clearly defined working relationship between the ACA meetings, the ACA WSO Board of Trustees, and its staff and committees, and thus ensuring their effective leadership, it is herein suggested that we endow each of these elements of service with the traditional Right of Decision.[3]

Concept IV

Throughout our structure, we maintain at all responsible levels a traditional Right of Participation.

Concept V

Throughout our structure, a Right of Petition prevails, thus assuring us that minority opinion will be heard and that petitions for the redress of grievances will be carefully considered.

Concept VI

On behalf of ACA as a whole, our Annual Business Conference has the principal responsibility for the maintenance of our world services, and it traditionally has the final decision respecting large matters of general policy and finance. But the Annual Business Conference also recognizes that the chief initiative and the active responsibility in most of these matters would be exercised primarily by the Trustee members of the World Service

HB

[3]The right of decision as defined herein refers to:

1) the right and responsibility of each trusted servant to speak and vote his/her own conscience, in the absence of any contrary mandate, on any issue regardless of the level of service;

2) the 12 Steps, 12 Traditions, and the Commitment to Service will be followed by trusted servants in decision making;

3) delegates to the Annual Business Conference are trusted servants and therefore equally guided by the 12 Steps, 12 Traditions, 12 Concepts, and the Commitment to Service;

4) standard practice that decisions made by subcommittees are subject to the authority of the service body which creates its mission and defines its parameters.

Organization when they act among themselves as the World Service Organization of Adult Children of Alcoholics.

Concept VII

The Annual Business Conference recognizes that the Articles of Incorporation and the Bylaws of the Adult Children of Alcoholics World Service Organization are legal instruments: that the Trustees are thereby fully empowered to manage and conduct all of the world service affairs of Adult Children of Alcoholics. It is further understood that our World Service Organization relies upon the force of tradition and the power of the ACA purse for its final effectiveness.

Concept VIII

The Trustees of the World Service Organization act in this primary capacity: with respect to the larger matters of over-all policy and finance, they are the principal planners and administrators. They and their primary committees directly manage these affairs.

Concept IX

Good service leaders, together with sound and appropriate methods of choosing them, are, at all levels, indispensable for our future functioning and safety. The primary world service leadership must necessarily be assumed by the Trustees of the Adult Children of Alcoholics World Service Organization.

Concept X

Every service responsibility should be matched by an equal service authority – the scope of such authority to be always well defined whether by tradition, by resolution, by specific job description, or by the Operating Policy and Procedures Manual and bylaws.

Concept XI

While the Trustees hold final responsibility for ACA's World Service administration, they should always have the assistance of the best possible standing committees, corporate trustees, executives, staffs, and consultants. Therefore the composition of these underlying committees and service boards, the personal qualifications of their members, the manner of their induction into service, the systems of their rotation, the way in which they are related to each other, the special rights and duties of our executives, staffs and consultants, together with a proper basis for the financial compensation of these special workers, will always be matters for serious care and concern.

Concept XII

In all its proceedings, Adult Children of Alcoholics World Service Organization shall observe the spirit of the ACA Twelve Traditions, taking great care that the conference never becomes the seat of perilous wealth or power; that sufficient operating funds, plus an ample reserve, be its prudent financial principle; that none of the Conference members shall ever be placed in a position of unqualified authority over any of the others; that all important decisions be reached by discussion vote and whenever possible, by substantial unanimity; that no WSO action ever be personally punitive or an incitement to public controversy; that though the WSO may act for the service of Adult Children of Alcoholics, it shall never perform any acts of government; and that, like the fellowship of Adult Children of Alcoholics which it serves, the WSO itself will always remain democratic in thought and action.

ACA World Service Organization

Adult Children of Alcoholics World Service Organization, Inc. (ACA WSO) is an organization of volunteer members elected to serve in the capacity of corporate trustees according to the laws of the State of California, U.S.A.

WSO provides a sense of common purpose, stability, and continuity for meetings, Intergroups, and Regions. By serving as a central point of group communication, the WSO encourages unity and similarity among ACA meetings. ACA WSO coordinates meeting information worldwide. It is one place where ACA groups and the general public can find information, literature, and locations of meetings.

The mission, the singleness of purpose, of WSO is to carry the message of recovery to all who suffer from being raised in an alcoholic or other dysfunctional environment.

ACA WSO maintains a telephone line, postal address, Internet website, and e-mail addresses as a stable communication base for the ACA program. ACA WSO committees prepare the literature for conference approval, prepare the *ComLine* newsletter, coordinate group outreach, and provide public information.

The ACA WSO Board of Trustees oversees WSO and its operations. The Board is made up of board members from ACA Regions, Intergroups, and meetings. The ACA trustees hold a monthly teleconference to conduct ACA business during the conference year. To listen in on the teleconference, one needs an access number that is available by contacting WSO or by locating that number on the WSO website. The ACA WSO Board of Trustees holds one in-person meeting a year. The trustees meet at the Annual Business Conference.

HB

Annual Business Conference

The ACA Annual Business Conference is held in April and is attended by Group Service Representatives and Intergroup Representatives discussing and voting on fellowship business.

That business can include literature development, public information practices, hospitals and institutions meetings, or other topics. The ACA WSO Board of Trustees hosts the annual meeting.

HB

Appendix A

Looking Back to Look Forward: ACA in the 21st Century

Using the Steps and the Traditions to Recover From Domestic Trauma

A Supplement to the ACA Identity Papers

This paper looks at the tripartite dysfunction/recovery model developed by the ACA Handbook Committee (body/mind/spirit) and offers some suggestions for organizing and arranging the important ideas and processes the committee has addressed as guides to achieving a fuller, more complete recovery. We also look back and see that the model is consistent with recovery concepts generated early in the program.

As ACA moves into the new millennium and we attempt to integrate into our program the vast amount of personal experiences, clinical research and written material about Adult Children and dysfunctional families, we think it's important to keep in mind a modification of KIS to KISC, Keep It Simple Conceptually. That is why we suggest adopting Bill W.'s notion of emotional sobriety/intoxication as a foundation, a guide, and a destination for recovery.

Recovery looks like something. It can be envisioned and eventually achieved. This appears to be a basic difference between ACA and other programs. While ACA uses the term disease to describe the cause and consequences of trauma, as The Problem states, it's a process of conditioning, or learned behavior. What can be learned can be unlearned even though reversing learned

Appendix A

helplessness and neophobia, the effects of developmental trauma, is an exacting process. Emotional sobriety, primary ontological security (Laing, 1965), openness to experience (Rogers, 1961), internal locus of control (Rotter, 1982), autonomy (Milgram, 1974), non-conformity (Asch, 1955), and phenomenological field independence (Witkin, 1965) are ways to describe being spiritually awake and happy, joyous, and free. They are, as well, ways to describe the manifestation of two therapeutic ideals: no excess tension in the body and a neutral reaction to symbolic associations and mental representations of trauma. Using the Steps and the Traditions to reach these ideals, to face and complete the past, is a full remembrance approach to recovery, and is Proustian in nature. The goal is to reach a place where the madeleines of trauma and the imagos of internal addiction no longer carry a sting. This would be a fulfillment of the second Promise: "We will not regret the past nor wish to shut the door on it."

When children struggle to control the devastating effects of domestic trauma, to avoid or at least minimize the damage, they are injured in three critical ways. First, they are corporeally compromised; the evidence of mechanical damage that comes from going 90 mph with the brake on, as described by Marge Toomim, is obvious and easily measured (Smith, 2005). This antagonism in the nervous system, the simultaneous impulse to stop and go, indicates the excruciating paralysis children experience when they are caught in a double-bind in an unsafe environment, unable to decide when and where to move or not move in order to protect themselves and be safe. Secondly, they are mentally fragmented. Associated symbolic fragments – phobias, obsessions, nightmares, fantasies, and taboos (the permission problems all Adult Children face, Claudia Black's three "don'ts" [1982] and the over-arching injunction, "don't remember") – are used to regulate the doses from the pharmacy inside (see the second Identity Paper's section on dissociation). They are an integral component of the corporeal regulation process, controlling the energy that

A

maintains the shaky balance between braking and accelerating an already dysregulated system. Too much brake and you risk rupturing the system and losing the prime (shock); too much accelerator and you risk having a stroke. Internal dosing, approaching and avoiding other people, and exogenous substances are all employed to keep the trauma-adjusted system limping along, an adjustment made to withstand the disintegrative forces first encountered in the home. It is a continuation of a sad and futile attempt to manage and correct the family dysfunction. Finally, children are spiritually dejected by their inability to manage the disintegrating family system and the constant threat to personal integrity. They are spiritually crushed and sometimes broken by the attitude and reality of the abuse they endure. They are reduced to what the AA Big Book calls a state of "pitiful and incomprehensible demoralization." This is the level of injury that has to be acknowledged and healed.

Pushing down and holding back the history of a lifetime of injury and hurt from consciousness is painful, not metaphorically or psychically painful, but physically agonizing. It's a matter of blood, tissue, nerves and bone. Bringing the history into consciousness is an exacting task because the symbolic representations of the initially unendurable experiences are used to dose and maintain the process of protective dissociation. There is considerable resistance to change.

Paradoxically, the solution is to concentrate on de-stressing the machine, to soothe and heal the pain-wracked body with all that that means psychologically and spiritually.

Hans Selye (1980), in an update of his general adaptation syndrome, wrote that the alarm stage could be divided into two phases: the shock phase and the countershock phase. In the shock phase, which he does not distinguish from the initial trauma phase, he lists the various signs of injury: "tachycardia, loss of muscle tone, decreased temperature, and decreased blood pressure." (p. 129) This is followed by the countershock phase which is "a rebound reaction marked by the mobilization of

[the] defensive phase." He adds that "most of the acute stress diseases correspond to these two phases of the alarm reaction." (p. 129) In the resistance stage that comes after the alarm reaction, there is a "full adaptation to the stressor" with "an improvement or disappearance of symptoms" and "a concurrent decrease in resistance to most other stimuli." (p. 129) This is a great description of dissociative denial and mirrors Marge Toomim's findings about paradoxical flattening (Toomim & Toomim, 1975). Exhaustion, collapse and death follow if the stress continues unabated.

Wayne Kritsberg (1985) uses a modified trauma, shock, rebound version of Selye's model to explain the ACA syndrome. He offers an insightful analysis although he does not specifically define the terms trauma, shock and resistance. In an early paper on post-traumatic stress and the loss of ontological security (Smith, 1987), trauma was defined as the maximal arousal of the sympathetic nervous system by pain or the threat of pain. A child's fight or flight response can go no higher. This definition allows the event of trauma to be tabulated, at least in theory, as it is in a lab experiment or ethological field study, whenever and wherever it occurs, in and outside the home, over days, weeks and years, and permits an exact calculation of when resistance and denial set in. Likewise, shock is defined in a way that is consistent with the medical definition – inadequate tissue perfusion to the brain. With both injury and the system-wide vaso-dilation that comes with emotional overload, the blood literally drains out of the brain. The conscious control of behavior is severely undermined or becomes impossible with a complete loss of consciousness.

R. D. Laing (1965) describes the loss of ontological security as beginning with a partial loss of relatedness to the synthetic self and other people, and ending with a descent into chaotic non-entity, or a total loss of connection to self and others. This psycho-philosophical description of the loss of fundamental security parallels a psycho-physiological description of traumatized people dropping into shock or going unconscious. It is not difficult to understand that if a system is pushed hard enough and long enough, or hard enough all at once, it will break or break down. This is particularly true for the delicate system of a child. Shifting the concept of losing basic security to a psycho-physical foundation (trauma and shock) provides a clear picture of the difference between pre- and post-trauma living. It also makes it possible to develop a measurable, biologically-based treatment methodology for restoring ontological security.

In "The Laundry List" (1991) Tony A. wrote:

> Recovery is a complex process. We cannot return to childhood and ask our parents to love us in the way we needed to be loved. It just can't be done. As ACoAs we need to learn how to nurture and fulfill ourselves. We need to look within, find the origins of our feelings and come to understand our difficulties and the role we play in causing them.
>
> This is all possible within the framework of the ACoA program. Those of us who have lived through the nightmare of family alcoholism need a safe and secure environment where we can unburden ourselves, be brought closer to our painful childhood feelings and learn that we are not alone in our struggle. As ACoAs *we have paid a tremendous price to reach this point of recovery.* (emphasis added, p. xvi)

Nevertheless, Tony says, "the recovery process works." (p. xvi) He cautioned, however, that at the time, a major difficulty in ACoA was a "limited grasp of the...process" which he sought to address.

Writing in the AA Big Book, Bill W., in the beginning of "A Vision for You" said, "As we became subjects of King Alcohol... the chilling vapor that is loneliness settled down" and if we continue to seek solace in drinking we awaken "to face the hideous Four Horsemen – Terror, Bewilderment, Frustration, Despair." (p. 151) He then wrote, however, that "[t]he age of miracles is still with us." (p. 153)

His second vision for AA, the next frontier of emotional sobriety, can now be the miracle of recovery for survivors of developmental trauma. Bill concluded "A Vision for You" by noting "we know only a little" and the answer to the question of what to do for those who still suffer will come only when "our own house is in order." (p. 164) We can't transmit what we don't have. What could not be transmitted at that time, because it was unknown, was how to use the Twelve Steps to recover from trauma.

Tony's recognition of the high price of recovery thus far in ACA points out how difficult it has been to push through the social and personal denial concerning family-generated PTSD (post-traumatic stress disorder). His faith that the recovery process works also points out that many people, starting with Bill and Dr. Bob, have put their house in order and opened themselves to the leading of a loving Higher Power. We now have gathered the knowledge and experience needed to transmit a vision for healing the injury and hurt caused by childhood trauma. As Bill recognized, if our relationship with God is right, then "great events will come to pass for [us] and countless others. This is the Great Fact for us." (p. 164)

In the coming years our experience with the re-integrative process described in this outline, first envisioned by Bill, Tony and Jack E. (author of The Problem), will show us more clearly how the Steps and Traditions can be broadened and deepened to restore wholeness in Adult Children.[1] The belief that we can be restored to or gain sanity which we are given in Step Two and the materialization of the Twelve Promises that occurs when we begin to make amends and set things right with ourselves and other people in the Ninth Step, are tremendous incentives for taking the Steps. Sharing our personal stories and experience of recovery with one another, and letting other Adult Children

[1] Bill, in a letter to friend, wrote about deepening AA's moral inventory to focus on what he called psychic damage: "...it may be that someday we shall devise some common denominator of psychiatry – of course, throwing away their much abused terminology – common denominators which neurotics could use on each other. The idea would be to extend the moral inventory of AA to a deeper level, making it an inventory of psychic damages, reliving in conversation episodes, etc. I suppose someday a Neurotics Anonymous will be formed and will actually do all this." He later suggests the inventory be about "actual episodes: inferiority, shame, guilt, anger" so they could be relived in the mind and their power reduced. The true, non-neurotic self could then emerge out of hiding. (Letters with commentary reprinted in Fitzgerald, R. (1995), The Soul of Sponsorship, Hazelden, Center City, MN, pp. 41–42.)

know that the pain and blurring of reality which come from constantly contending with insanity can end, and that it's possible to be spiritually awake, psychologically integrated, physically healed and ontologically secure, could galvanize the Program and give hope to countless Adult Children who still suffer.

Laura Russell (1984), Timmen Cermak (1985), and the first Identity Paper drew the link between ACAs and post-combat trauma reactions. However, it was the Tenth Characteristic of the Laundry List that focused on the traumatic nature of our childhoods and the post-childhood torment the trauma creates.

Michael Seabaugh, in his wonderful dissertation "The Vulnerable Self of the Adult Child of an Alcoholic" (1983), listed fourteen themes of vulnerability: 1) conflict over meeting the needs of another, 2) vulnerability to narcissistic injury, 3) emotional distress over the exposure of one's vulnerable self, 4) vulnerability to the powerfulness of another, 5) vulnerability to abandonment, 6) vulnerability to another's anger, 7) protection of the vulnerable self by withdrawal, 8) protection of the vulnerable self by withholding of difficult feelings, 9), protection of the vulnerable self by pleasing others, 10) protection of the vulnerable self through acts of aggression, 11) protection of the vulnerable self by willful control of the expansive self, 12) protection of the vulnerable self by controlling others, 13) protection of the vulnerable self by being "heroic," 14) protection of the vulnerable self by cognitively transforming reality.

Themes 1, 2 and 3 explain the nature and origin of the vulnerable self; themes 4, 5, and 6 examine how the vulnerable self is expressed in interpersonal relationships; themes 7, 8, 11, and 14 focus on how Adult Children protect themselves by re-directing energy back against themselves, while 10, 12, 9, and 13 look at how they protect themselves through acts of aggression and placation. Solving these problems and repairing the wear and tear caused by the stress and strain of resistance are the tasks that are the nuts and bolts of recovery. And even though

A

solving these tasks is crucial, what is paramount is remaining safely within the protective framework and comforting shelter of the Steps and Traditions.

The first Identity Paper focused on the hopelessness and despair that come with the futile effort to save the family and, by extension, save the self. The second Identity Paper emphasized the necessity for a complete internal separation, psychologically, emotionally and spiritually, from a sick family system. In this case there is no such thing as being a little intoxicated, a little bit drunk. The third Identity Paper examined the steep cost of surviving by hiding the vulnerable and wounded child in a prison of isolation, the high price of using the myriad methods we employ to protect the vulnerable self by staying emotionally intoxicated and numb.

In his "Next Frontier" article Bill wrote, "If we examine every disturbance we have, great or small, we will find at the root of it some unhealthy dependency and its consequent unhealthy demand. Let us, with God's help, continually surrender these hobbling demands. Then we can be set free to live and love; we may then be able to Twelfth Step ourselves and others into emotional sobriety." (p. 5) This certainly seems clear enough. We now need to see what this means in real-time, day-to-day terms.

A long-time member of our program, when she was new in recovery, said she felt liberated when her sponsor told her she "could walk away from crazy." This is a great message, one the Handbook can carry to the fellowship. It's important to remember, however, that not only can we walk away from crazy, we can walk toward sanity at the same time.

A

This paper grew out of conversations and correspondence between the chairperson of the ACA Handbook Committee, and Marty S. of the Identity Committee, about the future of ACA.

References

A., Tony & F., Dan (1991). The Laundry List. Pompano Beach, FL: Health Communications, Inc

Alcoholics Anonymous, Third Edition (1976). New York: AAWS

Asch, S. E. (1955). Opinions and Social Pressure. *Sci Am*, 193, 31–35

Black, C. (1982). It Will Never Happen To Me. Bainbridge Island, WA: M.A.C. Publishing

Cermak, T. (1985). A Primer on Adult Children of Alcoholics. Pompano Beach, FL: Health Communications, Inc

Identity Papers (1996). Torrance, CA: Adult Children of Alcoholics WSO

Kritsberg, W. (1985). The Adult Children of Alcoholics Syndrome. Deerfield Beach, FL: Health Communications, Inc

Laing, R. D. (1965). The Divided Self. Middlesex, UK: Penguin

Milgram, S. (1974). Obedience to Authority. New York: Harper & Row

Rogers, C. R. (1961). On Becoming a Person. Boston: Houghton Mifflin

Rotter, J. B. (1982). Generalized expectancies for internal versus external locus of control of reinforcement, in C. D. Spielberger, gen. ed., The Development and Applications of Social Learning Theory. New York: Praeger

Russell, L. (1984). Alcoholism and Child Abuse. Rutherford, NJ: Thomas W. Perrin, Inc

Seabaugh, M. O. L. (1983). The Vulnerable Self of The Adult Child of an Alcoholic: A Phenomenologically Derived Theory. Doctoral dissertation, USC

Selye, H. (1980). The Stress Concept Today, in I. Kutash and L. B. Schlesinger, eds., Handbook on Stress and Anxiety. San Francisco: Jossey–Bass

A

Smith, M. R. (1987). Post-Traumatic Stress and the Loss of Ontological Security: overcoming trauma-induced neophobia in adult children of alcoholics, in B. G. Braun, ed., *Proceedings of the Fourth International Conference on Multiple Personality/Dissociative States*, Chicago

Smith, M. R. (2005). Marjorie Toomim: A Remembrance. Biofeedback, 33 (2), 77–78

Toomim, M. & Toomim, H. (1975). GSR biofeedback in psychotherapy: some clinical observations. *Psychotherapy: Theory, Research and Practice*, 12 (1), 33–38

W., Bill (1958, January). The Next Frontier – Emotional Sobriety. *AA Grapevine*, 2–5

Witkin, H. A. (1965). Psychological differentiation and forms of pathology. *Journal of Abnormal Psychology*, 70 (5), 317–336.

A

Appendix B
Hearing a Fifth Step

"Admitted to God, to ourselves, and to another human being the exact nature of our wrongs."

$\mathcal{H}$earing or listening to another person's Fifth Step is an ultimate act of service coming from love. To hear a person's story, you should have completed your own Fifth Step and the remaining Twelve Steps. You should be working an active ACA program by attending meetings and changing your behavior in workable relationships.

The following guidelines are one method of listening to a Fifth Step given by an ACA member. These guidelines are consistent with the Fellow Traveler method of sponsorship. This guide is designed to match the exercises in the ACA basic text. In addition to offering tips on hearing a Fifth Step, this guide will help you assist the person with Steps Six through Eight as well.

This guide is designed for a sponsor and sponsee working the Twelve Steps of ACA. Typically, the Fifth Step is heard by the sponsor of the sponsee working the Steps. However, there are others who can hear a Fifth Step. These people can include counselors, spiritual advisors, and members of other Twelve Step fellowships. A person should not ask a spouse, parents, relatives, friends, or old lovers to hear his or her Fifth Step.

Appendix B

The person hearing the Fifth Step should have an understanding of the design and focus of the Twelve Steps of ACA. While ACA is similar to other Twelve Step fellowships, we have expanded the Fourth Step to include an inventory of the family system in addition to an inventory of one's self. That means ACA looks at the effects of parental behavior and some sibling behavior in addition to the behavior of the individual. The sponsee needs a listener who understands what he or she is trying to accomplish with the ACA Steps.

Step Five represents the courage of an individual to admit the exact nature of his or her wrongs without embellishing or minimizing the events. The person is telling his or her story to another person and to God. In Step Five, the ACA member trusts another to hear his or her life story without judgment. For many, this is the first time the adult child has told the most intimate details of his or her life to another. Trust of another person is one of the spiritual principles of Step Five. There is also the principle of self-honesty.

Your sponsee should have worked Steps One through Four before beginning Step Five. Ideally, you and the sponsee should work the first four Steps together. Chapter Seven is designed to help an ACA member work all of the Steps with a sponsor or counselor. The chapter is an excellent Twelve Step guide for these purposes. There are no timelines on completing the first four Steps of ACA, but usually a person should be making progress in finishing Steps One through Four within the first year of recovery. Some members will complete these Steps more quickly while others will take longer. There should be no rush to complete these early Steps; however, we should not procrastinate with the Steps.

B

Hearing Someone's Fifth Step Involves Three Basic Elements:

1. Understanding the sequence of the Steps and what the person is trying to achieve by working Steps Four and Five.

2. Listening with empathy and without judging the person.

3. Helping the person move onto Steps Six, Seven, and Eight, and the rest of the Steps after Step Five.

No. 1 – Understanding the sequence of the Steps and what the person is trying to achieve by working Steps Four and Five.

There is a specific sequence of the Twelve Steps that begins with the person hitting a bottom, asking for help, and admitting denial. The person doing his or her Fifth Step should have admitted powerlessness over the effects of family dysfunction in Step One followed by an equal admission of unmanageability. There should be a willingness to seek spiritual solutions in Step Two and Step Three. In Step Four and Step Five, there should be self-honesty and a willingness to speak openly with another person about one's life. These are the undercurrent of attitudes that we listen for as we listen to the main details of someone's Fifth Step.

The result the sponsee is trying to achieve in Step Four involves a searching and fearless inventory of himself or herself. The sponsee is exposing secrets, abuse, and false loyalty to a dysfunctional family system. The person is seeking clarity and a fair look at parental behavior that affected him or her as a child and continues to affect the person as an adult. The sponsee is also addressing his or her own selfish or harmful behavior.

As you listen to a Fifth Step, you should not overly identify with the victim or victimizer aspect of the sponsee. Most adult children have been victims, and they have victimized others.

B

As a listener you seek neutrality. In Step Five, we avoid the urge to rescue the sponsee as he or she relates some of the harrowing events of childhood. We can feel empathy and compassion for the sponsee while maintaining our neutrality.

In Step Five, we encourage our sponsee to tell everything, holding back nothing, so that the person can be free of secrets and carried shame. As the Fifth Step progresses, we may briefly share some of our own story to create identification, but we do not dominate the time. The Fifth Step is for the sponsee to talk and to share his or her story.

No. 2 – Listening with empathy and without judging the person.

Most adult children have never been listened to, so listening to another adult child without judgment is possibly one of the greatest gifts we can give another person. Listening with empathy adds spirituality to the gift.

At the same time, listening with empathy does not mean that we suspend our duty to point out problematic behavior. We can gently highlight where a person has wronged others. We can help the sponsee see the exact nature of the wrong. As a sponsor, we can listen to others without judgement but still offer our experience on where amends should be made. We can point out problematic behavior that could be inventoried in the future. We do not do this during the Fifth Step. We wait until the Fifth Step is done. At the end of Step Five, we offer the person a balanced assessment of his or her strong points and points that can be improved.

As the person shares his or her Fifth Step, we listen to the story with complete attention. We also listen for clues that the person has admitted powerlessness over the effects of family dysfunction in Step One. For example, do we hear the person still holding onto notions that he or she can control outcomes? Or is the person truly seeking to let go and focus on himself or herself? Is the person being honest? Is the person seeking help from a Higher Power?

No. 3 – Helping the person move onto Steps Six, Seven, and Eight, and the rest of the Steps after Step Five.

To hear a Fifth Step you will need a pen and paper and a quiet, comfortable place. On the day of the Fifth Step, the sponsee should arrive with numerous lists and worksheets from the Fourth Step guide in this book. The ACA Fourth Step contains 12 exercises. The lists need to be complete enough to present a searching and fearless inventory of the person's life. Listen to all the lists. Information about character defects and making amends will typically come from exercises No. 5, No. 7, and No. 9. Exercise No. 12 has a list of positive traits that will help you balance the problematic behaviors.

1. Inventory of Laundry List Traits (How traits developed)

2. Family Secrets

3. Shame List

4. Abandonment List

5. Harms Inventory

6. Stored Anger (Resentment)

7. Relationships (Romance, sexual, or friendships)

8. Sexual Abuse Inventory

9. Denial Inventory (Parent's behavior; Sponsee's behavior)

10. Post-Traumatic Stress Disorder worksheet

11. Feelings Exercise

12. Praise Work

B

These exercises represent a comprehensive Fourth Step that includes an inventory of the dysfunctional family system in addition to an inventory of the sponsee.

To begin, you should allow plenty of time for the Fifth Step to be completed. Before the Fifth Step begins, you may tell the sponsee that you will listen to him or her without judgment. You may also assure the person that you will treat his or her story with confidentiality. Everything that is said during the Fifth Step will remain between you and the sponsee. You can tell the sponsee that you will take brief notes while he or she talks. The notes will be used to help create a Sixth Step List and Eighth Step Amends List when Step Five is done. (Do not take a lot of notes since this can be distracting as the person talks out his or her Fifth Step.) Keep it simple.

Sixth Step List (defects of character)

On a piece of paper, before the Fifth Step begins, write "Sixth Step List" at the top of the page. Then write "assets" on the left-hand side of the page. On the right-hand side, write "defects of character" or "ineffectual behaviors." As the sponsee talks during the Fifth Step, write down positive behaviors and problematic behaviors that could be addressed by attending meetings, journaling, prayer, and further Step work. Helping a sponsee identify his or her character defects based on your own experience with the Steps, is well within the Fellow Traveler method of sponsorship. Think about your own Step work and how you addressed assets and defects of character. Help the sponsee identify his or her attributes as well. Most adult children can identify negative thoughts and behaviors but struggle with seeing their good traits. As a sponsor and fellow traveler, you can help the sponsee see positive qualities that the person possesses. You can simplify this list by limiting it to three or four examples.

For Example:
Sixth Step List

Assets:	Defects of Character or Ineffectual Behaviors:
Selflessness	Selfishness
Caring	Judgmental
Creative	Jealousy
Hard worker	Procrastinates

When the Fifth Step is done, you will use this list to help the person move on to Step Six and Step Seven (removal of defects of character). The key is to balance the behaviors. Each adult child has strong qualities and qualities that can be improved.

Eighth Step Amends List

Also, before the Fifth Step begins, use a separate piece of paper to create an Eighth Step Amends List. At the top of the page write "Eighth Step Amends List." As the sponsee talks, list names and incidents that should be addressed in Step Eight – "Made a list of all persons we had harmed and became willing to make amends to them all." Place the sponsee's name at the top of the list. We must make amends to ourselves and forgive ourselves before we can take action to do the same for others.

To keep it simple and to avoid distractions during the Fifth Step, just write down the name of the person who will receive an amends in the left-hand column. Fill in the "incident" and "amends type" after the Fifth Step is completed.

B

For Example:
Eighth Step Amends List

Name of Person receiving amends (fill in during Fifth Step)	Incident (fill in later)	Amends type (fill in later)

An Example of a Completed Eighth Step Amends List

Name	Incident	Amends
John (Sponsee)	self-hate, inner critic	learn to love myself
Sue	damaged her car in a fit of rage	pay to have car fixed
Mike	gossiped about him	stop gossiping
Father	cursed him in public	apologize for cursing him
Boss	stole from him	pay it back
My daughter	blamed her for my temper, my rage	living amends, ask for forgiveness

When the Fifth Step is done, you will use this list to help the person move onto Step Eight. You might set up time on another day to fill in the Step Eight list. In Step Eight we become willing to make amends. The actual amends are made in Step Nine. Have the sponsee read Step Eight in Chapter Seven for insight into willingness. Along with willingness, the key to making amends is making things right for harms we have done. Some amends are monetary amends in which we pay back money, while other amends are living amends in which we change our behavior one day at a time. Other amends can involve naming our behavior and asking for forgiveness from the person we have harmed. We usually say "I am making amends for my behavior and for harming you. It was wrong/selfish/hurtful (pick one or a combination of these). I am learning how to live differently. I am not making excuses for my behavior. I will try to not repeat my behavior. In the meantime, here is what I am doing to make it right."

We must back up this statement with program action such as attending meetings and helping others. We also change our behavior.

If there is a question about an amends, the weight of responsibility should lean toward the sponsee. We want to grow up, and that involves being responsible. We want to be free of harmful behavior that brings isolation and regret. Making amends with the support of ACA, even if the direction of harm is unsure, is better than living with open questions about the past. We make these amends and leave the results up to God, as we understand God.

Recap on Preparing to Hear a Fifth Step

1. Set a date to hear the Fifth Step.

2. Prepare for hearing the Fifth Step by reviewing the exercises in Step Four (Chapter Seven). These are the lists and worksheets the sponsee will be bringing to the Fifth Step.

3. On the day of the Fifth Step, before the sponsee arrives, get a notepad and make a Sixth Step List and Eighth Step List. Avoid taking a lot of notes during the Fifth Step, but take enough notes to sketch out character defects, positive traits, and individuals to receive an amends.

B

4.   When the sponsee arrives, explain that you will listen with empathy and fairness to the Fifth Step. Explain that Step Four and Step Five involve rigorous honesty and identifying the exact nature of his or her wrongs. Explain that you will help the sponsee identify positive traits and problematic traits as part of balancing the personal inventory and as part of preparing for Step Six and Step Seven.

5.   Begin Step Five.

6.   When the Fifth Step ends, review the Sixth Step List. Share your experience with identifying your own character defects and positive traits. Keep it simple when helping the sponsee do the same. Give three examples of positive traits and three examples of character defects that the sponsee possesses. This helps the sponsee avoid focusing only on defects, and he or she will not be overwhelmed by a lengthy list. (The list of character defects and positive traits at the end of these instructions will help you and the sponsee select items for the Sixth Step list.)

7.   Make plans to discuss the Eighth Step Amends List on another day.

8.   Instruct the sponsee to return home and read all of the section on Step Six in this book. He or she will find directions on how to proceed with Step Six and Step Seven in the reading. There will also be directions on integrating Laundry List traits.

B

For Use In Helping the Sponsee Determine Positive Traits and Defects of Character

Possible Defects of Character are:

Self-centeredness, judgmentalness, procrastination, perfectionism, envy, greed, lust, feeling superior, dishonesty, gossiping, and pettiness.

Positive Traits include:

strong	compassionate	spontaneous	trustworthy	prompt
humorous	courteous	creative	tenacious	kind
sensitive	talented	loving	judicious	hard working
willing	honest	a listener	accepting	a friend
intelligent	organized	spiritual	modest	an ACA member

A Discussion About Step Eight and Step Nine

Step Eight involves becoming willing to make amends to those we have harmed while Step Nine puts that willingness into action. As you help a sponsee create an Eighth Step Amends List, family situations must be considered. By their nature, some dysfunctional families can be violent or potentially violent. In other cases there can be demeaning remarks and hurtful denial. We try to not project how an amends will proceed, but the Steps do not require us to place ourselves in harm's way. We also do not use an amends to have a showdown with our parents or relatives. The amends involves our effort to repair harm we have caused and to forgive ourselves and others. We want to make amends to our family to the best of our ability while also protecting ourselves from potential harm.

We don't grovel or plead while making amends. We can feel good about what we are doing for ourselves. Our attitude is one of humility and a sincere desire to make amends for harms done.

B

Appendix B

Some people may accept our sincerity, and others may not, but we remain committed to our recovery. We have usually harmed other family members with remarks, judgments, and physical abuse in some cases. We may have struck someone, and we may have been struck back. Yet, we are focusing on our behavior so that we can go forward. We cannot make excuses for our behavior to avoid making amends.

At the same time, there can be incest, emotional abuse, and physical trauma perpetrated by the parents or other family members upon the sponsee. The sponsee is obviously not responsible for this behavior since he or she was a child. The child did not cause it and cannot cure it. However, the Twelve Steps require us to make amends for our selfish and destructive behavior as adults so that we can change from within and contribute to ACA and to society. There will be behavior by the sponsee that is clearly abusive to his or her family. In some cases it is retaliatory abuse in which the sponsee has actively sought to hurt the parents or family since the family harmed him or her. There could also be matters of money in which the sponsee uses guilt to get money from a perpetrating family member. It is an understood pay-off for secretive behavior. None of this is healthy, but it can be dealt with through honesty and a willingness to live life without secrets or dependence.

Asking an incest survivor to make amends to his or her perpetrating relative for harms the incest survivor has done after leaving the home must be discussed in greater detail. (Read Step Eight for more details.) We seek discernment in these circumstances since each one is different. We also seek fellowship experience. Some ACA members will not make amends to a violent or perpetrating family member for reasons that involve personal safety and retaining self-dignity. Some of these parents or family members remain unrepentant and sick. There is lust and perverseness and a complete rejection of the truth. The sponsee must protect himself or herself from such family members. Under these extreme conditions, a direct amends to the family is usually not appropriate; however, the sponsee can find freedom from the shame that surrounds the sexual abuse if he or she remains focused on the Twelve Steps and seeks guidance from a Higher Power. At the same time, the sponsee must continue on with amends to other people on the Eighth Step List. The bar must remain high so that we can make things right and claim personal freedom. This is a courageous and meaningful path that fulfills Step Eight and Step Nine.

In other cases, incest survivors in ACA have made face-to-face amends to a perpetrating parent or relative. The amends involved behavior committed by the incest survivor after leaving the home. With help, the person was able to judge the situation and discern the spiritual aim of Steps Eight and Nine and to balance that with retaining self-dignity. These members knew they were making amends for adult behaviors that have roots in the abuse visited upon them by the family. In essence, they release the shame surrounding the sexual abuse while taking responsibility for their adult behaviors. In some of these cases, full forgiveness for the perpetrator usually comes later rather than sooner.

These examples are our fellowship experience that we can rely upon, in addition to prayer and a sincere desire to not back down from Step work that can bring lasting and spiritual peace.

B

Appendix C
Our Fellowship Name

*W*hile there are different types of adult-child groups, there is only one Adult Children of Alcoholics. ACA is the original adult-child fellowship and the first to develop a Twelve Step program and specific literature addressing the effects of being raised in a dysfunctional home. The ACA fellowship also outlined The Solution.

In the past, questions have arisen about the wording of our fellowship name. There have been discussions on removing or adding words. A few groups have chosen to alter the ACA name in hopes of attracting more members to the fellowship. The results of these well-intentioned efforts are inconclusive and appear to be ineffective.

We believe that ACA World Services must honor our original name and our roots. We were founded as Adult Children of Alcoholics. To remain credible and to encourage adult children to find value in their past, we must honor our past and its value as well.

Our registered groups are overwhelmingly Adult Children of Alcoholics groups. Each group is autonomous, but we ask groups registering with ACA World Services to understand that they are part of Adult Children of Alcoholics. The consistency of the ACA name is essential for fellowship unity and for our ability to attract newcomers from a variety of dysfunctional family types. We believe that Adult Children of Alcoholics has successfully met the challenge of opening wide the doors of ACA to adult children from a variety of family situations while sustaining our original purpose and focus. This book and its writing are an example of that success.

In ACA, we are more alike than different. The common denominator among all adult children involves the sense that we have failed at fixing our families or that we helped cause our family problems. Believing we could have controlled outcomes or restored our family is a common error in thinking among adult children from all dysfunctional family types. Our common solution is a spiritual awakening brought by seeking a God of our Understanding through the Twelve Steps. We must also reparent ourselves and help others to continue our spiritual growth. These are the foundational truths of our fellowship put in place from the beginning. These experiences have sustained us and carried us as we enter our next decade as Adult Children of Alcoholics.

ACA Handbook (big book) Committee

Appendix D
The Laundry Lists and Their Flip Sides[1]

*W*hile the original Laundry List describes how we were affected by alcoholism and family dysfunction, we realize that as adults, we might, in turn, "act out"[2] those traits by becoming victimizers. In other words, adult children, by adopting their parents' behaviors, "become" their parents. This simple observation planted the seed for the development of **The Other Laundry List** and provides a fuller picture of how we are affected by the effects of alcoholism and family dysfunction.

The Other Laundry List is briefly mentioned on pp. 8-9, and a fuller explanation was presented at a convention in 2008. In addition, **The Flip Side of The Laundry List** and **The Flip Side of The Other Laundry List** were presented, detailing how, through reparenting and practicing the ACA Twelve Steps, we might be freed from these effects.

The Laundry Lists Workbook was published in 2015. It describes how dissociation[3] may appear in adult children, and provides a detailed landscape of all the areas we may travel on our journey to achieve wholeness.

---

[1] Adult Children of Alcoholics, *The Laundry Lists Workbook*, pp. viii, 168-174, Signal Hill: ACA WSO, 2015

[2] The term "acting out" is used by mental health professionals to denote that someone has a subconscious conflict that they "act out".

[3] The term "dissociation" refers to a mechanism that allows the mind to separate or compartmentalize certain memories or thoughts from normal consciousness. These split-off mental contents are not erased. They may resurface spontaneously or be triggered by objects or events in the person's environment. Additional terms used by mental health professionals include "learned dissociation", "continuum of dissociation", and "involuntary dissociation".

D

The Laundry List

1. We became isolated and afraid of people and authority figures.

2. We became approval seekers and lost our identity in the process.

3. We are frightened by angry people and any personal criticism.

4. We either become alcoholics, marry them, or both, or find another compulsive personality such as a workaholic to fulfill our sick abandonment needs.

5. We live life from the viewpoint of victims and we are attracted by that weakness in our love and friendship relationships.

6. We have an overdeveloped sense of responsibility and it is easier for us to be concerned with others rather than ourselves. This enables us not to look too closely at our own faults.

7. We get guilt feelings when we stand up for ourselves instead of giving in to others.

8. We become addicted to excitement.

9. We confuse love with pity and tend to "love" people who we can "pity" and "rescue".

10. We have stuffed our feelings from our traumatic childhoods and have lost the ability to feel or express our feelings because it hurts so much (denial).

11. We judge ourselves harshly and have a very low sense of self-esteem.

12. We are dependent personalities who are terrified of abandonment and will do anything to hold on to a relationship in order not to experience painful

abandonment feelings which we received from living with sick people who were never there emotionally for us.

13. Alcoholism is a family disease and we became para-alcoholics and took on the characteristics of the disease even though we did not pick up the drink.

14. Para-alcoholics are reactors rather than actors.

The Other Laundry List

1. To cover our fear of people and our dread of isolation we tragically become the very authority figures who frighten others and cause them to withdraw.

2. To avoid becoming enmeshed and entangled with other people and losing ourselves in the process, we become rigidly self-sufficient. We disdain the approval of others.

3. We frighten people with our anger and threat of belittling criticism.

4. We dominate others and abandon them before they can abandon us or we avoid relationships with dependent people altogether. To avoid being hurt, we isolate and dissociate and thereby abandon ourselves.

5. We live life from the standpoint of a victimizer, and are attracted to people we can manipulate and control in our important relationships.

6. We are irresponsible and self-centered. Our inflated sense of self-worth and self-importance prevents us from seeing our deficiencies and shortcomings.

7. We make others feel guilty when they attempt to assert themselves.

8. We inhibit our fear by staying deadened and numb.

D

9. We hate people who "play" the victim and beg to be rescued.

10. We deny that we've been hurt and are suppressing our emotions by the dramatic expression of "pseudo" feelings.

11. To protect ourselves from self punishment for failing to "save" the family we project our self-hate onto others and punish them instead.

12. We "manage" the massive amount of deprivation we feel, coming from abandonment within the home, by quickly letting go of relationships that threaten our "independence" (not too close).

13. We refuse to admit we've been affected by family dysfunction or that there was dysfunction in the home or that we have internalized any of the family's destructive attitudes and behaviors.

14. We act as if we are nothing like the dependent people who raised us.

The Flip Side of The Laundry List

1. We move out of isolation and are not unrealistically afraid of other people, even authority figures.

2. We do not depend on others to tell us who we are.

3. We are not automatically frightened by angry people and no longer regard personal criticism as a threat.

4. We do not have a compulsive need to recreate abandonment.

5. We stop living life from the standpoint of victims and are not attracted by this trait in our important relationships.

6. We do not use enabling as a way to avoid looking at our own shortcomings.

7. We do not feel guilty when we stand up for ourselves.

8. We avoid emotional intoxication and choose workable relationships instead of constant upset.

9. We are able to distinguish love from pity, and do not think "rescuing" people we "pity" is an act of love.

10. We come out of denial about our traumatic childhoods and regain the ability to feel and express our emotions.

11. We stop judging and condemning ourselves and discover a sense of self-worth.

12. We grow in independence and are no longer terrified of abandonment. We have interdependent relationships with healthy people, not dependent relationships with people who are emotionally unavailable.

13. The characteristics of alcoholism and para-alcoholism we have internalized are identified, acknowledged, and removed.

14. We are actors, not reactors.

The Flip Side of The Other Laundry List

1. We face and resolve our fear of people and our dread of isolation and stop intimidating others with our power and position.

2. We realize the sanctuary we have built to protect the frightened and injured child within has become a prison and we become willing to risk moving out of isolation.

3. With our renewed sense of self-worth and self-esteem we realize it is no longer necessary to protect ourselves by intimidating others with contempt, ridicule and anger.

D

Appendix D

4. We accept and comfort the isolated and hurt inner child we have abandoned and disavowed and thereby end the need to act out our fears of enmeshment and abandonment with other people.

5. Because we are whole and complete we no longer try to control others through manipulation and force and bind them to us with fear in order to avoid feeling isolated and alone.

6. Through our in-depth inventory we discover our true identity as capable, worthwhile people. By asking to have our shortcomings removed we are freed from the burden of inferiority and grandiosity.

7. We support and encourage others in their efforts to be assertive.

8. We uncover, acknowledge and express our childhood fears and withdraw from emotional intoxication.

9. We have compassion for anyone who is trapped in the "drama triangle" and is desperately searching for a way out of insanity.

10. We accept we were traumatized in childhood and lost the ability to feel. Using the 12 Steps as a program of recovery we regain the ability to feel and remember and become whole human beings who are happy, joyous and free.

11. In accepting we were powerless as children to "save" our family we are able to release our self-hate and to stop punishing ourselves and others for not being enough.

12. By accepting and reuniting with the inner child we are no longer threatened by intimacy, by the fear of being engulfed or made invisible.

13. By acknowledging the reality of family dysfunction we no longer have to act as if nothing were wrong or keep

denying that we are still unconsciously reacting to childhood harm and injury.

14. We stop denying and do something about our post-traumatic dependency on substances, people, places and things to distort and avoid reality.

Index

143, 168, 172, 177, 260, 271, 434,
438, 457, 558, 645
Betrayal: xxiii
Birthday (ACA Birthday – a
celebration of yearly recovery):
348, 567
Black-and-white thinking: see All-
or-nothing thinking
Blame (and Blaming): vii*n*, xxiii, 7,
15, 35, 158, 234, 238, *250*, 251,
298, 299, 421, 344
Blameless: xvi, 52, 109, 157, 159
Body, Mind, Spirit: see Disease
model
Body shame (and Voice shame): 441
Bottom (Hitting bottom): 65-73,
99, 123-124, 336, 579-580
Boundaries: 102, 123, 148, 250,
320, *373*, *413-414*, 419, 430, 443,
483; defined: 346-347; saying
"no": 329

C

Celebrating: 261, 324, 329, 348,
404, 477, 553
Challenges: 237, 240, 255, 286,
290, 393, 581
Changes: 252, 406-412, *414*, 415,
576, 578, 590
Childhood: vii, xxxvi, 7, *17*, 20*n*,
32, 33, 71, 83, 84, 94, 100, 154,
199-200, 204, 273, *279*, 296-297,
302, 334, 347, 417, 430, 434, 451,
625
Children of alcoholics (COAs):
475-476, 478, 483, 484, 486
Choice: 79, 147-148, 258-259; no
choice: 69, 103, 155-156, 255,
457; real choice: 95, 108, 256;
from denial to discernment: 148,
156, 256, 259

Clarity: *131-132*, 135-136, 238,
274, 306; see also Sanity
Codependence: 20, 60, 166, 402,
406, 438, 449, 456-457; defined:
6, 100, 335; see also Dependence
Common behaviors: see Laundry
List
Communicating (talking and
listening): *192*, 206, 214, 291,
367, *374*, 403-404, 405, 441, 547,
576; see also Sharing
Comparing: 204, 307, 308, 581
Compassion: *309*, 346, 634
Compulsion: 4, 69, 100, 124,
247-249, 288
Concepts (Twelve Concepts for
ACA World Service): see Twelve
Concepts
Connectedness: 265
Consciousness: 268, 284
Consistency: 60, 603, 609, 615
Control: xxii, 36, 39-43, 104, *138*,
143-147, 155, 258-259, 405
Counseling (and Therapy): 181,
333, 372, 447-448, 451-455, 564;
how to find a counselor: 455-456,
462-463; informed counseling:
xiii, 453; questions to ask:
462-463
Courage: 160, 171, 231, 242, 359,
459, 632
Creativity: xxiv, 155, 222, 225, 275,
278, 284, 296, 328
Crisis: 70, 137, 284, 291, 300, 336,
579
Critical inner parent/voice: 11, 35,
48-50, 115, 196, *207*, 254, 296,
298-299, 306-308, 337, 435, 581
Criticism: 15, 47, 156, 308, 366
Cross talk (and Cross-talk rule):
341-342, 564, 573-576

𝒟

Decision: 33, 79, 107, *138*, 142, 144, 145, 415

Defects of character: 188, *207-208*, 210, 215, 220-221, 225; distinguished from Laundry List traits: 111-112, *208-209*, 211; Sixth Step list: 214, 636-637

Denial: xi, xxiii, 22, 32, 53, 82, 96, 105, 124, 155, 201, 259, 448, 563; denial categories: 91-92, 344, 453-454, 580; denial inventory: 175-177

Dependence: 7, 20*n*, 83, 101, *130*, 154, 173, 265, 356

Dependent personality: 6, 17-18, 158

Depression: xxviii, 12, 17, 32, 143, 172, 182, 199

Desire: 50, 222, 242, 506; only requirement for ACA membership: 64, 338, 340, 346, 503-505

Desires: 430, 431, 433, 550

Discernment: 259, 308, 501; see also Choice

Discovery (versus recovery): *29*, 50-51, 367, 376

Disease of alcoholism: xxvii, xxxviii, 12-13, 25, 26, 56*n*, 458

Disease of family dysfunction: xxvi, xxxv, 22, 25, 27, 56, 67, 75, 96, 99, 105-106, 125, 143, 156, 170, 177, 544, 582, 621

Disease model (body, mind, spirit): xxvi, 17, 105, 544

Disease progression: 67, 582

Dissociation: 17, 87-88, 203, 253, 269, 459; defined: 344

Diversity: xiv, 60-61, 505, 514

Divided Self: see Self

"Doctor's Opinion": xxvii-xxx

Dreams: 285, 429-431, 432-433, 477, 481

Dysfunctional family types: 57-59, 338

ℰ

Effects: xxviii, 22-23, 31-32, 71, 111, 156, 196, 334, 339, 340, 358, 387, 448, 452, 506, 622-623

Effort: 9, 50, 71, 145, 210, 253, 286, 300, 303, 326, 438, *473*

Elections: 499-500, 529; group officers: 560, 606; Intergroups and Regions: 604

Emotional eating: 31, 65, 154, 391, 450

Emotional intoxication: 628

Emotional sobriety: 45, 90, 91, 155, 265-266, 347, 348, 367, 392, 431, 621, 628

Empathy: 60, *139*, 346, 365, 515, 573, 634

Enabling: 40-41, 290, 377, 438

Enmeshment: 14, 24, 180, 256, 274

Envy: 215, 221, 641

Equality: 334, 366, 369, 386, 483

Excitement: xxxiv, 16, 23, 69, 87, 158, 266, 273, 589

Expectations: 29, 36, 58, 182, 183, 297, *319*, 380

"Experience, Strength, and Hope": viii, xiv, *xxxix*, 117, 359, 360, 374, 510, *514*, 590

ℱ

Faith: xxv, 76-77, *78*, 79, 106-107, *130*, *133*, 142, 146, *281*, 291, 423, 581

𝒩

O

𝒫

Ten: 114, 115-116, 250-262, 307, 569; Step Eleven: 116, 263-278, 569; Step Twelve: *80*, 116-117, 279-294, *469*, *513*, 516, 528, 546, 569

Twelve Traditions of ACA: xxxvi, 79, 346, 489-490, 550, 566, 592; Tradition One: 491-496, 550, 585; Tradition Two: 497-502, 550; Tradition Three: 63-64, 503-507, 550; Tradition Four: 508-512, 551, 608; Tradition Five: 513-517, 551; Tradition Six: 518-521, 551; Tradition Seven: 522-526, 551, 565, 609, 610; Tradition Eight: 527-531, 551; Tradition Nine: 532-537, 551, 611; Tradition Ten: 538-541, 551; Tradition Eleven: 542-548, 551; Tradition Twelve: 549-554

U

Uniqueness: 96, 168, 285, 293
Unity: xiv, 491-495, *497*
Ultimate authority: 489, 497, 615
Unmanageability: 104, *120*, *121*, 136, 155, 333

V

Victim: 14, 24, 156, 158, 176, 201, 248, *279*, 349, 602, 633
Voice (finding one's voice): xxiv, 73, 116-117, 193, 441, 495; see also Critical inner parent/voice
Vulnerable: 6, 90, 105, *152*, 162, 210, 355, 356, 361, *471*, 627

W-X

Wants: see Needs

Wholeness: xxi, 75, 137, 143, 159, 221, 269, 271, 289, 303, 358, 590
Will: 144, 223, *264*, 376, 496; good use of the will : 212, 223
Willpower: 122-123, 215; see also Surrender
Willingness: 50, 146, 210, 223, 233, 285, 304, *313*, 369, 386, 454, 464, 506, 633, 641
Workplace: reenactment: 416, 417, *420*; roles: 421-422, 424; using the program at work: 402, 415, 423, *425*, 426-427, *542*
Workplace Laundry List: 416-419
Worry: 16, 24, 27, 243, 335, 581
Wound (and wounded): 71, 83, 199, 289, 434, 440, 535, 569; soul wound: 94, 124
Worth (and worthiness): 29, 72, 84, 86, 93, *151*, 169, 342, 363, 436
Wrong: 30, 105, 110, *152*, 162, 182, *250*, 342, *412*; assuming we always are: vii*n*, 15, *35*, 47, *138*, 196, *251*, 302
Wrongs: 115, 195, 197, *207*, *235*, 241, 440, 634; exact nature of: *190-191*, 197, 198-199, 205, 632; see also Amends, Harm

Y-Z

Youth: see ACA Teen, Children of alcoholics

Notes